中国司法部“法治建设与法学理论研究部级科研项目”子课题成果

家事法研究学术文库

当代中国民众财产继承观念与遗产处理习惯实证调查研究

（上卷）

主　编　**陈　苇**（课题负责人）

中国人民公安大学出版社

2019·北京

当代中国民众财产继承观念与遗产处理习惯实证调查研究

我国十省市被调查地区调查组组长、副组长

（以撰写章节先后为序）

重庆市调查组组长： 西南政法大学　陈苇教授

副组长： 西南政法大学　胡苷用副教授

上海市调查组组长： 华东政法大学　许莉教授

吉林省调查组组长： 吉林大学法学院　李洪祥教授

河北省调查组组长： 燕山大学　罗杰副教授

湖北省调查组组长： 中南财经政法大学　孟令志副教授

江西省调查组组长： 赣南师范大学　曹贤信副教授

广东省调查组组长： 中山大学法学院　卓冬青副教授

副组长： 广东工业大学政法学院　郭丽红教授

海南省调查组组长： 海南大学法学院　叶英萍教授

福建省调查组组长： 厦门大学法学院　何丽新教授

四川省调查组组长： 西南政法大学　陈苇教授

副组长： 西南政法大学　胡苷用副教授

当代中国民众财产继承观念与遗产处理习惯实证调查研究

撰稿人（以撰写章节先后为序）

陈　苇　陈　法　石　婷　白　玉　刘宇娇　李洪祥
苗艺璇　高　岩　马　旭　贺海燕　张　远　吴天宜
程藉瑶　许　莉　张　叶　柯婵娟　罗　杰　尹　鸽
孟令志　贾艳艳　李　想　王传印　元　雨　彭　锦
曹贤信　曾瑞玉　李　艳　卓冬青　郭丽红　黄蔚菁
胡明玉　叶英萍　王彦翔　文　灿　何丽新　孙　菁
余虹宇　王思颖　石　雷　郭庆敏　占泸霞

《家事法研究学术文库》顾问

（以姓氏笔画为序）

谨以此书献给我的家人

——我衷心地感谢你们30多年来对我工作的默默支持!

This work is dedicated to my family

—I sincerely thank you for your silent support of my work over the past 30 years.

目　　录

上　卷

前　言 …………………………………………………………… 陈　苇（ 1 ）
作者序 …………………………………………………………… 陈　苇（ 1 ）
鸣　谢 ……………………………………………………………………（ 1 ）
本书引用的主要法律、法规和司法解释的简称 ……………………………（ 1 ）
第一章　当代中国民众财产继承观念与遗产处理习惯实证调查概述 ………（ 1 ）
第一节　当代中国民众财产继承观念与遗产处理习惯实证调查的背景、对象和意义 …………………………………………………………（ 3 ）
一、实证调查的背景 ……………………………………………………（ 3 ）
二、实证调查的对象和意义 ……………………………………………（ 4 ）
第二节　当代中国民众财产继承观念与遗产处理习惯实证调查的实施概况 …………………………………………………………………（ 5 ）
一、实证调查的主要内容 ………………………………………………（ 5 ）
二、实证调查的情况简介 ………………………………………………（ 7 ）
三、实证调查报告的撰写方法 …………………………………………（ 9 ）
第二章　当代中国重庆市民众财产继承观念与遗产处理习惯实证调查研究 ………（ 12 ）
第一节　当代中国重庆市民众财产继承观念与遗产处理习惯实证调查概况 …………………………………………………………………（ 12 ）
一、被调查地区概况 ……………………………………………………（ 12 ）
二、实证调查情况简介 …………………………………………………（ 13 ）
三、被调查对象的基本情况 ……………………………………………（ 14 ）
第二节　当代中国重庆市民众财产继承观念与遗产处理习惯实证调查的数据统计情况 ……………………………………………………（ 16 ）
一、遗产范围界定之调查数据统计情况 ………………………………（ 16 ）
二、继承开始的通知和公告之调查数据统计情况 ……………………（ 18 ）
三、遗产管理之调查数据统计情况 ……………………………………（ 20 ）
四、法定继承之调查数据统计情况 ……………………………………（ 23 ）
五、遗嘱继承之调查数据统计情况 ……………………………………（ 30 ）

六、继承和遗赠的接受与放弃之调查数据统计情况 …………………………（33）
七、继承权的丧失、被继承人的宥恕与代位继承之调查数据统计情况 ……（37）
八、继承协议之调查数据统计情况 …………………………………………（39）
九、遗产债务清偿之调查数据统计情况 ……………………………………（43）
十、遗产分割之调查数据统计情况 …………………………………………（47）
十一、无人承受遗产之调查数据统计情况 …………………………………（53）
十二、遗产处理相关案例的简介与评析 ……………………………………（58）
第三节 当代中国重庆市民众财产继承观念与遗产处理习惯的特点与原因分析 ……………………………………………………………（68）
一、遗产范围界定之特点与原因分析 ………………………………………（68）
二、继承开始的通知和公告之特点与原因分析 ……………………………（73）
三、遗产管理之特点与原因分析 ……………………………………………（76）
四、法定继承之特点与原因分析 ……………………………………………（80）
五、遗嘱继承之特点与原因分析 ……………………………………………（86）
六、继承和遗赠的接受与放弃之特点与原因分析 …………………………（90）
七、继承权的丧失、被继承人的宥恕与代位继承之特点与原因分析 ………（94）
八、继承协议之特点与原因分析 ……………………………………………（97）
九、遗产债务清偿之特点与原因分析 ………………………………………（99）
十、遗产分割之特点与原因分析 ……………………………………………（104）
十一、无人承受遗产之特点与原因分析 ……………………………………（108）
第四节 当代中国重庆市民众财产继承观念与遗产处理习惯对中国民法典继承编制定的立法启示 ……………………………………………（112）
一、我国遗产范围界定制度之不足与立法完善建议 ………………………（112）
二、我国继承开始的通知和公告制度之不足与立法完善建议 ……………（113）
三、我国遗产管理制度之不足与立法完善建议 ……………………………（114）
四、我国法定继承制度之不足与立法完善建议 ……………………………（115）
五、我国遗嘱继承制度之不足与立法完善建议 ……………………………（116）
六、我国继承和遗赠的接受与放弃制度之不足与立法完善建议 …………（117）
七、我国继承权的丧失、被继承人的宥恕与代位继承制度之不足与立法完善建议 ……………………………………………………………（118）
八、我国遗赠扶养协议制度之不足与立法增补建议 ………………………（119）
九、我国遗产债务清偿制度之不足与立法完善建议 ………………………（119）
十、我国遗产分割制度之不足与立法完善建议 ……………………………（120）
十一、我国无人承受遗产制度之不足与立法完善建议 ……………………（121）
第三章 当代中国吉林省民众财产继承观念与遗产处理习惯实证调查研究 ………（123）
第一节 当代中国吉林省民众财产继承观念与遗产处理习惯实证调查概况 ……………………………………………………………（123）
一、被调查地区概况 …………………………………………………………（123）
二、实证调查情况简介 ………………………………………………………（124）

三、被调查对象的基本情况 …………………………………………………………… (125)
第二节　当代中国吉林省民众财产继承观念与遗产处理习惯实证调查的数据统计情况 …………………………………………………………… (127)
一、遗产范围界定之调查数据统计情况 ……………………………………… (127)
二、继承开始的通知和公告之调查数据统计情况 …………………………… (130)
三、遗产管理之调查数据统计情况 …………………………………………… (132)
四、法定继承之调查数据统计情况 …………………………………………… (136)
五、遗嘱继承之调查数据统计情况 …………………………………………… (142)
六、继承和遗赠的接受与放弃之调查数据统计情况 ………………………… (145)
七、继承权的丧失、被继承人的宥恕与代位继承之调查数据统计情况 …… (149)
八、继承协议之调查数据统计情况 …………………………………………… (150)
九、遗产债务清偿之调查数据统计情况 ……………………………………… (153)
十、遗产分割之调查数据统计情况 …………………………………………… (156)
十一、无人承受遗产之调查数据统计情况 …………………………………… (161)
十二、遗产处理相关案例的简介与评析 ……………………………………… (165)
第三节　当代中国吉林省民众财产继承观念与遗产处理习惯的特点与原因分析 ………………………………………………………………… (175)
一、遗产范围界定之特点与原因分析 ………………………………………… (175)
二、继承开始的通知和公告之特点与原因分析 ……………………………… (179)
三、遗产管理之特点与原因分析 ……………………………………………… (181)
四、法定继承之特点与原因分析 ……………………………………………… (184)
五、遗嘱继承之特点与原因分析 ……………………………………………… (190)
六、继承和遗赠的接受与放弃之特点与原因分析 …………………………… (192)
七、继承权的丧失、被继承人的宥恕与代位继承之特点与原因分析 ……… (195)
八、继承协议之特点与原因分析 ……………………………………………… (197)
九、遗产债务清偿之特点与原因分析 ………………………………………… (199)
十、遗产分割之特点与原因分析 ……………………………………………… (202)
十一、无人承受遗产的处理之特点与原因分析 ……………………………… (205)
第四节　当代中国吉林省民众财产继承观念与遗产处理习惯对中国民法典继承编制定的立法启示 ……………………………………………… (207)
一、我国遗产范围界定制度之不足与立法完善建议 ………………………… (207)
二、我国继承开始的通知和公告制度之不足与立法完善建议 ……………… (208)
三、我国遗产管理制度之不足与立法完善建议 ……………………………… (208)
四、我国法定继承制度之不足与立法完善建议 ……………………………… (209)
五、我国遗嘱继承制度之不足与立法完善建议 ……………………………… (210)
六、我国继承和遗赠的接受与放弃制度之不足与立法完善建议 …………… (211)
七、我国继承权的丧失、被继承人的宥恕与代位继承制度之不足与立法完善建议 ………………………………………………………………… (211)
八、我国遗赠扶养协议制度之不足与立法增补建议 ………………………… (212)

九、我国遗产债务清偿制度之不足与立法完善建议 ……………………（212）
十、我国遗产分割制度之不足与立法完善建议 …………………………（213）
十一、我国无人承受遗产的处理制度之不足与立法完善建议 …………（214）
第四章 当代中国上海市民众财产继承观念与遗产处理习惯实证调查研究 ………（215）
第一节 当代中国上海市民众财产继承观念与遗产处理习惯实证调查概况 ……………………………………………………………………………（215）
一、被调查地区概况 …………………………………………………（215）
二、实证调查情况简介 ………………………………………………（216）
三、被调查对象的基本情况 …………………………………………（217）
第二节 当代中国上海市民众财产继承观念与遗产处理习惯实证调查的数据统计情况 ……………………………………………………………（219）
一、遗产范围界定之调查数据统计情况 ……………………………（219）
二、继承开始的通知和公告之调查数据统计情况 …………………（222）
三、遗产管理之调查数据统计情况 …………………………………（224）
四、法定继承之调查数据统计情况 …………………………………（227）
五、遗嘱继承之调查数据统计情况 …………………………………（235）
六、继承和遗赠的接受与放弃之调查数据统计情况 ………………（238）
七、继承权的丧失、被继承人的宥恕与代位继承之调查数据统计情况 ……（242）
八、继承协议之调查数据统计情况 …………………………………（245）
九、遗产债务清偿之调查数据统计情况 ……………………………（248）
十、遗产分割之调查数据统计情况 …………………………………（252）
十一、无人承受遗产之调查数据统计情况 …………………………（257）
十二、遗产处理相关案例的简介与评析 ……………………………（262）
第三节 当代中国上海市民众财产继承观念与遗产处理习惯的特点与原因分析 ……………………………………………………………………（272）
一、遗产范围界定之特点与原因分析 ………………………………（272）
二、继承开始的通知和公告之特点与原因分析 ……………………（274）
三、遗产管理之特点与原因分析 ……………………………………（277）
四、法定继承之特点与原因分析 ……………………………………（280）
五、遗嘱继承之特点与原因分析 ……………………………………（286）
六、继承和遗赠的接受与放弃之特点与原因分析 …………………（289）
七、继承权的丧失、被继承人的宥恕与代位继承之特点与原因分析 ………（292）
八、继承协议之特点与原因分析 ……………………………………（293）
九、遗产债务清偿之特点与原因分析 ………………………………（295）
十、遗产分割之特点与原因分析 ……………………………………（298）
十一、无人承受遗产之特点与原因分析 ……………………………（301）
第四节 当代中国上海市民众财产继承观念与遗产处理习惯对中国民法典继承编制定的立法启示 ……………………………………………………（303）
一、我国遗产范围界定制度之不足与立法完善建议 ………………（303）

二、我国继承开始的通知和公告制度之不足与立法完善建议 …………… (304)
三、我国遗产管理制度之不足与立法完善建议 …………………… (304)
四、我国法定继承制度之不足与立法完善建议 …………………… (305)
五、我国遗嘱继承制度之不足与立法完善建议 …………………… (306)
六、我国继承和遗赠的接受与放弃制度之不足与立法完善建议 ………… (306)
七、我国继承权的丧失、被继承人的宥恕与代位继承制度之不足与立法完善建议 ……………………………………………………… (307)
八、我国遗赠扶养协议制度之不足与立法增补建议 ……………… (307)
九、我国遗产债务清偿制度之不足与立法完善建议 ……………… (308)
十、我国遗产分割制度之不足与立法完善建议 …………………… (309)
十一、我国无人承受遗产制度之不足与立法完善建议 …………… (309)
第五章 当代中国河北省民众财产继承观念与遗产处理习惯实证调查研究 ……… (310)
第一节 当代中国河北省民众财产继承观念与遗产处理习惯实证调查概况 ……………………………………………………… (310)
一、被调查地区概况 ……………………………………………… (310)
二、实证调查情况简介 …………………………………………… (311)
三、被调查对象的基本情况 ……………………………………… (312)
第二节 当代中国河北省民众财产继承观念与遗产处理习惯实证调查的数据统计情况 ……………………………………………… (314)
一、遗产范围界定之调查数据统计情况 ………………………… (314)
二、继承开始的通知和公告之调查数据统计情况 ……………… (316)
三、遗产管理之调查数据统计情况 ……………………………… (318)
四、法定继承之调查数据统计情况 ……………………………… (322)
五、遗嘱继承之调查数据统计情况 ……………………………… (328)
六、继承和遗赠的接受与放弃之调查数据统计情况 …………… (331)
七、继承权的丧失、被继承人的宥恕与代位继承的调查数据统计情况 …… (335)
八、继承协议之调查数据统计情况 ……………………………… (336)
九、遗产债务清偿之调查数据统计情况 ………………………… (339)
十、遗产分割之调查数据统计情况 ……………………………… (342)
十一、无人承受遗产之调查数据统计情况 ……………………… (347)
十二、遗产处理相关案例的简介与评析 ………………………… (350)
第三节 当代中国河北省民众财产继承观念与遗产处理习惯的特点与原因分析 ……………………………………………………… (364)
一、遗产的范围之特点与原因分析 ……………………………… (364)
二、继承开始的通知和公告之特点与原因分析 ………………… (366)
三、遗产管理之特点与原因分析 ………………………………… (369)
四、法定继承之特点与原因分析 ………………………………… (372)
五、遗嘱继承之特点与原因分析 ………………………………… (377)
六、继承和遗赠的接受与放弃之特点与原因分析 ……………… (380)

七、继承权的丧失、被继承人的宥恕与代位继承之特点与原因分析 ……… (383)
八、继承协议之特点与原因分析 ……… (385)
九、遗产债务清偿之特点与原因分析 ……… (388)
十、遗产分割之特点与原因分析 ……… (391)
十一、无人承受遗产之特点与原因分析 ……… (393)
第四节 当代中国河北省民众财产继承观念与遗产处理习惯对中国民法典继承编制定的立法启示 ……… (396)
一、我国遗产范围界定制度之不足与立法完善建议 ……… (396)
二、我国继承开始的通知和公告制度之不足与立法完善建议 ……… (397)
三、我国遗产管理制度之不足与立法完善建议 ……… (397)
四、我国法定继承制度之不足与立法完善建议 ……… (398)
五、我国遗嘱继承制度之不足与立法完善建议 ……… (399)
六、我国继承和遗赠的接受与放弃制度之不足与立法完善建议 ……… (400)
七、我国继承权的丧失、被继承人的宥恕与代位继承制度之不足与立法完善建议 ……… (400)
八、我国遗赠扶养协议制度之不足与立法增补建议 ……… (401)
九、我国遗产债务清偿制度之不足与立法完善建议 ……… (402)
十、我国遗产分割制度之不足与立法完善建议 ……… (403)
十一、我国无人承受遗产之不足与立法完善建议 ……… (403)
第六章 当代中国湖北省民众财产继承观念与遗产处理习惯实证调查研究 ……… (405)
第一节 当代中国湖北省民众财产继承观念与遗产处理习惯实证调查概况 ……… (405)
一、被调查地区概况 ……… (405)
二、实证调查情况简介 ……… (406)
三、被调查对象的基本情况 ……… (407)
第二节 当代中国湖北省民众财产继承观念与遗产处理习惯实证调查的数据统计情况 ……… (409)
一、遗产范围界定之调查数据统计情况 ……… (409)
二、继承开始的通知和公告之调查数据统计情况 ……… (412)
三、遗产管理之调查数据统计情况 ……… (414)
四、法定继承之调查数据统计情况 ……… (418)
五、遗嘱继承之调查数据统计情况 ……… (425)
六、继承和遗赠的接受与放弃之调查数据统计情况 ……… (429)
七、继承权的丧失、被继承人的宥恕与代位继承之调查数据统计情况 ……… (432)
八、继承协议之调查数据统计情况 ……… (434)
九、遗产债务清偿之调查数据统计情况 ……… (437)
十、遗产分割之调查数据统计情况 ……… (439)
十一、无人承受遗产之调查数据统计情况 ……… (445)
十二、遗产处理相关案例的简介与评析 ……… (450)

第三节 当代中国湖北省民众财产继承观念与遗产处理习惯的特点与原因分析 …………（459）
一、遗产范围界定之特点与原因分析 …………（459）
二、继承开始的通知和公告之特点与原因分析 …………（462）
三、遗产管理之特点与原因分析 …………（464）
四、法定继承之特点与原因分析 …………（467）
五、遗嘱继承之特点与原因分析 …………（472）
六、继承和遗赠的接受与放弃之特点与原因分析 …………（474）
七、继承权的丧失、被继承人的宥恕与代位继承之特点与原因分析 …………（477）
八、继承协议之特点与原因分析 …………（479）
九、遗产债务清偿之特点与原因分析 …………（481）
十、遗产分割之特点与原因分析 …………（483）
十一、无人承受遗产之特点与原因分析 …………（485）
第四节 当代中国湖北省民众财产继承观念与遗产处理习惯对中国民法典继承编制定的立法启示 …………（488）
一、我国遗产范围界定制度之不足与立法完善建议 …………（488）
二、我国继承开始的通知和公告制度之不足与立法完善建议 …………（488）
三、我国遗产管理制度之不足与立法完善建议 …………（489）
四、我国法定继承制度之不足与立法完善建议 …………（490）
五、我国遗嘱继承制度之不足与立法完善建议 …………（491）
六、我国继承和遗赠的接受与放弃制度之不足与立法完善建议 …………（492）
七、我国继承权的丧失、被继承人的宥恕与代位继承制度之不足与立法完善建议 …………（492）
八、我国遗赠扶养协议制度之不足与立法增补建议 …………（493）
九、我国遗产债务清偿制度之不足与立法完善建议 …………（493）
十、我国遗产分割制度之不足与立法完善建议 …………（494）
十一、我国无人承受遗产制度之不足与立法完善建议 …………（494）

下 卷

第七章 当代中国江西省民众财产继承观念与遗产处理习惯实证调查研究 …………（497）
第一节 当代中国江西省民众财产继承观念与遗产处理习惯实证调查概况 …………（497）
一、被调查地区概况 …………（497）
二、实证调查情况简介 …………（498）
三、被调查对象的基本情况 …………（499）
第二节 当代中国江西省民众财产继承观念与遗产处理习惯实证调查的数据统计情况 …………（501）

一、遗产范围界定之调查数据统计情况 …………………………………………（501）
二、继承开始的通知和公告之调查数据统计情况 ………………………………（504）
三、遗产管理之调查数据统计情况 ……………………………………………（506）
四、法定继承之调查数据统计情况 ……………………………………………（510）
五、遗嘱继承之调查数据统计情况 ……………………………………………（517）
六、继承和遗赠的接受与放弃之调查数据统计情况 …………………………（521）
七、继承权的丧失、被继承人的宥恕与代位继承之调查数据统计情况 ……（526）
八、继承协议之调查数据统计情况 ……………………………………………（528）
九、遗产债务清偿之调查数据统计情况 ………………………………………（533）
十、遗产分割之调查数据统计情况 ……………………………………………（537）
十一、无人承受遗产之调查数据统计情况 ……………………………………（544）
十二、遗产处理相关案例的简介与评析 ………………………………………（549）
第三节　当代中国江西省民众财产继承观念与遗产处理习惯的特点与原因分析 …………………………………………………………………………（559）
一、遗产范围界定之特点与原因分析 …………………………………………（559）
二、继承开始的通知和公告之特点与原因分析 ………………………………（562）
三、遗产管理之特点与原因分析 ………………………………………………（564）
四、法定继承之特点与原因分析 ………………………………………………（568）
五、遗嘱继承之特点与原因分析 ………………………………………………（573）
六、继承和遗赠的接受与放弃之特点与原因分析 ……………………………（576）
七、继承权的丧失、被继承人的宥恕与代位继承之特点与原因分析 ………（579）
八、继承协议之特点与原因分析 ………………………………………………（581）
九、遗产债务清偿之特点与原因分析 …………………………………………（583）
十、遗产分割之特点与原因分析 ………………………………………………（586）
十一、无人承受遗产之特点与原因分析 ………………………………………（588）
第四节　当代中国江西省民众财产继承观念与遗产处理习惯对中国民法典继承编制定的立法启示 ……………………………………………………（591）
一、我国遗产范围制度之不足与立法完善建议 ………………………………（591）
二、我国继承开始的通知和公告制度之不足与立法完善建议 ………………（592）
三、我国遗产管理制度之不足与立法完善建议 ………………………………（592）
四、我国法定继承制度之不足与立法完善建议 ………………………………（593）
五、我国遗嘱继承制度之不足与立法完善建议 ………………………………（594）
六、我国继承和遗赠的接受与放弃制度之不足与立法完善建议 ……………（595）
七、我国继承权的丧失、被继承人的宥恕与代位继承制度之不足与立法完善建议 ……………………………………………………………………（596）
八、我国遗赠扶养协议制度之不足与立法增补建议 …………………………（597）
九、我国遗产债务清偿制度之不足与立法完善建议 …………………………（597）
十、我国遗产分割制度之不足与立法完善建议 ………………………………（598）
十一、我国无人承受遗产制度之不足与立法完善建议 ………………………（599）

第八章　当代中国四川省民众财产继承观念与遗产处理习惯实证调查研究 ……… (600)
第一节　当代中国四川省民众财产继承观念与遗产处理习惯实证调查概况 …… (600)
一、被调查地区概况 …… (600)
二、实证调查情况简介 …… (601)
三、被调查对象的基本情况 …… (602)
第二节　当代中国四川省民众财产继承观念与遗产处理习惯实证调查的数据统计情况 …… (604)
一、遗产范围界定之调查数据统计情况 …… (604)
二、继承开始的通知和公告之调查数据统计情况 …… (607)
三、遗产管理之调查数据统计情况 …… (609)
四、法定继承之调查数据统计情况 …… (613)
五、遗嘱继承之调查数据统计情况 …… (620)
六、继承和遗赠的接受与放弃之调查数据统计情况 …… (624)
七、继承权的丧失、被继承人的宥恕与代位继承之调查数据统计情况 …… (628)
八、继承协议之调查数据统计情况 …… (630)
九、遗产债务清偿之调查数据统计情况 …… (634)
十、遗产分割之调查数据统计情况 …… (638)
十一、无人承受遗产之调查数据统计情况 …… (644)
十二、遗产处理相关案例的简介与评析 …… (648)
第三节　当代中国四川省民众财产继承观念与遗产处理习惯的特点与原因分析 …… (659)
一、遗产范围界定之特点与原因分析 …… (659)
二、继承开始的通知和公告之特点与原因分析 …… (663)
三、遗产管理之特点与原因分析 …… (666)
四、法定继承之特点与原因分析 …… (670)
五、遗嘱继承之特点与原因分析 …… (679)
六、继承和遗赠的接受与放弃之特点与原因分析 …… (683)
七、继承权的丧失、被继承人的宥恕与代位继承之特点与原因分析 …… (688)
八、继承协议之特点与原因分析 …… (690)
九、遗产债务清偿之特点与原因分析 …… (693)
十、遗产分割之特点与原因分析 …… (697)
十一、无人承受遗产之特点与原因分析 …… (702)
第四节　当代中国四川省民众财产继承观念与遗产处理习惯对中国民法典继承编制定的立法启示 …… (705)
一、我国遗产范围界定制度之不足与立法完善建议 …… (705)
二、我国继承开始的通知和公告制度之不足与立法完善建议 …… (706)
三、我国遗产管理制度之不足与立法完善建议 …… (707)
四、我国法定继承制度之不足与立法完善建议 …… (707)

五、我国遗嘱继承制度之不足与立法完善建议 …………………………… (709)
六、我国继承和遗赠的接受与放弃制度之不足与立法完善建议 ………… (709)
七、我国继承权的丧失、被继承人的宥恕与代位继承制度之不足与立法完善建议 …………………………………………………………………… (710)
八、我国遗赠扶养协议制度之不足与立法增补建议 ……………………… (711)
九、我国遗产债务清偿制度之不足与立法完善建议 ……………………… (712)
十、我国遗产分割制度之不足与立法完善建议 …………………………… (713)
十一、我国无人承受遗产制度之不足与立法完善建议 …………………… (714)
第九章　当代中国广东省民众财产继承观念与遗产处理习惯实证调查研究 ……… (715)
第一节　当代中国广东省民众财产继承观念与遗产处理习惯实证调查概况 …………………………………………………………………… (715)
一、被调查地区概况 ……………………………………………………… (715)
二、实证调查情况简介 …………………………………………………… (716)
三、被调查对象的基本情况 ……………………………………………… (717)
第二节　当代中国广东省民众财产继承观念与遗产处理习惯实证调查的数据统计情况 ……………………………………………………………… (719)
一、遗产范围界定之调查数据统计情况 ………………………………… (719)
二、继承开始的通知和公告之调查数据统计情况 ……………………… (722)
三、遗产管理之调查数据统计情况 ……………………………………… (724)
四、法定继承之调查数据统计情况 ……………………………………… (727)
五、遗嘱继承之调查数据统计情况 ……………………………………… (733)
六、继承和遗赠的接受与放弃之调查数据统计情况 …………………… (735)
七、继承权的丧失、被继承人的宥恕与代位继承之调查数据统计情况 …… (737)
八、继承协议之调查数据统计情况 ……………………………………… (739)
九、遗产债务清偿之调查数据统计情况 ………………………………… (743)
十、遗产分割之调查数据统计情况 ……………………………………… (745)
十一、无人承受遗产的处理之调查数据统计情况 ……………………… (749)
十二、遗产处理相关案例的简介与评析 ………………………………… (752)
第三节　当代中国广东省民众财产继承观念与遗产处理习惯的特点与原因分析 ……………………………………………………………………… (761)
一、遗产范围界定之特点与原因分析 …………………………………… (761)
二、继承开始的通知和公告之特点与原因分析 ………………………… (764)
三、遗产管理之特点与原因分析 ………………………………………… (767)
四、法定继承之特点与原因分析 ………………………………………… (770)
五、遗嘱继承之特点与原因分析 ………………………………………… (775)
六、继承和遗赠的接受与放弃之特点与原因分析 ……………………… (778)
七、继承权的丧失、被继承人的宥恕与代位继承之特点与原因分析 ……… (780)
八、继承协议之特点与原因分析 ………………………………………… (782)
九、遗产债务清偿之特点与原因分析 …………………………………… (784)

十、遗产分割之特点与原因分析 …………………………………………………… (786)
十一、无人承受遗产之特点与原因分析 ……………………………………………… (789)
第四节　当代中国广东省民众财产继承观念与遗产处理习惯对中国民法典继承编制定的立法启示 …………………………………………………… (791)
一、我国遗产范围界定之不足与立法完善建议 …………………………………… (791)
二、我国继承开始的通知和公告制度之不足与立法完善建议 …………………… (792)
三、我国遗产管理制度之不足与立法完善建议 …………………………………… (793)
四、我国法定继承制度之不足与立法完善建议 …………………………………… (793)
五、我国遗嘱继承制度之不足与立法完善建议 …………………………………… (794)
六、我国继承和遗赠的接受与放弃制度之不足与立法完善建议 ………………… (795)
七、我国继承权的丧失、被继承人的宥恕与代位继承制度之不足与立法完善建议 …………………………………………………………………… (795)
八、我国继承扶养协议制度之立法建议 …………………………………………… (796)
九、我国遗产债务清偿制度之不足与立法完善建议 ……………………………… (796)
十、我国遗产分割制度之不足与立法完善建议 …………………………………… (797)
十一、我国无人承受遗产制度之不足与立法完善建议 …………………………… (797)
第十章　当代中国海南省民众财产继承观念与遗产处理习惯实证调查研究 ……… (798)
第一节　当代中国海南省民众财产继承观念与遗产处理习惯实证调查概况 …………………………………………………………………… (798)
一、被调查地区概况 ………………………………………………………………… (798)
二、实证调查情况简介 ……………………………………………………………… (798)
三、被调查者的基本情况 …………………………………………………………… (800)
第二节　当代中国海南省民众财产继承观念与遗产处理习惯实证调查的数据统计情况 …………………………………………………………………… (801)
一、遗产范围界定之调查数据统计情况 …………………………………………… (801)
二、继承开始的通知和公告之调查数据统计情况 ………………………………… (804)
三、遗产管理之调查数据统计情况 ………………………………………………… (806)
四、法定继承之调查数据统计情况 ………………………………………………… (809)
五、遗嘱继承之调查数据统计情况 ………………………………………………… (815)
六、继承和遗赠的接受与放弃之调查数据统计情况 ……………………………… (819)
七、继承权的丧失、被继承人的宥恕与代位继承之调查数据统计情况 …… (822)
八、继承协议之调查数据统计情况 ………………………………………………… (824)
九、遗产债务清偿之调查数据统计情况 …………………………………………… (828)
十、遗产分割之调查数据统计情况 ………………………………………………… (831)
十一、无人承受遗产之调查数据统计情况 ………………………………………… (836)
十二、遗产处理相关案例的简介与评析 …………………………………………… (841)
第三节　当代中国海南省民众财产继承观念与遗产处理习惯的特点与原因分析 …………………………………………………………………… (851)
一、遗产范围界定之特点与原因分析 ……………………………………………… (851)

二、继承开始的通知和公告之特点与原因分析 …………………………… （854）
三、遗产管理之特点与原因分析 …………………………………………… （856）
四、法定继承之特点与原因分析 …………………………………………… （859）
五、遗嘱继承之特点与原因分析 …………………………………………… （865）
六、继承和遗赠的接受与放弃之特点与原因分析 ………………………… （867）
七、继承权的丧失、被继承人的宥恕与代位继承之特点与原因分析 ……… （871）
八、继承协议之特点与原因分析 …………………………………………… （873）
九、遗产债务清偿之特点与原因分析 ……………………………………… （875）
十、遗产分割之特点与原因分析 …………………………………………… （878）
十一、无人承受遗产之特点与原因分析 …………………………………… （882）
第四节　当代中国海南省民众财产继承观念与遗产处理习惯对中国民法典继承编制定的立法启示 …………………………………………… （884）
一、我国遗产范围界定制度之不足与立法完善建议 ……………………… （885）
二、我国继承开始的通知和公告制度之不足与立法完善建议 …………… （885）
三、我国遗产管理制度之不足与立法完善建议 …………………………… （886）
四、我国法定继承制度之不足与立法完善建议 …………………………… （887）
五、我国遗嘱继承制度之不足与立法完善建议 …………………………… （888）
六、我国继承和遗赠的接受与放弃制度之不足与立法完善建议 ………… （888）
七、我国继承权的丧失、被继承人的宥恕与代位继承制度之不足与立法完善建议 …………………………………………………………… （889）
八、我国继承扶养协议制度之立法建议 …………………………………… （890）
九、我国遗产债务清偿制度之不足与立法完善建议 ……………………… （890）
十、我国遗产分割制度之不足与立法完善建议 …………………………… （891）
十一、我国无人承受遗产制度之不足与立法完善建议 …………………… （891）
第十一章　当代中国福建省民营企业主财产继承观念与遗产处理习惯实证调查研究 ………………………………………………………………… （893）
第一节　当代中国福建省民营企业主财产继承观念与遗产处理习惯实证调查概况 …………………………………………………………… （893）
一、被调查地区概况 ………………………………………………………… （893）
二、实证调查情况简介 ……………………………………………………… （894）
三、被调查对象的基本情况 ………………………………………………… （896）
第二节　当代中国福建省民营企业主财产继承观念与遗产处理习惯实证调查的数据统计情况 ………………………………………………… （897）
一、遗产范围界定之调查数据统计情况 …………………………………… （897）
二、继承开始的通知和公告之调查数据统计情况 ………………………… （899）
三、遗产管理之调查数据统计情况 ………………………………………… （901）
四、法定继承之调查数据统计情况 ………………………………………… （904）
五、遗嘱继承之调查数据统计情况 ………………………………………… （910）
六、继承和遗赠的接受与放弃之调查数据统计情况 ……………………… （912）

七、继承权的丧失、被继承人的宥恕与代位继承的调查数据统计情况 …… (914)
八、继承协议之调查数据统计情况 …… (915)
九、遗产债务清偿之调查数据统计情况 …… (918)
十、遗产分割之调查数据统计情况 …… (920)
十一、无人承受遗产之调查数据统计情况 …… (923)
十二、遗产处理相关案例的简介与评析 …… (926)
第三节　当代中国福建省民营企业主财产继承观念与遗产处理习惯的特点与原因分析 …… (939)
一、遗产范围界定之特点与原因分析 …… (939)
二、继承开始的通知和公告之特点与原因分析 …… (942)
三、遗产管理之特点与原因分析 …… (944)
四、法定继承之特点与原因分析 …… (948)
五、遗嘱继承之特点与原因分析 …… (954)
六、继承和遗赠的接受与放弃之特点与原因分析 …… (957)
七、继承权的丧失、被继承人的宥恕与代位继承之特点与原因分析 …… (960)
八、继承协议之特点与原因分析 …… (961)
九、遗产债务清偿之特点与原因分析 …… (964)
十、遗产分割之特点与原因分析 …… (967)
十一、无人承受遗产的处理之特点与原因分析 …… (969)
第四节　当代中国福建省民营企业主财产继承观念与遗产处理习惯对中国民法典继承编制定的立法启示 …… (972)
一、我国遗产范围制度之不足与立法完善建议 …… (972)
二、我国遗产开始的通知与公告制度之不足与立法完善建议 …… (973)
三、我国遗产管理制度之不足与立法完善建议 …… (973)
四、我国法定继承制度之不足与立法完善建议 …… (974)
五、我国遗嘱继承制度之不足与立法完善建议 …… (975)
六、我国继承和遗赠的接受与放弃制度之不足与立法完善建议 …… (976)
七、我国继承权的丧失、被继承人的宥恕与代位继承制度之不足与立法完善建议 …… (977)
八、我国遗赠扶养协议制度之不足与立法增补建议 …… (977)
九、我国遗产债务清偿制度之不足与立法完善建议 …… (978)
十、我国遗产分割制度之不足与立法完善建议 …… (979)
十一、我国无人承受遗产制度之不足与立法完善建议 …… (980)
第十二章　当代中国川渝等地民营企业主财产继承观念与遗产处理习惯实证调查研究 …… (981)
第一节　当代中国川渝等地民营企业主财产继承观念与遗产处理习惯实证调查概况 …… (981)
一、实证调查背景 …… (981)
二、实证调查情况简介 …… (981)

三、被调查者的基本情况 …………………………………………………………… (983)
第二节　当代中国川渝等地民营企业主财产继承观念与遗产处理习惯实证调查的数据统计情况 …………………………………………………… (984)
一、遗产范围界定之调查数据统计情况 ……………………………………… (984)
二、继承开始的通知和公告之调查数据统计情况 …………………………… (987)
三、遗产管理之调查数据统计情况 …………………………………………… (989)
四、法定继承之调查数据统计情况 …………………………………………… (992)
五、遗嘱继承之调查数据统计情况 …………………………………………… (999)
六、继承和遗赠的接受与放弃之调查数据统计情况 ………………………… (1003)
七、继承权的丧失、被继承人的宥恕与代位继承之调查数据统计情况 …… (1007)
八、继承协议之调查数据统计情况 …………………………………………… (1009)
九、遗产债务清偿之调查数据统计情况 ……………………………………… (1013)
十、遗产分割之调查数据统计情况 …………………………………………… (1017)
十一、无人承受遗产之调查数据统计情况 …………………………………… (1022)
十二、遗产处理相关案例的简介与评析 ……………………………………… (1027)
第三节　当代中国川渝等地民营企业主财产继承观念与遗产处理习惯的特点与原因分析 ……………………………………………………………… (1038)
一、遗产范围界定之特点与原因分析 ………………………………………… (1038)
二、继承开始的通知和公告之特点与原因分析 ……………………………… (1041)
三、遗产管理之特点与原因分析 ……………………………………………… (1044)
四、法定继承之特点与原因分析 ……………………………………………… (1047)
五、遗嘱继承之特点与原因分析 ……………………………………………… (1054)
六、继承和遗赠的接受与放弃之特点与原因分析 …………………………… (1057)
七、继承权的丧失、被继承人的宥恕与代位继承之特点与原因分析 ……… (1060)
八、继承协议之特点与原因分析 ……………………………………………… (1062)
九、遗产债务清偿之特点与原因分析 ………………………………………… (1064)
十、遗产分割之特点与原因分析 ……………………………………………… (1068)
十一、无人承受遗产之特点与原因分析 ……………………………………… (1071)
第四节　当代中国川渝等地民营企业主财产继承观念与遗产处理习惯对中国民法典继承编制定的立法启示 …………………………………………… (1073)
一、我国遗产范围制度之不足与立法完善建议 ……………………………… (1074)
二、我国继承开始的通知和公告制度之不足与立法完善建议 ……………… (1074)
三、我国遗产管理制度之不足与立法完善建议 ……………………………… (1075)
四、我国法定继承制度之不足与立法完善建议 ……………………………… (1076)
五、我国遗嘱继承制度之不足与立法完善建议 ……………………………… (1077)
六、我国继承和遗赠的接受与放弃制度之不足与立法完善建议 …………… (1077)
七、我国继承权的丧失、被继承人的宥恕与代位继承制度之不足与立法完善建议 ……………………………………………………………………… (1078)
八、我国遗赠扶养协议制度之不足与立法增补建议 ………………………… (1079)

九、我国遗产债务清偿制度之不足与立法完善建议 …………………………（1079）
十、我国遗产分割制度之不足与立法完善建议 ……………………………（1080）
十一、我国无人承受遗产制度之不足与立法完善建议 ………………………（1081）
主要参考文献 ………………………………………………………………（1082）
附录
西南政法大学外国家庭法及妇女理论研究中心简介（中英文对照）…………（1086）
西南政法大学外国家庭法及妇女理论研究中心 2006~2012 年已出版书目…………（1090）

Contents

Volume One

Forword ·· CHEN Wei (1)
Author's Preface ·· CHEN Wei (1)
Acknowledgement ·· (1)
Abbreviations for the Major Laws, Regulations and Judicial Interpretations ······ (1)
Chapter One Overview of Empirical Investigation on People's Concepts of Property Inheritance and Habits of Heritage Disposal in Contemporary China ·· (1)
Section 1 Background, Object and Significance of Empirical Investigation on People's Concepts of Property Inheritance and Habits of Heritage Disposal in Contemporary China ·· (3)
1. Background of Empirical Investigation ·· (3)
2. Object and Significance of Empirical Investigation ·· (4)
Section 2 the Implementation of Empirical Investigation on People's Concepts of Property Inheritance and Habits of Heritage Disposal in Ten Provinces of Contemporary China ·· (5)
1. Main Contents of Empirical Investigation ·· (5)
2. Brief Introduction of Empirical Investigation ·· (7)
3. Method of Writing Empirical Investigation Report ·· (9)
Chapter Two Empirical Research on People's Concepts of Property Inheritance and Habits of Heritage Disposal in Chongqing Municipality of Contemporary China ·· (12)
Section 1 Overview of Empirical Investigation on People's Concepts of Property Inheritance and Habits of Heritage Disposal in Chongqing Municipality of Contemporary China ·· (12)
1. Overview of the Investigated Region ·· (12)
2. Brief Introduction of Empirical Investigation ·· (13)
3. Basic Situations of Respondents ·· (14)

Section 2 Statistics of Investigated Data for Empirical Investigation on People's Concepts of Property Inheritance and Habits of Heritage Disposal in Chongqing Municipality of Contemporary China ········ (16)
1. Statistics of Investigated Data on the Definition of Heritage Scope ··········· (16)
2. Statistics of Investigated Data on the Notice and Announcement of the Beginning of Succession ········· (18)
3. Statistics of Investigated Data on Administration of Heritage ········· (20)
4. Statistics of Investigated Data on Intestate Succession ········· (23)
5. Statistics of Investigated Data on Testate Succession ········· (30)
6. Statistics of Investigated Data on Acceptance and Abandonment of Succession and Bequest ········· (33)
7. Statistics of Investigated Data on Loss of Succession Rights, Forgiveness of the Deceased and Succession by Subrogation ········· (37)
8. Statistics of Investigated Data on Succession Agreements ········· (39)
9. Statistics of Investigated Data on Liquidation of Heritage Debt ········· (43)
10. Statistics of Investigated Data on Heritage Division ········· (47)
11. Statistics of Investigated Data on Disposal of Inheritance without Heirs and Beneficiaries ········· (53)
12. Brief Introduction and Evaluation of Cases Related to Heritage Disposal ··· (58)
Section 3 Analysis on the Characteristics and Causes to People's Concepts of Property Inheritance and Habits of Heritage Disposal in Chongqing Municipality of Contemporary China ····· (68)
1. Analysis on the Characteristics and Causes to the Definition of Heritage Scope ········· (68)
2. Analysis on the Characteristics and Causes to Notice of the Beginning of Succession and Anouncement ········· (73)
3. Analysis on the Characteristics and Causes to Heritage Administration ········· (76)
4. Analysis on the Characteristics and Causes to Intestate Succession ········· (80)
5. Analysis on the Characteristics and Causes to Testate Succession ········· (86)
6. Analysis on the Characteristics and Causes to Acceptance and Abandonment of Succession and Bequest ········· (90)
7. Analysis on the Characteristics and Causes to Loss of Succession Rights, Forgiveness of the Deceased and Succession by Subrogation ········· (94)
8. Analysis on the Characteristics and Causes to Succession Agreements ········· (97)
9. Analysis on the Characteristics and Causes to Liquidation of Heritage Debt ········· (99)
10. Analysis on the Characteristics and Causes to Heritage Division ········· (104)
11. Analysis on the Characteristics and Causes to Inheritance without Heirs and Beneficiaries ········· (108)

Section 4 The Legislative Enlightenment of People's Concepts of Property Inheritance and Habits of Heritage Disposal in Chongqing Municipality of Contemporary China to Succession Law of Chinese Civil Code …… (112)

1. The Inadequacy of Chinese Definition of Heritage Scope System and Legislative Suggestions for Improvements …… (112)
2. The Inadequacy of Chinese Notice and Announcement of the Beginning of Succession System and Legislative Suggestions for Improvements …… (113)
3. The Inadequacy of Chinese Administration of Heritage System and Legislative Suggestions for Improvements …… (114)
4. The Inadequacy of Chinese Intestate Succession System and Legislative Suggestions for Improvements …… (115)
5. The Inadequacy of Chinese Testate Succession System and Legislative Suggestions for Improvements …… (116)
6. The Inadequacy of Chinese Acceptance and Abandonment of Succession and Bequest System and Legislative Suggestions for Improvements …… (117)
7. The Inadequacy of Chinese Loss of Succession Rights, Forgiveness of the Deceased and Succession by Subrogation System and Legislative Suggestions for Improvements …… (118)
8. The Inadequacy of Chinese Maintenance Agreement by Will System and Legislative Suggestions for Supplement …… (119)
9. The Inadequacy of Chinese Liquidation of Heritage Debt System and Legislative Suggestions for Improvement …… (119)
10. The Inadequacy of Chinese Heritage Division System and Legislative Suggestions for Improvement …… (120)
11. The Inadequacy of Chinese Inheritance without Heirs and Beneficiaries Disposal System and Legislative Suggestions for Improvement …… (121)

Chapter Three Empirical Research on People's Concepts of Property Inheritance and Habits of Heritage Disposal in Jilin Province of Contemporary China …… (123)

Section 1 Overview of Empirical Investigation on People's Concepts of Property Inheritance and Habits of Heritage Disposal in Jilin Province of Contemporary China …… (123)

1. Overview of Investigated Regions …… (123)
2. Brief Introduction of Empirical Investigation …… (124)
3. Basic Situations of Respondents …… (125)

Section 2 Statistics of Investigated Data for Empirical Investigation on People's Concepts of Property Inheritance and Habits of Heritage Disposal in Jilin Province of Contemporary China …… (127)

1. Statistics of Investigated Data on the Definition of Heritage Scope ………… (127)
2. Statistics of Investigated Data on the Notice and Announcement of the Beginning of Succession ………… (130)
3. Statistics of Investigated Data on Administration of Heritage ………… (132)
4. Statistics of Investigated Data on Intestate Succession ………… (136)
5. Statistics of Investigated Data on Testate Succession ………… (142)
6. Statistics of Investigated Data on Acceptance and Abandonment of Succession and Bequest ………… (145)
7. Statistics of Investigated Data on Loss of Succession Rights, Forgiveness of the Deceased and Succession by Subrogation ………… (149)
8. Statistics of Investigated Data on Succession Agreements ………… (150)
9. Statistics of Investigated Data on Liquidation of Heritage Debt ………… (153)
10. Statistics of Investigated Data on Heritage Division ………… (156)
11. Statistics of Investigated Data on Disposal of Inheritance without Heirs and Beneficiaries ………… (161)
12. Brief Introduction and Evaluation of Cases Related to Heritage Disposal … (165)
Section 3 Analysis on the Characteristics and Causes to People's Concepts of Property Inheritance and Habits of Heritage Disposal in Jilin Province of Contemporary China ………… (175)
1. Analysis on the Characteristics and Causes to the Definition of Heritage Scope ………… (175)
2. Analysis on the Characteristics and Causes to Notice of the Beginning of Succession and Anouncement ………… (179)
3. Analysis on the Characteristics and Causes to Heritage Administration ………… (181)
4. Analysis on the Characteristics and Causes to Intestate Succession ………… (184)
5. Analysis on the Characteristics and Causes to Testate Succession ………… (190)
6. Analysis on the Characteristics and Causes to Acceptance and Abandonment of Succession and Bequest ………… (192)
7. Analysis on the Characteristics and Causes to Loss of Succession Rights, Forgiveness of the Deceased and Succession by Subrogation ………… (195)
8. Analysis on the Characteristics and Causes to Succession Agreements ………… (197)
9. Analysis on the Characteristics and Causes to Liquidation of Heritage Debt ………… (199)
10. Analysis on the Characteristics and Causes to Heritage Division ………… (202)
11. Analysis on the Characteristics and Causes to Inheritance without Heirs and Beneficiaries ………… (205)

Section 4 The Legislative Enlightenment of People's Concepts of Property Inheritance and Habits of Heritage Disposal in Jilin Province of Contemporary China to Succession Law of Chinese Civil Code ······ (207)

1. The Inadequacy of Chinese Definition of Heritage Scope System and Legislative Suggestions for Improvements ······ (207)
2. The Inadequacy of Chinese Notice and Announcement of the Beginning of Succession System and Legislative Suggestions for Improvements ······ (208)
3. The Inadequacy of Chinese Administration of Heritage System and Legislative Suggestions for Improvements ······ (208)
4. The Inadequacy of Chinese Intestate Succession System and Legislative Suggestions for Improvements ······ (209)
5. The Inadequacy of Chinese Testate Succession System and Legislative Suggestions for Improvements ······ (210)
6. The Inadequacy of Chinese Acceptance and Abandonment of Succession and Bequest System and Legislative Suggestions for Improvements ······ (211)
7. The Inadequacy of Chinese Loss of Succession Rights, Forgiveness of the Deceased and Succession by Subrogation System and Legislative Suggestions for Improvements ······ (211)
8. The Inadequacy of Chinese Maintenance Agreement by Will System and Legislative Suggestions for Supplement ······ (212)
9. The Inadequacy of Chinese Liquidation of Heritage Debt System and Legislative Suggestions for Improvement ······ (212)
10. The Inadequacy of Chinese Heritage Division System and Legislative Suggestions for Improvement ······ (213)
11. The Inadequacy of Chinese Inheritance without Heirs and Beneficiaries System and Legislative Suggestions for Improvement ······ (214)

Chapter Four Empirical Research on People's Concepts of Property Inheritance and Habits of Heritage Disposal in Shanghai Municipality of Contemporary China ······ (215)

Section 1 Overview of Empirical Investigation on People's Concepts of Property Inheritance and Habits of Heritage Disposal in Shanghai Municipality of Contemporary China ······ (215)

1. Overview of Investigated Regions ······ (215)
2. Brief Introduction of Empirical Investigation ······ (216)
3. Basic Situations of Respondents ······ (217)

Section 2 Statistics of Investigated Data for Empirical Investigation on People's Concepts of Property Inheritance and Habits of Heritage Disposal in Shanghai Municipality of Contemporary China ······ (219)

1. Statistics of Investigated Data on the Definition of Heritage Scope ………… (219)
2. Statistics of Investigated Data on the Notice and Announcement of the Beginning of Succession ……………………………………………………………… (222)
3. Statistics of Investigated Data on Administration of Heritage ………………… (224)
4. Statistics of Investigated Data on Intestate Succession ……………………… (227)
5. Statistics of Investigated Data on Testate Succession ………………………… (235)
6. Statistics of Investigated Data on Acceptance and Abandonment of Succession and Bequest ……………………………………………………………………… (238)
7. Statistics of Investigated Data on Loss of Succession Rights, Forgiveness of the Deceased and Succession by Subrogation ……………………………… (242)
8. Statistics of Investigated Data on Succession Agreements …………………… (245)
9. Statistics of Investigated Data on Liquidation of Heritage Debt ……………… (248)
10. Statistics of Investigated Data on Heritage Division ………………………… (252)
11. Statistics of Investigated Data on Disposal of Inheritance without Heirs and Beneficiaries ………………………………………………………………… (257)
12. Brief Introduction and Evaluation of Cases Related to Heritage Disposal … (262)
Section 3 Analysis on the Characteristics and Causes to People's Concepts of Property Inheritance and Habits of Heritage Disposal in Shanghai Municipality of Contemporary China …… (272)
1. Analysis on the Characteristics and Causes to the Definition of Heritage Scope ……………………………………………………………………………… (272)
2. Analysis on the Characteristics and Causes to Notice of the Beginning of Succession and Anouncement …………………………………………………… (274)
3. Analysis on the Characteristics and Causes to Heritage Administration ……… (277)
4. Analysis on the Characteristics and Causes to Intestate Succession ………… (280)
5. Analysis on the Characteristics and Causes to Testate Succession …………… (286)
6. Analysis on the Characteristics and Causes to Acceptance and Abandonment of Succession and Bequest ……………………………………………………… (289)
7. Analysis on the Characteristics and Causes to Loss of Succession Rights, Forgiveness of the Deceased and Succession by Subrogation ………………… (292)
8. Analysis on the Characteristics and Causes to Succession Agreements ……… (293)
9. Analysis on the Characteristics and Causes to Liquidation of Heritage Debt …… (295)
10. Analysis on the Characteristics and Causes to Heritage Division …………… (298)
11. Analysis on the Characteristics and Causes to Disposal of Inheritance without Heirs and Beneficiaries ……………………………………………………… (301)
Section 4 The Legislative Enlightenment of People's Concepts of Property Inheritance and Habits of Heritage Disposal in Shanghai Municipality of Contemporary China to Succession Law of Chinese Civil Code ……………………………………………… (303)

1. The Inadequacy of Chinese Definition of Heritage Scope System and Legislative Suggestions for Improvements (303)
2. The Inadequacy of Chinese Notice and Announcement of the Beginning of Succession System and Legislative Suggestions for Improvements (304)
3. The Inadequacy of Chinese Administration of Heritage System and Legislative Suggestions for Improvements (304)
4. The Inadequacy of Chinese Intestate Succession System and Legislative Suggestions for Improvements (305)
5. The Inadequacy of Chinese Testate Succession System and Legislative Suggestions for Improvements (306)
6. The Inadequacy of Chinese Acceptance and Abandonment of Succession and Bequest System and Legislative Suggestions for Improvements (306)
7. The Inadequacy of Chinese Loss of Succession Rights, Forgiveness of the Deceased and Succession by Subrogation System and Legislative Suggestions for Improvements (307)
8. The Inadequacy of Chinese Maintenance Agreement by Will System and Legislative Suggestions for Supplement (307)
9. The Inadequacy of Chinese Liquidation of Heritage Debt System and Legislative Suggestions for Improvement (308)
10. The Inadequacy of Chinese Heritage Division System and Legislative Suggestions for Improvement (309)
11. The Inadequacy of Chinese Inheritance without Heirs and Beneficiaries System and Legislative Suggestions for Improvement (309)

Chapter Five Empirical Research on People's Concepts of Property Inheritance and Habits of Heritage Disposal in Hebei Province of Contemporary China (310)

Section 1 Overview of Empirical Investigation on People's Concepts of Property Inheritance and Habits of Heritage Disposal in Hebei Province of Contemporary China (310)
1. Overview of Investigated Regions (310)
2. Brief Introduction of Empirical Investigation (311)
3. Basic Situations of Respondents (312)

Section 2 Statistics of Investigated Data for Empirical Investigation on People's Concepts of Property Inheritance and Habits of Heritage Disposal in Hebei Province of Contemporary China (314)
1. Statistics of Investigated Data on the Definition of Heritage Scope (314)
2. Statistics of Investigated Data on the Notice and Announcement of the Beginning of Succession (316)
3. Statistics of Investigated Data on Administration of Heritage (318)

4. Statistics of Investigated Data on Intestate Succession ………………………… (322)
5. Statistics of Investigated Data on Testate Succession ………………………… (328)
6. Statistics of Investigated Data on Acceptance and Abandonment of Succession and Bequest ……………………………………………………………………… (331)
7. Statistics of Investigated Data on Loss of Succession Rights, Forgiveness of the Deceased and Succession by Subrogation ……………………………… (335)
8. Statistics of Investigated Data on Succession Agreements ………………… (336)
9. Statistics of Investigated Data on Liquidation of Heritage Debt ……………… (339)
10. Statistics of Investigated Data on Heritage Division ………………………… (342)
11. Statistics of Investigated Data on Disposal of Inheritance without Heirs and Beneficiaries ……………………………………………………………………… (347)
12. Brief Introduction and Evaluation of Cases Related to Heritage Disposal … (350)
Section 3 Analysis on the Characteristics and Causes to People's Concepts of Property Inheritance and Habits of Heritage Disposal in Hebei Province of Contemporary China …………… (364)
1. Analysis on the Characteristics and Causes to the Definition of Heritage Scope ……………………………………………………………………………… (364)
2. Analysis on the Characteristics and Causes to Notice of the Beginning of Succession and Anouncement ……………………………………………… (366)
3. Analysis on the Characteristics and Causes to Heritage Administration ……… (369)
4. Analysis on the Characteristics and Causes to Intestate Succession ………… (372)
5. Analysis on the Characteristics and Causes to Testate Succession …………… (377)
6. Analysis on the Characteristics and Causes to Acceptance and Abandonment of Succession and Bequest ………………………………………………… (380)
7. Analysis on the Characteristics and Causes to Loss of Succession Rights, Forgiveness of the Deceased and Succession by Subrogation ………………… (383)
8. Analysis on the Characteristics and Causes to Succession Agreements ……… (385)
9. Analysis on the Characteristics and Causes to Liquidation of Heritage Debt ……………………………………………………………………………… (388)
10. Analysis on the Characteristics and Causes to Heritage Division …………… (391)
11. Analysis on the Characteristics and Causes to Disposal of Inheritance without Heirs and Beneficiaries …………………………………………………… (393)
Section 4 The Legislative Enlightenment of People's Concepts of Property Inheritance and Habits of Heritage Disposal in Hebei Province of Contemporary China to Succession Law of Chinese Civil Code ……………………………………………………………… (396)
1. The Inadequacy of Chinese Definition of Heritage Scope System and Legislative Suggestions for Improvements ……………………………………………… (396)

2. The Inadequacy of Chinese Notice and Announcement of the Beginning of Succession System and Legislative Suggestions for Improvements ············ (397)
3. The Inadequacy of Chinese Administration of Heritage System and Legislative Suggestions for Improvements ············ (397)
4. The Inadequacy of Chinese Intestate Succession System and Legislative Suggestions for Improvements ············ (398)
5. The Inadequacy of Chinese Testate Succession System and Legislative Suggestions for Improvements ············ (399)
6. The Inadequacy of Chinese Acceptance and Abandonment of Succession and Bequest System and Legislative Suggestions for Improvements ············ (400)
7. The Inadequacy of Chinese Loss of Succession Rights, Forgiveness of the Deceased and Succession by Subrogation System and Legislative Suggestions for Improvements ············ (400)
8. The Inadequacy of Chinese Maintenance Agreement by Will System and Legislative Suggestions for Supplement ············ (401)
9. The Inadequacy of Chinese Liquidation of Heritage Debt System and Legislative Suggestions for Improvement ············ (402)
10. The Inadequacy of Chinese Heritage Division System and Legislative Suggestions for Improvement ············ (403)
11. The Inadequacy of Chinese Inheritance without Heirs and Beneficiaries System and Legislative Suggestions for Improvement ············ (403)

Chapter Six Empirical Research on People's Concepts of Property Inheritance and Habits of Heritage Disposal in Hubei Province of Contemporary China ············ (405)

Section 1 Overview of Empirical Investigation on People's Concepts of Property Inheritance and Habits of Heritage Disposal in Hubei Province of Contemporary China ············ (405)
1. Overview of Investigated Regions ············ (405)
2. Brief Introduction of Empirical Investigation ············ (406)
3. Basic Situations of Respondents ············ (407)

Section 2 Statistics of Investigated Data for Empirical Investigation on People's Concepts of Property Inheritance and Habits of Heritage Disposal in Hubei Province of Contemporary China ············ (409)
1. Statistics of Investigated Data on the Definition of Heritage Scope ············ (409)
2. Statistics of Investigated Data on the Notice and Announcement of the Beginning of Succession ············ (412)
3. Statistics of Investigated Data on Administration of Heritage ············ (414)
4. Statistics of Investigated Data on Intestate Succession ············ (418)
5. Statistics of Investigated Data on Testate Succession ············ (425)

6. Statistics of Investigated Data on Acceptance and Abandonment of Succession and Bequest …… (429)
7. Statistics of Investigated Data on Loss of Succession Rights, Forgiveness of the Deceased and Succession by Subrogation …… (432)
8. Statistics of Investigated Data on Succession Agreements …… (434)
9. Statistics of Investigated Data on Liquidation of Heritage Debt …… (437)
10. Statistics of Investigated Data on Heritage Division …… (439)
11. Statistics of Investigated Data on Disposal of Inheritance without Heirs and Beneficiaries …… (445)
12. Brief Introduction and Evaluation of Cases Related to Heritage Disposal … (450)
Section 3 Analysis on the Characteristics and Causes to People's Concepts of Property Inheritance and Habits of Heritage Disposal in Hubei Province of Contemporary China …… (459)
1. Analysis on the Characteristics and Causes to the Definition of Heritage Scope. …… (459)
2. Analysis on the Characteristics and Causes to Notice of the Beginning of Succession and Anouncement …… (462)
3. Analysis on the Characteristics and Causes to Heritage Administration …… (464)
4. Analysis on the Characteristics and Causes to Intestate Succession …… (467)
5. Analysis on the Characteristics and Causes to Testate Succession …… (472)
6. Analysis on the Characteristics and Causes to Acceptance and Abandonment of Succession and Bequest …… (474)
7. Analysis on the Characteristics and Causes to Loss of Succession Rights, Forgiveness of the Deceased and Succession by Subrogation …… (477)
8. Analysis on the Characteristics and Causes to Succession Agreements …… (479)
9. Analysis on the Characteristics and Causes to Liquidation of Heritage Debt. …… (481)
10. Analysis on the Characteristics and Causes to Heritage Division …… (483)
11. Analysis on the Characteristics and Causes to Disposal of Inheritance without Heirs and Beneficiaries …… (485)
Section 4 The Legislative Enlightenment of People's Concepts of Property Inheritance and Habits of Heritage Disposal in Hubei Province of Contemporary China to Succession Law of Chinese Civil Code …… (488)
1. The Inadequacy of Chinese Definition of Heritage Scope System and Legislative Suggestions for Improvements …… (488)
2. The Inadequacy of Chinese Notice and Announcement of the Beginning of Succession System and Legislative Suggestions for Improvements …… (488)

3. The Inadequacy of Chinese Administration of Heritage System and Legislative Suggestions for Improvements (489)
4. The Inadequacy of Chinese Intestate Succession System and Legislative Suggestions for Improvements (490)
5. The Inadequacy of Chinese Testate Succession System and Legislative Suggestions for Improvements (491)
6. The Inadequacy of Chinese Acceptance and Abandonment of Succession and Bequest System and Legislative Suggestions for Improvements (492)
7. The Inadequacy of Chinese Loss of Succession Rights, Forgiveness of the Deceased and Succession by Subrogation System and Legislative Suggestions for Improvements (492)
8. The Inadequacy of Chinese Maintenance Agreement by Will System and Legislative Suggestions for Supplement (493)
9. The Inadequacy of Chinese Liquidation of Heritage Debt System and Legislative Suggestions for Improvement (493)
10. The Inadequacy of Chinese Heritage Division System and Legislative Suggestions for Improvement (494)
11. The Inadequacy of Chinese Inheritance without Heirs and Beneficiaries System and Legislative Suggestions for Improvement (494)

Volume Two

Chapter Seven Empirical Research on People's Concepts of Property Inheritance and Habits of Heritage Disposal in Jiangxi Province of Contemporary China (497)
Section 1 Overview of Empirical Investigation on People's Concepts of Property Inheritance and Habits of Heritage Disposal in Jiangxi Province of Contemporary China (497)
1. Overview of Investigated Regions (497)
2. Brief Introduction of Empirical Investigation (498)
3. Basic Situations of Respondents (499)
Section 2 Statistics of Investigated Data for Empirical Investigation on People's Concepts of Property Inheritance and Habits of Heritage Disposal in Jiangxi Province of Contemporary China (501)
1. Statistics of Investigated Data on the Definition of Heritage Scope (501)
2. Statistics of Investigated Data on the Notice and Announcement of the Beginning of Succession (504)
3. Statistics of Investigated Data on Administration of Heritage (506)
4. Statistics of Investigated Data on Intestate Succession (510)

5. Statistics of Investigated Data on Testate Succession …………………………… (517)
6. Statistics of Investigated Data on Acceptance and Abandonment of Succession and Bequest ………………………………………………………………………… (521)
7. Statistics of Investigated Data on Loss of Succession Rights, Forgiveness of the Deceased and Succession by Subrogation …………………………………… (526)
8. Statistics of Investigated Data on Succession Agreements …………………… (528)
9. Statistics of Investigated Data on Liquidation of Heritage Debt ……………… (533)
10. Statistics of Investigated Data on Heritage Division ……………………………… (537)
11. Statistics of Investigated Data on Disposal of Inheritance without Heirs and Beneficiaries ……………………………………………………………………… (544)
12. Brief Introduction and Evaluation of Cases Related to Heritage Disposal … (549)
Section 3 Analysis on the Characteristics and Causes to People's Concepts of Property Inheritance and Habits of Heritage Disposal in Jiangxi Province of Contemporary China …………… (559)
1. Analysis on the Characteristics and Causes to the Definition of Heritage Scope ………………………………………………………………………………… (559)
2. Analysis on the Characteristics and Causes to Notice of the Beginning of Succession and Anouncement ……………………………………………………… (562)
3. Analysis on the Characteristics and Causes to Heritage Administration ……… (564)
4. Analysis on the Characteristics and Causes to Intestate Succession ………… (568)
5. Analysis on the Characteristics and Causes to Testate Succession …………… (573)
6. Analysis on the Characteristics and Causes to Acceptance and Abandonment of Succession and Bequest ………………………………………………………… (576)
7. Analysis on the Characteristics and Causes to Loss of Succession Rights, Forgiveness of the Deceased and Succession by Subrogation ………………… (579)
8. Analysis on the Characteristics and Causes to Succession Agreements ……… (581)
9. Analysis on the Characteristics and Causes to Liquidation of Heritage Debt ………………………………………………………………………………… (583)
10. Analysis on the Characteristics and Causes to Heritage Division …………… (586)
11. Analysis on the Characteristics and Causes to Disposal of Inheritance without Heirs and Beneficiaries …………………………………………………… (588)
Section 4 The Legislative Enlightenment of People's Concepts of Property Inheritance and Habits of Heritage Disposal in Jiangxi Province of Contemporary China to Succession Law of Chinese Civil Code ……………………………………………………………… (591)
1. The Inadequacy of Chinese Definition of Heritage Scope System and Legislative Suggestions for Improvements …………………………………………………… (591)
2. The Inadequacy of Chinese Notice and Announcement of the Beginning of Succession System and Legislative Suggestions for Improvements …………… (592)

3. The Inadequacy of Chinese Administration of Heritage System and Legislative Suggestions for Improvements (592)
4. The Inadequacy of Chinese Intestate Succession System and Legislative Suggestions for Improvements (593)
5. The Inadequacy of Chinese Testate Succession System and Legislative Suggestions for Improvements (594)
6. The Inadequacy of Chinese Acceptance and Abandonment of Succession and Bequest System and Legislative Suggestions for Improvements (595)
7. The Inadequacy of Chinese Loss of Succession Rights, Forgiveness of the Deceased and Succession by Subrogation System and Legislative Suggestions for Improvements (596)
8. The Inadequacy of Chinese Maintenance Agreement by Will System and Legislative Suggestions for Supplement (597)
9. The Inadequacy of Chinese Liquidation of Heritage Debt System and Legislative Suggestions for Improvement (597)
10. The Inadequacy of Chinese Heritage Division System and Legislative Suggestions for Improvement (598)
11. The Inadequacy of Chinese Inheritance without Heirs and Beneficiaries System and Legislative Suggestions for Improvement (599)

Chapter Eight Empirical Research on People's Concepts of Property Inheritance and Habits of Heritage Disposal in Sichuan Province of Contemporary China (600)

Section 1 Overview of Empirical Investigation on People's Concepts of Property Inheritance and Habits of Heritage Disposal in Sichuan Province of Contemporary China (600)
1. Overview of Investigated Regions (600)
2. Brief Introduction of Empirical Investigation (601)
3. Basic Situations of Respondents (602)

Section 2 Statistics of Investigated Data for Empirical Investigation on People's Concepts of Property Inheritance and Habits of Heritage Disposal in Sichuan Province of Contemporary China (604)
1. Statistics of Investigated Data on the Definition of Heritage Scope (604)
2. Statistics of Investigated Data on the Notice and Announcement of the Beginning of Succession (607)
3. Statistics of Investigated Data on Administration of Heritage (609)
4. Statistics of Investigated Data on Intestate Succession (613)
5. Statistics of Investigated Data on Testate Succession (620)

6. Statistics of Investigated Data on Acceptance and Abandonment of Succession and Bequest …… (624)
7. Statistics of Investigated Data on Loss of Succession Rights, Forgiveness of the Deceased and Succession by Subrogation …… (628)
8. Statistics of Investigated Data on Succession Agreements …… (630)
9. Statistics of Investigated Data on Liquidation of Heritage Debt …… (634)
10. Statistics of Investigated Data on Heritage Division …… (638)
11. Statistics of Investigated Data on Disposal of Inheritance without Heirs and Beneficiaries …… (644)
12. Brief Introduction and Evaluation of Cases Related to Heritage Disposal …… (648)
Section 3 Analysis on the Characteristics and Causes to People's Concepts of Property Inheritance and Habits of Heritage Disposal in Sichuan Province of Contemporary China …… (659)
1. Analysis on the Characteristics and Causes to the Definition of Heritage Scope …… (659)
2. Analysis on the Characteristics and Causes to Notice of the Beginning of Succession and Anouncement …… (663)
3. Analysis on the Characteristics and Causes to Heritage Administration …… (666)
4. Analysis on the Characteristics and Causes to Intestate Succession …… (670)
5. Analysis on the Characteristics and Causes to Testate Succession …… (679)
6. Analysis on the Characteristics and Causes to Acceptance and Abandonment of Succession and Bequest …… (683)
7. Analysis on the Characteristics and Causes to Loss of Succession Rights, Forgiveness of the Deceased and Succession by Subrogation …… (688)
8. Analysis on the Characteristics and Causes to Succession Agreements …… (690)
9. Analysis on the Characteristics and Causes to Liquidation of Heritage Debt. …… (693)
10. Analysis on the Characteristics and Causes to Heritage Division …… (697)
11. Analysis on the Characteristics and Causes to Disposal of Inheritance without Heirs and Beneficiaries …… (702)
Section 4 The Legislative Enlightenment of People's Concepts of Property Inheritance and Habits of Heritage Disposal in Sichuan Province of Contemporary China to Succession Law of Chinese Civil Code …… (705)
1. The Inadequacy of Chinese Definition of Heritage Scope System and Legislative Suggestions for Improvements …… (705)
2. The Inadequacy of Chinese Notice and Announcement of the Beginning of Succession System and Legislative Suggestions for Improvements …… (706)

3. The Inadequacy of Chinese Administration of Heritage System and Legislative Suggestions for Improvements (707)
4. The Inadequacy of Chinese Intestate Succession System and Legislative Suggestions for Improvements (707)
5. The Inadequacy of Chinese Testate Succession System and Legislative Suggestions for Improvements (709)
6. The Inadequacy of Chinese Acceptance and Abandonment of Succession and Bequest System and Legislative Suggestions for Improvements (709)
7. The Inadequacy of Chinese Loss of Succession Rights, Forgiveness of the Deceased and Succession by Subrogation System and Legislative Suggestions for Improvements (710)
8. The Inadequacy of Chinese Maintenance Agreement by Will System and Legislative Suggestions for Supplement (711)
9. The Inadequacy of Chinese Liquidation of Heritage Debt System and Legislative Suggestions for Improvement (712)
10. The Inadequacy of Chinese Heritage Division System and Legislative Suggestions for Improvement (713)
11. The Inadequacy of Chinese Inheritance without Heirs and Beneficiaries System and Legislative Suggestions for Improvement (714)

Chapter Nine Empirical Research on People's Concepts of Property Inheritance and Habits of Heritage Disposal in Guangdong Province of Contemporary China (715)

Section 1 Overview of Empirical Investigation on People's Concepts of Property Inheritance and Habits of Heritage Disposal in Guangdong Province of Contemporary China (715)
1. Overview of Investigated Regions (715)
2. Brief Introduction of Empirical Investigation (716)
3. Basic Situations of Respondents (717)

Section 2 Statistics of Investigated Data for Empirical Investigation on People's Concepts of Property Inheritance and Habits of Heritage Disposal in Guangdong Province of Contemporary China (719)
1. Statistics of Investigated Data on the Definition of Heritage Scope (719)
2. Statistics of Investigated Data on the Notice and Announcement of the Beginning of Succession (722)
3. Statistics of Investigated Data on Administration of Heritage (724)
4. Statistics of Investigated Data on Intestate Succession (727)
5. Statistics of Investigated Data on Testate Succession (733)
6. Statistics of Investigated Data on Acceptance and Abandonment of Succession and Bequest (735)

7. Statistics of Investigated Data on Loss of Succession Rights, Forgiveness of the Deceased and Succession by Subrogation …… (737)
8. Statistics of Investigated Data on Succession Agreements …… (739)
9. Statistics of Investigated Data on Liquidation of Heritage Debt …… (743)
10. Statistics of Investigated Data on Heritage Division …… (745)
11. Statistics of Investigated Data on Disposal of Inheritance without Heirs and Beneficiaries …… (749)
12. Brief Introduction and Evaluation of Cases Related to Heritage Disposal …… (752)
Section 3 Analysis on the Characteristics and Causes to People's Concepts of Property Inheritance and Habits of Heritage Disposal in Guangdong Province of Contemporary China …… (761)
1. Analysis on the Characteristics and Causes to the Definition of Heritage Scope …… (761)
2. Analysis on the Characteristics and Causes to Notice of the Beginning of Succession and Anouncement …… (764)
3. Analysis on the Characteristics and Causes to Heritage Administration …… (767)
4. Analysis on the Characteristics and Causes to Intestate Succession …… (770)
5. Analysis on the Characteristics and Causes to Testate Succession …… (775)
6. Analysis on the Characteristics and Causes to Acceptance and Abandonment of Succession and Bequest …… (778)
7. Analysis on the Characteristics and Causes to Loss of Succession Rights, Forgiveness of the Deceased and Succession by Subrogation …… (780)
8. Analysis on the Characteristics and Causes to Succession Agreements …… (782)
9. Analysis on the Characteristics and Causes to Liquidation of Heritage Debt …… (784)
10. Analysis on the Characteristics and Causes to Heritage Division …… (786)
11. Analysis on the Characteristics and Causes to Disposal of Inheritance without Heirs and Beneficiaries …… (789)
Section 4 The Legislative Enlightenment of People's Concepts of Property Inheritance and Habits of Heritage Disposal in Guangdong Province of Contemporary China to Succession Law of Chinese Civil Code …… (791)
1. The Inadequacy of Chinese Definition of Heritage Scope System and Legislative Suggestions for Improvements …… (791)
2. The Inadequacy of Chinese Notice and Announcement of the Beginning of Succession System and Legislative Suggestions for Improvements …… (792)

3. The Inadequacy of Chinese Administration of Heritage System and Legislative Suggestions for Improvements (793)
4. The Inadequacy of Chinese Intestate Succession System and Legislative Suggestions for Improvements (793)
5. The Inadequacy of Chinese Testate Succession System and Legislative Suggestions for Improvements (794)
6. The Inadequacy of Chinese Acceptance and Abandonment of Succession and Bequest System and Legislative Suggestions for Improvements (795)
7. The Inadequacy of Chinese Loss of Succession Rights, Forgiveness of the Deceased and Succession by Subrogation System and Legislative Suggestions for Improvements (795)
8. Legislative Suggestions of Chinese Maintenance Agreement of Succession (796)
9. The Inadequacy of Chinese Liquidation of Heritage Debt System and Legislative Suggestions for Improvement (796)
10. The Inadequacy of Chinese Heritage Division System and Legislative Suggestions for Improvement (797)
11. The Inadequacy of Chinese Inheritance without Heirs and Beneficiaries System and Legislative Suggestions for Improvement (797)
Chapter Ten Empirical Research on People's Concepts of Property Inheritance and Habits of Heritage Disposal in Hainan Province of Contemporary China (798)
Section 1 Overview of Empirical Investigation on People's Concepts of Property Inheritance and Habits of Heritage Disposal in Hainan Province of Contemporary China (798)
1. Overview of Investigated Regions (798)
2. Brief Introduction of Empirical Investigation (798)
3. Basic Situations of Respondents (800)
Section 2 Statistics of Investigated Data for Empirical Investigation on People's Concepts of Property Inheritance and Habits of Heritage Disposal in Hainan Province of Contemporary China (801)
1. Statistics of Investigated Data on the Definition of Heritage Scope (801)
2. Statistics of Investigated Data on the Notice and Announcement of the Beginning of Succession (804)
3. Statistics of Investigated Data on Administration of Heritage (806)
4. Statistics of Investigated Data on Intestate Succession (809)
5. Statistics of Investigated Data on Testate Succession (815)
6. Statistics of Investigated Data on Acceptance and Abandonment of Succession and Bequest (819)

7. Statistics of Investigated Data on Loss of Succession Rights, Forgiveness of the Deceased and Succession by Subrogation …………………………… (822)
8. Statistics of Investigated Data on Succession Agreements …………………… (824)
9. Statistics of Investigated Data on Liquidation of Heritage Debt ……………… (828)
10. Statistics of Investigated Data on Heritage Division ………………………… (831)
11. Statistics of Investigated Data on Disposal of Inheritance without Heirs and Beneficiaries ……………………………………………………………………… (836)
12. Brief Introduction and Evaluation of Cases Related to Heritage Disposal … (841)
Section 3 Analysis on the Characteristics and Causes to People's Concepts of Property Inheritance and Habits of Heritage Disposal in Hainan Province of Contemporary China ……………………… (851)
1. Analysis on the Characteristics and Causes to the Definition of Heritage Scope ……………………………………………………………………………… (851)
2. Analysis on the Characteristics and Causes to Notice of the Beginning of Succession and Anouncement ……………………………………………………… (854)
3. Analysis on the Characteristics and Causes to Heritage Administration ……… (856)
4. Analysis on the Characteristics and Causes to Intestate Succession ………… (859)
5. Analysis on the Characteristics and Causes to Testate Succession …………… (865)
6. Analysis on the Characteristics and Causes to Acceptance and Abandonment of Succession and Bequest ……………………………………………………… (867)
7. Analysis on the Characteristics and Causes to Loss of Succession Rights, Forgiveness of the Deceased and Succession by Subrogation ………………… (871)
8. Analysis on the Characteristics and Causes to Succession Agreements ……… (873)
9. Analysis on the Characteristics and Causes to Liquidation of Heritage Debt ……………………………………………………………………………… (875)
10. Analysis on the Characteristics and Causes to Heritage Division …………… (878)
11. Analysis on the Characteristics and Causes to Inheritance without Heirs and Be ……………………………………………………………………………… (882)
Section 4 The Legislative Enlightenment of People's Concepts of Property Inheritance and Habits of Heritage Disposal in Hainan Province of Contemporary China to Succession Law of Chinese Civil Code ……………………………………………………………………… (884)
1. The Inadequacy of Chinese Definition of Heritage Scope System and Legislative Suggestions for Improvements ………………………………………………… (885)
2. The Inadequacy of Chinese Notice and Announcement of the Beginning of Succession System and Legislative Suggestions for Improvements …………… (885)
3. The Inadequacy of Chinese Administration of Heritage System and Legislative Suggestions for Improvements ………………………………………………… (886)

4. The Inadequacy of Chinese Intestate Succession System and Legislative Suggestions for Improvements (887)
5. The Inadequacy of Chinese Testate Succession System and Legislative Suggestions for Improvements (888)
6. The Inadequacy of Chinese Acceptance and Abandonment of Succession and Bequest System and Legislative Suggestions for Improvements (888)
7. The Inadequacy of Chinese Loss of Succession Rights, Forgiveness of the Deceased and Succession by Subrogation System and Legislative Suggestions for Improvements (889)
8. Legislative Suggestions of Chinese Maintenance Agreement of Succession (890)
9. The Inadequacy of Chinese Liquidation of Heritage Debt System and Legislative Suggestions for Improvement (890)
10. The Inadequacy of Chinese Heritage Division System and Legislative Suggestions for Improvement (891)
11. The Inadequacy of Chinese Inheritance without Heirs and Beneficiaries System and Legislative Suggestions for Improvement (891)

Chapter Eleven Empirical Research on Private Entrepreneurs' Concepts of Property Inheritance and Habits of Heritage Disposal in Fujian Province of Contemporary China (893)

Section 1 Overview of Empirical Investigation on Private Entrepreneurs' Concepts of Property Inheritance and Habits of Heritage Disposal in Fujian Province of Contemporary China (893)
1. Overview of Investigated Regions (893)
2. Brief Introduction of Empirical Investigation (894)
3. Basic Situations of Respondents (896)

Section 2 Statistics of Investigated Data for Empirical Investigation on Private Entrepreneurs' Concepts of Property Inheritance and Habits of Heritage Disposal in Fujian Province of Contemporary China (897)
1. Statistics of Investigated Data on the Definition of Heritage Scope (897)
2. Statistics of Investigated Data on the Notice and Announcement of the Beginning of Succession (899)
3. Statistics of Investigated Data on Administration of Heritage (901)
4. Statistics of Investigated Data on Intestate Succession (904)
5. Statistics of Investigated Data on Testate Succession (910)
6. Statistics of Investigated Data on Acceptance and Abandonment of Succession and Bequest (912)
7. Statistics of Investigated Data on Loss of Succession Rights, Forgiveness of the Deceased and Succession by Subrogation (914)

8. Statistics of Investigated Data on Succession Agreements …………………… (915)
9. Statistics of Investigated Data on Liquidation of Heritage Debt ……………… (918)
10. Statistics of Investigated Data on Heritage Division ………………………… (920)
11. Statistics of Investigated Data on Disposal of Inheritance without Heirs and Beneficiaries …………………………………………………………………… (923)
12. Brief Introduction and Evaluation of Cases Related to Heritage Disposal … (926)
Section 3 Analysis on the Characteristics and Causes to Private Entrepreneurs' Concepts of Property Inheritance and Habits of Heritage Disposal in Fujian Province of Contemporary China … (939)
1. Analysis on the Characteristics and Causes to the Definition of Heritage Scope …………………………………………………………………… (939)
2. Analysis on the Characteristics and Causes to Notice of the Beginning of Succession and Anouncement ……………………………………………… (942)
3. Analysis on the Characteristics and Causes to Heritage Administration ……… (944)
4. Analysis on the Characteristics and Causes to Intestate Succession ………… (948)
5. Analysis on the Characteristics and Causes to Testate Succession …………… (954)
6. Analysis on the Characteristics and Causes to Acceptance and Abandonment of Succession and Bequest ……………………………………………… (957)
7. Analysis on the Characteristics and Causes to Loss of Succession Rights, Forgiveness of the Deceased and Succession by Subrogation ………………… (960)
8. Analysis on the Characteristics and Causes to Succession Agreements ……… (961)
9. Analysis on the Characteristics and Causes to Liquidation of Heritage Debt …………………………………………………………………… (964)
10. Analysis on the Characteristics and Causes to Heritage Division …………… (967)
11. Analysis on the Characteristics and Causes to Disposal of Inheritance without Heirs and Beneficiaries ……………………………………………… (969)
Section 4 The Legislative Enlightenment of Private Entrepreneurs' Concepts of Property Inheritance and Habits of Heritage Disposal in Fujian Province of Contemporary China to Succession Law of Chinese Civil Code ……………………… (972)
1. The Inadequacy of Chinese Definition of Heritage Scope System and Legislative Suggestions for Improvements ……………………………………… (972)
2. The Inadequacy of Chinese Notice and Announcement of the Beginning of Succession System and Legislative Suggestions for Improvements …………… (973)
3. The Inadequacy of Chinese Administration of Heritage System and Legislative Suggestions for Improvements ……………………………………… (973)
4. The Inadequacy of Chinese Intestate Succession System and Legislative Suggestions for Improvements ……………………………………… (974)

5. The Inadequacy of Chinese Testate Succession System and Legislative Suggestions for Improvements ······ (975)
6. The Inadequacy of Chinese Acceptance and Abandonment of Succession and Bequest System and Legislative Suggestions for Improvements ······ (976)
7. The Inadequacy of Chinese Loss of Succession Rights, Forgiveness of the Deceased and Succession by Subrogation System and Legislative Suggestions for Improvements ······ (977)
8. The Inadequacy of Chinese Maintenance Agreement by Will System and Legislative Suggestions for Supplement ······ (977)
9. The Inadequacy of Chinese Liquidation of Heritage Debt System and Legislative Suggestions for Improvement ······ (978)
10. The Inadequacy of Chinese Heritage Division System and Legislative Suggestions for Improvement ······ (979)
11. The Inadequacy of Chinese Inheritance without Heirs and Beneficiaries System and Legislative Suggestions for Improvement ······ (980)

Chapter Twelve Empirical Research on Private Entrepreneurs' Concepts of Property Inheritance and Habits of Heritage Disposal in Sichuan, Chongqing and Other Provinces of Contemporary China ······ (981)

Section 1 Overview of Empirical Investigation on Private Entrepreneurs' Concepts of Property Inheritance and Habits of Heritage Disposal in Sichuan, Chongqing and Other Provinces of Contemporary China ······ (981)
1. Background of Investigation ······ (981)
2. Brief Introduction of Empirical Investigation ······ (981)
3. Basic Situations of Respondents ······ (983)

Section 2 Statistics of Investigated Data for Empirical Investigation on Private Entrepreneurs' Concepts of Property Inheritance and Habits of Heritage Disposal in Sichuan, Chongqing and Other Provinces of Contemporary China ······ (984)
1. Statistics of Investigated Data on the Definition of Heritage Scope ······ (984)
2. Statistics of Investigated Data on the Notice and Announcement of the Beginning of Succession ······ (987)
3. Statistics of Investigated Data on Administration of Heritage ······ (989)
4. Statistics of Investigated Data on Intestate Succession ······ (992)
5. Statistics of Investigated Data on Testate Succession ······ (999)
6. Statistics of Investigated Data on Acceptance and Abandonment of Succession and Bequest ······ (1003)
7. Statistics of Investigated Data on Loss of Succession Rights, Forgiveness of the Deceased and Succession by Subrogation ······ (1007)

8. Statistics of Investigated Data on Succession Agreements ………………… (1009)
9. Statistics of Investigated Data on Liquidation of Heritage Debt ……………… (1013)
10. Statistics of Investigated Data on Heritage Division ……………………… (1017)
11. Statistics of Investigated Data on Disposal of Inheritance without Heirs and Beneficiaries ……………………………………………………………… (1022)
12. Brief Introduction and Evaluation of Cases Related to Heritage Disposal … (1027)
Section 3 Analysis on the Characteristics and Causes to Private Entrepreneurs' Concepts of Property Inheritance and Habits of Heritage Disposal in Sichuan, Chongqing and Other Provinces of Contemporary China ……………………………………… (1038)
1. Analysis on the Characteristics and Causes to the Definition of Heritage Scope ……………………………………………………………………… (1038)
2. Analysis on the Characteristics and Causes to Notice of the Beginning of Succession and Announcement ……………………………………………… (1041)
3. Analysis on the Characteristics and Causes to Heritage Administration ……… (1044)
4. Analysis on the Characteristics and Causes to Intestate Succession ………… (1047)
5. Analysis on the Characteristics and Causes to Testate Succession …………… (1054)
6. Analysis on the Characteristics and Causes to Acceptance and Abandonment of Succession and Bequest ……………………………………………… (1057)
7. Analysis on the Characteristics and Causes to Loss of Succession Rights, Forgiveness of the Deceased and Succession by Subrogation ……………… (1060)
8. Analysis on the Characteristics and Causes to Succession Agreements ……… (1062)
9. Analysis on the Characteristics and Causes to Liquidation of Heritage Debt ……………………………………………………………………… (1064)
10. Analysis on the Characteristics and Causes to Heritage Division …………… (1068)
11. Analysis on the Characteristics and Causes to Disposal of Inheritance without Heirs and Beneficiaries ………………………………………………… (1071)
Section 4 The Legislative Enlightenment of Private Entrepreneurs' Concepts of Property Inheritance and Habits of Heritage Disposal in Sichuan, Chongqing and Other Provinces of Contemporary China to Succession Law of Chinese Civil Code ……………… (1073)
1. The Inadequacy of Chinese Definition of Heritage Scope System and Legislative Suggestions for Improvements ……………………………………… (1074)
2. The Inadequacy of Chinese Notice and Announcement of the Beginning of Succession System and Legislative Suggestions for Improvements ……………… (1074)
3. The Inadequacy of Chinese Administration of Heritage System and Legislative Suggestions for Improvements ……………………………………… (1075)
4. The Inadequacy of Chinese Intestate Succession System and Legislative Suggestions for Improvements ……………………………………… (1076)

5. The Inadequacy of Chinese Testate Succession System and Legislative Suggestions for Improvements …… (1077)
6. The Inadequacy of Chinese Acceptance and Abandonment of Succession and Bequest System and Legislative Suggestions for Improvements …… (1077)
7. The Inadequacy of Chinese Loss of Succession Rights, Forgiveness of the Deceased and Succession by Subrogation System and Legislative Suggestions for Improvements …… (1078)
8. The Inadequacy of Chinese Maintenance Agreement by Will System and Legislative Suggestions for Supplement …… (1079)
9. The Inadequacy of Chinese Liquidation of Heritage Debt System and Legislative Suggestions for Improvement …… (1079)
10. The Inadequacy of Chinese Heritage Division System and Legislative Suggestions for Improvement …… (1080)
11. The Inadequacy of Chinese Inheritance without Heirs and Beneficiaries System and Legislative Suggestions for Improvement …… (1081)

Bibliographies …… (1082)

Appendix

Introduction of the Research Center on Foreign Family Law and Women's Theory of Southwest University of Political Science and Law(SWUPL), China(Chinese and English) …… (1086)

Contents of the Books Published(2006 to 2012) by the Research Center on Foreign Family Law and Women's Theory of SWUPL, China …… (1090)

前　言

自1978年西南政法学院复办以来，我国著名的婚姻法专家、中国法学会婚姻法学研究会副总干事杨怀英教授担任我校婚姻法研究方向的学科带头人。1985年3月至7月，我校承担了司法部委托的全国法律专业婚姻法师资进修班的教学任务。当时全国著名的婚姻法专家巫昌祯、杨大文、王德意、李忠芳、任国钧等教授应邀前来我校，与我校杨怀英教授及胡平等教师共同为来自全国的婚姻法师资进修班学员上课，传授婚姻法学的理论知识和教学经验。如今，该婚姻法师资进修班学员大部分都成为了各高校婚姻法领域的知名专家学者和骨干教师，他们为国家培养了大批优秀的人才。因此，可以说，我校是我国婚姻法学人才培养的摇篮。在科研方面，杨怀英教授先后主编出版：《滇西南边疆少数民族婚姻家庭与法的研究》（法律出版社1988年出版）、《中国婚姻法论》（重庆出版社1989年出版，1991年荣获重庆市社科优秀科研成果三等奖）、《凉山彝族奴隶社会法律制度研究》（四川民族出版社1994年出版，1996年荣获四川省社科优秀科研成果二等奖）等专著和教材。1995年杨怀英教授去世后，由中国法学会婚姻法学研究会常务理事邓宏碧教授担任我校婚姻法研究方向的学科带头人。邓宏碧教授、胡平副教授等老教师带领讲授婚姻法课程的教师，继续努力进行教学和科研工作。尤其值得指出的是，邓宏碧教授主编的《中国少数民族人口政策研究》（国家社会科学“八五”规划重点科研项目，重庆出版社1998年出版），2001年荣获重庆市社会科学优秀科研成果一等奖。

薪火相传。本人于1979年9月考入西南政法学院法律系本科学习，1983年6月毕业任教一年后，于1984年9月考入西南政法学院攻读民法专业硕士研究生，师从杨怀英教授，主要研究方向为婚姻家庭继承法。1987年7月本人硕士研究生毕业后留校任教至今。我自1979年9月在母校学习法律知识、毕业后主要从事婚姻家庭继承法及妇女儿童老人权益法律保护的教学和科研工作，至今已近40年了。这近40年里，在母校各级领导和老师们的辛勤培养下，在本人的勤奋工作和刻苦钻研下，我由一名学生逐步成长为助教、讲师、副教授、教授、博士生导师、博士后合作导师；于1996年5月起担任民法教研室副主任，1999 年 5 月起担任民法教研室主任，2003 年 5 月起至今担任婚姻家庭继承法教研室主任。在婚姻法学界老一辈专家的辛勤培养下，本人于 1996 年 7 月起担任中国法学会婚姻法学研究会理事；于 1999 年 7 月起担任中国法学会婚姻法学研究会常务理事；于 2004 年 7 月起至今，担任中国法学会婚姻法学研究会副会长；于 2011 年 11 月起担任家庭法国际学会执行委员会委员；于 2014 年 8 月起至 2017 年 6 月，担任家庭法国际学会执行委员会委员兼学术委员会委员；于 2017 年 7 月至今，担任家庭法国际学会副主席兼学术委员会委员。必须说明，自 2011 年 11 月我由第十四届家庭法国际学会主席、澳大利亚悉尼大学法学院 Patrick Parkinson 教授[①]提名，经家庭法国际学会执行委员会研究同意后受聘担任家庭法国际学会执行委员会委员以来，我每年积极撰写论文，“以文参会”，先后到意大利、韩国、法国、英国、巴西、荷兰等国出席家庭法国际学会召开的执委会、地区性会议和世界大会，在会上积极发言，发出中国声音、阐述中国见解，增进了其他国家学者对中国婚姻家庭领域的新问题和最新修改立法的了解，扩大了中国婚姻家庭法学者在家庭法学术研究领域的国际影响力。2014 年 8 月，家庭法国际学会在巴西召开“第十五届家庭法世界大会”，会上我当选为家庭法国际学会执行委员会委员兼学术委员会委员。2017 年 7 月，家庭法国际学会在荷兰召开“第十六届家庭法世界大会”，会上我当选为家庭法国际学会副主席并继续兼任学术委员会委员。作为中国婚姻家庭法专家，在家庭法国际学会中我是第一位来自中国的副主席，为祖国争了光。从此，在这一家庭法国际学术交流的最高平台上，我可以讲述中国故事、提供中国观点、贡献中国智慧。这有利于进一步促进中外婚姻家庭继承法研究领域的国际学术交流，为各国婚姻家庭继承法律制度的改革提供参考，以造福于全人类的婚姻家庭。

在校内学术研究和人才培养平台方面。2003 年 12 月至 2004 年 12 月，本人受国家留学基金资助由教育部公派出国留学，作为访问学者到澳大利亚悉尼大学法学院进修外国家庭法一年。我留学回国后，于 2005 年 1 月向学校提出建立“西南政法大学外国家庭法及妇女理论研究中心”的书面申请。2005 年 4 月 1 日，西南政法大学校长办公会议批准同意该研究中心成立，任命我担任主任。自 2005 年 4 月该研究中心成立以来，本人夙夜忧虑，恐负厚望，带领研究中心的教师和研究生组成科研创新团队，勤奋科研，不敢懈怠。近年来，我担任项目负责人主持、带领团队成员共同完成并公开出版的中文著作和译著有 10 余部，主要有：《外国婚姻家庭法比较研究》（重庆市哲学社会科学“十五”规划项目，2006 年 1 月出版）、《加拿大家庭法汇编》（2006 年 1 月出版）、《中国大陆与港、澳、

① Patrick Parkinson 教授是我受中国国家留学基金资助以访问学者身份于 2003 年 12 月~2004 年 12 月在澳大利亚悉尼大学法学院进修外国家庭法的导师。

台继承法比较研究》(重庆市教育委员会人文社科项目，2007年1月出版)、《当代中国民众继承习惯调查实证研究》(国家社科基金项目子课题，2008年1月出版)、《澳大利亚家庭法（2008年修正）》(重庆市教育委员会人文社科重点项目，2009年1月出版)、《美国家庭法精要（第五版）》(2010年3月出版)、《改革开放三十年（1978~2008）中国婚姻家庭继承法研究之回顾与展望》(西南政法大学重点项目，2010年1月出版)、《中国婚姻家庭法立法研究》(第二版，2010年1月出版)、《外国继承法比较与中国民法典继承编制定研究》(国家社科基金项目结项成果著作，经专家匿名评审后被鉴定为“优秀”等级，2010年入选首届《国家哲学社会科学成果文库》，全国哲学社会科学办公室在“出版说明”中指出：入选成果代表当前相关领域学术研究的前沿水平，体现我国哲学社会科学界的学术创造力，按照“统一标识、统一封面、统一版式、统一标准”的总体要求组织出版。该著作于2011年3月出版)、《澳大利亚法律的传统与发展（第三版）》(2011年5月出版)、《当代中国内地与港、澳、台婚姻家庭法比较研究》(中国司法部“法治建设与法学理论研究”课题成果著作，2012年5月出版)、《中国继承法修改热点难点问题研究》(2013年10月出版)、《我国防治家庭暴力情况实证调查研究——以我国六省市被抽样调查地区防治家庭暴力情况为对象》(中国法学会部级法学研究课题，2014年5月出版)、《21世纪家庭法与家事司法：实践与变革》(2016年10月出版)、《中国妇女儿童权益法律保障情况实证调查研究——以中国五省市被抽样调查地区妇女儿童权益法律保障情况为对象（上、下卷）》(中国法学会部级法学研究课题，2017年3月出版)、《中国家事审判改革暨家事法修改理论与实务研究》(2018年4月出版)等。此外，本人应邀与美国、意大利学者合作撰写美国法学院比较家庭法英文教材1部：*Practical Global Family Law——United States，China and Italy*（2009年4月在美国出版）。

在国内学术研究和人才培养平台方面。为促进婚姻家庭继承法领域的学术研究和学术交流，本人于2005年起创办《家事法研究》学术论文集刊。自《家事法研究》2006年首卷面世以来，至2011年的六年间，先后出版了2005年卷至2010年卷共计六卷，推出了一批具有前沿性的学术论文，培养了一批学术新人，受到国内学术界同仁和实务界人士的肯定和好评，产生了良好的社会影响。为进一步扩大《家事法研究》的学术影响，经本人提出申请，中国法学会婚姻法学研究会常务理事会研究同意，《家事法研究》从2011年卷起转为“中国法学会婚姻法学研究会”的会刊。可以相信，在该研究会的精心主办下，《家事法研究》将在法学理论研究与司法实务探索相结合的沃土中更加茁壮成长，枝繁叶茂！

长江后浪推前浪。为继续推进我国婚姻家庭继承法学理论与实务研究，培养更多的学术新人，自2012年起本人主编出版《家事法研究学术文库》丛书。此文库丛书作为学术研究和学术交流的平台，遴选出版婚姻家庭继承法研究领域具有前沿性、创新性的博士学位论文和学术著作，每年拟出版 2~3 本。本文库丛书的出版目的，旨在通过婚姻家庭继承法学研究领域最新学术著作的出版，推出一批前沿理论和实务问题研究的新作，促进我国婚姻家庭继承法学研究朝着更深、更广的方向发展，以更多的优秀研究成果为我国民众处理婚姻家庭继承问题提供参考，为国家完善立法、改进司法服务。至 2018 年年底，本文库已出版著作 19 部，在 2019 年拟将出版《中国民法典编纂视野下家事审判改革暨家事法修改研究》、《中国遗产处理制度系统化构建研究》、《当代中国民众财产继承观念与遗产处理习惯实证调查研究》（上、下卷）、《中国婚姻家庭法理论与实践研究》、《中国继承法理论与实践研究》、《我国成年人监护制度立法完善研究》、《未成年人监护制度研究》，以飨读者。

最后，我衷心感谢编辑老师们对本文库丛书出版所付出的辛勤劳动！

陈　苇

《家事法研究学术文库》主编

2019 年 2 月 28 日

作者序

《当代中国民众财产继承观念与遗产处理习惯实证调查研究》是西南政法大学陈苇教授主持完成的司法部科研项目“我国遗产处理制度系统化构建研究”（编号16SFB2036）的子课题成果。

为适应和调整社会主义市场经济关系、婚姻家庭关系新情况新问题的需要，2014年10月中国共产党的十八届四中全会通过的《中共中央关于全面推进依法治国若干重大问题的决定》提出了编纂“民法典”的重要任务。调整财产继承关系的“民法分则继承编”是民法典的重要组成部分。为保护继承人的财产权益和实现家庭的扶养职能，维护第三人的利益和交易安全，促进我国经济发展、家庭幸福与社会和谐稳定，“民法典继承编”的编纂被我国立法机关提上了工作日程。2016年11月，西南政法大学陈苇教授主持申报的司法部科研项目“我国遗产处理制度系统化构建研究”（编号16SFB2036）被批准立项。为了给开展本项目的理论研究和制度研究提供基本国情资料，必须了解当代中国民众的财产继承观念与遗产处理习惯；为推进科学立法、民主立法，为我国“民法典继承编”的编纂提供基本国情资料，也必须了解当代中国民众的财产继承观念与遗产处理习惯，在此时代背景下，我们组织开展“当代中国民众财产继承观念与遗产处理习惯实证调查研究”这一司法部项目的子课题研究。

继承法是调整一国民众的财产继承关系之法律规范的总和。财产继承关系，涉及千家万户、男女老少的切身利益，也涉及第三人的利益和交易安全。自1949年10月中华人民共和国成立以来，我国已出版一部《当代中国民众继承习惯调查实证研究》的著作（群众出版社2008年出版），但此著作是以2005年8月至2006年7月期间进行的“中国民众继承习惯实证调查”的统计数据为基础撰写的，距今已有十余年之久。为此，我们选取“当代中国民众财产继承观念与遗产处理习惯”这一重要现实问题作为实证调查的研究对象，开展1949年中华人民共和国成立以来我国第二次全国较大范围的民众继承习惯调查。考虑到本课题组人力、物力的限制和选择具有合作意向的部分高校教师共同进行社会调查的可能性，课题负责人陈苇教授选择我国以下十省市作为被调查地区，包括东北部的吉林省、东部的上海市、北部的河北省、中部的湖北省和江西省、南部的广东省和海南省、东南部的福建省、西南部的重庆市和四川省，然后联系确定了十省市高校的教师担任各省市调查组组长，共同组织进行“当代中国民众财产继承观念与遗产处理习惯实证调查研究”这一子课题。本次参加实地调查和调查数据统计汇总的师生合计有1295人次，通过入户访问调查，发放了5739份调查问卷供被调查者填写，同时还进行了个人访谈，以收集遗产纠纷的典型案例。十省市调查组撰写完成的 11 份调查研究报告，共同构成了本课题成果著作的内容。本著作既可以填补中国当代民众继承习惯实证调查的理论空白，又可以为修改和完善我国《继承法》和“中国民法典继承编”的编纂提供第一手国情资料，还可以为我国司法机关释法和执法、为法律服务工作者和财产继承关系当事人处理遗产问题提供参考，因此具有重要的学术价值、理论意义和实际应用价值。

2017 年 10 月 1 日作为民法典重要组成部分的我国《民法总则》已经实施。2018 年 9 月，我国立法机关已经公布“民法分则各编（草案）”（包括继承编草案），征求社会各界意见。2019 年 7 月 5 日“民法典继承编”（草案二次审议稿）已经在中国人大网公布，正在征求社会公众意见。习近平总书记指出：全面推进依法治国总目标是建设中国特色社会主义法治体系、建设社会主义法治国家。要把体现人民利益、反映人民愿望、维护人民权益、增进人民福祉落实到依法治国全过程，使法律及其实施充分体现人民意志。要推进科学立法、民主立法、依法立法，使每一项立法都符合宪法精神、反映人民意志、得到人民拥护。要坚持“立改废释”并举，增强法律法规的及时性、系统性、针对性、有效性。我们认为，《当代中国民众财产继承观念与遗产处理习惯实证调查研究》的 11 份调查研究报告各自在一定程度上反映了我国十省市被调查民众包括部分地区民营企业主的财产继承观念和遗产处理习惯，各章作者基于自己的研究结论所提的立法建议也不尽相同，它的出版可以为我国立法机关编纂“中国民法典继承编”提供不同视角立法观点的参考，有利于推进“科学立法、民主立法”。

回顾本课题的研究过程，自 2016 年 11 月起至 12 月，课题负责人陈苇教授组织设计调查问卷、遴选我国十省市作为被调查地区、联系确定十省市调查组组长，十省市调查组组长负责召集、遴选本省市籍的学生调查员，组织学生调查员参加“社会调查动员暨培训会”；自 2017 年 1 月至 2 月，十省市学生调查员各自在自己的家乡开展“入户访问调查”，发放调查问卷供被调查者填写和进行个人访谈以收集遗产纠纷案例；自 2017 年 3 月至 4 月，十省市调查组组长组织学生统计员进行本省市调查数据的录入统计，制作完成本省市调查统计数据汇总表的定稿。2017 年 4 月，陈苇教授撰写完成“当代中国民众财产继承观念与遗产处理习惯实证调查研究的写作提纲和写作要求”发送给十省市调查组组长。从 2017 年 5 月起，十省市调查组组长根据此写作提纲与要求，各自组织本地作者以本省市的调查统计数据汇总表为基础，收集相关参考文献，并在中国裁判文书网等下载各级人民法院对遗产纠纷案件的司法裁判文书，合作撰写本省市民众财产继承观念与遗产处理习惯实证调查研究稿件的初稿、第二稿、第三稿（有的省市先后修改撰写了第四、五、六、七、八稿不等）。其间，根据陈苇教授的历次修改补充建议和中期评审专家的意见，各省市调查组组长对本省市调查研究报告稿件多次进行了相应的修改和补充，至 2018 年 12 月底十省市调查组组长全部向陈苇教授提交了本省市调查研究报告的定稿。从 2019 年 1 月起，陈苇教授继续对我国十省市调查研究报告稿件进行审阅和修改补充，然后组织重庆地区调查组的博士生对这些稿件统一进行了三次修改补充，最终于 2019 年 6 月底完成了我国十省市调查研究报告的 11 份定稿（其中，有 9 份为我国九省市各自的民众继承习惯调查研究报告，还有 2 份分别为福建省民营企业主继承习惯调查研究报告和川渝等地民营企业主继承习惯调查研究报告），共计150余万字。回顾自2016年11月初起至2019年6月底止，历时两年零八个月，我们为完成《当代中国民众财产继承观念与遗产处理习惯实证调查研究》这一司法部项目的子课题，经常夜以继日地写作，对十省市稿件多次进行修改和补充（有的省市稿件进行修改补充达10次以上），可谓竭尽全力，终于把本著作奉献在读者的面前。但由于我们的学识有限，本著作可能还存在某些不足，恳请各位长辈和同仁不吝指正，对此我们表示衷心的感谢！

本著作共计十二章，各章撰稿人如下（按撰写章节先后为序）：

第一章：陈苇、陈法

第二章：陈苇、石婷、白玉、刘宇娇

第三章：李洪祥、苗艺璇、高岩、马旭、贺海燕、张远、吴天宜、程藉瑶

第四章：许莉、白玉、张叶、柯婵娟

第五章：罗杰、贺海燕、尹鸽

第六章：孟令志、白玉、贾艳艳、李想、王传印、元雨、彭锦

第七章：曹贤信、贺海燕、曾瑞玉

第八章：陈苇、李艳、白玉、刘宇娇

第九章：卓冬青、郭丽红、黄蔚菁、白玉

第十章：胡明玉、叶英萍、贺海燕、王彦翔、文灿

第十一章：何丽新、贺海燕、孙菁、余虹宇、王思颖

第十二章：陈苇、石雷、贺海燕、郭庆敏、占泸霞

最后，我代表全体作者，对我指导的博士研究生白玉、刘宇娇、郭庆敏、贺海燕四位同学为本书稿件的辛勤修改补充和校对工作表示衷心的感谢！对中国人民公安大学出版社的编辑老师们对本书出版的辛勤编辑工作表示衷心的感谢！！

陈　苇

2019年7月26日

鸣　谢

我们向参加《当代中国民众财产继承观念与遗产处理习惯实证调查》的入户问卷调查和个人访谈、调查问卷的统计和复核工作的师生们表示衷心的感谢！参加本次我国十省市（包括重庆市、上海市、吉林省、河北省、湖北省、江西省、广东省、海南省、福建省和四川省）实地调查和调查数据统计汇总的师生合计1295人次。

一、我国十省市被调查地区的调查组组长、副组长名单（排名不分先后）

重庆市调查组组长：西南政法大学陈苇教授
副组长：西南政法大学胡苷用副教授
上海市调查组组长：华东政法大学许莉教授
吉林省调查组组长：吉林大学李洪祥教授
河北省调查组组长：燕山大学罗杰副教授
湖北省调查组组长：中南财经政法大学孟令志副教授
江西省调查组组长：赣南师范大学曹贤信副教授
广东省调查组组长：中山大学卓冬青副教授
副组长：广东工业大学郭丽红教授
海南省调查组组长：海南大学叶英萍教授
福建省调查组组长：厦门大学何丽新教授
四川省调查组组长：西南政法大学陈苇教授
副组长：西南政法大学胡苷用副教授

二、参加本次我国十省市民众财产继承观念与遗产处理习惯实证调查的调查员和统计员师生名单（排名不分先后，总计1295人次）

（一）重庆市的调查员和统计员师生合计148人次

1. 重庆市的社会调查人员名单（合计119人）

（1）组织开展社会调查的教师名单（合计6人）

西南政法大学民商法学院：陈苇教授（教师组长）、胡苷用副教授（教师副组长）、党总支书记张伟莉副教授、李兆玉副院长、年级辅导员蒋莉老师、李扬副教授

（2）参加社会调查的学生名单（合计113人）

参加实地调研和提交调查问卷的调查员（合计113人）

西南政法大学法学院2014级法学本科学生（50人）：

第一组：熊玲（大组长）、周锐、陶明月、张旭、谭华蓉、冉雪莲、詹智涵、谭妍妮、秦梦琪、田其娇

第二组：向文丽（小组长）、黄栏馨、何宜璘、杨秀瑛、喻灵香、邓馨、牟红平、钱艳月、郑润洁、陈鹏

第三组：卞先银（小组长）、夏梓棋、周琳皓、蒋佳琪、姚玲、梁九平、文江斌、曾陆林、温碧莹、石庆柱

第四组：黄月婷（小组长）、张嘉艺、饶菁、王颖鸿、任清林、杨欣谊、任虹霓、赵煦阳、祁渝松、邱雅欣

第五组：刘海洋（小组长）、王枝枝、雷华容、鲜路、黄文舒、屈柯辛、李杰、王双双、张军、蒋桢

西南政法大学民商法学院2014级法学本科学生（50人）：

第一组：曾子洋（小组长）、刘磊、冯琴秋、帅雅绮、潘小洪、谢婷、肖红、唐雪佼、王江杨、周林

第二组：陈琪琦（小组长）、米钦、徐攀、黄茜、周宇婷、王雨琪、谭双、赵丹丹、费文志、李琪

第三组：陈源媛（小组长）、周游、李春芳、马惠敏、邓茜文、刘天颖（大组长）、王益为、易侠伶、匡润发、李晓冬

第四组：陆巧（小组长）、姜雨宏、黄镜璇、胡玉洁、张瀚文、张雪、刘睿杰、秦思、张兴建、廖铭琪

第五组：黄啸（小组长）、蒋艳林、陈若诗、傅先明、钟玉婕、邓天翊、丁姝月、冉建渝、黄佳雯、陈倩

西南政法大学民商法学院2015级法学本科学生（13人）：张粲敏（小组长）、文智慧、吕丹、姚卓杭、田柔、余志勇、邓若杨、李秋吉、杨松蕾、吴瑶瑶、冉丽、田振华、申诗语

2. 重庆市的调查数据统计人员名单（合计29人）

（1）组织进行调查数据统计的教师名单（合计2人）

西南政法大学民商法学院：陈苇教授（教师组长）、胡苷用副教授（教师副组长）

（2）参加调查数据统计的学生名单（合计27人）

西南政法大学民商法学院博士研究生（1人）：陈钊（大组长）

西南政法大学民商法学院2015级硕士研究生（3人）：吕德天、刘宇娇、张文彩

西南政法大学民商法学院2016级硕士研究生（12人）：李睿、郑静文、张林玉、石雨杭、孙铃铃、肖雅兰、姜丽媛、余玲峰、林宁、王雪、王瑞寒、田玉华

西南政法大学法学院2014级本科生（10人）：熊玲、向文丽、卞先银、黄月婷、刘海洋、王海铃、王文玥、裴丽娟、朱萌越、黄诗樾

西南政法大学法学院2016级本科生（1人）：梁梓韵

（二）上海市的调查员和统计员师生合计83人次

1. 上海市社会调查人员名单（合计77人）

（1）组织开展社会调查的教师名单（合计1人）

华东政法大学法律学院许莉教授（教师组长）

（2）参加社会调查学生名单（合计 76 人）

参加实地调研和提交调查问卷的调查员（合计 76 人）

华东政法大学 2014 级本科学生（48 人）：

第一组：桂航、金麟、袁琦、徐含哲、高逸炜

第二组：孙川、许博闻、李悦、金鹏玮、潘盈

第三组：姜泽州、段禹成、陈谦益、汤沛佑、鞠天童、陈云仪、王佳颖、孙尧尧、郭欣然

第四组：殷敦辉、施觊文、王婕琼

第五组：戴培尧（小组长）、孙瑜（小组长）、陆晨豪、万蘅、王尚逸、王欣、薛钰、蔡丁佳、张立权、苏展、龚萌悦、董嘉琦

第六组：查汝玲（小组长）、刘中亮、何玉妍、江思嘉、张世泽、叶尧、张亦扬、王清源、许多曦、范裴玲、施添、陆晨、张露、陈天纯

华东政法大学 2015 级本科学生（18 人）：吴逸轩（小组长）、王怡之（小组长）、钱彧妮、陈浩、金奕欣、楼丝琪、张艺馨、邱雨桐、陈政、陆天盈、仇韵舒、屠珍妮、王若禹、万欣吉、杨星亮、伊肖伟、陆澄澄、郑雨婷

华东政法大学 2014 级研究生（3 人）：邬演嘉、朱培、陈希

华东政法大学 2015 级研究生（4 人）：朱舒倩（小组长）、陈婉青、姚佳、陈嘉仪

华东政法大学 2016 级研究生（3 人）：蒋雨达、陆楠、李天奇

2. 上海市调查数据统计人员名单（合计 6 人）

（1）组织进行调查数据统计的教师名单（合计 1 人）

华东政法大学法律学院许莉教授（教师组长）

（2）参加调查数据统计的学生名单（合计 5 人）

华东政法大学 2015 级研究生（2 人）：朱舒倩、王茜

华东政法大学 2016 级研究生（3 人）：柯婵娟、郑佳颖、张叶

（三）吉林省的调查员和统计员师生合计 110 人次

1. 吉林省社会调查人员名单（合计 88 人）

（1）组织开展社会调查的教师名单（合计 4 人）

吉林大学法学院李洪祥教授（教师组长），吉林大学法学院学生工作办公室主任、团委书记高岩老师，吉林大学妇委会副主任、副研究员苗艺璇老师，吉林大学法学院辅导员、讲师马旭老师

（2）参加社会调查学生名单（合计 84 人）

参加实地调研和提交调查问卷的调查员（合计 84 人）

吉林大学法学院 2014 级法学本科学生（42 人）：

第一组：卢琪瑶（小组长）、刘泓池、李官锦、田恒宇、王超、林星彤、徐航、王涵、李君怡、刘睿盈

第二组：罗媛（小组长）、刘苏仪、高春英、宫雯、姜懿莹、包文蕾、周泳、侯彦竹、李姿莹、白天宇

第三组：高昕（小组长）、朴昭瑛、孙雪婷、冯天禹、卓然、张云珊、朴河颖、马金池、姜肇祺、张乃方、周萌、杨姗

第四组：温砚琪（小组长）、马一鸣、司耕旭、齐乃萱、龚越、芦珊、邬童、胡馨方、朴夏景、尚小贺

吉林大学法学院 2015 级硕士研究生（35 人）：

第一组：朱芳凝（小组长）、周金明、王岩、冯艾琳、牧琪、谭婷婷、吕梦蝶、张羽超、聂朝阳

第二组：安晓玉（小组长）、佘圣男、夏文闻、卞小月、杜楠、谷美蕙、赵任伟、张伟佳

第三组：张远（小组长）、柳佩莹、杨拓、孟婉婷、李乐、吴婉晨、张舒、孟祥森、石晶

第四组：邱胜华（小组长）、王祉涵、尹美丹、谢文静、范思宇、胡雪莹、吴博、刘娜、冯月晓

吉林大学法学院 2016 级硕士研究生（7 人）：刘冬卉（小组长）、孙煜、吴天宜、刘欣阳、唐伟元、郭凯莉、冯胜男

2. 吉林省调查数据统计人员名单（合计 22 人）

（1）组织进行调查数据统计的教师名单（合计 1 人）

吉林大学法学院李洪祥教授（教师组长）

（2）参加调查数据统计的学生名单（合计 21 人）

吉林大学法学院 2016 级博士（2 人）：徐聪、都青

吉林大学法学院 2014 级硕士研究生（3 人）：刘倩、张燕、徐英

吉林大学法学院 2015 级硕士研究生（6 人）：朱芳凝、王岩、安晓玉、谢文静、石晶、白晓航

吉林大学法学院 2016 级硕士研究生（9 人）：刘冬卉、吴天宜、孙煜、关秋蕾、关悦、王惠、韩爽、段昕彤、蔡文蕾

吉林大学法学院 2014 级法学本科学生（1 人）：徐曦文

（四）河北省的调查员和统计员师生合计 137 人次

1. 河北省社会调查人员名单（合计 126 人）

（1）组织开展社会调查的教师名单（合计 1 人）

燕山大学文法学院罗杰副教授（教师组长）

（2）参加社会调查学生名单（合计 125 人）

参加实地调研和提交调查问卷的调查员（合计 125 人）

燕山大学 2014 级法学本科生（47 人）：李艳萍、李帅、马泽群、黄云龙、齐双、孙爽、谢姗珊、康诗涵、赵星晖、丁玉、白兰鑫、张彬彬、许悦、崔燕的、宋红岩、张博文、邓钰琛、江进帅、房中乐、曹嘉文、黄一希、丁铃、吕玉瑶、孙璇、王超亚、戴文星、辛玉涛、许红、胡双双、张倩、廉春雨、简柯杏、刘畅、宇文亚茹、王蒙、赵冉、李碧瑶、夏双双、田然、赵乾宇、李宇航、董亚峰、孙启汉、魏子豪、李绿铭、李慧、贤明秀

燕山大学辅修法学双学位本科生（6 人）：高圣雅、丁磊、孙嘉傲、胡靖怡、张琴、田雨彤

燕山大学里仁学院 2014 级法学本科生（41 人）：杨畅、郝安娜、万里、尚凯、马丹、

赵楠、宋清蔚、范思文、赵菊、冯晓丽、韩云飞、王茜茜、杨石惠、肖馨敏、王晨光、王国栋、夏天、吴美欢、张朝梦、侍小琳、王鹏、武新星、苏松渤、戈晓祯、王若琪、杨一楠、智雨池、周金山、刘东南、曹凤至、闫璐璐、闫浩宇、魏娟、李慧峰、王若男、刘伟、贾平川、郎立杰、刘浩、马斌、史晓宇

燕山大学 2016 级法学研究生（诉讼法学法律硕士）（31 人）：刘悦、党悦、刘丰、冯爱迪、薛菲、郭东栋、刘爽、柳琪、孔菲菲、周静、朱文珊、王邓超、都保旺、张莉敏、平泽丽、赵令艳、吴保川、潘沫涵、杨伯乔、周放、许臣臣、艾玉娇、吴海婷、李光霞、张境原、李金越、王伟伟、赵丽新、房文秀、周放、崔甜梦

2. 河北省调查数据统计人员名单（合计 11 人）

（1）组织进行调查数据统计的教师名单（合计 1 人）

燕山大学文法学院罗杰副教授（教师组长）

（2）参加调查数据统计的学生名单（合计 10 人）

燕山大学文法学院 2016 级硕士研究生（2 人）：尹鸽、冯爱迪

燕山大学文法学院 2014 级法学本科学生（7 人）：康诗涵、谢珊珊、李慧、许悦、李帅、齐双、董亚峰

燕山大学里仁学院 2014 级法学本科生（1 人）：肖馨敏

（五）湖北省的调查员和统计员师生合计 145 人次

1. 湖北省社会调查人员名单（合计 131 人）

（1）组织开展社会调查的教师名单（5 人）

中南财经政法大学法学院：孟令志副教授（教师组长）、夏昊晗老师，年级辅导员王瑄老师、徐金花老师、危晓燕老师

（2）参加社会调查学生名单（合计 126 人）

学生组织：中南财经政法大学法学院志愿者协会、“巾帼维权”大学生法律服务团

2013 级志愿者的学生调查员（17 人）：李静菱、贺超、郑晓、文玉洁、曹志、张兆书、陈嘉帝、张梦灵、汪鑫林、翁佳立、饶迪、杨双发、袁菁敏、陈俊鹏、李钰、张明耀、李垚林

2014 级志愿者的学生调查员（64 人）：何春阳、黄书迪、李兰、孙悦、章维薇、易雅琪、任炳光、张思雨、周云曦、刘业、向靖铭、胡娴婧、赵钰漫、韩聪、丁燚荧、黄佳佳、吴金阳、韦逸平、王俊辉、马雅莉、戴岭、肖奔、尹丽娟、徐玲、杨馨莹、蔡子盎、陈进、刘琦薇、段小姁、王瑶、黄丽芳、王紫君、龙佳女、付世文、李奥琦、张琪、祁子沐、方俊鑫、管苏扬、汪思敏、邓思垚、张一帆、杨柯清、顾代君、廖锡龙、张梦捷、赵敏、曹庭枝、汪明昕、陈石、曾祥由、刘会容、柯雅、胡春花、李宗亿、霍峰、明康琪、秦丹萍、陈琴韵、周云曦、方莹、章秀学、刘雨兮、梁胜阳

2015 级志愿者的学生调查员（43 人）：杨新虎、谭金哲、黄宇杰、袁宝琦、陈阳、方孝天、周君良、李洁、齐天宇、任捧利、刘雨兮、杨尧、郑绪佳、杨书越、杨房宜、魏慕颖、閤成鑫、王鹏、向建成、王聪聪、肖文静、叶娟、吕佳俊、黄冠男、赵锦楸、张雨馨、鲍遥思、杨粤、张帅群、江芷悦、刘倩、蔡齐、马静文、王琪瑶、向婷、朱美华、刘兰欣、刘璇、胡玥、张婉秋、李晨昊、李成微、靳翠茹

2015 级法律硕士研究生（1 人）：邓敏

2016级法律硕士研究生（1人）：彭锦

2. 湖北省调查数据统计人员名单（合计14人）

（1）组织进行调查数据统计的教师名单（1人）

中南财经政法大学法学院孟令志副教授（教师组长）

（2）参加调查数据统计的中南财经政法大学学生名单（合计13人）

法学院2015级民商法硕士研究生（5人）：潘芳芳、龚琳、王小雪、褚晶晶、周长泳

2015级法律硕士研究生（2人）：邓敏、许梅

法学院2016级民商法硕士研究生（4人）：李想、贾艳艳、元雨、张敏

2016级法律硕士研究生（2人）：彭锦、王传印

（六）江西省的调查员和统计员师生合计142人次

1. 江西省调查人员名单（合计109人）

（1）组织开展社会调查的教师名单（合计2人）

赣南师范大学政治与法律学院：曹贤信副教授（教师组长）、辅导员郭冠斌老师

（2）参加社会调查学生名单（合计107人）

法学本科生调查员（94人）：

第一组（宜春，9人）：袁金萍、胡娴、袁媛、金薇、罗邱兰、梅心荃、胡恒胜、伍雯青、徐丰

第二组（上饶，7人）：胡紫荆、俞静、王财仙、李莉、叶骏、陈蒙、吴娟

第三组（新余、萍乡、抚州，9人）：胡雪、柳慧玲、梁盼、章文、谢欣怡、罗东、涂也清、李增超、贺新莹

第四组（九江，8人）：雷芳芳、江文洁、许偲、张鑫鑫、陈晴晴、王寅莹、何亚霖、涂金林

第五组（南昌、景德镇，9人）：段洋娜、洪小敏、查焰玲、周琴、付姗姗、甘海妹、邓文清、熊成龙、朱阳阳

第六组（吉安，9人）：钟鑫、彭佳丽、赵林、李乐、肖阳阳、欧阳艳、段屹甲、江霖、姚龙

第七组（安远、信丰、会昌、寻乌、全南、定南、大余，13人）：缪莹、梅慧婷、汪越、赖琳琪、袁慧、邝慧蓉、甘雅玉、陈晓凤、赖如燕、卢娜、曹健、郭福雨、肖云

第八组（龙南、南康、于都，11人）：邱娜、黄桥英、谢康玲、温云超（大组长）、刘志明、肖鹏英、谢金明、黄晨阳、刘青云、林宇、刘龙飞

第九组（宁都、瑞金、上犹、石城、兴国，8人）：李泽鸿、陈思琪、黄雅妮、温唤春、吴洁、邹林、王丽、刘林香

第十组（赣州章贡区，11人）：刘昕、朱赞栋、施燕、薛文怡、刘心怡、杜香清、吴小芳、刘珊珊、赖嘉明、黄天雯、陈文芳

硕士研究生调查员（13人）：曾瑞玉、何远健、吴娟梅、邓云园、雷桑、凌材峰、邓奕明、陈飞、邹亮、钟宝平、罗爱梅、陈伟华、李婷

2. 江西省调查数据统计人员名单（合计33人）

（1）法学本科生统计人员名单（25人）

罗世丽、单婷婷、张天然、张婷妮、吴冯云、曹健、黄天雯、邹林、郭福雨、谢康

玲、肖云、伍雯肖、林宇、姚龙、刘龙飞、王财仙、叶骏、李泽鸿、段洋娜、袁金萍、许偲、梅心荃、陈文芳、贺新莹、陈蒙

（2）硕士研究生统计人员名单（8人）

曾瑞玉（大组长）、邓奕明、刘凯、陈飞、吴倩倩、钟宝平、邹亮、罗爱梅

（七）广东省的调查员和统计员师生合计143人次

1. 广东省社会调查人员名单（合计139人）

（1）组织开展社会调查的教师名单（合计1人）

广东工业大学政法学院郭丽红教授（教师组长）

（2）参加社会调查学生名单（合计138人）

参加实地调研和提交调查问卷的调查员（合计138人）

广东工业大学政法学院2013级法学本科学生（8人）：黄元俊、李考玲、林燕旋、罗慧嫦、罗小燕、王钰莹、陈嘉豫、文美谊

广东工业大学政法学院2015级法学本科学生（130人）：

第一组：邓潇龙、黄德铨、赖泽荣、刘波、刘健文、龙海东、苏武博、肖宇轩、许杰闻、杨铮、曾志添、陈煜珊、单丹、黄淑闲、蓝柔静、李衍颀、李子灵、梁雅莉、梁颖华、凌嘉敏、卢雅琳、彭彩菊、丘楚瑶、丘欣霖、肖婉君、叶云姗、张金敏、张丽婷、张琴、郑健燕、朱纯梓、朱月琼

第二组：蔡金宇、戴正言、冯康平、甘志权、高志鹏、何佳杰、黄恒宪、李剑波、刘如浩、罗杰、欧阳锦涛、彭振楠、陈橙、邓嘉仪、冯嘉棋、黄晓惠、黄钰茵、江梦凡、廖嘉曼、刘晓莉、卢美恩、彭利美、石桂花、吴悠铮、许倩、叶丽琴、余颖蕾、曾雯姗、张佳婷、郑婉莹、邹馨瑜

第三组：杜旭锋、胡潇鹏、赖威、黎烽、李浩明、欧超杰、潘俊明、唐仲伟、薛浩、姚沛通、余经纬、张焯霖、朱启立、陈晓欣、陈云婷、邓立媚、黄锦红、黄晓丹、赖碧莹、梁月明、廖舒婷、刘蕙珊、刘婉莹、卢诗娟、邱观梅、曲飞宇、王金雨、温紫晴、徐紫瑶、叶绮君、曾靖寓、张妙慧、朱翠玉

第四组：何伟宏、黄赐龙、黄润贤、李裕文、李泽锴、林根源、林溧欣、林跃、卢成捷、邱均兴、覃厚儒、王丕再、王铮宇、吴桐、陈静燕、陈至欣、冯诗琪、辜佳慧、黄美芬、黄瑞琪、黄曦、黎倩莹、林万华、刘正绩、罗洁钊、莫蕙维、邵婉仪、佘锦燕、汤诗敏、肖嘉丽、谢绮桦、曾嘉祺、郑依纯、钟雪莹

2. 广东省调查数据统计人员名单（合计4人）

（1）组织进行调查数据统计的教师名单（合计1人）

广东工业大学政法学院郭丽红教授（教师组长）

（2）参加调查数据统计的学生名单（合计3人）

广东工业大学政法学院2015级法学本科学生（3人）：邹馨瑜、叶云姗、王金雨

（八）海南省的调查员和统计员师生合计116人次

1. 海南省社会调查人员名单（合计104人）

（1）组织开展社会调查的教师名单（合计4人）

海南大学法学院叶英萍教授（教师组长）、胡明玉讲师、罗旭南教授，海南师范大学法学院唐欣瑜讲师

（2）参加社会调查学生名单（合计100人）

参加实地调研和提交调查问卷的调查员（合计100人）

海南大学法学院2014级法学本科学生（20人）：

第一组：陈群（小组长）、王紫、黄倩、符丽婷、符京菁、庄伟伟、张靖、郭海丹、傅愉惠、王小乔

第二组：梁菁（小组长）、李俊锐、陈备名、陈惠媚、苏凡、卢星霞、王可敏、邓丽香、高菲、王小钰

海南大学法学院2015级法学本科学生（8人）：

第一组：羊香慧（小组长）、王艺铮、姚丹丹、陈编

第二组：黄润凡（小组长）、何翘然、许晨颜、林匀婷

海南大学法学院2016级法学本科学生（14人）：

第一组：王敏（小组长）、林佳嘉、王发乐、黄华兴、劳鹏、陈境梵

第二组：林琤（小组长）、陈德声、杨楠、车钰莹、许开新、庄惠雯、杨海英、符馨尹

海南大学法学院2016级硕士研究生（7人）：

陈积雪（小组长）、陈晴燕、陈伟彬、陈文婷、黄骁、罗贻丽、朱馨

海南师范大学法学院法学本科学生（51人）：

学生大组长（1人）：黄冠宇

2014级法学本科学生（21人）：羊丽金、蒋文欣、符贵园、符天娱、郭仁平、黄彩虹、黎梦仪、李奶丽、李雪颖、林海韵、林婷婷、沈子佳、王惠芬、王莹莹、吴琼风、吴淑俊、许铭桃、杨兴莹、余永多、郑铭瑶、周源

2015级法学本科学生（29人）：陈亚芬、陈宗蕃、蒋雅洁、黎慧玲、李秀慧、梁薇、梁晓彤、麦世娴、潘翔、孙倩倩、吴丽珠、冼远康、虞惠滢、张继威、常敏敏、陈善烁、陈小靓、陈泽奇、邓玉梅、冯才颜、符晓达、高宜、韩佳琪、康丹丹、谭志群、吴来馨、吴小婷、朱兰芝、庄惠婷

2. 海南省调查数据统计人员名单（合计12人）

（1）组织进行调查数据统计的教师名单（合计1人）

海南大学法学院胡明玉讲师

（2）参加调查数据统计的学生名单（合计11人）

海南大学法学院2016级硕士研究生（11人）：王彦翔、文灿、张烜东、王佩、伊雅茜、包葵、彭英捷、王谋明、于思维、李冰、李惊雷

（九）福建省社会调查和统计的师生合计33人次

1. 福建省社会调查人员名单（合计29人）

（1）组织开展社会调查的教师名单（合计1人）

厦门大学法学院何丽新教授（教师组长）

（2）参加社会调查学生名单（合计28人）

参加实地调研并提交调查问卷的调查员（合计28人）

厦门大学法学院本科生（14人）：方林颖彦、许佳颖、颜佳艺、束嘉希、黄泽南、颜海晏、蔡银铃、蔡文君、黄真真、张珑、孙睿琪、吴建茜、林怡佳、陈华忍

厦门大学法学院研究生（13人）：陈静颖、曹超、孙菁、余虹宇、王思颖、叶妮妮、陈京、徐彦婷、林俐辰、詹秀清、林鑫、陈义、冯周敏

厦门大学公共事务学院研究生（1人）：叶艳艳

2. 福建省调查数据统计人员名单（合计4人）

（1）组织进行调查数据统计的教师名单（合计1人）

厦门大学法学院何丽新教授（教师组长）

（2）参加调查数据统计的学生名单（合计3人）

厦门大学法学院研究生：孙菁、余虹宇、王思颖

（十）四川省的调查员和统计员师生合计145人次

1. 四川省社会调查人员名单（合计118人）

（1）组织开展社会调查的教师名单（合计4人）

西南政法大学民商法学院陈苇教授（教师组长）、胡苷用副教授（教师副组长），西南政法大学法学院党总支书记梅传强教授、年级辅导员黄娥老师

（2）参加社会调查学生名单（合计114人）

参加实地调研和提交调查问卷的调查员（合计114人）

西南政法大学法学院2014级法学本科学生（51人）：

第一组：王海铃（大组长）、邹倪珈、张云仪、刘俊秀、胡馨梅、陶倩茹、江静、王思敏、陈俊宏、何俊龙

第二组：王文玥（小组长）、鲜冬梅、韩瑞、宋佩耘、费志平、王迪、游霞、邓子林、米俊岑、陈栎文

第三组：裴丽娟（小组长）、刘芸、李小炜、刘夏、袁煜棠、谢瑞、赵承尧、刘馨宇、冯娟、王诗琪、余溢婷

第四组：朱萌越（小组长）、王美玲、明蕊、王雅卉、王心怡、王虹又、文艺程、马美瑶、胡艺、廖珊珊

第五组：黄诗樾（小组长）、何婷婷、闵浩南、李莼、吴小玲、刘七萍、赵紫荆、刘钰力、王柔柔、马至诚

西南政法大学民商法学院2014级法学本科学生（59人）：

第一组：阙婷婷（小组长）、何龙江、肖贝、周桃、王韵洁、徐小雨、王师沁、梁霜、陈光庭、何倪鲜

第二组：陈洁玲（小组长）、丁云斐、谢方陈、黄可、毛彦钧、胡鑫、柯辰羽、周清清、李小飞、刘琳

第三组：李志然（小组长）、唐静、李明露、曾婷婷、弋鹏飞、陈敏、罗子薇、徐诗尧、黎倩、冉茂璋

第四组：刘静雨（小组长）、黄巍、贾滨菡、叶艾果、廖珍、张銮、鲜素华、陈琳静、吴霞（大组长）

第五组：郑璟（小组长）、曾佐玥、杨培松、侯怡伶、王云倩、兰玥、王洋、贺丹、周霞、陈聪

西南政法大学民商法学院2015级本科生（4人）：王艳婷（小组长）、曹瑞玥、车讯、肖莎莎

2. 四川省调查数据统计人员名单（合计 27 人）

（1）组织进行调查数据统计的教师名单（合计 2 人）

西南政法大学民商法学院陈苇教授（教师组长）、胡苷用副教授（教师副组长）

（2）参加调查数据统计的学生名单（合计 25 人）

西南政法大学民商法学院博士研究生（1 人）：李艳（大组长）

西南政法大学民商法学院硕士研究生（14 人）：

西南政法大学 2014 级硕士研究生（1 人）：梁明凤

西南政法大学 2015 级硕士研究生（3 人）：杨超、李文娟、郭庆敏

西南政法大学 2016 级硕士研究生（10 人）：占泸霞、邓孟姣、郝玉凯、潘娅、邢美玲、丁婷婷、李说、郭辉、李荣花、石会娟

西南政法大学民商法学院 2014 级法学本科学生（10 人）：张銮、杨桠楠、包雨婷、王子君、蔡腾飞、曹佳姗、吴姵雯、徐小雨、张兴建、萧婷婷

（十一）川渝等地区民营企业组的调查员和统计员师生合计 93 人次

1. 川渝等地区民营企业组社会调查人员名单（合计 57 人）

（1）组织开展社会调查的教师名单（合计 2 人）

西南政法大学民商法学院陈苇教授（教师组长）、胡苷用副教授（教师副组长）

（2）参加社会调查学生名单（合计 55 人）

参加实地调研并提交调查问卷的调查员（合计 55 人）

西南政法大学民商法学院 2014 级硕士研究生（4 人）：林英、泽绒拥珍、赵孟亚、强米米

西南政法大学民商法学院 2015 级硕士研究生（12 人）：李文娟、鲁瀚阳、刘宇娇、吕德天、张文彩、杨超、郭庆敏、欧忆虹、胡杨、周立里、吴丹、黄耀

西南政法大学民商法学院 2016 级硕士研究生（36 人）：石雨杭、肖雅兰、孙铃、郑静文、张林玉、梅婷、石会娟、茹晴晴、潘亚、邢美玲、梁明凤、华溪、樊利涛、杨洋、程婕、冯嘉敏、王瑞寒、邓孟姣、丁婷婷、李睿、李荣花、张霞、蒋忻如、田梅、李说、郭辉、占泸霞、蒲芸芸、张冬雪、姜丽媛、余玲峰、郝玉凯、林宁、杨晓宇、许欣、王雪

西南政法大学民商法学院 2015 级博士研究生（2 人）：陈钊、董思远

西南政法大学民商法学院 2016 级博士研究生（1 人）：李艳

2. 川渝等地区民营企业组参加调查数据统计人员名单（合计 36 人）

（1）组织进行调查数据统计的教师名单（合计 3 人）

西南政法大学民商法学院陈苇教授（教师组长）、胡苷用副教授（教师副组长）、石雷讲师

（2）参加调查数据统计的学生名单（合计 33 人）

西南政法大学民商法学院 2015 级博士生（1 人）：董思远（大组长）

西南政法大学民商法学院 2016 级博士生（1 人）：李艳

西南政法大学民商法学院 2015 级硕士研究生（8 人）：田梅、杨超、郭庆敏、张文彩、刘宇娇、周迁凤、汪鹏、王可

西南政法大学民商法学院 2016 级硕士研究生（16 人）：茹晴晴、郑静文、张林玉、潘娅、邢美玲、李说、丁婷婷、邓孟娇、王瑞寒、占泸霞、肖雅兰、张霞、普思佳、蒋忻

如、姜丽媛、许欣

西南政法大学民商法学院 2015 级本科生（7 人）：周利、王艳婷、文智慧、漏玲蓉、周佳城、刘雨浓、刘媛

本书引用的主要法律、法规和司法解释的简称

一、中国法

1.《中华人民共和国宪法》（2018年3月11日通过第五次修正，并公布施行），简称：我国现行《宪法》。

2.《中华人民共和国民法通则》（1987年1月1日起施行，2009年修正），简称：我国《民法通则》。

3.《中华人民共和国继承法》（1985年10月1日起施行），简称：我国《继承法》。

4.《最高人民法院关于贯彻执行〈中华人民共和国继承法〉若干问题的意见》（1985年9月11日起施行），简称：1985年《执行继承法意见》。

5.《中华人民共和国婚姻法》（2001年4月28日修正和公布，自公布之日起施行），简称：我国现行《婚姻法》。

6.《中华人民共和国收养法》（1998年11月4日修正，1999年4月1日起施行），简称：我国现行《收养法》。

7.《中华人民共和国老年人权益保障法》（2018年12月29日第三次修正，于2018年12月29日施行），简称：我国现行《老年人权益保障法》。

8. 我国司法部《遗赠扶养协议公证细则》（1991年4月3日起施行），简称：我国司法部《遗赠扶养协议公证细则》。

9.《中华人民共和国物权法》（2007年10月1日起施行），简称：我国《物权法》。

10.《中华人民共和国民事诉讼法》（2017年6月27第三次修正，自2017年7月1日起实施），简称：我国现行《民事诉讼法》。

11.《中华人民共和国企业破产法》（2007年6月1日起施行），简称：我国《企业破产法》。

12.《中华人民共和国民法总则》（2017年10月1日起实施），简称：我国《民法总则》。

13.《中华人民共和国合同法》（1999年10月1日起施行），简称：我国《合同法》。

14.《中华人民共和国保险法》（2015年4月24日第三次修正），简称：我国现行《保险法》。

15.《中华人民共和国侵权责任法》（自2010年7月1日起施行），简称：我国《侵权责任法》。

16. 《最高人民法院关于适用〈中华人民共和国民事诉讼法〉的解释》（2015年2月4日起施行），简称：我国2015年《关于适用民事诉讼法的解释》。

17. 《最高人民法院关于审理人身损害赔偿案件适用法律若干问题的解释》（2004年5月1日起施行），简称：我国2004年《关于审理人身损害赔偿案件适用法律若干问题的解释》。

18. 《最高人民法院关于确定民事侵权精神损害赔偿责任若干问题的解释》（2001年3月10日起施行），简称：我国2001年《关于确定民事侵权精神损害赔偿责任若干问题的解释》。

19. 《工伤保险条例》（2003年4月27日公布，2010年12月20日修订），简称：我国现行《工伤保险条例》。

20. 《遗嘱公证细则》（2000年3月24日公布，2000年7月1日起施行），简称：我国司法部《遗嘱公证细则》。

二、外国法

21. 罗结珍译：《法国民法典》（北京大学出版社2010年版），简称：《法国民法典》（特别引用另有说明的除外）。

22. 陈卫佐译：《德国民法典》（第4版）（法律出版社2015年版），简称：《德国民法典》（特别引用另有说明的除外）。

23. 戴永盛译：《瑞士民法典》（法律出版社2016年版），简称：《瑞士民法典》（特别引用另有说明的除外）。

24. 刘士国、牟宪魁、杨瑞贺译：《日本民法典》（中国法制出版社2018年版），简称：《日本民法典》（特别引用另有说明的除外）。

25. 费安玲、丁玫、张宓译：《意大利民法典》（中国政法大学出版社2004年版），简称：《意大利民法典》（特别引用另有说明的除外）。

26. 黄道秀译：《俄罗斯联邦民法典》（北京大学出版社2007年版），简称：《俄罗斯联邦民法典》（特别引用另有说明的除外）。

27. 谢怀栻译：《德意志联邦共和国民事诉讼法》（中国法制出版社2001年版），简称：《德国民事诉讼法》（特别引用另有说明的除外）。

28. 唐晓晴等译：《葡萄牙民法典》（北京大学出版社2009年版），简称：《葡萄牙民法典》（特别引用另有说明之处除外）。

29. 薛军译：《埃塞俄比亚民法典》（法制出版社2002年版），简称：《埃塞俄比亚民法典》（特别引用另有说明之处除外）。

30. 孙建江、郭站红、朱亚芬译：《魁北克民法典》（中国人民大学出版社2005年版），简称：《魁北克民法典》（特别引用另有说明之处除外）。

31. 崔吉子编译：《韩国最新民法典》（北京大学出版社2010年版），简称：《韩国民法典》（特别引用另有说明之处除外）。

32. 潘灯、成琴译：《西班牙民法典》（中国政法大学出版社2013年版），简称：《西班牙民法典》（特别引用另有说明之处除外）。

33. 徐涤宇译：《智利共和国民法典》（2000年修订本）（北京大学出版社2014年

版)，简称：《智利共和国民法典》(特别引用另有说明之处除外)。

34. Uniform Probate Code (amended in 2010), USA，简称：美国《统一遗嘱检验法典》或 Uniform Probate Code。

第一章　当代中国民众财产继承观念与遗产处理习惯实证调查概述*

"社会经济的发展，必然要求法律的调整和保护。"① 继承法律制度是调整继承关系的法律规范的总和。继承关系既涉及家庭的生产、生活关系，也涉及社会的经济关系。恩格斯指出："历史中的决定性因素，归根结底是直接生活的生产和再生产。"② 法律制度属于经济基础决定的上层建筑，继承法也不例外。美国学者摩尔根认为，原始社会的经济条件决定人们的生活方式和死者财产的转移方式，人类原始社会共经历了以下"三种继承法"：第一种是氏族继承法，即在本氏族内部成员中分配死者遗留的财产。第二种是同宗继承法，即仅限于在氏族成员的同宗亲属中分配死者遗留的财产，而将其余氏族的成员排除在外。第三种是子女继承法，即死者遗留的财产限于在死者的子女中分配。摩尔根分析指出："罗马十二铜表法包括了当时已经确立的继承法。财产首先由子女继承，死者之妻是与子女处于同等地位的继承人；若无子女且世系为男系，则由归近的同宗继承；若无同宗继承，则由氏族成员继承。这里我们又一次发现法律的根本基础是财产必须留在氏族之内。"③ 在欧洲，根据早期日耳曼法的规定，"大多数财产属于家庭或部落，不能在一个成员死亡时加以分配。"④ 在人类社会进入阶级社会以后，人类社会主要经历了"两种继承法"：第一种是古代社会的身份继承法。在古代小农社会的经济条件下，奴隶社会和封建社会的家庭都是人们生产、生活的基本单位，为统一组织家庭生产活动和维持家庭成员的生活，需要实行家长制。在家长制下，家长为一家之主，统领家庭成员，家庭成员则处于从属、依附家长的地位。我国有学者认为，古代继承法最主要的特色是"合身份继承与财产继承为一体"⑤，以家长身份继承为主，家庭财产继承为辅。例如，在古罗马，"继承人准确地说曾是宗亲集团或家族最高权力的接班人，而且只是作为其结果，才也作为财产的继受人"。"遗产继承是向新的主体转移对家庭的主权。""遗产继承最初不是用来进行财产转移的，而是用来转移罗马家庭的最高权力的。"⑥ 在我国，自父系家长制以后，就

---

* 作者简介：陈苇，女，西南政法大学民商法学院博士生导师、教授；陈法，男，重庆大学法学院民商法博士研究生、重庆市潼南区人民法院法官助理。

① 张晋藩：《中国法律的传统与近代转型（第三版）》，法律出版社2009年版，第555页。

② 恩格斯：《家庭、私有制和国家的起源（第一版）》，人民出版社1972年版，序言，第3页。

③ 参见［美］路易斯·亨利·摩尔根著：《古代社会》（下册），杨东莼、马雍、马巨译，商务印书馆1983年版，第533~535、537~538、542~555页。

④ ［美］哈罗德·J. 伯尔曼：《法律与革命——西文法律传统的形成》，贺卫方、高鸿钧、张志铭、夏勇译，中国大百科全书出版社1993年版，第279页。

⑤ 刘素萍主编：《继承法》，中国人民大学出版社1988年版，第18页。

⑥ ［意］彼德罗·彭梵得：《罗马法教科书》，黄风译，中国政法大学出版社1992年版，第421、426、433页。

出现了家庭财产。“古代的家长，专指父亲，家长财产权是父亲的财产权。”① 这是就家长一人独自掌握家庭财产和享有处置家庭财产权的角度而言的。我国有学者指出：“家庭财产，父在为父所有，父殁为母管理；必要时，其母有权利处置，子不可提出异议。”②“《盟水斋存牍》中有不少判例显示出，晚明的法律规定和司法实践中保护宗族的经济秩序特别是家长的财产所有权。只要未分家，儿子就无权占有家里的财产，更不可擅自加以处置。”③ 但我国另有学者认为，中国传统的家产是所有家庭成员的共同财产，而不是家父的个人财产。因此，没有财产所有权的让渡，只有家产管理者的换届。④ 也就是说，此“换届”首先是家长身份的继承，而继承家庭身份者，当然也就是家产的管理者。总之，对于古代家长身份的继承或者“换届”而言，继承人与被继承人之间必须具有特定的身份关系，其才能够成为合法的继承人或者说才能具有继承资格，才能继承被继承人在家族和社会中的政治地位与权利及其遗留的财产并承担相应的义务。⑤ 第二种是近代、现代社会的财产继承法。人类社会发展到近代社会，随着社会经济的发展，资本主义生产条件下人身依附关系弱化，天赋人权、个人主义等思想兴起，发生了“从身份到契约”的转变。正如法国学者所言，“1789 年法国《人权宣言》和 1804 年《拿破仑法典》以及其他一切近代民法典都是以个人主义的理念为基础的”⑥，均把个人权利放在首位，强调自由的意思自治。在此社会背景下，近代、现代社会的财产继承法均废除了身份继承而专行财产继承。例如，在国外，作为近代社会民法典代表的 1804 年《拿破仑法典》第 711 条规定：“财产所有权，因继承、生前赠与、遗赠以及债的效力而取得或转移。”⑦ 1900 年《德国民法典》第 1922 条第 1 款也规定，继承自被继承人死亡时开始，其财产全部转移给其一名或数名的继承人。⑧ 1907 年制定的《瑞士民法典》第 481 条亦规定：“被继承人在其自由处分权的范围内，可以通过遗嘱或者继承契约处分其全部或部分财产。继承人不得处分的部分，归属于法定继承人。”⑨ 在我国，中华民国时期《民法继承编》（1930 年）第 1148 条规定：“继承人自继承开始时，除本法另有规定外，承受被继承人财产上之一切权利、义务。但权利、义务专属于被继承人本身者，不在此限。”⑩ 此项规定在我国台湾地区被沿用至今。在我国大陆地区，1985 年《继承法》第 3 条规定：“遗产是公民死亡时遗留的个人合法财产。”

纵观人类社会继承法发展史，我们可以发现，不同历史时期的社会经济条件决定和制约着人们的财产继承观念与遗产处理习惯，这种财产继承观念与遗产处理习惯又决定着不

---

① 程维荣：《中国继承制度史》，中国出版集团东方出版中心 2006 年版，第 231、235~236 页。

② 吴之屏：《民法继承编论》，上海法政学社 1933 年版，第 15 页，转引自程维荣：《中国继承制度史》，中国出版集团东方出版中心 2006 年版，第 236 页。

③ 程维荣：《中国继承制度史》，中国出版集团东方出版中心 2006 年版，第 236 页。

④ 高其才主编：《当代中国分家析产习惯法》，中国政法大学出版社 2014 年版，第 198~199 页。

⑤ 参见李双元、温世扬主编：《比较民法学》，武汉大学出版社 1998 年版，第 958 页。

⑥ 参见［法］莱昂·狄骥：《〈拿破仑法典〉以来私法的普通变迁》，徐砥平译，中国政法大学出版社 2003 年版，第 7 页。

⑦ 李浩培、吴传颐、孙鸣岗译：《拿破仑法典》（《法国民法典》），商务印书馆 1983 年版，第 94 页。

⑧ 郑冲、贾红梅译：《德国民法典》，法律出版社 1999 年版，第 447 页。

⑨ 殷生根、王燕译：《瑞士民法典》，中国政法大学出版社 1999 年版，第 132 页。

⑩ 1930 年“中华民国民法”第五编继承，载杨立新主编：《中国百年民法典汇编》，中国法制出版社 2011 年版，第 513~514 页。

同历史时期继承法的性质。法国学者指出：每一种继承习惯都以自己的方式代表着一种解决办法，一方面是希望要公平；另一方面是要保证家产延续，这两个方面相妥协的解决办法。[①] 我国学者认为："法律是社会的产物，是社会制度之一。它与风俗习惯有密切的关系，它维护着现存的制度和道德、伦理等价值观念，它反映某一时期、某一社会的社会结构，法律与社会的关系极为密切……任何社会的法律都是为了维护并巩固其社会制度和社会秩序而制定的，只有充分了解产生某一种法律的社会背景，才能了解这些法律的意义和作用。"[②] 美国学者认为："对过去来说，法律是文明的一种产物；对现在来说，法律是维系文明的一种工具；对未来来说，法律是增进文明的一种工具。"而且"法律的目的，就是最大限度地满足人类的需求。"[③] 我们认为，现代继承法必须根据现代社会的经济条件，适时进行"立、改、废"，才能适应现代社会民众的家庭生活和生产经营的现实需要。而现代继承法要适时进行"立、改、废"，就必须考察当代社会经济条件决定的民众财产继承观念及遗产处理习惯，将其中符合家庭职能要求和社会经济发展的内容反映在最新立法之中，才能最大限度地满足社会民众的现实需要，实现法律"维系文明、增进文明"之目的。

本章研究和阐述的主要内容包括：第一节当代中国民众财产继承观念与遗产处理习惯实证调查的背景、对象与意义；第二节当代中国民众财产继承观念与遗产处理习惯实证调查的实施概况。

第一节　当代中国民众财产继承观念与遗产处理习惯实证调查的背景、对象和意义

一、实证调查的背景

在我国，为了适应和调整社会主义市场经济关系、婚姻家庭关系新情况新问题的需要，2014 年 10 月中国共产党的十八届四中全会审议通过的《中共中央关于全面推进依法治国若干重大问题的决定》提出了编纂"民法典"的重要任务。财产继承关系与婚姻家庭关系一样，涉及男女老少、千家万户的切身利益。继承法律制度是我国民事法律制度的重要组成部分，完善和发展继承法律制度是我国社会主义法制建设的重要内容之一。[④] 调整财产继承关系的"继承编"是民法典不可或缺的重要组成部分。为保护继承人的财产权益和实现家庭的扶养职能，维护第三人的利益和交易安全，促进我国经济发展、家庭幸福与社会和谐稳定，"民法典继承编"的编纂被我国立法机关提上了工作日程。2016 年 11 月，西南政法大学陈苇教授主持申报的司法部科研项目"我国遗产处理制度系统化构

① ［法］安德烈·比尔基埃、［法］克里蒂斯亚娜·克拉比什-朱伯尔、［法］玛尔蒂娜·雪伽兰、［法］弗朗索瓦兹·佐纳邦德：《家庭史　现代化的冲击》（第二卷），袁树仁等译，生活·读书·新知三联出版社 1997 年版，第 90 页。

② 瞿同祖：《中国法律与中国社会》导论，商务印书馆 2010 年版，第 1 页。

③ ［美］罗斯科·庞德：《法律史解释》，邓正来译，中国法制出版社 2002 年版，第 212~213 页。

④ 陈苇、王歌雅：《改革开放三十年中国继承法制建设之回顾与展望》，载陈苇（项目负责人）：《改革开放三十年（1978~2008）中国婚姻家庭继承法研究之回顾与展望》，中国政法大学出版社 2010 年版，第 349 页。

建研究”（编号 16SFB2036）被批准立项。“实践对理论的选择是最好的检验。”① 为了给开展本项目的理论研究和制度研究提供基本国情资料，必须了解当代中国民众的财产继承观念与遗产处理习惯；为推进科学立法、民主立法，为我国“民法典继承编”的编纂提供基本国情资料，也必须了解当代中国民众的财产继承观念与遗产处理习惯，在此时代背景下，我们组织进行了“当代中国民众财产继承观念与遗产处理习惯实证调查研究”这一司法部科研项目的子课题。

二、实证调查的对象和意义

在现代社会，继承法是调整一国民众的财产继承关系之法律规范的总和。财产继承关系，涉及千家万户、男女老少的切身利益，也涉及第三人的利益和交易安全。目前，我国虽然已出版《当代中国民众继承习惯调查实证研究》，但此著作是以 2005 年 8 月至 2006 年 7 月我国民众继承习惯调查数据为基础撰写的，距今已有十余年之久。为此，我们选取“当代中国民众财产继承观念与遗产处理习惯”这一重要现实问题作为实证调查对象，开展 1949 年中华人民共和国成立以来我国第二次全国较大范围的民众继承习惯调查。

必须说明，在 2005 年 10 月至 2007 年 7 月，陈苇教授作为 2005 年度国家社科基金项目负责人，为完成《外国继承法比较与中国民法典继承编制定研究》课题，曾经主持进行过 1949 年中华人民共和国成立以来我国首次“中国民众继承习惯调查”。当时在北京市、重庆市、武汉市和山东省四地开展此社会调查，参加实地调查和调查数据统计汇总的师生合计有 411 人次。② 时隔 11 年之后，陈苇教授针对开展 2016 年立项的司法部科研项目“我国遗产处理制度系统化构建研究”的需要，为收集我国更多地区民众的继承习惯资料，扩大了被调查地区的范围，同时考虑到课题组人力、物力的限制和选择部分具有合作意向的高校教师共同进行社会调查的可能性，在我国选择了以下十省市作为被调查地区，包括重庆市、吉林省、上海市、河北省、湖北省、江西省、广东省、海南省、福建省和四川省，开展“当代中国民众财产继承观念与遗产处理习惯实证调查研究”这一子课题，参加实地调查和调查数据统计汇总的师生合计有 1295 人次，通过入户访问调查，发放了 5739 份调查问卷供被调查者填写，同时还进行了个人访谈。本次调查的统计汇总数据，可以为我国立法机关了解当代中国更多地区民众的财产继承观念与遗产处理习惯提供第一手基本国情资料。

目前，我国已是世界第二经济大国。根据中央电视台的新闻报道，民营企业在我国经济体系中已是“三分天下有其一”，在我国经济体系中占据重要地位。民营企业主死亡时留下的企业遗产依法适当处理的问题，既涉及民营企业的继续经营发展，也涉及我国经济的可持续发展。同时，我国已逐渐步入老龄化社会，据民政部的统计数据，截至 2017 年年底，全国 60 周岁及以上老年人口达 24090 万人，占总人口的 17.3%，其中 65 周岁及以上老年人口达 15831 万人，占总人口的 11.4%。2017 年火化遗体 482 万具，火化率为

① 张中秋：《中西法律文化比较研究》（第 4 版），法律出版社 2009 年版，第 346 页。

② 参见陈苇主编：《当代中国民众继承习惯调查实证研究》的“中国民众继承习惯调查”之调查人员简介，群众出版社 2008 年版，第 6 页。

48.9%，即当年死亡人数已达985万以上。[①] 在被继承人去世后，其遗留的债权与债务之适当处理的问题，既涉及继承人的财产权益保障，也涉及与之交易的债权人利益的保护与交易安全的维护，对于上述基本国情我国立法机关在编制“民法典继承编”时必须予以关注。为编制一部具有时代特点、符合中国国情、具有前瞻性的“民法典继承编”，需要进行“当代中国民众财产继承观念与遗产处理习惯实证调查研究”，从而为立法机关提供第一手国情资料。当然，我们“对民事习惯的积极和消极作用应当有比较全面的认识”，[②] 并且应当注意发挥法律对不良继承习惯如重男轻女、否认出嫁女儿继承权的旧传统继承习惯等的引导改革作用。我们应当在立法中贯彻男女平等基本国策，在“民法典继承编”应当继续规定“继承权男女平等”，以保障妇女的财产继承权益。总之，只有进行“科学立法、民主立法”“体现人民利益、反映人民愿望、维护人民权益、增进人民福祉”，才能符合中国国情，满足当代中国民众处理财产继承问题的实际需要，达到既维护继承人、受遗赠人等的合法权益，也维护第三人的利益和交易安全，促进我国经济发展，增进人民群众生活幸福的目的。

综上所述，《当代中国民众财产继承观念与遗产处理习惯实证调查研究》的出版，既可以填补中国当代民众继承习惯实证调查的理论空白，又可以为修改与完善我国《继承法》和“民法典继承编”的编纂提供第一手国情资料，还可以为我国司法机关释法和执法、为法律服务工作者及财产继承关系当事人处理遗产问题提供参考，因此具有重要的学术价值、理论意义和实际应用价值。

第二节 当代中国民众财产继承观念与遗产处理习惯实证调查的实施概况

一、实证调查的主要内容

本次实证调查调查问卷的主要内容，包括当代中国民众财产继承观念与遗产处理习惯十二个方面的问题、理由或情况，对于我国十省市被调查民众财产继承观念与遗产处理的行为习惯及其理由的调查，可以为分析当代中国民众财产继承观念与遗产处理习惯的特点及其原因打下基础。

本次实证调查的调查问卷之主要内容如下：（1）遗产范围的界定，实地调查两个问题：遗产的种类、被继承人生前特种赠与财产的归扣；（2）继承开始的通知和公告，实地调查三个问题：继承开始的通知和公告的主体、继承开始的通知和公告的方式、继承开始的通知和公告的期间；（3）遗产管理，实地调查三个问题：遗产管理人的确定、遗产管理人的职责与报酬、遗产管理人的损害赔偿责任；（4）法定继承，实地调查五个问题：法定继承人的范围与顺序、配偶与血亲继承人的法定应继份、配偶对遗产中家庭住房的先

---

① 民政部：2017年社会服务发展统计公报，载 http://www.mca.gov.cn/article//sj/tjgb/201808/20180800010446.shtml，访问日期：2019年6月30日。

② 徐国栋：《认真地反思民间习惯与民法典的关系》，载徐国栋：《认真地对待民法典》，中国人民大学出版社2004年版，第44页。

取权和终生使用权、后顺序特殊法定继承人对遗产中原使用的住房及日常生活用品的终生使用权、尽了主要赡养义务的丧偶的儿媳或女婿的遗产分配方式；（5）遗嘱继承，实地调查三个问题：公证遗嘱与其他形式遗嘱的效力、遗嘱自由的限制——特留份、夫妻共同遗嘱；（6）继承和遗赠的接受与放弃，实地调查三个问题：继承的接受与放弃的时间和方式、遗赠的接受与放弃的方式和效力、继承的放弃与债权人的撤销权；（7）继承权的丧失、被继承人的宥恕与代位继承，实地调查两个问题：继承权的丧失与被继承人的宥恕、继承权的丧失与代位继承；（8）继承协议，实地调查两个问题：继承协议的订立主体与方式、继承协议的变更方式及效力；（9）遗产债务清偿，实地调查三个问题：遗产债务清偿责任的类型、被继承人丧葬费的支付、遗产债务的清偿顺序；（10）遗产分割，实地调查两个问题：遗产分割的自由与限制、遗产分割瑕疵的担保责任；（11）无人承受遗产，实地调查两个问题：无人承受遗产的归属、无人承受遗产的处理；（12）遗产纠纷的典型案例。

在此必须说明以下四个问题：

第一，由于本次实证调查的内容，涉及被继承人生前对部分法定继承人的特种赠与财产（包括因分家、结婚、营业等赠与的财产）即对该继承人应继份的预付问题，故采用“遗产处理”一词，而不用“遗产继承”一词。

第二，在本次实证调查研究的十二个方面的问题中，遗产范围界定的立法模式与归扣，遗产管理制度的构建，法定继承制度中法定继承人的范围与顺序、生存配偶和部分特殊继承人对遗产中家庭住房的先取权或终生使用权，遗嘱继承制度中的特留份、继承协议（或称继承扶养协议、在国外立法中称为继承合同或继承契约），遗产债务的清偿顺序及遗产分割的瑕疵担保责任等均是我国《继承法》没有规定的，而在本次“民法典继承编”的编纂中是迫切需要研究解决的热点和难点问题。

第三，本次实证调查研究的“归扣”概念的内涵与归扣财产的性质。所谓归扣又称遗产归扣，是指依据法律的规定，参加继承的部分或全部法定继承人，如果在被继承人生前获得了某些特殊赠与财产（包括因结婚、分家、营业等获得的赠与财产），在继承开始时其应将此特种赠与财产与现有遗产合并计算出待继承财产的总额，再依此总额计算各继承人的应继份，然后在应继份中将该继承人获得的特种赠与财产扣除，最后所得财产数额即为该继承人的应继财产。这样，能够实现在共同继承人之间公平地分配被继承人的遗产。即该继承人在被继承人生前获得的特种赠与财产被视为其应继承份的预付，就此而言，该归扣的财产在性质上可以被认为属于遗产的组成部分。但为了尊重被继承人的意愿，法律规定，如被继承人生前明确表示免除归扣的，则该特种赠与财产不予以归扣。所以，我国有学者认为，此特种赠与财产不属于完全意义上的遗产，故对其应称为“不完全遗产”。[①] 正如法国学者所言：“实际上，家产传递的策略应该与潜在的平等需求相适应。”[②] 也就是说，我们研究在我国设立归扣制度，主要是为了保障在共同继承人中公平地分配被继承人的遗产，尤其是在我国大力倡导和推进“一带一路”中外经济共同发展

① 参见陈苇主编：《外国继承法比较与中国民法典继承编制定研究》，北京大学出版社2011年版，第233页。

② ［法］安德烈·比尔基埃、［法］克里蒂斯亚娜·克拉比什-朱伯尔、［法］玛尔蒂娜·雪伽兰、［法］弗朗索瓦兹·佐纳邦德：《家庭史：现代化的冲击》（第二卷），袁树仁等译，生活·读书·新知三联出版社1997年版，第90页。

的新时代社会背景下，涉外婚姻增多，涉外婚姻家庭继承纠纷也会增多，研究在我国设立归扣制度有利于保障涉外继承关系的共同继承人间公平地分配被继承人的遗产。

第四，本次实证调查研究的继承协议（又称继承扶养协议），属于狭义的继承协议。狭义的继承协议是指：被继承人与法定继承人中的一人或数人通过协商，对被继承人（受扶养人）的扶养与扶养人对受扶养人之遗产的继承或放弃等事项达成的协议。可见，此狭义的继承协议的性质属于一种双务、有偿的合同。在国外，继承协议被称为继承合同（或称继承契约）。国外的继承合同是指：被继承人与继承人、其他自然人、法人和其他组织等就继承权或者受遗赠权的取得或消灭及相应义务承担等而达成的合意。[①] 根据继承合同的不同内容，可分为两种类型：一是被继承人与其他民事主体就继承、遗赠的取得或消灭达成的合意，继承人、受遗赠人取得继承或受遗赠有财产无须履行相应的义务，即属于单务、无偿合同；二是被继承人与其他民事主体就继承、遗赠的取得或消灭达成合意，同时约定继承人、受遗赠人应履行相应的义务，即属于双务、有偿合同。[②] 在我国，目前有部分民众承认被继承人与自己的法定继承人双方协商后签订以扶养和继承为内容的继承扶养协议。本次实地调查发现，在我国现实生活中，不少地区的民间都存在采取签订继承协议的方式将养老与遗产继承同时处理的习惯。因此，研究在我国设立继承扶养协议制度，可以回应我国部分民众以遗产继承解决老人赡养问题的现实需要。

二、实证调查的情况简介

为了解当代中国民众的财产继承观念与遗产处理习惯，2016 年 11 月初至 2019 年 6 月底，历时两年零八个月，我们组织开展完成了“当代中国民众财产继承观念与遗产处理习惯实证调查研究”的实地调查、统计数据的汇总和十省市调查研究报告的撰写工作。现将本次实证调查的组织实施概况简介如下。

（一）被调查地区的选取与调查组组长的确定

为了给 2016 年 11 月立项的司法部科研项目“我国遗产处理制度系统化构建研究”提供实证调查研究的基础资料，课题负责人陈苇教授于 2016 年 11 月初开始组织进行“当代中国民众财产继承观念与遗产处理习惯实证调查研究”司法部项目的子课题。陈苇教授考虑到我国不同地区的社会经济发展程度有一定差异，不同地区民众的继承观念和遗产处理习惯也有所不同，并考虑到课题组人力、物力资源的限制，选择确定我国以下十省市作为被调查地区，包括东北部的吉林省、东部的上海市、北部的河北省、中部的湖北省和江西省、南部的广东省和海南省、东南部的福建省、西南部的重庆市和四川省。然后，陈苇教授分别联系我国十省市部分高校具有合作进行本课题研究意向的教师，确定了我国十省市被调查地区的调查组组长如下（排名不分先后）：吉林省调查组组长为吉林大学法学院李洪祥教授；上海市调查组组长为华东政法大学许莉教授；河北省调查组组长为燕山大学罗杰副教授；湖北省调查组组长为中南财经政法大学孟令志副教授；江西省调查组组长为赣南师范大学曹贤信副教授；广东省调查组组长、副组长为中山大学法学院卓冬青副教

① 从签订协议的主体范围来看，国外继承合同的主体范围不限于被继承人与法定继承人之间。参见陈苇主编：《外国继承法比较与中国民法典继承编制定研究》，北京大学出版社 2011 年版，第 433 页。

② 参见陈苇主编：《中国遗产处理制度系统化构建研究》，中国人民公安大学出版社 2019 年版，第 230 页。

授和广东工业大学政法学院郭丽红教授；海南省调查组组长为海南大学法学院叶英萍教授；福建省调查组组长为厦门大学法学院何丽新教授；重庆市和四川省两省市的调查组组长、副组长分别为西南政法大学陈苇教授和西南政法大学胡苷用副教授。

（二）调查问卷的设计和学生调查员的召集与培训

2016 年 11 月中旬，陈苇教授组织重庆市项目组成员分工合作，设计制作当代中国民众财产继承观念与遗产处理习惯实证调查的“调查问卷”，至同年 12 月中旬完成了调查问卷的设计工作。然后，陈苇教授把“调查问卷”通过电子邮件发送给十省市调查组组长，以供各省市开展实地调查时统一使用。同年 12 月下旬，根据陈苇教授撰写的“当代中国民众继承观念与遗产处理习惯社会调查动员和培训会”的说明书，十省市调查组组长各自在本地高校召集、遴选本省籍的学生调查员 100 名左右，然后各自组织召开本省市的“社会调查动员和培训会”对学生调查员进行社会调查的动员和知识培训。在会上，各省市调查组组长首先对学生调查员发放调查问卷，然后讲解本次社会调查的目的意义、主要内容、调查问题的要点和具体的调查方法，说明被调查者必须是男女各 3 名，分为老、中、青（61 岁以上、41~60 岁、20~40 岁）三个年龄段，并且最好具有不同的职业背景。每名学生调查员将利用 2017 年的寒假在自己家乡开展“入户访谈”的实地社会调查，要求每人发放和回收 6 份调查问卷。

（三）实地社会调查的方式

2017 年 1 月至 2 月，十省市高校的学生调查员们同时在 2017 年的寒假在自己的家乡开展实地社会调查。本次调查主要采取学生调查员“入户问卷调查”和“个人访谈”的方式进行。

一是入户问卷调查。要求学生调查员在 2017 年 1 月至 2 月的寒假期间回到自己的家乡，在当地民众中进行入户问卷调查。根据培训会说明的本次被调查对象的选取要求，每位调查员选取的被调查对象有 6 名，要求选取的被调查者必须涉及不同性别、不同年龄段、不同文化程度、不同社会职业，而每位被调查者只能填写一份调查问卷。学生调查员入户首先向被调查者讲解说明本次调查的目的意义和调查问卷填写的相关问题，采取被调查者自己填写问卷或者学生调查员向被调查者提问后代为填写两种方式完成调查问卷的填写。

二是个人访谈调查。要求采取“一对一”的个人访谈调查方式，以收集与遗产继承有关的纠纷或案例。本次实地调查要求学生调查员采取“一对一”的个人访谈调查方式，除要求调查问卷由学生调查员在讲解说明本次调查的问题后由被调查者亲自填写或学生调查员代为填写问卷外，还要求辅以“一对一”的个人访谈，以便学生调查员能够收集和详细记录典型的继承纠纷或相关案例的内容。因为，本次调查问卷涉及客观选择与主观理由两部分内容，采取“一对一”的个人访谈方式，可以避免被调查者受到他人的影响，便于更客观深入地了解被调查民众的真实想法。

（四）调查问卷数据的录入、统计汇总、复核与写作提纲的撰写

2017 年 3 月开学后，十省市调查组组长各自组织统一回收本省市的调查问卷与典型案例的访谈记录，然后组织学生统计员对调查问卷进行数据统计，剔除其中的无效问卷，根据有效问卷进行调查数据的录入、制作统计汇总表，并且进行统计汇总数据的复核工作。本次我国十省市实地调查共计发放调查问卷 5739 份，收回有效问卷 5085 份，有效问

卷率为88.60%。至2017年4月底，十省市调查组组长先后组织完成了本省市调查问卷统计数据汇总表的定稿。2017年4月，陈苇教授撰写了《当代中国民众财产继承观念与遗产处理习惯实证调查研究》的写作提纲和写作要求，以电子邮件发送给十省市调查组组长。十省市调查组组长根据此写作提纲和写作要求，负责组织本省市的作者撰写各省市本次实证调查研究报告。

在此，我们诚挚地向参加“当代中国民众财产继承观念与遗产处理习惯实证调查”的我国十省市实地调查和调查数据统计汇总工作的全体师生表示衷心的感谢！（全体师生的名单，详见鸣谢）

三、实证调查报告的撰写方法

本次十省市实证调查研究报告共计以下11份：（1）当代中国重庆市民众财产继承观念与遗产处理习惯实证调查研究；（2）当代中国吉林省民众财产继承观念与遗产处理习惯实证调查研究；（3）当代中国上海市民众财产继承观念与遗产处理习惯实证调查研究；（4）当代中国河北省民众财产继承观念与遗产处理习惯实证调查研究；（5）当代中国湖北省民众财产继承观念与遗产处理习惯实证调查研究；（6）当代中国江西省民众财产继承观念与遗产处理习惯实证调查研究；（7）当代中国四川省民众财产继承观念与遗产处理习惯实证调查研究；（8）当代中国广东省民众财产继承观念与遗产处理习惯实证调查研究；（9）当代中国海南省民众财产继承观念与遗产处理习惯实证调查研究；（10）当代中国福建省民营企业主财产继承观念与遗产处理习惯实证调查研究；（11）当代中国川渝等地民营企业主财产继承观念与遗产处理习惯实证调查研究。

我国学者指出：“研究法律自离不开条文的分析，这是研究的根据。但仅仅研究条文是不够的，我们也应注意研究法律的实效问题……社会现实与法律条文之间，往往存在着一定的差距。如果只注重条文，而不注意实施情况，只能说是条文的、形式的、表面的研究，而不是活动的、功能的研究。我们应该知道法律在社会上的实施情况，是否有效，推行的程度如何，对人民的生活有什么影响等。”① 因此，我们在研究本次民众继承习惯实证调查的统计汇总数据资料时，既要考察法律文本和学者观点，也要研究法律在社会民众中的实施情况和在司法实践中的适用情况，进行“活动的、功能的研究”。因此，对于“当代中国民众财产继承观念与遗产处理习惯实证调查研究”之调查研究报告的撰写，我们主要采取以下五种研究方法：

第一，个人访问调查研究法，包括“入户问卷调查”和“个人访谈”。我们组织学生调查员对我国东北部的吉林省、东部的上海市、北部的河北省、中部的湖北省和江西省、南部的广东省和海南省、东南部的福建省、西南部的重庆市和四川省共计十省市的5739名被调查民众，开展了“当代中国民众财产继承观念与遗产处理习惯实证调查研究”的实地调查，采取个人访问调查研究法，包括“入户问卷调查”和“个人访谈”的方式，了解我国十省市被调查民众对于遗产范围的界定与归扣（又称遗产归扣）、继承开始的通知和公告、遗产管理、法定继承、遗嘱继承、继承和遗赠的接受与放弃、继承权的丧失与被继承人的宥恕、继承权的丧失与代位继承、继承协议、遗产债务清偿、遗产分割、无人

① 瞿同祖：《中国法律与中国社会》（导论），商务印书馆2010年版，第2页。

承受遗产等方面的民众观念和遗产处理习惯，收集遗产纠纷案例，进行调查资料的统计汇总，为本研究报告的撰写提供第一手国情资料。

第二，统计数据研究法。根据我国十省市被调查民众对于遗产范围的界定、继承开始的通知和公告、遗产管理、法定继承、遗嘱继承、继承和遗赠的接受与放弃、继承权的丧失与被继承人的宥恕、继承权的丧失与代位继承、继承协议、遗产债务清偿、遗产分割、无人承受遗产的财产继承观念和遗产处理习惯的调查问卷，统计相关调查数据，制作调查统计数据汇总表，然后对统计汇总数据进行分析研究，总结归纳我国十省市被调查民众的财产继承观念与遗产处理习惯各自的特点，并且主要根据被调查民众填写的理由来分析这些特点产生的原因，为进一步分析我国《继承法》各项具体制度的优点与不足打下基础。

第三，案例研究法。在开展“当代中国民众财产继承观念与遗产处理习惯实证调查”中，一方面通过实地“入户访谈”收集继承纠纷案例，另一方面在撰写调查研究报告过程中在中国裁判文书网收集和选取我国人民法院近年审理继承纠纷案件的判决书进行研究与分析，考察法律“在社会上的实施情况”是否有效，其在司法审判的实践中被适用的情况如何，“对人民群众的生活有什么影响”，从而总结司法实践中反映的我国《继承法》各项具体制度立法的优点与不足，为提出相关立法建议提供社会实践效果和法律适用情况的参考。

第四，比较研究法。针对涉及遗产处理的各项具体制度，包括遗产范围的界定、继承开始的通知和公告、遗产管理、法定继承、遗嘱继承、继承和遗赠的接受与放弃、继承权的丧失与被继承人的宥恕、继承权的丧失与代位继承、继承协议、遗产债务清偿、遗产分割、无人承受遗产制度进行比较研究。我们主要在两个领域进行比较研究：一是外国继承法的比较研究，主要考察大陆法系国家和英美法系国家的相关立法，总结其中有益的立法经验；二是我国诸继承法学者建议稿的立法观点的比较研究，包括考察研究我国学者公开发表的以下七部继承法学者建议稿[①]：梁慧星等学者建议稿（本书以下各章简称“梁稿”）[②]、徐国栋等学者建议稿（本书以下各章简称“徐稿”）[③]、何丽新等学者建议稿（本书以下各章简称“何稿”）[④]；王利明等学者建议稿（本书以下各章简称“王稿”）[⑤]、张玉敏等学者建议稿（本书以下各章简称“张稿”）[⑥]、陈苇等学者建议稿（本

① 本书各章所列的我国继承法学者建议稿，按照各学者建议稿的出版或发表时间的先后排序。

② 梁慧星（课题负责人）：《中国民法典草案建议稿》，法律出版社 2003 年版；梁慧星（课题负责人）：《中国民法典草案建议稿附理由·继承编》，法律出版社 2013 年版，本书所引用的“梁稿”条文均出自此书，但特别注明为其他版本的除外。

③ 徐国栋主编：《绿色民法典草案》，社会科学文献出版社 2004 年版，本书所引用的“徐稿”条文均出自此书。

④ 何丽新、谢美山、熊良敏等：《民法典草案继承法编修改建议稿》，载《厦门大学法律评论》2004 年第 2 期，第 251~301 页（以下简称“何稿”），本书所引用的“何稿”条文均出自此文。

⑤ 王利明（项目主持人）：《中国民法典学者建议稿及立法理由·人格权编、婚姻家庭编、继承编》，法律出版社 2005 年版，本书所引用的“王稿”条文均出自此书。

⑥ 张玉敏（课题负责人）：《中国继承立法建议稿及立法理由》，人民出版社 2006 年版，本书所引用的“张稿”条文均出自此书。

书以下各章简称“陈稿”)①、杨立新等学者建议稿（本书以下各章简称“杨稿”)② 的主要观点，在此基础上进行比较评析，比较分析其异同，吸取其中有益的立法经验和理论观点，为提出相关立法完善建议提供法律文献和法学理论的基础。

第五，文献研究法。对涉及遗产继承制度的著作和论文等参考文献进行研究，尤其注意对近年我国学者出版发表的有关“民法典继承编”立法与实践研究的学术著作和论文进行研究，以吸取前人的研究成果，为修改和完善我国《继承法》、为“中国民法典继承编”的编纂提出相关立法建议，提供学术观点的参考。

2017 年 5 月起，根据陈苇教授撰写的《当代中国民众财产继承观念与遗产处理习惯实证调查研究》的写作提纲和写作要求，十省市调查组组长各自组织本地作者以本省市的调查统计数据汇总表为基础，并且收集相关参考文献和在中国裁判文书网等下载各级人民法院对于遗产纠纷案件的司法裁判文书，采取以上五种研究方法，合作撰写本省市民众财产继承观念与遗产处理习惯实证调查研究稿件的初稿、第二稿、第三稿（有的省市先后修改撰写了第四、五、六、七、八稿不等)，其间，根据陈苇教授的历次修改补充建议和中期评审专家的意见，各省市调查组组长对本省市调查研究报告稿件多次进行了相关修改和补充，至 2018 年 12 月十省市调查组组长全部向课题负责人陈苇教授提交了本省市调查研究报告的定稿。从 2019 年 1 月起，陈苇教授继续对我国十省市调查研究报告稿件进行审阅和修改补充，然后组织重庆地区调查组的博士生对这些稿件统一进行了三次修改补充，最终于 2019 年 6 月底完成了 11 份定稿（其中，有 9 份为我国九省市各自的民众继承习惯之调查研究报告，还有 2 份分别为福建省民营企业主继承习惯之调查研究报告和川渝等地民营企业主继承习惯之调查研究报告)，共同构成了本课题成果著作的主要内容，共计 100 余万字。

① 陈苇（项目负责人)：《〈中华人民共和国继承法〉修正案（学者建议稿）》，本建议稿全文摘自陈苇主编：《外国继承法比较与中国民法典继承编制定研究》，北京大学出版社 2011 年版，载陈苇主编：《中国继承法修改热点难点问题研究》，群众出版社 2013 年版，本书所引用的“陈稿”条文均出自此书。

② 杨立新、杨震等：《〈中华人民共和国继承法〉修正草案建议稿》，载《河南财经政法大学学报》2012 年第 5 期，第 14~26 页，本书所引用的“杨稿”的条文均出自此文。

第二章　当代中国重庆市民众财产继承观念与遗产处理习惯实证调查研究*

第一节　当代中国重庆市民众财产继承观念与遗产处理习惯实证调查概况

一、被调查地区概况

（一）重庆市社会经济发展水平情况

2018 年全市实现地区生产总值 20363.19 亿元，比上年增长 6.0%。按常住人口计算，全市人均地区生产总值达 65933 元，比上年增长 5.1%。全员劳动生产率为 118647 元/人，比上年增长 6.6%。①

（二）重庆市人口结构情况

关于重庆市的城乡人口结构，2018 年全市常住人口 3101.79 万人，比上年增加 26.63 万人，其中城镇人口 2031.59 万人，占常住人口比重（常住人口城镇化率）为 65.50%；乡村人口有 1070.20 万人，占常住人口比重为 34.50%。关于重庆市的人口性别结构，全市男性人口 1563.43 万人，占总人口比重为 50.40%，女性人口 1538.36 万人，占总人口比重为 49.60%。关于重庆市的人口年龄结构，少儿人口（0~15 周岁人口）有 562.29 万人，占总人口的 18.10%；青壮年人口（15~59 周岁人口）有 1901.12 万人，占总人口的 61.30%；老年人口（60 周岁及以上人口）有 1075.73 万人，占总人口的 34.70%。②

（三）重庆市城乡人口的年均收入情况

2018 年全市居民人均可支配收入 26386 元，比上年增长 9.2%。按常住地分，城镇居民人均可支配收入 34889 元，增长 8.4%；农村居民人均可支配收入 13781 元，增长 9.0%。③

---

* 作者简介：陈苇，女，西南政法大学外国家庭法及妇女理论研究中心主任、民商法学院教授、博士生导师；石婷，女，法学博士，西南政法大学民商法学院讲师；白玉，女，西南政法大学 2017 级民商法博士研究生；刘宇娇，女，西南政法大学 2018 级民商法博士研究生。

① 参见中国统计信息网：《重庆市 2018 年国民经济和社会发展统计公报》，载 http://www.tjcn.org/tjgb/22cq/35817.html，访问时间：2019 年 5 月 22 日。

② 参见中国统计信息网：《重庆市 2018 年国民经济和社会发展统计公报》，载 http://www.tjcn.org/tjgb/22cq/35817.html，访问时间：2019 年 5 月 22 日。

③ 参见中国统计信息网：《重庆市 2018 年国民经济和社会发展统计公报》，载 http://www.tjcn.org/tjgb/22cq/35817.html，访问时间：2019 年 5 月 22 日。

二、实证调查情况简介

2016 年 11 月，西南政法大学陈苇教授主持申报的司法部科研项目“我国遗产处理制度系统化构建研究”被批准立项。为给此项目的理论研究和制度研究提供国情资料，必须了解当代中国民众的财产继承观念和遗产处理习惯。考虑到课题组的人力、物力的限制，陈苇教授选择我国十省市包括东北部的吉林省、东部的上海市、北部的河北省、中部的湖北省和江西省、南部的广东省和海南省、东南部的福建省、西南部的重庆市和四川省作为被调查地区，然后联系并确定了各省市调查组组长共同组织开展本项目的子课题“当代中国民众的财产继承观念与遗产处理习惯实证调查研究”。本次当代中国“重庆市民众财产继承观念与遗产处理习惯实证调查研究”是西南政法大学陈苇教授主持的“当代中国民众财产继承观念与遗产处理习惯实证调查研究”的组成部分之一，由西南政法大学民商法学院陈苇教授担任重庆地区调查组组长，由西南政法大学民商法学院胡苷用副教授担任副组长。

（一）调查问卷的设计和学生调查员的召集与培训

2016 年 11 月中旬，陈苇教授组织重庆市课题组成员分工合作，设计制作“当代中国民众财产观念与遗产处理习惯实证调查”的调查问卷，至同年 12 月中旬完成了调查问卷的设计工作。然后，陈苇教授把该调查问卷通过电子邮件发送给参与本次实证调查的十省市调查组组长，以供开展实地调查时十省市被调查地区统一使用。同年 12 月下旬，根据陈苇教授撰写的“当代中国民众财产继承观念与遗产处理习惯社会调查动员和培训会”的说明书，陈苇教授作为重庆市调查组组长，分别联系了西南政法大学民商法学院党总支张伟莉书记、年级辅导员蒋莉老师和商法教研室李杨老师，在她们的动员和协助下，在民商法学院共计召集了 113 名重庆籍学生志愿者担任社会调查员。2016 年 12 月 28 日，陈苇教授和胡苷用副教授共同组织召开“当代中国重庆市民众财产继承观念与遗产处理习惯实证调查动员暨社会调查知识培训会”。在会上，陈苇教授给每位学生调查员发放了 6 份调查问卷，首先向学生调查员讲解说明此次社会调查的目的和意义，然后对学生调查员进行社会调查知识培训。她详细介绍了本次问卷调查的各项问题、调查的方法和具体要求，向学生调查员逐一讲解本次调查知识的要点，要求在 6 名被调查者中，有 20~40 岁的青年人 2 名、41~60 岁的中年人 2 名或 3 名和 60 岁以上老年人 1 名或 2 名，且男女各 3 名。在 2017 年 1 月的寒假期间学生调查员回到自己的家乡，开展重庆市民众财产继承观念与遗产处理习惯的实地调查。

（二）实地社会调查的方式

2017 年 1 月至 2 月的寒假期间，重庆市学生调查员在其家乡开展实地社会调查。本次调查主要采取学生调查员“入户问卷调查”和“个人访谈”的方式。

一是入户问卷调查。学生调查员在 2017 年的寒假期间回到自己的家乡，向当地民众进行入户问卷调查。每位被调查对象必须符合培训会的条件要求，而且其只能填写一份调查问卷。学生调查员入户后，首先向被调查者讲解说明调查的目的意义和调查问卷询问的问题，然后让被调查者自己填写问卷或者学生调查员向被调查者询问后代为填写的方式完成问卷填写。

二是个人访谈。要求采取“一对一”的个人访谈方式，以收集与遗产继承有关的纠纷或案例。本次实地调查，除填写调查问卷外，还要求辅以“一对一”的个人访谈，收集和记录典型的继承纠纷或相关案例的内容。因为调查问卷涉及客观选择与主观理由两部分内容，采取“一对一”的个人访谈方式，可以避免被调查者受到他人的影响，便于客观深入地了解被调查民众的真实想法。

（三）调查问卷数据的录入、统计汇总、复核与撰写调查研究报告

2017 年 3 月开学后，重庆市调查组教师组织统一回收了调查问卷与典型案例的访谈记录，然后组织学生统计员对调查问卷进行数据统计工作。本次调查实际发放调查问卷 678 份，回收有效问卷为 634 份，有效回收率达 93.51%。随后，根据有效问卷进行调查数据的录入、制作统计汇总表，再进行统计汇总数据的复核工作。2017 年 4 月底完成了《〈当代中国民众财产继承观念与遗产处理习惯实证调查问卷〉重庆市民众实证调查统计数据汇总表》的定稿。我们在此需要特别说明，关于各项调查问题之统计人数的合计，凡单选题的人数合计均为 100%，合计在统计表中；凡多选题的人数合计均超过 100%，故不予进行合计统计。本调查报告就是根据此次调查统计数据汇总表进行分析和研究而成的。在此，特向所有参与此次调查活动的老师和同学表示衷心的感谢!①

2017 年 4 月，陈苇教授拟定了“当代中国民众财产继承观念与遗产处理习惯实证调查研究的写作提纲与写作要求”。2017 年 5 月起，我们根据此写作提纲和写作要求，进入参考文献资料的收集和调查报告的写作与修改阶段。本章“当代中国重庆市民众财产继承观念与遗产处理习惯实证调查研究”由西南政法大学陈苇教授、石婷博士共同撰写初稿至第四稿，其间，根据陈苇教授对初稿至第四稿的历次修改意见和中期评审专家的评审意见，多次对稿件进行了相应的修改和补充，最后向课题负责人陈苇教授交稿。2019 年 1 月，陈苇教授对重庆市调查研究报告继续进行审阅和修改补充，然后组织重庆市调查组博士生对重庆市调查研究报告统一进行了三次修改补充，最终于 2019 年 6 月完成定稿。

三、被调查对象的基本情况

本次调查的对象为重庆市常住人口，我们根据 634 份有效问卷，对 634 名被调查者的性别、年龄和职业情况统计如下：

（一）被调查者的性别情况

表 2-1　被调查者的性别情况统计

性别	人数	比例
男	319	50.32%
女	315	49.68%
合计	634	100%

关于本次被调查者的性别情况，调查统计数据显示，在 634 名被调查者中，男性有 319 人（50.32%）；女性有 315 人（49.68%）。可见，被调查者的男女性别占比大体

① 参与重庆市民众财产继承观念与遗产处理习惯的实地调查以及调查数据统计汇总等工作的师生名单，详见“鸣谢”。

持平。

（二）被调查者的年龄情况

表 2-2　被调查者的年龄情况统计

年龄	人数	比例
20-30 岁	168	26.50%
31-40 岁	78	12.30%
41-50 岁	138	21.77%
51-60 岁	83	13.09%
61-70 岁	85	13.40%
71 岁以上	82	12.94%
合计	634	100%

关于本次被调查者的年龄情况，调查统计数据显示，在 634 名被调查者中，青年人（20~40 岁）有 246 人（38.80%）；中年人（41~60 岁）有 221 人（34.86%）；老年人（61 岁以上）有 167 人（26.34%）。可见，在本次被调查对象中，青年人和中年人的人数大体相当，两者占比合计为 73.66%，而老年人的人数较之前二者约少一成，只占 26.34%，即被调查者以中青年为主体。

（三）被调查者的职业情况

表 2-3　被调查者的职业情况统计

职业	人数	比例
农民	163	25.71%
工人	63	9.94%
经商	56	8.83%
公务员及企事业单位人员	137	21.61%
其他	215	33.91%
合计	634	100%

关于本次被调查者的职业情况，调查统计数据显示，在 634 名被调查者中，农民有 163 人（25.71%）；公务员及企事业单位人员有 137 人（21.61%）；工人有 63 人（9.94%）；商人有 56 人（8.83%）；其他职业有 215 人（33.91%）。可见，在被调查者的职业情况中，其他职业的占比最高，占近三成半（33.91%）；农民和工人合计占三成半（35.65%）；公务员及企事业单位职工合计占两成（21.61%）；经商的只占近一成（8.83%）。

综上所述，本次被调查者的男女性别比大体持平，老、中、青各年龄段者均有，但以中青年为主体，而且他们的职业涉及广泛，基本能够反映不同性别、年龄和职业被调查者的财产继承观念与遗产处理习惯。

第二节　当代中国重庆市民众财产继承观念与遗产处理习惯实证调查的数据统计情况

一、遗产范围界定之调查数据统计情况

关于遗产范围界定之调查数据统计，我们主要从遗产的种类和被继承人生前特种赠与财产的归扣两个方面进行调查数据的统计情况汇总分析。

（一）遗产的种类

问题【一、（一）】“2016年2月某甲因车祸死亡，经清理某甲个人名下的遗物如下，您认为，哪些属于某甲的遗产？A. 住房一套；B. 小汽车一辆；C. 家庭日常生活用品若干；D. 存款10万元；E. 股票10万元；F. 某甲以其姓名注册的邮箱、QQ账号等；G. 单位出租给某甲的午休住房一间；H. 某甲向某公司购货的欠款5万元；I. 某甲因交通事故死亡获得50万元赔偿金。（多选）”

表2-4　属于遗产种类的民众观念情况统计（多选）

选项	人数	比例
A. 住房一套	632	99.68%
B. 小汽车一辆	621	97.95%
C. 家庭日常生活用品若干	421	66.40%
D. 存款10万元	603	95.11%
E. 股票10万元	532	83.91%
F. 某甲以其姓名注册的邮箱、QQ账号等	125	19.72%
G. 单位出租给某甲的午休住房一间	50	7.89%
H. 某甲向某公司购货的欠款5万元	220	34.70%
I. 某甲因交通事故死亡获得50万元赔偿金	479	75.55%

关于属于遗产种类的民众观念，调查统计数据显示，在634名被调查者中，（1）选择A、B、D、E项，认为房屋（99.68%）、汽车（97.95%）、存款（95.11%）、股票（83.91%）属于遗产的，均占八成至九成以上；认为G项“单位出租给某甲的午休住房”不属于遗产的，占九成以上（92.11%）[①]；（2）选择C、H、I项，认为家庭日常生活用品若干（66.40%）、欠款（34.70%）和死亡赔偿金（75.55%）属于遗产的，各占三成和六成半以上；（3）选择F项，认为“某甲以其姓名注册的邮箱、QQ账号等”属于遗产的占近两成（19.72%），但其是否属于遗产我国现行法无规定。

① 认为“单位出租给某甲的午休住房”属于遗产的仅占7.89%，即有九成以上（92.11%）的人认为其不属于遗产。

（二）被继承人生前特种赠与财产的归扣

1. 被继承人生前特种赠与财产是否应归入遗产范围的民众观念情况统计

问题【一、（二）1.】“张老汉有三个儿子，在10年前大儿子甲结婚时，张老汉给其资助购买婚房的现金20万元；二儿子乙一直未结婚，但5年前在其开办豆腐坊时，张老汉资助其营业资金10万元。在两年前小儿子丙结婚时，张老汉为其购买一套价值30万元的房屋（产权登记在小儿子丙名下）；2016年1月张老汉去世时遗留有个人所有的住房一套和50万元存款。请问上述哪些财产应当计算入遗产？A. 张老汉生前给三个儿子不同资助的财产与死亡时其遗留的住房、存款，均应当合并计算为遗产；B. 张老汉去世时遗留的个人所有的住房和50万元存款，才可以计算为遗产；C. 其他。（单选）”

表2-5 被继承人生前特种赠与财产是否应归入遗产范围的民众观念情况统计（单选）

选项	人数	比例
A. 张老汉生前给三个儿子不同资助的财产与死亡时其遗留的住房、存款，均应当合并计算为遗产	110	17.35%
B. 张老汉去世时遗留的个人所有的住房和50万元存款，才可以计算为遗产	448	76.97%
C. 其他	36	5.68%
合计	634	100%

关于被继承人生前资助的财产是否应归入遗产范围的民众观念，调查统计数据显示，在634名被调查者中，（1）选择B项遗产的范围应仅以被继承人死亡时遗留的财产为限，不包括被继承人生前对子女的特种赠与财产的，占七成半以上（76.97%）；（2）选择A项被继承人生前对子女继承人的特种赠与财产与死亡时其遗留的住房、存款，均应当合并计算为遗产的，占近两成（17.35%）。

2. 归扣遗产的价值计算时间的民众观念情况统计

问题【一、（二）2.】“如果上述答案您选A，请问张老汉为小儿子丙买房的价值应该按何时计算？A. 买房时；B. 张老汉去世时；C. 实际分割遗产时；D. 其他。（单选）”

表2-6 归扣遗产的价值计算时间的民众观念情况统计（单选）

选项	人数	比例
A. 买房时	24	21.82%
B. 张老汉去世时	21	19.09%
C. 实际分割遗产时	37	33.64%
D. 其他	28	25.45%
合计	110	100%

关于归扣遗产的价值计算时间的民众观念，统计数据显示，在填写本问题的110名被调查者中，（1）选择C项应按实际分割遗产时计算的，占三成以上（33.64%）；（2）选择A项应按购置该财产时计算的，占两成以上（21.82%）；（3）选择B项应按被继承人去世时计算的，占不到两成（19.09%）。即认为应按实际分割遗产时计算归扣遗产价值的占比居第一位。

3. 生前特种赠与财产是否归扣纳入遗产范围的民间习惯情况统计

问题【一、（二）3.】“在您所在地区，如果发生上述张老汉生前给三个儿子不同资助财产的情况，在继承遗产时这些资助财产是否被合计到遗产范围内？A. 是；B. 不是。（单选）”

表2-7　生前特种赠与财产是否归扣纳入遗产范围的民间习惯情况统计（单选）

选项	人数	比例
A. 是	168	26.50%
B. 不是	466	73.50%
合计	634	100%

关于生前特种赠与财产是否归扣纳入遗产范围的民间习惯，调查统计数据显示，634名被调查者所在地区的继承习惯是：（1）B项没有此归扣习惯的，占七成以上（73.50%）；（2）A项有该习惯的，占近三成（26.50%）。

4. 生前特种赠与财产不归入遗产情况下的分配方式之民间习惯统计

问题【一、（二）4.】“上一题如果您选择B项，即这些资助财产不是被合计到遗产范围内，三个儿子是如何分配父亲张老汉的遗产的？A. 平均分配；B. 乙应该适当多分；C. 其他。（单选）”

表2-8　生前特种赠与财产不归入遗产情况下的分配方式之民间习惯统计（单选）

选项	人数	比例
A. 平均分配	281	60.30%
B. 乙应该适当多分	133	28.54%
C. 其他	52	11.16%
合计	466	100%

关于生前特种赠与财产不归入遗产情况下的分配方式之民间习惯，调查统计数据显示，填写本问题的466名被调查者所在地区的继承习惯是：（1）A项有平均分配习惯的，占六成（60.30%）；（2）B项有乙应当适当多分习惯的，占近三成（28.54%）。

二、继承开始的通知和公告之调查数据统计情况

关于继承开始的通知和公告之调查数据统计，我们主要从继承开始的通知和公告的主体、继承开始的通知和公告的方式、继承开始的通知和公告的期间三个方面进行调查数据

的统计情况汇总分析。

（一）继承开始的通知和公告的主体

问题【二、（一）】“被继承人死亡后，在您所在的地区一般由下列哪些人通知涉及遗产分配的相关人员？A. 知道被继承人死亡的继承人；B. 保管遗产的继承人；C. 知道被继承人死亡的单位、村（居）委会；D. 处理被继承人死亡事件的机构，如公安交警部门；E. 其他。（多选）”

表 2-9　继承开始的通知和公告的主体的民间习惯情况统计（多选）

选项	人数	比例
A. 知道被继承人死亡的继承人	458	72. 24%
B. 保管遗产的继承人	418	65. 93%
C. 知道被继承人死亡的单位、村（居）委会	283	44. 64%
D. 处理被继承人死亡事件的机构，如公安交警部门	252	39. 75%
E. 其他	37	5. 84%

关于继承开始的通知和公告的主体的民间习惯，调查统计数据显示，被调查者所在地区的继承习惯是：（1）A、B 两项由继承人作为通知主体的，各占六成至七成以上，具体包括：“知道被继承人死亡的继承人”（72. 24%）和“保管遗产的继承人”（65. 93%）；（2）C 项由知道被继承人死亡的单位、村（居）委会为通知主体的，占近四成半（44. 64%）；（3）D 项由处理被继承人死亡事件的机构为通知主体的，占近四成（39. 75%）。

（二）继承开始的通知和公告的方式

问题【二、（二）】“被继承人死亡后，您所在地区的人们一般采取以下哪些方式通知涉及遗产处理的相关人员？A. 口头、电话、微信等方式通知；B. 信件、告知函等书面通知；C. 在报纸、电视、网络等平台上发布被继承人死亡的公告；D. 在被继承人所在地的村（居）委会公告栏公告；E. 申请人民法院以公告程序进行公告；F. 其他。（多选）”

表 2-10　继承开始的通知和公告的方式的民间习惯情况统计（多选）

选项	人数	比例
A. 口头、电话、微信等方式通知	514	81. 07%
B. 信件、告知函等书面通知	320	50. 47%
C. 在报纸、电视、网络等平台上发布被继承人死亡的公告	141	22. 24%
D. 在被继承人所在地的村（居）委会公告栏公告	212	33. 44%
E. 申请人民法院以公告程序进行公告	167	26. 34%
F. 其他	14	2. 21%

关于继承开始的通知和公告的方式的民间习惯，调查统计数据显示，634 名被调查者所在地区的继承习惯是：（1）A、B 两项分别由口头、电话、微信等通知（81.07%）和信件、告知函等书面通知（50.47%）的，各占五成至八成以上；（2）C、D、E 三项，分别在报纸、电视、网络等平台上发布被继承人死亡的公告（22.24%）、在被继承人所在地的村（居）委会公告栏公告（33.44%）和申请人民法院以公告程序进行公告（26.34%）的，各占二成至三成以上。

（三）继承开始的通知和公告的期间

问题【二、（三）】“您认为，通知人应在被继承人死亡后几日内发出通知？A. 3 日；B. 7 日；C. 15 日；D. 30 日；E. 其他。（单选）”

表 2-11　继承开始的通知和公告期间的民众观念情况统计（单选）

选项	人数	比例
A. 3 日	245	38.64%
B. 7 日	160	25.24%
C. 15 日	127	20.03%
D. 30 日	76	11.99%
E. 其他	26	4.10%
合计	634	100%

关于继承开始的通知和公告期间的民众观念，调查统计数据显示，在 634 名被调查者中，（1）选择 A、B 两项应在 7 日内的较短期间发出通知和公告的，合计占六成以上（占 63.88%）；（2）选择 C、D 两项应在 15 至 30 日内发出通知和公告的，合计占三成多（32.02%）。

三、遗产管理之调查数据统计情况

关于遗产管理之调查数据统计，我们主要从遗产管理人的确定、遗产管理人的职责与报酬、遗产管理人的损害赔偿责任三个方面进行调查数据的统计情况汇总分析。

（一）遗产管理人的确定

问题【三、（一）】“您所在地区人们处理遗产继承时，一般由谁清点和管理遗产？A. 死者的法定继承人：配偶、子女、父母、兄弟姐妹、孙子女或外孙子女、祖父母或外祖父母；B. 死者的儿媳或女婿；C. 死者家族中的德高望重者；D. 死者的其他亲戚朋友；E. 死者所在的单位或村/居委会；F. 其他。（多选）理由是什么？”

1. 关于遗产管理人的确定的民间习惯情况统计

表 2-12　关于遗产管理人的确定的民间习惯情况统计（多选）

<table>
<tr><th colspan="2">选项</th><th colspan="2">人数</th><th colspan="2">比例</th></tr>
<tr><td rowspan="6">A. 死者的法定继承人：配偶、子女、父母、兄弟姐妹、孙子女或外孙子女、祖父母或外祖父母</td><td>配偶</td><td rowspan="6">633</td><td>312</td><td rowspan="6">99.84%</td><td>49.21%</td></tr>
<tr><td>子女</td><td>300</td><td>47.31%</td></tr>
<tr><td>父母</td><td>268</td><td>42.27%</td></tr>
<tr><td>兄弟姐妹</td><td>111</td><td>17.51%</td></tr>
<tr><td>孙子女或外孙子女</td><td>52</td><td>8.2%</td></tr>
<tr><td>祖父母或外祖父母</td><td>26</td><td>4.1%</td></tr>
<tr><td colspan="2">B. 死者的儿媳或女婿</td><td colspan="2">167</td><td colspan="2">26.34%</td></tr>
<tr><td colspan="2">C. 死者家族中的德高望重者</td><td colspan="2">268</td><td colspan="2">42.27%</td></tr>
<tr><td colspan="2">D. 死者的其他亲戚朋友</td><td colspan="2">140</td><td colspan="2">22.08%</td></tr>
<tr><td colspan="2">E. 死者所在的单位或村/居委会</td><td colspan="2">161</td><td colspan="2">25.39%</td></tr>
<tr><td colspan="2">F. 其他</td><td colspan="2">16</td><td colspan="2">2.52%</td></tr>
</table>

关于遗产管理人的确定的民间习惯，调查统计数据显示，634 名被调查者所在地区的继承习惯是：（1）A 项由死者的法定继承人作为遗产管理人的，占九成以上（99.84%）；（2）B、C、D、E 四项，分别由“死者的儿媳或女婿”（26.34%）、“死者家族中的德高望重者”（42.27%）、“死者的其他亲戚朋友”（22.08%）和“死者所在的单位或村/居委会”（25.39%）作为遗产管理人的，各占二成至四成以上。其中，选择 A 项“死者的法定继承人”担任遗产管理人的 633 名被调查中，认为应由法定继承人中的配偶（49.21%）、子女（47.31%）和父母（42.27%）担任遗产管理人的，各占四成以上。

2. 关于遗产管理人的确定的民间习惯之理由情况统计

表 2-13　关于遗产管理人的确定的民间习惯之理由情况统计

项目	人数	比例
A. 遗产管理人一般由法定继承人来担任，便于清点和妥善管理遗产	138	74.59%
B. 遗产管理人一般由法定继承人之外的人或组织来担任，可以防止遗产被隐藏、转移，有利于保护遗产相关人的合法权益	30	16.22%
C. 其他理由	17	9.19%
合计	185	100%

关于遗产管理人的确定的民间习惯之理由，调查统计数据显示，有 185 名被调查者填写了理由，（1）认为遗产管理人一般由法定继承人来担任的理由是，A 项便于清点和妥善管理遗产的，占近七成半（74.59%）；（2）认为遗产管理人一般由法定继承人之外的人或组织来担任的理由是，B 项可以防止遗产被隐藏、转移，有利于保护遗产相关人合法

权益的，占一成半以上（16.22%）。

（二）遗产管理人的职责与报酬

1. 遗产管理人的职责的民众观念情况统计

问题【三、（二）1.】“您认为，遗产管理人的职责有哪些？A. 清查遗产，制作遗产清单；B. 妥善保管遗产；C. 查明被继承人生前的债权和债务，积极地追讨债权或清偿债务；D. 查明被继承人是否留有遗嘱，并且确定遗嘱是否真实合法；E. 可以原告或被告的身份参加因遗产引起的诉讼；F. 定期制作遗产管理报告，向继承人报告遗产管理的情况；G. 其他。（多选）”

表 2-14 遗产管理人的职责的民众观念情况统计（多选）

选项	人数	比例
A. 清查遗产，制作遗产清单	556	88.96%
B. 妥善保管遗产	570	91.20%
C. 查明被继承人生前的债权和债务，积极地追讨债权或清偿债务	449	71.84%
D. 查明被继承人是否留有遗嘱，并且确定遗嘱是否真实合法	353	56.48%
E. 可以原告或被告的身份参加因遗产引起的诉讼	501	80.16%
F. 定期制作遗产管理报告，向继承人报告遗产管理的情况	366	58.56%
G. 其他	10	1.60%

关于遗产管理人的职责的民众观念，调查统计数据显示，填写该问题的625名被调查者中，认为遗产管理人的职责包括A、B、C、D、E、F六项，即“清查遗产，制作遗产清单”（88.96%）、“妥善保管遗产”（91.20%）、“查明被继承人生前的债权和债务，积极地追讨债权或清偿债务”（71.84%）、“查明被继承人是否留有遗嘱，并且确定遗嘱是否真实合法”（56.48%）、“可以原告或被告的身份参加因遗产引起的诉讼”（80.16%）和“定期制作遗产管理报告，向继承人报告遗产管理情况”（58.56%）的，各占五成至九成以上。

2. 遗产管理人是否有权取得报酬的民间习惯情况统计

问题【三、（二）2.】“您所在地区，负责管理遗产的人是否可以获得报酬？A. 继承人担任遗产管理人的，不能请求给付报酬；B. 法院指定的遗产管理人，有权请求给付报酬；C. 继承人选任的第三人作为遗产管理人，是否给付报酬，应当由继承人决定；D. 继承人选任的第三人作为遗产管理人，一律有权请求给付报酬；E. 其他。（多选）”

表 2-15 遗产管理人是否有权取得报酬的民间习惯情况统计（多选）

选项	人数	比例
A. 继承人担任遗产管理人的，不能请求给付报酬	296	46.69%
B. 法院指定的遗产管理人，有权请求给付报酬	426	67.19%
C. 继承人选任的第三人作为遗产管理人，是否给付报酬，应当由继承人决定	290	45.74%
D. 继承人选任的第三人作为遗产管理人，一律有权请求给付报酬	261	41.17%
E. 其他	25	3.94%

关于遗产管理人是否有权取得报酬的民间习惯，调查统计数据显示，被调查者所在地区的继承习惯是：（1）B 项法院指定的遗产管理人有权请求给付报酬的，六成半以上（67.19%）；（2）A 项继承人担任遗产管理人的不能请求给付报酬的，四成半以上（46.69%）；（3）C、D 两项继承人选任的第三人作为遗产管理人，其中，C 项是否给付报酬应当由继承人决定的，占四成半（45.74%）；D 项一律有权请求给付报酬的，占四成以上（41.17%）。

（三）遗产管理人的损害赔偿责任

问题【三、（三）】“在您所在地区，负责管理遗产的人对因其过错造成的较大财产损失，是否承担赔偿责任？A. 只有故意或重大过失的，才承担赔偿责任；B. 无论是故意或重大过失或一般轻过失的，都要承担赔偿责任；C. 其他。（单选）”

表 2-16　遗产管理人的损害赔偿责任之民间习惯情况统计（单选）

选项	人数	比例
A. 只有故意或重大过失的，才承担赔偿责任	359	56.62%
B. 无论是故意或重大过失或一般轻过失的，都要承担赔偿责任	256	40.38%
C. 其他	19	3.00%
合计	634	100%

关于遗产管理人的损害赔偿责任之民间习惯，调查统计数据显示，634 名被调查者所在地区的继承习惯是：（1）A 项只有遗产管理人有故意或重大过失，才承担损害赔偿责任的，占五成半以上（56.62%）；（2）B 项无论遗产管理人是故意、重大过失或一般轻过失的，都要承担损害赔偿责任的，占四成（40.38%）。

四、法定继承之调查数据统计情况

关于法定继承之调查数据统计，我们主要从法定继承人的范围与顺序、配偶与血亲继承人的法定应继份、配偶对遗产中家庭住房的先取权与终生使用权、后顺序特殊法定继承人对遗产中原使用的住房及日常生活用品的终生使用权、尽了主要赡养义务的丧偶儿媳或女婿的遗产分配方式五个方面进行调查数据的统计情况汇总分析。

（一）法定继承人的范围与顺序

1. 法定继承人的范围与顺序的民众观念情况统计

问题【四（一）1.】“下列亲属，您认为哪些应当作为法定继承人？他们各自的继承顺序如何？请根据您认为适当的先后顺序填写数字：1. 2. 3. ……例如，父母（1）；子女（2）；祖父母、外祖父母（3）。如果您认为应当在同一顺序的人，可以填写相同的数字，例如，配偶（1）；父母（1）；子女（1）；祖父母、外祖父母（1）。”

配偶（ ）	父母（ ）	儿子（ ）女儿（ ）
孙子女（ ）外孙子女（ ）	祖父母（ ）外祖父母（ ）	兄弟（ ）姐妹（ ）
侄子女（ ）外甥子女（ ）	伯叔姑舅姨（ ）	堂兄弟姐妹（ ）
表兄弟姐妹（ ）	其他亲属（称谓）（ ）	其他亲属（称谓）（ ）

表 2-17　法定继承人的范围与顺序的民众观念情况统计（多选）

亲属名称	第一顺序		第二顺序		第三顺序		第四顺序		第四顺序以上	
	人数	比例	人数	比例	人数	比例	人数	比例	人数	比例
配偶	552	87.07%	27	4.26%	17	2.68%	0	0%	0	0%
父母	404	63.72%	135	21.29%	63	9.94%	5	0.79%	0	0%
子	456	71.92%	131	20.66%	47	7.41%	0	0%	0	0%
女	416	67.19%	121	19.09%	50	7.88%	0	0%	0	0%
孙子女	7	1.10%	318	50.10%	150	23.66%	29	4.57%	32	5.05%
外孙子女	7	1.10%	298	47.00%	125	19.72%	29	4.57%	32	5.05%
祖父母	10	1.58%	316	49.84%	138	19.72%	51	8.04%	37	5.84%
外祖父母	10	1.58%	303	47.79%	127	21.77%	48	7.57%	40	6.31%
兄弟	10	1.58%	264	41.64%	134	20.03%	50	7.89%	39	6.15%
姐妹	10	1.58%	257	40.54%	139	21.14%	50	7.89%	39	6.15%
侄子女	1	0.16%	4	0.63%	159	25.08%	58	9.15%	71	11.20%
外甥子女	1	0.16%	5	0.63%	154	24.29%	63	9.94%	71	11.20%
伯叔姑	0	0%	5	0.79%	162	25.55%	69	10.88%	73	11.51%
舅姨	0	0%	5	0.79%	162	25.55%	69	10.88%	73	11.51%
堂兄弟	1	0.16%	5	0.79%	156	24.61%	66	10.41%	63	9.94%
堂姐妹	1	0.16%	5	0.79%	156	24.61%	66	10.41%	63	9.94%
表兄弟	0	0%	3	4.73%	96	15.14%	70	11.04%	85	13.41%
表姐妹	0	0%	3	4.73%	96	15.14%	70	11.04%	85	13.41%
其他亲属	0	0%	1	0.16%	14	2.21%	0	0%	0	0%

关于法定继承人的范围与顺序的民众观念，各顺序以被调查者选择占比最高的作为统计依据，调查统计数据显示，被调查者较认可的法定继承人的范围与顺序是：（1）第一顺序配偶（87.07%）、父母（63.72%）、子（71.92%）、女（67.19%）；（2）第二顺序孙子女（50.10%）、外孙子女（47.00%）、祖父母（49.84%）、外祖父母（47.79%）、兄弟（41.64%）、姐妹（40.54%）；（3）第三顺序侄子女（25.08%）、外甥子女（24.29%）、伯叔姑舅姨（25.55%）、堂兄弟姐妹（24.61%）、表兄弟姐妹（15.14%）。

2. 配偶与血亲继承人顺序的民众观念情况统计

问题【四、（一）2.】“以下三种法定配偶继承人的范围和顺序，您认为哪一个更为适当？（单选）”

A	B	C
第一顺序：子女	第一顺序：子女	第一顺序：配偶、子女、父母
第二顺序：父母	第二顺序：父母	第二顺序：兄弟姐妹、祖父母、外祖父母
第三顺序：兄弟姐妹、祖父母、外祖父母 兄弟姐妹的子女（侄子女、外甥子女为代位继承人）	第三顺序：兄弟姐妹、祖父母、外祖父母 兄弟姐妹的子女（侄子女、外甥子女为代位继承人）	第三顺序：侄子女、外甥子女
配偶无固定顺序，能够参与第一顺序、第二顺序、第三顺序的继承	配偶无固定顺序，能够参与第一顺序、第二顺序的继承	配偶有固定顺序，只能参与第一顺序的继承

表 2-18　配偶与血亲继承人顺序的民众观念情况统计（单选）

选项	人数	比例
A. 配偶无固定顺序，可以参与第一、二、三顺序继承	77	12.15%
B. 配偶无固定顺序，可以参与第一、二顺序继承	81	12.78%
C. 配偶固定第一顺序	476	75.07%
合计	634	100%

关于配偶与血亲继承人顺序的民众观念，调查统计数据显示，在634名被调查者中，（1）选择C项第一顺序：配偶、子女、父母；第二顺序：兄弟姐妹，祖父母、外祖父母；第三顺序：侄子女、外甥子女；配偶有固定顺序，其属于第一顺位继承人的，占七成半（75.07%）。（2）选择A、B两项顺序为：第一顺序为子女；第二顺序为父母；第三顺序为兄弟姐妹、祖父母、外祖父母、兄弟姐妹的子女（侄子女、外甥子女为代位继承人）；配偶无固定的继承顺序，可分别与第一、第二（或第三）顺序的法定继承人共同继承的，合计占近二成半（24.93%）。

（二）配偶与血亲继承人的法定应继份

问题【四、（二）】“配偶与血亲继承人共同继承各取得遗产的份额，您认为以下哪一项更为适当？（单选）”

A. 配偶无固定继承顺序	B. 配偶无固定继承顺序	C. 配偶有固定继承顺序	D. 其他
配偶与第一顺序的子女共同继承时，其取得遗产的一半。另一半由子女按人数平均继承	配偶与第一顺序的子女共同继承时，其取得遗产的一半，另一半由子女按人数平均继承	第一顺序继承人为配偶、子女、父母，共同继承时按人数均分遗产	

续表

A. 配偶无固定继承顺序	B. 配偶无固定继承顺序	C. 配偶有固定继承顺序	D. 其他
配偶与第二顺序的父母共同继承时，其取得遗产的三分之二。另外三分之一由父母平均继承	配偶与第二顺序的父母共同继承时，其取得遗产的三分之二，另外三分之一由父母平均继承	无第一顺序血亲继承人时，配偶继承全部遗产	
配偶与第三顺序的兄弟姐妹、祖父母和外祖父母共同继承时，其取得遗产的四分之三。另外四分之一由兄弟姐妹、祖父母、外祖父母，按人数平均继承	无第一、第二顺序血亲继承人时，配偶继承全部遗产		
无上述三个顺序血亲继承人时，配偶取得全部遗产			

表 2-19　配偶与血亲继承人的法定应继份的民众观念情况统计（单选）

选项	人数	比例
A. 配偶无固定继承顺序，参与前三顺位继承并取得不同份额；无上述三个顺序血亲继承人时，配偶取得全部遗产	152	23.97%
B. 配偶无固定继承顺序，参与前二顺序继承并取得不同份额；无第一、第二顺序血亲继承人时，配偶继承全部遗产	133	20.98%
C. 配偶有固定继承顺序，与第一顺序继承人共同继承并均分遗产	338	53.31%
D. 其他	11	1.74%
合计	634	100%

关于配偶与血亲继承人的法定应继份之民众观念，调查统计数据显示，在634名被调查者中，（1）选择C项配偶应按固定顺序继承并均分遗产的，占近五成半（53.31%）；（2）选择A、B两项认为配偶应为无固定顺序继承的，可参与前三顺序或前二顺序继承，并取得不同份额的，合计占近四成半（44.95%）。值得注意的是，在前述对于配偶的法定继承顺序的民众观念统计中，认为配偶应无固定继承顺序的，A、B两项合计只占近二成半（24.93%）（见表2-18）。然而，在关于配偶与血亲继承人的法定应继份的统计中，却有近四成半（44.95%）的被调查者认为配偶应不固定继承顺序，与不同顺序的血亲继承人共同继承且在不同的继承顺序取得不同的遗产份额，占比上升了二成（20.02%）。

（三）配偶对遗产中家庭住房的先取权与终生使用权

1. 配偶对遗产中家庭住房的先取权与终生使用权的民间习惯情况统计

问题【四、（三）1.】“甲乙是夫妻，育有一子丙。甲因病去世时留下的遗产包括：价值50万元的住房一套（原由甲乙夫妻共同居住，丙已结婚分家另过）、价值10万元小汽车一辆和20万元存款。如果上述情况发生在您所在的地区，被继承人甲的妻子乙是否可以优先继承这套房屋（配偶先取权）？A. 是；B. 否。（单选）”

表2-20　配偶对遗产中家庭住房的先取权与终生使用权的民间习惯情况统计（单选）

选项	人数	比例
A. 是	544	85.80%
B. 否	90	14.20%
合计	634	100%

关于配偶对遗产中家庭住房的先取权与终生使用权的民间习惯，调查统计数据显示，634名被调查者所在地区的继承习惯是：（1）A项有该习惯的，占八成半（85.80%）；（2）B项无此习惯的，占近一成半（14.20%）。

2. 配偶对遗产中家庭住房的先取与终生使用是否付费的民间习惯情况统计

问题【四、（三）2.】“如果甲的妻子乙可以优先继承这套房屋，但该住房的价值超过其应当继承的遗产份额40万元，您所在地区是按照下列哪种情况处理的？A. 乙有权继承该住房，且无须向其他共同应召继承人丙进行补偿；B. 如果乙有经济补偿能力，则应当向其他共同应召继承人丙适当进行补偿；C. 其他。（单选）”

表2-21　配偶对遗产中家庭住房的先取与终生使用是否付费的民间情况统计（单选）

选项	人数	比例
A. 乙有权继承该住房，且无须向其他共同应召继承人丙进行补偿	217	34.22%
B. 如果乙有经济补偿能力，则应当向其他共同应召继承人丙适当进行补偿	407	64.20%
C. 其他	10	1.58%
合计	634	100%

关于配偶对遗产中家庭住房的先取与终生使用是否付费的民间习惯，调查统计数据显示，634名被调查者所在地区的继承习惯是：（1）B项有适当补偿习惯的，占近六成半（64.20%）；（2）A项没有该习惯即无须进行补偿的，只占近三成半（34.22%）。也就是说，如配偶无经济补偿能力的，可不予补偿而终生使用此房屋。

（四）后顺序特殊法定继承人对遗产中原使用的住房及日常生活用品的终生使用权

关于后顺序特殊法定继承人对遗产中原使用的住房及日常生活用品的终生使用权，也可称为后顺序特殊法定继承人对特殊遗产的终生使用权。

1. 后顺序特殊法定继承人对遗产中原使用的住房及日常生活用品的终生使用权的民间习惯情况统计

问题【四、（四）1.】“某甲死亡时遗留下若干遗产，其中包括一套三室一厅的住房（其中一间房屋一直由某甲的祖父居住）。由于某甲的祖父属于后顺序继承人而不能参加继承，遗产全部由某甲的第一顺序继承人即其配偶及子女等继承。请问：在您所在地区，如果发生了上述情况，有哪些处理方式？某甲的祖父对该供其居住的房屋，是否可以继续居住？A. 是；B. 否。（单选）”

表 2-22　后顺序特殊法定继承人对特殊遗产的终生使用权的民间习惯情况统计（单选）

选项	人数	比例
A. 是	554	87.38%
B. 否	80	12.62%
合计	634	100%

关于后顺序特殊法定继承人对特殊遗产是否享有终生使用权的民间习惯，调查统计数据显示，634 名被调查者所在地区的继承习惯是：（1）A 项有该习惯的，占近九成（87.38%）；（2）B 项没有该习惯的，占一成以上（12.62%）。

2. 后顺序特殊法定继承人对遗产中原使用的住房及日常生活用品的终生使用是否付费的民间习惯情况统计

问题【四、（四）2.】“如果某甲的祖父可以继续居住，是否其可以不交租金？A. 是；B. 否。（单选）”

表 2-23　后顺序特殊法定继承人对特殊遗产终生使用是否付费的民间习惯情况统计（单选）

选项	人数	比例
A. 是	554	87.38%
B. 否	80	12.62%
合计	634	100%

关于后顺序特殊法定继承人对特殊遗产的终生使用是否付费的民间习惯，调查统计数据显示，634 名被调查者所在地区的继承习惯是：（1）A 项没有支付租金习惯的，占近九成（87.38%）；（2）B 项有支付租金习惯的，占一成以上（12.62%）。

3. 后顺序特殊法定继承人对遗产中原使用的住房及日常生活用品的终生使用权之期限的民间习惯情况统计

问题【四、（四）3.】“如果某甲的祖父可以继续居住，是否可以居住到其死亡时为止（终生使用权）？A. 是；B. 否。（单选）”

表 2-24　后顺序特殊法定继承人对特殊遗产的终生使用权之期限的民间习惯情况统计（单选）

选项	人数	比例
A. 是	483	84.15%
B. 否	91	15.85%
合计	574	100%

关于后顺序特殊法定继承人对特殊遗产的终生使用权之期限的民间习惯，调查统计数据显示，填写该问题的574名被调查者所在地区的继承习惯是：（1）A项享有此终生使用权的，占近八成半（84.15%）；（2）B项不享有终生使用权的，占一成半（15.85%）。

（五）尽了主要赡养义务的丧偶儿媳或女婿的遗产分配方式

问题【四、（五）】"村民某甲，老伴因病早年去世，膝下有两个儿子乙和丙。2003年乙与丁结婚后和某甲共同生活。2012年1月乙因交通事故死亡，但乙的妻子丁仍然一直照料公公某甲的晚年生活，直至2015年1月某甲去世。请问：在您所在的地区，如发生上述情况，因乙的妻子丁对公公某甲尽了主要赡养义务，如何处理某甲的遗产分配问题？A. 丁可以与某甲的二儿子丙共同继承，并且平均分配遗产；B. 丁不能与某甲的二儿子丙共同继承，但其可分得适当的遗产；C. 其他。（单选）理由是什么？"

1. 尽了主要赡养义务的丧偶儿媳或女婿的遗产分配方式的民间习惯情况统计

表2-25　尽了主要赡养义务的丧偶儿媳或女婿的遗产分配方式的民间习惯情况统计（单选）

选项	人数	比例
A. 丁可以与某甲的二儿子丙共同继承，并且平均分配遗产	429	67.67%
B. 丁不能与某甲的二儿子丙共同继承，但其可分得适当的遗产	188	29.65%
C. 其他	17	2.68%
合计	634	100%

关于尽了主要赡养义务的丧偶儿媳或丧偶女婿遗产分配方式的民间习惯，调查统计数据显示，634名被调查者所在地区的继承习惯是：（1）A项尽了主要赡养义务的丧偶儿媳或女婿可以作为第一顺序继承人共同继承且平均分配遗产的，占近七成（67.67%）；（2）B项尽了主要赡养义务的丧偶儿媳或女婿不能作为第一顺序继承人，但可以酌情分得遗产的，占近三成（29.65%）。

2. 尽了主要赡养义务的丧偶儿媳或丧偶女婿的遗产分配方式的民间习惯之理由情况统计

表2-26　尽了主要赡养义务的丧偶儿媳或女婿的遗产分配方式的民间习惯之理由情况统计

项目	人数	比例
A. 作为儿媳妇，丁孝敬公公，已经尽了赡养义务，符合中国的孝道文化和道德观念，因此有权在第一顺位继承遗产	425	67.03%
B. 虽然丁一直照顾公公的晚年生活，但毕竟不是甲的子女，与甲不具有血缘关系	180	28.39%
C. 其他理由	29	4.58%
合计	634	100%

关于尽了主要赡养义务的丧偶儿媳或女婿的遗产分配方式的民间习惯之理由，调查统计数据显示，634 名被调查者中，（1）认为儿媳丁可以与某甲的儿子共同继承遗产的理由是，A 项认为儿媳丁孝敬公公，已经尽了赡养义务，符合中国的孝道文化和道德观念，因此有权作为第一顺位人取得继承遗产的，占六成半以上（67.03%）；（2）认为儿媳丁仅可分得适当遗产的理由是，B 项认为虽然儿媳丁一直照顾公公的晚年生活，但毕竟不是甲的子女，与甲不具有血缘关系，因此不能作为第一顺位继承的，占近三成（28.39%）。

五、遗嘱继承之调查数据统计情况

关于遗嘱继承之调查数据统计，我们主要从公证遗嘱与其他形式遗嘱的效力、遗嘱自由的限制——特留份、夫妻共同遗嘱三个方面进行调查数据的统计情况汇总分析。

（一）公证遗嘱与其他形式遗嘱的效力

问题【五、（一）】“退休职工甲有一套个人住房，其于 2011 年 2 月立了一份遗嘱，写明由其妻子乙一人继承该住房，并将该遗嘱进行了公证。后来，甲改变了主意，他重新写了一份遗嘱，写明由其妻子乙和儿子丙共同继承该房屋。2016 年 3 月甲住院病危期间，当着两位医生在现场立下口头遗嘱，指定其个人住房由儿子丙继承，两个小时后其抢救无效死亡。请问：您认为，甲的个人住房应该由谁继承？A. 乙；B. 乙和丙；C. 丙。（单选）理由是什么？”

1. 公证遗嘱与其他形式遗嘱适用效力的民众观念情况统计

表 2-27　公证遗嘱与其他形式遗嘱适用效力的民众观念情况统计（单选）

选项	人数	比例
A. 乙（公证遗嘱有效）	185	29.18%
B. 乙和丙（后成立的未公证书面遗嘱有效）	206	32.49%
C. 丙（最后的口头遗嘱有效）	243	38.33%
合计	634	100%

关于公证遗嘱与其他形式遗嘱适用效力的民众观念，调查统计数据显示，在 634 名被调查者中，（1）选择 B、C 两项后遗嘱的适用效力优先于前一公证遗嘱的，合计占七成（70.82%）；（2）而选择 A 项公证遗嘱适用效力优先的，占近三成（29.18%）。

2. 公证遗嘱与其他形式遗嘱适用效力的民众观念之理由情况统计

表 2-28　公证遗嘱与其他形式遗嘱适用效力的民众观念之理由情况统计

项目	人数	比例
A. 公证遗嘱的程序规范，具有较强的公示效力和证明效力	154	24.29%
B. 书面遗嘱（即第二份遗嘱）比较正式，容易取证，且其订立在公证遗嘱之后，反映了被继承人的真实意愿	137	21.61%

续表

项目	人数	比例
C. 口头遗嘱形式灵活，且有证人作证，能够反映被继承人的最后真实意愿	227	35.80%
D. 口头遗嘱形式不固定，很难准确、完全地反映被继承人的真实意愿，且有被篡改或修改的可能性	15	2.37%
E. 其他理由	101	15.93%
合计	634	100%

关于公证遗嘱与其他形式遗嘱适用效力的民众观念之理由，调查统计数据显示，在634名被调查者中，（1）认为公证遗嘱适用效力优先的理由是，A项公证遗嘱的程序规范，具有较强的公示效力和证明效力的，占近二成半（24.29%）；（2）认为后成立的书面遗嘱应优先适用的理由是，B项书面遗嘱（即第二份遗嘱）比较正式，容易取证，且其订立在公证遗嘱之后，反映了被继承人真实意愿的，占二成以上（21.61%）；（3）认为最后的口头遗嘱应优先适用的理由是，C项口头遗嘱形式灵活，且有证人作证，能够反映被继承人的最后真实意愿的，占三成半（35.80%）；但是，还有不到半成（2.37%）的人填写的理由是，D项口头遗嘱形式不固定，很难准确、完全地反映被继承人的真实意愿，且有被篡改或修改的可能性；（4）填写E项其他理由的，占一成半（15.93%）。

（二）遗嘱自由的限制——特留份

问题【五、（二）】“甲生前立了一份遗嘱，将自己死后遗留下的财产全部赠给他的一个好朋友乙，而他的配偶和子女不能取得甲的任何遗产。请问：您认为甲的这一做法是否适当？A. 适当；B. 不适当；C. 其他。（单选）理由是什么？”

1. 以遗嘱将个人遗产全部赠给他人的民众观念情况统计

表2-29　以遗嘱将个人遗产全部赠给他人之民众观念情况统计（单选）

选项	人数	比例
A. 适当	240	38.03%
B. 不适当	371	58.80%
C. 其他	20	3.17%
合计	631	100%

关于以遗嘱将个人遗产全部赠给他人的民众观念，调查统计数据显示，在631名被调查者中，对于被继承人将遗产全部赠与他人的行为，（1）选择B项不适当的，即主张对被继承人以遗嘱处分个人财产的行为予以适当限制的，占近六成（58.80%）；（2）选择A项适当的，占近四成（38.03%）。

2. 以遗嘱将个人遗产全部赠给他人的民众观念之理由情况统计

表 2-30　以遗嘱将个人遗产全部赠给他人的民众观念之理由情况统计

项目	人数	比例
A. 甲对自己的财产，享有自由处分的权利，其他人无权干涉	165	40.34%
B. 此行为易造成家庭财产外流，不利于保障甲的配偶及其子女的生活，同时也不符合风俗习惯，为常人难以接受	236	57.71%
C. 其他理由	8	1.95%
合计	409	100%

关于从以遗嘱将个人遗产全部赠给他人的民众观念之理由，调查统计数据显示，有409名被调查者填写了选择理由，（1）认为该行为不适当的理由是，B项此行为易造成家庭财产外流，不利于保障甲的配偶及其子女的生活，同时也不符合风俗习惯，为常人难以接受的，占近六成（57.71%）；（2）认为上述行为适当的理由是，A项认为被继承人对自己的财产，享有自由处分的权利，其他人无权干涉的，占四成（40.34%）。

（三）夫妻共同遗嘱

1. 夫妻共同遗嘱的民众观念与理由情况统计

问题【五、（三）1.】“甲乙是夫妻，双方在生前共同设立一份遗嘱，对死后的遗产处理进行安排。甲乙双方在遗嘱中约定，不管谁先去世，另一方都不得改变此遗嘱对遗产的处理安排。请问：您是否认同甲乙夫妻双方共同设立遗嘱的此约定？A. 赞同；B. 不赞同。（单选）理由是什么？”

（1）夫妻共同遗嘱的民众观念情况统计。

表 2-31　夫妻共同遗嘱的民众观念情况统计（单选）

选项	人数	比例
A. 赞同	465	73.34%
B. 不赞同	169	26.66%
合计	634	100%

关于夫妻共同遗嘱的民众观念，调查统计数据显示，在634名被调查者中，对于夫妻设立共同遗嘱，①选择A项赞成的，占近七成半（73.34%）；②选择B项不赞成的，占二成半以上（26.66%）。

（2）夫妻共同遗嘱的民众观念之理由情况统计。

表 2-32 夫妻共同遗嘱的民众观念之理由情况统计

项目	人数	比例
A. 该遗嘱为甲乙双方共同设立，反映了双方的共同意愿，理应为双方所遵守	305	77.02%
B. 该遗嘱无法应对出现的新情况和新问题，限制了双方对各自财产的处分权	90	22.73%
C. 其他理由	1	0.25%
合计	396	100%

关于夫妻能否设立共同遗嘱的民众观念之理由，调查统计数据显示，有 396 名被调查者选择了具体理由，①赞同设立的理由是，A 项该遗嘱为甲乙双方共同设立，反映了夫妻双方的共同意愿，理应为双方所遵守的，占近八成（77.02%）；②不赞同设立的理由是，B 项该遗嘱无法应对出现的新情况和新问题，限制了夫妻双方对各自财产的处分权的，占二成以上（22.73%）。

2. 夫妻共同遗嘱存在的民间习惯情况统计

问题【五、(三) 2.】“在您所在地区，有无夫妻共同设立遗嘱的情况发生？A. 有；B. 无。(单选)”

表 2-33 夫妻共同遗嘱存在的民间习惯情况统计（单选）

选项	人数	比例
A. 有	119	21.60%
B. 无	432	78.40%
合计	551	100%

关于夫妻共同遗嘱存在的民间习惯，调查统计数据显示，填写该问题的 551 名被调查者所在地区的继承习惯是：（1）B 项没有设立夫妻共同遗嘱习惯的，占近八成（78.40%）；（2）A 项有该习惯的，占二成以上（21.60%）。值得注意的是，关于夫妻间能否设立共同遗嘱的民众观念统计数据中，尽管近七成半（73.34%）的多数被调查者赞同设立夫妻共同遗嘱（见表 2-31），但在关于夫妻共同遗嘱存在的民间习惯统计数据中，却有近八成（78.40%）的多数被调查者所在地区并没有该习惯。

六、继承和遗赠的接受与放弃之调查数据统计情况

关于继承和遗赠的接受与放弃之调查数据统计，我们主要从继承的接受与放弃的时间与方式、遗赠的接受与放弃的方式与效力、继承的放弃与债权人的撤销权三个方面进行调查数据的统计情况汇总分析。

（一）继承的接受与放弃的时间与方式

问题【六、（一）】“对于继承人放弃继承的时间，您认为下列哪一个更为适当？A. 继承人放弃继承的，应在知道继承开始的两个月内作出放弃继承的表示；B. 继承开始后继承人放弃继承的，应当在遗产处理前，作出放弃继承的意思表示。（单选）请问您所在地区的民众是如何接受与放弃继承的理由是什么？”

1. 继承的接受与放弃的时间之民众观念情况统计

表 2-34　继承的接受与放弃的时间之民众观念情况统计（单选）

选项	人数	比例
A. 继承人放弃继承的，应在知道继承开始的两个月内作出放弃继承的意思表示	245	38.80%
B. 继承开始后继承人放弃继承的，应当在遗产处理前，作出放弃继承的意思表示	389	61.20%
合计	634	100%

关于继承的接受与放弃的时间之民众观念，调查统计数据显示，在 634 名被调查者中，（1）选择 B 项继承人放弃继承，应当在遗产处理前作出放弃继承意思表示的，占六成以上（61.20%）；（2）选择 A 项继承人放弃继承，应在知道继承开始的两个月内作出放弃继承意思表示的，占近四成（38.80%）。

2. 继承的接受与放弃的方式之民间习惯情况统计

表 2-35　继承的接受与放弃的方式之民间习惯情况统计（单选）

选项	人数	比例
A. 依据书面凭证	245	62.34%
B. 依据口头声明	50	12.73%
C. 口头声明与书面凭证皆可	98	24.93%
合计	393	100%

关于继承的接受与放弃的方式之民间习惯，调查统计数据显示，填写该问题的 393 名被调查者所在地区的继承习惯是：（1）A 项依据书面凭证接受继承的，占六成以上（62.34%）；（2）C 项口头声明与书面凭证皆可接受继承的，占近二成半（24.93%）；（3）B 项依据口头声明接受继承的，占一成以上（12.73%）。

（二）遗赠的接受与放弃的方式与效力

问题【六、（二）】“甲生前设立一份遗嘱，在甲死后，将一辆小汽车赠给其侄子乙。后来甲去世，乙得知遗嘱的内容后，对此遗赠没有作出任何意思表示，既没有说接受，也没有说放弃。您认为下列哪一项更为适当？A. 乙无权取得该小汽车，乙的行为应该被视为放弃该遗赠；B. 乙有权取得该小汽车，乙的行为应该被视为接受该遗赠。（单选）请问您所在地区的民众是如何接受遗赠的?”

1. 遗赠的接受与放弃的方式与效力的民众观念情况统计

表 2-36　遗赠的接受与放弃的方式与效力的民众观念情况统计（单选）

选项	人数	比例
A. 乙无权取得该小汽车，乙的行为应该被视为放弃该遗赠	149	23.61%
B. 乙有权取得该小汽车，乙的行为应该被视为接受该遗赠	482	76.39%
合计	631	100%

关于遗赠的接受与放弃的方式与效力的民众观念，调查统计数据显示，在填写该问题的631名被调查者中，对于受遗赠人未作任何意思表示的行为，（1）选择B项应认定为接受遗赠的，占七成半以上（76.39%）；（2）选择A项应认定为放弃遗赠的，占近二成半（23.61%）。

2. 遗赠的接受与放弃的方式与效力的民间习惯情况统计

表 2-37　遗赠的接受与放弃的方式与效力的民间习惯情况统计（单选）

选项	人数	比例
A. 乙无权取得该小汽车，乙的行为应该被视为放弃该遗赠	148	57.36%
B. 乙有权取得该小汽车，乙的行为应该被视为接受该遗赠	110	42.64%
合计	258	100%

关于遗赠的接受与放弃的方式与效力的民间习惯，对于受遗赠人未作任何意思表示的行为，调查统计数据显示，填写该问题的258名被调查者所在地区的继承习惯是：（1）A项视为放弃遗赠的，占近六成（57.36%）；（2）B项视为接受遗赠的，占四成以上（占42.64%）。

（三）继承的放弃与债权人的撤销权

问题【六、（三）】“甲为乙的父亲，2015年年底，乙因病住院治疗，医治无效去世，留下遗产5万元及房屋一套。此时，甲经营的摩配厂已经负债累累，拖欠工人的工资已有10个月，但他考虑儿媳在其丈夫乙去世后独自抚养年幼的女儿有经济困难，于是主动提出放弃继承儿子乙的遗产。甲的债权人却认为甲不应该放弃继承其儿子的遗产，这实际上是逃避债务，侵犯了债权人的利益。为此，甲的债权人起诉至人民法院，要求撤销甲放弃继承儿子乙遗产的行为。您认为下列哪一项更为恰当？A. 甲放弃继承乙遗产的行为，可以被撤销；B. 甲放弃继承乙遗产的行为，不可以被撤销。（单选）请问您所在地区的人们是如何处理此类行为的？理由是什么？”

1. 继承的放弃能否被债权人撤销的民众观念情况统计

表 2-38　继承的放弃能否被债权人撤销的民众观念情况统计（单选）

选项	人数	比例
A. 甲放弃继承乙遗产的行为，可以被撤销	323	51.11%
B. 甲放弃继承乙遗产的行为，不可以被撤销	309	48.89%
合计	632	100%

关于继承人放弃继承的行为是否可以被撤销的民众观念，调查统计数据显示，在填写该问题的632名被调查者中，对于继承人放弃继承的行为，（1）选择A项认为可以被债权人撤销的，占五成以上（51.11%）；（2）选择B项认为不可以被债权人撤销的，占近五成（48.89%）。

2. 继承的放弃能否被债权人撤销的民间习惯及理由情况统计

（1）继承的放弃能否被债权人撤销的民间习惯情况统计。

表 2-39　继承的放弃能否被债权人撤销的民间习惯情况统计（单选）

选项	人数	比例
A. 甲放弃继承乙遗产的行为，可以被撤销	106	51.71%
B. 甲放弃继承乙遗产的行为，不可以被撤销	99	48.29%
合计	205	100%

关于继承的放弃能否被债权人撤销的民间习惯，对于继承人放弃继承的行为，调查统计数据显示，填写该问题的205名被调查者所在地区的民间习惯是：①选择A项可以被债权人撤销的，占五成以上（51.71%）；②选择B项不可以被债权人撤销的，占近五成（48.29%）。

（2）继承的放弃能否被债权人撤销的民间习惯之理由情况统计。

表 2-40　继承的放弃能否被债权人撤销的民间习惯之理由情况统计

项目	人数	比例
A. 可以被撤销，甲的债权人利益也需要被考虑，符合法律的规定	106	51.71%
B. 不可以被撤销，这有利于照顾其儿媳及孙女的生活，她们是弱势群体，理应获得优先照顾	99	48.29%
合计	205	100%

关于继承的放弃能否被债权人撤销的民间习惯之理由，调查统计数据显示，在填写了理由的205名被调查者中，①认为该行为可以被撤销的理由是，A项债权人利益也需要被

考虑，这是符合法律规定的，占五成以上（51.71%）；②认为该行为不可以被撤销的理由是，B 项有利于照顾儿媳及其孙女的生活，她们是弱势群体，理应获得优先照顾的，占近五成（48.29%）。

七、继承权的丧失、被继承人的宥恕与代位继承之调查数据统计情况

关于继承权的丧失、被继承人的宥恕与代位继承之调查数据统计，我们主要从继承权的丧失与被继承人的宥恕、继承权的丧失与代位继承两个方面进行调查数据的统计情况汇总分析。

（一）继承权的丧失与被继承人的宥恕

问题【七、（一）】"某甲如果以欺诈或者胁迫的手段，迫使或者妨碍其父乙设立、变更或者撤销遗嘱，情节较为严重，但后来其获得乙的原谅。您认为以下哪一种处理更为适当？A. 某甲有资格继承其父遗产；B. 某甲仍然不能继承其父遗产。（单选）理由是什么？在您所在的地区，人们是如何处理此类行为的？"

1. 继承权的丧失与被继承人的宥恕的民众观念及理由情况统计

（1）继承权的丧失与被继承人的宥恕的民众观念情况统计。

表 2-41　继承权的丧失与被继承人的宥恕的民众观念情况统计（单选）

选项	人数	比例
A. 某甲有资格继承其父的遗产	456	72.04%
B. 某甲仍然不能继承其父的遗产	177	27.96%
合计	633	100%

关于继承权的丧失与被继承人的宥恕的民众观念，调查统计数据显示，在填写本问题的 633 名被调查者中，对于继承人因欺诈或者胁迫而丧失继承权，可以因被继承人宥恕而恢复的，①选择 A 项可以恢复继承权的，占七成以上（72.04%）；②选择 B 项不可以恢复继承权的，占近三成（27.96%）。

（2）继承权的丧失与被继承人的宥恕的民众观念之理由情况统计。

表 2-42　继承权的丧失与被继承人的宥恕的民众观念之理由情况统计

项目	人数	比例
A. 乙有权处分自己的遗产，如果乙已经原谅了某甲，则可以恢复某甲的继承权	145	53.71%
B. 某甲的行为造成恶劣影响，导致其丧失继承权，即使乙原谅了某甲，也不能恢复某甲的继承权	125	46.29%
合计	270	100%

关于继承权的丧失与被继承人的宥恕的民众观念之理由，调查统计数据显示，在填写了选择理由的270名被调查者中，①认为继承权可以恢复的理由是，A项被继承人有权处分自己的遗产，如果被继承人已经原谅了某甲，则可以恢复某甲继承权的，占近五成半（53.71%）；②认为继承权不可以恢复的理由是，B项认为某甲的行为造成恶劣影响，导致其丧失继承权，即使被继承人原谅了某甲，也不能恢复某甲的继承权，占四成半以上（46.29%）。

2. 继承权的丧失与被继承人的宥恕的民间习惯情况统计

表2-43　继承权的丧失与被继承人的宥恕的民间习惯情况统计（单选）

选项	人数	比例
A. 可以恢复某甲的继承权	145	53.71%
B. 不可以恢复某甲的继承权	125	46.29%
合计	270	100%

关于继承权丧失后可否因被继承人的原谅而恢复继承权的民间习惯，对于被继承人宥恕后继承人是否可以恢复继承权，调查统计数据显示，填写该问题的270名被调查者所在地区的继承习惯是：（1）A项可以恢复继承权的，占近五成半（53.71%）；（2）B项不可以恢复继承权的，占四成半以上（46.29%）。

（二）继承权的丧失与代位继承

问题【七、（二）】“村民甲死亡后，其子乙因实施伪造遗嘱的行为导致丧失了对其父甲的继承权，乙的儿子丙能否代替其父亲乙去继承祖父甲的遗产，您认为以下哪一种处理更为适当？A. 丙能够代替其父亲乙继承祖父甲的遗产；B. 丙不能代替其父亲乙继承祖父甲遗产。（单选）请问：在您所在地区的人们是如何处理此类情况的？理由是什么？”

1. 继承权丧失的效力是否及于代位继承人的民众观念情况统计

表2-44　继承权丧失的效力是否及于代位继承人的民众观念情况统计（单选）

选项	人数	比例
A. 丙能够代替其父亲乙继承祖父甲的遗产	262	41.32%
B. 丙不能代替其父亲乙继承祖父甲的遗产	372	58.68%
合计	634	100%

关于继承权丧失的效力是否及于代位继承人的民众观念，调查统计数据显示，在634名被调查者中，对于被代位人丧失继承权是否可以代位继承，（1）选择B项不可以代位继承的，占近六成（58.68%）；（2）选择A项可以代位继承的，占四成以上（41.32%）。

2. 继承权丧失的效力是否及于代位继承人的民间习惯及理由情况统计

（1）继承权丧失的效力是否及于代位继承人的民间习惯情况统计。

表 2-45　继承权丧失的效力是否及于代位继承人的民间习惯情况统计（单选）

选项	人数	比例
A. 丙能够代替其父亲乙继承祖父甲的遗产	165	53.23%
B. 丙不能代替其父亲乙继承祖父甲的遗产	145	46.77%
合计	310	100%

关于继承权丧失的效力是否及于代位继承人的民间习惯，调查统计数据显示，对于继承权丧失的效力是否及于代位继承人，填写该问题的 310 名被调查者所在地区的继承习惯是：（1）A 项不及于代位继承人的，占近五成半（53.23%）；（2）B 项及于代位继承人的，占四成半以上（46.77%）。

（2）继承权丧失的效力是否及于代位继承人的民间习惯之理由情况统计。

表 2-46　继承权丧失的效力是否及于代位继承人的民间习惯之理由情况统计

项目	人数	比例
A. 丙作为独立的民事主体，可以孙子的身份来继承祖父甲的遗产，与乙丧失继承权没有关系	160	52.98%
B. 乙已经丧失继承权，导致丙代替乙继承的前提丧失，所以，丙不能代替乙继承甲的遗产	142	47.02%
合计	302	100%

关于继承权丧失的效力是否及于代位继承人的民间习惯之理由，调查统计数据显示，有 302 名被调查者填写了选择理由，①认为不及于代位继承人的理由是，A 项孙子丙作为独立的民事主体，可以孙子的身份来继承祖父的遗产，与其父乙丧失继承权没有关系的，占五成以上（52.98%）；②认为及于代位继承人的理由是，B 项其父乙已经丧失继承权，导致丙代替乙继承的前提丧失，所以丙不能代替乙继承遗产的，占近五成（47.02%）。

八、继承协议之调查数据统计情况

必须说明，本节研究的对象是狭义的继承协议（又称继承扶养协议），是被继承人与继承人之间，就扶养与继承事项签订的协议。关于继承协议之调查数据统计，我们主要从继承协议的订立主体与方式、继承协议的变更方式及效力两个方面进行调查数据的统计情况汇总分析。

（一）继承协议的订立主体与方式

问题【八、（一）1.】“王某，现年 70 岁，有长子王一，次女王二，两个子女均已成家且分家另过。王某的老伴因患癌症花费了大量医药费后去世，老夫妻的共同财产现所剩无几，仅有郊区的一套住房是王某个人财产。虽然王某退休金不多，但身体没有大病，基本生活还是能够维持的。由于长子王一长期在外地工作，为解决父亲王某的养老送终问题，您认为，以下三种做法哪一做法较为妥当？A. 父亲王某与次女王二，双方协商并签订协议，由次女王二一人承担赡养父亲王某的义务，王某的全部遗产指定由王二继承。B. 父亲王某与子女王一、王二，三人协商并签订协议，由次女王二一人承担赡养父亲王某的义务，王某的全部遗产商定由王二继承；王一放弃对父亲王某遗产的继承权。C. 子女王一与王二，两人协商并签订协议，由次女王二一人承担赡养父亲王某的义务，王某的全部遗产商定由王二继承；王一放弃对父亲王某遗产的继承权。（单选）理由是什么？”

1. 继承协议的订立主体与方式的民众观念与理由情况统计

（1）继承协议的订立主体与方式的民众观念情况统计。

表 2-47　继承协议的订立主体与方式的民众观念情况统计（单选）

选项	人数	比例
A. 父亲王某与次女王二协商一致即可签订协议（第一种方式）	81	12.84%
B. 父亲王某需与全部继承人协商共同签订协议（第二种方式）	462	72.81%
C. 共同继承人间签订协议而无须被继承人知晓或同意（第三种方式）	91	14.35%
合计	634	100%

关于继承协议的订立主体与方式的民众观念，调查统计数据显示，在 634 名被调查者中，对于继承协议的订立，①选择 B 项应由被扶养人与全部继承人共同协商签订的，占七成以上（72.81%）；②选择 C 项应由共同继承人间协商签订即可，无须被扶养人知晓或同意的，占近一成半（14.35%）；③选择 A 项应由被扶养人与扶养人协商签订的，占一成以上（12.84%）。

（2）继承协议的订立主体与方式的民众观念之理由情况统计。

表 2-48　继承协议的订立主体与方式的民众观念之理由情况统计

项目	A.			B.	C.
理由	发生遗产继承的双方当事人签订协议即可	王某有权处理自己的财产	尽了赡养义务才可分得财产	全体当事人协商更公平，可以避免发生矛盾	继承人间进行协商更为公平
人数	11	4	4	134	18
比例	6.51%	2.30%	2.30%	78.36%	10.53%

关于继承协议的订立主体与方式的民众观念之理由，调查统计数据显示，有 171 名被调查者填写了选择理由，对于继承协议的订立，①认为被继承人与全体继承人协商一致签订协议的理由是，B 项由全体当事人协商签订，这样更公平，可以避免发生矛盾的，占近八成（78.36%）；②认为继承人间签订协议即可，无须被继承人知晓或同意的理由是，C

项这样更为公平的，占一成以上（10.53%）；③认为协议应由被扶养人和扶养人协商签订的理由是，A 项王某有权处理自己的财产（2.30%）和尽了赡养义务才可分得财产（2.30%）等。

2. 继承协议的民间习惯情况统计

问题【八、（一）2.】“您过去是否听说或者经历过有以上类似的情况？A. 听说过或经历过；B. 从没听说或经历过以上情况。（单选）在听说过或经历过签订继承协议的人中，听说或经历过的方式是哪一种？A. 第一种方式；B. 第二种方式；C. 第三种方式。（多选）”

（1）继承协议的民间习惯情况统计。

表 2-49　继承协议的民间习惯情况统计（单选）

选项	人数	比例
A. 听说过或经历过	291	45.90%
B. 从没听说或经历过以上情况	343	54.10%
合计	634	100%

关于继承协议的民间习惯，调查统计数据显示，634 名被调查者所在地区的民间习惯是：①B 项从没听说或经历过签订继承协议情况的，占近五成半（54.10%）；②A 项听说过或经历过以上情况的，占四成半（45.90%）。

（2）听说过或经历过签订继承协议方式的民间习惯情况统计。

表 2-50　听说过或经历过签订继承协议方式的民间习惯情况统计（多选）

选项	人数	比例
A. 第一种方式	76	26.12%
B. 第二种方式	188	64.60%
C. 第三种方式	94	32.30%

关于听说过或经历过签订继承协议方式的民间习惯，调查统计数据显示，填写该问题的 291 名被调查者所在地区的继承习惯是：对于继承协议的订立，①B 项由被扶养人与全部继承人共同协商签订的，占近六成半（64.60%）；②C 项由继承人间签订协议即可，无须被继承人知晓或同意的，占三成以上（32.30%）；③A 项由被扶养人与扶养人协商签订的，占二成半以上（26.12%）。

（二）继承协议的变更方式及效力

问题【八、（二）】“王某，现年 70 岁，有长子王一，次女王二，三子王三，三个子女均已成家且分家另过。王某的老伴因患癌症花费了大量医疗费后去世，现有郊区的一套住房是王某个人财产，市场价约为 30 万元，王某有少量退休金。王某与王二协商并签订继承协议，由王二主要赡养父亲王某，王某的所有遗产由王二继承。协议签订后，王二全家与父亲王某共同生活了 5 年，后王二因意外交通事故死亡。王二全家在与王某共同生活期间已为王某花费生活费、医疗费等扶养费共 9 万元。为解决王某的养老，您同意下列哪些做法？A. 王二的儿子有继续扶养外祖父王某的能力，王某也愿意与王二的儿子共同生活，应当由王二的儿子继续履行扶养义务，并继承王某的全部遗产；B. 王一、王三共同补偿王二家人 6 万元扶养费后（另有 3 万元扶养费属于应当由王二承担的），如果王一与父亲王某签订新的继承协议，并与王某共同生活一直扶养至其去世，就由王一继承王某的全部遗产；C. 对王二已经支付的扶养费不予补偿，如果王一与父亲王某签订新的继承协议，并与王某共同生活一直扶养至其去世，就由王一继承王某的全部遗产；D. 王一、王三共同补偿王二家人 6 万元扶养费后，由两人共同扶养父亲王某；E. 其他。（单选）您作出以上选择的理由是什么？”

1. 继承协议的变更方式与效力的民众观念情况统计

表 2-51 继承协议的变更方式与效力的民众观念情况统计（单选）

选项	人数	比例
A. 原扶养人的子女有扶养能力，在双方自愿的情况下，由原扶养人的子女继续扶养被扶养人，并继承全部遗产	219	34.54%
B. 原签订的继承协议效力终止，补偿原扶养人一定费用后，由某一有扶养能力的法定继承人，在双方自愿的情况下签订新协议，继续扶养被扶养人，并继承遗产	180	28.39%
C. 原签订的继承协议效力终止，对原扶养人无须补偿，由某一有扶养能力的法定继承人与被扶养人签订新协议，在双方自愿的情况下，继续扶养被扶养人，并继承全部遗产	40	6.31%
D. 原签订的继承协议效力终止，补偿原扶养人一定费用后，应由有扶养能力的全体法定继承人共同依法对被扶养人尽扶养义务，并依法定继承取得遗产	191	30.13%
E. 其他	4	0.63%
合计	634	100%

关于继承协议的变更方式与效力的民众观念，调查统计数据显示，在 634 名被调查者中，（1）选择 A 项，认为该协议可有条件继续履行，如原扶养人的子女有扶养能力的，在原扶养人的子女和被扶养人双方同意的情况下，可由原扶养人的子女继续履行该继承协议的，此即代位扶养的，占近三成半（34.54%）。（2）选择 B、C 两项，认为该协议效力终止，须签订新的继承协议，由新的扶养人履行扶养义务并继承遗产的，合计占近三成半（34.70%）。但 B、C 两项的区别在于，B 项应补偿原扶养人一定费用，而 C 项对原扶养人无须补偿。其中，B 项认为需要对原扶养人的继承人补偿超过其扶养义务部分费用的，占近三成（28.39%），C 项认为不需要对原扶养人的继承人补偿超过其扶养义务部分费用的，占不到一成（6.31%）。（3）选择 D 项，认为该协议效力终止，应向原扶养人的继承人补偿超过其扶养义务部分费用后，由所有法定继承人共同扶养的，即实行法定赡养的，占三成（30.13%）。可见，重庆市被调查者对于代位扶养的认可度最高，占近三成半。

2. 继承协议的变更方式与效力的民众观念之理由情况统计

表 2-52　继承协议的变更方式与效力的民众观念之理由情况统计

项目	人数	比例
A. 由王二的儿子继续扶养王某，可以使继承协议继续履行，避免产生不必要的纠纷，王某可以安享晚年	116	36. 14%
B. 赡养王某是王一和王三的法定义务，由于法律规定法定扶养义务人应平等承担赡养义务，王一、王三应当补偿王二家人 6 万元	144	44. 86%
C. 其他理由	61	19. 00%
合计	321	100%

关于继承协议的变更方式与效力的民众观念之理由，调查统计数据显示，321 名被调查者填写了选择理由，（1）认为应补偿王二家人 6 万元的理由是，B 项赡养王某是子女王一和王三的法定义务，由于法律规定法定扶养义务人应平等承担赡养义务，王一、王三应当补偿王二家人 6 万元的，占近四成半（44. 86%）；（2）认为继承协议继续有效（即代位扶养）的理由是，A 项由王二的儿子继续扶养王某，可以使继承协议继续履行，避免产生不必要的纠纷，以保障王某可以安享晚年的，占三成半以上（36. 14%）；（3）填写 C 项其他理由的，占近二成（19. 00%）。

九、遗产债务清偿之调查数据统计情况

关于遗产债务清偿之调查数据统计，我们主要从遗产债务清偿责任的类型、被继承人丧葬费的支付、遗产债务的清偿顺序三个方面进行调查数据的统计情况汇总分析。

（一）遗产债务清偿责任的类型

问题【九、（一）】“对于‘继承遗产，应当清偿被继承人的债务’，您是怎么理解这句话的？A. 对被继承人的生前所有债务，继承人都应当予以偿还；B. 对被继承人的生前所有债务，继承人应先用所有遗产偿还债务，不足部分由继承人以个人财产偿还；C. 对被继承人的生前所有债务，继承人只以继承的遗产为限予以偿还；D. 对被继承人的生前所有债务，继承人如果存在转移遗产、隐瞒遗产的情形，则其应当负责以遗产和其个人财产偿还所有的债务。（多选）在您所在的地区，人们遇到继承人有转移遗产、隐瞒遗产的情况时，一般是如何处理的？为什么？”

1. 遗产债务清偿责任的类型之民众观念情况统计

表 2-53　遗产债务清偿责任的类型之民众观念情况统计（多选）

选项	人数	比例
A. 对被继承人的生前所有债务，继承人都应当予以偿还	222	35. 02%
B. 对被继承人的生前所有债务，继承人应先用所有遗产偿还债务，不足部分由继承人以个人财产偿还	253	39. 91%

续表

选项	人数	比例
C. 对被继承人的生前所有债务，继承人只以继承的遗产为限予以偿还	371	58.52%
D. 对被继承人的生前所有债务，继承人如果存在转移遗产、隐瞒遗产的情形，则其应当负责以遗产和其个人财产偿还所有的债务	306	48.26%

关于遗产债务清偿责任的类型之民众观念，调查统计数据显示，在634名被调查者中，对于被继承人生前欠下的所有债务，(1) 选择A、B两项主张实行自愿的无限清偿责任的，合计占近七成半（74.93%）；(2) 选择C项主张实行有限清偿责任的，占近六成（58.52%）；(3) 选择D项主张对有侵害遗产违法行为者应当实行强制的无限清偿责任的，占近五成（48.26%）。

2. 继承人侵害遗产的法律责任之民间习惯及理由情况统计

(1) 继承人侵害遗产的法律责任之民间习惯情况统计。

表2-54 继承人侵害遗产的法律责任之民间习惯情况统计（单选）

选项	人数	比例
A. 应承担返还遗产及其相应责任	15	31.92%
B. 交给司法、行政等相关部门处置	18	38.30%
C. 剥夺继承权，不分遗产	14	29.78%
合计	47	100%

关于继承人侵害遗产的法律责任之民间习惯，调查统计数据显示，填写该问题的47名被调查者所在地区的继承习惯是：①A、C两项继承人应承担返还遗产的法律责任、剥夺继承权不分遗产的，合计占六成以上（61.70%）；②B项交给司法、行政等相关部门处置的，占近四成（38.30%）。

(2) 继承人侵害遗产的法律责任的民间习惯之理由情况统计。

表2-55 继承人侵害遗产的法律责任的民间习惯之理由情况统计

项目	人数	比例
A. 继承人转移或隐瞒遗产，主观恶性大，导致侵害遗产利害关系人的财产权益，为了表示惩戒，该继承人不能分得遗产或少分遗产	13	33.33%
B. 交给司法、行政等相关部门处置，能够体现公平	16	41.03%
C. 根据当地习俗，应当剥夺继承权，不分遗产	10	25.64%
合计	39	100%

关于继承人侵害遗产的法律责任的民间习惯之理由，统计数据显示，在填写选择理由的39名被调查者中，①填写B项认为交给司法、行政等相关部门处置，能够体现公平的，占四成以上（41.03%）；②填写A项认为继承人转移或隐瞒遗产，主观恶性大，导致侵害遗产利害关系人的财产权益，为了表示惩戒，该继承人不能分得遗产或少分遗产的，占近三成半（33.33%）；填写C项认为根据当地习俗，应当剥夺继承权，不分遗产的，占二成半（25.64%）。

（二）被继承人丧葬费的支付

问题【九、（二）】“在您所在地区，死者的丧葬费一般是如何支付的？A. 由全体继承人共同支付；B. 从被继承人的遗产中支付；C. 其他。（单选）”

表2-56　被继承人丧葬费的支付民间习惯情况统计（单选）

选项	人数	比例
A. 由全体继承人共同支付	337	53.15%
B. 从被继承人遗产中支付	261	41.17%
C. 其他	36	5.68%
合计	634	100%

关于被继承人丧葬费支付的民间习惯，调查统计数据显示，634名被调查者所在地区的民间习惯是：（1）A项由全体继承人共同支付的，占近五成半（53.15%）；（2）B项从被继承人的遗产中支付的，占四成以上（41.17%）。

（三）遗产债务的清偿顺序

问题【九、（三）】“在您所在地区，对被继承人死亡后遗留的以下费用，一般是按照哪种先后顺序进行清偿的？（1）民间习惯的处理方式；（2）您认为，按照哪种先后顺序进行清偿才比较合理？（多选）”

A. 丧葬费用	D. 欠付的工资	G. 对被继承人扶养较多的人之酌情分配遗产份额
B. 遗产管理等费用	E. 受被继承人扶养人的生活费	H. 遗赠扶养协议写明遗赠的遗产
C. 欠债	F. 税款	

1. 遗产债务清偿顺序的民间习惯情况统计

表2-57　遗产债务清偿顺序的民间习惯情况统计（多选）

费用	第一顺序		第二顺序		第三顺序		第四顺序		第五顺序		第六顺序		第七顺序		第八顺序	
	人数	比例%	人数	比例%	人数	比例%	人数	比例%	人数	比例%	人数	比例%	人数	比例%	人数	比例%
A.	386	60.88	33	5.20	26	4.10	35	5.52	22	3.47	25	3.94	20	3.15	20	3.15

续表

费用	第一顺序		第二顺序		第三顺序		第四顺序		第五顺序		第六顺序		第七顺序		第八顺序	
	人数	比例%	人数	比例%	人数	比例%	人数	比例%	人数	比例%	人数	比例%	人数	比例%	人数	比例%
B.	23	3.62	153	24.13	59	9.30	63	9.94	73	11.51	29	4.57	28	4.42	21	3.31
C.	36	5.68	126	19.87	191	30.13	94	14.83	38	5.99	26	4.10	15	2.37	14	2.21
D.	66	10.41	135	21.29	119	18.77	108	17.03	31	4.89	10	1.58	10	1.58	1	0.16
E.	9	1.42	47	7.41	54	8.52	71	11.20	116	18.30	91	14.35	49	7.73	17	2.68
F.	48	7.57	36	5.68	77	12.15	76	11.99	59	9.31	64	10.09	24	3.79	46	7.26
G.	3	0.47	14	2.21	35	5.52	42	6.62	53	8.36	102	16.09	133	20.98	81	12.78
H.	5	0.79	12	1.89	22	3.47	30	4.73	72	11.36	74	11.67	100	15.77	111	17.51

关于遗产债务清偿顺序的民间习惯，调查统计数据显示，各顺序以被调查者选择占比最高的作为统计依据，在被调查者所在地区，遗产债务按如下顺序清偿：（1）第一顺序为A项“丧葬费用”（60.88%）；（2）第二顺序为B项“遗产管理等费用”（24.13%）和D项“欠付的工资”（21.29%）；（3）第三顺序为C项“欠债”（30.13%）和F项“税款”（12.15%）；（4）第四顺序为E项“受被继承人扶养人的生活费”（18.30%）；（5）第五顺序为G项“对被继承人扶养较多的人之酌情分配遗产份额”（20.98%）；（6）第六顺序为H项“遗赠扶养协议写明遗赠的遗产”（17.51%）。①

2. 遗产债务清偿顺序的民众观念情况统计

表2-58 遗产债务清偿顺序的民众观念情况统计（多选）

费用	第一顺序		第二顺序		第三顺序		第四顺序		第五顺序		第六顺序		第七顺序		第八顺序	
	人数	比例%	人数	比例%	人数	比例%	人数	比例%	人数	比例%	人数	比例%	人数	比例%	人数	比例%
A.	326	51.42	52	8.20	38	5.99	47	7.41	42	6.62	26	4.10	18	2.84	11	1.74
B.	29	4.57	143	22.56	55	8.68	97	15.30	89	14.04	48	7.57	22	3.47	19	3.00
C.	47	7.41	131	20.66	186	29.34	81	12.78	20	3.15	23	3.63	14	2.21	6	0.95
D.	65	10.25	157	24.76	148	23.34	124	19.56	32	5.05	15	2.37	8	1.26	10	1.58
E.	12	1.89	44	6.94	30	4.73	75	11.83	104	16.40	98	15.46	58	9.15	38	5.99
F.	87	13.72	43	6.78	77	12.15	65	10.25	70	11.04	54	8.25	26	4.10	43	6.78
G.	6	0.95	7	1.10	21	3.31	34	5.36	65	10.25	82	12.93	152	23.97	119	18.77
H.	8	1.26	6	0.95	20	3.15	36	5.68	63	9.94	117	18.45	98	15.46	112	17.67

① 必须说明，各顺序原则上以被调查者选择占比最高的作为统计依据，但如各顺序依次排序时，前一顺序后面的顺序占比数不是最高的，则以该后面顺序占比最高的为准，其顺序与原顺序就不一致。例如，在表2-57中，G项占比最高的在第七顺序（20.98%），其顺序被调整后为第五顺序。本章以后各章节中的遗产债务清偿顺序表的统计数据，均是依此规则制作的统计数据说明。

关于遗产债务清偿顺序的民众观念，调查统计数据显示，以各顺序被调查者选择占比最高的作为统计依据，被调查者认可的遗产债务清偿顺序是：（1）第一顺序为A项“丧葬费用”（51.42%）和F项“税款”（13.72%）；（2）第二顺序为B项“遗产管理等费用（22.56%）”和D项“欠付的工资”（24.76%）；（3）第三顺序为C项“被继承人的欠债”（29.34%）；（4）第四顺序为E项“受被继承人扶养人的生活费”（16.40%）；（5）第五顺序为H项“遗赠扶养协议写明遗赠的遗产”（18.45%）；（6）第六顺序为G项“对被继承人扶养较多的人之酌情分配遗产份额”（23.97%）。

十、遗产分割之调查数据统计情况

关于遗产分割之调查数据统计，我们主要从遗产分割的自由与限制、遗产分割瑕疵的担保责任两个方面进行调查数据的统计情况汇总分析。

（一）遗产分割的自由与限制

问题【十、（一）1.】“按您当地的民间习惯，一般如何开始分割遗产？A. 由各继承人共同协商后进行分割；B. 只要有继承人要求分割遗产，就得进行分割；C. 对于被继承人以遗嘱禁止分割的遗产，不得进行分割；D. 其他。（多选）”理由是什么？

1. 遗产分割自由与限制的民间习惯及理由情况统计

（1）遗产分割自由与限制的民间习惯情况统计。

表2-59　遗产分割自由与限制的民间习惯情况统计（多选）

选项	人数	比例
A. 由各继承人共同协商后进行分割	567	89.43%
B. 只要有继承人要求分割遗产，就得进行分割	209	32.97%
C. 对于被继承人以遗嘱禁止分割的遗产，不得进行分割	352	55.52%
D. 其他	0	0%

关于遗产分割自由与限制的民间习惯，调查统计数据显示，634名被调查者所在地区的继承习惯是：①A项共同协商后分割遗产的，占近九成（89.43%）；②C项遗嘱禁止分割则不得分割的，占五成半（55.52%）；③B项只要有继承人要求分割遗产，就得进行分割的，占三成以上（32.97%）。

（2）遗产分割自由与限制的民间习惯之理由情况统计。

表2-60　遗产分割自由与限制的民间习惯之理由情况统计

项目	人数	比例
A. 遗产由各继承人共同所有，遗产分割关系各继承人的利益，故遗产的分割由各遗产继承人共同协商	349	55.05%
B. 每位继承人享有的继承权受法律保护，同时基于效率原则考虑，故继承开始后，基于继承人的要求就可以分割遗产	107	16.88%

续表

项目	人数	比例
C. 遗产是被继承人死亡时遗留下来的个人财产，当然有权通过遗嘱决定遗产的归属和分割	139	21.92%
D. 其他理由	39	6.15%
合计	634	100%

关于遗产分割自由与限制的民间习惯之理由，调查统计数据显示，在634名被调查者中，①认为由各继承人共同协商后进行分割的理由是，A项遗产为各继承人共同所有，遗产分割关系各继承人的利益，故遗产的分割由各遗产继承人共同协商的，占五成半（55.05%）；②认为对被继承人以遗嘱禁止分割的遗产，不得进行分割的理由是，C项遗产是被继承人死亡时遗留下来的个人财产，当然有权通过遗嘱决定遗产归属和分割的，占二成以上（21.92%）；③认为只要有继承人要求分割遗产，就得进行分割的理由是，B项每个继承人享有的继承权受法律保护，同时基于效率原则考虑，故继承开始后，基于继承人的要求就可以分割遗产的，占一成半以上（16.88%）。

2. 提出遗产分割请求时间的民间习惯及理由情况统计

问题【十、（一）2.】“老王去世时留有一套家庭居住的房屋（价值50万元）、存款20万元以及小汽车一辆（价值10万元）。老王去世时，其配偶和唯一的儿子小王均在世。请问：如果在您所在的地区，老王去世后，其儿子小王是否会马上向其母亲提出分割遗产的请求？A. 会；B. 不会；C. 会提出分割其他遗产的请求，但对其母正在居住的房屋的分割需等其母去世后进行；D. 其他。（单选）理由是什么？”

（1）提出遗产分割请求时间的民间习惯情况统计。

表2-61　提出遗产分割请求时间的民间习惯情况统计（单选）

选项	人数	比例
A. 会	54	8.52%
B. 不会	498	78.55%
C. 会提出分割其他遗产的请求，但对其母正在居住的房屋的分割需等其母去世后进行	80	12.61%
D. 其他	2	0.32%
合计	634	100%

关于提出遗产分割请求时间的民间习惯，调查统计数据显示，634名被调查者所在地区的继承习惯是：①B项不会提出上述请求的，占近八成（78.55%）；②A项会提出上述请求的，仅占不到一成（8.52%）；③还有一成以上（12.61%）的人选择了C项，认为会提出分割其他遗产的请求，但对其母正在居住房屋的分割需等其母去世后进行。可见，

主张对其母正在居住的房屋在其生存期间不予分割的，B、C 两项合计占九成以上（91.16%）。

（2）提出遗产分割请求时间的民间习惯之理由情况统计。

表 2-62　提出遗产分割请求时间的民间习惯之理由情况统计

项目	人数	比例
A. 遗产是由小王及其母亲共同继承的，继承开始后，小王有权根据法律规定提出遗产分割的请求，并且有利于防止日后发生不必要的纠纷	57	8.99%
B. 根据当地观念，小王的父亲去世遗留下的财产就应该由其母亲全部继承，故小王不能向其母亲提出遗产分割的请求，如果提出，会被视作不孝敬老人的表现	287	45.27%
C. 为体现孝敬老人，保证老人的晚年生活，小王可以提出分割其他遗产，但对其母正在居住房屋的分割需等其母去世后进行	197	31.07%
D. 其他	93	14.67%
合计	634	100%

关于提出遗产分割请求时间的民间习惯之理由，调查统计数据显示，在 634 名被调查者中，①认为不会提出分割遗产请求的理由是，B 项根据当地观念，小王的父亲去世遗留下的财产就应该由其母亲全部继承，故小王不能向其母亲提出遗产分割的请求，如果提出该遗产分割，会被视作不孝敬老人的，占四成半（45.27%）；②认为会提出分割其他遗产的请求，但对其母正在居住的房屋需等其去世后进行分割的理由是，C 项为体现孝敬老人，保证老人的晚年生活，小王可以提出分割其他遗产，但对其母正在居住房屋的分割需等其母去世后进行的，占三成以上（31.07%）；③认为会提出遗产分割请求的理由是，A 项遗产是由小王及其母亲共同继承的，继承开始后，小王有权根据法律规定提出遗产分割的请求，并且有利于防止日后发生不必要纠纷的，仅占不到一成（8.99%）。

3. 遗产分割是否受遗嘱限制的民众观念与理由情况统计

（1）遗产分割是否受遗嘱限制的民众观念情况统计。

问题【十、（一）3.（1）】“甲乙是夫妻，育有一子丙。甲系个体工商户，他生前立了一份遗嘱，指定由乙和丙共同继承遗产，但其死后遗产中的商铺门面房和家庭住房在 20 年内不能进行分割。甲死亡时留下的遗产有：商铺门面房一间（价值 100 万元）；一套三室一厅的家庭住房（价值 50 万元）、存款 20 万元以及小汽车一辆（价值 10 万元）。您认为，甲是否可以在遗嘱中写明在其死后上述商铺门面房和住房在一定期间内不能进行分割？A. 可以；B. 不可以。（单选）理由是什么？”

①遗产分割是否受遗嘱限制的民众观念情况统计。

表 2-63　遗产分割是否受遗嘱限制的民众观念情况统计（单选）

选项	人数	比例
A. 可以	553	87.22%
B. 不可以	81	12.78%
合计	634	100%

关于遗产分割是否受遗嘱限制的民众观念，调查统计数据显示，在 634 名被调查者中，Ⅰ. 选择 A 项认为可以限制的，占近九成（87.22%）；Ⅱ. 选择 B 项认为不可以限制的，仅占一成以上（12.78%）。

②遗产分割是否受遗嘱限制的民众观念之理由情况统计。

表 2-64　遗产分割是否受遗嘱限制的民众观念之理由情况统计

项目	人数	比例
A. 这些遗产是甲生前的个人财产，在设立遗嘱时有权决定遗产的分配及其分割等问题	188	29.65%
B. 甲在遗嘱中指定商铺门面房和住房在 20 年内不能分割，不利于发挥物的效用及价值，而且容易发生纠纷	220	34.70%
C. 其他理由	226	35.65%
合计	634	100%

关于遗产分割是否受遗嘱限制的民众观念之理由，调查统计数据显示，在 634 名被调查者中，Ⅰ. 认为遗嘱不可以限制遗产分割的理由是，B 项认为被继承人在遗嘱中指定店铺和住房在 20 年内不能分割，不利于发挥物的效用及价值，且容易发生纠纷的，占近三成半（34.70%）；Ⅱ. 认为遗嘱可以限制遗产分割的理由是，A 项认为这些遗产是甲生前的个人财产，在设立遗嘱时有权决定遗产的分配及其分割等问题的，占近三成（29.65%）；Ⅲ. 还有三成半（35.65%）的人填写了其他理由。

（2）被继承人立遗嘱限制遗产分割的具体期限之民众观念情况统计。

问题【十、（一）3.（2）】“在上题中，如果您选择 A 选项，那么该期限多久合适？A. 5 年；B. 10 年；C. 15 年；D. 其他。（单选）”

表 2-65　被继承人立遗嘱限制遗产分割的具体期限之民众观念情况统计（单选）

选项	人数	比例
A. 5 年	255	47.84%
B. 10 年	162	30.39%
C. 15 年	90	16.90%
D. 其他	26	4.87%
合计	533	100%

关于被继承人立遗嘱限制遗产分割的具体期限之民众观念，调查统计数据显示，在填写该问题的533名被调查者中，①选择A项在5年以内的，占近五成（47.84%）；②选择B项在10年以内的，占三成（30.39%）；③选择C项在15年以内的，占一成半以上（16.90%）。

（3）继承人协商能否变更遗嘱限制的民间习惯及理由情况统计。

问题【十、（一）3.（3）】“在您所在地区，如果乙和丙一致同意分割上述财产，那么，他们是否可以不遵守甲的遗嘱在一定期限内禁止分割上述房产的规定而进行分割？A. 可以不遵守遗嘱；B. 不可以不遵守遗嘱。（单选）理由是什么？”

①继承人协商能否变更遗嘱限制的民间习惯情况统计。

表 2-66　继承人能否变更遗嘱对遗产分割限制的民间习惯情况统计（单选）

选项	人数	比例
A. 可以不遵守遗嘱	304	47.95%
B. 不可以不遵守遗嘱	330	52.05%
合计	634	100%

关于继承人协商能否变更遗嘱限制的民间习惯，对于遗嘱对遗产分割的限制是否可以不遵守，调查统计数据显示，634名被调查者所在地区的继承习惯是：Ⅰ. B项不可以不遵守的，占五成以上（52.05%）；Ⅱ. A项可以不遵守的，占近五成（47.95%）。

②继承人协商能否变更遗嘱限制的民间习惯之理由情况统计。

表 2-67　继承人能否变更遗产分割时间限制的民间习惯之理由情况统计

项目	人数	比例
A. 乙和丙共同继承这些遗产，共同享有所有权，二人有权决定分割这些遗产，同时也有利于发挥物的效用价值	158	24.92%
B. 乙和丙根据甲设立的遗嘱享有继承权，对于遗产的分割问题，也应该依据遗嘱，不能选择性地修改遗嘱	127	20.03%

续表

项目	人数	比例
C. 遵守遗嘱，有利于保障被继承人配偶的老年生活	349	55.05%
合计	634	100%

关于继承人协商能否变更遗嘱限制的民间习惯之理由，调查统计数据显示，在634名被调查者中，Ⅰ. 认为不可变更的理由是，C项认为遵守遗嘱，有利于保障被继承人配偶老年生活的，占五成半（55.05%）；B项继承人乙和丙根据甲设立的遗嘱享有继承权，对于遗产的分割，也应该依据遗嘱，不能选择性修改遗嘱的占二成（20.03%）；Ⅱ. 认为可变更的理由是，A项继承人乙和丙共同继承这些遗产，共同享有所有权，二人有权决定分割这些遗产，同时也有利于发挥物之效用价值的，占近二成半（24.92%）。

（二）遗产分割瑕疵的担保责任

问题【十、（二）】“村民老王于2016年12月10日因病去世，死亡时留有50只羊。老王有两个儿子甲和乙，故老王死后，甲、乙各分得25只羊。但在双方分完羊两天之后，乙分得的25只羊中就有2只暴病死亡，这2只羊的死亡原因是在兄弟俩分割前就已经得了羊痘（一种急性传染病）。请问：在您所在地区，如果出现此种情况，这2只羊死亡的损失应该由谁承担？A. 由乙自行承担，羊群已分配完毕，乙分到了2只病羊，应该自认倒霉；B. 由甲和乙共同承担，甲应再分给乙1只羊或按照1只羊的价格进行补偿；C. 甲按1只羊的价格进行补偿，但乙承担大部分损失，甲承担小部分损失；D. 其他。（单选）理由是什么？”

1. 遗产分割瑕疵的担保责任的民间习惯情况统计

表2-68　遗产分割瑕疵的担保责任的民间习惯情况统计（单选）

选项	人数	比例
A. 由乙自行承担，羊群已分配完毕，乙分到了2只病羊，应该自认倒霉	294	46.37%
B. 由甲和乙共同承担，甲应再分给乙1只羊或按照1只羊的价格进行补偿	247	38.96%
C. 甲按1只羊的价格进行补偿，但乙承担大部分损失，甲承担小部分损失	91	14.35%
D. 其他	2	0.32%
合计	634	100%

关于遗产分割瑕疵的担保责任的民间习惯，调查统计数据显示，634名被调查者所在地区的民间习惯是：对于遗产分割的瑕疵，（1）B、C两项两名继承人分担遗产分割瑕疵担保责任的，合计占近五成半（53.31%）；（2）A项由“乙自行承担”，即共同继承人相互间不分担遗产分割瑕疵担保责任的，占四成半以上（46.37%）。

2. 遗产分割瑕疵的担保责任的民间习惯之理由情况统计

表 2-69　遗产分割瑕疵的担保责任的民间习惯之理由情况统计

项目	人数	比例
A. 乙分得的 25 只羊是随机分配的，事先甲乙两人都不知道，因此，对于 2 只病羊的损失，与甲无关，只能由乙自己承担	164	51.74%
B. 50 只羊是由甲和乙共同继承的，对于 2 只病羊的损失也应该由甲和乙共同承担；如果让乙一个人承担，则有悖公平原则	153	48.26%
合计	317	100%

关于遗产分割瑕疵的担保责任的民间习惯之理由，调查统计数据显示，317 名被调查者填写了选择理由，（1）共同继承人间不会共同承担的理由是，A 项乙分得的 25 只羊是随机分配的，事先甲乙两人都不知情，因此对于 2 只病羊的损失与甲无关，只能由乙自己承担的，占五成以上（51.74%）；（2）共同继承人间会共同承担的理由是，B 项 50 只羊是由甲和乙共同继承的，对于 2 只病羊的损失也应该由甲和乙共同承担；如果让乙一个人承担，则有悖公平原则的，占近五成（48.26%）。

十一、无人承受遗产之调查数据统计情况

关于无人承受遗产之调查数据统计，我们主要从无人承受遗产的归属和无人承受遗产的处理两个方面进行调查数据的统计情况汇总分析。

（一）无人承受遗产的归属

1. 城镇居民无人承受遗产的归属主体的民众观念与理由情况统计

问题【十一、（一）1.】“甲生前系城镇居民，其生前未婚且无其他继承人，其死后留下部分遗产，属于无人承受的遗产。您认为甲的遗产归属于下列哪一主体更合适？A. 国家；B. 死者生前所在地的国库；C. 死者生前所在地民政部门的社会福利机构；D. 死者生前所在的居委会；E. 不是继承人的其他亲属；F. 其他。（单选）理由是什么？”

（1）城镇居民无人承受遗产的归属主体的民众观念情况统计。

表 2-70　城镇居民无人承受遗产的归属主体的民众观念情况统计（单选）

选项	人数	比例
A. 国家	223	35.17%
B. 死者生前所在地的国库	53	8.36%
C. 死者生前所在地民政部门的社会福利机构	106	16.72%
D. 死者生前所在的居委会	49	7.73%
E. 不是继承人的其他亲属	172	27.13%
F. 其他	31	4.89%
合计	634	100%

关于城镇居民无人继承遗产的归属主体的民众观念，调查统计数据显示，在634名被调查者中，①选择A、B、C、D四项，认为城镇居民无人继承遗产应收归社会公共组织（包括归属于国家、死者生前所在地的国库、死者生前所在地民政部门的社会福利机构和死者生前所在地的居委会）的，合计占近七成（67.98%）；②选择E、F两项，认为城镇居民无人继承遗产应归自然人（归不是继承人的其他亲属等）的，合计占三成以上（32.02%）。

（2）城镇居民无人承受遗产的归属主体的民众观念之理由情况统计。

表2-71　城镇居民无人承受遗产的归属主体的民众观念之理由情况统计

项目	人数	比例
A. 甲的遗产没有人继承，为规范财产秩序，甲的遗产应归国家所有，同时，这也与部分国家的做法相一致	117	54.17%
B. 甲的遗产应归甲生前所在地的国库，有利于对遗产的清算、管理和利用	9	4.16%
C. 甲的其他亲属是与甲有一定亲属关系且有较密切联系的人，甲的遗产归其他亲戚所有，符合情理	90	41.67%
合计	216	100%

关于城镇居民无人承受遗产的归属主体的民众观念之理由，调查统计数据显示，216名被调查者填写了选择理由，①选择归属社会公共组织的主要理由分别为，A项为规范财产秩序，甲的遗产应归国家所有，这也与部分国家的做法相一致（占54.17%）和B项甲的遗产应归甲生前所在地的国库，有利于对遗产的清算、管理和利用（占4.16%）。②选择归属自然人的主要理由为，C项甲的其他亲属是与甲有一定亲属关系且有较密切联系的人，甲的遗产归其他亲戚所有符合情理（占41.67%）。

2. 农村居民无人承受遗产的归属主体的民众观念及理由情况统计

问题【十一、（一）2.】“甲生前系农村居民，其生前未婚且无其他继承人，其死后留下部分遗产，属于无人承受的遗产。您认为甲的遗产归属于下列哪一主体更合适？A. 死者生前所在地的国库；B. 死者生前所在地民政部门的社会福利机构；C. 死者生前所在的集体经济组织；D. 死者生前所在的村委会；E. 死者生前所在的村民小组；F. 不是继承人的其他亲属；G. 其他（您认为更合适的归属主体）。（单选）理由是什么？”

（1）农村居民无人承受遗产的归属主体的民众观念情况统计。

表2-72　农村居民无人承受遗产的归属主体的民众观念情况统计（单选）

选项	人数	比例
A. 死者生前所在地的国库	165	26.03%
B. 死者生前所在地民政部门的社会福利机构	85	13.41%

续表

选项	人数	比例
C. 死者生前所在的集体经济组织	54	8.52%
D. 死者生前所在的村委会	73	11.51%
E. 死者生前所在的村民小组	40	6.31%
F. 不是继承人的其他亲属	176	27.76%
G. 其他	41	6.46%
合计	634	100%

关于农村居民无人继承遗产归属主体的民众观念，调查统计数据显示，在634名被调查者中，①选择A、B、C、D、E五项，认为农村居民无人继承遗产应收归社会公共组织（包括死者生前所在地的国库、死者生前所在地民政部门的社会福利机构和死者生前所在的集体经济组织、村委会或村民小组）的，合计占六成半以上（65.78%）；②选择F、G两项，认为农村居民无人继承遗产应归自然人的，合计占近三成半（34.22%）。

（2）农村居民无人承受遗产的归属主体的民众观念之理由情况统计。

表2-73 农村居民无人承受遗产的归属主体的民众观念之理由情况统计（单选）

项目	人数	比例
A. 甲的遗产应归甲生前所在地的集体经济组织，有利于对遗产的清算、管理和利用	65	22.58%
B. 甲的其他亲属是与甲有较密切联系的人，甲的遗产归其他亲戚所有，符合情理	91	31.59%
C. 无人承受遗产应为国家等有关机关做贡献	132	45.83%
合计	288	100%

关于农村居民无人承受遗产的归属主体的民众观念之理由，调查统计数据显示，有288名被调查者填写了选择理由，①选择归属社会公共组织的主要理由分别为，A项甲的遗产应归甲生前所在地的集体经济组织，有利于对遗产的清算、管理和利用（占22.58%）和C项应为国家做贡献（占45.83%）。②选择归属自然人的主要理由为，B项甲的其他亲属是与甲有较密切联系的人，甲的遗产归其他亲戚所有，这符合情理（占31.59%）。

（二）无人承受遗产的处理

1. 无人承受遗产的管理人的产生方式的民众观念与民间习惯情况统计

问题【十一、（二）1.】“对于无人继承遗产的管理人，您认为下列哪一种产生方式更合适？A. 死者户籍所在地的居委会、村委会或所在单位指定遗产管理人；B. 人民法院指定遗产管理人；C. 民政部门指定遗产管理人。（单选）请问：在您所在地区的人们一般如何确定无人承受遗产的管理人，理由是什么?”

（1）无人承受遗产的管理人的产生方式之民众观念情况统计。

表 2-74　无人承受遗产管理人的产生方式之民众观念情况统计（单选）

选项	人数	比例
A. 死者户籍所在地的居委会、村委会或所在单位指定遗产管理人	350	55.20%
B. 人民法院指定遗产管理人	215	33.91%
C. 民政部门指定遗产管理人	69	10.89%
合计	634	100%

关于无人承受遗产的管理人的产生方式之民众观念，调查统计数据显示，在 634 名被调查者中，①选择 A 项认为应由死者户籍所在地的居委会、村委会或所在单位指定遗产管理人的，占五成半（55.20%）；②选择 B、C 两项认为应由人民法院或民政部门指定遗产管理人的，合计占近四成半（44.80%）。

（2）无人承受遗产管理人的产生方式之民间习惯与理由情况统计。

①无人承受遗产管理人的产生方式之民间习惯情况统计。

表 2-75　无人承受遗产管理人的产生方式之民间习惯情况统计（单选）

选项	人数	比例
A. 居委会、村委会或所在单位指定	96	40.51%
B. 法院指定	69	29.12%
C. 民政部门指定	26	10.97%
D. 其他亲属指定	16	6.76%
E. 有威望者指定	15	6.32%
F. 政府指定	15	6.32%
合计	237	100%

关于无人承受遗产管理人的产生方式之民间习惯，调查统计数据显示，填写该问题的 237 名被调查者所在地区的民间习惯是：Ⅰ. A、B、C、F 四项，遗产管理人由居委会、村委会、所在单位、民政部门和政府等组织指定的，合计占八成半以上（86.92%）；Ⅱ. D、E 两项遗产管理人由其他亲属和有威望者指定的，合计占近一成半（13.08%）。

②无人承受遗产管理人的产生方式的民间习惯之理由情况统计。

表 2-76　无人承受遗产管理人的产生方式的民间习惯之理由情况统计

项目	人数	比例
A. 死者户籍所在地的居委会、村委会或所在单位对死者及其遗产的情况比较清楚，由其指定遗产管理人，有利于对遗产进行清算、管理和利用	186	66.19%
B. 人民法院通过法定程序，对遗产进行清算和管理，由其指定遗产管理人，有利于公平保护相关债权人的利益	92	32.74%
C. 人民法院办案压力大，无暇顾及遗产管理人的指定	3	1.07%
合计	281	100%

关于无人承受遗产管理人的产生方式的民间习惯之理由，调查统计数据显示，在填写本题的281名被调查者中，Ⅰ. 遗产管理人由居委会、村委会、所在单位等组织指定的理由是，A项死者户籍所在地的居委会、村委会或所在单位对死者及其遗产的情况比较清楚，由其指定遗产管理人，有利于对遗产进行清算、管理和利用的，占六成半以上(66.19%)；Ⅱ. 遗产管理人由人民法院指定的理由是，B项人民法院通过法定程序，对遗产进行清算和管理，由其指定遗产管理人，有利于公平保护相关债权人利益的，占三成以上（32.74%）；Ⅲ. 遗产管理人由其他亲属和有威望者指定的理由是，C项人民法院办案压力大，可能无暇顾及遗产管理人的指定的，占不到一成（1.07%）。

2. 无人承受遗产的酌分请求权主体的民众观念与民间习惯情况统计

问题【十一、(二) 2.】“您认为下列哪些人可以酌情分得无人继承的遗产？A. 依靠死者扶养的人；B. 与死者共同生活的人；C. 与死者有密切联系且对其帮助较多的人；D. 其他。(多选) 请问：您所在地区的人们一般是如何分配此类遗产的？”

(1) 无人承受遗产的酌分请求权主体的民众观念情况统计。

表 2-77　无人承受遗产的酌分请求权主体的民众观念情况统计（多选）

选项	人数	比例
A. 依靠死者扶养的人	502	79.18%
B. 与死者共同生活的人	365	57.57%
C. 与死者关系密切且对其帮助较多的人	480	75.71%
D. 其他	11	1.74%

关于无人承受遗产的酌分请求权主体的民众观念，调查统计数据显示，在634名被调查者中，选择A、B、C三项，认为“依靠死者扶养的人”（79.18%）、“与死者共同生活的人”（57.57%）和“与死者关系密切且对其帮助较多的人”（75.71%）可以成为无人承受遗产之酌分请求权主体的，各占五成至七成以上。

（2）无人承受遗产的酌分请求权主体的民间习惯情况统计。

表 2-78　无人承受遗产的酌分请求权主体的民间习惯情况统计（单选）

选项	人数	比例
A. 近亲属或有扶养关系的人	136	80.00%
B. 居/村委会	16	9.41%
C. 国家	18	10.59%
合计	170	100%

关于无人承受遗产的酌分请求权主体的民间习惯，调查统计数据显示，回答该问题的170名被调查者所在地区的民间习惯是：①A项近亲属是无人承受遗产之酌分请求权主体的，占八成（80.00%）；②B、C两项，国家或居（村）委会是无人承受遗产之酌分请求权主体的，合计占二成（20.00%）

十二、遗产处理相关案例的简介与评析

（一）涉及遗产范围界定案例的简介与评析

案情简介：被告樊某甲与被告姚某乙育有一子，樊某乐。2003年5月3日，陈某某与樊某乐登记结婚，2004年1月6日生育一女樊某某（本案原告）。2007年12月6日，陈某某与樊某乐二人登记离婚。2013年3月24日，樊某乐在工地施工过程中意外身故。后事故方赔偿樊某乐丧葬费、被扶养人生活费、死亡赔偿金、精神抚慰金等共计620000元，转至被告樊某甲名下的存折。2013年10月16日，原告樊某某诉至法院，要求继承樊某乐的遗产，要求与樊某甲、姚某乙两被告分割死者樊某乐的死亡赔偿金。被告樊某甲辩称，原告系樊某乐之女属实，樊某乐死亡后由其女儿樊某某经办赔偿事宜，赔偿款620000元在其妻姚某乙名下保存。樊某乐的赔偿款应先扣除丧葬费及处理事故花费共计25000元，再扣除樊某甲与姚某乙及原告樊某某的被扶养人生活费后，剩余部分按照三人进行分配。被告姚某乙同意被告樊某甲的辩称意见，另外，她从赔偿款中已支取了160000元，用于偿还樊某乐生前购买一辆奥龙卡车所欠的债务。

法院审理后认为，樊某乐意外身故所获得的工伤死亡赔偿款620000元扣除丧葬费等费用后实际所剩595000元，该款是在受害人死亡后由侵权人支付的，不属于死者遗留的财产，不属于遗产范围。但在法律没有对死亡赔偿金的分配作出明确规定的情况下，可参照遗产继承合理进行分配，死者的近亲属具备受领赔偿款权利人资格。原告系死者的女儿，被告樊某甲、姚某乙是死者的父母，均属死者樊某乐的第一顺序继承人，依法有权获得樊某乐的上述赔偿款。①

适用法律分析：本案的争议焦点在于樊某乐的死亡赔偿金是否属于樊某乐的遗产，樊

① 参见中国裁判文书网：（2013）长×第×号，《樊某某与樊某甲、姚某乙财产分割纠纷一审民事判决书》，载http://wenshu.court.gov.cn/content/content? DocID=1b8001a2-0842-413a-8418-674a018cb237&KeyWord=长×第×号，访问日期：2019年3月8日。限于本章篇幅，作者对原案情内容有酌情删改。

某某的请求可否得到支持？我国 2001 年《关于确定民事侵权精神损害赔偿责任若干问题的解释》第 9 条将死亡赔偿金界定为“精神损害抚慰金”。参照最高人民法院就广东省高级人民法院《关于死亡赔偿金能否作为遗产处理的请示》做出的（2004）民一他字第 26 号《关于死亡赔偿金能否作为遗产处理的复函》，该复函指出“空难死亡赔偿金是基于死者死亡对死者近亲属所支付的赔偿。获得空难死亡赔偿金的权利人是死者近亲属，而非死者。故空难死亡赔偿金不宜认定为遗产。”法院审理本案后认为，樊某乐意外身故所获得的死亡赔偿款 620000 元减除丧葬费等费用后实际剩余 595000 元，该款是在受害人死亡后由侵权人支付给死者近亲属的赔偿金，不是死者遗留的财产。因此，此款项不属于遗产，不应当按照法定继承顺序进行分配，而应当由死者具有赔偿请求权资格的全体近亲属协商进行分配。原告是死者樊某乐的女儿，被告樊某甲、姚某乙是死者樊某乐的父母，均属樊某乐的近亲属，依法享有死者的赔偿金请求权，所以他们有权参与分配获得樊某乐的死亡赔偿款。

可见，现实生活中被调查民众对被继承人的死亡赔偿金是否属于遗产的认识不一，本次重庆市遗产处理观念调查统计中，有七成半（75.55%）的被调查者认为交通事故死亡赔偿金应纳入遗产范围（见表 2-4）。根据前述司法解释，死亡赔偿金是在死者死亡后产生的，以填补受害人近亲属因受害人死亡导致的生活资源减少的特殊财产，不属于死者的遗产范围，这是人民法院审判此类案件的依据。我们认为，被调查民众对于死亡赔偿金是否属于遗产有误解，主要原因是我国《继承法》尚无对遗产范围的反面排除规定，此为立法之不足。

（二）涉及继承开始的通知和公告案例的简介与评析

案情简介：王某与丈夫何某英生育子女三人，即大儿子何某甲、二儿子何某乙及女儿何某丙。2008 年 3 月王某与丈夫何某英离婚，2010 年 4 月 23 日王某去世，去世后其丧事由二儿子何某乙料理。何某乙通知了其妹何某丙及其父何某英，何某英向王某单位表示王某的丧葬后事由何某乙全权处理，但何某乙并未通知另一继承人何某甲。此后何某乙向王某生前所在的某单位领取了丧葬补助费、一次性抚恤金、一次性困难补助费以及王某在工商银行的存款 80000 元，同时在 2010 年 3 月何某乙通过房屋中介出租王某名下 60 平方米的房屋，已收取租金 3000 元。后何某甲起诉至法院，要求重新分割 60 平方米的房屋与租金、丧葬补助费、一次性抚恤金、一次性困难补助费以及王某在工商银行的存款 80000 元，并请求何某乙承担不通知其他继承人、隐瞒转移遗产的法律责任。何某乙认为，何某甲没有对其母王某生前尽到做子女的责任，其应该不分或少分遗产，并且自己没有通知何某甲参与继承的义务。

法院审理后认为，何某乙认为何某甲没有对其母王某尽到做子女的责任，自己对被继承人王某尽了主要扶养义务，但均没有提供相关的证据。由于何某乙在没有通知何某甲的情况下，领取了丧葬补助费、银行存款和房屋租金等费用并据为己有，侵害了何某甲的继承权。因此王某的遗产应按照法定继承，由其同一顺序继承人何某乙、何某丙、何某甲均等继承。但对于何某甲主张的应追究何某乙不通知其他继承人的法律责任，人民法院不予支持。①

适用法律分析：本案的焦点主要在于继承人何某乙负有通知其他继承人的义务而未通知的，是否应当承担相应的法律后果。对于继承开始的通知，我国《继承法》第23条规定："继承开始后，知道被继承人死亡的继承人应当及时通知其他继承人和遗嘱执行人。继承人中无人知道被继承人死亡或者知道被继承人死亡而不能通知的，由被继承人生前所在单位或者住所地的居民委员会、村民委员会负责通知。"但是对于负有通知义务的人，没有按照法律规定履行通知义务，是否应该承担法律责任，我国法律无规定。在本案中，受理法院认为虽然何某乙认为何某甲和何某丙没有对其母王某尽到做子女的责任，自己对被继承人王某尽了主要扶养义务，但均没有提供相关的证据，因此王某的遗产应按照法定继承，由其同一顺序继承人何某乙、何某丙、何某甲原则上均等继承。至于是否应该对何某乙没有通知继承开始的行为予以一定的惩罚，即由其承担一定法律责任，由于法律无规定，审理法院对此亦没有做出处罚。我们认为，我国《继承法》对继承开始的通知和公告之程序、法律责任等内容尚无规定，此为立法之不足。

（三）涉及遗产管理案例的简介与评析

案情简介：张某泉与王某育有子女张某1、张某2，二人于2016年2月4日离婚。张某奎为张某泉的父亲。张某泉于2016年6月1日在原告陈某处借款人民币70600元，用于购买钻井设备，并于当日出具了欠据一份。后张某泉于2017年5月26日病故。张某泉生前个人所有平房一套，该房屋一直由其父亲张某奎居住使用。后债权人陈某将张某奎和张某1、张某2告上法庭，要求他们承担清偿死者张某泉所欠债务的责任。在法院的庭审中，三被告明确表示放弃对张某泉的遗产继承权。

法院审理后认为，公民的合法债权受法律保护，现张某泉已经死亡，故原告陈某的债权应在张某泉的遗产范围内得到清偿。三被告明确放弃对张某泉财产及债权的继承权，但被告张某奎现一直居住使用张某泉所有的平房，可认定被告张某奎为张某泉的遗产管理人，有义务用其子张某泉的遗产对其子生前所欠债务承担清偿责任。因此该法院判决，依照我国《合同法》第60条以及我国现行《民事诉讼法》第64条规定，被告张某奎作为遗产管理人，在其管理张某泉遗产范围内偿还原告陈某借款人民币70600元。被告张某1、张某2不承担清偿责任。②

适用法律分析：本案的焦点主要在于张某奎和张某1、张某2是否应承担张某泉生前所欠债务的清偿责任，以及遗产管理人的确定与职责。目前，我国《继承法》第33条规定："继承遗产应当清偿被继承人依法应当缴纳的税款和债务，缴纳税款和清偿债务以他的遗产实际价值为限。超过遗产实际价值部分，继承人自愿偿还的不在此限。"本案中，审理法院依照我国《合同法》第60条以及我国现行《民事诉讼法》第64条的规定，认

① 参见中国裁判文书网：（2013）温×民初字第×号，《何某甲与何某乙继承纠纷一审民事判决书》，载 http://wenshu.court.gov.cn/content/content? DocID=e76f6d47-7047-4997-9f39-5c26a8762520&KeyWord=温×民初字第×号，访问日期：2019年3月8日。限于本章篇幅，作者对原案情内容有酌情删改。

② 参见中国裁判文书网：（2017）内×民初×号，《陈某与张某1、张某2等被继承人债务清偿纠纷一审民事判决书》，载 http://wenshu.court.gov.cn/content/content? DocID=6b3fe0fb-ceca-4a61-b005-a82c01174140&KeyWord=内×民初×号，访问日期：2019年3月8日。限于本章篇幅，作者对原案情内容有酌情删改。

为公民的合法债权受法律保护，死者张某泉生前向原告陈某借款，三被告又未提出相反的证据证实不存在该笔债务，故应认定此借据合法有效。虽然三被告明确放弃对张某泉遗产的继承权，但被告张某奎现一直居住使用张某泉生前个人所有的平房即遗产房屋之中，可认定被告张某奎为张某泉的遗产管理人，依法应当用其子张某泉的遗产对该债务承担清偿责任。

我们认为，本案中，为了保障遗产债权人的利益，法院在没有遗产管理法律规定的情况下，依据我国《合同法》第60条的规定，即当事人应当按照约定全面履行自己的义务。该合法的债权受法律保护，并认定一直居住使用张某泉生前个人所有房屋的张某奎为遗产管理人，这是合理的。目前我国《继承法》没有规定遗产管理制度，没有确立遗产管理人的资格、产生方式、职责等，但是现实生活中较多继承案件都涉及遗产管理的问题。确立遗产管理制度对于保全遗产、保障继承人以及遗产债权人的利益和使人民法院审理案件有法可依都具有重要的意义。[①] 我国《继承法》尚未设立该制度，是立法之不足。

（四）涉及法定继承案例的简介与评析

案情简介：被继承人刘某与前妻何某先后生育了四子女，即本案的被告。刘某与前妻何某在婚内出资购买建筑面积为60.60平方米的房屋（2000年7月，原房屋扩建后的住房面积为101平方米）。前妻何某于2000年12月3日去世。2001年11月，原告王某与刘某办理结婚登记并共同生活。2014年2月19日，刘某因病去世，留有遗产：（1）60.60平方米的住房；（2）生前银行存款54485.6元。刘某去世后，被继承人刘某的配偶王某与刘某的四个子女就其留下的房屋的继承权以及刘某生前的54485.6元存款的分配发生争议，王某将刘某的四个子女诉至法院，向法院请求：（1）判决原告对讼争的房屋拥有30平方米（约50000元）的产权面积；（2）判决夫妻共同财产54485.6元存款归原告分割一半。

法院审理后认为，我国目前法律虽然没有明确居住权的概念，但对一些特定身份的自然人，依然设置了某些保护其居住权益的规范性条文，我国现行《老年人权益保障法》第16条规定，赡养人应当妥善安排老年人的住房，不得强迫老年人居住或迁居条件低劣的房屋。原告王某基于与被继承人刘某夫妻关系这一特定身份，其提出要求继续居住遗产中的住房，理应予优先考虑原告的居住权，但原告主张对该房屋确认享有15平方米的继承份额的请求不予支持。关于银行存款54485.6元的问题。该存款为原告与刘某婚姻关系存续期间的工资收入，根据我国现行《婚姻法》第17条规定，夫妻在婚姻关系存续期间所得的工资、奖金，归夫妻共同所有，即银行存款54485.6元属于原告与刘某的共有财产。依据《继承法》第26条第1款规定："夫妻在婚姻关系存续期间所得的共同所有的财产，除有约定的以外，如果分割遗产，应当先将共同所有的财产的一半分出为配偶所有，其余的为被继承人的遗产。"故法院判决：（1）原告对讼争房屋享有终生的居住权和6平方米左右份额；（2）原告王某对二人的夫妻共同财产54485.6元的银行存款应享有一半的所有权。所以，原告王某的应得份额为32691元。[②]

---

① 陈苇、石婷：《我国设立遗产管理制度的社会基础及其制度构建》，载《河北法学》2013年第7期，第13页。

② 参见中国裁判文书网：（2014）新×民初字第×号，《王某与刘某甲、刘某乙、刘某丙、刘某丁继承纠纷一审民事判决书》，载 http://wenshu.court.gov.cn/content/content? DocID = 63d5a5bb - 518d - 42a1 - 9bab - fd34e9118dc3&KeyWord = （2014）新×民初字第×号，访问日期：2019年3月8日。限于本章篇幅，作者对原案情内容有酌情删改。

适用法律分析：本案的焦点在于是否确认原告对讼争的60.60平方米房屋是否享有居住权以及如何确认法定继承中各继承人的遗产份额。我国《继承法》第26条第1款规定："夫妻在婚姻关系存续期间所得的共同所有的财产，除有约定的以外，如果分割遗产，应当先将共同所有的财产的一半分出为配偶所有，其余的为被继承人的遗产。"我国现行《老年人权益保障法》第16条规定："赡养人应当妥善安排老年人的住房，不得强迫老年人居住或者迁居条件低劣的房屋。"在本案中，受理法院确认原告对讼争房屋享有终生的居住权和6平方米左右份额。法院认为，我国法律虽然没有明确居住权的概念，但对一些特定身份的自然人，依然设置了保护其居住权益的规范性条文，如我国现行《老年人权益保障法》第16条的规定，因此原告王某基于与被继承人刘某夫妻关系这一特定身份，其提出要求居住，符合相关法律规定，应予优先考虑原告的居住权。关于银行存款54485.6元的问题。该存款为原告与刘某婚姻关系存续期间的工资收入，根据我国现行《婚姻法》第17条规定，属于原告与刘某的共有财产。依据《继承法》第26条第1款规定，原告王某对54485.6元的银行存款应得份额为32691元。

我国司法实践中多有一方配偶死亡，而另一方配偶因房屋居住问题引发的继承纠纷。我们认为，虽然我国《继承法》没有明确配偶居住权的条款，但我国现行《老年人权益保障法》第16条有相关保护老年人居住权的规定。本案法院在审理案件中，综合考量各种因素，优先确认保护配偶对遗产中家庭房屋享有居住权，以保障生存配偶老有所居，这是符合法律规定，也是符合情理的。这与重庆市八成半（85.80%）的被调查者都认同配偶享有遗产住房先取权和终生居住权的继承观念相符合（见表2-20）。但我国《继承法》尚未设立配偶继承人对于遗产中供其居住的房屋享有先取权和终生使用权制度，是其立法之不足。

（五）涉及遗嘱继承案例的简介与评析

案情简介：陈某、何某系夫妻关系，双方共生育二子原告陈某甲、被告陈某乙。2013年12月26日，陈某与何某共同作出内容为打印的夫妻共同遗嘱一份，遗嘱内容为夫妻双方经过协商达成一致，决定夫妻共有一套40.20平方米房产，若夫妻一方先去世，则该房产属于先去世一方的份额由后去世的一方继承；待夫妻双方都去世后，再由长子陈某甲继承。遗嘱中明确订立该遗嘱期间遗嘱人神志清醒，且就订立本遗嘱未受到任何胁迫、欺诈，遗嘱为本人自愿作出，是其内心真实意思的表示。陈某与何某两人在上述遗嘱上签字及捺印的经过，由原、被告的表姐刘某在场，刘某的女儿王某录像记录，遗嘱的内容经陈某阅读捺印后，何某表示对遗嘱的内容无异议并在遗嘱上捺印、签名。陈某于2014年1月29日去世，何某于2014年5月5日去世。陈某甲、陈某乙因遗产分配问题诉至法院。原告陈某甲诉称：请求人民法院依遗嘱判令原告继承位于××村房屋一套。被告陈某乙辩称：请求驳回原告的全部诉讼请求。原告陈某甲出示的父亲陈某和母亲何某于2013年12月26日所立遗嘱为打印的，而非其父母亲笔书写，称其父母家中也无电脑及打印设备，也不懂电脑操作。并且，该遗嘱上没有代书人及其他见证人签名，故应为无效遗嘱。

法院审理后认为，公民可以立遗嘱处分个人财产，而且我国法律没有禁止以共同遗嘱的形式设立遗嘱，因此可以设立夫妻共同遗嘱。本案中的夫妻遗嘱，虽系立遗嘱人陈某、何某提供的打印遗嘱，但遗嘱的内容由陈某阅读、捺印并经何某认可后捺印、签名，且整个订立遗嘱的过程由在场人刘某、王某在场见证并由王某录像记录，其内容应视为立遗嘱人陈某、何某的真实意思表示，应视为有效。陈某乙认为其父母出具的遗嘱未有见证人签字，不符合代书遗嘱的形式要件的抗辩，不予采信，对于被告认为其父母受到胁迫、欺骗等抗辩，依据不足，亦不予采信。法院判决，陈某与何某订立的夫妻共同遗嘱有效，根据该遗嘱，系争房屋由原告陈某甲继承。①

适用法律分析：本案的争议焦点在于陈某与何某订立的夫妻共同遗嘱是否有效？我国《继承法》第 16 条规定："公民可以依照本法规定立遗嘱处分个人财产，并可以指定遗嘱执行人。"第 19 条规定："遗嘱应当对缺乏劳动能力又没有生活来源的继承人保留必要的遗产份额。"但是我国《继承法》和 1985 年《执行继承法意见》均未对夫妻共同遗嘱的效力作出规定。在本案中，受理该案的法院认为，公民可以立遗嘱处分个人财产，我国法律没有禁止以共同遗嘱的形式设立遗嘱，因此夫妻可以设立共同遗嘱。本案中的夫妻共同遗嘱，虽系立遗嘱人陈某、何某提供的打印遗嘱，但遗嘱的内容由陈某阅读、捺印并经何某认可后捺印、签名，且整个订立遗嘱的过程由在场人刘某、王某在场见证并由王某录像记录，其内容应视为立遗嘱人陈某、何某的真实意思表示，不能因没有见证人签字就认定为无效。在立遗嘱人陈某、何某去世后，其继承人陈某甲、陈某乙应依照遗嘱的内容执行。可见，虽然我国《继承法》和 1985 年《执行继承法意见》均未对夫妻共同遗嘱作出明确规定，但是实际生活中确实存在夫妻共同设立遗嘱的情况。

我们认为，遗嘱自由是私法自治原则的体现，我国《继承法》第 16 条、第 19 条已经对自然人设立个人遗嘱处分个人所有财产有所规定。但对于我国《继承法》是否规定夫妻共同遗嘱，应当慎重考虑。本次调查中虽然有近七成半的被调查者认同夫妻共同遗嘱具有法律效力（见表 2-31），但现实生活中夫妻共同立遗嘱的却很少见，仅有二成以上的被调查者所在地区有夫妻共同设立遗嘱的习惯（见表 2-33）。究其主要原因在于，夫妻在订立共同遗嘱时虽然有双方的意思表示一致，但在夫妻一方死亡后，生存配偶由于生活条件的变化，可能需要单方改变共同遗嘱，却因其为共同遗嘱而不能单方予以改变，这就限制了生存配偶的遗嘱自由。因此，我国未来的立法不仅要考虑多数被调查民众认可夫妻共同订立遗嘱的意愿，更应当考虑生存配偶因现实生活变化之需要变更共同遗嘱的要求，故不宜规定夫妻共同遗嘱。

（六）涉及继承和遗赠的接受与放弃案例的简介与评析

案情简介：金某梅系陈某甲母亲。1990 年，被告陈某甲分别向三原告借款。2008 年，原告王某 1、管某 2、戴某 3 分别向法院起诉，要求被告陈某甲归还借款本金及利息。由于被告陈某甲无财产可供执行，经申请执行人同意后法院于 2009 年作出民事裁定书，终结有关调解书的执行。2014 年 8 月 22 日，被告母亲金某梅因病去世。2014 年 8 月 26 日，被告陈某甲向×市公证处申请办理公证，陈某甲表示放弃对被继承人金某梅位于×市×街道×路×号房产遗产的继承权，公证处经审查后于 2014 年 9 月 18 日作出公证书。为此，原告特提起诉讼，认为被告陈某甲为逃避债务而放弃了继承权，该行为严重侵害了其合法权益，请求确定被告陈某甲放弃被继承人房屋继承份额的民事行为无效。被告辩称，其自从

---

① 参见中国裁判文书网：（2015）熟×民初字第×号，《陈某甲与陈某乙继承纠纷一审民事判决书》，载 http://wenshu.court.gov.cn/content/content? DocID=0a029598-3c6d-480b-b3ae-d1dd60745621&KeyWord=（2015）熟×民初字第×号，访问日期：2019 年 3 月 8 日。限于本章篇幅，作者对原案情内容有酌情删改。

单位辞职以来，生活一直非常拮据，难以维持，也无力照顾母亲，故出于愧疚才放弃母亲留下的房屋的继承权。

法院审理后认为，依据1985年《执行继承法意见》第46条规定："继承人因放弃继承权，致其不能履行法定义务的，放弃继承权的行为无效。"本案中被告欠原告的债务被法院已生效的法律文书予以确认，且由法院立案执行，故被告所负债务已上升为应付之法定义务。然被告放弃了对被继承人金某梅遗产继承的权利，被告这种明知负有还款义务而依然放弃继承权的行为，不仅反映出其有恶意损害原告债权的主观故意，事实上也致使其丧失了与可继承遗产部分等值的履行能力，且被告陈某甲事实上没有其他财产可用于偿还债务，故其放弃继承权行为与其不能履行法定义务的后果之间具有法律上的因果关系。原告请求确定被告陈某甲放弃继承的民事行为无效的诉讼请求于法有据，予以支持。①

适用法律分析：本案的争议焦点在于陈某甲放弃继承权的行为是否可以被债权人予以撤销。审理法院依据1985年《执行继承法意见》第46条认为，被告放弃了对被继承人金某梅遗产继承的权利，被告这种明知负有还款义务而依然放弃继承权的行为，不仅反映出其有恶意损害原告债权的主观故意，事实上也致使其丧失了与可继承遗产部分等值的履行能力，且被告陈某甲事实上没有其他财产可用于偿还债务，故该放弃继承行为可以被撤销。但是借款合同之债，系约定之债，而非"法定义务"，并且放弃继承权行为具有身份性质，在现代社会不能"强制继承"，而放弃继承之标的，也非欠债继承人的固有的财产，并没有损害债权人的利益。② 所以，我们认为，我国《继承法》没有对放弃继承权的行为是否可以被债权人予以撤销作出规定，是其立法不足。

（七）涉及继承权的丧失、被继承人的宥恕与代位继承案例的简介与评析

案情简介：陈某、李某系夫妻关系，双方共生育一子陈甲和一女陈乙，陈乙有先天残疾。李某于2008年1月5日去世，陈某于2013年5月5日去世，当时，其子和女均已成年。该父母在去世前，考虑到女儿有残疾，留下遗嘱，把遗产中的三分之二留给女儿陈乙，三分之一留给儿子陈甲。老人去世以后，儿子陈甲收拾老人的房间时，发现了这份遗嘱，就把这份遗嘱的两个继承人的名字改了，把三分之二的遗产份额改为自己继承，把三分之一的遗产份额改为妹妹继承。这份遗嘱后来被鉴定机关鉴定确认为是经篡改过的遗嘱。妹妹陈乙遂向法院起诉，要求法院确认父母的遗产由自己继承，哥哥丧失继承权。被告辩称，其虽然篡改了遗嘱，但是并非情节严重，故应该享有继承权。

法院审理后认为，依据我国《继承法》第7条规定，继承人伪造、篡改或者销毁遗嘱，情节严重的，丧失继承权。根据1985年《执行继承法意见》第14条规定，继承人伪造、篡改或者销毁遗嘱，侵害了缺乏劳动能力又无生活来源的继承人的利益，并造成其生活困难的，应认定其行为情节严重。由于陈甲篡改了遗嘱，造成陈乙的生活困难，其行

---

① 参见中国裁判文书网：（2015）×民初字第×号，《陈某甲与王某1、管某2、戴某3债务清偿纠纷一审民事裁定书》，载 http://wenshu.court.gov.cn/content/content? DocID = 9437aff6 - af49 - 4923 - a81e - a1cdaf57765e&KeyWord =（2013）广×民初字第×号，访问日期：2019年3月8号。限于本章篇幅，作者对原案情内容有酌情删改。

② 参见陈苇、王巍：《论放弃继承行为不能成为债权人撤销权的标的》，载《甘肃社会科学》2015年第5期，第163~165页。

为属于情节严重，故法院判决陈甲丧失继承权，其父母的遗产全部由妹妹陈乙继承。①

适用法律分析：本案的争议焦点在于继承人篡改遗嘱侵害其他继承人权益的，是否应丧失继承权？我国《继承法》第7条规定，继承人伪造、篡改或者销毁遗嘱，情节严重的，丧失继承权。1985年《执行继承法意见》第14条规定，继承人伪造、篡改或者销毁遗嘱，侵害了缺乏劳动能力又无生活来源的继承人的利益，并造成其生活困难的，应认定其行为情节严重。1985年《执行继承法意见》第9条规定，在遗产继承中，继承人之间就是否丧失继承权发生纠纷，诉讼到人民法院的，由人民法院根据我国《继承法》第7条的规定，判决确认其是否丧失继承权。本案审理法院根据现有法律规定，认定陈甲丧失继承权，其父母的遗产全部由妹妹陈乙继承。我们认为，本案中，哥哥陈甲为多分遗产而篡改了遗嘱，侵害了无劳动能力又无生活来源的继承人妹妹陈乙的继承权益，导致陈乙生活困难。因此，妹妹陈乙作为原告向法院起诉主张哥哥陈甲丧失继承权，法院判决由原告陈乙继承父母的全部遗产，这是有法律依据的。但是至于"伪造、篡改、销毁或隐匿遗嘱"是否需要以情节严重为条件。我们认为，现实中符合严重情节的情况较少，而且对遗嘱的伪造、篡改等行为就已经严重侵害被继承人的遗嘱自由权利，本身属于情节严重的行为，此为我国立法之不足。

（八）涉及继承协议案例的简介与评析

案情简介：郝某策与吕某兰系夫妻关系，两人共生育有郝某1、郝某2、郝某3、郝某4、郝某5、郝某6、郝某7七个子女。郝某策于2010年5月21日病故。2010年6月20日，吕某兰与七个子女协商后签订一份《母亲扶养及遗产继承协议书》，约定吕某兰由郝某7赡养至去世，其余六人放弃对吕某兰和郝某策所有遗产的继承权。协议签订后，郝某7依照协议的约定，与妻子共同照顾母亲吕某兰的日常生活至2012年2月17日吕某兰去世。后因其余六人不协助办理遗产过户手续，因此郝某7以其余六人为被告，诉至法院，要求认定其与被告签订的《母亲扶养及遗产继承协议书》有效。被告郝某1、郝某3、郝某5、郝某6经本院传票传唤，无正当理由拒不到庭。被告郝某4辩称，诉争的房产是郝某策与吕某兰的夫妻共同财产，吕某兰只能处分属于她的那部分财产，另一半财产只能由吕某兰与其他继承人平分继承。其他被告未作答辩。

法院审理后认为，依照我国《继承法》第2条、第3条、第5条、第10条、第11条、第26条、第29条、第33条，我国现行《婚姻法》第17条、第24条，我国现行《民事诉讼法》第64条第1款、第144条之规定，判决认定原告郝某7签订的母亲扶养及遗产继承协议书以及放弃各自继承权的部分合法有效，被告应当按协议履行。②

适用法律分析：本案争议的焦点在于吕某兰与郝某7等七人共同签订的母亲扶养及遗产继承协议书是否有效。审理法院认为，原告郝某7与被告签订的《母亲扶养及遗产继承协议书》以及放弃各自继承权的部分合法有效，被告应当按协议履行。可见，现实生活中确实存在被继承人（受扶养人）与其法定继承人（扶养义务人）签订继承协议的情

① 参见中国裁判文书网：（2016）化×民初字第×号，载 http://wenshu.court.gov.cn/Index，访问日期：2019年3月8日。限于本章篇幅，作者对原案情内容有酌情删改。

② 参见中国裁判文书网：（2014）×民初字第×号，载 http://wenshu.court.gov.cn/Index，访问日期：2019年3月8日。

况，对此协议目前有的法院承认其效力，有的法院认为继承权不得事前放弃而不承认此类协议的效力。从本次重庆市民众继承习惯实证调查情况来看，有四成半的被调查者表示听说或者经历过被继承人（受扶养人）与其法定继承人（扶养义务人）签订继承协议的情况（见表2-49）。我们认为，目前我国遗赠扶养协议的主体范围较窄，即将法定继承人排除在外，并且也没有规定继承协议制度，是为我国立法之不足。

（九）涉及遗产债务清偿案例的简介与评析

案情简介：1996 年，李某 1 与王某 2 同居生活，2005 年 6 月 8 日补办了结婚登记，领取结婚证。李某 1 于 2008 年 5 月 19 日死亡。原告李某甲系李某 1 与前妻的婚生之女。李某乙系李某 1 与王某 2 所生之子。李某 1 死亡后遗留的财产一直未予以分割。并且，夫妻尚未偿还的共同债务为房屋贷款 30266. 55 元。后王某 2、李某甲、李某乙三人因债务清偿问题产生纠纷，诉至法院。李某甲认为其不与父亲共同生活，也不应承担上述债务。

法院审理后认为，根据我国《继承法》第 33 条规定，继承遗产应当清偿被继承人依法应当缴纳的税款和债务，缴纳税款和清偿债务以他的遗产实际价值为限。超过遗产实际价值部分，继承人自愿偿还的不在此限。也就是说，继承人依法应当在继承遗产范围内承担被继承人的债务之清偿责任，并且各继承人之间按照各自继承遗产的份额承担清偿责任。案件中争议债务的其中一半属于被继承人的个人债务。故法院判决，此属于被继承人个人债务部分应由三位继承人按照继承遗产的比例清偿。①

适用法律分析：本案中的焦点在于，被继承人的遗产债务应如何清偿。审理法院认为，本案争议债务的其中一半属于被继承人的个人债务，此属于被继承人个人债务部分应由三位继承人按照各自继承遗产的比例清偿。这是以我国《继承法》第 33 条作为裁判依据，符合法律规定。

（十）涉及遗产分割案例的简介与评析

案情简介：李某与邹某于 1992 年结婚，双方均系再婚。李某 1、李某 2、李某 3 系李某与前妻所生子女。李某与邹某均为农民，双方靠从事皮蛋加工生意及农业生产为生，李某 1、李某 2、李某 3 未按月给付李某赡养费用，且邹某为残疾等级肆级的残疾人。2013 年 11 月 3 日，李某病故，李某银行账户有存款 102390 元，邹某银行账户有存款 30510 元，夫妻二人共计银行存款 132900 元。李某离世前未留下遗嘱，李某 1、李某 2、李某 3 认为他们对父亲李某均尽了赡养义务，故对其遗产依法应由其继承人按法定继承进行分割，但是邹某拒不分割李某的遗产，强占李某留下的房屋一套，并故意隐匿、转移其银行存款，为此，三人将邹某诉至法院，请求依法对李某的遗产进行分割。被告邹某辩称，原告诉称的涉案房产是客观存在的，但是该房屋没有办理产权登记，且原告方对该房屋的估价过高。对于邹某的银行存款，分割时应当按照照顾被告的原则进行分配，所以涉案的所有财产应当归被告所有。

一审和二审人民法院认为，首先，夫妻二人银行存款共计 132900 元，该款项依法属于夫妻共同财产。在李某生病住院及办理丧葬事宜期间所需必要医药费用及办理丧葬事宜

---

① 参见中国裁判文书网：（2014）扬×第×号，《王某 2、李某乙与李某甲继承纠纷二审民事判决书》，载 http://wenshu. court. gov. cn/content/content? DocID=24ce0b3d-cb62-40f1-ae5b-838fba530687&KeyWord=扬×第×号，访问日期：2019 年 3 月 8 日。限于本章篇幅，作者对原案情内容有酌情删改。

费用均由被告邹某支付，为此，邹某支出 30000 元。其次，一审、二审法院在综合考虑各继承人对被继承人的扶养或赡养具体情况以及各继承人经济状况、劳动能力、住房条件等客观因素情况下，根据我国《继承法》第 13 条、第 29 条，认定被告邹某属于应当酌情多分遗产份额的继承人及本案住房宜由邹某个人居住使用，并其余遗产中的存款酌情确定由李某 1、李某 2、李某 3 各继承 10000 元。三原告不服一审和二审终审判决，向法院申请再审。

再审法院认为，本案主要争议焦点在于如何确定各继承人对李某遗产房屋和银行存款的继承份额。再审法院查明，在被继承人李某生病住院及其丧葬事宜中所需必要医药费用及办理丧葬事宜费用的绝大部分为被告邹某支付，为此，有理由认定邹某的 30000 元存款用于支付李某生病期间的花销，而非恶意转移财产。另外，李某 1 等子女于日常生活中曾探望老人，给予李某亲情照顾和精神关怀，尽到了一定的赡养义务，但是，鉴于邹某与李某系老年再婚，两人共同生活了 20 余年，且邹某只有此一处居所，故一审、二审人民法院认定该房不宜分割，由邹某居住的判决是正确的。此外，对于遗产中的存款邹某作为残疾人，并对被继承人尽了较多照顾义务，理应多分。[①] 所以，再审法院判决维持原判。

适用法律分析：本案的争议焦点在于如何确定遗产分割中各继承人应继承的遗产份额。首先，由于李某生前并未立下遗嘱，根据我国《继承法》第 5 条的规定，本案应当适用法定继承。根据我国《继承法》第 26 条规定："夫妻在婚姻关系存续期间所得的共同所有的财产，除有约定的以外，如果分割遗产，应当先将共同所有的财产的一半分出为配偶所有，其余的为被继承人的遗产。"本案中二人的住房及银行存款中的一半，应为邹某个人财产，另一半属于李某遗产。析产后应对李某的个人财产进行分割。李某的遗产依法应由其第一顺序继承人即配偶邹某、子女李某 1、李某 2、李某 3 继承。其次，根据我国《继承法》第 13 条："同一顺序继承人继承遗产的份额，一般应当均等。对生活有特殊困难的缺乏劳动能力的继承人，分配遗产时，应当予以照顾。对被继承人尽了主要扶养义务或者与被继承人共同生活的继承人，分配遗产时，可以多分。"本案邹某年事已高且有残疾人证，应认定其属于生活困难及缺乏劳动能力的人，依法应当判决予以照顾多分。鉴于邹某与李某系老年再婚夫妻，双方共同独立生活长达 20 余年之久，尽到了夫妻扶养之义务，因邹某无他处可居，且系残疾人，本着照顾弱者利益原则和保障生存配偶生存权的需要，故判决本案住房不宜分割。综上，我们认为，一审、二审和再审的人民法院在综合考虑各继承人对被继承人的扶养或赡养具体情况以及各继承人经济状况、劳动能力、住房条件等客观因素情况下所作的判决适用法律正确，是合理的，体现了遗产分割原则中的均等分配、公平分割与照顾弱者利益原则。但目前我国《继承法》对于生存配偶之遗产中家庭住房的先取权和居住权无规定，这是立法之不足。

（十一）涉及无人承受遗产案例的简介与评析

案情简介：被继承人陈某与何某显结婚，没有生育、收养子女，何某显于 1952 年死亡。陈某的父母及祖父母均早于其死亡，陈某没有兄弟姐妹。何某 1 是陈某的堂侄，陈某

① 参见中国裁判文书网：（2015）川×第×号，《李某 1、李某 2、李某 3 与邹某继承纠纷申请再审民事裁定书》，载 http://wenshu.court.gov.cn/content/content? DocID = 14a7a695-d190-40ea-b2be-32ea12910beb&KeyWord = 川×第×号，访问日期：2019 年 3 月 8 日。限于本章篇幅，作者对原案情内容有酌情删改。

自1992年长期在×村定居直到终老，其间，多由何某1照顾。陈某于1996年3月死亡，其丧葬事宜也由何某1处理。陈某死亡时留有遗产房屋一间。2016年10月，×村委会在村内张贴公示，上述遗产为无人承受遗产的，将由村委会取得。2016年12月14日，何某1提起诉讼要求继承该房屋。被告答辩称，何某1不属于法定继承人的范围，且被继承人陈某生前没有留下遗嘱，故其遗产应当属于无人承受遗产，应归村委会所有。

法院审理后认为，本案中被继承人陈某没有配偶、子女等法定继承人，何某1提供其持有的涉案房屋的房地产权证原件、骨灰存放证原件，还有街坊证明等，能证实何某1属于继承人以外的对被继承人照顾扶养较多的人。因此，依照我国《继承法》第14条规定："对继承人以外的依靠被继承人扶养的缺乏劳动能力又没有生活来源的人，或者继承人以外的对被继承人扶养较多的人，可以分配给他们适当的遗产。"因此，法院判决陈某的上述遗产房屋酌情分配给何某1所有。[①]

适用法律分析：本案的争议焦点在于陈某的堂侄是否有权取得陈某的遗产房屋。我国《继承法》第32条规定："无人继承又无人受遗赠的遗产，归国家所有；死者生前是集体所有制组织成员的，归所在集体所有制组织所有。"1985年《执行继承法意见》第57条规定："遗产因无人继承收归国家或集体组织所有时，按继承法第十四条规定可以分给遗产的人提出取得遗产的要求，人民法院应视情况适当分给遗产。"本案中，被继承人陈某没有配偶、子女等任何顺序的法定继承人，何某1提供其持有的涉案房屋的房地产权证原件、骨灰存放证原件，还有街坊证明等，能证实何某1属于继承人以外的对被继承人照顾扶养较多的人。因此，依照我国《继承法》第14条规定："对继承人以外的依靠被继承人扶养的缺乏劳动能力又没有生活来源的人，或者继承人以外的对被继承人扶养较多的人，可以分配给他们适当的遗产。"法院判决将陈某的上述遗产房屋依法酌情分配给何某1取得。本案审理法院依据我国《继承法》第14条的规定作出判决，符合法律规定。

第三节　当代中国重庆市民众财产继承观念与遗产处理习惯的特点与原因分析

根据本次调查统计数据情况的汇总分析，重庆市被调查者对前述十一个问题所体现出的财产继承观念与遗产处理习惯之特点与原因分析如下：

一、遗产范围界定之特点与原因分析

（一）遗产的种类之特点与原因分析

关于属于遗产种类的民众观念，统计数据显示的特点是，（1）认为房屋（99.68%）、汽车（97.95%）、存款（95.11%）、股票（83.91%）属于遗产的，均占八成至九成以上；认为"单位出租给某甲的午休住房"不属于遗产的，占九成以上（92.11%），即此认识与我国现行法的规定相一致；（2）认为家庭日常生活用品（66.40%）、欠款（34.70%）和死亡赔偿金（75.55%）属于遗产的，各占六成半、三成和七成以上，即此

① 参见中国裁判文书网：（2016）粤×民初第×号，载 http://wenshu.court.gov.cn/Index，访问日期：2019年3月8日。限于本章篇幅，作者对原案情内容有酌情删改。

认识与我国现行法的规定不一致；（3）认为“家庭日常生活用品”属于遗产的，占六成半以上（66.40%）；（4）认为“某甲以其姓名注册的邮箱、QQ账号等”属于遗产的占近二成（19.72%），但其是否属于遗产，我国现行法无规定（见表2-4）。

以上特点的原因分析，（1）与我国《继承法》规定的遗产范围认识一致的原因分析。八成至九成以上的重庆市被调查者认为，“房屋”、“汽车”、“存款”和“股票”属于遗产，“单位出租给某甲的午休住房”不属于遗产，与我国《继承法》的规定相一致。这说明多数被调查者对部分遗产的范围有较为清晰的认识，其原因可能是受我国立法影响，我国《继承法》采用列举加概括兜底条款的方式规定遗产范围，遗产的主要种类包括公民的收入、储蓄、房屋、债权等。

（2）与我国《继承法》规定的遗产范围认识不一致的原因分析。其一，六成半以上的重庆市被调查者认为家庭日常生活用品属于遗产，此种观念与我国现行法的规定不一致。可能是因为被继承人也在使用家庭日常生活用品，所以应当属于其遗产。但此认识有误，因为“家庭日常生活用品”中只有属于被继承人的份额部分，才能属于遗产。其二，近三成半的重庆市被调查者认为被继承人遗留的欠款属于遗产，但是我国《继承法》第3条并没有将遗产债务列入遗产的范围，并且《继承法》第33条明确规定：“继承遗产应当清偿被继承人依法应当缴纳的税款和债务，缴纳税款和清偿债务以他的遗产实际价值为限。超过遗产实际价值部分，继承人自愿偿还的不在此限。”可见，目前我国对于遗产债务已明确规定不属于遗产范围。那么，遗产债务是否应当被纳入遗产范围？我们认为，在我国《继承法》中虽然遗产与债务均属于继承的客体，但遗产仅指被继承人遗留的积极财产，并不包括消极财产①，即将遗产仅限定于积极财产与其他继承客体分开，此具有历史的和现实的社会基础。无论出于民众对遗产内涵的理解和认识需要，还是出于司法实务的统一理解和执法的需要，都应尊重这一历史传统。② 其三，七成半以上的重庆市被调查者认为交通事故死亡赔偿金属于遗产，其原因可能是被调查民众对我国的遗产范围欠缺了解。但此认识与法律规定不一致，对于死亡赔偿金的性质，根据我国2004年《关于审理人身损害赔偿案件适用法律若干问题的解释》第1条第2款规定：“本条所称‘赔偿权利人’，是指因侵权行为或者其他致害原因直接遭受人身损害的受害人、依法由受害人承担扶养义务的被扶养人以及死亡受害人的近亲属。”第17条第3款规定：“受害人死亡的，赔偿义务人除应当根据抢救治疗情况赔偿本条第一款规定的相关费用外，还应当赔偿丧葬费、被扶养人生活费、死亡补偿费以及受害人亲属办理丧葬事宜支出的交通费、住宿费和误工损失等其他合理费用。”以上规定中表明，死者的人身损害死亡补偿费是对死亡受害人的近亲属的补偿费，其不属于遗产。

（3）对我国《继承法》尚无明确规定的遗产范围之民众观念分析。只有近二成重庆市被调查者认为“某甲以其姓名注册的邮箱、QQ账号等”属于遗产，其原因可能是：其一，我国法律无明文规定；其二，它们具有私人使用性质，涉及个人隐私，故不能作为遗产来继承。由于我国《继承法》在制定时，我国正处于计划经济时期，社会经济发展较慢，公民财富积累少，遗产种类也相对较少。因此我国《继承法》第3条对遗产范围的

---

① 参见陈苇、宋豫：《中国大陆与港、澳、台继承法比较研究》，群众出版社2007年版，第193、221页。

② 参见陈苇、魏小军：《论我国遗产范围立法的完善》，载《河南财经政法大学学报》2013年第6期。

立法，采取的以“遗产是公民死亡时遗留的个人合法财产”的概括性规定和“包括具体七项遗产范围”的列举加其他合法财产的兜底规定相结合的立法模式。这可以适应社会发展遗产种类增加的需要。目前，随着社会经济的发展，我国有学者已经提出应将虚拟财产作为遗产继承。① 然而，我们认为，被继承人以其姓名注册的邮箱、QQ 账号等如果其本人自愿出售则具有财产价值。如其未出售的，因具有人身性和隐私性，则不宜作为遗产来继承。

关于遗产的种类之我国立法，我国《继承法》第 3 条规定，遗产是公民死亡时遗留的个人合法财产，遗产的范围包括公民的收入，公民的房屋、储蓄和生活用品，公民的林木、牲畜和家禽，公民的文物、图书资料，法律允许公民所有的生产资料，公民的著作权、专利权中的财产权利，公民的其他合法财产等。1985 年《执行继承法意见》第 4 条还规定：“承包人死亡时尚未取得承包收益的，可把死者生前对承包所投入的资金和所付出的劳动及其增值和孳息，由发包单位或者接续承包合同的人合理折价、补偿，其价额作为遗产。”

从域外立法例看，域外有些国家对遗产的范围确定采取的是正面列举式与排除式相结合的模式，如《葡萄牙民法典》中列举了四类属于遗产的财产，并将基于性质或法律规定随主体死亡而消灭的排除在外。② 有的国家采取的是正面概括加反面排除式相结合的模式，如《日本民法典》第 896 条规定，继承开始时，继承人继承被继承人财产的所有权利义务。但是，专属于被继承人自身的权利义务，不在此限。

从我国诸继承法学者建议稿看，对于遗产范围的立法模式主要有以下两种建议：一是概括式和排除式相结合类型，即仅作原则性规定，法律未明确规定排除的均属遗产。例如，“陈稿”第 25 条规定，遗产是被继承人死亡时遗留的个人所有财产。与被继承人人身不可分割的财产和法律规定不得继承的财产，不属于遗产。其理由主要是列举财产类型的方式难以穷尽遗产的范围。二是概括式、列举式和排除式相结合类型。如“杨稿”第 7 条和第 8 条规定，遗产是被继承人死亡时遗留的个人财产，包括：（1）房屋、林木、牲畜、储蓄等不动产或动产的所有权；（2）个人享有的土地承包经营权和承包收益；（3）建设用地使用权；（4）可继承的财产债权及其担保；（5）有价证券载有的财产权利；（6）股权或合伙中的财产权益；（7）知识产权中的财产权益；（8）被继承人享有的人格衍生的财产利益；（9）互联网络中的虚拟财产；（10）被继承人的其他财产权益。被继承人的专属性权利和法律规定不得继承的权利不属于遗产。涉及被继承人个人信息权、隐私权的互联网络虚拟财产不属于遗产。经济适用房的继承人不符合申购条件的，可以继承由政府回购所得价款，也可以按照规定标准向政府交纳土地收益等相关款项后，继承房屋。因被继承人死亡而获得，但未指定受益人的保险金，比照法定继承人的规定确定权利人。遗体、骨灰、灵牌、墓地等特殊遗产的继承不得违反公序良俗。无遗嘱的，由继承人协商处理；协商不成的，依习惯；无习惯的，可在继承人中合理确定管理人，不进行分割。祖传物的继承与分割，无遗嘱的，由继承人协商处理；协商不成的，依习惯；无习惯的，可在继承人中合理确定管理人，不进行分割。未经全体继承人同意，不能采取拍卖、变价等处分所有权的方式分割。其理由主要是认

① 参见梅夏英、许可：《虚拟财产继承的理论与立法问题》，载《法学家》2013 年第 6 期。

② 参见《葡萄牙民法典》第 2025 条、第 2069 条。

为单纯的概括模式比较抽象，不能明确回答现实中突出的急需回答的问题；而概括式和排除式相结合也不能正面明确回应，即其认为这样的立法模式既能够有针对性地回应现实问题，又避免了遗漏。①

我们认为，现代社会的民事财产权利是一个开放的体系，会随着社会经济的发展不停地增添新内容。如果对遗产的正面规定采取列举式，难免会存在立法漏洞或不明确。② 我国对遗产范围的界定采取此种方式，这是立法之不足。目前，有一些域外国家也对遗产的范围采取了同时从正面和反面作出规定的立法模式。所以，应对我国现行遗产范围的立法模式进行修改，以使遗产范围更加明确。关于遗产范围的界定，以上概括规定与反面排除规定相结合的重庆市被调查民众的观念、日本立法例和“陈稿”的观点，可供我国立法参考。

（二）被继承人生前特种赠与财产的归扣之特点与原因分析

关于被继承人生前特种赠与财产的归扣的民众观念与民间习惯，统计数据显示的特点如下：(1) 关于被继承人生前资助的财产是否应归扣纳入遗产范围的民众观念，在重庆市被调查者中，认为遗产的范围应仅以被继承人死亡时遗留的财产为限，不包括被继承人生前对子女的特种赠与财产的，占七成半以上（76.97%）；认为被继承人生前对子女继承人的特种赠与财产与死亡时其遗留的住房、存款，均应当合并计算为遗产的，占近二成（17.35%）（见表2-5）。(2) 关于归扣遗产价值计算时间的民众观念，在重庆市被调查者中，认为应按实际分割遗产时计算的，占三成以上（33.64%）；认为应按购置该财产时计算的，占二成以上（21.82%）；认为应按被继承人去世时计算的，占不到二成（19.09%）。即认为应按实际分割遗产时计算价值的占比居于第一位（见表2-6）。(3) 关于生前特种赠与财产是否归扣纳入遗产范围的民间习惯，在重庆市被调查者所在地区，没有此归扣习惯的，占七成以上（73.50%）；有该习惯的，占近三成（26.50%）（见表2-7）。(4) 关于生前特种赠与财产不归入遗产情况下的分配方式之民间习惯，在重庆市被调查者所在地区，有平均分配习惯的，占六成（60.30%）；有“乙应当适当多分”习惯的，占近三成（28.54%）（见表2-8）。

以上特点的原因分析，(1) 关于被继承人生前资助的财产是否应归扣纳入遗产范围的民众观念与民间习惯特点之原因，其一，七成半以上的重庆市被调查者认为遗产不包括被继承人生前对子女的特种赠与财产，七成以上的该市被调查地区没有此种习惯，其原因可能是我国并没有规定归扣制度，被调查民众主要凭着自己的生活阅历、生活经验及被继承人死亡后遗留的财产才是遗产的朴素思想，按照民间的习惯来选择，因此很少出现将被继承人生前赠与继承人的财产计入遗产总额并分配的情况。但本次重庆市被调查民众中有近三成的民众认为，没有获得生前特种赠与财产的子女，应适当多分遗产。这反映了在共同继承人中公平分配遗产的理念，这是我国建立遗产归扣制度的民意。其二，近二成的重庆市被调查者认为被继承人生前对子女继承人的特种赠与财产应扣入遗产范围，近三成的该市被调查者所在地区有此种习惯，其原因可能是将被继承人生前对子女等的特定赠与财产计入遗产总额，能达到在共同继承人中公平分配遗产之目的。(2) 关于归扣遗产价值

① 参见孙毅：《继承法修正中的理论变革与制度创新——对〈继承法〉修正草案建议稿的展开》，载《北方法学》2012年第5期。

② 参见陈苇、魏小军：《论我国遗产范围立法的完善》，载《河南财经政法大学学报》2013年第6期。

计算时间的民众观念特点之原因，其一，三成以上的重庆市被调查者认为按实际分割遗产时计算，其原因可能是认为这样分割更符合公平原则。其二，二成以上的重庆市被调查者认为应按购置财产时计算，其原因可能是这样更能体现被继承人的意愿。其三，不到二成的重庆市被调查者认为按被继承人去世时计算，其原因可能是这样有利于确定遗产的价值，尽快实现遗产分割。(3) 关于生前特种赠与财产不归扣纳入遗产情况下的分配方式之民间习惯特点之原因，其一，六成的重庆市被调查者所在地区有平均分配的习惯，其原因可能是这样分配有利于减少纠纷，提高遗产分割的效率。其二，近三成的重庆市被调查者所在地区有乙适当多分的习惯，其原因可能是这样分配遗产更符合公平原则。

关于被继承人生前特种赠与财产制度之我国立法，我国《继承法》对此无规定。

从域外立法例看，《德国民法典》第 2050 条规定，作为法定继承人继承的晚辈直系血亲有义务在相互间分割遗产时，将他们在被继承人生前已经从被继承人处作为婚嫁立业资财取得的标的算入遗产，但是以被继承人在给予时不另作指示为限。为用作收入而给予的补贴，以及为职业培训而支出的费用，在它们超出与被继承人财产状况相当的程度的限度内，必须进行归扣。被继承人已在给予时指示进行归扣的，其他的生前给予也必须予以归扣。《法国民法典》第 843 条、《瑞士民法典》第 626 条以及《日本民法典》第 903 条也都分别规定有遗产归扣制度。

从我国诸继承法学者建议稿看，也有不少学者建议稿提出，我国应当设立遗产归扣制度。例如，“陈稿”第 78 条规定：(1) 遗产归扣的主体。在法定继承中遗产分割时，被继承人的子女在被继承人生前接受特种赠与财产的，为归扣义务人。除此义务人以外的其他参加继承的人，为归扣的权利主体。在代位继承时，由代位继承人承担该被代位人的归扣义务。归扣义务人，即使放弃继承或因法定事由丧失继承权的，仍然应当承担归扣义务。(2) 归扣义务人，在被继承人生前所受的特种赠与财产，包括因结婚、分居、生产经营所受赠与财产；大学本科以上的教育费用；成年以后的职业教育或培训费用；储蓄性人寿保险金。(3) 遗产归扣义务的免除。被继承人可以订立遗嘱或者通过公证的文件，明确表示免除归扣义务人无过错的，该财产不计入归扣财产的范围。(4) 遗产归扣的方法。遗产分割时，归扣义务人应当将其所受被继承人生前特种赠与财产原物或其价值返还归并于遗产总额之中，然后计算各共同继承人的应继份。生前特种赠与财产的价值，依继承开始时的价值计算。该生前特种赠与财产在继承开始后到遗产分割前的增值，应当计入归扣标的的价值，但计算该财产在受赠后的增值仅限于自然增值的价值。返还，得通过扣减应继份为之。如果生前特种赠与财产的价值，超过归扣的义务人应继份的，归扣义务人应当对其他继承人进行补偿，但被继承人有相反意思表示的除外。

我们认为，关于被继承人生前特种赠与财产的归扣制度，我国立法未规定，这是其立法之不足。在此次调查中，我国重庆市只有近二成的被调查民众在观念上认可遗产归扣制度，并且重庆市只有近三成的被调查者所在地区实行归扣行为的习惯。然而，遗产归扣制度在域外立法中已经在许多国家中被设立，我国学界对该制度在我国设立也有较高的呼声。该制度是否应当在我国设立，除应当考虑我国各地区被调查民众对遗产归扣行为的认识观念与行为习惯外，还应当考虑此制度的功能。其一，此制度能够“在同一顺序的特殊应召共同继承人中公平地分配遗产。”目前，我国已经是世界第二经济大国，随着我国经济的发展，民众的财富积累日益增多，不少父母在生前对子女结婚、分家、营业等的赠与财产也在增多，此即属于父母在生前将其遗产提前分配给子女（应继份预付）的民间习惯。①其二，此制度在涉外继承中能够平等地保护中外各方共同继承人的利益。尤其应当考虑，在全球化的背景下，在我国大力倡导“一带一路”建设，促进各国经济共同发展的情况下，涉外婚姻继承关系的数量必然会逐步增加。遗产归扣制度的设立，能够保障实现在涉外继承中对我国公民与外国公民的财产继承权益的平等保护。②法律，不仅是社会现实生活需要的反映，也是引导社会生活发展的调节器。因此，我国应在慎重考虑该制度的立法功能与可行性基础上，将遗产归扣制度增设在我国的“民法典继承编”之中。以上主张设立遗产归扣制度的重庆市被调查民众的观念与习惯、域外立法例和“陈稿”的观点，可供我国立法参考。

二、继承开始的通知和公告之特点与原因分析

（一）继承开始的通知和公告的主体之特点与原因分析

关于继承开始的通知和公告的主体的民间习惯，统计数据显示的特点是，在重庆市被调查者所在地区，（1）由继承人作为通知主体的各占六成半至七成以上，具体包括：“知道被继承人死亡的继承人”（72.24%）和“保管遗产的继承人”（65.93%）；（2）由知道被继承人死亡的单位、村（居）委会为通知主体的，占近四成半（44.64%）；（3）由处理被继承人死亡事件的机构为通知主体的，占近四成（39.75%）（见表2-9）。

以上特点的原因分析，在重庆市被调查者的继承习惯中，对于发出继承开始通知的主体比较多样化，并不限于我国《继承法》规定的知道被继承人死亡的继承人、被继承人生前所在单位或者居住地的（村）居民委员会，还包含了遗产保管人、处理被继承人死亡事件的机构，如公安交警部门等，其原因可能是民众从便利和快捷通知的角度进行选择，因此通知和公告的主体比较多样化。

关于继承开始的通知主体之我国立法，我国《继承法》第23条规定：“继承开始后，知道被继承人死亡的继承人应当及时通知其他继承人和遗嘱执行人。继承人中无人知道被继承人死亡或者知道被继承人死亡而不能通知的，由被继承人生前所在单位或者住所地的居民委员会、村民委员会负责通知。”2015年《民诉法解释》第55条规定：“在诉讼中，一方当事人死亡，需要等待继承人表明是否参加诉讼的，裁定中止诉讼。人民法院应当及时通知继承人作为当事人承担诉讼，被继承人已经进行的诉讼行为对承担诉讼的继承人有效。”即我国继承开始的法定通知义务主体，包括知道被继承人死亡的继承人、被继承人生前所在单位、居住地的居民委员会、居住地的村民委员会和法院共计五类主体。但对于继承开始的公告制度，我国《继承法》无规定。

从域外立法例看，国外负有通知义务的主体一般包括继承人、遗产法院（德国）、主管庭官（瑞士）、家庭法院（日本）或其选任的管理人、遗产保佐人（德国、意大利）、遗产代理人（英美）。③例如，《德国民法典》第1964、2061条分别规定，继承人不在适当的期间内被查明的，遗产法院必须确定不存在除国库义务的继承人。各共同继承人可以

① 参见陈苇主编：《外国继承法比较与中国民法典继承编制定研究》，北京大学出版社2011年版，第625、636页。

② 参见陈苇主编：《中国遗产处理制度系统化构建研究》，中国人民公安大学出版社2019年版，第439页。

③ 参见陈苇主编：《外国继承法比较与中国民法典继承编制定研究》，北京大学出版社2011年版，第636页。

公开催告遗产债权人在6个月内向该共同继承人或遗产法院申报他们的债权。该项催告已经进行的，各共同继承人在遗产分割后，仅对某项债权之与其应继份相当的那部分责任，但申报未在期间届满前发生，或该项债权在遗产分割时未为所知的为限。该项催告必须以《联邦公报》和为遗产法院发布公告而指定的报纸予以公布。该期间自最后刊登时起算。

从我国诸继承法学者建议稿看，对于继承开始的通知和公告主体有相应的建议：如"杨稿"第54条主张遗嘱执行人为通知主体。第70条规定继承人和遗嘱执行人均不知道被继承人死亡或者无能力通知的，由负责处理被继承人死亡事件的部门或基层组织通知。"王稿"第547条规定，继承开始后，知道被继承人死亡的继承人应当采用适当的方式及时通知其他继承人。继承人中无人知道被继承人死亡或知道被继承人死亡而不能通知的，由被继承人生前所在单位或者住所地的居民委员会、村民委员会负责通知。负有通知义务的继承人或单位，如果故意隐瞒继承开始的事实，造成其他继承人或受遗嘱人损失的，应当承担损害赔偿责任。继承人有无不明的，按照无人承受的遗产的处理执行。

我们认为，我国《继承法》欠缺继承开始的公告制度，这是立法之不足。在未来立法中，可适当扩大通知继承开始主体的范围，由可以履行通知职责的多个主体通知与告知继承开始的事项，有利于尽早地进行遗产分割。关于继承开始的通知和公告的义务主体，以上重庆市被调查民众的习惯、域外立法例和我国学者建议稿的观点，可供我国立法参考。

（二）继承开始的通知和公告的方式之特点与原因分析

关于继承开始的通知和公告的方式的民间习惯，统计数据显示的特点是，在被调查者所在地区，（1）通过口头、电话、微信等通知（81.07%）和信件、告知函等书面通知（50.47%）的，各占五成至八成以上；（2）在报纸、电视、网络等平台上发布被继承人死亡的公告（22.24%）、在被继承人所在地的村（居）委会公告栏公告（33.44%）和申请人民法院以公告程序进行公告（26.34%）的，各占二成至三成以上（见表2-10）。

以上特点的原因分析，重庆市被调查者所在地区的民间习惯是发出继承开始通知的方式多样化且便利化，人们最常采取的通知涉及遗产处理的相关人员的方式为"口头、电话、微信"等通知方式，其次才为信件、告知函等书面通知，其原因可能是随着社会通信技术的不断进步，手机、电话的普及和微信、QQ等通信工具在民众中得到广泛的应用，因此出现继承开始通知的方式多样化且便利化，电话、微信等通知方式选择比例大，而信件、告知函等书面通知方式选择比例小的结果。

关于继承开始的通知的具体方式之我国立法，我国《继承法》无规定。并且，也没有设立继承开始的公告方式规定。

从域外立法例看，大陆法系的德国、瑞士、日本和意大利等国均规定在继承人有无不明时，应发布寻找继承人的公告，催告权利人在一定期限内申明其继承权。[①] 例如，《意大利民法典》第498条规定，按遗产清单接受继承的继承人，如果知晓债权人和受遗赠人的住所或居所，则申报债权的通知应当用挂号信直接送达，同时，还应当将申报的债权的通知刊登在省级法律公报上。

从我国诸继承法学者建议稿看，"陈稿"第85条主张，继承人有无不明的，对于继

① 参见《德国民法典》第1965条；《瑞士民法典》第555条；《日本民法典》第958条。

承开始通知的，遗产管理人可在村或社区公告栏公告或在省一级报纸登报公告或申请人民法院公告。“杨稿”第92条主张，继承人有无不明的，遗产管理人应当在接受指定后十日内发出寻找遗产承受权利人、遗产债权人的公告。

我们认为，我国立法欠缺继承开始的通知和公告的方式，这是其立法之不足。继承开始的通知和公告的方式可以多样化，立法只需作概括性规定“及时通知”或“公告”即可，但对未知被通知对象的继承开始的通知和公告，立法须规定具体的方式，以引导通知和公告的义务主体依法履行义务。以上重庆市被调查民众的习惯、域外立法例和我国学者建议稿的观点，可供我国立法参考。

（三）继承开始的通知和公告的期间之特点与原因分析

关于继承开始的通知和公告期间的民众观念，统计数据显示的特点是，在重庆市被调查者中，（1）认为应在7日以内的较短期间发出通知和公告的，合计占六成以上（占63.88%）；（2）认为应在15日至30日以内发出通知和公告的，仅占三成多（32.02%）（见表2-11）。

以上特点的原因分析，（1）六成以上的重庆市被调查者认为应在7日以内的较短期间发出通知和公告，其原因可能是希望能知道被继承人死亡的人，能够在第一时间通知其他继承人被继承人死亡的事实，因此，继承开始的通知和公告期间不宜过长，应该尽快完成通知与公告。（2）三成多的重庆市被调查者认为应在15日至30日以内的较短期间发出通知和公告，其原因可能是认为需要较长的时间通知相关遗产利害关系人。

关于继承开始的通知和公告的期间之我国立法，我国《继承法》第23条仅规定“及时”发出继承开始的通知，并没有明确规定继承开始的通知期间。关于无主财产的公告程序，我国现行《民事诉讼法》第191、192条对于认定财产无主公告的期间规定为1年。另外，关于公示催告程序，根据我国现行《民事诉讼法》第219条有关票据遗失、被盗等的公告程序规定，人民法院决定受理申请，应在3日内发出公告，催促利害关系人申报权利。公示催告的期间，由人民法院根据情况决定，但不得少于60日。

从域外立法例看，对于继承开始的公告期间，德国、意大利等均在继承的接受或放弃、催告遗产债权人的期间中有所体现。[①] 例如，《意大利民法典》规定，继承人应当自接到异议通知之日起1个月内，由继承开始地的公证人确定的不少于30日的期限内，召集债权人和受遗赠人进行债权申报。任何利害关系人均可请求司法机构为有权取得遗产的人确定一个表示接受或拒绝接受继承的期限。德国规定通过公示催告遗产债权人的期间是6个月。

从我国诸继承法学者建议稿看，对于继承人有无不明时的催告期间，例如，“王稿”第662条规定，人民法院决定受理申请，应在3日内发出公告，催促继承人、受遗赠人、债权人等其他利害关系人申报、登记。公示催告的期间，由人民法院根据情况决定，但不得少于60日。“张稿”第67条、“陈稿”第85条、“杨稿”第92条规定公告期限不得少于6个月。对于公示催告债权人申报债权的期间，“梁稿”第2017条、“王稿”第662条、“杨稿”第81条规定，法院公示催告期间不得少于3个月。

我们认为，我国现行立法并未规定继承开始的通知的具体期间，这是立法之不足。关

① 参见《德国民法典》第1965、2061条；《意大利民法典》第481、498、650条。

于继承开始的通知和公告期间，在未来立法中，应该结合实际区分不同的情形，给予不同的期间，如通常情况下，继承开始后通知义务人的通知期；法院依据相关申请后公示催告遗产利害关系人的期间；无人继承情况下的催告期间。以上主张 7 日内发出通知和公告的重庆市被调查民众的观念、域外立法例和我国学者建议稿的观点，可供我国立法参考。

三、遗产管理之特点与原因分析

（一）遗产管理人的确定之特点与原因分析

关于遗产管理人的确定的民间习惯，统计数据显示的特点是，在重庆市被调查者所在地区，（1）由死者的法定继承人作为遗产管理人的，占九成以上（99.84%）；（2）由死者的儿媳或女婿（26.34%）、死者家族中的德高望重者（42.27%）、死者的其他亲戚朋友（22.08%）和死者所在的单位或村/居委会（25.39%）作为遗产管理人的，各占二成至四成以上（见表 2-12）。

以上特点的原因分析，根据遗产管理人的确定的民间习惯之理由（见表 2-13），（1）九成以上的重庆市被调查者所在地区有由继承人担任遗产管理人的习惯，其原因是法定继承人是遗产继承的法定权利主体，且都是与被继承人的近亲属，由其担任遗产管理人，可以便于清点和妥善管理遗产。（2）四成以上的重庆市被调查者（排在第二位）所在地区有由死者家族中的德高望重者作为遗产管理人的习惯，其原因是由德高望重者担任遗产管理人，可以有效地防止遗产被隐藏、转移，有利于保护遗产相关人的合法权益。

关于遗产管理人制度之我国立法，我国《继承法》缺乏系统的遗产管理制度，只是在《继承法》第三章“遗嘱继承和遗赠”之第 16 条①、第四章“遗产的处理”之第 24 条②、1985 年《执行继承法意见》“关于遗产的处理部分”之第 44 条③中原则性地规定了遗产执行和遗产保管的部分内容，但缺乏对遗产管理制度中遗产管理人的确定、职责及报酬等内容的系统性规定。

从域外立法例看，许多国家都设立有遗产管理制度，并明确规定了遗产管理人的确定问题，如德国、日本、意大利立法等。例如，《德国民法典》规定，遗产管理人的确立有三种情况：一是遗嘱指定遗产管理人。如被继承人在遗嘱中确立了遗嘱执行人的，则由其承担管理遗产的职责。二是继承人担任遗产管理人。继承人在接受继承后对遗产享有权利和负担义务，继承人有多人的，则由其共同管理遗产。三是法院指定遗产管理人。法院可以根据继承人以享受限定继承利益为目的的申请，或者根据遗产债权人以其权利受到继承人的行为方式或者资产情况的不良影响为由的申请，发布指定遗产管理人对遗产进行管理的命令。另外，当不确定是否有继承人或不能明确继承人已接受继承的，法院应依法为待

① 我国《继承法》第 16 条规定：“公民可以依照本法规定立遗嘱处分个人财产，并可以指定遗嘱执行人。公民可以立遗嘱将个人财产指定由法定继承人的一人或者数人继承，公民可以立遗嘱将个人财产赠给国家、集体或者法定继承人以外的人。”

② 我国《继承法》第 24 条规定：“存有遗产的人，应当妥善保管遗产，任何人不得侵吞或者争抢。”

③ 1985 年《执行继承法意见》第 44 条规定：“人民法院在审理继承案件时，如果知道有继承人而无法通知的，分割遗产时，要保留其应继承的遗产，并确定该遗产的保管人或保管单位。”

继承遗产选任遗产管理人。① 另外，《意大利民法典》② 和《日本民法典》③ 也规定，遗产管理人的确定主要有遗嘱指定、继承人担任、法院指定三种方式。

从我国诸继承法学者建议稿看，对于遗产管理人的确定都主张可以遗嘱指定和继承人本人担任遗产管理人。争议之处则主要在于，无遗嘱指定遗产管理人又无继承人担任遗产管理人的情况下遗产管理人如何确定问题，不同继承法学者建议稿对于法院指定、村（居）委会担任、民政部门指定有不同的建议。如"张稿"第25条、"陈稿"第7条第2款规定由法院指定遗产管理人。"王稿"第661条规定由村（居）委会作为遗产管理人。"杨稿"第91条规定，继承人有无不明的，由民政部门指定遗产管理人。

我们认为，我国《继承法》缺乏系统的遗产管理制度，这是其立法之不足。关于遗产管理人的确定，以上重庆市被调查民众的习惯、域外立法例和我国学者建议稿的观点，可供我国立法参考。

（二）遗产管理人的职责与报酬之特点与原因分析

第一，遗产管理人职责的民众观念之特点与原因分析。

关于遗产管理人职责的民众观念，统计数据显示的特点是，在重庆市被调查者中，认为遗产管理人的职责包括"清查遗产，制作遗产清单"（88.96%）、"妥善保管遗产"（91.20%）、"查明被继承人生前的债权和债务，积极地追讨债权或清偿债务"（71.84%）、"查明被继承人是否留有遗嘱，并且确定遗嘱是否真实合法"（56.48%）、"可以原告或被告的身份参加因遗产引起的诉讼"（80.16%）和"定期制作遗产管理报告，向继承人报告遗产管理的情况"（58.56%）的，各占五成至九成以上（见表2-14）。

以上特点的原因分析，被调查民众认为遗产管理人应承担较为广泛的职责，其原因可能是被调查民众认识到遗产管理人的重要性，遗产管理人职责的设置关系着整个遗产管理程序的顺利进行，只有在明确遗产管理人各项具体职责的基础上，才能保障遗产管理任务的履行。

关于遗产管理人的具体职责之我国立法，我国《继承法》第24条规定："存有遗产的人，应当妥善保管遗产，任何人不得侵吞或者争抢。"但对于遗产管理人的具体职责无规定。

从域外立法例看，域外国家对遗产管理人规定有较为全面的职责。例如，《意大利民法典》规定，遗产管理人的职责主要如下：其一，遗产管理人应编制并执行遗产清册。其二，适当的处分和管理遗产，如将处理遗产收获的现金存放在指定的金融机构。其三，催告遗产债权人和受遗赠人在一定期间内申报权利。其四，对债权人和受遗赠人承担报告管理遗产账目的义务，债权人和受遗赠人还可以为其指定一个报告账目的期限。其五，在遗产状况有必要的情况下，以原告的身份向法院提起诉讼，或者以被告的身份加入因遗产引起的诉讼。其六，在公证人的协助下编制清偿顺序表并进行公示，按照债权人各自享有的先取特权顺序进行清偿。④

---

① 《德国民法典》第1959~1961条、第1981条、第2032条、第2038条、第2197条、第2205条。

② 《意大利民法典》第460条、第508~509条、第528条、第703条。

③ 《日本民法典》第918条、第926条、第936条、第952条、第1006条、第1012条。

④ 《意大利民法典》第485条、第486条、第496条、第502条、第528~531条。

从我国诸继承法学者建议稿看，大部分建议稿对于遗产管理人的职责有较为全面的规定，如“陈稿”第8条、第87~88条规定遗产管理人有如下职责：一是收集遗产，编写遗产清册。二是对遗产的管理应忠实且谨慎。三是公示催告。四是报告遗产管理情况。五是清偿债务。六是交付剩余遗产，同时应保留失踪人的继承份额，如超过20年没人主张的，则认定为无人承受遗产。七是负责与待继承遗产有关的起诉和应诉。“杨稿”第74条规定，遗产管理人应当勤勉谨慎地履行以下职责：一是，查明被继承人是否留有遗嘱，并且确定遗嘱是否真实合法；二是，查明并通知遗产承受权利人、被继承人的债权人、债务人；三是，管理遗产，制作遗产清单并公证；四是，清偿遗产债务；五是，分割、移交遗产；六是，在管理权限之内，可以采取必要的措施或通过诉讼保全遗产；七是，进行与管理遗产有关的其他必要行为。“徐稿”第四分编第51条也对此有规定。

我们认为，我国《继承法》对于遗产管理人的具体职责无规定，这是其立法之不足。关于遗产管理人的具体职责，以上重庆市被调查民众的观念、意大利立法例和我国学者建议稿的观点，可供我国立法参考。

第二，遗产管理人是否有权取得报酬的民间习惯之特点与原因分析。

关于遗产管理人是否有权取得报酬的民间习惯，统计数据显示的特点是，在重庆市被调查者中，（1）法院指定的遗产管理人有权请求给付报酬的，六成半以上（67.19%）；（2）继承人担任的遗产管理人不能请求给付报酬的，四成半以上（46.69%）；（3）继承人选任的第三人担任的遗产管理人，其中，是否给付报酬由继承人决定的，占四成半（45.74%），一律有权请求给付报酬的，占四成以上（41.17%）（见表2-15）。

以上特点的原因分析，（1）四成半以上的重庆市被调查地区有继承人担任遗产管理人的则不享有报酬，如遗产管理人是继承人选任的，是否有报酬由继承人决定的习惯，其原因可能是在被调查者观念中，作为遗产管理人的继承人通常情况下与被继承人关系密切，且会继承遗产，因此由继承人担任管理遗产人不应享有报酬。（2）六成半以上的重庆市被调查者所在地区有对于法院指定的遗产管理人，可以请求给付报酬的习惯，其原因可能是该遗产管理人需要为管理遗产付出自己的时间、精力和劳动，应该给予一定的遗产管理费用，这不仅是对遗产管理劳动价值的承认，也符合权利与义务相一致的原则。（3）四成半的重庆市被调查者所在地区有由继承人选任第三人作为遗产管理人的，是否给付报酬由继承人决定的习惯，但是，四成以上的重庆市被调查者所在地区在此种情况下，有一律给付报酬的习惯，其原因可能是如存在多个继承人或者继承人不愿意担任遗产管理人时，那么继承人选任遗产管理人时，需由其协商解决遗产管理人的报酬问题，这样既符合前述继承人担任遗产管理人需付报酬的原则，又给予继承人是否担任遗产管理人的自由选择权利。

关于遗产管理人是否有权取得报酬之我国立法，我国《继承法》对此无规定。

从域外立法例看，一些国家的遗产管理制度中都对遗产管理人的报酬予以明确规定，如《德国民法典》规定，遗产管理人可以为其职务的履行而请求适当的报酬，但是对于遗嘱执行人的报酬被继承人生前在遗嘱中另作规定的除外。[①]《日本民法典》规定，遗产管理人的报酬可以由法院依据遗产管理人与被继承人的关系或者其他的正当理由予以确

① 《德国民法典》第1987条、第2215条第5项、第2221条。

定。对于遗嘱执行人的报酬，如遗嘱确定了报酬事项的，就依据遗嘱而定，如没有确定，可以由法院依据遗产的具体情况或其他状况而定。[①] 可见，原则上遗产管理人可以获得适当的报酬，但遗嘱人或遗嘱有例外规定的除外。

从我国诸继承法学者建议稿看，关于遗产管理人的报酬，“梁稿”第1995条规定，遗嘱人可以在遗嘱中确定遗嘱执行人的报酬。遗嘱人未确定遗嘱执行人报酬的，遗嘱执行人不得请求报酬，但继承人或受遗赠人自愿支付报酬的除外。“王稿”第639条、“陈稿”第9条也规定了遗产管理人的报酬请求权。

我们认为，关于遗产管理人是否有权取得报酬，我国《继承法》对此无规定，这是其立法之不足。因此，有必要赋予遗产管理人获得遗产管理报酬的权利。关于遗产管理人是否有权取得报酬，以上区别不同情况确定是否给予遗产管理者报酬的重庆市被调查民众的习惯，德国、日本立法例和我国学者建议稿的观点，可供我国立法参考。

（三）遗产管理人的损害赔偿责任之特点与原因分析

关于遗产管理人的损害赔偿责任之民间习惯，统计数据显示的特点是，在重庆市被调查者所在地区，（1）遗产管理人有故意或重大过失，才承担损害赔偿责任的，占五成半以上（56.62%）；（2）无论遗产管理人有故意、重大过失或一般轻过失，都要承担损害赔偿责任的，占四成（40.38%）（见表2-16）。

以上特点的原因分析，（1）五成半以上的重庆市被调查者所在地区有遗产管理人有故意或重大过失，才承担损害赔偿责任的习惯，其原因可能是在被调查者的观念中，认为遗产管理人需要承担的职责较多，而且继承人担任遗产管理人还没有报酬，为使其能够勇于担任遗产管理人的职责，有必要去除其会因轻度过失而需承担严重责任的担忧，而且遗产管理人负有善良管理人的义务，其在具有故意或者重大过失的情况下才承担赔偿责任较为合理。（2）四成的重庆市被调查者所在地区有无论遗产管理人有故意、重大过失或一般轻过失都要承担损害赔偿责任的习惯，其原因可能是要严格规范遗产管理人的行为，以防止其滥用权利。

关于遗产管理人的损害赔偿责任之我国立法，我国《继承法》对此无规定。

从域外立法例看，域外有些国家也规定遗产管理人有故意或重大过失才承担赔偿责任。例如，《意大利民法典》第491条规定，享有遗产清单利益的继承人在遗产管理中只对重大过失承担责任。《日本民法典》第934条第1款规定，限定承认人怠于按照法律规定进行公告或者催告，或者因在同条第一款的期间内向遗产债权人或受遗嘱人清偿，而无法向其他遗产债权人或者受遗嘱人清偿时，对由此发生的损害负赔偿责任。违反公告期间届满后的清偿、期限前债务等的清偿、对受遗赠人清偿等规定而为的清偿，亦同。

从我国诸继承法学者建议稿看，各建议稿都主张遗产管理人在违反法律规定的情况下应承担相应的责任。例如，“张稿”第50条规定，遗嘱执行人因故意或重大过失给继承人、受遗赠人或其他利害关系人造成损失的，应承担赔偿责任。但遗嘱执行人系有偿执行遗嘱的，应对自己的一切过失所造成的损失承担赔偿责任。两个或两个以上的遗嘱执行人，应对全部遗嘱执行事务共同承担责任，但遗嘱执行人按照遗嘱人的指示各自独立执行职务的除外。

---

① 《日本民法典》第918条、第1018条、第1021条。

我们认为，我国《继承法》没有规定遗产管理人的损害赔偿责任，这是其立法之不足。关于遗产管理人的损害赔偿责任，应当针对不同情形，规定继承人的损害赔偿责任。以上故意或重大过失造成遗产损害应承担赔偿责任的重庆市被调查民众的习惯，意大利立法例和“张稿”的观点，可供我国立法参考。

四、法定继承之特点与原因分析

（一）法定继承人的范围与顺序之特点与原因分析

关于法定继承人的范围与顺序，统计数据显示的特点如下：（1）关于法定继承人范围与顺序的民众观念，各以被调查者选择占比最高的顺序作为统计依据，重庆市被调查者较认可的法定继承顺序为第一顺序配偶（87.07%）、父母（63.72%）、子（71.92%）、女（67.19%）；第二顺序孙子女（50.10%）、外孙子女（47.00%）、祖父母（49.84%）、外祖父母（47.79%）、兄弟（41.64%）、姐妹（40.54%）；第三顺序侄子女（25.08%）、外甥子女（24.29%）、伯叔姑舅姨（25.55%）、堂兄弟姐妹（24.61%）、表兄弟姐妹（15.14%）（见表2-17）。可见，被调查者认可的法定继承人范围较广，除我国《继承法》第10条已规定的父母、子女、兄弟姐妹、祖父母、外祖父母、孙子女、外孙子女属于外，还包括伯叔姑舅姨、侄子女外甥子女、堂兄弟姐妹、表兄弟姐妹。（2）关于配偶与血亲继承人顺序的民众观念，在重庆市被调查者中，其一，认为配偶应为固定的第一顺序继承人的，占七成半（75.07%）；其二，认为配偶无固定继承顺序的，合计占近二成半（24.93%）（见表2-18）。

以上特点的原因分析，（1）关于法定继承人范围与顺序的民众观念特点之原因，重庆市被调查者认定的法定继承人范围较广，其原因可能是：其一，传统的多人口家庭结构已经转变为少人口的家庭结构的影响。我国自20世纪80年代开始实施“提倡一对夫妻只生一个孩子”的计划生育政策以来，已经有30多年的时间。我国目前以一对夫妻及其未成年子女的“核心家庭”居多①，而且独生子女家庭中没有兄弟姐妹。在“核心家庭”中，通常兄弟姐妹数量少或无兄弟姐妹，同时，伯叔姑舅姨、侄子女、外甥子女等血亲人数也相应减少。在此情况下，如果仅仅依据我国《继承法》规定的法定继承人范围，可能有被继承人死亡后出现遗产无人继承的情况。其二，我国已进入老龄化社会，到21世纪30年代中国将进入老龄化的高峰期，并持续近40年时间。② 目前我国老年人的养老方式仍是以“家庭养老”为主，在老年人的子女不在身边或子女先于老年人去世的情况下，老年人通常会受其他血缘关系较近的亲属（侄子女、外甥子女）的慰藉与照料。③ 其三，受中国传统的“家财不外流”的观念影响。我国传统观念中，通常财产须在家庭内部传承，并承担着赡养、抚养及保证家庭门户延续等功能。④ 我国目前法定继承人的范围较

① 在1990年、2000年，我国由一对夫妻与其未成年子女组成的核心家庭分别占全部家庭的67.31%和56.02%。参见周福林：《我国家庭结构的变迁》，经济管理出版社2016年版，第179页。

② 参见财经国家周刊：《老龄化加剧养老难题：2050年1.5个职工养1个退休者》，载http://guba.eastmoney.com/news,cjpl,95828497.html,访问日期：2017年11与5日。

③ 陈苇、冉启玉：《完善我国法定继承人范围和顺序立法的思考》，载《法学论坛》2013年第2期，第52~57页。

④ 焦垣生、张维：《中国传统家文化下的财产继承》，载《西安交通大学学报（社会科学版）》2008年第6期，第65~70页。

窄，被继承人的遗产可能出现没有法定继承人的情况，根据我国《继承法》第32条的规定，该无人继承的遗产将被收归国家或集体所有。因此，被调查者多认为应当适当扩大法定继承人的范围，增加其他血缘关系较近的亲属参与继承，以保护自然人的个人财产所有权。

（2）关于配偶与血亲继承人顺序的民众观念特点之原因，其一，七成半的重庆市被调查者认为配偶应为固定的第一顺序继承人，其原因可能是受我国《继承法》第10条之规定影响，第一顺序法定继承人为配偶、子女、父母，长期以来该规定已深入人心。而且在家庭成员中，配偶、子女、父母是与被继承人关系最为亲密的人。其二，近二成半的重庆市被调查者认为配偶无固定顺序，可以参与前二顺序或者前三顺序的继承，其原因可能是这样更符合遗产向下传承的规律。

关于法定继承人的范围与顺序之我国立法，我国《继承法》第10条规定："遗产按照下列顺序继承：第一顺序：配偶、子女、父母。第二顺序：兄弟姐妹、祖父母、外祖父母。继承开始后，由第一顺序继承人继承，第二顺序继承人不继承。没有第一顺序继承人继承的，由第二顺序继承人继承。"

从域外立法例看，对于继承人的范围与顺序，大陆法系的德国、法国、俄罗斯等国立法中，血亲继承人范围和继承顺序都比我国更广和更多。例如，《德国民法典》规定的法定继承人范围和顺序如下：第一顺序为直系晚辈血亲；第二顺序为父母及其直系晚辈血亲；第三顺序为祖父母、外祖父及其直系晚辈血亲；第四顺序为曾祖父母及其直系晚辈血亲、曾外祖父母及其直系晚辈血亲；第五和更远的顺序为辈分更大的祖先及其直系晚辈血亲；配偶无固定继承顺序，可参与第一、第二、第三顺序的继承。①《法国民法典》规定的法定继承人之范围和顺序如下：第一顺序为子女及其直系卑血亲；第二顺序为父母、兄弟姐妹及其直系卑亲；第三顺序为父母之外的直系尊血亲；第四顺序为除兄弟姐妹及其直系卑亲以外的其他六亲等内的旁系亲属；配偶无固定的继承顺序，其与被继承人的子女及其直系卑血亲或父母共同继承。② 可见，德国和法国立法的血亲继承人范围都宽于我国，继承顺序也多于我国，而且子女及其直系晚辈血亲的顺序都优先于父母的顺序。这体现了保证遗产尽可能被集中传承于被继承人的晚辈直系血亲，以发挥遗产的育幼职能。

从我国诸继承法学者建议稿看，学者们对于法定继承人的范围与顺序有不同建议。第一种观点认为，应继续坚持我国《继承法》现行规定（"徐稿"）。其建议稿第495条规定法定继承人的范围和顺序如下：第一顺序为配偶、子女、父母；第二顺序为兄弟姐妹、祖父母、外祖父母。第二种观点认为，应将我国法定继承人的范围扩大至其他四亲等以内的亲属（"梁稿"、"王稿"、"杨稿"）。其建议的法定继承人范围和顺序如下：第一顺序为配偶、子女、父母；第二顺序为兄弟姐妹、祖父母、外祖父母；第三顺序为其他四亲等以内的亲属。"杨稿"的第三顺序为曾祖父母、外曾祖父母、伯、叔、姑、舅、姨、堂兄弟姐妹、表兄弟姐妹、侄子女、外甥子女等四亲以内的其他直系或者旁系血亲。第三种观点认为，应增加兄弟姐妹的子女（侄子女、外甥子女）作为法定继承人，并将晚辈直系血亲直接列入第一顺序法定继承人的范围。例如，"张稿"第28条、"陈稿"第45条规

① 《德国民法典》第1922~1931条。

② 《法国民法典》第734、756、757-1、757-2、757-3条。

定的继承人之范围和顺序如下：第一顺序为子女及其晚辈直系血亲；第二顺序为父母；第三顺序为兄弟姐妹及其子女；第四顺序为祖父母，包括父系祖父母和母系祖父母；配偶可以与任一顺序或前三顺序的血亲继承人共同继承。

我们认为，关于法定继承人的范围与顺序的确定，我国现行法规定的法定继承人范围较窄，配偶为固定继承顺序不科学，这是其立法之不足。对此问题，以上重庆市被调查民众的观念，德国、法国立法例和“张稿”及“陈稿”的观点，可供我国立法参考。

（二）配偶与血亲继承人的法定应继份之特点与原因分析

关于配偶与血亲继承人法定应继份的民众观念，统计数据显示的特点是，在重庆市被调查者中，（1）认为配偶应按固定顺序继承并均分遗产的占近五成半（53.31%）；（2）认为配偶应为无固定顺序继承，可参与前三顺序或前二顺序继承，并取得不同份额的，合计占近四成半（44.95%）（见表2-19）。

以上特点的原因分析，（1）近五成半的重庆市被调查者认为配偶应按固定顺序继承并均分遗产，其原因可能是受我国现行法的影响。（2）近四成半的重庆市被调查者认为配偶应为无固定顺序继承，可参与前三顺序或前二顺序继承，并取得不同份额的，其原因可能是这样有利于保护其他继承人的利益，更符合遗产向下传承的规律。

关于配偶与血亲继承人的法定应继份之我国立法，我国《继承法》第10条将配偶作为第一顺序法定继承人与其他第一顺序法定继承人父母、子女共同继承遗产。第13条规定，同一顺序继承人继承遗产的份额，一般应当均等。对生活有特殊困难的缺乏劳动能力的继承人，分配遗产时，应当予以照顾。对被继承人尽了主要扶养义务或者与被继承人共同生活的继承人，分配遗产时，可以多分。有扶养能力和有扶养条件的继承人，不尽扶养义务的，分配遗产时，应当不分或者少分。继承人协商同意的，也可以不均等。

从域外立法例看，对配偶的继承顺序主要有两种不同的立法例，一是配偶无固定继承顺序。如《德国民法典》第1931条规定，配偶可与第一、第二、第三顺序的血亲继承人共同继承遗产。《法国民法典》第765条规定，配偶与子女及其直系卑亲、父母共同继承遗产。二是配偶有固定继承顺序。例如，《俄罗斯联邦民法典》第1142条规定，配偶仅与第一顺序的血亲继承人共同继承遗产。

从我国诸继承法学者建议稿看，各建议稿也存在前述两种不同的体例，一是“梁稿”第1946条、“王稿”第564条、“杨稿”第57条都规定配偶有固定继承顺序，配偶仅与第一顺序的血亲继承人共同继承遗产。二是“张稿”第28条和“陈稿”第45条规定配偶无固定继承顺序，配偶可与任一顺序的血亲继承人或前三个顺序的血亲继承人共同继承遗产。

我们认为，我国未规定配偶无固定继承顺序且与任一顺序的血亲继承人共同继承，这是其立法之不足。我国宜采取“配偶无固定继承顺序且与任一顺序的血亲继承人共同继承”的立法模式，这样可以兼顾保护配偶及血亲继承人的继承权。关于配偶与血亲继承人的法定应继份，以上主张配偶无固定顺序且与其他顺序的血亲继承人共同继承的重庆市被调查民众的观念，德国、法国立法例和“张稿”及“陈稿”的观点，可供我国立法参考。

（三）配偶对遗产中家庭住房的先取权与终生使用权之特点与原因分析

关于配偶对遗产中家庭住房的先取权与终生使用权，统计数据显示的特点是，

(1) 关于配偶对遗产中家庭住房先取权与终生使用权的民间习惯，在重庆市被调查者所在地区，有该习惯的占八成半（85.80%）；无此习惯的占近一成半（14.20%）（见表2-20）。(2) 关于配偶对遗产中家庭住房的先取与终生使用是否付费的民间习惯，在重庆市被调查者所在地区，有适当补偿习惯的，占近六成半（64.20%）；没有该习惯即无须进行补偿的，只占近三成半（34.22%）。也就是说，如配偶无经济补偿能力的，可不予补偿而终生使用此房屋（见表2-21）。

以上特点的原因分析，(1) 关于配偶对遗产中家庭住房先取权与终生使用权的民间习惯特点之原因，其一，八成半的重庆市被调查者所在地区有该习惯，其原因可能是大部分的被调查者认为家庭住房是对生存配偶提供生活保障的重要物质基础。而且，该房屋是被继承人生前与其配偶共同生活的场所，夫妻双方都共同为家庭做出了贡献，当被继承人死亡后，原本属于夫妻共同财产的家庭住房，尤其是该住房为夫妻唯一所有的房屋情况下，如果该房屋因继承而被分割，将使生存配偶不能维持其一贯的生活方式，这不利于保障生存配偶的利益。① 其二，近一成半的重庆市被调查者所在地区无此习惯，其原因可能是认为遗产应及时分割，以防止后续发生纠纷。(2) 关于配偶对遗产中家庭住房的先取与终生使用是否付费的民间习惯特点之原因，其一，近六成半的重庆市被调查者所在地区有适当补偿的习惯，其原因可能是这样符合民法中的公平原则。其二，近三成半的重庆市被调查者所在地区无适当补偿的习惯，其原因可能是这更有利于保证生存配偶一方的生活，保护其合法权益。

关于家庭住房先取权与终生使用权制度之我国立法，我国《继承法》对此无规定。

从域外立法例看，为保障生存配偶的基本生存权和居住权，瑞士、德国、法国都规定配偶对其居住的遗产房屋享有先取权或居住权。例如，《瑞士民法典》规定，夫妻双方居住的房屋、公寓或使用的家具属于遗产的，生存配偶可以请求获得该房屋、公寓或家具的所有权，计入其继承份额。同时规定配偶也可以选择不取得上述房屋、公寓或家具的所有权，而是取得使用权或居住权。②《法国民法典》规定，除被继承人有相反表示外，有继承权的配偶对其实际占用并作为主要住宅的原属于夫妻双方或全部属于遗产的住房享有居住权，并对住房内属于遗产的家具享有使用权，直至其本人死亡。③

从我国诸继承法学者建议稿看，对于配偶就遗产中家庭住房的先取权问题，学者们观点不一致。“梁稿”、“杨稿”和“徐稿”等都没有规定配偶对遗产中家庭住房的先取权。“王稿”第580条中规定了配偶用益权的内容，即配偶尚生存且没有自己住房的，如果没有继承遗产中的房屋，则对遗产中的房屋享有法定用益物权。“张稿”第32条中规定设立配偶先取权，配偶对遗产中供自己使用的住房和日常生活用品有先取特权，若配偶的先取特权超过其应继份，则以先取特权作为其应继份。“陈稿”第48条规定设立配偶的先取权，并同时设立配偶对特殊遗产的使用权和居住权，即生存配偶对遗产中的婚姻住宅和家庭日常生活用品享有先取权，如其继承份额小于这些财产的价值时，可选择对家庭日常生活用品的使用权和对婚姻住宅的终身居住权。

---

① 参见陈苇、宋豫主编：《中国大陆与港、澳、台继承法比较研究》，群众出版社2007年版，第294页。

② 《瑞士民法典》第612条。

③ 《法国民法典》第764条。

我们认为，我国《继承法》没有规定家庭住房先取权与终生使用权制度，这是其立法之不足。设立此制度对于生存配偶维持一贯的生活方式而保持生活的稳定性，对于保障受生存配偶抚养的未成年子女的健康成长，具有重要的现实意义。以上主张生存配偶可以优先继承遗产中的家庭住房的重庆市被调查民众的习惯、域外立法例和“张稿”、“陈稿”的观点，可供我国立法参考。

（四）后顺序特殊法定继承人对遗产中原使用的住房及日常生活用品的终生使用权之特点与原因分析

关于后顺序特殊法定继承人对特殊遗产的终生使用权，统计数据显示的特点如下：（1）关于后顺序特殊法定继承人对特殊遗产的终生使用权的民间习惯，在重庆市被调查者所在地区，有该习惯的占近九成（87.38%）；没有该习惯的只占一成以上（12.62%）（见表2-22）。（2）关于后顺序特殊法定继承人对特殊遗产的终生使用是否付费的民间习惯，在重庆市被调查者所在地区，没有支付租金习惯的，占近九成（87.38%）；有支付租金习惯的，占一成以上（12.62%）（见表2-23）。（3）关于后顺序特殊法定继承人对特殊遗产的终生使用权之期限的民间习惯，在重庆市被调查者所在地区，享有此终生使用权习惯的，占近八成半（84.15%）；不享有终生使用权习惯的，占一成半（15.85%）（见表2-24）。

以上特点的原因分析，（1）关于后顺序特殊法定继承人对特殊遗产的终生使用权的民间习惯特点之原因，近九成的重庆市被调查者所在地区有此习惯，其原因可能是，如果被继承人死亡，存在有第一顺序继承人，那么与被继承人生前共同生活的继承顺序在后的近亲属继承人，如祖父母、外祖父母就不能继承遗产。因此，设立这些后顺序特殊法定继承人的居住权，能够使其保持一贯的生活方式而安度晚年。同时，这样不仅是我国尊老养老传统美德的彰显，也是对与被继承人共同生活的而未参与继承的祖父母、外祖父母之特殊后顺序继承人的照顾，符合我国《继承法》的照顾弱者利益原则。[①]（2）关于后顺序特殊法定继承人对特殊遗产的终生使用是否付费的民间习惯特点之原因，其一，近九成的重庆市被调查者所在地区有后顺序特殊法定继承人对原居住的遗产住房无须支付租金的习惯，其原因可能是他们与被继承人有血缘关系，要求其支付租金不利于保障该特殊继承人的利益。其二，一成以上的重庆市被调查者所在地区有后顺序特殊法定继承人对原居住的遗产住房享支付租金的习惯，其原因可能是这样可以保护其他法定继承人的权益，符合公平原则。（3）关于后顺序特殊法定继承人对特殊遗产的终生使用权之期限的民间习惯特点之原因，其一，近八成半的重庆市被调查者所在地区有该特殊继承人享有此终生使用权的习惯，其原因可能是这样可以更能保障特定后顺序法定继承人的基本生活；其二，一成半的重庆市被调查者所在地区无享有此终生使用权的习惯，其原因可能是可以避免后顺序法定继承人损害其他前顺序法定继承人的利益。

关于后顺序特殊法定继承人对特殊遗产的终生使用权之我国立法，我国《继承法》对此无规定。

从域外立法例看，域外有国家规定后顺序特殊法定继承人对原使用的遗产住房及日常

① 参见陈苇、董思远：《民法典编纂视野下法定继承制度的反思与重构》，载《河北法学》2017年第7期，第2~19页。

生活用品的享有使用权。如《德国民法典》第1969条规定，继承人有义务在继承开始后最初30日内，向在被继承人死亡时属于被继承人的家具并受其扶养的被继承人家属给予扶养费，并许可使用住宅和家庭用具。

从我国诸继承法学者建议稿和学者的论文看，有学者提出，“依靠被继承人扶养的法定继承人在未参加应召顺序继承时，对遗产中供其个人日常生活使用的物品和住房，享有使用权，直至其死亡时为止”。[①] “张稿”第33条规定，父母因顺序在后未参加继承时，对遗产中供其个人日常生活使用的住房和其他物品有终生使用权。“陈稿”第48条规定，依靠被继承人扶养的法定继承人在未参加继承时，对遗产中供其个人日常生活使用的物品和住房享有终生使用权。

我们认为，我国《继承法》未规定后顺序特殊法定继承人对特殊遗产的终生使用权制度，这是其立法之不足。关于后顺序特殊法定继承人对特殊遗产的终生使用权，以上主张设立此制度的重庆市被调查民众的习惯、德国立法例和我国学者建议稿及相关论文的观点，可供我国立法参考。

（五）尽了主要赡养义务的丧偶儿媳或女婿的遗产分配方式之特点与原因分析

关于尽了主要赡养义务的丧偶儿媳或女婿的遗产分配方式的民间习惯，统计数据显示的特点是，在重庆市被调查者所在地区，（1）尽了主要赡养义务的丧偶儿媳或女婿可以与第一顺序继承人共同继承且平均分配遗产的，占近七成（67.67%）；（2）尽了主要赡养义务的丧偶儿媳或女婿不能作为第一顺序继承人，但可以酌情分得遗产的，占近三成（29.65%）（见表2-25）。

以上特点的原因分析，根据尽了主要赡养义务的丧偶儿媳或女婿遗产分配方式的民间习惯之理由（见表2-26），（1）近七成的重庆市被调查者所在地区有尽了主要赡养义务的丧偶儿媳或女婿可以与第一顺序继承人共同继承的习惯，其原因是儿媳和女婿赡养老人符合中国的孝道文化和道德观念，而且赋予尽赡养义务的丧偶儿媳或女婿作为第一顺序继承人，可以对其起到鼓励的作用，而且也符合权利义务相一致原则。（2）近三成的重庆市被调查者所在地区有尽了主要赡养义务的丧偶儿媳或女婿可以酌情分得遗产的习惯，其原因是被调查者认为丧偶儿媳或女婿与被继承人毕竟不具有血缘关系，“外人”不能作为第一顺序继承人。

关于尽了主要赡养义务的丧偶儿媳或女婿的遗产分配方式之我国立法，我国《继承法》第12条规定：“丧偶儿媳对公、婆，丧偶女婿对岳父、岳母，尽了主要赡养义务的，作为第一顺序继承人。”我国1985年《执行继承法意见》第29条规定，丧偶儿媳对公婆、丧偶女婿对岳父、岳母，无论其是否再婚，依继承法第12条规定作为第一顺序继承人时，不影响其子女代位继承。

从域外立法例看，在世界上绝大多数国家的立法中，姻亲间无法定的权利义务关系，继承权只能因婚姻关系或血缘关系取得。[②]

从我国诸继承法学者建议稿看，“杨稿”第60条规定丧偶儿媳（或女婿）对公婆

① 陈苇、杜江涌：《我国法定继承制度的立法构想》，载《现代法学》2002年第3期，第97页。

② 参见陈苇主编：《外国继承法比较与中国民法典继承编制定研究》，北京大学出版社2011年版，第409、417~418页。

（或岳父母）尽了主要赡养义务的，作为第一顺序继承人；“王稿”第569条规定丧偶儿媳（或女婿）对公婆（或岳父母）尽了主要赡养义务的，没有代位继承人时，作为第一顺序继承人；“陈稿”第50条规定，丧偶儿媳（或女婿）对公婆（或岳父母）尽了主要赡养义务的，可以酌情分给适当财产；“梁稿”、“徐稿”和“张稿”则均笼统规定继承人以外的对被继承人扶养较多的人，可以分给适当的财产。①

我们认为，我国《继承法》将尽了主要赡养义务的丧偶的儿媳或女婿作为第一顺序法定继承人，此立法存在不合理之处。关于尽了主要赡养义务的丧偶儿媳或女婿的遗产分配方式，结合我国继承法多数学者建议稿主张尽了主要赡养义务的丧偶的儿媳或女婿不宜纳入继承顺序，宜作为遗产酌分请求权人取得遗产的观点，建议对于尽了主要赡养义务的丧偶儿媳（或女婿）可不作为第一顺序法定继承人，而将他们作为酌情分配遗产请求权人，在参与不同顺序的法定继承中可请求酌情分得适当遗产。这样既有利于鼓励他们发扬敬老、养老的传统美德，也能够避免他们作为第一顺序继承人在无其他应召共同继承人时有可能独自取得全部遗产，而后顺序的血亲继承人却被排除在外，这不利于保护血亲继承人之继承权。② 为加强酌情分配遗产的可操作性，有必要细化丧偶的女婿或儿媳对公婆的遗产请求酌情分配时，必须具备的一定条件。一是应达到最低的年限要求，为维护家庭伦理道德和防止居心不良之人谋取家庭财物；二是明确规定认定赡养义务的标准，应综合参考其平时是否对公婆、岳父母进行了必要的经济供养、生活照顾和精神慰藉等行为。③

五、遗嘱继承之特点与原因分析

（一）公证遗嘱与其他形式遗嘱的效力之特点与原因分析

关于公证遗嘱与其他形式遗嘱适用效力的民众观念，统计数据显示的特点是，在重庆市被调查者中，（1）认为后遗嘱的适用效力优先于前一公证遗嘱的，合计占七成（70.82%）；（2）认为公证遗嘱适用效力优先的，占近三成（29.18%）（见表2-27）。

以上特点的原因分析，根据公证遗嘱与其他形式遗嘱适用效力的民众观念之理由（见表2-28），（1）七成的重庆市被调查者认为后遗嘱的适用效力优先于前一公证遗嘱，其一，三成以上的该市被调查者认为后成立的书面遗嘱有效，其原因是书面遗嘱（第二份遗嘱）比较正式，取证容易。其二，近四成的该市被调查者认为最后的口头遗嘱有效，其原因是口头遗嘱是在最后设立的，且有证人作证，最能反映被继承人的最后真实意愿。但是，有的认为，口头遗嘱形式不固定，很难准确、完全地反映被继承人的真实意愿，且有被篡改或修改的可能性。（2）有近三成的重庆市被调查者认为公证遗嘱适用效力优先，其原因是公证遗嘱的程序规范，具有较强的公示效力和证明效力。

关于公证遗嘱与其他形式遗嘱的适用效力之我国立法，我国《继承法》第20条明确规定，遗嘱人可以撤销、变更自己所立的遗嘱。立有数份遗嘱，内容相抵触的，以最后的遗嘱为准。自书、代书、录音、口头遗嘱，不得撤销、变更公证遗嘱。1985年《执行继

① 参见“梁稿”第1956条；“徐稿”第四分编第497条；“张稿”第61条。但“张稿”在理由说明中，解释说明将尽了主要赡养义务的丧偶儿媳或女婿作为酌分遗产请求权人。参见张玉敏：《中国民法典继承编立法建议稿及立法理由》，人民出版社2006年版，第162页。

② 参见陈苇、杜江涌：《我国法定继承制度的立法构想》，载《现代法学》2002年第3期。

③ 参见石婷：《冲突与协调：苗族女性继承习惯与继承权的双重探析》，载《河北法学》2016年第7期。

承法意见》第42条也规定，遗嘱人以不同形式立有数份内容相抵触的遗嘱，其中有公证遗嘱的，以最后所立公证遗嘱为准；没有公证遗嘱的，以最后所立的遗嘱为准。

从域外立法例看，域外一些国家对于遗嘱的适用效力有相关规定，均采取“后遗嘱优先于前遗嘱”的原则。例如，《瑞士民法典》第511条规定，如被继承人未明确废除原遗嘱而又重新订立新遗嘱，只要不能肯定新遗嘱为原遗嘱的补充，应视新遗嘱为原遗嘱的替代。同样，被继承人对同一物有两个遗嘱，如前后有抵触，后者代替前者。《德国民法典》第2231、2248条、《日本民法典》第1022~1023条也有类似规定。

从我国诸继承法学者建议稿看，有部分主张以“后遗嘱优先于前遗嘱”为原则，如“张稿”第42条规定，遗嘱人可以另立遗嘱明确表示撤回变更自己以前所立的遗嘱，立有数份遗嘱，内容相抵触的，以最后的遗嘱为准。“陈稿”第38条规定，遗嘱人有权变更先前遗嘱，立有数份遗嘱，且内容相互抵触的，以最后的遗嘱为准，先前的遗嘱视为被撤回。“杨稿”第33条规定，遗嘱人可以另立遗嘱明确表示撤回变更自己以前所立的遗嘱，遗嘱人故意销毁遗嘱的，视为撤回……立有数份遗嘱，内容相抵触的，以最后的遗嘱为准，前遗嘱抵触部分视为撤回。

我们认为，我国《继承法》规定公证遗嘱的适用效力优先，不能反映被继承人的真实意愿，这是其立法之不足。虽然公证遗嘱相较其他遗嘱形式有更为严格的制定程序，更能保障遗嘱人意思表示的真实性。但是我国《继承法》确定公证遗嘱具有最高效力，而且只能采用公证的形式进行变更，其存在不合理之处。因为，赋予财产继承人设立遗嘱的最根本目的是准确按照遗嘱人的意愿，在其死后把遗产交给指定的继承人。如果对公证遗嘱的变更只能以公证的方式进行，这既违背了继承法的立法精神与目的，而且与设立遗嘱继承的自由原则背道而驰，不能维护遗嘱人设立、变更遗嘱的合法权益。因此，关于公证遗嘱与其他形式遗嘱的适用效力，以上主张“后遗嘱优先于前遗嘱”的重庆市被调查民众的观念、域外立法例和我国学者建议稿的观点，可供我国立法参考。

（二）遗嘱自由的限制——特留份之特点与原因分析

关于以遗嘱将个人遗产全部赠给他人的民众观念，统计数据显示的特点是，在重庆市被调查者中，对于被继承人将遗产全部赠与他人的行为，（1）认为不适当的，即主张对被继承人以遗嘱处分个人财产的行为予以适当限制的，占近六成（58.80%）；（2）认为适当的，占近四成（38.03%）（见表2-29）。

以上特点的原因分析，根据关于以遗嘱将个人遗产全部赠给他人的民众观念之理由（见表2-30），（1）近六成的重庆市被调查者认为该行为不适当，其原因是被调查民众认为该做法会造成家庭财产外流，不利于保障甲的配偶及其子女的生活，同时也不符合风俗习惯，为常人所难接受。（2）近四成的重庆市被调查者认为该行为是适当的，其原因是认为个体对自己的财产享有自由处分的权利，其他人无权干涉。

关于遗嘱自由的限制之我国立法，我国《继承法》第19条明确规定：“遗嘱应当对缺乏劳动能力又没有生活来源的继承人保留必要的遗产份额。”1985年《执行继承法意见》第37条也规定：“遗嘱人未保留缺乏劳动能力又没有生活来源的继承人的遗产份额，遗产处理时，应当为该继承人留下必要的遗产，所剩余的部分，才可参照遗嘱确定的分配原则处理。”

从域外立法例看，很多国家的继承法对遗嘱处分个人所有财产都有特留份制度之限制。例如，《瑞士民法典》规定，被继承人，有直系血亲卑亲属、父母、配偶、登记的同性伴侣为继承人者，对其财产，为继承人保留特留份后，得为死因处分。[①]《日本民法典》规定，兄弟姐妹以外的继承人，作为特留份，按照以下各项所列之区分，各自接受所使用各项相应比例的数额：（1）只有直系尊亲属为继承人的情形，为被继承人财产的三分之一；（2）前项所列情形外，为被继承人财产的二分之一。[②]

从我国诸继承法学者建议稿看，根据"陈稿"第32~33条的规定，主张增设特留份制度，并同时保留必留份制度，即采取双轨制。遗嘱人以遗嘱处分财产，应当为配偶、晚辈直系血亲、父母保留特定的遗产份额。对于我国特留份权利人的范围的确定，我们主张其权利人的范围不宜过大，可限于被继承人的配偶、子女（包括胎儿）和父母作为特留份权利主体。正如我国学者所言，从当今中国社会的现状看，父母与未成年子女组成的核心家庭占有主导地位。将特留份的权利主体限于关系最为密切的配偶、子女及父母，更能充分发挥特留份制度的立法功能。而且这一权利主体范围也与多数国家的立法相同。[③]同时，我国也需要保留必留份制度，将特留份主体之外的被继承人的兄弟姐妹、直系尊亲属和直系卑亲属等法定继承人中，无劳动能力又无经济来源者有条件地作为必留份请求权人。我们认为，为使受被继承人扶养的其他继承人能够取得适当的遗产，需要放宽请求必留份的条件，即只要他们属于受被继承人扶养的继承人，而无论其是否属于我国《继承法》第19条规定的"无劳动能力又没有生活来源的继承人"，都应要求遗嘱人为其保留必留份。也就是说，我们主张设立特留份的同时保留必留份，采取双轨制的主要理由如下：第一，特留份与必留份，两者的主体范围不同。前者的主体范围窄，仅包括家庭关系最为亲密的配偶、子女（包括胎儿）和父母；后者的主体范围宽，包括除配偶、子女（包括胎儿）和父母之外的受被继承人扶养但不论其有无劳动能力或有无经济来源（放宽条件情况下）的其他法定继承人。第二，特留份与必留份，两者请求权的取得条件不同。前者是依据婚姻关系或血缘关系而享有特留份请求权，无须考虑当事人的受扶养状况和经济情况；后者只需属于受被继承人扶养的人这一条件，不论其有无劳动能力或有无经济来源均可请求取得必留份。第三，两种制度的功能不同，特留份体现了法律基于伦理、亲情和权利义务关系的考量，对家庭中最基本成员的继承权益的特殊保护[④]；必留份体现了法律对受扶养的继承人之继续维持其一贯的生活方式的保障。

我们认为，我国《继承法》规定的必留份制度的条件过于严格，缺少特留份制度，这是其立法之不足。鉴于特留份与必留份，两种制度各自的权利主体范围不同、请求权的取得条件不同、各自的功能亦不同，因此建议我国增设特留份制度，同时保留必留份制度，并放宽请求必留份的条件。两种制度相辅相成，共同发挥作用。关于遗嘱自由的限制，以上主张对遗嘱自由进行适当限制的重庆市被调查民众的观念、域外立法例和我国学者建议稿的观点，可供我国立法参考。

---

① 参见《瑞士民法典》第470条；《法国民法典》第913~916条；《日本民法典》第1028条；《德国民法典》第2303条。

② 参见《日本民法典》第1028条。

③ 许莉：《我国继承法应增设特留份制》，载《法学》2012年第8期。

④ 参见陈苇主编：《外国继承法比较与中国民法典继承编制定研究》，北京大学出版社2011年版，第345、350、358~359页。

（三）夫妻共同遗嘱之特点与原因分析

关于夫妻共同遗嘱，统计数据显示的特点如下：（1）关于夫妻间能否设立共同遗嘱的民众观念，在重庆市被调查者中，赞成设立夫妻共同遗嘱的，占近七成半（73.34%）；不赞成设立夫妻共同遗嘱的，占二成半以上（26.66%）（见表2-31）。（2）关于夫妻共同遗嘱存在的民间习惯，在重庆市被调查者所在地区，没有设立夫妻共同遗嘱习惯的，占近八成（78.40%）；有该习惯的占二成以上（21.60%）（见表2-33）。

以上特点的原因分析，关于夫妻间能否设立共同遗嘱的民众观念与民间习惯特点之原因，根据关于夫妻共同遗嘱的能否设立的民众观念之理由（见表2-32），（1）近七成半的重庆市被调查者赞同设立夫妻共同遗嘱，二成以上的该市被调查者所在地区存在此种习惯，其原因是他们认为夫妻双方共同设立遗嘱，反映了双方的共同意愿。（2）占二成半的重庆市被调查者不赞同设立夫妻共同遗嘱，近八成的该市被调查者所在地区存在此种习惯，其原因是该遗嘱无法应对出现的新情况和新问题，限制了配偶各自对本人财产的处分权。同时，由于共同遗嘱须双方协商才能变更，而且须双方死亡才能生效。如果一方配偶死亡，生存配偶无权单方变更共同遗嘱，这就限制了生存配偶自由处分其个人财产的权利，尤其是如果基于情势变更，生存配偶需要变更该遗嘱的意愿无法实现。因此，实践中夫妻共同设立遗嘱的情况较少。

关于夫妻共同遗嘱之我国立法，我国《继承法》和1985年《执行继承法意见》均未对夫妻共同遗嘱作出规定。但我国《遗嘱公证细则》第15条规定："两个以上的遗嘱人申请办理共同遗嘱公证的，公证处应当引导他们分别设立遗嘱。遗嘱人坚持申请办理共同遗嘱公证的，共同遗嘱中应当明确遗嘱变更、撤销及生效的条件。"

从域外立法例看，大陆法系和英美法系国家立法对于夫妻共同遗嘱主要有两种立法例：一是承认夫妻共同遗嘱，如德国。《德国民法典》第2265~2269条规定，夫妻可以订立共同遗嘱。夫妻双方在其据以相互指定为继承人的共同遗嘱中，规定生存配偶死亡后，双方的遗产应归属于第三人的，有疑义时，必须认为该第三人系就全部遗产而被指定为最后死亡的配偶的继承人。可见，德国立法承认共同遗嘱的效力，且共同遗嘱的主体仅限于夫妻。二是否定夫妻共同遗嘱，如法国和日本。《法国民法典》第968条规定，二人或二人以上不得以同一证书订立遗嘱。《日本民法典》第957条规定，二人以上者，不得以同一文书立遗嘱。

从我国诸继承法学者建议稿看，学术界对夫妻共同遗嘱的认识存在一定的分歧，主要有以下两方面的观点：（1）否定说。该学说不认同夫妻共同遗嘱的效力，代表学者如王利明、张平华、刘耀东、秦伟等。[①] 例如，"王稿"两人以上不得订立同一遗嘱。[②] 另外，"张稿"、"陈稿"中也没有规定夫妻共同遗嘱。其主要原因在于：一是，夫妻共同遗嘱有违遗嘱的基本原理，遗嘱是单方法律行为，其设立、撤销、更改应由遗嘱人的单方意愿进行，而设立夫妻共同遗嘱，一方死亡后，就会阻碍这些方式的实现。二是，夫妻一方死亡后，另一方生存配偶因为各种原因可能需要撤销或者变更原来所立的夫妻共同遗嘱，导致

① 参见王利明（项目主持人）：《中国民法典学者建议稿及立法理由·人格权编、婚姻家庭编、继承编》，法律出版社2005年版，第86页；张平华、刘耀东：《继承法原理》，中国法制出版社2009年版，第307页；秦伟：《继承法》，上海人民出版社2001年版，第194页。

② 参见"王稿"第597条。

原来所指定的继承人或受遗赠人与新的继承人或受遗赠人之间发生继承纠纷。因此，有学者提出应该立法明确禁止夫妻共同遗嘱，以减少不必要的纠纷。[①]（2）肯定说。该学说认为，应当确立共同遗嘱的法律地位，提倡夫妻二人采用合立遗嘱的形式处分共同财产。这一学说的主要代表学者是徐国栋、刘春茂、刘文等。[②] 如“徐稿”第四分编第 60~61 条就承认夫妻共同遗嘱，并对其形式、自动失效等作了规定，但不承认其他任何形式的共同遗嘱。其主要理由在于，共同遗嘱与我国民众的传统习惯吻合。现实生活中，许多家庭都习惯在父母双方都逝世后，才对全部遗产进行分割处理。设立夫妻共同遗嘱，有利于维持生存配偶的正常生活和保护处于弱势地位的年纪尚幼的子女权益，从而避免家庭成员争夺遗产，维护家庭的和睦与稳定。

我们认为，关于夫妻共同遗嘱，通过结合以上重庆市被调查民众的观念与习惯的调查，考察综合域外国家的立法和我国学界的争议观点，我们赞同“否定说”。原因在于，其一，重庆市近八成的被调查者所在地区没有设立夫妻共同遗嘱的习惯，尽管大部分被调查民众主观上对夫妻共同遗嘱持认可态度，但现实生活中实际上很少见到夫妻双方订立共同遗嘱的实例。其二，域外多数国家的立法亦否认或不予规定夫妻共同遗嘱的效力，以保障夫妻各方独立行使遗嘱自由的权利。其三，我国民间确实存在父母一方死亡后子女一般不开始继承遗产的习惯，许多家庭都习惯在父母双方都逝世后，才对全部遗产进行分割处理，但这与是否设立共同遗嘱无关，这是民众的传统继承习惯。并且，我国今后的继承立法可以借鉴前述法国立法例，通过设立特殊继承人对遗产中家庭住房的先取权和居住权，达到维持生存配偶的正常生活和保护未成年子女的继承权益之目的。因此，以上否定设立夫妻共同遗嘱的重庆市被调查民众的观念与习惯，法国、日本立法例和“王稿”的观点，可供我国立法参考。

六、继承和遗赠的接受与放弃之特点与原因分析

（一）继承的接受与放弃的时间与方式之特点与原因分析

第一，继承的接受与放弃的时间之民众观念之特点与原因分析。

关于继承的接受与放弃的时间之民众观念，统计数据显示的特点是，在重庆市被调查者中，（1）认为继承人放弃继承，应当在遗产处理前作出放弃继承意思表示的，占六成以上（61.20%）；（2）认为继承人放弃继承，应在知道继承开始的 2 个月内作出放弃继承意思表示的，占近四成（38.80%）（见表 2-34）。

以上特点的原因分析，（1）超过六成的重庆市被调查者认为继承人放弃继承应当在遗产处理前作出，其原因可能是受我国现行法的影响。（2）近四成的重庆市被调查者认为继承人放弃继承，应在知道继承开始的 2 个月内作出放弃继承意思表示，其原因可能是：其一，可以避免遗产处理程序的复杂化，保障遗产分配的顺利进行。其二，为避免遗产归属长期处于确定状态，须及时明确其继承主体。

关于继承的接受与放弃的时间之我国立法，我国《继承法》第 25 条第 1 款规定：

① 参见张华贵：《利益平衡与立法选择：论立法应当禁止夫妻共同遗嘱》，载《山东女子学院学报》2013 年第 3 期。

② 参见刘春茂主编：《中国民法·财产继承》，人民法院出版社 2008 年版，第 299 页；刘文：《继承法比较研究》，中国人民公安大学出版社第 2004 年版，第 235 页。

“继承开始后，继承人放弃继承的，应当在遗产处理前，作出放弃继承的表示。没有表示的，视为接受继承。”

从域外立法例看，关于继承的接受与放弃之时间、方式和效力，不少大陆法系国家都有明确的规定。关于放弃继承的时间，《日本民法典》第915条规定，放弃继承的期限为3个月，且从继承人知道有继承开始时起算。《德国民法典》第1944条的规定，放弃继承的期限一般为6个星期，但若被继承人只在国外有最后住所或继承人期间开始时在国外居住的，期间为6个月，且该期间从继承人知悉遗产的归属和指定继承的理由时开始起算。

从我国诸继承法学者建议稿看，“张稿”第9~13条及“陈稿”第11~13条都规定，继承开始后，继承人可自知道其为继承人或自遗嘱开启2个月内，声明放弃或接受继承。继承人在国外的为6个月。以采取制作遗产清册的方式接受有条件的限定责任继承。没有做出声明或没有制作遗产清册的，视为无条件的概况继承。“杨稿”第12条规定，继承人应当自知道或者应当知道继承开始并有资格继承遗产之日起3个月内，作出是否接受继承的表示，逾期未表示或者已经接受遗产分配的，视为接受继承，接受或者视为接受继承后不得再放弃继承。接受或放弃继承的表示附条件附期限的无效。

我们认为，我国《继承法》没有规定继承的接受与放弃的具体期限，这是其立法之不足。由于继承开始时，被继承人的财产状况尚未明确，放弃继承对其他继承人以及遗产债权人的利益关系重大，一方面继承人需一定的时间对遗产状况作调查方能决定是否放弃继承，另一方面时间过长又会使继承关系处于不稳定状态。因此，关于继承的接受与放弃的时间，以上继承人应在继承开始后2个月内作出放弃继承意思表示的重庆市被调查民众的观念和“张稿”、“陈稿”的观点，可供我国立法参考。

第二，继承的接受与放弃的方式之民间习惯的特点与原因分析。

关于继承的接受与放弃的方式之民间习惯，统计数据显示的特点是，在重庆市调查者所在地区，(1) 依据书面凭证接受继承的占六成以上（62.34%）；(2) 口头声明与书面凭证皆可接受继承的地区占近二成半（24.93%）；(3) 依据口头声明接受继承的地区占一成以上（12.73%）(见表2-35)。

以上特点的原因分析，(1) 六成以上的重庆市被调查者所在地区有依据书面凭证接受继承的习惯，其原因可能是他们认为书面凭证，具有直观性和内容的确信性，因此可以作为证明的凭据。(2) 近二成半的重庆市被调查者所在地区有口头声明与书面凭证皆可接受继承的习惯，其原因可能是采用两种方式可灵活使用，适用不同情况。(3) 一成以上的重庆市被调查者所在地区有依据口头声明接受继承的习惯，其原因可能是口头声明方式更为便捷。

关于继承的接受与放弃的方式之我国立法，1985年《执行继承法意见》第47条规定：“继承人放弃继承应当以书面形式向其他继承人表示。用口头方式表示放弃继承，本人承认，或有其他充分证据证明的，也应当认定其有效。”可见，重庆市大部分被调查者以书面凭证的形式确定放弃继承的习惯与我国司法解释的规定精神相一致。

从域外立法例看，法国、日本、德国的立法都明确规定继承的接受与放弃的方式须为要式行为。如《法国民法典》第804条规定，全部概括继承人或部分概括继承人放弃继承，应当向继承开始地的大审法院书记室为之，才能对抗第三人。《日本民法典》第938条规定，要放弃继承的人，须将其意思向家庭法院申述。《德国民法典》1944~1945条规定，放弃遗产应向遗产法院表示，该表示必须以遗产法院的记录或者公证认证的方式作出。

从我国诸继承法学者建议稿看，“张稿”第12条规定，放弃继承的声明应当以书面的形式向继承人、遗产管理人或法院作出。“杨稿”第13条规定，放弃继承的表示应当以书面形式向其他继承人遗产管理人或遗嘱执行人作出，用口头方式表示放弃继承，本人承认，或有其他证据证明的，应当认定为有效。没有或者不知其他继承人遗产管理人或遗嘱执行人的，放弃继承受遗赠的意思表示向民政部门作出或者以公证的方式作出。

我们认为，我国《继承法》规定的继承的接受与放弃的方式存在不足，有待于进一步完善。继承的接受与放弃的方式，既关系到继承人的权益，也关系到遗产债权人的利益。因此，以上重庆市被调查民众的习惯、域外立法例和我国学者建议稿的观点，可供我国立法参考。

（二）遗赠的接受与放弃的方式与效力之特点与原因分析

关于遗赠的接受与放弃的方式与效力，统计数据显示的特点如下：（1）关于遗赠的接受与放弃的方式与效力之民众观念，在重庆市被调查者中，认为放弃遗赠应明示，未为表示的视为接受遗赠的占七成半以上（76.39%）；认为接受遗赠的应明示，未为表示的视为放弃遗赠的占近二成半（23.61%）（见表2-36）。（2）关于遗赠的接受与放弃的方式与效力的民间习惯，在重庆市被调查者所在地区，对于受遗赠人未作任何意思表示的行为，视为放弃遗赠的，占近六成（57.36%）；视为接受遗赠的，占四成以上（占42.64%）（见表2-37）。

以上特点的原因分析，关于遗赠的接受与放弃的方式与效力之民众观念与民间习惯的特点之原因，（1）七成半以上的重庆市被调查者认为，放弃遗赠应明示，未为表示视为接受遗赠，近四成以上的该市被调查者所在地区存在此种习惯，其原因可能是被调查民众认为接受遗赠是一种纯获利行为，不表示即应视为接受。（2）二成半的重庆市被调查者认为接受遗赠的应明示，未为表示视为放弃遗赠，近六成的该市被调查者所在地区存在此种习惯，其原因可能是被调查民众认为受遗赠人有权选择是否接受或者放弃遗赠，明确表示更能直接有效的反映被遗赠人的真实意愿。

关于遗赠的接受与放弃的方式与效力之我国立法，我国《继承法》第25条规定第2款规定：“受遗赠人应当在知道受遗赠后两个月内，作出接受或者放弃受遗赠的表示。到期没有表示的，视为放弃受遗赠。”

从域外立法例看，根据《日本民法典》第986、987条规定，受遗赠人，在遗嘱人死亡以后，可以随时放弃遗赠。遗赠的放弃，溯及遗嘱人死亡之时发生其效力。遗赠义务人及其他利害关系人，可以设定相当期间，催告受遗赠人应在该期间内作出对遗赠的承认或放弃。如果受遗赠人在其期间内，未对遗赠义务表示其意思时，视为已承认其遗赠。即对于遗赠的接受，日本采明示与非明示并行的双轨制。

从我国诸继承法学者建议稿看，“陈稿”第59条规定，受遗赠人在遗赠人死亡以后可表示放弃接受遗赠。放弃的意思表示应在知道或者应当知道受遗赠后1年内作出，1年内未作出的视为接受遗赠。遗嘱义务人及其他利害关系人可催告受遗赠人在2个月内作出接受或放弃的表示，未表示的视为接受遗赠。“杨稿”第12~13条规定，受遗赠人在知道或者应当知道受遗赠后未作出放弃表示的，视为接受遗赠。放弃继承受遗赠的效力，溯及于继承开始之时。放弃应当以书面形式向其他继承人遗产管理人或遗嘱执行人作出，没有前述主体的，可向民政部门或者以公证的方式作出。

我们认为，关于遗赠的接受与放弃的方式与效力，我国《继承法》规定受遗赠人未作出表示的，视为放弃遗赠，这是其立法之不足。但重庆市七成半以上多数被调查者认可以未为表示的方式表示接受遗赠，这与我国《继承法》规定是不相符合的。既然接受遗赠所接受的是一种财产权益，与接受继承是接受包括财产权利和财产义务的遗产不同。依照民法的基本理念，对于财产权益权利人没有表示放弃的，应当视为接受而不是放弃。①因此，以上未表示则推定为接受遗赠的重庆市被调查民众的观念与习惯、日本立法例和“陈稿”、“杨稿”的观点，可供我国立法参考。

（三）继承的放弃与债权人的撤销权之特点与原因分析

关于继承的放弃与债权人的撤销权，统计数据显示的特点如下：（1）关于继承的放弃能否被债权人予以撤销的民众观念，在重庆市被调查者中，对于继承人放弃继承的行为，认为可以被债权人撤销的，占五成以上（51.11%）；认为不可以被债权人撤销的，占近五成（48.89%）（见表2-38）。（2）关于继承的放弃能否被债权人撤销的民间习惯，在重庆市被调查者所在地区，可以被债权人撤销的，占五成以上（51.71%）；不可以被债权人撤销的，占近五成（48.29%）（见表2-39）。

以上特点的原因分析，关于继承的放弃能否被债权人予以撤销的民众观念与民间习惯的特点之原因，根据关于继承的放弃能否被债权人撤销的民间习惯之理由（见表2-40），（1）五成以上的重庆市被调查者认为继承人放弃继承的行为可以被债权人撤销，五成以上的该市被调查者所在地区存在此种习惯，其原因是继承人为照顾家庭中的妇女、儿童的生存需要而放弃继承的未获得被调查者认可，这是为保护债权人的利益。（2）近五成的重庆市被调查者认为继承人放弃继承的行为不可以被债权人撤销，近五成的该市被调查者所在地区存在此种习惯，其原因是有利于优先保护弱势群体，也体现了私法自治原则，即对继承人自愿选择是否继承意愿的尊重。

关于继承的放弃与债权人的撤销权之我国立法，我国《继承法》对此无规定。

从域外立法例看，主要有两种立法例：一是肯定债权人有撤销权。例如，《瑞士民法典》第578条规定，债务超过继承财产的继承人，以妨害债权人的利益为目的而抛弃继承权时，债权人或破产管理人可在6个月内提起撤销抛弃继承权之诉。但其债权得到担保的，不在此限。《法国民法典》第788条规定，继承人放弃继承有损债权人利益时，债权人可以请求法院准许其以债务人的名义，代替其地位接受继承，且得为债权人的利益，在债权额的限度内对继承人的放弃行为予以撤销。二是对于放弃继承行为债权人的撤销权无规定，如德国、日本等均对此无规定。

从我国诸继承法学者建议稿看，“王稿”第562条规定，继承人放弃继承损害其债权人利益的，债权人可以在知道或者应当知道继承人放弃继承之日起6个月内申请人民法院撤销继承人的放弃行为。

我们认为，关于继承的放弃与债权人的撤销权，我国《继承法》对此无规定，这是

① 参见吴国平、吴琨：《我国大陆地区遗赠接受与放弃制度的立法完善》，载《福建行政学院学报》2013年第1期。

其立法之不足。由于接受继承和放弃继承行为兼具财产行为和身份行为双重属性，是法律赋予继承人的单方法律行为，直接涉及继承人的人格自由和尊严。在现代社会，基于私法自治原则，继承法规定实行自愿继承，允许继承人自愿选择接受继承或放弃继承。债权人撤销权制度设立的目的，在于保全债权，防止债务人的责任财产不当减少，损害其债权。债务人的责任财产应当是其个人的固有财产，而被继承人的遗产并不是继承人的固有财产。并且，债权人行使撤销权的前提是债务人的行为使责任财产不当减少，有危及自身的债权之虞。[①] 或者说，如果债权人实施不当减少其责任财产的行为而侵害债权时，债权人就有权撤销该行为，以保证实现其债权。[②] 由于继承人放弃继承并没有减少其本身的固有财产，并没有损害债权人的债权，因此债权人不应当享有对放弃继承遗产行为的撤销权。否则，如果承认债权人享有对放弃继承行为的撤销权，这实际上就是承认强制继承，这有悖现代继承立法自愿继承的立法理念，不符合现代民法的私法自治原则。因此，关于继承的放弃与债权人的撤销权，以上否定债权人之撤销权的重庆市被调查民众的观念与习惯，可供我国立法参考。

七、继承权的丧失、被继承人的宥恕与代位继承之特点与原因分析

（一）继承权的丧失与被继承人的宥恕之特点与原因分析

关于继承权的丧失与被继承人的宥恕，统计数据显示的特点如下：对于继承人因欺诈或者胁迫而丧失继承权的，获得被继承人宥恕后，（1）关于继承权丧失与被继承人宥恕的民众观念，在重庆市被调查者中，认为可以恢复继承权的，占七成以上（72.04%）；认为不可以恢复继承权的，占近三成（27.96%）（见表2-41）。（2）关于继承权丧失与被继承人宥恕的民间习惯，在重庆市被调查者所在地区，可以恢复继承权的，占近五成半（53.71%）；不可以恢复继承权的，占四成半以上（46.29%）（见表2-43）。

以上特点的原因分析，关于继承权丧失与被继承人宥恕的民众观念与民间习惯的特点之原因，根据关于继承权的丧失与被继承人宥恕的民众观念之理由（见表2-42），（1）七成以上的重庆市被调查者认为获得被继承人宥恕后可以恢复继承权，近五成半的该市被调查者所在地区存在此种习惯，其原因是被继承人作为遗产的所有者，有权自由决定如何处分自己的遗产。如果继承人丧失继承权后，又获得被继承人的原谅，基于尊重被继承人的意愿，就应当恢复该继承人的继承权。（2）近三成的重庆市被调查者认为即使获得被继承人的宥恕也不可以恢复继承权，近四成半以上的该市被调查者所在地区存在此种习惯，其原因是继承人的行为造成了恶劣影响，即使其已经获得了被继承人的原谅，也需要对继承人的过错行为应予以一定惩戒。

关于继承权的丧失与被继承人的宥恕之我国立法，我国《继承法》第7条规定，继承人有下列行为之一的丧失继承权：故意杀害被继承人的；为争夺遗产而杀害其他继承人的；遗弃被继承人的，或者虐待被继承人情节严重的；伪造、篡改或者销毁遗嘱，情节严重的。关于继承人继承权的恢复，1985年《执行继承法意见》第13条规定，继承人虐待

① 参见张玉敏：《继承法律制度研究》，法律出版社1999年版，第105页。

② 参见陈苇、王巍：《论放弃继承行为不能成为债权人撤销权的标的》，载《甘肃社会科学》2015年第5期，第164页。

被继承人情节严重的，或者遗弃被继承人的，如以后确有悔改表现，而且被虐待人、被遗弃人生前又表示宽恕，可不确认其丧失继承权。然而，对于采用欺诈或胁迫行为妨碍被继承人设立、变更或者撤销遗嘱而继承权丧失者如获得被继承人的原谅是否可以恢复，我国《继承法》和 1985 年《执行继承法意见》尚无规定。

从域外立法例看，关于继承权丧失之法定情形，《德国民法典》第 2339 条规定继承人有下列情况之一，丧失其继承权：故意和违法地致被继承人死亡，或使被继承人直至死亡时为止处于无能力为死因处分或撤销死因处分的状况者；故意或违法的妨碍被继承人为死因或撤销死因处分者；以恶意欺诈或违法地以胁迫促使被继承人为死因处分或撤销死因处分者；犯伪造公务罪者。《意大利民法典》第 463 条规定，继承人因下列情形丧失继承权：因杀害继承人或被继承人配偶、卑亲属或尊亲属的；犯诬告罪；诈欺或胁迫被继承人撤销或修改遗嘱的；销毁、隐匿、伪造遗嘱；制作假遗嘱或知道是假遗嘱仍使用。对于继承人继承权丧失之恢复，《德国民法典》第 2343 条规定，如被继承人已宽恕丧失继承权者，撤销权即被排除。《意大利民法典》第 466 条规定，如被继承人在遗嘱或公证中明确表示恢复无资格人的继承权的，则继承人可参加继承。

从我国诸继承法学者建议稿看，各建议稿对于丧失继承权的法定情形均有规定。例如，“王稿”规定，继承人有下列行为之一的，丧失继承权：（1）故意杀害被继承人；（2）为争夺遗产而杀害其他继承人；（3）遗弃被继承人或者虐待被继承人情节严重的；（4）伪造、篡改或者销毁、隐匿遗嘱的；（5）以欺诈或者胁迫的手段，迫使或者妨碍被继承人设立、变更或者撤销遗嘱，情节严重的。继承人有前款第（3）（4）（5）种情形丧失继承权，如经被继承人宽恕的，可确认其丧失继承权。被继承人知道继承人除前款（1）（2）项外的丧失继承资格的事由，仍然在遗嘱中指定其为继承人或对其为遗赠，视为宽恕。继承权丧失的事由准用于受遗赠权的丧失。[①] 至于“伪造、篡改、销毁或隐匿遗嘱”、“以欺诈或者胁迫的手段，迫使或者妨碍被继承人设立、变更或者撤销遗嘱”作为丧失继承权的法定情形，则诸继承法学者建议稿对其是否需要以“情节严重”为条件有所不同。我国学者指出，对遗嘱的伪造、篡改等行为就已经严重侵害被继承人的遗嘱自由权利，本身属于情节严重的行为，因此不必增加“情节严重”的条件。[②] 而且域外一些国家都将遗嘱的伪造、篡改等行为规定为丧失继承权的行为之一，并没有“情节严重”的要求。我们赞同不以“情节严重”为条件的观点，此值得我国借鉴。

我们认为，对于丧失继承权的法定事由的确定，我国立法获得被继承人宥恕的情形较少，这是其立法之不足。在未来立法中，我国应该以是否能维护亲属间伦理道德和继承秩序稳定为考量依据，对于严重违反伦理道德的继承人应该取消继承资格，增补为继承权丧失的法定情形。对于因宽恕而恢复继承权问题，我们认为，“王稿”的规定可以借鉴。正如我国学者所言，对于宽恕的范围应该区别对待，如故意杀害继承人或被继承人的，无论既遂或者未遂，应该不可以被宽恕，因为故意杀害行为是一种极为严重的犯罪行为，如果杀害已遂，则往往继承开始时，继承人已被缉拿在案或开始服刑，继承的意义不大。如果杀害未遂，虽然继承尚未开始，杀害行为得到宽恕可能会影响到服刑改造的效果。并且杀

① 参见“杨稿”第 11 条；“王稿”第 532 条；“陈稿”第 17 条；“张稿”第 6 条；“徐稿”第四分编第 18~24 条。

② 参见张玉敏（课题负责人）：《中国继承法立法建议稿及立法理由》，人民出版社 2006 年版，第 37 页。

害行为导致继承权绝对丧失与整体社会道德风尚的形成及伦理秩序的建构是相契合的。①因此，关于继承权的丧失与被继承人的宥恕，以上主张相对丧失与绝对丧失相结合的重庆市被调查民众的观念与习惯、域外立法例和“王稿”的观点，可供我国立法参考。

（二）继承权的丧失与代位继承之特点与原因分析

关于继承权的丧失与代位继承，统计数据显示的特点如下：（1）关于继承权丧失的效力是否及于代位继承人的民众观念，在重庆市被调查者中，对于继承权丧失的效力是否及于代位继承人，认为及于代位继承人的，占近六成（58.68%）；认为不及于代位继承人的，占四成以上（41.32%）（见表2-44）。（2）关于继承权丧失的效力是否及于代位继承人的民间习惯，在重庆市被调查者所在地区，有不及于代位继承人习惯的，占近五成半（53.23%）；有及于代位继承人习惯的，占四成半（46.77%）（见表2-45）。

以上特点的原因分析，关于继承权丧失的效力是否及于代位继承人的民众观念与民间习惯的特点之原因，根据继承权丧失的效力是否及于代位继承人的民间习惯之理由（见表2-46），（1）四成以上的重庆市被调查者认为继承权丧失的效力不及于代位继承人，近五成半的该市被调查者所在地区存在此种习惯，其原因是虽然继承人已经丧失继承权，其子女仍然享有其固有的代位继承权，因而代位继承遗产的基础丧失，所以丧失继承权的继承人子女能够代替丧失继承权的继承人而继承遗产。（2）近六成的重庆市被调查者认为继承权丧失的效力及于代位继承人，四成半以上的该市被调查者所在地区存在此种习惯，其原因是代位继承人作为独立的民事主体，可以自己固有的代位继承人的身份继承被继承人的遗产，与被代位人丧失继承权没有关系。

关于继承权丧失的效力是否及于代位继承人之我国立法，我国《继承法》第11条规定，被继承人的子女先于被继承人死亡的，由被继承人的子女的晚辈直系血亲代位继承。代位继承人一般只能继承他的父亲或者母亲有权继承的遗产份额。1985年《执行继承法意见》第28条规定，继承人丧失继承权的，其晚辈直系血亲不得代位继承。如该代位继承人缺乏劳动能力又没有生活来源，或对被继承人尽赡养义务较多的，可适当分给遗产。

从域外立法例看，《意大利民法典》第465条规定，丧失继承权的父母，其子女仍可以代位继承遗产，父母不再享有法律赋予的用益权和管理权。《日本民法典》第887条规定，被继承人的子女，在继承开始前，因欠缺资格或者因废除而丧失其继承权时，该人的子女代位其成为继承人。但是，非继承人的直系卑亲属的人，不在此限。

从我国诸继承法学者建议稿看，“徐稿”第四分编第31条规定，因被取消继承权的父母，其子女仍可以代位继承遗产，但是父母不再享有法律赋予的用益权和管理权。“陈稿”第19条规定，继承人丧失继承权的，其晚辈直系血亲仍得以代位继承，但该继承人不得对其子女继承的遗产享有用益权。

我们认为，我国被代位继承人丧失继承权的效力及于其晚辈直系血亲，这是其立法之不足。在现代社会，法律应当引导人们向善，应当坚持让不法行为人本人承担其不法行为的责任，而不能株连其后代，让其后代承担该不法行为的后果。如果把父母丧失继承权之后果延伸至其子女的代位继承权，这是不公平、不合理的。这不符合现代民法的“自己

① 参见王利明：《中国民法典学者建议稿及立法理由——婚姻家庭·继承编》，法律出版社2005年版，第465页。

责任原则”和1989年联合国《儿童权利公约》倡导的“子女最大利益原则”。① 因此，我们主张继承人丧失继承权的，不能导致其晚辈直系血亲丧失代位继承。关于继承人丧失继承权后其子女能否代位继承遗产，以上主张被代位继承人丧失继承权的效力不及于代位继承人的重庆市被调查民众的观念与习惯、意大利、日本立法例和“陈稿”的观点，可供我国立法参考。

八、继承协议之特点与原因分析

(一) 继承协议的订立主体与方式之特点与原因分析

关于继承协议的订立主体与方式，统计数据显示的特点如下：(1) 关于继承协议的订立主体与方式的民众观念，在重庆市被调查者中，认为继承协议应由被扶养人与全部继承人共同协商签订的，占七成以上（72.81%）；认为继承人间协商签订继承协议即可，无须被扶养人知晓或同意的，占近一成半（14.35%）；认为继承协议应由被扶养人与扶养人协商签订的，占一成以上（12.84%）（见表2-47）。(2) 关于继承协议的民间习惯，在重庆市被调查者所在地区，从没听说或经历过签订继承协议情况的，占近五成半（54.10%）；听说过或经历过以上情况的，占四成半（45.90%）（见表2-49）。(3) 关于听说过或经历过签订继承协议方式的民间习惯，在重庆市被调查者所在地区，继承协议由被扶养人与全部继承人共同协商签订的，占近六成半（64.60%）；继承协议由继承人间签订协议即可，无须被继承人知晓或同意的，占三成以上（32.30%）；继承协议由被扶养人与扶养人协商签订的，占二成半以上（26.12%）（见表2-50）。

以上特点的原因分析，(1) 关于继承协议的订立主体与方式的民众观念与民间习惯的特点之原因，其一，七成以上的重庆市被调查者认为继承协议应由被扶养人与全部继承人共同协商签订，近六成半的该市被调查者所在地区存在此习惯，其原因可能是由全体当事人协商签订，这样更公平，可以避免发生矛盾。其二，近一成半的重庆市被调查者认为继承人之间协商签订继承协议即可，无须被扶养人知晓或同意，三成以上的该市被调查者所在地区也存在此种习惯，其原因可能是这样更为公平。其三，一成以上的重庆市被调查者认为继承协议应由被扶养人与扶养人协商签订，二成半以上的该市被调查者所在地区也存在此习惯，其原因可能是被继承人有权处理自己的财产，并且只有尽了赡养义务才能分得遗产。(2) 关于继承协议的民间习惯的特点之原因，其一，近五成半的重庆市被调查者表示从没听说或经历过签订继承协议情况，其原因可能是我国《继承法》没有规定继承协议制度，民众签订此协议于法无据。其二，近四成半的重庆市被调查者听说过或经历过以上签订继承协议的情况，其原因可能是现实社会中民众对此协议的签订和履行有实际需要。

关于继承协议制度之我国立法，我国《继承法》第31条规定：“公民可以与扶养人签订遗赠扶养协议。按照协议，扶养人承担该公民生养死葬的义务，享有受遗赠的权利。”但我国立法没有规定继承协议，必须注意，遗赠扶养协议与继承协议的扶养义务人范围不同，前者的范围只能是被扶养人与法定继承人以外的自然人和集体组织；后者的范围是法定继承人与被继承人。但我国现行立法对继承协议尚无规定。

① 参见陈苇主编：《外国继承法比较与中国民法典继承编制定研究》，北京大学出版社2011年版，第220~221页。

从域外立法例看，域外立法对于继承协议主要有两种立法例：第一种持肯定态度的立法例，如德国、瑞士。《德国民法典》第2274~2280条明确规定，具有完全民事行为能力的被继承人和继承人只能通过公证的方式亲自订立继承合同，继承合同适用于夫妻或未婚夫妻之间，家庭成员之间也适用。《瑞士民法典》第468条、第495~497条、第512条对此也有承认继承协议效力的规定。第二种持否定态度的立法例，如《法国民法典》第1130条规定，任何人都不能对尚未开始的继承作出放弃的意思表示，也不得订立以放弃继承资格为内容的任何条款，即使在被继承人的同意之下也无效。

从我国诸继承法学者建议稿看，对于继承协议，"陈稿"第61条规定，自然人、法人和其他组织，可以与被继承人签订继承合同，按照继承合同，自然人、法人和其他组织作为扶养义务人，承担对被继承人生养死葬的义务，享有依照继承合同继承遗产或接受遗赠的权利。"徐稿"第四分编第503条、"杨稿"第69条、"张稿"第54条第1款对此也有规定。

我们认为，目前我国遗赠扶养协议的主体范围较窄，不能满足现实生活中部分被继承人与其法定继承人订立继承协议的现实需要，这是其立法之不足。我国立法可以借鉴域外立法经验及我国继承法学者建议稿的建议，在保留遗赠扶养协议的基础上，设立与遗赠扶养协议并行的继承协议制度，即采取"双轨制"。因为，在本次调查中，重庆市被调查者的建议占比最高的就是"为尊重老人意愿，其可与子女进行协商订立继承协议，这样有利于避免矛盾"。继承协议由被继承人与法定继承人双方协商订立，约定协议当事人的赡养义务和继承遗产的权利，即以明确的主体、形式及方式对被继承人进行赡养。[①] 因此，履行扶养义务的主体可以按照约定享有接受遗产的权利，符合权利义务相一致原则。在我国人口老年化程度加剧的社会背景下，在保留适用于被继承人与非法定继承人的遗赠扶养协议制度的基础上，增加适用于被继承人与法定继承人的继承协议制度，两者相辅相成，共同发挥作用，可以满足部分民众尤其是老年人与其法定继承人签订继承协议的现实需要，有利于减少赡养义务人之间相互推诿的情况，有助于解决老年人的养老问题。所以，以上承认继承协议的重庆市被调查民众的观念与习惯，德国、瑞士立法例和"陈稿"的观点，可供我国立法参考。

（二）继承协议的变更方式及效力之特点与原因分析

关于继承协议的变更方式与效力的民众观念，统计数据显示的特点是，在重庆市被调查者中，（1）认为继承协议继续有效（代位扶养），原扶养人的子女有扶养能力，在双方自愿的情况下，由原扶养人的子女继续扶养被扶养人，并继承全部遗产的，占近三成半（34.54%）；（2）认为原签订的继承协议终止，应由某一有扶养能力的法定继承人，在双方自愿的情况下，签订新的继承协议，继续扶养被扶养人并继承遗产的，合计占近三成半（34.70%）；（3）补偿原扶养人一定费用后，原签订的继承协议效力终止，应由有扶养能力的全体法定继承人，共同依法对被扶养人尽扶养义务，并依法定继承遗产的，占三成（30.13%）（见表2-51）。

以上特点的原因分析，根据继承协议的变更方式与效力的民众观念之理由（见表2-52），（1）近三成半的重庆市被调查者认为，该种情况继承协议继续有效（代位扶

① 参见张玉敏（课题负责人）：《中国继承法立法建议稿及立法理由》，人民出版社2006年版，第150页。

养)，其原因是他们认为在继承人死亡的情况下，由其子女代替履行赡养义务，这样不仅可以使继承协议继续履行，避免产生不必要的纠纷，而且还可以使老年人在不改变原有生活环境的情况下，安度晚年。(2) 近三成半的重庆市被调查者认为，继承协议履行过程中，如扶养人去世，则该继承协议效力终止，应重新签订继承协议，其原因是扶养行为具有特定的身份属性，因此，在继承协议中约定的扶养人去世后，该协议的效力即终止，应由被扶养人与其他主体签订新的继承协议以解决其赡养与继承问题。(3) 三成的重庆市被调查者认为原签订的继承协议效力终止，应由有扶养能力的全体法定继承人，共同依法对被扶养人尽扶养义务，其原因是他们认为赡养被继承人是其子女的法定义务，应由被继承人的其他子女对其履行赡养义务。

关于继承协议的变更方式及效力之我国立法，我国《继承法》对此无规定。但是，我国现行《婚姻法》第 21 条规定，子女对父母有赡养扶助的义务。子女不履行赡养义务时，无劳动能力的或生活困难的父母，有要求子女付给赡养费的权利。我国现行《老年人权益保障法》第 19、20 条分别规定，赡养人不得以放弃继承权或者其他理由，拒绝履行赡养义务。赡养人不履行赡养义务，老年人有要求赡养人付给赡养费的权利。经老年人同意，赡养人之间可以就履行赡养义务签订协议。赡养协议的内容不得违反法律的规定和老年人的意愿。基层群众性自治组织、老年人组织或者赡养人所在单位监督协议的履行。关于继承协议的解除后果，我国《继承法》无规定，但是，对于遗赠扶养协议解除的事由及后果，我国司法解释有规定。1985 年《执行继承法意见》第 56 条规定，扶养人或集体组织与公民订有遗赠扶养协议，扶养人或集体组织无正当理由不履行，致协议解除的，不能享有受遗赠的权利，其支付的供养费用一般不予补偿；遗赠人无正当理由不履行，致协议解除的，则应偿还扶养人或集体组织已支付的供养费用。可见，依据我国前述法律的规定，赡养父母是每个子女的责任与义务，不能以放弃继承权或以其他理由拒绝履行赡养义务。但赡养义务人之间可以就履行赡养义务签订协议。

从域外立法例看，对于继承协议的变更与效力，在继承人先于被继承人死亡的情况下继承协议的效力，《瑞士民法典》第 515 条规定，当继承人先于被继承人死亡时，协议自行丧失效力，对本应由继承人受益的财产，该继承人有权向原继承协议的被继承人以不当得利返还为由提出请求。

从我国诸继承法学者建议稿看，“张稿”第 55 条规定，继承合同可因义务人不按约定履行赡养义务，或因死亡或丧失赡养能力不能继承履行合同义务，被继承人可以解除合同，义务人已经支付的赡养费用应当在共同继承人之间进行结算。“徐稿”第四分编第 516 条，“陈稿”第 64 条、第 65 条对此也有相关规定。

我们认为，我国《继承法》未规定继承协议的变更方式与效力，这是其立法之不足。关于继承协议的变更方式与效力，以上重庆市被调查民众的观念、瑞士立法例和我国学者建议稿的观点，可供我国立法参考。

九、遗产债务清偿之特点与原因分析

(一) 遗产债务清偿责任的类型之特点与原因分析

关于遗产债务清偿责任的类型，统计数据显示的特点如下：(1) 关于遗产债务清偿责任的类型之民众观念，在重庆市被调查者中，主张实行自愿的无限责任继承的合计占近

七成半（74.93%）；主张实行有限责任继承的占近六成（58.52%）；主张对有侵害遗产违法行为者应当实行强制的无限责任继承的占近五成（48.26%）（见表2-53）。（2）关于继承人侵害遗产的法律责任之民间习惯，在重庆市被调查者所在地区，侵害人应返还遗产并承担相应责任或剥夺继承权不分遗产的，合计占六成以上（61.70%）；会交给司法、行政等相关部门处置的，占近四成（38.30%）（见表2-54）。

以上特点的原因分析，（1）关于遗产债务清偿责任的类型之民众观念特点之原因，其一，近七成半的重庆市被调查者认为继承人对于被继承人的债务应全部予以偿还的，即主张实行自愿的无限清偿责任，其原因可能是我国存在“父债子还”的传统观念。其二，近六成的重庆市被调查者主张实行有限责任继承，即对被继承人债务仅以遗产承担有限清偿责任，其原因可能是受我国立法之影响，认为这样对继承人才是公平的。其三，近五成的重庆市被调查者认为，继承人如果存在转移遗产、隐瞒遗产的情形，则其应当以遗产和其个人财产偿还所有的债务，其原因可能是无限清偿责任的惩罚方式可以防止继承人转移和隐瞒遗产的情况发生，有利于保护遗产债权人及相关权利人的利益。（2）关于继承人侵害遗产的法律责任之民间习惯特点之原因，根据继承人侵害遗产法律责任的民间习惯之理由（见表2-55），其一，近四成的重庆市被调查者所在地区，有交给司法、行政等相关部门处置的习惯，其原因是这样能够体现公平。其二，六成以上的重庆市被调查者所在地区，有侵害人应返还遗产并承担相应责任或剥夺继承权不分遗产的习惯，其原因是：一是继承人转移或隐瞒遗产，主观恶性大，导致侵害遗产利害关系人的财产权益，对其应予惩戒，该继承人不能分得遗产或少分遗产；二是根据当地的习俗，其应丧失继承权，不分遗产。

关于遗产债务清偿责任的类型之我国立法，我国《继承法》第33条规定，继承遗产应当清偿被继承人依法应当缴纳的税款和债务，缴纳税款和清偿债务以他的遗产实际价值为限。超过遗产实际价值部分，继承人自愿偿还的不在此限。可见，对于被继承人的遗产债务清偿，我国《继承法》规定了无条件的有限清偿责任和自愿承担的无限清偿责任。但未规定对继承人存在转移遗产、隐瞒遗产行为的强制无限清偿责任。

从域外立法例看，对于遗产债务的清偿责任类型，依据其是否以遗产的实际价值为限进行清偿，可分为有限责任与无限责任。① 有限责任是指继承人仅以继承的遗产为限清偿被继承人的债务。② 无限责任是指继承人以其继承的遗产和个人的固有财产清偿被继承人的债务。并且，根据此无限责任是由继承人自愿选择的或法律强制的，可分为自愿的无限清偿责任（自愿的无限责任继承）和强制的无限清偿责任（强制的无限责任继承）。例如，根据《法国民法典》第782~785条的规定，首先，关于有条件的有限责任继承，继承人应在法定期限内向法院提交忠实而明确的遗产清册，然后声明限定继承或放弃继承。其次，关于自愿的无限责任继承，无条件接受继承的方式得为明示或不作为表示的方式。无条件接受继承的概括继承人，对遗产的债务承担无限清偿责任。最后，关于强制的无限责任继承，如果继承人不在法定期限内声明放弃继承或声明限定继承并提交遗产清册，或

① 参见陈苇主编：《外国继承法比较与中国民法典继承编制定研究》，北京大学出版社2011年版，第501页。

② 参见陈苇主编：《外国继承法比较与中国民法典继承编制定研究》，北京大学出版社2011年版，第502页；杜江涌：《遗产债务法律制度研究》，群众出版社2013年版，第60页。

编制遗产清册不忠实，则须对遗产债务负无限责任。《瑞士民法典》第550~601条对此也有规定。

从我国诸继承法学者建议稿看，各建议稿都规定了以遗产为限清偿债务的有限责任，但“徐稿”、“张稿”、“陈稿”还具体规定了承担有限清偿责任的法定条件与承担强制的无限清偿责任之法定情形。首先，对于有限责任继承，如“梁稿”第2014条规定，继承人以其所接受遗产的实际价值为限对遗产债务承担责任。超过遗产实际价值部分，继承人自愿偿还的，不在此限。继承人放弃继承的，对被继承人依法应当缴纳的税款和债务不承担偿还责任。其次，对于承担有限清偿责任的法定条件与强制的无限清偿责任的法定情形。例如，“陈稿”第69条规定，继承人选择有条件限定继承且依法制作遗产清册的，仅以遗产为限清偿债务。继承人自愿选择无条件概括继承的，以继承的遗产和个人财产清偿遗产债务。已全部或部分处分遗产，或未在法定期间制作遗产清册的，或故意未将遗产计入遗产清册的，承担无限清偿责任。

我们认为，我国《继承法》规定的无条件的有限责任继承，此立法存在不足。目前，世界上许多国家的立法对遗产债务的清偿责任均分为有限清偿责任、自愿的无限清偿责任和强制的无限清偿责任，对于有限清偿责任都是有条件的，如前所述的法国立法例，这样可以公平地保护继承人和被继承人的债权人的合法权益。而我国实行无条件的有限责任继承，虽然继承人的利益不会受损，但却往往可能损害被继承人的债权人的利益。[①] 正如我国学者所指出的，我国立法没有规定任何一项保证遗产首先被用于清偿被继承人债务的措施，忽视了对被继承人的债权人利益的保护，这与民法的公平原则是相悖的。[②] 因此，关于遗产债务清偿责任的类型，以上重庆市被调查民众的观念与习惯、法国立法例和“陈稿”的观点，可供我国立法参考。

(二) 被继承人丧葬费的支付之特点与原因分析

关于被继承人丧葬费支付的民间习惯，统计数据显示的特点是，在被调查者所在地区，对于丧葬费，(1) 由全体继承人共同支付的，占近五成半（53.15%）；(2) 从被继承人的遗产中支付的，占四成以上（41.17%）（见表2-56）。

以上特点的原因分析，(1) 近五成半的重庆市被调查者所在地区有丧葬费由全体继承人共同支付的习惯，其原因可能是被调查民众认为子女应当担负对父母的养老送终即生养死葬的责任，这不仅是我国传统的家庭道德的要求，也是民间一直以来的习惯。(2) 四成以上的重庆市被调查者所在地区有丧葬费从被继承人的遗产中支付的习惯，其原因可能是认为从遗产中支付丧葬费用对各继承人更为公平。

关于被继承人丧葬费的支付方式之我国立法，我国现行立法对此无规定。

从域外立法例看，对于丧葬费用是否从遗产中支付，域外主要有两种立法例，第一，肯定说。立法承认被继承人死亡宣告费用和丧葬费属于继承费用，应该从遗产中支付。例如，《俄罗斯联邦民法典》第1174条规定，遗产在第一顺位清偿被继承人的疾病和丧葬所支出的费用。《埃塞俄比亚民法典》规定，遗产债务清偿的第一顺位为丧葬费。[③] 第二，

① 参见陈苇主编：《外国继承法比较与中国民法典继承编制定研究》，北京大学出版社2011年版，第557页。

② 参见梁慧星（课题负责人）：《中国民法典草案建议稿》，法律出版社2003年版，第247~248页。

③ 参见《埃塞俄比亚民法典》第1014条。

否定说。立法不承认丧葬费用从遗产中支付。因为殡葬被继承人是继承人应尽的义务，应由其承担。例如，《德国民法典》第1968条明确规定，被继承人与其社会地位相称的殡葬费用，由继承人负担。

从我国诸继承法学者建议稿看，对此主要有两种观点：第一，否定说。例如，“王稿”第651条规定，被继承人的、与其社会地位相称的丧葬费用，由继承人负担。第二，肯定说。例如，“杨稿”第83条、“陈稿”第71条都规定，遗产债务清偿的第一顺序包括合理的丧葬费用、遗产管理费用、遗嘱执行费用等继承费用。

我们认为，我国现行立法对被继承人丧葬费的支付方式无规定，这是其立法之不足。丧葬费用可以有条件地从遗产中支付，诚然，丧葬费用不属于被继承人的债务，既然殡葬被继承人是继承人应尽的义务，那么支付丧葬费也属于继承人应当负担的义务。从本次实证调查结果来看，有超过五成的被调查者认为丧葬费用由继承人承担更为合理。虽然，也有占四成以上的被调查民众认为丧葬费用可以由遗产中支付。从尊重我国多数被调查民众意愿的角度考量：我们认为，原则上丧葬费应当由继承人负担，但无人承受的遗产之被继承人的丧葬费应由遗产支付。从现实生活中看，如果属于无人承受的遗产，将丧葬费从被继承人的遗产中支付，是合理的。对此问题的处理，以上主张由继承人负担丧葬费的重庆市被调查民众的习惯、德国立法例和“王稿”的观点，可供我国立法参考。

（三）遗产债务的清偿顺序之特点与原因分析

关于遗产债务的清偿顺序，统计数据显示的特点如下：（1）关于遗产债务清偿顺序的民间习惯，在重庆市被调查者所在地区，遗产债务按如下顺序清偿：第一顺序为“丧葬费用”（60.88%）；第二顺序为“遗产管理等费用”（24.13%）和“欠付的工资”（21.29%）；第三顺序为“欠债”（30.13%）和“税款”（12.15%）；第四顺序为“受被继承人扶养人的生活费”（18.30%）；第五顺序为“对被继承人扶养较多的人之酌情分配遗产份额”（20.98%）；第六顺序为“遗赠扶养协议写明遗赠的遗产”（17.51%）（见表2-57）。（2）关于遗产债务清偿顺序的民众观念，以各顺序被调查者选择占比最高的作为统计依据，被调查者认可的遗产债务清偿顺序是：第一顺序为“丧葬费用”（51.42%）和“税款”（13.72%）；第二顺序为“遗产管理等费用（22.56%）”和“欠付的工资”（24.76%）；第三顺序为“被继承人的欠债”（29.34%）；第四顺序为“受被继承人扶养人的生活费”（16.40%）；第五顺序为“遗赠扶养协议写明遗赠的遗产”（18.45%）；第六顺序为“对被继承人扶养较多的人之酌情分配遗产份额”（23.97%）（见表2-58）。

以上特点的原因分析，（1）关于遗产债务清偿顺序的民间习惯特点之原因，在被调查者所在地区，遗产债务按如下顺序清偿：其一，对于第一顺序的丧葬费用，可能是基于中国民间流传的“死者为大”的传统观念，遗产首先应该用于支付丧葬费用，以保障被继承人能入土为安。① 其二，对于第二顺序“遗产管理费用和欠付的工资”，可能是因为遗产管理是对被继承人遗产处理的前提，遗产管理费用属于共益费用，其应当被优先受偿，这有利于继承事务的及时处理，符合全体继承关系当事人的利益；而欠付的工资则直

① 必须说明，我们认为，此处丧葬费用作为第一顺位的清偿债务，与前述的丧葬费用应该由共同继承人承担并不矛盾。因为，对于丧葬费用的清偿顺序，在调查问卷中是必选项，排除负担丧葬费用应当作为继承人的法定义务情况外，如果被继承人没有继承人负担其丧葬费的情形下，根据民间习俗，其遗产首先应该保障被继承人的顺利安葬。

接关系到与被继承人生前产生劳动关系的相关主体的生计，因此也被排在第二顺序。其三，对于第三顺序的“欠债”，其是被继承人生前从事民事活动与一般民事主体发生的债务关系，为了维护社会市场交易秩序的稳定，以彰显民法的诚实信用原则，将其排在第三顺序。对于“税款”，其是被继承人生前与国家发生的公法上的债务关系，国家相对于普通的民事主体，其债务承担能力更强，而且税款是公法上的义务，居于普通债务之后可保障其他遗产债权人的利益。其四，对于第四顺序的“受被继承人扶养人的生活费”，则主要体现了对弱势群体的关怀。其五，对于排在第五顺序的“遗赠扶养协议写明遗赠的遗产”和第六顺序的“对被继承人扶养较多的人之酌情分配遗产份额”，则主要是因为，前者属于被继承人生前所欠的有对价的债务，且已经明确约定其标的为遗赠遗产；后者不属于履行法定扶养义务，仅属于道义上的扶养，因此前者应当优先于后者受到清偿。[①]

（2）关于遗产债务清偿顺序的民众观念特点之原因，被调查者所认可的遗产债务清偿顺序与其所在地区的民间习惯差别不大。前者与后者的主要区别在于，其一，“税款”的清偿顺序不同。被调查者更认同将“税款”作为第一顺序清偿，可能是认为缴纳税款是公民的法定义务，国家利益高于个人利益。其二，在被调查者观念中，更认可将“遗赠扶养协议写明遗赠的遗产”排在第五顺序，而将“对被继承人扶养较多的人之酌情分配遗产份额”排在第六顺序，可能是因为被调查者认为在遗赠扶养协议中是存在对价的，这样更有利于保护受遗赠人的合法权益。

关于遗产债务的清偿顺序之我国立法，我国《继承法》对此无规定，但对遗产债务的清偿责任，采取的是有限清偿责任。我国《继承法》第33条规定，继承遗产应当清偿被继承人依法应当缴纳的税款和债务，缴纳税款和清偿债务以他的遗产实际价值为限。超过遗产实际价值部分，继承人自愿偿还的不在此限。继承人放弃继承的，对被继承人依法应当缴纳的税款和债务可以不负偿还责任。

从域外立法例看，域外一些国家立法对于遗产债务的清偿顺序有相应的规定，如《日本民法典》第306条规定，因下列各项原因产生的债权者，于债务人的总财产上有先取特权：一是共益费用；二是受雇人的报酬；三是殡葬费用；四是日用品的供给。第309条规定，殡葬费用的先取特权的对象为，存在于为债务人举办殡葬的费用中的相当额度。前项的先取特权的对象，也包括为债务人应扶养的亲族而举办的殡葬的费用中的相当额度。《俄罗斯联邦民法典》第1174条规定，第一顺序补偿被继承人的疾病和丧葬所支出的费用；第二顺序补偿保护遗产和管理遗产所支出的费用；第三顺序补偿与执行遗嘱有关的费用。第1138条规定，被遗嘱人责成负有遗赠义务的继承人，应在转移给他的遗产价值范围内扣除他应支付的遗嘱人的债务后执行遗赠。可见，上述两个国家都将丧葬费用列入了遗产清偿的债务范围。此外，因日本对丧葬费用是与其他优先权债务并列为优先清偿债务的，其为第一顺序，与俄罗斯相同。

从我国诸继承法学者建议稿看，关于遗产债务的清偿顺序有所规定，如“王稿”第650条规定，继承人对遗产按下列次序进行清偿：一继承费用；（因继承人和遗产管理人过失而支出的费用不属于继承费用，由负有过失的继承人和遗产管理人承担）二遗产税；三被继承人生前欠下的债务；四遗产酌给债务；五因特留份扣减权、遗赠等产生的债务。

① 参见陈苇：《我国遗产债务清偿顺序的立法构建》，载《法学》2012年第8期，第41~42页。

对遗产享有担保物权的债权人可申请就担保物优先受偿。“杨稿”第83条规定，遗产按下列顺序清偿：一合理的丧葬费用、遗产管理费用、遗嘱执行费用等继承费用；二税款；三债务；四遗赠扶养协议与继承扶养协议中扶养人取得遗产的权利；五受遗赠人取得遗赠的权利。遗产不足以清偿全部遗产债务时，同一顺序的债权按比例受偿。有缺乏劳动能力又没有生活来源的继承人的，即使遗产不足清偿债务和税款，也应在清偿前为其保留必要遗产份额。“梁稿”[①]、“张稿”[②] 和“陈稿”[③] 对此也有相关规定。

我们认为，我国《继承法》对遗产债务的清偿顺序无规定，这是其立法之不足。遗产债务清偿顺序的确立，涉及继承人、遗产债务人及相关利害关系人的财产权益保护。有必要结合现代民法确立的保护弱者利益原则、公平原则、诚信原则、维护第三人利益和交易安全原则等。关于遗产债务清偿顺序，应根据遗产债务发生的时间及遗产债务的性质和目的[④]，增补我国的此项制度。以上重庆市被调查民众的观念与习惯、域外立法例和我国学者建议稿的观点，可供我国立法参考。

十、遗产分割之特点与原因分析

（一）遗产分割的自由与限制之特点与原因分析

第一，遗产分割自由与限制的民间习惯之特点与原因分析。

关于遗产分割自由与限制的民间习惯，统计数据显示的特点是，在重庆市被调查者所在地区，（1）共同协商后分割遗产的，占近九成（89.43%）；（2）遗嘱禁止分割不可分割的，占五成半（55.52%）；（3）继承人要求分割遗产，就进行分割的，占三成以上（32.97%）（见表2-59）。

以上特点的原因分析，根据关于遗产分割自由与限制的民间习惯之理由（见表2-60），（1）近九成的重庆市被调查者所在地区有共同协商后分割遗产的习惯，其原因是在被调查者的观念和习惯中，遗产由各继承人共同所有，遗产分割关系各继承人的利益，故遗产的分割应该由各遗产继承人共同协商。（2）五成半的重庆市被调查者所在地区有遗嘱禁止分割则不可分割的习惯，其原因是遗产是被继承人死亡时遗留下来的个人财产，对该财产享有自由处分权，其当然有权通过遗嘱决定遗产的归属和分割，其他继承人应该遵循被继承人的遗愿。（3）还有三成以上的重庆市被调查者所在地区，只要有继承人要求分割遗产，就得进行分割的习惯，原因是每个继承人享有的继承权受法律保护，同时基于效率原则考虑，故继承开始后，基于继承人的要求就可以分割遗产，以保障继承人的遗产

---

① “梁稿”第2016条规定，遗产首先应当用于清偿遗产债务。清偿遗产债务后有剩余的，应当按遗嘱继承办理；仍有剩余的再由法定继承人按法律规定的比例分配遗产。同一顺序继承人有数人时，应当按其应得份额的比例进行分配，法律另有规定的除外。依前两款规定完成遗产处理程序可能导致缺乏劳动能力又没有生活来源的继承人难以维持生活的，应当在遗产处理前为其保留维持6个月生活所必要的费用。

② “张稿”第20条规定，遗产债务按下列顺序清偿：一遗产管理费用；二被继承人生前扶养的、无劳动能力的人的必要生活费用；三被继承人生前所负债务；四遗赠。即使遗产不足以清偿第三顺序债务，也必须为无劳动能力又无其他生活来源的继承人保留必要的生活费。

③ “陈稿”第71条规定，遗产债务按如下顺序依次清偿：一继承费用；二有优先清偿权的债务；三必留份、确为维持生存所需的酌给遗产；四劳动工资；五税款及普通债务；六遗赠扶养协议之债；七特留份之债；八遗赠之债。

④ 参见陈苇：《我国遗产债务清偿顺序的立法构建》，载《法学》2012年第8期。

分割自由。①

关于遗产分割的自由与限制之我国立法，我国《继承法》第 15 条明确规定："继承人应当本着互谅互让、和睦团结的精神，协商处理继承问题。遗产分割的时间、办法和份额，由继承人协商确定。协商不成的，可以由人民调解委员会调解或向人民法院提起诉讼。"此规定体现了遗产分割自由原则。对于遗产分割的方法，我国《继承法》第 29 条规定："遗产分割应当有利于生产和生活需要，不损害遗产的效用。不宜分割的遗产，可以采取折价、适当补偿或者共有等方法处理。"并且该法第 5 条规定："继承开始后，按照法定继承办理；有遗嘱的，按照遗嘱继承或者遗赠办理；有遗赠扶养协议的，按照协议办理。"

从域外立法例看，遗产分割自由原则已经为许多国家的继承立法所承认。许多国家的继承立法均明确规定，继承开始后，继承人可以随时请求分割遗产。例如，《德国民法典》第 2042 条规定，以第 2043 条至第 2045 条不另有规定为限，各共同继承人可以随时请求分割遗产。《日本民法典》第 907 条规定，共同继承人，除规定由被继承人以遗嘱禁止的情形外，可以随时以协议分割遗产。《意大利民法典》第 713 条规定，共同继承人，无论何时，均可请求分割遗产。可见，上述国家都主张除有特别规定的情况外，继承人都可随时分割遗产。关于遗产分割的限制，《意大利民法典》第 713 条规定，全体或部分继承人是未成年人，遗嘱人可以规定在最后出生的继承人达到成年年龄后的 1 年内，不得进行遗产分割。遗嘱人还可以规定在遗嘱人死亡后不超过 5 年的期间内不得对遗产或某些遗产进行分割。

从我国诸继承法学者建议稿看，"王稿"、"梁稿"、"陈稿"和"张稿"均规定，继承开始后，继承人得随时请求分割遗产，但遗嘱另有规定或共同继承人有约定或法律另有规定的除外。② 例如，"陈稿"规定，继承开始后，继承人得随时请求分割遗产，其他继承人有协助的义务，但有下列情况的除外：（1）被继承人以遗嘱指定在一定期间内不得分割遗产，但被继承人以遗嘱禁止分割遗产的期限不得超过 5 年；（2）共同继承人协议确定在一定期间内不分割某遗产或永久不分割某遗产；（3）遗产分割将严重损害遗产的价值和功能的，经共同继承人申请，人民法院可判决暂缓分割；（4）继承人中有尚未出生的胎儿的，遗产分割的时间应当延缓至胎儿出生以后；（5）遗产债务尚未清偿的，遗产分割的时间应当延缓至遗产债务清偿完毕以后，但有不能及时清偿该债务的合理理由的除外；（6）继承人身份关系尚未确定的，遗产分割的时间应当延缓至继承人身份关系确定以后。并且，"梁稿"、"王稿"、"杨稿"、"陈稿"、"张稿"和"徐稿"均规定各继承人约定不予分割的遗产不得分割。③

我们认为，重庆市近九成的被调查者所在地区存在须经各继承人协商同意才能分割遗产的民间习惯，这与我国《继承法》的规定是一致的。但我国《继承法》没有规定继承人协商分割遗产的限制情形，此为立法之不足。以上主张适当限制遗产分割自由的重庆市

① 遗产分割自由，是指继承人可以随时请求分割遗产，任何继承人不得拒绝。否则请求分割遗产的继承人可通过诉讼程序请求分割遗产。参见郭明瑞、房绍坤、关涛：《继承法研究》，中国人民大学出版社 2003 年版，第 168 页。

② 参见"王稿"第 645 条；"梁稿"第 2021 条；"陈稿"第 74 条；"张稿"第 58 条。

③ 参见"梁稿"第 2021 条；"王稿"第 645 条；"杨稿"第 85 条；"陈稿"第 74 条；"张稿"第 58 条；"徐稿"第四分编第 406 条。

被调查民众的习惯、域外立法例和我国学者建议稿的观点，可供我国立法参考。

第二，提出遗产中住房分割请求时间的民间习惯之特点与原因分析。

关于提出遗产分割请求时间的民间习惯，统计数据显示的特点是，对于遗产中其母正在居住的房屋之分割，在重庆市被调查者所在地区，（1）不会提出请求的，占近八成（78.55%）；（2）会提出请求的，仅占不到一成（8.52%）；（3）会提出分割其他遗产，但对其母正在居住房屋的分割需等其母去世后进行的，占一成以上（12.61%）（见表2-61）。

以上特点的原因分析，根据关于提出遗产中住房分割请求时间之理由（见表2-62），（1）近八成的重庆市被调查者所在地区有不会提出请求遗产分割的习惯，其原因是根据当地观念，父母一方去世遗留下的财产就应该由另一方全部继承，故子女不能向其生存父母一方提出遗产分割的请求，如果提出该遗产分割，会被视作不孝敬老人。有学者认为，按照中国家庭中传统的"同居共财"的生活模式与夫妻共同财产的观念，如果其中夫妻中有一方死亡，另一方生存配偶仍会继续维持原有的家产现状。[①] 而且，对于父母一方尚在世，其子女不进行分割遗产的行为，也体现了对死者的尊敬及对生者的安慰与孝顺。（2）不到一成的重庆市被调查者所在地区有提出请求分割遗产中家庭住房的习惯，其原因是遗产是由被继承人的子女和生存配偶共同继承，继承开始后，子女有权根据法律规定提出遗产分割的请求，并且这也有利于防止日后发生不必要的纠纷。（3）一成以上的重庆市被调查者所在地区有会提出分割其他遗产，但对其母正在居住房屋的分割需要等其母去世后进行的习惯，其原因是这样体现了孝敬老人，可以保证老人的晚年生活。

关于提出遗产中住房分割请求时间之我国立法，我国《继承法》无此规定。

从域外立法例看，关于提出遗产中住房分割请求时间，有些国家的立法有此规定。例如，根据《法国民法典》第822条的规定，为未成年人或生存配偶的利益，经其请求，均可以请求继续维持财产的共有。如果涉及的是居住场所，健在配偶在被继承人死亡时应是在此居住。《日本民法典》第907条第3款规定，家事法院在有特别事由时，可以规定在一定期间内，就遗产的全部或部分禁止分割。

从我国诸继承法学者建议稿看，关于提出遗产中住房分割请求时间，有的学者建议稿作出了规定。例如，"陈稿"第48条规定，生存配偶对遗产中的婚姻住宅和家庭日常生活用品享有先取权。如其继承的份额小于该家庭日常生活用品的价值时，其也可以选择对其日常生活用品享有终身使用权。生存配偶对遗产中的婚姻住宅享有优先扣除其继承遗产份额的权利，如其继承的遗产份额小于该婚姻住宅的价值时，其也可以选择对婚姻住宅有终身居住权。

我们认为，我国《继承法》并未规定继承人提出遗产中住房分割请求时间的限制，这是其立法之不足。有关生存配偶在世期间对遗产中家庭住房不予分割，此即受生存配偶居住权的限制，以上重庆市被调查民众的习惯、法国、日本立法例和"陈稿"的观点，可供我国立法参考。

第三，被继承人是否可在遗嘱中限制遗产分割之特点与原因分析。

关于被继承人是否可在遗嘱中限制遗产分割，统计数据显示的特点如下：（1）关于

① 参见［日］滋贺秀三：《中国家族法原理》，张建国等译，商务印书馆2013年版，第142~143页。

被继承人是否可在遗嘱中限制遗产分割的民众观念，在重庆市被调查者中，认为可以限制分割的占近九成（87.22%）；认为不可以限制分割的仅占一成以上（12.78%）（见表2-63）。（2）关于被继承人立遗嘱限制遗产分割的具体期限之民众观念，在重庆市被调查者中，认为在5年以内的，占近五成（47.84%）；认为在10年以内的，占三成（30.39%）；认为在15年以内的，占一成半以上（16.90%）（见表2-65）。（3）关于继承人协商能否变更遗嘱限制的民间习惯，在重庆市被调查者所在地区，对于遗嘱对遗产分割的限制是否可以不遵守，不可以不遵守的，占五成以上（52.05%）；可以不遵守的，占近五成（47.95%）（见表2-66）。

以上特点的原因分析，（1）关于遗产分割是否受遗嘱限制的民众观念之理由（见表2-64），其一，近九成的重庆市被调查者认为遗嘱可以限制遗产分割，其原因是这些遗产是被继承人生前的个人财产，在设立遗嘱时有权决定遗产的分配及其分割等问题。其二，一成以上的重庆市被调查者认为遗嘱不可以限制遗产分割，其原因是被继承人在遗嘱中指定部分遗产在一定的期限内不能分割，不利于发挥物的效用及价值，而且容易发生纠纷。（2）关于遗嘱限制遗产分割的具体期限之民众观念特点的原因，近五成的重庆市被调查者认为被继承人立遗嘱限制遗产分割的期限应在5年以内，其原因可能是被继承人虽然有遗嘱自由权，但是每个继承人享有的继承权受法律保护，同时基于发挥遗产效用原则的考虑，对遗产禁止分割的限定期过长，不利于发挥遗产的效用。（3）关于继承人协商能否变更遗嘱限制的民间习惯特点之原因，根据于继承人协商能否变更遗嘱限制的民间习惯之理由（见表2-67），其一，五成以上的重庆市被调查者所在地区有不可变更的习惯，其原因是继承人根据被继承人设立的遗嘱享有继承权，对于遗产的分割，也应该依据遗嘱，不能选择性地修改遗嘱；其二，近五成的重庆市被调查者所在地区有可以变更的习惯，其原因是继承人共同继承遗产，共同享有所有权，其当然有权决定分割这些遗产，同时也有利于发挥物的效用价值。

关于被继承人是否可在遗嘱中限制遗产分割之我国立法，我国《继承法》对此无规定。

从域外立法例看，关于被继承人是否可在遗嘱中限制遗产分割，域外许多国家都有相应的规定，如《意大利民法典》第713条规定，遗嘱人还可规定其死亡后在5年内不得分割遗产。《法国民法典》第815条规定，任何人不得被强制维持遗产共有的状态，即使有相反的合意与禁止，仍可随时请求分割遗产。继承人之间可确立不超过5年的期限不分割遗产的契约。

从我国诸继承法学者建议稿看，各建议稿都规定了遗产分割的自由及限制的内容。例如，“梁稿”第2021条规定，继承人得随时请求分割遗产，但遗嘱指定于一定期间不得分割，此期间不超过5年，超过5年的，缩短为5年。“王稿”第654条、“陈稿”第74条对此也有相关规定。

我们认为，我国现行立法并未规定被继承人是否可以在遗嘱中限制遗产分割，这是立法之不足。以上被继承人可在遗嘱中限制遗产分割及其限制期限不超过5年的重庆市被调查民众的观念与习惯、域外立法例和我国学者建议稿的观点，可供我国立法参考。

（二）遗产分割瑕疵的担保责任之特点与原因分析

关于遗产分割瑕疵的担保责任之民间习惯，统计数据显示的特点是，在重庆市被调查者所在地区，（1）共同继承人间相互承担遗产分割瑕疵担保责任的，合计占近五成半（53.31%）；（2）共同继承人间相互不分担遗产分割瑕疵担保责任的，占四成半以上（46.37%）（见表2-68）。

以上特点的原因分析，根据关于遗产分割瑕疵的担保责任的民间习惯之理由（见表2-69），（1）四成半以上的重庆市被调查者所在地区有共同继承人间相互不承担遗产分割瑕疵担保责任的习惯，其原因是认为遗产分割是随机的，当无法预见分割的遗产质量时，如果经分割的遗产已经归属于各继承人所有，那么应该由继承人自行承担遗产的瑕疵责任。（2）近五成半的重庆市被调查者所在地区有共同继承人间相互承担遗产分割瑕疵担保责任的习惯，其原因是遗产是所有继承人共同继承的，如果只让一个人承担遗产的瑕疵损失，有悖民法中的公平原则，应当让其他继承人平均分担损失，才能达到在共同继承人之间公平分配遗产之目的。

关于遗产分割瑕疵的担保责任之我国立法，我国《继承法》对此无规定。

从域外立法例看，对于分割后的遗产瑕疵责任承担，许多国家立法都有相应的规定。例如，《日本民法典》第911~912条规定，各共同继承人，对其他共同继承人与出卖人相同，按其应继份负担保责任。并就其他共同继承人因分割而受的债权，按其应继份担保债务人于分割时的资力。《瑞士民法典》第637条规定，共同继承人在分割终了后，对遗产互负卖方及买方的义务。共同继承人在分割时，对归属于各自的债权的成立，互为担保，并在算定的债权额内，对于债务人的支付能力负有与普通保证人相同的义务。但有市价的有价证券不在此限。①

从我国诸继承法学者建议稿看，诸学者建议稿都明确规定，共同继承人在遗产分割后，应就遗产的瑕疵以及遗产上权利的瑕疵承担担保责任。例如，“梁稿”第2025条规定，遗产分割后，各继承人以其所得的遗产份额为限，对其他继承人分得的遗产，负与出卖人同样的担保责任。受遗赠人所接受的遗产为种类物的，有权要求继承人承担前款规定的责任。各继承人对其他继承人分得的债权，就遗产分割时债务人的支付能力，负担保责任。“陈稿”第79条对此也有规定。

我们认为，我国《继承法》欠缺遗产分割之共同继承人瑕疵担保责任制度，这是其立法之不足。针对此立法空白，关于遗产分割瑕疵的担保责任，以上是主张共同继承人相互承担遗产瑕疵担保责任的重庆市被调查民众的习惯，日本、瑞士立法例和“梁稿”与“陈稿”的观点，可供我国增补此制度时参考。

十一、无人承受遗产之特点与原因分析

（一）无人承受遗产的归属之特点与原因分析

关于无人承受遗产的归属主体之民众观念，统计数据显示的特点是，无论是城镇居民还是农村居民的无人承受遗产，（1）认为其应归社会公共组织所有的，各占近七成（67.98%、65.78%）；（2）认为其应归自然人所有的，各占三成以上（32.02%、34.22%）（见表2-70、

---

① 在理论上，瑕疵担保责任是从共有到各个所有中必然设立的制度，其根源在于原共有人的共有权范围至遗产各部分，遗产的分割就是共有人相互交换应有部分，已达到各个所有的过程，过程类似于特殊买卖合同中的互易，故买卖法中的瑕疵担保责任理应适用于遗产分割中。参见史尚宽：《继承法论》，中国政法大学出版社2000年版，第249页。

表2-72)。

以上特点的原因分析，根据关于城镇居民或农村居民无人承受遗产的归属主体的民众观念之理由（见表2-71、表2-73)，(1) 在近七成的重庆市被调查者认为城镇居民或农村居民的无人承受的遗产应归属于社会公共组织，其原因是以便用于社会公共事业建设，使全体民众受益。并且，这也与部分国家的做法相一致。(2) 有三成以上的重庆市被调查者认为应归属于自然人，即归属于被继承人不在法定继承范围内的其他近亲属，其原因是认为个人的私有财产不应轻易被收归国有，将无人继承的遗产归属于被继承人的非继承人的其他亲属，符合情理。

关于无人承受遗产的归属之我国立法，我国《继承法》第32条规定："无人继承又无人受遗赠的遗产，归国家所有；死者生前是集体所有制组织成员的，归所在集体所有制组织所有"。可见，近七成的被调查民众认为城镇居民或农村居民的无人承受的遗产应归社会公共组织，与我国《继承法》第32条规定的无人继承又无人受遗赠的遗产归国家所有，两者在主张"归公"上是基本一致的。

从域外立法例看，域外许多国家都对无人承受遗产的归属进行了规定。例如，《日本民法典》第959条规定，未能依据第958-3条规定的对特别关系人处分的无人继承财产，归属于国库。《瑞士民法典》第466条规定，被继承人无继承人的，其遗产归属于其最后住所地的州，或归属于依州立法享有权利的乡镇。《德国民法典》第1964条规定，在法定期间内没能查明继承人，遗产法院应该确定除国库之外不存在其他继承人；以此推定国库为法定继承人。但是国家作为继承人应该按照公示催告程序催告债权、受赠人申报权利，清算后有剩余的才归国库所有。正如我国学者所指出的，在无人承受遗产的最后归属上，两大法系的法国、德国、瑞士、日本、英国、美国都将清偿债务后的剩余财产归属于国家（国库）所有。[①]

从我国诸继承法学者建议稿看，"王稿"第660条规定，公告期满，无继承人承认继承时，其遗产在清偿债权并交付遗赠物后，如有剩余，由遗产管理人移交有关部门上缴国库所有；如果死者生前是集体所有制组织成员的，则应移交所在的集体所有制组织并归其所有。"梁稿"第2029条、"张稿"第70条、"陈稿"第87条第2款、"杨稿"第94条均对无人承受的遗产之归属主体有所规定，并且，前述诸学者建议稿都规定遗产在清偿债务、执行遗赠后有剩余的，应该归属于国家，如果死者生前是集体所有制组织成员的，则应移交所在的集体所有制组织并归其所有。

我们认为，关于无人承受遗产的归属，我国现行法区分城乡居民的身份而确定其遗产的归属，这是其立法之不足。以上主张无人承受遗产"归公"即归属国库或集体组织所有的重庆市被调查民众的观念、域外立法例和我国学者建议稿的观点，表明我国立法是适合我国国情的。但是，由于现在集体所有制组织具有地方性，在范围和地域上都比较受限，故不宜再作为无人承受遗产的归属主体。所以，对其可更改为被继承人死亡前最后住所地的国库。

（二）无人承受遗产的处理之特点与原因分析

第一，无人承受遗产管理人的产生方式之特点与原因分析。

① 参见陈苇主编：《中国遗产处理制度系统化构建研究》，中国人民公安大学出版社2019年版，第521页。

关于无人承受遗产管理人的产生方式，统计数据显示的特点如下：（1）关于无人承受遗产管理人产生方式的民众观念，在重庆市被调查者中，认为应由死者户籍所在地的居委会、村委会或所在单位指定遗产管理人的，占五成半（55.20%）；认为应由人民法院或民政部门指定遗产管理人的，合计占近四成半（44.80%）（见表2-74）。（2）关于无人承受遗产管理人的产生方式之民间习惯，在重庆市被调查者所在地区，遗产管理人由居委会、村委会、所在单位、民政部门和政府等组织指定的，合计占八成半以上（86.92%）；遗产管理人由其他亲属和有威望者指定的，合计占近一成半（13.08%）（见表2-75）。

以上特点的原因分析，关于无人承受遗产管理人产生方式的民众观念与民间习惯特定之原因，根据关于无人承受遗产管理人的产生方式的民间习惯之理由（见表2-76），（1）五成半的重庆市被调查者认为应由死者户籍所在地的居委会、村委会或所在单位指定遗产管理人，近四成半的该市被调查者认为应由人民法院或民政部门指定遗产管理人，八成半以上的该市被调查者所在地区存在这些习惯，其原因是：其一，死者户籍所在地的居委会或村委会或所在单位对死者及其遗产的情况比较清楚，且是与群众接触最密切的基层组织，由其指定遗产管理人，有利于对遗产进行清算、管理和利用。其二，由人民法院通过指定遗产管理人，对遗产进行清算和管理，有利于公平保护相关债权人的利益。（2）近一成半的重庆市被调查者所在地区有由其他亲属和有威望者指定的习惯，原因是被调查民众认为人民法院办案压力大，可能无暇顾及遗产管理人的指定。

关于无人承受遗产的管理之我国立法，目前我国缺乏无人承受遗产的管理制度，也没有具体规定遗产管理人的产生方式。

从域外立法例看，《德国民法典》第1960条特设遗产的保全和遗产保佐人或保护人制度，即在接受继承前，以有需要为限，遗产法院应负责保全遗产；继承人不明或不能肯定其是否接受遗产的，应设立遗产保佐人并对遗产进行保全。《法国民法典》第811~812条规定，无人主张继承遗产，也无已知的继承人，或已知的继承人抛弃继承时，该遗产为无人承认继承的遗产。继承开始地法院得依据利害关系人或检察官的请求，选任财产管理人。《日本民法典》第951~952条规定，继承人有无不明时继承财产为法人，家庭法院因利害关系人或检察官的请求应选任继承财产管理人。

从我国诸继承法学者建议稿看，“梁稿”第2002条规定，没有继承人或者继承人下落不明，而遗嘱中又未指定遗嘱执行人的，经利害关系人申请，法院可以指定遗产管理人。“王稿”第661条规定，继承开始时，有无继承人不明时，由村委会或居委会作为遗产管理人。遗产管理人应该从速申请人民法院按公示催告程序，公告通知可能存在的继承人、受遗赠人、债权人等其他利害关系人前来法院申报登记。“张稿”第67条、第70条，“陈稿”第83条，“杨稿”第91条对此也有规定。

我们认为，我国欠缺无人承受遗产的管理制度，也无该遗产管理人的指定方式规定，这是其立法之不足。因此，关于无人承受遗产管理人的产生方式，以上重庆市被调查民众的观念与习惯、域外立法例和我国学者建议稿的观点，可供我国立法参考。

第二，无人承受遗产之酌分请求权主体的民众观念与民间习惯之特点与原因分析。

关于无人承受遗产之酌分请求权主体的民众观念与民间习惯，统计数据显示的特点如下：（1）关于无人承受遗产的酌分请求权主体的民众观念，在重庆市被调查者中，认为

“依靠死者扶养的人”（79.18%）、“与死者共同生活的人”（57.57%）和“与死者关系密切且对其帮助较多的人”（75.71%）可以成为无人承受遗产之酌分请求权主体的，各占五成至七成以上（见表2-77）。（2）关于无人承受遗产的酌分请求权主体的民间习惯，在重庆市被调查者所在地区，近亲属是无人承受遗产之酌分请求权主体的，占八成（80.00%）；国家或居（村）委会是无人承受遗产之酌分请求权主体的，合计占二成（20.00%）（见表2-78）。

以上特点的原因分析，目前中国的许多家庭因受实施30多年的计划生育政策影响，家庭规模和家庭人口数量相对缩小，能继承被继承人财产的亲属也相应减少，遗产归公的可能性增大。因此，许多被调查的民众认为，为了尽量使民众的遗产免于归国有或集体所有，避免家庭中的财产归公，凡属于依靠死者扶养的人、与死者共同生活的人、与死者有密切联系且对其帮助较多的人都可酌情分得遗产，以充分发挥遗产的经济扶养功能和可利用价值。

关于无人承受遗产的酌分请求权人之我国立法，根据1985年《执行继承法意见》第57条的规定，遗产因无人继承收归国家或集体组织所有时，按《继承法》第14条规定可以分给遗产的人提出取得遗产的要求，人民法院应视情况适当分给遗产。① 可见，对于无人继承遗产的酌分请求权主体，我国《继承法》仅限于“对继承人以外依靠被继承人扶养的缺乏劳动能力又没有生活来源的人”和“继承人以外的对被继承人扶养较多的人”两种类型。从重庆市被调查者的观念和地区习惯看，认可的酌分无人继承遗产的前三名主体是“依靠死者扶养的人”、“与死者有密切联系且对其帮助较多的人”、“与死者共同生活的人”，此处的第三种人与现行立法的规定不一致。

从域外立法例看，有国家的立法明确规定对与被继承人有密切关系者可以酌情分配遗产。例如，《日本民法典》第958-3条规定，遗产无人继承时，家庭法院因与被继承人共谋生计者、悉心治疗护养被继承人者及其他与被继承人有特别关系者的请求，可以向其分配清算后剩余财产的全部或一部分。

从我国诸继承法学者建议稿看，“张稿”第70条规定，财产无人继承后，清偿债务和执行遗赠后剩余的财产，法院可将其全部或部分分配给与被继承人共同生活或精心照顾被继承人的人。“陈稿”第87条规定，无人承受遗产，经清偿债务、执行遗赠后有剩余的，遗产管理人经书面请求居民委员会或村民委员会主任并获同意及签字后，遗产管理人可依情况将遗产的全部或部分酌情分配给依靠被继承人扶养的人、对被继承人扶养较多的人、与被继承人一同生活的人或其他与被继承人有密切关系的人。可见，“张稿”和“陈稿”都规定无人承受的遗产之全部或部分可酌情分配给与被继承人有密切关系的但非法定酌分遗产请求权主体。

我们认为，我国现行法规定的无人承受遗产的酌分请求权人主体范围较窄，这是其立法之不足。因为在对无人承受遗产的分配中，应该注重遗产私有权的保护，保障遗产经济扶养功能的有效发挥。目前，随着我国社会老龄化结构的加剧，在实际生活中，确实存在受被继承人扶养或精心照顾被继承人的人，如被继承人不具有法定继承权的其他亲属、没

① 我国《继承法》第14条规定：“对继承人以外的依靠被继承人扶养的缺乏劳动能力又没有生活来源的人，或者继承人以外的对被继承人扶养较多的人，可以分给他们适当的遗产。”

有办理结婚登记而长期以夫妻名义生活的老年伴侣、长期精心照顾被继承人的保姆等。[①]因此，我国修订《继承法》时，对于无人承受的遗产酌分请求权主体范围可适当扩大。以上重庆市被调查民众的观念与习惯、域外立法例和我国学者建议稿的观点，可供我国立法参考。

第四节　当代中国重庆市民众财产继承观念与遗产处理习惯对中国民法典继承编制定的立法启示

以上，我们根据重庆市被调查者的财产继承观念与遗产处理习惯实证调查的统计汇总数据，分析归纳了其特点，研究其特点的产生原因，并考察我国司法实践相关案例，分析我国继承法律制度的适用情况，进而结合考察域外立法例和我国诸继承法学者建议稿的观点，总结我国《继承法》相关制度的优点和剖析其不足。以下，我们将以重庆市被调查者的财产继承观念与遗产处理习惯为参考基础，从中国实际出发，借鉴域外立法例和我国诸继承法学者建议稿的有益观点，对我国“民法典继承法编”编纂中相关继承制度的修改完善或予以保留，提出立法建议，以供我国立法机关参考。

一、我国遗产范围界定制度之不足与立法完善建议

（一）我国遗产范围界定制度之不足

我国《继承法》的遗产范围界定制度，主要存在两个方面的不足：第一，对于遗产的范围，仅有正面列举与概括相结合的规定，欠缺反面排除的规定，这导致民众对遗产的范围认识发生偏差。从属于遗产种类的民众观念看，七成半的重庆市被调查者认为死亡赔偿金属于遗产，还有近三成半的被调查者认为欠款属于遗产，容易引起纠纷（见表 2-4）。前述涉及遗产范围界定制度的案例之司法审判实践中，也反映出我国遗产范围界定制度存在不足。第二，对于遗产总额的确定，欠缺被继承人生前特种赠与财产的归扣制度。从被继承人生前资助的财产是否应归扣纳入遗产范围的民众观念与民间习惯看，尽管重庆市有超过七成半的被调查者不认同遗产归扣（见表 2-5），并且，七成以上的该市被调查者所在地区没有遗产归扣的习惯（见表 2-7）。但是，我国欠缺遗产归扣制度，这既不利于在共同继承人中公平分配遗产，也不利于在全球化背景下平等保护涉外继承关系中各方共同继承人的合法继承权益。[②]

（二）我国遗产范围界定制度之立法完善建议

针对以上不足，我们提出以下两方面立法完善建议：

1. 遗产范围界定模式之立法建议

遗产，是指被继承人死亡时遗留的个人所有财产。但与被继承人人身不可分割的财产和法律规定不得继承的财产，不属于遗产。

2. 被继承人生前特种赠与财产的归扣之立法建议

在法定继承中遗产分割时，被继承人的子女在被继承人生前接受特种财产赠与的，为归

---

① 参见张玉敏（课题负责人）：《中国继承法立法建议稿及立法理由》，人民出版社 2006 年版，第 184 页。

② 参见陈苇主编：《外国继承法比较与中国民法典继承编制定研究》，北京大学出版社 2011 年版，第 257~258 页。

扣义务人，其他参加共同继承的人为归扣权利人。

归扣义务人，在被继承人生前所受的特种赠与财产，包括因结婚、分家、生产经营所受赠与财产或免除债务；大学本科以上的教育费用；成年以后的职业教育或培训费用；储蓄性人寿保险金。

遗产分割时，归扣义务人应当将其所受被继承人生前特种赠与财产的原物或其价值合并计算于遗产总额之中，然后对此遗产总额计算各共同继承人的应继份。但如果被继承人已经明确表示免除该继承人归扣义务的，不在此限。

生前特种赠与财产的价值，依赠与时的价值计算。①

二、我国继承开始的通知和公告制度之不足与立法完善建议

（一）我国继承开始的通知和公告制度之不足

我国《继承法》的继承开始的通知和公告制度，主要存在三个方面的不足：第一，欠缺继承开始的公告制度，并且继承开始的通知的义务主体范围狭窄，这不利于继承人和遗产利害关系人及时获知继承开始的信息。从继承开始的通知和公告的主体的民间习惯看，对于发出继承开始通知的主体比较多样化，并不限制于我国《继承法》规定的知道被继承人死亡的继承人、被继承人生前所在单位或者居住地的（村）居民委员会，还包含遗产保管人、处理被继承人死亡事件的机构如公安交警部门（见表2-9）。第二，欠缺继承开始通知与公告的具体方式，不利于指导民众履行通知义务。从继承开始的通知和公告方式的民间习惯看，重庆市被调查者发出继承开始通知的方式具有多样化且便利化，人们最常采取的通知涉及遗产处理的相关人员为“口头、电话、微信”等通知方式，其次才为信件、告知函等书面通知（见表2-10）。第三，欠缺继承通知与公告期间的规定，不利于继承人与遗产利害关系人在确定的时间范围内确认权利，容易引发继承纠纷。从继承开始的通知和公告期间的民众观念看，六成以上的重庆市被调查者认为应在7日以内的较短期间发出通知和公告（见表2-11）。

（二）我国继承开始的通知和公告制度之立法完善建议

针对以上立法之不足，我们提出以下三方面立法完善建议：

1. 继承开始的通知和公告的主体之立法建议

增补继承开始的通知和公告的义务主体。知道被继承人死亡的继承人为继承开始通知和公告的义务人。继承人中无人知道被继承人死亡或者知道被继承人死亡因无民事行为能力等原因而不能通知的，被继承人生前所在单位或者住所地的居民委员会、村民委员会为继承开始通知和公告的义务人。其他利害关系人，如遗产保管人、受遗赠人、处理被继承人死亡事件的机构等，知道继承开始的事实的，也应担负通知或公告的职责。

2. 继承开始的通知和公告的方式之立法建议

对通知的方式可分不同情况规定：继承开始通知与公告主体的义务，对于已知的继承人及遗产利害关系人，可依据实际情况采取适当的方式进行通知。例如，继承关系当事人遗产利害关系情况不明，可在省一级报纸登报公告或申请人民法院进行公告。

① 参见陈苇主编：《中国遗产处理制度系统化构建研究》，中国人民公安大学出版社2019年版，第492~493页。

3. 继承开始的通知和公告的期间之立法建议

凡负有继承开始的通知或公告义务的主体，应当在得知继承开始的事实之日起 7 日内将此事实通知其明知或应当知道被通知的对象。在被通知对象不明、不知下落或用其他方式无法通知时，应在 7 日内在被继承人生前住所地村（居）民委员会公告栏中公告，并且在省一级报纸、电视、网络上公告，或申请被继承人生前住所地或遗产的不动产所在地的人民法院进行公示催告，公告期间不少于 60 日。如果被继承人遗留的遗产不足以支付公示催告费用的，可以不进行公告。

三、我国遗产管理制度之不足与立法完善建议

（一）我国遗产管理制度之不足

我国的遗产管理制度，主要存在以下不足：我国《继承法》只是原则性地规定了遗产执行和遗产保管的部分内容，缺乏对遗产管理人的确定、遗产管理人的职责，遗产管理人的报酬等遗产管理制度内容较为系统、全面的规定。从遗产管理人的确定的民间习惯看，在重庆市被调查地区，存在由死者的法定继承人、死者的儿媳或女婿、死者家族中的德高望重者、死者的其他亲戚朋友和死者所在的单位或村/居委会作为遗产管理人的，各占二成至四成以上（见表 2-12）；从遗产管理人职责的民众观念看，重庆市被调查民众认为遗产管理人应承担较为广泛的职责（见表 2-14）；从遗产管理人是否有权取得报酬的民间习惯看，法院指定遗产管理人的，六成半以上的重庆市被调查者所在地区有可以请求给付报酬的习惯（见表 2-15）；从遗产管理人的损害赔偿责任之民间习惯看，五成半以上的重庆市被调查者所在地区有遗产管理人有故意或重大过失，才承担损害赔偿责任的习惯（见表 2-16）。在前述涉及遗产管理人制度的案例之司法审判实践中，也反映出我国遗产管理人的资格、产生方式、职责等制度存在不足。

（二）我国遗产管理制度之立法完善建议

针对以上立法之不足，我们提出以下三方面立法完善建议：

1. 遗产管理人的确定之立法建议

建议遗产管理人的产生规定为：有遗嘱执行人的，由其担任遗产管理人。无遗嘱执行人时，由继承人担任遗产管理人或由继承人协商推选其他主体管理遗产。继承人有多人的，可以由多名继承人共同管理遗产，也可以推选其中一人或第三人担任遗产管理人。依据当地习俗，继承人也可以推选家庭中德高望重者担任遗产管理人。例如，继承人对推选有异议的，可以申请人民法院指定遗产管理人，也可以依据遗产利害关系人的申请由人民法院指定遗产管理人，可视情况在被继承人的生存配偶、子女及其直系卑血亲、父母、兄弟姐妹及其直系卑血亲、祖父母中指定或者在基层村（居）委会组织成员中指定。①

2. 遗产管理人的管理职责与报酬之立法建议

遗产管理人的职责如下：收集遗产，编写遗产清册；对遗产进行妥善管理；及时发出继承开始的通知或公告；报告遗产管理情况；清偿被继承人的债务；参与与遗产有关的诉讼及处理其他遗产管理需要的行为；交付剩余遗产。

明确规定遗产管理人取得报酬的具体情形：在法定继承的情形下，除继承人担任遗产管

---

① 参见石婷：《遗产管理制度研究》，群众出版社 2017 年版，第 213~215 页。

理人外，其他遗产管理人有权请求给予适当的报酬。但如果继承人管理的遗产数额大、类型复杂的，也可以请求给予适当的报酬。

遗嘱指定的遗嘱执行人，由遗嘱人指明是否给予其适当的报酬。

3. 遗产管理人的法律责任之立法建议

非继承人担任遗产管理人的，因故意或重大过失违反管理义务或遗产的限制性规定，损害遗产权利人利益的，应当承担损害赔偿责任。①

继承人担任遗产管理人的，如有藏匿遗产或在遗产清册中记载不实债务或有其他损害遗产债权人利益行为的，应对遗产债务承担无限清偿责任。

四、我国法定继承制度之不足与立法完善建议

（一）我国法定继承制度之不足

我国的法定继承制度，主要存在五个方面的不足：第一，我国法定继承人的范围较窄且顺序较少，可能容易出现被继承人死亡后遗产无人继承的情况。从法定继承人的范围与顺序的民众观念看，重庆市被调查者认定的法定继承人范围较广，除我国《继承法》第10条已规定的父母、子女、兄弟姐妹、祖父母、外祖父母、孙子女、外孙子女外，还包括伯叔姑舅姨、侄子女外甥子女、堂兄弟姐妹、表兄弟姐妹（见表2-17）。第二，配偶为固定继承顺序，这不利于保障配偶继承权及后顺序的兄弟姐妹等近血亲的继承权。从配偶与血亲继承人顺序的民众观念看，近二成半的重庆市被调查者认为配偶为无固定顺序（见表2-18）；从配偶与血亲继承人法定应继份的民众观念看，占近四成半的重庆市被调查者认为配偶应为无固定顺序继承，可参与前三顺序或前二顺序继承，并取得不同份额（见表2-19）。第三，没有规定配偶对遗产中家庭住房的先取权和居住权，不利于保障生存配偶的基本生存权，从配偶对遗产中家庭住房先取权与终生使用权的民间习惯看，八成半以上的重庆市被调查者所在地区有配偶可以优先继承遗产中原居住的家庭房屋的习惯（见表2-20）。在前述涉及法定继承制度的案例之司法实践审判中，也反映出我国尚未设立配偶继承人对于遗产中家庭住房先取权与终生使用权制度，是为立法之不足。第四，没有规定后顺序特殊法定继承人对原使用的遗产住房及日常生活用品的终生使用权，从后顺序特殊法定继承人对特殊遗产的终生使用权的民间习惯看，近九成的重庆市被调查者所在地区存在被继承人对原使用的遗产住房及日常生活用品享有终生使用权的习惯（见表2-22）。第五，我国尽了主要赡养义务的丧偶儿媳（或女婿）作为第一顺序法定继承人的规定不够科学，不利于保护后顺序血亲继承人之继承权。

（二）我国法定继承制度之立法完善建议

针对以上立法之不足，我们提出以下五方面立法完善建议：

1. 法定继承的范围与顺序之立法建议

建议扩大法定继承人的范围，修改和增加法定继承人的顺序：第一顺序为子女及其晚辈直系血亲；第二顺序为父母；第三顺序为兄弟姐妹及其子女；第四顺序为祖父母与外祖父母。

---

① 参见陈苇、石婷：《我国设立遗产管理制度的社会基础及其制度构建》，载《河北法学》2013年第7期，第21页。

配偶作为无固定顺序的继承人，其可以与前面三个顺序的继承人共同继承。

2. 配偶与血亲继承人的法定应继份之立法建议

建议修改规定配偶作为无固定顺序的法定继承人，其可以与各个顺序的血亲继承人共同继承。配偶与不同顺序的血亲继承人共同继承时，各自取得不同的遗产份额。配偶与第一顺序血亲继承人共同继承时，各继承人应继份均等；配偶与第二顺序血亲继承人共同继承时，其应继份为二分之一；配偶与第三顺序血亲继承人共同继承时，其应继份为三分之二；配偶与第四顺序血亲继承人共同继承时，其应继份为四分之三。无血亲继承人时，配偶继承全部遗产。

3. 配偶对遗产中的家庭住房的先取权与终生使用权之立法建议

增补生存配偶对遗产中的婚姻住宅和家庭日常生活用品享有先取权。如其继承份额小于这些财产的价值时，可选择对家庭日常生活用品的终生使用权和对婚姻住宅的终生居住权。

4. 后顺序特殊法定继承人对遗产中原使用的住房及日常生活用品的终生使用权之立法建议

增补与被继承人共同生活的而未参与继承的父母（如其被改为第二顺序）、祖父母、外祖父母之特殊后顺序继承人在未参加继承时，对遗产中供其个人日常生活使用的物品和住房享有终生使用权。

5. 尽了主要赡养义务的丧偶儿媳或女婿的遗产分配之立法建议

建议删除尽了主要赡养义务的丧偶儿媳（或女婿）作为第一顺序法定继承人的规定，将他们列入酌情分配遗产请求权人，其有权根据所尽扶养义务的情况，请求酌情分配适当的遗产。

五、我国遗嘱继承制度之不足与立法完善建议

（一）我国遗嘱继承制度之不足

我国遗嘱继承制度，主要存在两个方面的不足和一个立法空白：第一，公证遗嘱具有优先适用的效力，且只能采用公证的形式进行变更，不利于实现遗嘱人设立、变更遗嘱的自由。从公证遗嘱与其他形式遗嘱适用效力的民众观念看，七成以上的重庆市被调查者认为后遗嘱的适用效力优先于前一公证遗嘱（见表2-27）。第二，必留份主体范围较窄，欠缺特留份制度，不利于防止遗嘱自由的滥用和遗产养老育幼及维系亲情伦理之功能的发挥，从以遗嘱将个人遗产全部赠给他人的民众观念看，近六成的重庆市被调查者主张对遗嘱处分个人财产应适当限制（见表2-29）。第三，无夫妻共同遗嘱立法，从夫妻间能否设立共同遗嘱的民众观念与民间习惯看，虽然近七成半的重庆市被调查者赞成设立夫妻共同遗嘱，但只有二成的该市被调查者所在地区有夫妻设立共同遗嘱的习惯（见表2-31、表2-33）。在前述涉及遗嘱继承制度的案例之司法审判实践中，也反映出我国不宜设立夫妻共同遗嘱制度。

（二）我国遗嘱继承制度之立法完善建议

针对以上立法之不足，我们提出以下三方面立法完善建议：

1. 公证遗嘱与其他形式遗嘱的适用效力之立法建议

建议修正公证遗嘱的适用效力位阶和不同形式遗嘱的变更方式。

遗嘱人先后立有自书遗嘱、代书遗嘱、公证遗嘱等不同形式遗嘱，且它们的内容相抵触的，以最后所立的遗嘱为准。

遗嘱的变更，可采取公证、书面等形式的遗嘱进行。

2. 遗嘱自由的限制——特留份之立法建议

建议增设特留份制度，保留必留份制度，并修改放宽享有必留份的条件。

特留份权利人，为被继承人的配偶、子女（包括胎儿）和父母。同时，明确规定特留份的份额、完善特留份扣减权及诉讼时效等具体制度。

除配偶、子女（胎儿）和父母外，凡依靠被继承人扶养的继承人，包括被继承人的兄弟姐妹、直系尊亲属和直系卑亲属，均作为必留份请求权主体。遗嘱应当为受被继承人扶养的继承人，保留必要的遗产份额。（无论其是否属于我国《继承法》第19条规定的“无劳动能力又没有生活来源的继承人”，遗嘱都应为其保留必留份，以保障维持其基本生活。）

3. 夫妻共同遗嘱之立法建议

关于我国对夫妻共同遗嘱的立法空白，我们认为，我国不宜设立夫妻共同遗嘱。本次实证调查发现，重庆市被调查者所在地区只有占二成的地区有设立夫妻共同遗嘱的习惯，尽管有占七成的大部分被调查民众在观念上都认同夫妻共同遗嘱（见表2-31、表2-33）。诚然，夫妻共同遗嘱也体现了遗嘱自由的精神。但是，考虑到生存配偶一方可能因现实生活的变化，需要单方变更共同遗嘱，而共同遗嘱却不允许单方变更，这会限制生存配偶之遗嘱自由权的行使。并且，配偶一方去世后，如果允许生存配偶可以因情势变更而单方变更共同遗嘱中自己处分的部分遗产，则该共同遗嘱已失去部分效力，其不符合共同遗嘱的本意。因此，为满足生存配偶因现实生活的变化，要求单方变更遗嘱的需要，保障其实现遗嘱自由，并减少因单方变更共同遗嘱引发的纠纷，我国未来“民法典继承编”不宜规定夫妻共同遗嘱。

六、我国继承和遗赠的接受与放弃制度之不足与立法完善建议

（一）我国继承和遗赠的接受与放弃制度之不足

我国的继承和遗赠的接受与放弃制度，主要存在三个方面的不足：第一，对继承的接受与放弃的表示期间与方式不完善。从继承的接受与放弃的时间之民众观念看，近四成的重庆市被调查者认为继承人放弃继承，应在知道继承开始的两个月内作出放弃继承意思表示（见表2-34）；从继承的接受与放弃的方式之民间习惯看，在重庆市被调查者所在地区，存在书面凭证接受、口头与书面相结合、口头接受等多种方式（见表2-35）。第二，我国须以明示方式接受遗赠，以未为表示接受的视为放弃遗赠，不利于保护当事人的合法权利。从遗赠的接受与放弃的方式与效力看，七成半以上的重庆市被调查者认为受遗赠人只要没有明确拒绝，未为表示的应视被为接受遗赠的（见表2-36）。第三，对于债权人撤销继承人放弃继承的行为未予明确否定。该行为实为“强制继承”，不符合自愿继承的立法理念和现代民法的私法自治原则，而继承人放弃继承并未损及自己的固有财产（债务人的责任财产）。从继承的放弃能否被债权人予以撤销的民众观念与民间习惯看，近五成的重庆市被调查者认为继承人放弃继承的行为不可以被债权人撤销，并且近五成的该市被调查者所在地区存在此种习惯（见表2-38、表2-39）。在前述涉及继承和遗赠的接受与放弃制度的案例之司法审判实践中，也反映出我国未规定继承人放弃继承权的行为是否可以被继承人撤销，存在不足。

（二）我国继承和遗赠的接受与放弃制度之立法完善建议

针对以上立法之不足，我们提出以下三方面立法完善建议：

1. 继承的接受与放弃的时间与方式之立法建议

继承开始后，继承人可自知道其为继承人或自遗嘱开启两个月内，声明放弃继承。继承人在国外的为6个月。逾期未作放弃之意思表示的，视为接受继承。

放弃继承的声明须以书面的形式向继承人、遗产管理人或法院作出。

接受和放弃继承不得附条件和期限。

2. 遗赠的接受与放弃的方式与效力之立法建议

继承开始后，受遗赠人放弃遗赠的意思表示应在知道或者应当知道受遗赠后2个月内以书面形式作出，逾期未作出放弃遗赠意思表示的视为接受遗赠。

遗嘱执行人及其他利害关系人可催告受遗赠人在两个月内作出接受或放弃的表示，未表示的视为接受遗赠。

3. 继承的放弃与债权人的撤销权之立法建议

建议明确规定继承人的债权人无权撤销继承人之放弃继承的行为。

七、我国继承权的丧失、被继承人的宥恕与代位继承制度之不足与立法完善建议

（一）我国继承权的丧失、被继承人的宥恕与代位继承制度之不足

我国有关继承权的丧失、被继承人的宥恕与代位继承制度，主要存在两个方面的不足：第一，我国继承权丧失的法定情形规定仍有不足，其中对于采用欺诈或胁迫行为妨碍被继承人设立、变更或者撤销遗嘱而继承权丧失后如获得被继承人的原谅是否可以恢复，尚无规定。从关于继承权丧失与被继承人的宥恕的民众观念与民间习惯看，七成以上的重庆市被调查者认为获得被继承人的宥恕后可以恢复继承权，近五成半的该市被调查者所在地区存在此种习惯（见表2-41、表2-43）。在前述涉及继承权的丧失、被继承人的宥恕与代位继承制度的案例之司法审判实践中，也反映出继承权丧失的法定情形存在不足。第二，我国继承人丧失继承权的，其晚辈直系血亲不得代位继承，这不符合现代民法的“自己责任原则”和“子女最大利益原则”。从关于继承权丧失的效力是否及于代位继承人的民众观念与民间习惯看，四成以上的重庆市被调查者认为继承权丧失的效力不及于代位继承人，并且，近五成半的该市被调查者所在地区存在此种习惯（见表2-44、表2-45）。

（二）我国继承权的丧失、被继承人的宥恕与代位继承制度之立法完善建议

针对以上立法之不足，我们提出以下两方面立法完善建议：

1. 继承权的丧失与被继承人的宥恕之立法建议

（1）增补继承权丧失的法定情形。

继承人因下列情况丧失继承权：一是故意杀害被继承人的；二是为争夺遗产而杀害其他继承人的；三是故意使被继承人丧失遗嘱能力的；四是遗弃被继承人或虐待被继承人情节严重的；五是伪造、篡改、隐匿或者销毁遗嘱；六是以欺诈或胁迫的手段，迫使或者妨碍被继承人设立变更或者撤销遗嘱的。

（2）修改补充被继承人宽恕而恢复继承权的条件。

继承人因上述第三项至第六项规定而丧失继承权后，如确有悔改表现，被继承人生前以书面或口头形式表示宽恕的，可恢复其继承权。

被继承人知道继承人有丧失继承权的其他事由，仍然在遗嘱中指定其为继承人的，视为宽恕，但具有第一项和第二项的情形除外。

2. 继承权的丧失与代位继承之立法建议

修改丧失继承权的继承人子女不得代位继承的立法为：被代位继承人丧失继承权的，不影响其子女的代位继承。凡丧失继承权者对其子女代位继承取得的遗产，不享有用益权。

八、我国遗赠扶养协议制度之不足与立法增补建议

（一）我国遗赠扶养协议制度之不足

我国的继承协议制度，其不足主要是：目前我国遗赠扶养协议的主体范围较窄，即其不适用于法定继承人，尚未设立适用于法定继承人的继承扶养协议制度，这无法满足被扶养人要求与其法定继承人订立继承扶养协议的现实需要，尤其不利于解决老年人的养老问题。从继承协议的订立主体与方式的民众观念看，七成以上的多数重庆市被调查者认为，继承协议应由被扶养人与全部继承人共同协商签订，并且近六成半的该市被调查者所在地区存在此种习惯（见表2-47、表2-50）；从关于继承协议的民间习惯看，四成半的重庆市被调查者听说过或经历过签订继承协议的情况（见表2-49）。在前述涉及继承协议制度的案例之司法实践审判中，也反映出我国继承扶养协议制度之不足。

（二）我国继承扶养协议制度之立法增补建议

针对以上立法之不足，我们提出以下两方面立法完善建议：

1. 继承扶养协议的订立主体与方式之立法建议

继承扶养协议的订立主体为被继承人与其法定继承人。

被继承人可以与法定继承人中的一人或数人订立继承扶养协议，约定扶养人一人或数人轮流承担扶养（赡养）被继承人的义务，享有依照协议继承指定遗产的权利。

订立继承扶养协议的人均应具有完全民事行为能力。

继承扶养协议的订立，必须采取书面形式，并有两名以上无利害关系的见证人在场进行见证或公证。继承扶养协议的内容不得违反法律和社会公共利益。

2. 继承扶养协议的变更及效力之立法建议

因扶养人死亡继承扶养协议终止。因扶养人丧失扶养能力不能继续履行约定义务，双方当事人可以协议解除继承扶养协议。协议解除的，可诉请人民法院判决解除。但如果受扶养人同意接受已经死亡的扶养人之继承人继续承担扶养义务，该继承人有负担能力且自愿继续履行扶养义务的，该继承扶养协议可以继续履行。

因正当理由或因死亡而解除协议的，受扶养人对扶养人已经履行的扶养义务中超出其法定扶养义务部分的费用应予适当补偿。受扶养人对此补偿支付的赡养费有权向其他法定扶养义务人追偿。

九、我国遗产债务清偿制度之不足与立法完善建议

（一）我国遗产债务清偿制度之不足

我国《继承法》的遗产债务清偿制度，主要存在两个方面的不足：第一，我国实行无条件的限定继承，并且没有规定继承人强制承担无限清偿责任之法定情形，不利于保护继承人及遗产债权人的利益。从遗产债务清偿责任的类型之民众观念看，近六成的重庆市被调查者主张实行有限责任继承，近五成的该市被调查者主张对有侵害遗产违法行为者应当实行强制的无限责任继承（见表2-53）。第二，对遗产债务的清偿顺序没有规定，不利于保障遗产

权利人利益的有效实现。从关于遗产债务清偿顺序的民间习惯看，在重庆市被调查者所在地区，遗产债务按如下顺序清偿：第一顺序为丧葬费用；第二顺序为遗产管理等费用和欠付的工资；第三顺序为欠债和税款；第四顺序为受被继承人扶养人的生活费；第五顺序为对被继承人扶养较多的人之酌情分配遗产份额；第六顺序为遗赠扶养协议写明遗赠的遗产（见表2-57）。从遗产债务清偿顺序的民众观念看，重庆市被调查者认可的遗产债务清偿顺序是：第一顺序为丧葬费用、税款；第二顺序为遗产管理等费用、欠付的工资；第三顺序为被继承人的欠债；第四顺序为受被继承人扶养人的生活费；第五顺序为遗赠扶养协议写明遗赠的遗产；第六顺序为对被继承人扶养较多的人之酌情分配遗产份额（见表2-58）。

（二）我国遗产债务清偿制度之立法完善建议

针对以上立法之不足，我们提出以下三方面立法完善建议：

1. 遗产债务清偿责任的类型之立法建议

（1）增补有条件的有限责任继承与保留现行自愿的无限责任继承。

对于被继承人的债务，继承人自愿声明选择实行有条件的限定继承，且依法制作忠实的遗产清册的，仅以遗产为限进行清偿。

对于被继承人的债务，继承人自愿选择实行无条件的无限责任继承的，以继承的遗产和个人所有的财产进行清偿。

（2）确立强制无限责任继承的法定情形。

继承人如已全部或部分处分遗产的，或未在法定两个月期间内向其他遗产权利人书面声明实行有限责任继承并制作遗产清单的，或有故意未将遗产计入遗产清单、伪造遗产债务等侵害遗产行为的，对被继承人的债务应当承担无限清偿责任。

2. 被继承人丧葬费的支付之立法建议

被继承人的与其社会地位相称的丧葬费，由继承人负担。但如属于无人承受的遗产，则被继承人的丧葬费，从遗产中支付。

3. 遗产债务的清偿顺序之立法建议

建议规定被继承人债务的清偿顺序如下：（1）无人承受遗产的被继承人的合理的丧葬费用、遗产管理费用及遗嘱执行费用等继承费用；（2）税款；（3）普通债务；（4）继承扶养协议中约定扶养人取得的遗产标的；（5）必留份、受被继承人扶养的人之酌分遗产份额；（6）对被继承人扶养较多的人之酌分遗产份额；（7）特留份；（8）遗赠。遗产不足以清偿全部遗产债务时，同一顺序的债权按比例受偿。

有优先权的担保债务，应当就其担保的财产优先受偿，不足清偿的部分作为普通债务受偿。

有缺乏劳动能力又没有生活来源的继承人的，即使遗产不足清偿债务和税款，也应在清偿前为其保留必要遗产份额。

十、我国遗产分割制度之不足与立法完善建议

（一）我国遗产分割制度之不足

我国的遗产分割制度，主要存在两个方面的不足：第一，没有明确规定遗产分割的请求时间和限制遗产分割的条件与期间。从提出遗产分割请求时间的民间习惯看，九成以上的重庆市被调查者所在地区有不会提出请求遗产分割的习惯（见表2-61）；从被继承人是否可在

遗嘱中限制遗产分割的民众观念看，近九成的重庆市被调查者认为被继承人可以在遗嘱中限制遗产分割（见表2-63）；从被继承人立遗嘱限制遗产分割的具体期限之民众观念看，近五成的重庆市被调查者认为被继承人立遗嘱限制遗产分割的期限应在5年以内（见表2-65）；从继承人协商能否变更遗嘱限制的民间习惯看，五成以上的重庆市被调查者所在地区有不可变更的习惯（见表2-66）。在前述涉及遗产分割制度的案例司法实践审判中，也反映出我国欠缺对于生存配偶之遗产中家庭住房的先取权和居住权制度之不足。第二，欠缺遗产分割之共同继承人瑕疵担保责任制度，不利于公平的保护各共同继承人的继承权益。从遗产分割瑕疵的担保责任之民间习惯看，近五成半的重庆市被调查者所在地区有共同继承人间相互承担遗产分割瑕疵担保责任的习惯（见表2-68）。

（二）我国遗产分割制度之立法完善建议

针对以上立法之不足，我们提出以下两方面立法完善建议：

1. 遗产分割的自由与限制之立法建议

补充遗产分割的请求时间和限制遗产分割的条件与期间。继承开始后，继承人可随时请求分割遗产，其他继承人有协助的义务。但有下列情形的除外：（1）遗产债务尚未清偿完毕的。（2）遗嘱指定于一定期间不得分割的，但此期间不得超过5年，超过5年的，缩短为5年。（3）继承人协商约定在一定期间内不分割遗产的。（4）胎儿未出生的，遗产分割时应为胎儿保留其应继份。经胎儿的母亲请求延缓分割的，可以延缓至胎儿出生后分割遗产。（5）对特定遗产分割会严重损害其价值的，人民法院经继承人申请，可判决暂缓分割。（6）依法律规定禁止分割的。[①]

2. 遗产分割瑕疵的担保责任之立法建议

增设遗产分割的瑕疵担保责任。遗产分割后，各继承人以其所得的遗产份额为限，对其他继承人分得的遗产，负与出卖人同样的担保责任。各共同继承人对其他继承人分得的未届清偿期的债权及附停止条件的债权，就清偿时债务人之支付能力，承担担保责任。如有继承人无支付能力不能偿还其分担份额的，由其他继承人按比例分担，因该继承人自身原因所致不能支付的除外。

十一、我国无人承受遗产制度之不足与立法完善建议

（一）我国无人承受遗产制度之不足

我国无人承受遗产制度，主要存在两个方面的不足：第一，欠缺无人承受遗产的管理制度，这不利于对该类遗产进行及时清点、妥善保管和以该遗产清偿被继承人的债务。从无人承受遗产管理人产生方式的民众观念与民间习惯看，五成半的重庆市被调查者认为应由死者户籍所在地的居委会、村委会或所在单位指定遗产管理人，八成半以上的该市被调查者所在地区存在此种习惯，近一成半的该市被调查者所在地区有由其他亲属和有威望者指定的习惯（见表2-74、表2-75）。第二，我国无人承受遗产的酌分请求权人主体范围较窄，不利于发挥遗产的扶养功能。从无人承受遗产的酌分请求权主体的民众观念看，在被调查者中，认为依靠死者扶养的人、与死者有密切联系且对其帮助较多的人和与死者共同生活的人可酌情分得无人继承遗产的，各占五至七成以上（见表2-77）；从无人承受遗产的酌分请求权主体的

① 例如，对于生存配偶之遗产住房限制分割的规定。

民间习惯看，八成的重庆市被调查者所在地区有近亲属是无人承受遗产之酌分请求权主体的习惯，二成的该市被调查者所在地区有国家或居（村）委会是无人承受遗产之酌分请求权主体的习惯（见表2-78），即酌分请求权主体较我国现行规定更广泛。

（二）我国无人承受遗产制度之立法完善建议

针对以上立法之不足，我们提出以下两方面立法完善建议：

1. 无人承受遗产的处理之立法建议

设立无人承受遗产的管理人。如遗产有无人继承人和受遗赠人不明时，应当由死者户籍所在地的居委会或村委会或所在单位指定遗产管理人；遗产利害关系人可以申请人民法院指定遗产管理人。

遗产管理人对无人承受的遗产，应当发出寻找无人承受遗产继承人及其他遗产利害关系人的公告①，及时清点并制作遗产清册，妥善管理遗产，在清偿债务、酌情分配遗产后，剩余遗产归属被继承人死亡前最后住所地②的国库，用于社会公益事业。

2. 无人承受遗产的酌分请求权主体之立法建议

增加无人承受遗产的酌情分配请求权主体。无人承受遗产在清偿债务后有剩余的，遗产管理人经受被继承人扶养、或与其共同生活、或对其扶养较多的关系密切的人的书面请求，报请无人承受遗产所在地村委会、居委会审查批准后，可以酌情将遗产的部分或全部分配给他们。

---

① 公告的方式、期间及效力详见继承开始的通知和公告的立法建议。

② 我国《民法总则》第25条："自然人以户籍登记或者其他有效身份登记记载的居所为住所；经常居所与住所不一致的，经常居所视为住所。"

第三章　当代中国吉林省民众财产继承观念与遗产处理习惯实证调查研究*

第一节　当代中国吉林省民众财产继承观念与遗产处理习惯实证调查概况

一、被调查地区概况

（一）吉林省社会经济发展水平情况

吉林省位于中国东北地区的中部，2018 年全省实现地区生产总值（GDP）15074.62 亿元。其中第一、第二、第三产业分别实现增加值 1160.75 亿元、6410.85 亿元和 7503.02 亿元，同比分别增长 2.0%、4.0%和 5.5%。①

（二）吉林省人口结构情况

2018 年年末全省总人口为 2704.06 万人，其中城镇常住人口 1555.65 万人，占总人口比重（常住人口城镇化率）为 57.53%，比上年年末提高 0.88 个百分点。人口性别比为 102.41（以女性为 100）。该省人口年龄结构，0~15 岁（含不满 16 周岁）的人有 352.61 万人，占总人口的 13.04%；16~59 岁（含不满 60 周岁）的人有 1822.27 万人，占总人口的 67.39%；60 周岁及以上的人有 529.18 万人，占总人口的 19.57%。②

（三）吉林省城乡人口的年均收入情况

2018 年全年全省城镇常住居民人均可支配收入达到 30172 元，比上年增长 6.5%；农村常住居民人均可支配收入达到 13748 元，比上年增长 6.2%。

---

* 作者简介：李洪祥，男，吉林大学法学院教授（负责本章第三节、第四节部分内容的撰写和全章初稿、第二稿和第三稿的修改补充统稿工作）。苗艺璇，女，吉林大学妇委会主任、副研究员；高岩，男，吉林大学法学院学生办公室主任（现任研究生办公室主任）、团委书记、讲师；马旭，女，吉林大学法学院辅导员、讲师（三位老师负责调查问卷发放、收回、调查员培训、调查数据统计以及第一节内容的撰写）。贺海燕，女，西南政法大学 2017 级民商法博士研究生（负责全章内容的修改补充）。张远，女，吉林大学法学院 2015 级民商法学硕士研究生；吴天宜，女，吉林大学法学院 2016 级法律硕士；程藉瑶，女，吉林大学法学院 2017 级民商法学硕士研究生（三位同学负责部分调查数据统计以及第二节、第三节、第四节部分内容的撰写）。

① 参见《吉林省 2018 年国民经济和社会发展统计公报》，载 http://www.jl.gov.cn/sj/sjcx/nbcx/tjgb/201904/t20190430_5832406.html，访问日期 2019 年 6 月 2 日。

② 参见《吉林省 2018 年国民经济和社会发展统计公报》，载 http://www.jl.gov.cn/sj/sjcx/nbcx/tjgb/201904/t20190430_5832406.html，访问日期 2019 年 6 月 2 日。

二、实证调查情况简介

2016年11月，西南政法大学陈苇教授主持申报的司法部科研项目“我国遗产处理制度系统化构建研究”被批准立项。为了给本项目的理论研究和制度研究提供国情资料，必须调查了解当代中国民众的财产继承观念和遗产处理习惯。考虑到课题组人力、物力的限制，陈苇教授选择我国十省市包括东北部的吉林省、东部的上海市、北部的河北省、中部的湖北省和江西省、南部的广东省和海南省、东南部的福建省、西南部的重庆市和四川省作为被调查地点，然后联系确定了各省市调查组组长共同组织开展本项目的子课题“当代中国民众财产继承观念与遗产处理习惯实证调查研究”。本次“当代中国吉林省民众财产继承观念与遗产处理习惯实证调查研究”是西南政法大学陈苇教授主持的“当代中国民众财产继承观念与遗产处理习惯实证调查研究”的组成部分之一，吉林省调查组组长为吉林大学法学院李洪祥教授。

（一）调查问卷的设计和学生调查员的召集与培训

2016年11月中旬，陈苇教授组织重庆市课题组成员分工合作，设计制作“当代中国民众财产继承观念与遗产处理习惯实证调查研究”的调查问卷，至同年12月中旬完成了调查问卷的设计工作。然后，陈苇教授把调查问卷通过电子邮件发送给参与本次实证调查的十省市调查组组长，以供开展实地调查时十省市被调查地区统一使用。同年12月下旬，根据陈苇教授撰写的“当代中国民众财产继承观念与遗产处理习惯社会调查动员和培训会”说明书，吉林省调查组组长李洪祥教授负责召集、遴选吉林省籍的学生调查员104名，然后组织召开“当代中国吉林省民众继承观念和遗产处理习惯实证调查动员暨社会调查知识培训会”。在会上，李洪祥教授给每位学生调查员发放了6份调查问卷，针对问卷的问题，逐一讲解调查要点和具体的调查方法，要求被调查者应当具有吉林省户籍，且必须是男女各3名，分为老、中、青（61岁以上、41~60岁、20~40岁）三个年龄段，并且要求每名学生调查员利用2017年的寒假期间各自在家乡开展实地社会调查。

（二）实地社会调查的方式

2017年1月至2月的寒假期间，吉林大学法学院的本省籍学生调查员们回到各自家乡开展实地社会调查。本次调查主要采取学生调查员“入户问卷调查”和“个人访谈”的方式。

一是入户问卷调查。学生调查员在2017年的寒假期间回到自己的家乡，对当地的民众进行入户问卷调查。每位被调查对象必须符合培训会说明的条件要求，而且其只能填写一份调查问卷。学生调查员入户后首先向被调查者讲解说明本次调查的目的意义和调查问卷填写的相关问题，采取被调查者自己填写问卷或者学生调查员向被调查者询问后代为填写，这两种方式完成问卷的填写。

二是个人访谈。要求采取“一对一”的个人访谈方式，以收集与遗产继承有关的纠纷或案例。本次实地调查，除填写调查问卷外，还要求辅以“一对一”的个人访谈，收集和记录典型的继承纠纷或相关案例的内容。因为，调查问卷涉及客观选择与主观理由两部分内容，采取“一对一”的个人访谈方式，可以避免被调查者受到他人的影响，以便能够较为客观深入地了解被调查民众的真实想法。

（三）调查问卷数据的录入、统计汇总、复核与撰写调查研究报告

2017年3月开学后，本调查组统一回收调查问卷与典型案例的访谈记录，然后组织学

生统计员进行数据统计工作。本次实地调查实际发放问卷609份，剔除无效问卷后，共计回收有效问卷600份，有效问卷率为98.52%。随后，根据有效问卷进行调查数据的录入、制作统计汇总表，并且进行统计汇总数据的复核。2017年4月底完成《〈当代中国民众财产继承观念与遗产处理习惯实证调查问卷〉吉林省民众实证调查统计数据汇总表》的定稿。我们在此需要特别说明，关于各项调查问题之统计人数的合计，凡单选题的人数合计均为100%，均合计在统计表中；凡多选题的人数合计均超过100%，故不予进行合计的统计。本调查报告的撰写就是根据此次调查统计数据汇总表作为基础资料进行分析和研究而成的。在此，特向所有参与此次调查活动的老师和同学表示衷心感谢![①]

2017年4月，陈苇教授拟定了“当代中国民众财产继承观念与遗产处理习惯实证调查研究的写作提纲和写作要求”。2017年5月起，我们据此写作提纲和写作要求，进入参考文献的收集和调查报告的写作阶段。本章“当代中国吉林省民众财产继承观念与遗产处理习惯实证调查研究”由李洪祥教授和苗艺璇、高岩、马旭和张远等师生共同撰写初稿至第六稿。其间，根据陈苇教授对初稿至第六稿的历次修改意见和中期评审专家意见，对稿件进行了相应的多次修改和补充，最后向课题负责人陈苇教授交稿。2019年1月，陈苇教授继续对吉林省调查研究报告进行审阅和修改补充，然后组织重庆市调查组博士研究生对吉林省调查研究报告统一进行了三次修改补充，最终于2019年6月完成定稿。

三、被调查对象的基本情况

本次调查的对象均为吉林省常住人口，我们对600名被调查者的性别、年龄和职业情况进行了如下统计：

（一）被调查者的性别情况

表3-1　被调查者的性别情况统计

性别	人数	比例
男性	279	46.50%
女性	321	53.50%
合计	600	100%

关于被调查者的性别，调查统计数据显示，在600名被调查者中，男性有279人（占46.50%）；女性有321人（占53.50%）。可见，被调查者性别比例大体相当。

① 参与吉林省民众财产继承观念与遗产处理习惯的实地调查以及调查数据统计汇总等工作的师生名单详见“鸣谢”。

（二）被调查者的年龄情况

表 3-2 被调查者的年龄情况统计

年龄	人数	比例
20~30 岁	286	47.67%
31~40 岁	90	15%
41~50 岁	153	25.50%
51~60 岁	43	7.17%
61~70 岁	22	3.66%
71 岁以上	6	1%
合计	600	100%

关于被调查者的年龄，调查统计数据显示，在 600 名被调查者中，20~40 岁青年人占六成（62.67%）、41~60 岁的中年人占三成以上（32.67%），而 60 岁以上的老年人，合计约占半成（4.66%）。

（三）被调查者的职业情况

表 3-3 被调查者的职业情况统计

职业	人数	比例
农民	59	9.83%
工人	92	15.33%
经商	57	9.50%
公务员、企事业单位员工	179	29.84%
其他（打工等不固定职业）	213	35.50%
合计	600	100%

关于被调查者的职业，调查统计数据显示，在 600 名被调查者中，农民占近一成（9.83%）；工人占一成半（15.33%）；经商的占近一成（9.50%）；公务员和企事业单位职工合计占近三成（29.83%）；其他（打工等不固定职业）合计占三成半（35.50%）。

综上，本次被调查者的性别比例大体持平，老、中、青各年龄段的均有，但以中青年为主体，且他们的职业分布广泛，本次调查数据基本上能够反映不同性别、年龄和职业的被调查者的意愿。

第二节　当代中国吉林省民众财产继承观念与遗产处理习惯实证调查的数据统计情况

一、遗产范围界定之调查数据统计情况

关于遗产范围界定之调查数据统计，我们主要从遗产的种类和被继承人生前特种赠与财产的归扣两个方面进行调查数据的统计情况汇总分析。

（一）遗产的种类

问题【一、（一）】“2016年2月某甲因车祸死亡，经清理某甲个人名下的遗物，您认为，以下哪些属于某甲的遗产：A. 住房一套；B. 小汽车一辆；C. 家庭日常生活用品若干；D. 存款10万元；E 股票10万元；F. 某甲以其姓名注册的邮箱、QQ账号等；G. 单位出租给某甲的午休住房一间；H. 某甲向某公司购货的欠款5万元；I. 某甲因交通事故死亡获得50万元赔偿金。（单选）”

表3-4　属于遗产种类的民众观念情况统计（单选）

选项	遗产	
	人数	比例
A. 住房一套	543	90.50%
B. 小汽车一辆	554	92.33%
C. 家庭日常生活用品若干	408	68.00%
D. 存款10万元	538	89.67%
E. 股票10万元	479	79.83%
F. 某甲以其姓名注册的邮箱、QQ账号等	322	53.67%
G. 单位出租给某甲的午休住房一间	48	8.00%
H. 某甲向某公司购货的欠款5万元	269	44.83%
I. 某甲因交通事故死亡获得50万元赔偿金	361	60.17%

关于属于遗产种类的民众观念，调查统计数据显示，在600名被调查者中，（1）近八成至九成的人认为A项住房（90.50%）、B项汽车（92.33%）、D项存款（89.67%）和E项股票（79.83%）属于遗产。（2）近一成至七成的人认为C项家庭日常生活用品（68.00%）、I项交通事故死亡赔偿金（60.17%）、H项欠款（44.83%）和G项单位出租给被继承人的午休住房（8.00%）属于遗产。（3）五成以上的人认为F项以被继承人的姓名注册的邮箱、QQ账号等（53.67%）属于遗产。

（二）被继承人生前特种赠与财产的归扣

1. 被继承人生前特种赠与的财产是否应归入遗产范围的民众观念情况统计

问题【一、（二）1.】“张老汉有三个儿子，在10年前大儿子甲结婚时，张老汉给其资

助购买婚房的现金 20 万元；二儿子乙一直未结婚，但 5 年前在其开办豆腐坊时，张老汉资助其营业资金 10 万元。在 2 年前小儿子丙结婚时，张老汉为其购买一套价值 30 万元的房屋（产权登记在小儿子丙名下）；2016 年 1 月张老汉去世时遗留有个人所有的住房一套和 50 万元存款。您认为，上述哪些财产应当计算入遗产：A. 张老汉生前给三个儿子不同资助的财产与死亡时遗留的住房、存款，均应当合并计算为遗产；B. 张老汉去世时遗留的个人所有的住房和 50 万元存款，才可以计算为遗产；C. 其他。（单选）”

表 3-5　被继承人生前特种赠与的财产是否应归入遗产范围的民众观念情况统计（单选）

选项	人数	比例
A. 张老汉生前给三个儿子不同资助的财产与死亡时遗留的住房、存款，均应当合并计算为遗产	96	16.00%
B. 张老汉去世时遗留的个人所有的住房和 50 万元存款，才可以计算为遗产	447	74.50%
C. 其他	57	9.50%
合计	600	100%

关于被继承人生前特种赠与的财产是否应归入遗产范围的民众观念，调查统计数据显示，在 600 名被调查者中，（1）选择 B 项持否定观点的，占近七成半（74.50%）；（2）选择 A 项持肯定观点的，只占一成半以上（16.00%）。

2. 归扣遗产价值计算时间的民众观念情况统计

问题【一、（二）2.】“如果上述答案您选 A，请问张老汉为小儿子丙买房的价值应该按何时计算？A. 买房时；B. 张老汉去世时；C. 实际分割遗产时；D. 其他。（单选）”

表 3-6　归扣遗产价值计算时间的民众观念情况统计（单选）

选项	人数	比例
A. 买房时	27	28.13%
B. 张老汉去世时	20	20.83%
C. 实际分割遗产时	47	48.96%
D. 其他	2	2.08%
合计	96	100%

关于归扣遗产价值计算时间的民众观念，调查统计数据显示，在填写该问题的 96 名被调查者中，根据其占比高低排序如下：（1）选择 C 项认为应以分割遗产时为准的，占近五成（48.96%）；（2）选择 A 项认为应以赠与时为准的，占近三成（28.13%）；（3）选择 B 项认为以张老汉去世时为准的，占二成（20.83%）。即认为应以分割遗产时计算归扣财产价值的占比居第一位。

3. 生前特种赠与财产是否归入遗产范围的民间习惯情况统计

问题【一、(二) 3.】"在您所在地区，如果发生上述张老汉生前给三个儿子不同资助财产的情况，在继承遗产时这些资助财产是否被合计到遗产范围内？A. 是；B. 不是；C. 不清楚。(单选)"

表 3-7 生前特种赠与财产是否归入遗产范围的民间习惯情况统计（单选）

选项	人数	比例
A. 是	213	35.50%
B. 不是	378	63.00%
C. 不清楚	9	1.50%
合计	600	100%

关于生前特种赠与财产是否归入遗产范围的民间习惯，调查统计数据显示，600 名被调查者所在地区的习惯是：(1) B 项不是，即无归扣习惯的，占六成以上（63.00%）；(2) A 项是，即有归扣习惯的，占三成半（35.50%）。

4. 生前特种赠与财产不归入遗产情况下的分配方式之民间习惯与理由情况统计

(1) 生前特种赠与财产不归入遗产情况下的分配方式之民间习惯情况统计。

问题【一、(二) 4.】"如果您选择 B 项即这些资助财产不是被合计到遗产范围内，三个儿子是如何分配父亲张老汉的遗产的？A. 平均分配；B. 乙应该适当多分；C. 其他。(单选)"

表 3-8 生前特种赠与财产不归入遗产情况下的分配方式之民间习惯情况统计（单选）

选项	人数	比例
A. 平均分配	239	63.22%
B. 乙应该适当多分	100	26.46%
C. 其他	39	10.32%
合计	378	100%

关于生前特种赠与财产不归入遗产情况下的分配方式之民间习惯，调查统计数据显示，填写该问题的 378 名被调查者所在地区的习惯是：①A 项继承人之间平均分配的，占六成以上（63.22%）；②B 项获得被继承人生前特种赠与较少的继承人可以多分的，占二成半以上（26.46%）。

（2）生前特种赠与财产不归入遗产情况下的分配方式之理由情况统计。

表 3-9　生前特种赠与财产不归入遗产情况下的分配方式之理由统计

<table>
<tr><th colspan="2">项目</th><th>人数</th><th>比例</th></tr>
<tr><td colspan="2">A. 不考虑张老汉生前给三个儿子财产的情况，死后平均分配所留遗产，有利于遗产的分割</td><td>220</td><td>58.20%</td></tr>
<tr><td colspan="2">B. 因为张老汉生前给乙的财产较少，在其死后乙应多分些，这体现公平原则</td><td>148</td><td>39.15%</td></tr>
<tr><td rowspan="2">C. 其他</td><td>符合公众认知</td><td>3</td><td>0.80%</td></tr>
<tr><td>按照法定继承</td><td>7</td><td>1.85%</td></tr>
<tr><td colspan="2">合计</td><td>378</td><td>100%</td></tr>
</table>

关于生前特种赠与财产不归入遗产情况下的分配方式之理由，调查统计数据显示，在填写了该理由的378名被调查者中，①认为遗产分配采取平均分配方式的理由是，A项有利于遗产分割的，占近六成（58.20%）；②认为未获得特种财产赠与的继承人应多分遗产的理由是，B项可体现公平原则的，占近四成（39.15%）。

二、继承开始的通知和公告之调查数据统计情况

关于继承开始的通知和公告之调查数据统计，我们主要从继承开始的通知和公告的主体、继承开始的通知和公告的方式、继承开始的通知和公告的期间，这三个方面进行调查数据的统计情况汇总分析。

（一）继承开始的通知和公告的主体

问题【二、（一）】“被继承人死亡后，在您所在地区一般由下列哪些人通知涉及遗产分配的相关人员？A. 知道被继承人死亡的继承人；B. 保管遗产的继承人；C. 知道被继承人死亡的单位、村（居）委会；D. 处理被继承人死亡事件的机构，如公安交警部门；E. 其他。（多选）”

表 3-10　继承开始的通知和公告的主体的民间习惯统计情况（多选）

<table>
<tr><th colspan="2">选项</th><th colspan="2">人数</th><th colspan="2">比例</th></tr>
<tr><td colspan="2">A. 知道被继承人死亡的继承人</td><td colspan="2">203</td><td colspan="2">33.83%</td></tr>
<tr><td colspan="2">B. 保管遗产的继承人</td><td colspan="2">441</td><td colspan="2">73.50%</td></tr>
<tr><td colspan="2">C. 知道被继承人死亡的单位、村（居）委会</td><td colspan="2">310</td><td colspan="2">51.67%</td></tr>
<tr><td colspan="2">D. 处理被继承人死亡事件的机构，如公安交警部门</td><td colspan="2">255</td><td colspan="2">42.50%</td></tr>
<tr><td rowspan="2">E. 其他</td><td>法院保管</td><td rowspan="2">112</td><td>87</td><td rowspan="2">18.67%</td><td>14.50%</td></tr>
<tr><td>专门机构保管</td><td>25</td><td>4.17%</td></tr>
</table>

关于继承开始的通知和公告的主体的民间习惯，调查统计数据显示，在600名被调查者填写的所在地区的习惯分别是：(1) A项由知道被继承人死亡的继承人发出的，占三成以上(33.83%)；(2) B项由保管遗产的继承人发出的，占七成以上（73.50%)；(3) C项由知道被继承人死亡的单位、村（居）委会发出的，占五成以上（51.67%)；(4) D项由处理被继承人死亡事件的机构（如公安交警部门）发出的，占四成以上（42.50%)。

（二）继承开始的通知和公告的方式

问题【二、(二)】“被继承人死亡后，您所在地区的人们一般采取以下哪些方式通知涉及遗产处理的相关人员：A. 口头、电话、微信等；B. 信件、告知函等书面通知；C. 在报纸、电视、网络等平台上发布被继承人死亡的公告；D. 在被继承人所在地的村（居）委会公告栏公告；E. 申请人民法院以公告程序进行公告；F. 其他。(多选)”

表3-11　继承开始的通知和公告的方式的民间习惯情况统计（多选）

选项	人数	比例
A. 口头、电话、微信等	444	74.00%
B. 信件、告知函等书面通知	276	46.00%
C. 在报纸、电视、网络等平台上发布被继承人死亡的公告	124	20.67%
D. 在被继承人所在地的村（居）委会公告栏公告	180	30.00%
E. 申请人民法院以公告程序进行公告	179	29.83%
F. 其他	21	3.50%

关于继承开始的通知和公告的方式的民间习惯，调查统计数据显示，600名被调查者填写的所在地区的习惯是：(1) A项使用口头、电话、微信等方式的，占近七成半(74.00%)；(2) B项使用书信、告知函等方式的，占四成半以上（46.00%)；(3) D项采用在村（居）委会公告栏公告方式的，占三成（30.00%)；(4) C项使用在报纸、电视、网络等平台上发布被继承人的死亡公告方式的，占二成（20.67%)；(5) E项采用申请人民法院以公告程序进行公告方式的，占近三成（29.83%)。

（三）继承开始的通知和公告的期间

问题【二、(三)】“您认为，通知人应在被继承人死亡后几日内发出通知：A. 3日；B. 7日；C. 15日；D. 30日；E. 其他。(单选)”

表3-12　继承开始的通知和公告的期间之民众观念的情况统计（单选）

选项	人数	比例
A. 3日	134	22.33%
B. 7日	157	26.17%
C. 15日	153	25.50%

续表

选项	人数	比例
D. 30 日	152	25. 33%
E. 其他	4	0. 67%
合计	600	100%

关于继承开始的通知和公告的期间之民间观念，调查统计数据显示，在600名被调查者中，对于被继承人死亡后发出继承开始的通知的时间，（1）选择A项和B项认为应在7日内发出的，合计占近五成（48. 50%）；（2）选择C项和D项认为应在15日或30日内发出的，合计占五成（50. 83%）。

三、遗产管理之调查数据统计情况

关于遗产管理之调查数据统计，我们主要从遗产管理人的确定、遗产管理人的职责与报酬、遗产管理人的损害赔偿责任，这三个方面进行调查数据的统计情况汇总分析。

（一）遗产管理人的确定

问题【三、（一）】“您所在地区人们处理遗产继承时，一般是由谁清点和管理遗产？A. 死者的法定继承人：配偶、子女、父母、兄弟姐妹、孙子女或外孙子女、祖父母或外祖父母；B. 死者的儿媳或女婿；C. 死者家族中的德高望重者；D. 死者的其他亲戚朋友；E. 死者所在的单位或村（居）委会；F. 其他。（多选）其理由是什么？”

1. 关于遗产管理人的确定的民间习惯情况统计

表3-13　关于遗产管理人的确定的民间习惯情况统计（多选）

<table>
<tr><th colspan="2">选项</th><th colspan="2">人数</th><th colspan="2">比例</th></tr>
<tr><td rowspan="6">A. 死者的法定继承人：
配偶、子女、父母、兄弟姐妹、孙子女或外孙子女、祖父母或外祖父母</td><td>配偶</td><td rowspan="6">513</td><td>377</td><td rowspan="6">85. 50%</td><td>62. 83%</td></tr>
<tr><td>子女</td><td>310</td><td>51. 67%</td></tr>
<tr><td>父母</td><td>332</td><td>55. 33%</td></tr>
<tr><td>兄弟姐妹</td><td>112</td><td>18. 67%</td></tr>
<tr><td>孙子女或外孙子女</td><td>151</td><td>25. 17%</td></tr>
<tr><td>祖父母或外祖父母</td><td>93</td><td>15. 50%</td></tr>
<tr><td colspan="2">B. 死者的儿媳或女婿</td><td colspan="2">131</td><td colspan="2">21. 83%</td></tr>
<tr><td colspan="2">C. 死者家族中的德高望重者</td><td colspan="2">207</td><td colspan="2">34. 50%</td></tr>
<tr><td colspan="2">D. 死者的其他亲戚朋友</td><td colspan="2">87</td><td colspan="2">14. 50%</td></tr>
<tr><td colspan="2">E. 死者所在的单位或村（居）委会</td><td colspan="2">156</td><td colspan="2">26. 00%</td></tr>
</table>

续表

选项		人数		比例	
F. 其他	专门机构	23	10	3.83%	1.67%
	其他亲属		13		2.16%

关于遗产管理人的确定的民间习惯，调查统计数据显示，600 名被调查者填写的所在地区的习惯排在前两位的是：（1）选择 A 项由死者的法定继承人担任的，占八成半（85.50%）；（2）选择 C 项由死者家族中的德高望重者担任的，占近三成半（34.50%）。

2. 关于遗产管理人的确定的民间习惯之理由情况统计

表 3-14　关于遗产管理人的确定的民间习惯之理由情况统计

项目	人数	比例
A. 遗产管理人一般由法定继承人来担任，便于清点和妥善管理遗产	33	8.19%
B. 遗产管理人一般由法定继承人之外的人或组织来担任，可以防止遗产被隐藏、转移，有利于保护遗产相关人的合法权益	81	20.10%
C. 遗产管理人由继承人之外的人或组织来担任，是自愿协商	76	18.86%
D. 遗产管理人由继承人来担任，符合风俗习惯	213	52.85%
合计	403	100%

关于遗产管理人的确定的民间习惯之理由，调查统计数据显示，在填写了理由的 403 名被调查者所在地区，（1）由法定继承人作为遗产管理人的理由是，D 项符合风俗习惯的，占五成以上（52.85%），A 项便于清点和妥善管理遗产的，占近一成（8.19%）；（2）由法定管理人之外的人或组织担任遗产管理人的理由是，C 项自愿协商的，占近二成（18.86%），B 项可以防止遗产被隐藏、转移，有利于保护遗产相关人的合法权益的，占二成（20.10%）。

（二）遗产管理人的职责与报酬

1. 遗产管理人职责

问题【三、（二）1.】"您认为，遗产管理人的职责有哪些？A. 清查遗产，制作遗产清单；B. 妥善保管遗产；C. 查明被继承人生前的债权和债务，积极地追讨债权或清偿债务；D. 查明被继承人是否留有遗嘱，并且确定遗嘱是否真实合法；E. 可以原告或被告的身份参加因遗产引起的诉讼；F. 定期制作遗产管理报告，向继承人报告遗产管理的情况；G. 其他。（多选）"

表 3-15　对遗产管理人管理职责的民众观念情况统计（多选）

选项	人数	比例
A. 清查遗产，制作遗产清单	548	91.33%
B. 妥善保管遗产	550	91.67%
C. 查明被继承人生前的债权和债务，积极地追讨债权或清偿债务	433	72.17%
D. 查明被继承人是否留有遗嘱，并且确定遗嘱是否真实合法	341	56.83%
E. 可以原告或被告的身份参加因遗产引起的诉讼	431	71.83%
F. 定期制作遗产管理报告，向继承人报告遗产管理的情况	367	61.17%
G. 其他	27	4.50%

关于对遗产管理人管理职责的民众观念，调查统计数据显示，在600名被调查者中，占五至九成的人认为主要职责包括：A项清查遗产，制作遗产清单的，占91.33%；B项妥善保管遗产的，占91.67%；C项查明被继承人生前的债权和债务，积极地追讨债权或清偿债务的，占72.17%；E项可以原告或被告的身份参加因遗产引起的诉讼的，占71.83%；F项定期制作遗产管理报告，向继承人报告遗产管理的情况的，占61.17%；D项查明被继承人是否留有遗嘱，并且确定遗嘱是否真实合法的，占56.83%。

2. 遗产管理人是否可取得报酬的民间习惯与理由情况统计

问题【三、（二）2.】"您所在地区，负责管理遗产的人是否可以获得报酬？A. 继承人担任遗产管理人的，不能请求给付报酬；B. 法院指定的遗产管理人，有权请求给付报酬；C. 继承人选任的第三人作为遗产管理人，是否给付报酬，应当由继承人决定；D. 继承人选任的第三人作为遗产管理人，一律有权请求给付报酬；E. 其他。（多选）其理由是什么？"

（1）遗产管理人是否取得报酬的民间习惯情况统计。

表 3-16　遗产管理人是否可以获得报酬的民间习惯情况统计（多选）

选项	人数	比例
A. 继承人担任遗产管理人的，不能请求给付报酬	293	48.83%
B. 法院指定的遗产管理人，有权请求给付报酬	396	66.00%
C. 继承人选任的第三人作为遗产管理人，是否给付报酬，应当由继承人决定	217	36.17%
D. 继承人选任的第三人作为遗产管理人，一律有权请求给付报酬	268	44.67%
E. 其他	27	4.50%

关于遗产管理人是否可以获得报酬的民间习惯，调查统计数据显示，600名被调查者填写的所在地区的习惯是：①A项继承人担任的管理人不可以取得报酬的，占近五成（48.83%）；②B项法院指定担任的管理人可以取得报酬的，占六成半以上（66.00%）；

③继承人选任的第三人担任的管理人，其中，D 项一律可以取得报酬的，占近四成半（44.67%），C 项是否可以取得报酬由继承人决定的，占三成半以上（36.17%）。

（2）遗产管理人是否取得报酬的民间习惯之理由情况统计。

表 3-17　遗产管理人是否可以获得报酬的民间习惯之理由情况统计

项目	人数	比例
A. 遗产管理人在多数情况下与被继承人关系密切，具有亲情关系，同时，其作为继承人又继承遗产，因此，其不需要报酬	77	26.92%
B. 遗产管理人为管理遗产付出了自己的劳动，占用了自己的时间，应该给予一定的费用	42	14.69%
C. 遗产管理人是否可取得报酬，应由继承人和遗产管理人协商确定	81	28.32%
D. 为了维持社会秩序的公平，应当给予报酬	86	30.07%
合计	286	100%

关于遗产管理人是否可以获得报酬的民间习惯之理由，调查统计数据显示，在填写该理由的 286 名被调查者中，①遗产管理人可以获得报酬的民间习惯之理由是，B 项和 D 项，遗产管理人为管理遗产付出了劳动和时间与为了维持社会秩序的公平的，占近四成半（44.76%）；②遗产管理人不可获得报酬的民间习惯之理由是，A 项遗产管理人与被继承人关系密切且其作为继承人可继承遗产的，占二成半以上（26.92%）；③遗产管理人是否取得报酬，C 项应由继承人和遗产管理人协商确定的，占近三成（28.32%）。

（三）遗产管理人的损害赔偿责任

问题【三、（三）】“在您所在地区，负责管理遗产的人对因其过错造成的较大财产损失，是否承担赔偿责任？A. 凡有故意或重大过失的，才承担赔偿责任；B. 无论是故意或重大过失或一般轻过失的，都要承担赔偿责任；C. 其他。（单选）”

表 3-18　遗产管理人是否承担赔偿责任的民间习惯情况统计（单选）

选项	人数	比例
A. 凡有故意或重大过失的，才承担赔偿责任	418	69.66%
B. 无论是故意或重大过失或一般轻过失的，都要承担赔偿责任	178	29.67%
C. 其他	4	0.67%
合计	600	100%

关于遗产管理人是否承担赔偿责任的民间习惯，调查统计数据显示，600 名被调查者填写的所在地区的习惯是：（1）A 项凡有故意或重大过失才承担赔偿责任的，占近七成（69.66%）；（2）B 项无论是故意或重大过失或一般轻过失的，都要承担赔偿责任的，只占近三成（29.67%）。

四、法定继承之调查数据统计情况

关于法定继承之调查数据统计，我们主要从法定继承人的范围与顺序、配偶与血亲继承人的法定应继份、配偶对遗产中家庭住房的先取权和终生使用权、后顺序特殊法定继承人对遗产中原使用的住房及日常生活用品的终生使用权、尽了主要赡养义务的丧偶的儿媳或女婿的遗产分配方式，这五个方面进行调查数据的统计情况汇总分析。

(一) 法定继承人的范围与顺序

1. 法定继承人的范围与顺序的民众观念的情况统计

问题【四、(一) 1.】"下列亲属，您认为哪些应当作为法定继承人？他们各自的继承顺序如何？请根据您认为适当的先后顺序填写数字：1. 2. 3. ……，例如，父母 (1)；子女 (2)；祖父母、外祖父母 (3)。如果您认为应当在同一顺序的人，可以填写相同的数字，如配偶 (1)；父母 (1)；子女 (1)；祖父母、外祖父母 (1)。"

配偶 ( )	父母 ( )	儿子 ( ) 女儿 ( )
孙子女 ( ) 外孙子女 ( )	祖父母 ( ) 外祖父母 ( )	兄弟 ( ) 姐妹 ( )
侄子女 ( ) 外甥子女 ( )	伯叔姑舅姨 ( )	堂兄弟姐妹 ( )
表兄弟姐妹 ( )	其他亲属 (称谓) ( )	其他亲属 (称谓) ( )

表 3-19 法定继承人的范围与顺序的民众观念情况统计 (多选)

亲属名称	第一顺序		第二顺序		第三顺序		第四顺序		第四顺序以上	
	人数	比例 (%)	人数	比例 (%)	人数	比例 (%)	人数	比例 (%)	人数	比例 (%)
配偶	565	94.17	25	4.17	3	0.50	7	1.17	0	0
父母	325	54.17	165	27.50	100	16.67	7	1.17	0	0
子女	347	57.83	126	21.00	117	19.50	0	0	3	0.50
孙子女、外孙子女	4	0.67	278	46.33	56	9.33	152	25.33	82	13.67
祖父母、外祖父母	4	0.67	275	45.83	53	8.83	87	14.50	159	26.50
兄弟姐妹	6	1.00	238	39.67	78	13.00	35	5.83	210	35.00
侄子女、外甥子女	1	0.17	5	0.83	198	33.00	44	7.33	258	43.00
伯叔姑舅姨	1	0.17	4	0.67	182	30.33	39	6.50	266	44.33
堂兄弟姐妹	0	0	5	0.83	180	30.00	32	5.33	273	45.50
表兄弟姐妹	0	0	3	0.50	96	16.00	84	14.00	281	46.83
其他亲属	0	0	0	0	2	0.33	21	3.50	220	36.67

关于法定继承人的范围与顺序的民众观念，各顺序以被调查者选择占比最高的作为统计依据，600 名被调查者较认可的法定继承范围为：第一顺序为配偶 (94.17%)、父母 (54.17%)、子女 (57.83%)；第二顺序为孙子女、外孙子女 (46.33%)，祖父母、外祖父母 (45.83%) 和兄弟姐妹 (39.67%)；第三顺序为侄子女、外甥子女 (33.00%)，伯

叔姑舅姨（30.33%）；第四顺序为堂兄弟姐妹（45.50%）、表兄弟姐妹（15.08%）。

2. 配偶与血亲继承人顺序的民众观念情况统计

问题【四、（一）2.】“以下三种法定继承人的范围和顺序，您认为哪一个更为适当：（单选）”

A	B	C
第一顺序：子女	第一顺序：子女	第一顺序：配偶、子女、父母
第二顺序：父母	第二顺序：父母	第二顺序：兄弟姐妹、祖父母、外祖父母
第三顺序：兄弟姐妹、祖父母、外祖父母 兄弟姐妹的子女（侄子女、外甥子女为代位继承人）	第三顺序：兄弟姐妹、祖父母、外祖父母 兄弟姐妹的子女（侄子女、外甥子女为代位继承人）	第三顺序：侄子女、外甥子女
配偶无固定顺序，可以参与第一、第二、第三顺序继承	配偶无固定顺序，可以参与第一、第二顺序继承	

表 3-20　配偶与血亲继承人顺序之民众观念情况统计（单选）

选项	人数	比例
A. 配偶无固定顺序，可以参与第一、第二、第三顺序继承	43	7.17%
B. 配偶无固定顺序，可以参与第一、第二顺序继承	45	7.50%
C. 配偶与子女、父母同为第一顺序，共同继承	512	85.33%
合计	600	100%

关于配偶与血亲继承人顺序之民众观念，调查统计数据显示，在600名被调查者中，（1）选择C项顺序为：第一顺序：配偶、子女、父母；第二顺序：兄弟姐妹、祖父母外祖父母；第三顺序：侄子女、外甥子女；配偶有固定顺序，其属于第一顺位继承人的，占八成半（85.33%）。（2）选择A、B两项顺序为：第一顺序为子女；第二顺序为父母；第三顺序为兄弟姐妹、祖父母、外祖父母、兄弟姐妹的子女（侄子女、外甥子女为代位继承人）；配偶无固定的继承顺序，可分别与第一、第二（或第三）顺序的法定继承人共同继承的，合计只占近一成半（14.67%）。

（二）配偶与血亲继承人的法定应继份

问题【四、（二）】“配偶与血亲继承人共同继承各取得遗产的份额，您认为以下哪一项更为适当？（单选）”

A. 配偶无固定继承顺序	B. 配偶无固定继承顺序	C. 配偶有固定继承顺序	D. 其他（您认为适当的配偶继承份额）
配偶与第一顺序的子女共同继承时，其取得遗产的一半，另一半由子女按人数平均继承	配偶与第一顺序的子女共同继承时，其取得遗产的一半，另一半由子女、按人数平均继承	第一顺序继承人为配偶、子女、父母，共同继承时按人数均分遗产	
配偶与第二顺序的父母共同继承时，其取得遗产的三分之二，另外三分之一由父母平均继承	配偶与第二顺序的父母共同继承时，其取得遗产的三分之二，另外三分之一由父母平均继承	无第一顺序血亲继承人时，配偶继承全部遗产	
配偶与第三顺序的兄弟姐妹、祖父母和外祖父母共同继承时，其取得遗产的四分之三，另外四分之一由兄弟姐妹、祖父母、外祖父母，按人数平均继承	无第一、第二顺序血亲继承人时，配偶继承全部遗产		
无上述三个顺序血亲继承人时，配偶取得全部遗产			

表 3-21　配偶与血亲继承人的法定应继份的民众观念的情况统计（单选）

选项	人数	比例
A. 配偶无固定继承顺序，参与前三顺序的继承并取得不同份额；无上述三个顺序血亲继承人时，配偶取得全部遗产	234	39.00%
B. 配偶无固定继承顺序，参与前二顺序的继承并取得不同份额；无第一、第二顺序血亲继承人时，配偶继承全部遗产	107	17.83%
C. 配偶有固定继承顺序并均分遗产，与第一顺序继承人共同继承	249	41.50%
D. 其他	10	1.67%
合计	600	100%

关于配偶与血亲继承人的法定应继份的民众观念，调查统计数据显示，在 600 名被调查者中，（1）选择 A 项和 B 项配偶为无固定继承顺序，可参与第一、第二（或第三）顺序且在不同顺序其应继份不同的，合计占五成半以上（56.83%）；（2）选择 C 项配偶为有固定顺序的继承人，与第一顺序的继承人共同继承并平均分配遗产的，占四成以上（41.50%）。

（三）配偶对遗产中家庭住房的先取权与终生使用权

1. 配偶对遗产中家庭住房的先取权与终生使用权的民间习惯情况统计

问题【四、（三）1.】“甲乙是夫妻，育有一子丙。甲因病去世时留下的遗产包括：

价值50万元住房一套（原由甲乙夫妻共同居住，丙已结婚分家另过）、价值10万元小汽车一辆和20万元存款。如果上述情况发生在您所在地区，被继承人甲的妻子乙是否可以优先继承这套房屋（配偶先取权）？A. 是；B. 否。（单选）”

表3-22　配偶对遗产中家庭住房的先取权与终生使用权的民间习惯情况统计（单选）

选项	人数	比例
A. 是	277	46.17%
B. 否	323	53.83%
合计	600	100%

关于配偶对遗产中家庭住房的先取权与终生使用权的民间习惯，调查统计数据显示，600名被调查者填写的所在地区的习惯是：（1）A项是，即有该习惯的，占四成半以上（46.17%）；（2）B项否，即无此习惯的，占五成以上（53.83%）。

2. 配偶对遗产中家庭住房的先取权与终生使用权是否付费的民间习惯与理由情况统计

问题【四、（三）2.】“如果甲的妻子乙可以优先继承这套房屋，但该住房的价值超过其应当继承的遗产份额40万元，在您所在地区是否按照下列情况处理？A. 乙有权继承该住房，且无须向另一法定继承人丙进行补偿；B. 如果乙有经济补偿能力，则应当向另一法定继承人丙适当进行补偿；C. 其他。（单选）其理由是什么？”

（1）配偶对遗产中家庭住房的先取权与终生使用权是否付费之民间习惯情况统计。

表3-23　配偶对遗产中家庭住房的先取权与终生使用权是否付费之民间习惯情况统计（单选）

选项	人数	比例
A. 乙有权继承该住房，且无须向其他共同应召继承人丙进行补偿	327	54.50%
B. 如果乙有经济补偿能力，则应当向其他共同应召继承人丙适当进行补偿	257	42.83%
C. 其他（协商是否补偿）	16	2.67%
合计	600	100%

关于配偶对遗产中家庭住房的先取权与终生使用权是否付费之民间习惯，调查统计数据显示，600名被调查者填写的所在地区的习惯是：①A项配偶无须进行补偿的，占五成半（54.50%）；②B项如果配偶有经济补偿能力则需要补偿费用的，占四成以上（42.83%）。

（2）配偶对遗产中家庭住房的先取权与终生使用是否付费之理由情况统计。

表 3-24　配偶对遗产中家庭住房的先取权与终生使用是否付费之理由情况统计

项目	人数	比例
A. 首先保证乙有居住之所，同时，丙是乙的儿子，将来乙的遗产也会由丙来继承，所以，乙无须向丙进行补偿	36	10.94%
B. 由乙向丙进行补偿，符合法律规定，体现公平精神	132	40.12%
C. 其他（基于共同享有该遗产所有权，故无须补偿）	161	48.94%
合计	329	100%

关于配偶对遗产中家庭住房的先取权与终生使用是否付费之理由，在填写此问题的 329 名被调查者所在地区，①配偶无须进行补偿的理由是，A 项和 C 项，保证生存配偶有居住之所，且将来其子女可以继承该生存配偶遗产或是基于共同继承人对该遗产享有所有权故无须补偿的，合计占近六成（59.88%）；②如果配偶有经济补偿能力则需要补偿的理由是，B 项符合法律规定并体现公平精神的，占四成（40.12%）。

（四）后顺序特殊法定继承人对遗产中原使用的住房及日常生活用品的终生使用权

后顺序特殊法定继承人对遗产中原使用的住房及日常生活用品的终生使用权，也可称为后顺序特殊法定继承人对特殊遗产的终生使用权。

1. 后顺序特殊法定继承人对遗产中原使用的住房及日常生活用品的终生使用权的民间习惯情况统计

问题【四、（四）1.】“某甲死亡时遗留下若干遗产，其中包括一套三室一厅的住房（其中的一间房屋一直由某甲的祖父居住）。由于某甲的祖父属于后顺序继承人而不能参加继承，遗产全部由某甲的第一顺序继承人配偶及其子女等继承。请问：在您所在地区，如果发生了上述情况，有哪些下列处理方式？某甲的祖父对该供其居住的房屋，是否可以继续居住？A. 是；B. 否。（单选）”

表 3-25　后顺序特殊法定继承人对特殊遗产的终生使用权之民间习惯情况统计（单选）

选项	人数	比例
A. 是	486	81.00%
B. 否	114	19.00%
合计	600	100%

关于后顺序特殊法定继承人对特殊遗产的终生使用权之民间习惯，调查统计数据显示，600 名被调查者填写的所在地区的习惯是：（1）A 项是，即有此习惯的，占八成以上（81%）；（2）B 项否，即无此习惯的，占近二成（19.00%）。

2. 后顺序特殊法定继承人对遗产中原使用的住房及日常生活用品的终生使用是否付费的民间习惯情况统计

问题【四、（四）2.】“如果某甲的祖父可以继续居住，是否其可以不交租金？A. 是；B. 否。（单选）”

表 3-26　后顺序特殊法定继承人对特殊遗产的终生使用是否付费的民间习惯情况统计（单选）

选项	人数	比例
A. 是	383	63.83%
B. 否	217	36.17%
合计	600	100%

关于后顺序特殊法定继承人对特殊遗产的终生使用是否付费的民间习惯，调查统计数据显示，600 名被调查者填写的所在地区的习惯是：（1）A 项是，即无须支付费用的，占近六成半（63.83%）；（2）B 项否，即需要支付费用的，占三成半以上（36.17%）。

3. 后顺序特殊法定继承人对遗产中原使用的住房及日常生活用品的终生使用权之期限的民间习惯情况统计

问题【四、（四）3.】“如果甲的祖父可以继续居住，是否可以居住到其死亡时为止（终生使用权）。A. 是；B. 否。（单选）”

表 3-27　后顺序特殊法定继承人对特殊遗产的终生使用权之期限的民间习惯情况统计（单选）

选项	人数	比例
A. 是	422	70.33%
B. 否	178	29.67%
合计	600	100%

关于后顺序特殊法定继承人对特殊遗产的终生使用权之期限的民间习惯，调查统计数据显示，600 名被调查者填写的所在地区的习惯是：（1）A 项是，即有此习惯的，占七成（70.33%）；（2）B 项否，即无此习惯的，占近三成（29.67%）。

（五）尽了主要赡养义务的丧偶儿媳或女婿的遗产分配方式

问题【四、（五）】“村民某甲，老伴因病早年去世，膝下有两个儿子乙和丙。2003 年乙与丁结婚后与某甲共同生活。2012 年 1 月乙因交通事故死亡，但乙的妻子丁仍然一直照料公公某甲的晚年生活，直至 2015 年 1 月某甲去世。请问：在您所在地区，如发生上述情况，因乙的妻子丁对公公某甲尽了主要赡养义务，如何处理某甲的遗产分配问题？A. 丁可以与某甲的二儿子丙共同继承，并且平均分配遗产；B. 丁不能与某甲的二儿子丙共同继承，但其可分得适当的遗产；C. 其他。（单选）”

表 3-28　尽了主要赡养义务的丧偶儿媳或女婿的遗产分配方式的民间习惯情况统计（单选）

选项	人数	比例
A. 丁可以与某甲的二儿子丙共同继承，并且平均分配遗产	365	60.84%
B. 丁不能与某甲的二儿子丙共同继承，但其可分得适当的遗产	224	37.33%
C. 其他	11	1.83%
合计	600	100%

关于尽了主要赡养义务的丧偶儿媳或女婿的遗产分配方式的民间习惯，调查统计数据显示，600 名被调查者填写的所在地区的习惯是：（1）A 项其与被继承人其他子女共同继承并且平均分配遗产的，占六成（60.84%）；（2）B 项其不可与被继承人其他子女共同继承但其可分得适当遗产的，占三成半以上（37.33%）。

五、遗嘱继承之调查数据统计情况

关于遗嘱继承之调查数据统计，我们主要从公证遗嘱与其他形式遗嘱的效力、遗嘱自由的限制——特留份、夫妻共同遗嘱，这三个方面进行调查数据的统计情况汇总分析。

（一）公证遗嘱与其他形式遗嘱的效力

问题【五、（一）】“退休职工甲有一套个人住房，他于 2011 年 2 月立了一份遗嘱，写明由其妻子乙一人继承该住房，并将该遗嘱进行了公证。后来，甲改变了主意，他重新写了一份遗嘱，写明其妻子乙和儿子丙共同继承该房屋。2016 年 3 月甲住院病危期间，当着二位医生在现场立下口头遗嘱，指定其个人住房由儿子丙继承，两个小时后其抢救无效死亡。请问：您认为，甲的个人住房应该由谁继承？A. 乙；B. 乙和丙；C. 丙。（单选）其理由是什么？”

1. 公证遗嘱与其他形式遗嘱的适用效力的民众观念情况统计

表 3-29　公证遗嘱与其他形式遗嘱的适用效力的民众观念情况统计（单选）

选项	人数	比例
A. 乙（公证遗嘱有效）	195	32.50%
B. 乙和丙（后成立的未公证书面遗嘱有效）	182	30.33%
C. 丙（最后的口头遗嘱有效）	223	37.17%
合计	600	100%

关于公证遗嘱与其他形式遗嘱的适用效力的民众观念，调查统计数据显示，在 600 名被调查者中，（1）选择 B 项和 C 项后遗嘱优先于前一遗嘱（包括公证遗嘱）适用的，合计占六成半以上（67.50%）；（2）选择 A 项公证遗嘱应当优先适用的，占三成以上（32.50%）。

2. 公证遗嘱与其他形式遗嘱的适用效力的民众观念的理由情况统计

表 3-30 公证遗嘱与其他形式遗嘱的适用效力的民众观念的理由情况统计

项目	人数	比例
A. 公证遗嘱的程序规范，具有较强的公示效力和证明效力	234	39.00%
B. 书面遗嘱（第二份遗嘱）比较正式，容易取证，且其订立在公证遗嘱之后，反映了被继承人最后的意愿	72	12.00%
C. 口头遗嘱形式灵活，且有证人作证，能够反映被继承人的最后真实意愿	210	35.00%
D. 口头遗嘱形式不固定，很难准确、完全地反映被继承人的最后真实意愿，且有被篡改或修改的可能性	11	1.83%
E. 其他理由	73	12.17%
合计	600	100%

关于公证遗嘱与其他形式遗嘱的适用效力的民众观念的理由，调查统计数据显示，在600名被调查者中，(1) 认为后遗嘱应当优先于前一遗嘱（包括公证遗嘱）适用的理由是，B项和C项，后遗嘱更能反映遗嘱人最后真实意愿的，合计占近五成（47.00%）；(2) 认为公证遗嘱应当优先适用的理由是，A项公证遗嘱程序规范，具有较强的公示公信力和证明效力的，占近四成（39.00%）。

（二）遗嘱自由的限制——特留份

问题【五、(二)】"甲生前立了一份遗嘱，将自己死后遗留下的财产全部赠给他的一个好朋友乙，而他的配偶和子女不能取得甲的任何遗产。请问：您认为甲的这一做法是否适当？A. 适当；B. 不适当；C. 其他。(单选) 其理由是什么？"

1. 以遗嘱将个人遗产全部赠给他人之民众观念的情况统计

表 3-31 以遗嘱将个人遗产全部赠给他人之民众观念的情况统计（单选）

选项	人数	比例
A. 适当	158	26.33%
B. 不适当	427	71.17%
C. 其他	15	2.50%
合计	600	100%

关于以遗嘱将个人遗产全部赠给他人的民众观念，调查统计数据显示，在600名被调查者中，(1) 选择B项该行为不适当，即应对遗嘱的自由予以限制的，占七成以上(71.17%)；(2) 选择A项该行为适当，即不应对遗嘱的自由予以限制的，仅占二成半以上（26.33%）。

2. 以遗嘱将个人遗产全部赠给他人之民众观念的理由情况统计

表 3-32　以遗嘱将个人遗产全部赠给他人之民众观念的理由情况统计

项目	人数	比例
A. 甲对自己的财产，享有自由处分的权利，其他人无权干涉	311	51. 83%
B. 造成家庭财产外流，不利于保障甲的配偶及其子女的生活，同时也不符合风俗习惯，为常人所难接受	212	35. 33%
C. 其他理由	77	12. 84%
合计	600	100%

关于以遗嘱将个人遗产全部赠给他人之民众观念的理由，调查统计数据显示，在 600 名被调查者中，(1) 认为该行为适当的理由是，A 项被继承人对自己的财产享有自由处分的权利，其他人无权干涉的，占五成以上（51. 83%）；(2) 认为该行为不适当的理由是，B 项该做法会造成家庭财产外流，不利于保障被继承人的生存配偶及其子女的生活，同时也不符合风俗习惯，为常人所难接受，即应对其遗嘱处分个人财产的自由进行限制的，占三成半（35. 33%）。

（三）夫妻共同遗嘱

1. 夫妻共同遗嘱的民众观念与理由情况统计

问题【五、(三) 1.】“甲乙是夫妻，双方在生前共同设立一份遗嘱，对死后的遗产处理进行安排。甲乙双方在遗嘱中约定，不管谁先去世，另一方都不得改变此遗嘱对遗产的处理安排。请问：您是否认同甲乙夫妻双方共同设立遗嘱的此约定？A. 赞同；B. 不赞同。(单选) 其理由是什么?”

(1) 夫妻共同遗嘱的民众观念情况统计。

表 3-33　夫妻共同遗嘱的民众观念情况统计（单选）

选项	人数	比例
A. 赞同	465	77. 50%
B. 不赞同	135	22. 50%
合计	600	100%

关于夫妻共同遗嘱的民众观念，调查统计数据显示，在 600 名被调查者中，①选择 A 项持赞成态度的，占七成半以上（77. 50%）；②选择 B 项持不赞同态度的，占二成以上（22. 50%）。

（2）夫妻共同遗嘱的民众观念之理由情况统计。

表 3-34　夫妻共同遗嘱的民众观念之理由情况统计

项目	人数	比例
A. 该遗嘱为甲乙双方共同设立，反映了双方的共同意愿，理应为双方所遵守	62	10.33%
B. 该遗嘱无法应对出现的新情况和新问题，限制了双方对自己财产的处分权	500	83.33%
C. 其他理由	38	6.33%
合计	600	100%

关于夫妻共同遗嘱的民众观念之理由，调查统计数据显示，在 600 名被调查者中，①认可夫妻共同遗嘱的理由是，B 项该遗嘱反映了双方的共同意愿故应为双方遵守的，占八成以上（83.33%）；②不赞同夫妻共同遗嘱的理由是，A 项该遗嘱无法应对出现的新情况和新问题且限制了双方对各自财产的处分权的，占一成（10.33%）。

2. 夫妻共同遗嘱的民间习惯情况统计

问题【五、（三）2.】"在您所在地区，有无夫妻共同设立遗嘱的情况发生？A. 有；B. 无。（单选）"

表 3-35　夫妻共同遗嘱的民间习惯情况统计（单选）

选项	人数	比例
A. 有	435	72.50%
B. 无	165	27.50%
合计	600	100%

关于夫妻共同遗嘱的民间习惯，调查统计数据显示，600 名被调查者填写的所在地区的习惯是：①A 项有该习惯的，占七成以上（72.50%）；②选择 B 项无该习惯的，占二成半以上（27.50%）。

六、继承和遗赠的接受与放弃之调查数据统计情况

关于继承和遗赠的接受与放弃之调查数据统计，我们主要从继承的接受与放弃的时间与方式、遗赠的接受与放弃的方式与效力、继承的放弃与债权人的撤销权，这三个方面进行调查数据的统计情况汇总分析。

（一）继承的接受与放弃的时间与方式

问题【六、（一）】"继承人放弃继承的时间，您认为下列哪一个更为适当？A. 继承人放弃继承的，应在知道继承开始的 2 个月内作出放弃继承的意思表示；B. 继承开始后继承人放弃继承的，应当在遗产处理前，作出放弃继承的意思表示。（单选）其理由是

什么?”

1. 继承的接受与放弃的时间与方式的民众观念情况统计

表 3-36 继承的接受与放弃的时间与方式的民众观念情况统计（单选）

选项	人数	比例
A. 继承人放弃继承的，应在知道继承开始的 2 个月内作出放弃继承的意思表示	197	32.83%
B. 继承开始后继承人放弃继承的，应当在遗产处理前，作出放弃继承的意思表示	403	67.17%
合计	600	100%

关于继承的接受与放弃的时间与方式的民众观念，调查统计数据显示，在 600 名被调查者中，(1) 选择 B 项继承人应在遗产处理前作出放弃继承的意思表示的，占六成半以上 (67.17%)；(2) 选择 A 项继承人应在知道继承开始的 2 个月内作出放弃继承的意思表示的，仅占三成以上 (32.83%)。

2. 继承的接受与放弃的时间与方式的民众观念之理由情况统计

表 3-37 继承的接受与放弃的时间与方式的民众观念之理由情况统计

项目	人数	比例
A. 2 个月的时间较为合适，可以让继承人有一定的时间去考虑是否放弃继承权，同时，又可以督促继承人积极行使权利	197	32.83%
B. 在遗产处理前，继承人都可以放弃继承权，这样既不影响其他继承人的利益，又可以保证继承人行使放弃继承的权利	403	67.17%
合计	600	100%

关于继承的接受与放弃的时间与方式的民众观念之理由，调查统计数据显示，在 600 名被调查者中，(1) 认为继承人应当在遗产处理前作出放弃继承的意思表示之理由是，B 项这样既不影响其他继承人的利益，又可以保证继承人行使放弃继承的权利的，占六成半以上 (67.17%)；(2) 认为继承人应在知道继承开始的 2 个月内作出放弃继承的表示之理由是，A 项 2 个月的时间较为合适，可以让继承人有一定的时间去考虑是否放弃继承权，同时又可以督促继承人积极行使权利的，占三成以上 (32.83%)。

(二) 遗赠的接受与放弃的方式与效力

问题【六、(二)】“甲生前设立了一份遗嘱，其内容为：在甲死后，将一辆小汽车赠给其侄子乙。后来甲去世，乙得知遗嘱的内容后，对此遗赠没有作出任何意思表示，既没有说接受，也没有说放弃。您认为下列哪一项更为适当？A. 乙无权取得该小汽车，乙的行为应该被视为放弃该遗赠；B. 乙有权取得该小汽车，乙的行为应该被视为接受该遗赠。(单选) 其理由是什么?”

1. 遗赠的接受与放弃的方式与效力的民众观念情况统计

表 3-38　遗赠的接受与放弃的方式与效力的民众观念情况统计（单选）

选项	人数	比例
A. 乙无权取得该小汽车，乙的行为应该被视为放弃该遗赠	199	33.17%
B. 乙有权取得该小汽车，乙的行为应该被视为接受该遗赠	401	66.83%
合计	600	100%

关于遗赠的接受与放弃的方式与效力的民众观念，调查统计数据显示，在 600 名被调查者中，（1）选择 B 项受遗赠人未作表示应认定为接受遗赠的，占六成半以上（66.83%）；（2）选择 A 项受遗赠人未作表示应认定为放弃遗赠的，占三成以上（33.17%）。

2. 遗赠的接受与放弃的方式与效力的民众观念之理由情况统计

表 3-39　遗赠的接受与放弃的方式与效力的民众观念之理由情况统计

项目	人数	比例
A. 接受遗赠毕竟是一种纯获利行为，乙不表示，就应该视为接受；如其不接受，那他早就作出不接受的表示了	401	66.83%
B. 乙有权选择是否接受甲的遗赠，如乙没有表示，就应该视为放弃遗赠，这与现行法规定一致	199	33.17%
合计	600	100%

关于遗赠的接受与放弃的方式与效力的民众观念之理由，调查统计数据显示，在 600 名被调查者中，（1）受遗赠人未作表示应推定为接受遗赠的理由是，A 项接受遗赠是一种纯获利行为的，占六成半以上（66.83%）；（2）受遗赠人未作表示应推定为放弃遗赠的理由是，B 项与现行法规定一致的，占三成以上（33.17%）。

（三）继承的放弃与债权人的撤销权

问题【六、（三）】“甲为乙的父亲，2015 年年底，乙因病住院治疗，医治无效去世，留下遗产 5 万元及房屋一套。此时甲经营的摩配厂已经负债累累，拖欠工人的工资已有 10 个月，但他考虑儿媳在其丈夫乙去世后个人抚养年幼的女儿有经济困难，于是主动提出放弃继承儿子乙的遗产。甲的债权人却认为甲不应放弃继承儿子的遗产，这实际上是逃避债务，侵犯了债权人利益。为此，甲的债权人起诉至法院，要求撤销甲放弃继承儿子乙遗产的行为。您认为下列哪一项更为适当？A. 甲放弃继承乙遗产的行为，可以被撤销；B. 甲放弃继承乙遗产的行为，不可以被撤销。（单选）其理由是什么？请问：您所在地区的人们是如何处理此类行为的？”

1. 继承的放弃行为能否被债权人撤销的民众观念情况统计

表 3-40 继承的放弃行为能否被债权人撤销的民众观念情况统计（单选）

选项	人数	比例
A. 甲放弃继承乙遗产的行为，可以被撤销	289	48.17%
B. 甲放弃继承乙遗产的行为，不可以被撤销	311	51.83%
合计	600	100%

关于继承的放弃行为能否被债权人撤销的民众观念，调查统计数据显示，在600名被调查者中，（1）选择A项持肯定态度的，占近五成（48.17%）；（2）选择B项持否定态度的，占五成以上（51.83%）。

2. 继承的放弃能否被债权人撤销的民众观念之理由情况统计

表 3-41 继承的放弃能否被债权人撤销的民众观念之理由情况统计

项目	人数	比例
A. 不可以被撤销，因为这有利于照顾儿媳及其孙女的生活，她们是弱势群体，理应获得优先照顾	138	53.28%
B. 可以被撤销，因为甲的债权人利益需要被保护	121	46.72%
合计	259	100%

关于继承的放弃能否被债权人撤销的民众观念之理由，调查统计数据显示，在填写该问题的259名被调查者中，（1）认为继承的放弃不可以被债权人撤销的理由是，A项放弃继承的行为有利于照顾其他继承人（特别是被继承人的生存配偶或子女等弱势群体）的利益、继承人有权决定是否继承的，占五成以上（53.28%）；（2）认为继承放弃的行为可以被债权人撤销的理由是，B项继承人的债权人利益需要被保护的，占四成半以上（46.72%）。

3. 继承的放弃能否被债权人撤销的民间习惯情况统计

表 3-42 继承的放弃能否被债权人撤销的民间习惯情况统计（单选）

选项	人数	比例
A. 可以撤销	43	21.29%
B. 不可以撤销	35	17.33%
C. 依据规定诉至法院	124	61.39%
合计	202	100%

关于继承人放弃的行为能否被债权人撤销的民间习惯，调查统计数据显示，在填写该问题的202名被调查者所在地区的习惯是：（1）选择A项和C项可以被撤销的，合计占八成以上（82.68%）；（2）选择B项不可以被撤销的，占一成半以上（17.33%）。

七、继承权的丧失、被继承人的宥恕与代位继承之调查数据统计情况

关于继承权的丧失、被继承人的宥恕与代位继承之调查数据统计，我们主要从继承权的丧失与被继承人的宥恕、继承权的丧失与代位继承，这两个方面进行调查数据的统计情况汇总分析。

（一）继承权的丧失与被继承人的宥恕

问题【七、（一）】“某甲如果以欺诈或者胁迫的手段，迫使或者妨碍其父乙设立、变更或者撤销遗嘱，情节较为严重，但后来其获得乙的原谅。您认为以下哪一种处理更为适当？A. 某甲有资格继承其父遗产；B. 某甲仍然不能继承其父遗产。（单选）”

表3-43　继承权的丧失与被继承人的宥恕的民间观念情况统计（单选）

选项	人数	比例
A. 某甲有资格继承其父遗产	454	75.67%
B. 某甲仍然不能继承其父遗产	146	24.33%
合计	600	100%

关于继承权的丧失与被继承人的宥恕的民众观念，即因欺诈、胁迫行为丧失继承权的，如获得被继承人谅解其继承权是否可以恢复，调查统计数据显示，在600名被调查者中，（1）选择A项可以恢复的，占七成半（75.67%），（2）选择B项不可以恢复的，占近二成半（24.33%）。

（二）继承权的丧失与代位继承

问题【七、（二）】“村民甲死亡后，其子乙因实施伪造遗嘱的行为导致丧失了对其父甲的继承权，乙的儿子丙能否代父乙去继承祖父甲的遗产，您认为以下哪一种处理更为适当？A. 丙能够代父乙继承祖父甲遗产；B. 丙不能代父乙继承祖父甲遗产。（单选）”

表3-44　继承权的丧失的效力是否及于代位继承人的民众观念情况统计（单选）

选项	人数	比例
A. 丙能够代父乙继承祖父甲遗产	165	27.50%
B. 丙不能代父乙继承祖父甲遗产	435	72.50%
合计	600	100%

关于继承权的丧失的效力是否及于代位继承人的民众观念，调查统计数据显示，在600名被调查者中，（1）选择B项不可以代位继承的，占七成以上（72.50%）；（2）选择A项可以代位继承的，占近三成（27.50%）。

八、继承协议之调查数据统计情况

必须说明，本节研究的对象是狭义的继承协议（又称继承扶养协议）。关于继承协议之调查数据统计，我们主要从继承协议的订立主体与方式、继承协议的变更方式及效力，这两个方面进行调查数据的统计情况汇总分析。

（一）继承协议的订立主体与方式

1. 继承协议的订立主体与方式的民众观念情况统计

问题【八、（一）1.】“王某，现年70岁，有长子王一，次女王二，两个子女均已成家且分家另过。王某的老伴因患癌症花费了大量医药费后去世，老夫妻的共同财产现所剩无几，现有郊区的一套住房是王某个人财产。虽然王某退休金不多，但身体没有大病，基本生活还是能够维持的。由于长子王一长期在外地工作，为解决父亲王某的养老送终问题，您认为，如下三种做法哪种较为妥当？A. 父亲王某与次女王二，双方协商并签订协议，由次女王二一人承担赡养父亲王某的义务，王某的全部遗产指定由王二继承；B. 父亲王某与子女王一、王二，三人协商并签订协议，由次女王二一人承担赡养父亲王某的义务，王某的全部遗产商定由王二继承；王一放弃对父亲王某遗产的继承权；C. 子女王一与王二，两人协商并签订协议，由次女王二一人承担赡养父亲王某的义务，王某的全部遗产商定由王二继承；王一放弃对父亲王某遗产的继承权。（单选）”

表3-45 继承协议的订立主体与方式的民众观念情况统计（单选）

选项	人数	比例
A. 父亲王某与次女王二协商一致即可签订协议（第一种方式）	127	21.17%
B. 父亲王某需与全部继承人协商，共同签订协议（第二种方式）	344	57.33%
C. 共同继承人间签订协议即可，无须被继承人知晓或同意（第三种方式）	129	21.50%
合计	600	100%

关于继承协议订立主体与方式的民众观念，调查统计数据显示，在600名被调查者中，对于继承协议的订立，（1）选择B项由被继承人与全体法定继承人共同订立的，占近六成（57.33%）；（2）选择C项由继承人之间签订而无须被继承人知晓或同意的，占二成以上（21.50%）；（3）选择A项由被扶养人与扶养义务人共同签订的，占二成以上（21.17%）。

2. 继承协议的民间习惯情况统计

问题【八、（一）2.】“您过去是否听说或者亲历过有以上类似的情况？A. 听说过或经历过；B. 从没听说或经历过以上情况。（单选）在听说过或经历过签订继承协议的人中，听说过或经历过的方式是哪一种？A. 第一种方式；B. 第二种方式；C. 第三种方式。（多选）”

（1）关于继承协议的民间习惯情况统计。

表 3-46 继承协议的民间习惯情况统计（多选）

选项	人数	比例
A. 听说过或经历过	315	52.50%
B. 从没听说或经历过以上情况	285	47.50%
合计	600	100%

关于继承协议的民间习惯，对于继承协议的签订，调查统计数据显示，600 名被调查者填写的所在地区的习惯是：①A 项听说过或经历过的，占五成以上（52.50%）；②B 项从没有听说或经历过的，占四成半以上（47.50%）。

（2）关于听说过或经历过签订继承协议的方式的民间习惯情况统计。

表 3-47 听说过或经历过签订继承协议的方式的民间习惯情况统计（多选）

选项	人数	比例
A. 第一种方式	127	27.02%
B. 第二种方式	230	48.94%
C. 第三种方式	113	24.04%

关于听说过或经历过签订继承协议的方式之民间习惯，对于继承协议的签订方式，调查统计数据显示，填写该问题的 315 名被调查者所在地区的习惯是：①B 项第二种方式，由被继承人与全体法定继承人共同订立的，占近五成（48.94%）；②A 项第一种方式，由被扶养人与扶养义务人共同签订的，占二成半以上（27.02%）；③C 项第三种方式，由继承人之间签订的，占近二成半（24.04%）。

（二）继承协议的变更方式及效力

1. 继承协议的变更方式与效力的民众观念情况统计

问题【八、（二）】"王某，现年 70 岁，有长子王一，次女王二，三子王三，三个子女均已成家且分家另过。王某的老伴因患癌症花费了大量医药费后去世，现有郊区的一套住房是王某个人财产，市场价约为 30 万元，王某有少量退休金。王某与王二协商并签订继承协议，由王二主要赡养父亲王某，王某的所有遗产由王二继承。协议签订后，王二全家与父亲王某共同生活了 5 年后的一天，王二因意外交通事故死亡。王二全家在与王某共同生活的期间已为王某花费生活费、医疗费等扶养费共 9 万元。为解决王某的养老，您同意下列哪些做法？A. 王二的儿子有继续扶养外祖父王某的能力，王某也愿意与王二的儿子共同生活，应当由王二的儿子继续履行扶养义务，并继承王某的全部遗产；B. 王一、王三共同补偿王二家人 6 万元扶养费后（另有 3 万元扶养费属于应当由王二承担的），如果王一与父亲王某签订新的继承协议，并与王某共同生活一直扶养至其去世，就由王一继承王某的全部遗产；C. 对王二已经支付的扶养费不予补偿，如果王一与父亲王某签订新的继承协议，并与王某共同生活一直扶养至其去世，就由王一继承王某的全部遗产；

D. 王一、王三共同补偿王二家人6万元扶养费后，由两人共同扶养父亲王某；E. 其他。（单选）其理由是什么？”

表3-48 继承协议的变更方式与效力的民众观念情况统计（单选）

选项	人数	比例
A. 原扶养人的子女有扶养能力，在双方自愿的情况下，由原扶养人的子女继续扶养被扶养人，并继承全部遗产	192	32.10%
B. 原签订的继承协议效力终止，补偿原扶养人一定费用后，由某一有扶养能力的法定继承人，在双方自愿的情况下签订新协议，继续扶养被扶养人，并继承遗产	212	35.29%
C. 原签订的继承协议效力终止，对原扶养人无须补偿，应由某一有扶养能力的法定继承人与被扶养人，在双方自愿的情况下签订新协议，继续扶养被扶养人并继承全部遗产	41	6.89%
D. 原签订的继承协议效力终止，补偿原扶养人一定费用后，应由有扶养能力的全体法定继承人，共同依法对被扶养人尽扶养义务，并依法定继承取得遗产	151	25.21%
E. 其他	4	0.51%
合计	600	100%

关于继承协议的变更方式与效力的民众观念，即在继承协议的履行中，如扶养人先于被扶养人去世，被调查者对于该协议的变更方式与效力的认识，统计数据显示，在600名被调查者中，（1）选择A项，认为该协议可有条件继续履行，如原扶养人的子女有扶养能力，在原扶养人的子女和被扶养人双方同意的情况下，可由原扶养人的子女继续履行该继承协议的，此即代位扶养的，占三成以上（32.10%）；（2）选择B项和C项，认为该协议终止，须签订新的继承协议，由新的扶养人履行扶养义务并继承遗产的，合计占四成以上（42.18%），其中，B项认为需要对原扶养人的继承人补偿超过其扶养义务部分费用的，占三成半（35.29%），C项认为不需要对原扶养人的继承人补偿超过其扶养义务部分费用的，占不到一成（6.89%）；（3）选择D项，认为该协议终止，应对原扶养人补偿超过其扶养义务部分费用后，由所有法定继承人共同扶养的，即实行法定赡养的，占二成半（25.21%）。可见，吉林省被调查者对于该协议终止且应重新签订继承协议的认可度最高，B、C两项合计占四成以上。

2. 继承协议的变更方式与效力的民众观念之理由情况统计

表 3-49　继承协议的变更方式与效力的民众观念之理由情况统计

项目	人数	比例
A. 由王二的儿子继续扶养王某，可以使继承协议继续履行，避免产生不必要的纠纷，有利于维持被扶养人一贯的生活方式而安享晚年	276	54.44%
B. 赡养王某是王一和王三的法定义务，根据权利义务相一致原则，王一、王三应当补偿王二家人 6 万元	231	45.56%
合计	507	100%

关于继承协议的变更方式与效力的民众观念之理由，即在继承协议履行过程中，如扶养人先于被扶养人去世，调查统计数据显示，在填写该理由的 507 名被调查者中，(1) 认可原扶养人的子女有扶养能力，在原扶养人的子女和被扶养人双方同意的情况下，可由该子女继续履行该继承协议的理由是，A 项这样可以避免产生不必要的纠纷，有利于维持被扶养人一贯的生活方式而安享晚年的，占近五成半（54.44%）；(2) 认为该继承协议因扶养人死亡已终止，被扶养人的其他法定扶养义务人对已去世的扶养人支付的超出其法定扶养义务的扶养费进行合理补偿的理由是，B 项基于公平原则的，占四成半（45.56%）。

九、遗产债务清偿之调查数据统计情况

关于遗产债务清偿之调查数据统计，我们主要从遗产债务清偿责任的类型、被继承人丧葬费的支付、遗产债务的清偿顺序，这三个方面进行调查数据的统计情况汇总分析。

（一）遗产债务清偿责任的类型

问题【九、(一)】“继承遗产，应当清偿被继承人的债务，您是怎么理解这句话的？A. 对被继承人的生前所有债务，继承人都应当予以偿还；B. 对被继承人的生前所有债务，继承人应先用所有遗产偿还债务，不足部分由继承人以个人财产偿还；C. 对被继承人的生前所有债务，继承人只以继承的遗产为限予以偿还；D. 对被继承人的生前所有债务，继承人如果存在转移遗产、隐瞒遗产的情形，则其应当负责以遗产和其个人财产偿还所有的债务。(多选) 在您所在的地区，人们遇到继承人有转移遗产、隐瞒遗产的情况时，一般是如何处理的？”

1. 继承人遗产债务清偿责任类型的民众观念情况统计

表 3-50　继承人遗产债务清偿责任类型的民众观念情况统计（多选）

选项	人数	比例
A. 对被继承人的生前所有债务，继承人都应当予以偿还	215	35.83%
B. 对被继承人的生前所有债务，继承人应先用所有遗产偿还债务，不足部分由继承人以个人财产偿还	177	29.50%

续表

选项	人数	比例
C. 对被继承人的生前所有债务，继承人只以继承的遗产为限予以偿还	475	79.17%
D. 对被继承人的生前所有债务，继承人如果存在转移遗产、隐瞒遗产的情形，则其应当负责以遗产和其个人财产偿还所有的债务	340	56.67%

关于继承人清偿遗产债务责任类型的民众观念，对于被继承人的债务清偿责任，调查统计数据显示，在600名被调查者中，（1）选择C项，认为只以其继承的遗产承担有限清偿责任的，占近八成（79.17%）；（2）选择A项和B项，认为应承担自愿的无限清偿责任的，合计占六成半（65.33%）；（3）选择D项，认为继承人如有侵害遗产的行为应承担强制的无限清偿责任的，占五成半以上（56.67%）。

2. 继承人侵害遗产的法律责任的民间习惯情况统计

表3-51　继承人侵害遗产的法律责任的民间习惯情况统计（单选）

选项	人数	比例
A. 一般不予以处理	21	58.33%
B. 起诉由法院处理	9	25.00%
C. 以遗产和个人财产偿还所有债	6	16.67%
合计	36	100%

关于继承人侵害遗产的法律责任的民间习惯，即继承人有转移遗产、隐瞒遗产的应如何处理，调查统计数据显示，填写该问题的36名被调查者所在地区的习惯是：（1）A项一般不予以处理的，占近六成（58.33%）；（2）C项起诉由法院处理的，占二成半（25.00%）；（3）B项即对遗产债务承担无限清偿责任的，占一成半以上（16.67%）。

（二）被继承人丧葬费的支付

问题【九、（二）】“在您所在地区，死者的丧葬费一般是如何支付的？A. 由全体继承人共同支付；B. 从被继承人的遗产中支付；C. 其他。（单选）”

表3-52　被继承人丧葬费的支付民间习惯情况统计（单选）

选项	人数	比例
A. 全体继承人共同支付	305	50.83%
B. 从被继承人遗产中支付	292	48.67%
C. 其他	3	0.50%
合计	600	100%

关于被继承人丧葬费的民间支付的民间习惯，调查统计数据显示，600 名被调查者填写的所在地区的习惯是：（1）A 项由全体继承人共同支付的，占五成（50.83%）；（2）B 项从被继承人的遗产中支付的，占近五成（48.67%）。

（三）遗产债务的清偿顺序

问题【九、（三）】“在您所在地区，对被继承人死亡后遗留的以下费用，一般是按哪种先后次序进行清偿的？（1）对民间习惯的处理方式，请填写；（2）您认为，按照哪种进行先后次序进行清偿才比较合理。（多选）”

A. 丧葬费用	D. 欠付的工资	G. 对被继承人扶养较多的人之酌情分配遗产份额
B. 遗产管理等费用	E. 受被继承人扶养人的生活费	H. 遗赠扶养协议写明遗赠的遗产
C. 欠债	F. 税款	

1. 遗产债务清偿顺序的民间习惯情况统计

表 3-53　遗产债务清偿顺序的民间习惯情况统计（多选）

费用	第一顺序		第二顺序		第三顺序		第四顺序		第五顺序		第六顺序		第七顺序		第八顺序	
	人数	比例%	人数	比例%	人数	比例%	人数	比例%	人数	比例%	人数	比例%	人数	比例%	人数	比例%
A.	379	63.17	14	2.33	11	1.83	4	0.67	4	0.67	0	0	9	1.50	0	0
B.	78	13.00	140	23.33	57	9.50	20	3.33	11	1.83	4	0.67	139	23.17	13	2.17
C.	77	12.83	163	27.17	54	9.00	22	3.67	19	3.17	7	1.17	2	0.33	48	8.00
D.	61	10.17	66	11.00	149	24.83	148	24.67	20	3.33	12	2.00	2	0.33	3	0.50
E.	38	6.33	5	0.80	16	2.67	127	21.17	23	3.83	82	13.67	14	2.33	8	1.33
F.	53	8.83	14	2.33	27	4.50	29	4.83	69	11.50	17	2.83	8	1.33	94	15.67
G.	54	9.00	6	1.00	57	9.50	13	2.17	95	15.83	12	2.00	31	5.17	40	6.67
H.	36	6.00	34	5.67	6	1.00	55	9.17	21	3.50	105	17.50	33	5.50	25	4.17

关于遗产债务清偿顺序的民间习惯，各顺序以被调查者选择占比最高的作为统计依据，调查统计数据显示，600 名被调查者填写的所在地区的遗产债务清偿顺序的习惯是：第一顺序“A. 丧葬费用”（占 63.17%）；第二顺序“B. 遗产管理等费用”（占 23.33%）和“C. 欠债”（占 27.17%）；第三顺序“D. 欠付的工资”（占 24.83%）；第四顺序“E. 受被继承人扶养人的生活费”（占 21.17%）；第五顺序“F. 税款”（占 11.50%）和“G. 对被继承人扶养较多的人之酌情分配遗产份额”（占 15.83%）；第六顺序“H. 遗赠扶养协议写明遗赠的遗产”（占 17.50%）。

2. 遗产债务清偿顺序的民众观念情况统计

表 3-54 遗产债务清偿顺序的民众观念情况统计（多选）

费用	第一顺序		第二顺序		第三顺序		第四顺序		第五顺序		第六顺序		第七顺序		第八顺序	
	人数	比例%	人数	比例%	人数	比例%	人数	比例%	人数	比例%	人数	比例%	人数	比例%	人数	比例%
A.	308	51.33	16	2.67	10	1.67	8	1.33	10	1.67	6	1.00	3	0.50	64	10.67
B.	66	11.00	82	13.67	29	4.83	21	3.50	15	2.50	3	0.50	144	24.00	3	0.50
C.	74	12.33	120	20.00	58	9.67	32	5.33	18	3.00	54	9.00	2	0.33	0	0.00
D.	60	10.00	21	3.50	110	18.33	40	6.67	74	12.33	19	3.17	14	2.33	2	0.33
E.	63	10.50	2	0.33	8	1.33	102	17.00	36	6.00	62	10.33	12	2.00	60	10.00
F.	74	12.33	22	3.67	78	13.00	55	9.17	26	4.33	80	13.33	6	1.00	23	3.83
G.	46	7.67	115	19.17	6	1.00	42	7.00	35	5.83	17	2.83	29	4.83	67	11.17
H.	84	14.00	5	0.83	14	2.33	16	2.67	71	11.83	33	5.50	50	8.33	32	5.33

关于遗产债务清偿顺序的民众观念，各顺序以被调查者选择占比最高作为统计依据，调查统计数据显示，600 名被调查者观念中的遗产债务清偿顺序如下：第一顺序“A. 丧葬费用”（占 51.33%）和“H. 遗赠扶养协议写明遗赠的遗产”（占 14.00%）；第二顺序“C. 欠债”（占 20.00%）和“G. 对被继承人扶养较多的人之酌情分配遗产份额”（占 19.17%）；第三顺序“D. 欠付的工资”（占 18.33%）；第四顺序“E. 受被继承人扶养人的生活费”（占 17.00%）；第五顺序“F. 税款”（13.33%）；第六顺序“B. 遗产管理等费用”（占 24.00%）。

十、遗产分割之调查数据统计情况

关于遗产分割之调查数据统计，我们主要从遗产分割的自由与限制、遗产分割瑕疵的担保责任，这两个方面进行调查数据的统计情况汇总分析。

（一）遗产分割的自由与限制

1. 遗产分割的自由与限制的民间习惯与理由情况统计

问题【十、（一）1.】“按您当地的民间习惯，对遗产一般如何开始分割的？A. 由各继承人共同协商后进行分割；B. 只要有继承人要求分割遗产，就得进行分割；C. 对于被继承人以遗嘱禁止分割的遗产，不得进行分割；D. 其他。（多选）其理由是什么？”

（1）遗产分割的自由与限制的民间习惯情况统计。

表 3-55 遗产分割的自由与限制的民间习惯情况统计（多选）

选项	人数	比例
A. 由各继承人共同协商后进行分割	378	63.00%
B. 只要有继承人要求分割遗产，就得进行分割	107	17.83%
C. 对于遗嘱禁止分割的遗产，不得进行分割	99	16.50%
D. 其他	16	2.67%

关于遗产分割的自由与限制的民间习惯，调查统计数据显示，600 名被调查者填写的所在地区的习惯是：①A 项由各继承人共同协商后进行遗产分割的，占六成以上（63.00%）；②B 项只要有继承人要求分割遗产就得进行分割的，占近二成（17.83%）；③C 项当遗嘱禁止分割遗产则不得分割遗产的，占一成半以上（16.50%）。

（2）遗产分割的自由与限制的民间习惯之理由情况统计。

表 3-56 遗产分割的自由与限制的民间习惯之理由情况统计

项目	人数	比例
A. 遗产由各继承人共同继承，遗产分割涉及各继承人的利益，故遗产的分割应共同协商	504	84.00%
B. 每位继承人享有的继承权受法律保护，同时基于效率原则考虑，故继承开始后，基于继承人的要求就可以分割遗产	136	22.67%
C. 遗产是被继承人死亡时遗留下来的个人财产，当然有权通过遗嘱决定遗产的归属和分割	207	34.50%
D. 其他	45	7.5%

关于遗产分割的自由与限制的民间习惯之理由，调查统计数据显示，在填写该理由的被调查者所在地区，①遗产的分割应当由各遗产继承人共同协商的理由是，A 项遗产由各继承人共同继承，遗产分割涉及到各继承人的利益的，占近八成半（84.00%）；②遗嘱人有权通过遗嘱禁止分割遗产的理由是，C 项遗产是被继承人死亡时遗留下来的个人财产，其有权自由处分包括一定期限内禁止分割的，占近三成半（34.50%）；③继承开始后基于继承人的要求就可以分割遗产的理由是，B 项每个继承人享有的继承权受法律保护且也是基于效率原则考虑的，占二成以上（22.67%）。

2. 提出遗产分割请求时间的民间习惯与理由情况统计

问题【十、（一）2.】“老王去世时留有一套家庭居住的房屋（价值 50 万元）、存款 20 万元以及小汽车一辆（价值 10 万元）。老王去世时，其配偶和唯一的儿子小王均在世。请问：如果在您所在地区，老王去世后，其儿子小王是否会马上向其母亲提出分割遗产的请求？A. 会；B. 不会；C. 会提出分割其他遗产的请求，但对其母正在居住房屋的分割需等其母去世后进行；D. 其他。(单选)”

(1) 提出遗产分割请求时间的民间习惯情况统计。

表 3-57 提出遗产分割请求时间的民间习惯的情况统计（单选)

选项	人数	比例
A. 会	77	12.92%
B. 不会	481	80.70%
C. 会提出分割其他遗产的请求，但对其母正在居住房屋的分割需等其母去世后进行	35	5.87%
D. 其他	3	0.50%
合计	596	100%

关于提出遗产分割请求时间的民间习惯，即当被继承人死亡后，其子女继承人是否可以向其母亲（被继承人的生存配偶）提出分割遗产请求，调查统计数据显示，在填写该问题的596名被调查者所在地区的习惯是：①B项不会，即不可提出遗产分割请求的，占八成（80.70%）；②A项和C项会，即可以提出遗产分割请求的，合计占近二成(18.79%)。

(2) 提出遗产分割请求时间的民间习惯之理由情况统计。

表 3-58 提出遗产分割请求时间的民间习惯之理由情况统计

项目	人数	比例
A. 遗产是由小王及其母亲共同继承的，继承开始后，小王有权根据法律规定提出遗产分割的请求，并且有利于防止日后发生不必要的纠纷	245	41.11%
B. 根据当地观念，小王的父亲的遗产就应该由其母亲全部继承，故小王不能向其母亲提出遗产分割的请求，如果提出，会被视作不孝敬老人的表现	178	29.87%
C. 体现孝敬老人，保证老人的晚年生活，小王可以提出分割其他遗产，但对其母正在居住房屋的分割需等其母去世后进行	373	62.53%

关于提出遗产分割请求时间的民间习惯之理由，即当被继承人死亡后，关于其子女可否与母亲提出分割遗产的理由，调查统计数据显示，在填写该理由的被调查者所在地区，①有可以提出遗产分割遗产习惯的，其中：其一，可有条件地提出遗产分割习惯，即其子女不可以提出分割母亲正在居住的房屋但可提出分割其他遗产的理由是，C项体现孝敬老人，保证老人的晚年生活，但对其母正在居住房屋的分割需等其母去世后进行的，占六成以上（62.53%)；其二，可无条件提出遗产分割习惯的理由是，A项符合法律规定并且有利于防止日后发生不必要的纠纷的，占四成以上（41.11%)；②不可以提出遗产分割之

习惯的理由是，B 项根据当地观念，被继承人的遗产就应该由其生存配偶全部继承，故其子女不能向母亲提出遗产分割的请求，如果提出会被视作不孝敬老人的表现的，占近三成（29.87%）。

3. 遗嘱可否限制遗产分割的民众观念与理由情况统计

（1）遗嘱可否限制遗产分割的民众观念与理由情况统计。

问题【十、（一）3.（1）】“甲乙是夫妻，育有一子丙。甲生前立了一份遗嘱，指定由乙和丙共同继承遗产。甲死亡时留下一套家庭住房（价值 50 万元）、存款 20 万元以及小汽车一辆（价值 10 万元）。您认为，甲是否可以在遗嘱中写明在其死后上述房屋在一定期间内不能进行分割？A. 可以；B. 不可以。（单选）其理由是什么？”

①遗嘱可否限制遗产分割的民众观念情况统计。

表 3-59 遗嘱可否限制遗产分割的民众观念的统计情况（单选）

选项	人数	比例
A. 可以	475	79.97%
B. 不可以	119	20.03%
合计	594	100%

关于遗嘱可否限制遗产分割的民众观念，调查统计数据显示，在填写该问题的 594 名被调查者中，Ⅰ. 选择 A 项主张可以的，占近八成（79.97%）；Ⅱ. 选择 B 项主张不可以的，只占二成（20.03%）。

②遗嘱限制遗产分割的理由情况统计。

表 3-60 遗嘱限制遗产分割的民众观念的理由情况统计

项目	人数	比例
A. 这些遗产是甲生前的个人财产，在设立遗嘱时有权决定遗产的分配及其分割	302	92.35%
B. 如果甲在遗嘱中的住房在 20 年内不能分割，不利于发挥物的效用及价值，而且容易发生纠纷	19	5.81%
C. 其他	6	0.92%
合计	327	100%

关于遗嘱限制遗产分割的民众观念的理由，调查统计数据显示，在填写该理由的 327 名被调查者中，Ⅰ. 主张遗嘱可以限制遗产分割的理由是，A 项遗产是被继承人生前的个人财产，在设立遗嘱时有权决定遗产的分配及其分割的，占九成以上（92.35%）；Ⅱ. 主张遗嘱不可以限制遗产分割的理由是，B 项如果被继承人在遗嘱中指定特定遗产在 20 年内不能分割，这不利于发挥物的效用及价值，即遗嘱限制分割的时间不能太长的，占不到一成（5.81%）。

（2）遗嘱限制遗产分割之具体期限的民众观念情况统计。

问题【十、（一）3.（2）】“在上题中，如果您选择A选项，那么该期限多久合适？A. 5年；B. 10年；C. 15年；D. 其他。（单选）”

表3-61　遗嘱限制遗产分割之具体期限的民众观念情况统计（单选）

选项	人数	比例
A. 5年	168	28. 72%
B. 10年	166	28. 38%
C. 15年	55	9. 40%
D. 其他	196	33. 50%
合计	585	100%

关于遗嘱限制遗产分割之具体期限的民众观念，调查统计数据显示，在填写该问题的585名被调查者中，①选择A项5年之内的，占近三成（28. 72%）；②选择B项10年之内的，占近三成（28. 38%）；③选择C项15年之内的，占近一成（9. 40%）；④选择D项其他的，占三成以上（33. 50%）。

（3）继承人协商能否变更遗嘱限制的民间习惯及理由情况统计。

问题【十、（一）3.（3）】“在您所在地区，如果乙和丙一致同意分割上述财产，那么，他们是否可以不遵守甲的遗嘱在一定期间内禁止分割该房屋的规定而进行分割？A. 可以不遵守遗嘱；B. 不可以不遵守遗嘱。（单选）”

表3-62　继承人协商能否变更遗嘱限制的民间习惯情况统计（单选）

选项	人数	比例
A. 可以不遵守遗嘱	271	45. 55%
B. 不可以不遵守遗嘱	324	54. 45%
合计	595	100%

关于继承人协商能否变更遗嘱限制的民间习惯，对于遗嘱对遗产分割的限制是否可以不遵守，调查统计数据显示，填写该问题的595名被调查者所在地区的习惯是：①A项可以不遵守的，占四成半（45. 55%）；②B项不可以不遵守遗嘱的，占近五成半（54. 45%）。

（二）遗产分割瑕疵的担保责任

问题【十、（二）】“村民老王于2016年12月10日因病去世，死亡时他留有50只羊。老王有两个儿子甲和乙，故老王死后，甲、乙各分得25只羊。但在双方分完羊两天之后，乙分得的25只羊中就有2只暴病死亡，这2只羊死亡的原因是在兄弟俩分割前就已经得了羊痘（一种急性传染病）。请问，在您所在地区，如果出现此种情况，这2只羊死亡的损失应该由谁承担？A. 由乙自行承担，羊群已分配完毕，乙分到了2只病羊，应该自认倒霉；B. 由甲和乙共同承担，甲应再分给乙 1 只羊或按 1 只羊的价格进行补偿；C. 按 1 只羊的价格进行补偿，但乙承担大部分损失，甲承担小部分损失；D. 其他。（单选）”

表 3-63　遗产分割瑕疵的担保责任民间习惯情况统计（单选）

选项	人数	比例
A. 由乙自行承担，羊群已分配完毕，乙分到了 2 只病羊，应该自认倒霉	349	58.17%
B. 由甲和乙共同承担，甲应再分给乙 1 只羊或按 1 只羊的价格进行补偿	176	29.33%
C. 按 1 只羊的价格进行补偿，但乙承担大部分损失，甲承担小部分损失	67	11.17%
D. 其他	8	1.33%
合计	600	100%

关于遗产分割瑕疵的担保责任的民间习惯，对于遗产分割的瑕疵，调查统计数据显示，600 名被调查者填写的所在地区的习惯是：（1）B 项和 C 项由共同继承人相互承担的，合计占四成（40.50%）；（2）A 项由分得瑕疵遗产的继承人自行承担，即继承人间不相互承担遗产分割瑕疵担保责任的，占近六成（58.17%）。

十一、无人承受遗产之调查数据统计情况

关于无人承受的遗产之调查数据统计，我们主要从无人承受遗产的归属和无人承受遗产的处理，这两个方面进行调查数据的统计情况汇总分析。

（一）无人承受遗产的归属

1. 城镇居民无人承受遗产的归属主体的民众观念与理由情况统计

问题【十一、（一）1.】“甲生前系城镇居民，其生前未婚且无其他继承人，其死后留下部分遗产，属于无人继承的遗产。您认为甲的遗产归属于下列哪一主体更合适？A. 国家；B. 死者生前所在地的国库；C. 死者生前所在地民政部门的社会福利机构；D. 死者生前所在地的居委会；E. 不是继承人的其他亲属；F. 其他。（单选）”

（1）城镇居民无人承受遗产的归属主体的民众观念情况统计。

表 3-64　城镇居民无人承受遗产的归属主体的民众观念情况统计（单选）

选项	人数	比例
A. 国家	281	46.83%
B. 死者生前所在地的国库	35	5.83%
C. 死者生前所在地民政部门的社会福利机构	59	9.84%

续表

选项	人数	比例
D. 死者生前所在地的居委会	114	19.00%
E. 不是继承人的其他亲属	103	17.17%
F. 其他	8	1.33%
合计	600	100%

关于城镇居民无人承受遗产的归属主体的民众观念，调查统计数据显示，在600名被调查者中，①选择A、B、C、D四个选项，即主张归属主体为社会公共组织（包括归属于国家、死者生前所在地的国库、死者生前所在地民政部门的社会福利机构和死者生前所在地的居委会）的，合计占八成以上（81.50%）；②选择E项，即主张归属主体为自然人（归属于不是继承人的其他亲属）的，占一成半以上（17.17%）。

（2）城镇居民无人承受遗产的归属主体的民众观念之理由情况统计。

表3-65　城镇居民无人承受遗产的归属主体的民众观念之理由情况统计

项目	人数	比例
A. 甲的遗产没有人继承，为规范财产秩序，甲的遗产只能归国家所有，同时，这也与部分国家的做法相一致	32	20.91%
B. 甲的遗产归甲生前所在地的国库，有利于对遗产的清算、管理和利用	41	26.80%
C. 甲的其他亲属是与甲有一定亲属关系且有较密切联系的人，甲的遗产归其他亲戚所有，符合情理	72	47.06%
D. 其他（回馈社会）	8	5.23%
合计	153	100%

关于城镇居民无人承受遗产的归属主体的民众观念之理由，调查统计数据显示，在填写该理由的153名被调查者中，①主张归属主体为社会公共组织，其一，归国家所有的理由是，A项可以规范财产秩序，也与部分国家的做法相一致，占二成（20.91%）；其二，归生前所在地的国库的理由是，B项有利于对遗产的清算、管理和利用，占二成半以上（26.80%）；②主张归属主体为自然人的理由是，C项归不是继承人的其他亲戚所有符合情理，占四成半以上（47.06%）。

2. 农村居民无人承受遗产的归属主体的民众观念情况统计

问题【十一、（一）2.】“甲生前系农村居民，其生前未婚且无其他继承人，其死后留下部分遗产，属于无人继承的遗产。您认为甲的遗产归属于下列哪一主体更合适？A. 死者生前所在地的国库；B. 死者生前所在地民政部门的社会福利机构；C. 死者生前所在的集体经济组织；D. 死者生前所在地的村委会；E. 死者生前所在的村民小组；

F. 不是继承人的其他亲属；G. 其他。（单选）”

表 3-66　农村居民无人承受遗产的归属主体的民众观念情况统计（单选）

选项	人数	比例
A. 死者生前所在地的国库	93	15.50%
B. 死者生前所在地民政部门的社会福利机构	124	20.67%
C. 死者生前所在的集体经济组织	108	18.00%
D. 死者生前所在地的村委会	152	25.33%
E. 死者生前所在的村民小组	7	1.17%
F. 不是继承人的其他亲属	107	17.83%
G. 其他	9	1.50%
合计	600	100%

关于农村居民无人承受遗产的归属主体的民众观念，调查统计数据显示，在 600 名被调查者中，(1) 选择 A、B、C、D、E 五个选项，即归属主体为社会公共组织（包括归属于国家、死者生前所在地的国库、死者生前所在地民政部门的社会福利机构和死者生前所在的集体经济组织、村委会或村民小组）的，合计占八成（80.67%）；(2) 选择 F 项不是继承人的其他亲属，即主张归属主体为自然人的，占一成半以上（17.83%）。

（二）无人承受遗产的处理

1. 无人承受遗产的管理人的产生方式的民众观念及理由情况统计

(1) 无人承受遗产的管理人的产生方式的民众观念情况统计。

问题【十一、（二）1.】“对于无人继承遗产的管理人，您认为下列哪一种产生方式更合适？A. 死者户籍所在地的居委会、村委会或所在单位指定遗产管理人；B. 人民法院指定遗产管理人；C. 民政部门指定遗产管理人；D. 其他。（单选）其理由是什么？”

表 3-67　无人继承遗产管理人产生方式的民众观念情况统计（单选）

选项	人数	比例
A. 死者户籍所在地的居委会、村委会或所在单位指定遗产管理人	181	30.17%
B. 人民法院指定遗产管理人	320	53.33%
C. 民政部门指定遗产管理人	88	14.67%
D. 其他	11	1.83%
合计	600	100%

关于无人继承遗产的管理人产生方式的民众观念，调查统计数据显示，在600名被调查者中，①选择B项由人民法院指定的，占五成以上（53.33%）；②选择A项由死者户籍所在地的居委会、村委会或所在单位指定的，占三成（30.17%）；③选择C项由民政部门指定的，占近一成半（14.67%）。

（2）无人承受遗产的管理人的产生方式的民众观念的理由统计。

表3-68　无人继承遗产的管理人产生方式的民众观念的理由统计

项目	人数	比例
A. 死者户籍所在地的居委会、村委会或所在单位对死者及其遗产的情况比较清楚，由其指定遗产管理人，有利于对遗产进行清算、管理和利用	92	79.31%
B. 人民法院通过法定程序，对遗产进行清算和管理，由其指定遗产管理人，有利于公平保护相关债权人的利益	21	18.10%
C. 人民法院无暇顾及	3	2.59%
合计	116	100%

关于无人继承遗产的管理人产生方式的民众观念之理由，调查统计数据显示，在填写该理由的116名被调查者中，①认为由死者户籍所在地的居委会、村委会或所在单位指定遗产管理人的理由是，A项上述单位对死者及其遗产的情况比较清楚，由其指定遗产管理人有利于对遗产进行清算、管理和利用的，占近八成（79.31%）；②认为由人民法院指定遗产管理人的理由是，B项有利于公平保护相关债权人的利益，占近二成（18.10%）。

2. 无人承受遗产酌分请求权主体的民众观念及民间习惯情况统计

（1）无人承受遗产酌分请求权主体的民众观念情况统计。

问题【十一、（二）2.】“您认为下列哪些人可以酌情分得无人继承的遗产？A. 依靠死者扶养的人；B. 与死者共同生活的人；C. 与死者关系密切且对其帮助较多的人；D. 其他。（多选）请问：您所在地区人们一般是如何分配此类遗产的？”

表3-69　无人承受遗产酌分请求权主体的民众观念情况统计（多选）

选项	人数	比例
A. 依靠死者扶养的人	467	77.83%
B. 与死者共同生活的人	377	62.83%
C. 与死者关系密切且对其帮助较多的人	418	69.67%
D. 其他	38	6.33%

关于无人承受遗产酌分请求权主体的民众观念，调查统计数据显示，在600名被调查者中，有六成至七成的人主张无人承受的遗产的酌分请求权人包括：A项依靠死者扶养的人（占77.83%）；B项与死者共同生活的人（占62.83%）；C项与死者关系密切且对其

帮助较多的人（占 69.67%）。

（2）无人承受遗产酌分请求权主体的民间习惯情况统计。

表 3-70 无人承受遗产酌分请求权主体的民间习惯情况统计（单选）

选项	人数	比例
A. 尽主要赡养义务的人	18	66.67%
B. 依靠死者扶养的人	2	7.41%
C. 非继承人的亲戚	7	25.92%
合计	27	100%

关于无人承受遗产酌分请求权主体的民间习惯，调查统计数据显示，填写该问题的 27 名被调查者所在地区的习惯是：①A 项酌分给尽主要赡养义务的人，占六成半以上（66.67%）；②B 项酌分给依靠死者扶养的人，占不到一成（7.41%）；③C 项酌分给非继承人的亲戚，占二成半多（25.92%）。

十二、遗产处理相关案例的简介与评析

（一）涉及遗产范围界定案例的简介与评析

案情简介：被继承人唐某于 2015 年 2 月 12 日死亡，原告崔某系唐某的母亲，被告计某系唐某的妻子，被告唐某 1 系唐某的女儿。某号出租车系被继承人唐某与计某婚姻关系存续期间取得，现该车由计某管理。因就遗产分割事宜产生纠纷，原告崔某遂诉至法院，要求与被告计某、唐某 1 分割唐某生前留下的出租车及其运营手续。被告计某辩称，出租车是计某婚前个人购买，不属于唐某的遗产，不涉及继承问题。被告唐某 1 称，遵从崔某的意见，要求分割遗产。

法院审理后认为，关于被继承人唐某遗产范围，对于该出租车及其运营手续总价值 30 万元。被告计某称某号出租车及其运营手续的价值系其婚前购买，应属其个人财产，未提供证据证明，且据该车车籍登记记载，该车购买于计某与唐某结婚之后，且产权登记于唐某名下，应认定为计某与唐某夫妻共同财产，即某号出租车及其运营手续的价值系被继承人唐某与计某婚姻关系存续期间所得的共同所有的财产，其中一半价值 15 万元应为被告计某所有，另一半价值 15 万元系被继承人唐某生前个人合法财产应属于唐某的遗产。故法院判决，被继承人唐某遗产价值 15 万元的某号出租车及其运营手续归被告计某所有，被告计某扣除本人应继份 5 万元价值外，自本判决生效之日起 3 日内给付原告崔某人民币 5 万元、给付被告唐某 1 人民币 5 万元。[①]

适用法律分析：本案的争议焦点是遗产范围的认定，即出租车营运手续是否属于遗产。我国《继承法》第 3 条规定："遗产是公民死亡时遗留的个人合法财产，包括：（一）公民

① 参见中国裁判文书网：（2016）吉×民初×号，《崔某与计某、唐某法定继承纠纷一审民事判决书》，载 http://wenshu.court.gov.cn/content/content? DocID=16954c1b-8a56-4544-b929-a7a100a203f7，访问日期：2019 年 2 月 9 日。限于本章篇幅，作者对原案情内容有酌情删改。

的收入；（二）公民的房屋、储蓄和生活用品；（三）公民的林木、牲畜和家禽；（四）公民的文物、图书资料；（五）法律允许公民所有的生产资料；（六）公民的著作权、专利权中的财产权利；（七）公民的其他合法财产。”即我国《继承法》采取列举加兜底的立法模式规定了遗产的种类。但针对本案争议的焦点问题，即出租车的营运手续价值是否为遗产，我国立法中无规定。可见，我国《继承法》中对遗产范围采用列举和兜底结合的立法模式，其优点在于，列举式便于民众认定遗产种类，且兜底式可以为立法中未明确列举为遗产种类的财产权益之认定提供法律依据。

（二）涉及继承开始的通知和公告案例的简介与评析

案情简介：于某（原告）、于某1（被告）系兄妹关系，两人的父亲于某某于1996年3月因病去世，母亲即被继承人姜某某于2006年5月22日去世。姜某某在其丈夫去世后于1999年年初通过房改购得住房一套（涉案房屋），房产部门于2000年1月12日向其颁发了房屋所有权证。姜某某生前于2004年3月22日在某市某区公证处立有一份公证遗嘱，具体内容为“我现住某住房（涉案房屋），原属单位宿舍，房改时我于2000年年初买下产权，我现年事已高，以后怕发生纠纷，所以我立遗嘱。在我去世后，把此房给我的儿子于某继承”。在2006年5月22日姜某某去世后，被告于某1通过吉林省某市某公证处以“姜某某未收养其他子女，故姜某某的上述遗产由其长女于某1继承”为由出具了某号《继承权公证书》。某市住房保障和房地产管理局据此公证书将上述房屋于2006年10月变更至被告于某1名下，并于2006年10月9日向其发放了涉案房屋的新的所有权证。现原告于某诉至法院，要求继承涉案房产。被告于某1辩称，原告于某出国近20年，不但拿走了父母的所有积蓄，在此期间对母亲也不闻不问，没有尽到任何赡养义务，而被告于某1对母亲全心全意照料和赡养，直至母亲去世。故请求法院本着公平正义的法律原则，判决由被告继承房屋总价值中的20万元。

法院审理后认为，依据我国《继承法》第5条“继承开始后，按照法定继承办理；有遗嘱的，按照遗嘱继承或者遗赠办理”及第16条“公民可以依照本法规定立遗嘱处分个人财产”、第17条“公证遗嘱由遗嘱人经公证机关办理”的规定，被继承人姜某某在生前立有一份公证遗嘱，明确其个人所有的涉案房产由原告继承。该遗嘱有被继承人姜某某签字及手印，有某公证处出具的公证书，符合相关法律规定，应当认定合法有效。对于被告于某1主张的其在原告出国期间一直负责照顾姜某某，应当获得相应的遗产。对此，本院认为，被告在姜某某去世后，在没有通知其他继承人即原告的情况下，故意隐瞒事实致使房产部门作出错误的房产变更登记，造成姜某某所留遗产由其一人继承，侵害了其他继承人即原告的合法权益，故对被告该项主张本院亦不予支持。依据被继承人所立的公证遗嘱，故法院判决被继承人姜某某生前所留遗产即涉案房产由原告于某继承。[①]

适用法律分析：本案争议的焦点为继承开始的通知主体未履行通知义务应承担何种责任。我国《继承法》第23条规定：“继承开始后，知道被继承人死亡的继承人应当及时通知其他继承人和遗嘱执行人。继承人中无人知道被继承人死亡或者知道被继承人死亡而

---

① 参见中国裁判文书网：（2017）吉×民初×号，《于某1与于某2继承纠纷一审民事判决书》，载 http://wenshu.court.gov.cn/content/content? DocID=7031529f-758d-4c72-95eb-a81700dcadfb，访问日期：2019年2月9日。限于本章篇幅，作者对原案情内容有酌情删改。

不能通知的，由被继承人生前所在单位或者住所地的居民委员会、村民委员会负责通知”。在本案中，作为继承人之一的被告于某1故意隐瞒被继承人死亡的事实，不通知其他继承人参与继承，并隐瞒共同继承人的存在，办理遗产继承人公证书后变更了涉案房产的登记，导致其他继承人的继承权益受到侵害。该审理法院根据我国《继承法》第5条和第17条的规定，按照被继承人所立公证遗嘱，判决涉案遗产房屋由原告于某继承，于法有据。通过上述案例分析可以发现，我国《继承法》存在以下不足：第一，未规定继承开始的通知之方式和期间；第二，立法没有规定通知主体因故意或重大过失不履行继承开始的通知义务的法律责任，不利于公平保障继承人和其他遗产利害关系人的权益。

（三）涉及遗产管理案例的简介与评析

案情简介：被继承人赵某某向原告孙某某陆续借款多笔，2010年11月14日，赵某某出具借据一份，借据内容为今借孙某某现金贰拾捌万柒仟元整。同日，孙某某作为甲方与赵某某作为乙方签订还款协议书一份，约定赵某某从孙某某处借现金28.7万元，到2011年5月底一次性还清。2013年4月9日，赵某某向孙某某出具还款计划，上载明：在孙某某借款和利息在某法院判决后马上还清。赵某某于2014年死亡，赵某某与前妻于1999年离婚。赵某某父母均先于赵某某死亡。赵某某与前妻共育有赵1、赵2、赵3、赵4、赵5五名子女，赵某某死亡时，留有坐落于某小区某号楼房屋（涉案房屋）。原告孙某某迫于无奈只能诉请法院判决赵某某的五名继承人偿还本金和利息。

本案在诉讼过程中，五名被告赵1、赵2、赵3、赵4、赵5于2017年11月17日向受理法院书面作出放弃继承房屋的意思表示，并辩称五名被告均已放弃继承，故无须承担清偿赵某某生前的债务。

法院审理后认为，赵某某向孙某某借款28.7万元事实，有协议书、借据、还款计划予以证实。合法的借贷关系受法律保护。借贷期满后，赵某某应当履行归还欠款的义务。赵某某因病去世后，赵1、赵2、赵3、赵4、赵5作为赵某某法定继承人，虽在遗产处理前表示放弃继承，但仍应作为赵某某的遗产管理人，并应承担以其所管理的遗产的实际价值为限偿还被继承人债务的责任。故法院判决，被告赵1、赵2、赵3、赵4、赵5应以遗产实际价值为限偿还被继承人债务。①

适用法律分析：本案的争议焦点是在被继承人死亡后，所有法定继承人均表示放弃继承时，遗产管理人的确定以及其是否应当履行清偿被继承人生前债务的义务。我国《继承法》第24条规定：“存有遗产的人，应当妥善保管遗产，任何人不得侵吞或者争抢。”且第33条规定：“继承遗产应当清偿被继承人依法应当缴纳的税款和债务，缴纳税款和清偿债务以他的遗产实际价值为限。超过遗产实际价值部分，继承人自愿偿还的不在此限。继承人放弃继承的，对被继承人依法应当缴纳的税款和债务可以不负偿还责任。”在本案中，全部法定继承人均表示放弃继承，在遗产无人继承且债务无人偿还的情况下，法院判令放弃继承权的继承人仍应作为遗产管理人，并以其管理的遗产的实际价值为限偿还被继承人的债务，是合理的。但由本案可见我国《继承法》存在以下不足：第一，缺少

---

① 参见中国裁判文书网：（2016）吉×民初×号，《原告孙某某诉被告赵某某民间借贷纠纷案》，载 http://wenshu.court.gov.cn/content/content? DocID=3036e02b-b53d-4419-8ebb-0940bf0fa093，访问日期：2019年2月10日。限于本章篇幅，作者对原案情内容有酌情删改。

对遗产管理人的选任的规定；第二，缺少对遗产管理人的具体职责与权利的规定，不能依法引导遗产管理人履行管理职责，不利于保护遗产债权人等遗产利害关系人的合法权益。

（四）涉及法定继承案例的简介与评析

案情简介：被告唐某某与被继承人王某某系夫妻关系，被告王某甲、王某乙系两人的女儿，王某丙系两人的儿子，原告李某某与王某丙系夫妻关系，被告王某丁系李某某与王某丙的婚生女儿，被继承人王某某的孙女。王某丙于2011年3月21日因病去世，被继承人王某某于2011年9月17日因病去世。2010年6月至2013年10月居住在王某乙家中，两人日常花销及住院花费均不用儿女负担。2011年3月21日原告李某某在丈夫王某丙因病去世后，原告李某某与王某丁一直前往医院悉心照料二老的日常饮食，对时常癌症病发住院的被继承人也是尽心尽力服侍及精神抚慰，履行着主要赡养责任。原告一直照料到被继承人2011年9月17日因肺癌去世。原告作为被继承人的丧偶儿媳，以对两位老人尽了主要赡养义务为由，请求法院确认原告与四名被告共同作为被继承人王某某的第一顺序继承人参与遗产分配。四名被告辩称：原告从未与王某某和唐某某一起生活，更没尽到赡养义务，不具继承人资格。

法院审理后认为：我国《继承法》第12条规定，“丧偶儿媳对公、婆，丧偶女婿对岳父、岳母尽了主要赡养义务的，作为第一顺序继承人”。1985年《执行继承法意见》第30条规定：“对被继承人生活提供了主要经济来源，或在劳务等方面给予了主要扶助的，应当认定其尽了主要赡养义务或主要扶养义务。”本案原告及被告均认可，被继承人王某某经济独立，原告李某某及王某乙、王某甲等均不需在经济来源方面提供帮助，被继承人王某某与被告唐某某多年来住在女儿王某乙家中，不与原告同住，虽然可以认定在王某丙去世后，原告李某某仍然前往医院照顾过因病住院的王某某，但是不能提供证据证明其尽到了主要的赡养义务，其要求确认为第一顺序继承人没有事实和法律依据。遂法院判决驳回原告李某某的诉讼请求。①

适用法律分析：本案的争议焦点是如何认定丧偶儿媳或丧偶女婿尽了主要赡养义务。在本案中，作为丧偶儿媳的李某某以其对被继承人尽了主要赡养义务为由请求作为第一顺序继承人参与继承，但法院认为尽了主要赡养义务是指对被继承人生活提供了主要经济来源，或在劳务等方面给予了主要扶助等情况，因而驳回了原告的诉讼请求。

我们认为，通过上述的案例分析，可见我国《继承法》存在以下不足：第一，对尽了主要赡养义务的定义没有明确规定。虽然1985年《执法继承法意见》第30条规定：“对被继承人生活提供了主要经济来源，或在劳务等方面给予了主要扶助的，应当认定其尽了主要赡养义务或主要扶养义务。”但该规定并未被广大民众所了解，以致在现实生活中容易发生此类的继承纠纷。第二，将对公、婆，丧偶女婿对岳父、岳母尽了主要赡养义务的丧偶儿媳或女婿作为第一顺序继承人，可能会导致遗产分配不公。因为该规定忽略了在现实生活中该丧偶儿媳或女婿的子女依然可以作为代位继承人参与第一顺序的继承，按照在继承人间平均分配遗产的规则，丧偶儿媳或女婿及其子女就可能获得双份遗产份额，

① 参见中国裁判文书网：（2015）宽民初字第×号，《李某某与唐某某、王某甲、王某乙、王某丙继承纠纷一审民事判决书》，载 http://wenshu. court. gov. cn/content/content? DocID=896acb66-ec91-4bb3-825c-fd18b8c8102d，访问日期：2019年2月9日。限于本章篇幅，作者对原案情内容有酌情删改。

有失遗产的公平分配。此外，特别是在被继承人无其他第一顺序继承人的情况下，丧偶儿媳或女婿有可能一人继承所有遗产，不利于保护被继承人第二顺位的血亲继承人继承利益。第三，忽略了我国民众被继承人遗产不外传的传统继承习惯。丧偶儿媳或女婿作为与被继承人无血缘关系的继承人，其继承遗产后有权带产再婚，导致被继承人的遗产流出家庭之外，这很难被其他法定继承人接受。综上，我国此立法有待修正。

（五）涉及遗嘱继承案例的简介与评析

案情简介：郎某某与赵某某于1963年10月登记结婚，婚后生育长子赵某甲、长女被告赵某乙、次女原告赵某丙。1976年，双方登记离婚。2003年5月23日，赵某某购买了一套职工住房（涉案房屋）。2009年8月5日，赵某某立公证遗嘱一份，内容为：赵某某于2003年10月工伤退休，因公致残不能自理，一直与赵某丙共同生活，由其护理；赵某某自愿将房屋（涉案房屋，现闲置，已列于搬迁安置房屋，待安置）及终年后的抚恤金由赵某丙继承；如安置新区房屋也归赵某丙所有；遗嘱写明以赵某丙为其养老送终为条件。赵某某的房屋拆迁后，某市人民政府为其安置位于某路某单元63.37平方米楼房，该房屋被登记在赵某某名下，由原告赵某丙与赵某某共同生活居住。赵某某于2013年2月6日搬到被告赵某乙家居住。赵某某于2013年3月2日向人民法院提起诉讼，要求原告赵某丙腾出房屋，返还房屋产权证书、户口簿、身份证、工资本、医保卡等物品。其间，赵某某于2013年3月9日挂失补办工资本、4月9日又公告补办了房屋产权证书。同年5月14日，赵某某立代书遗嘱一份，指定其名下的位于某路某单元63.37平方米楼房及抚恤金由赵某乙继承。赵某某向受理法院提起的民事案件于2013年8月21日开庭审理。因赵某某于2013年8月30日突发疾病经抢救无效死亡，受理法院裁定该案终结诉讼。赵某某去世后，原告赵某丙与被告赵某乙共同操办了丧事，出席了葬礼。被告赵某乙领取了赵某某单位支付的一次性抚恤金31339.48元。被告用该款支付了合理的丧葬费6251元，并于2014年8月3日交付给郎某某（被继承人的前妻）1.2万元。遂原告赵某丙诉至法院，要求法院确认赵某某于2009年8月5日所立的遗嘱有效，按照遗嘱继承涉案房产，并分割抚恤金。被告赵某乙辩称：2009年8月5日的公证遗嘱内容与赵某某的生前行为相抵触，应依法推定为撤销公证遗嘱；并应按照2013年5月14日赵某某的代书遗嘱继承遗产，且赵某某的抚恤金在性质上不是遗产，不能继承。

法院审理后认为，赵某某于2009年8月5日所立的公证遗嘱及2013年5月14日所立代书遗嘱均为赵某某的真实意思表示，故该两份遗嘱中关于房屋的遗嘱均合法有效。因抚恤金不属于遗产，故该两份遗嘱中有关抚恤金的遗嘱无效。赵某某的生前起诉行为不能推定为撤销其所立的公证遗嘱。根据1985年《执行继承法意见》第39条："遗嘱人生前的行为与遗嘱的意思表示相反，而使遗嘱处分的财产在继承开始前灭失、部分灭失或所有权转移、部分转移的，遗嘱视为被撤销或部分被撤销"和第42条："遗嘱人以不同形式立有数份内容相抵触的遗嘱，其中有公证遗嘱的，以最后所立公证遗嘱为准；没有公证遗嘱的，以最后所立的遗嘱为准"的规定，虽然赵某某于2013年3月2日向某市人民法院提起诉讼，要求原告腾出房屋，返还房屋产权证书、户口簿、身份证、工资本、医保卡等物品，但该部分主张系基于物权主张，并未明确行使撤销公证遗嘱，该起诉行为并不能导致上述的财产在继承开始前灭失、部分灭失或所有权转移、部分转移法律事实的发生，故不能据此推定赵某某撤销了其所立的公证遗嘱。公证遗嘱效力优于代书遗嘱，原告赵某丙对被继承人赵某某履行了养老送终的义务，应由原告赵某丙继承争议房屋。依据被继承人的公证遗嘱，故法院判决，涉案房产归原告赵某丙所有。[①]

适用法律分析：本案争议焦点为被继承人所立的两份遗嘱是否有效且其生前的起诉行为能否撤销其所立的公证遗嘱。我国《继承法》第 20 条第 2 款规定："自书、代书、录音、口头遗嘱，不得撤销、变更公证遗嘱。" 1985 年《执行继承法意见》第 42 条，"遗嘱人以不同形式立有数份内容相抵触的遗嘱，其中有公证遗嘱的，以最后所立公证遗嘱为准"。在本案中，被继承人生前先后立有公证遗嘱与代书遗嘱两份遗嘱，被继承人去世前曾向法院起诉要求公证遗嘱的继承人腾出房屋，返还房屋产权证书、户口簿、身份证、工资本、医保卡等物品。法院依据我国《继承法》的规定认定公证遗嘱效力优于代书遗嘱，且被继承人生前起诉行为不能撤销其所立的公证遗嘱。

我们认为，通过上述的案例分析可发现，我国《继承法》关于遗嘱效力的规定存在以下不足：第一，对公证遗嘱最高效力的规定不合理。在被继承人生前立有多份遗嘱的情况下，认为公证遗嘱的最高效力，这会导致不能实现被继承人最后的遗嘱处分意愿。第二，公证遗嘱一旦设立，其变更、撤销只能在公证机关经由公证程序办理。在被继承人对遗产分配意图发生变动时，在现实中变更、撤销公证遗嘱既耗时又费力，极易引起纠纷。

（六）涉及继承和遗赠的接受与放弃案例的简介与评析

案情简介：肇某 1 与肇某 2 系表兄弟关系。被继承人肇某某系肇某 2 的父亲、亦是肇某 1 的叔叔。孙某与被继承人肇某某系夫妻关系，双方于 1986 年 11 月 20 日登记结婚，双方均为再婚。2008 年 5 月 19 日，被继承人肇某某立遗嘱一份，载明"……我今年 76 岁，为了在我去世后，在财产分割上不发生纠纷，特立此遗嘱：1. 涉案房屋 1 号（房改房）；2. 涉案房屋 2 号。上述两套房屋属于我和后妻子孙某的共有财产，在我去世后，两套房屋的一半由肇某 1（我的侄子）继承"。肇某某于 2016 年 1 月 25 日因病去世。孙某曾于 2016 年 9 月 18 日作为原告起诉肇某 2 继承纠纷一案诉讼至受理法院，2016 年 12 月 21 日，孙某与肇某 2 之间的继承纠纷案件经法院开庭审理，当时孙某申请撤诉。当日原告肇某 1 才从被告肇某 2 处得知叔叔肇某某生前立下自书遗嘱，并将两套房屋的各一半部分遗赠给原告肇某 1。2017 年 1 月 4 日，原告肇某 1 以孙某和肇某 2 为被告诉至法院，请求依法认定肇某某于 2008 年 5 月 19 日立下的自书遗嘱合法有效；并依法认定涉案房屋 1 号和涉案房屋 2 号中肇某某的个人部分（两套房屋各一半份额）按照遗嘱，要求两被告执行遗赠，由原告肇某 1 取得该遗赠房产。被告孙某辩称，原告接受遗赠的表示已超时效，应视为放弃受遗赠。

法院审理后认为：公民可以立遗嘱将个人财产赠给国家、集体或者法定继承人以外的人，故本案应按遗赠办理。至于孙某认为肇某 1 未在知道受遗赠后 2 个月内，作出接受遗赠的表示，视为放弃受遗赠的抗辩理由。受理法院合议庭认为，继承开始后，受遗赠人应

① 参见无讼网：（2014）蛟民一初字第×号，《赵某某、赵某甲、郎某某与被告赵某乙遗嘱继承纠纷一审民事判决书》，载 https://www.itslaw.com/detail? judgementId = fc558ab9 - 1605 - 40f4 - bdd4 - 614e74248031&area = 0&index = 1&sortType = 1&count = 35&conditions = searchWord%2B%E8%A2%AB%E5%91%8A%E8%B5%B5%E6%9F%90%E4%B9%99%2B1%2B%E8%A2%AB%E5%91%8A%E8%B5%B5%E6%9F%90%E4%B9%99&conditions = searchWord%2B%E5%85%AC%E8%AF%81%E9%81%97%E5%98%B1%2B1%2B%E5%85%AC%E8%AF%81%E9%81%97%E5%98%B1，访问日期：2019 年 2 月 9 日。限于本章篇幅，作者对原案情内容有酌情删改。

当在知道受遗赠后 2 个月内，作出接受的表示。到期没有表示的，视为放弃受遗赠。被继承人肇某某去世后，2016 年 12 月 21 日，在孙某与肇某 2 的继承纠纷案件中肇某 2 出示遗嘱，孙某才得知肇某某写有遗嘱一事，肇某 2 则表示是在该案孙某撤诉后才告知肇某 1，孙某无证据证明肇某 1 事先知道遗嘱一事，且肇某 1 已向法院起诉，作出接受遗赠的表示，故孙某的抗辩理由不成立。故法院判决，被继承人肇某某于 2008 年 5 月 19 日所立的自书遗嘱合法有效，涉案房屋 1 号和涉案房屋 2 号中各属于遗嘱人肇某某的 50%的份额由原告肇某 1 取得。[①]

适用法律分析：本案争议的焦点为接受或放弃遗赠的方式及效力问题。我国《继承法》第 25 条规定，“继承开始后，受遗赠人应当在知道受遗赠后两个月内，作出接受或者放弃受遗赠的表示。到期没有表示的，视为放弃受遗赠”。在本案中，被告称受遗赠人在遗赠开始后的 2 个月内没有作出接受遗赠的意思表示，即为放弃受遗赠。而受遗赠人称其此前不知自己受到遗赠的事实，且被告无法证明其已告知肇某 1 遗赠的情况。故受理法院的判决于法有据。

我们认为，通过此案例分析可发现，我国《继承法》对接受或放弃遗赠的规定之不足：一是遗赠作为单方民事行为，被继承人表示遗赠的意思即成立并在继承开始后生效，除非受遗赠人明确表示放弃遗赠，否则立法不宜推定受遗赠人的未作表示的即为放弃遗赠之表示。二是未规定任何主体有义务通知受遗赠人关于继承开始的事宜或其受遗赠的事项。因此，在实现生活中，继承人为了避免遗产落入受遗赠人之手，常常隐瞒被继承人关于遗赠之遗嘱，而受遗赠人对该遗赠往往也不知晓。因此，立法要求受遗赠人在其应当在知道受遗赠后 2 个月内作出接受或放弃遗赠的表示，否则推定为放弃受遗赠，缺乏合理性。

（七）涉及继承权的丧失、被继承人的宥恕与代位继承案例的简介与评析

案情简介：刘某某生前共生育四子，即长子刘某甲、次子刘某乙、三子刘某丙、四子刘某丁。刘某丁曾因销毁刘某某自书遗嘱情节严重而丧失继承权。但刘某某生病期间，刘某丁对刘某某百般照顾。刘某某在临终前口头表示允许刘某丁与刘某甲、刘某乙、刘某丙共同继承其唯一的遗产房屋。刘某某于 2001 年死亡，涉案房产一直未分割。上述涉案房屋于 2014 年 6 月 24 日被拆迁。该房估价为 130529 元。刘某甲与某市土地房屋征收管理办公室签订了一份房屋产权调换协议，调换了一处楼房。现原告刘某丁要求参与继承，并请求三被告即刘某甲、刘某乙、刘某丙立即支付原告刘某丁拆迁补偿款 32632. 25 元而诉至法院。三被告刘某甲、刘某乙、刘某丙辩称，刘某丁因销毁刘某某遗嘱且情节严重而丧失继承权，故无权分得拆迁补偿款。

法院审理后认为，根据我国《继承法》第 7 条规定，继承人“伪造、篡改或者销毁遗嘱，情节严重的”丧失继承权。1985 年《执行继承法意见》第 13 条规定：“继承人虐待被继承人情节严重的，或者遗弃被继承人的，如以后确有悔改表现，而且被虐待人、被遗弃人生前又表示宽恕，可不确认其丧失继承权。”但立法并未规定，如果继承人实施了

---

① 参见中国裁判文书网：（2017）吉×民初×号，《肇某 1 与孙某、肇某 2 遗赠纠纷一审民事判决书》，载 http://wenshu. court. gov. cn/content/content? DocID=d552e263-02ea-43b4-8007-a82a00b3b8a9，访问日期：2019 年 2 月 10 日。限于本章篇幅，作者对原案情内容有酌情删改。

“伪造、篡改或者销毁遗嘱，情节严重的”行为而丧失继承权后，在获得被继承人的宽恕后其继承权是否可以恢复。刘某丁因销毁刘某某自书遗嘱情节严重而丧失继承权，恢复继承权于法无据。

故法院判决驳回原告刘某丁的诉讼请求。宣判后，刘某丁不服，向受理法院提起上诉。二审法院查明的事实与原审认定的事实一致，判决维持原判。①

适用法律分析：本案争议焦点是刘某丁是否可以恢复继承权。我国《继承法》第7条规定，继承人因故意杀害被继承人、或为争夺遗产而杀害其他继承人的遗弃被继承人、或虐待被继承人情节严重、或伪造、篡改或者销毁遗嘱情节严重的均丧失继承权。但从法理上分析，继承人虐待被继承人情节严重的，或者遗弃被继承人的（该情节较为严重，涉及侵害被继承人的生命权）行为性质比伪造、篡改或者销毁遗嘱情节严重的行为（该情节相对较轻，只妨碍了被继承人的遗嘱自由权）更为恶劣，立法规定“继承人虐待被继承人情节严重的，或者遗弃被继承人如以后确有悔改表现，而且被虐待人、被遗弃人生前又表示宽恕，可不确认其丧失继承权”，却没有规定“因伪造、篡改或者销毁遗嘱情节严重而丧失继承权的”可否因为被继承人的宽恕而恢复继承权。因此，我们认为，我国《继承法》未规定此情形下继承人丧失继承权后可恢复继承权，此为立法之不足。

（八）涉及继承协议案例的简介与评析

案情简介：刘某某、殷某某生前共抚育了四个子女，分别为刘某1、刘某2、刘某3、刘某4。涉案房屋一套登记在刘某某名下，共有人为殷某某。刘某某去世后，殷某某也于2016年2月3日去世。2016年1月30日，刘某1、刘某2、刘某3、刘某4共同签署《协议书》一份，主要内容为：父亲刘某某已去世，母亲殷某某现由儿子刘某3赡养送终；父母房屋一套，各协议人同意该处房产以后由刘某3继承，协议人均自愿同意放弃对该处房产的继承权。事后，原告刘某1、刘某2向法院起诉，要求继承父母涉案房屋遗产的三分之二继承权，理由是签订继承协议时，存在胁迫情节，非上诉人真实意思表示；并且继承协议签订时，殷某某尚未去世，未征得殷某某同意就对其财产进行处理，明显违反法律规定，该协议不具备法律效力。被告刘某3辩称，该继承协议是继承人对遗产进行处分的真实意思表示，符合民事法律意思自治原则，也不违反法律强制性规定，为有效的法律行为，继承人应予以遵守。

一审法院另查明，刘某4已明确表示放弃对涉案房屋的继承权。

一审法院审理后认为，关于双方争议的房屋，第一顺序继承人在该房屋全部转化为遗产之前，已经通过协议的方式共同事先约定由刘某3继承，该协议并不违反法律、行政法规的强制性规定，在被继承人全部去世后对协议的各方均具有法律约束力。刘某1、刘某2虽诉称协议签订时并非自己真实意思表示，但未能提供确实充分的证据予以佐证，且刘某3对此亦不予认可，故法院不予采信。

故一审法院判决驳回刘某2、刘某1的诉讼请求。刘某1、刘某2不服一审判决，上诉至二审法院。二审法院审理查明的事实与一审法院查明的事实一致，判决驳回上诉，维

① 参见中国裁判文书网：(2016) 吉×民终×号，《刘某甲、刘某乙、刘某丙与刘某戊继承纠纷二审民事判决书》，载 http://wenshu.court.gov.cn/content/content? DocID = 63d73417 - 76e9 - 48e8 - a9a0 - 3f9d8ef8281b，访问日期：2019年2月9日。限于本章篇幅，作者对原案情内容有酌情删改。

持原判。①

适用法律分析：本案争议焦点是该《协议书》是否有效。在本案中，法定继承人相互间签订继承协议对被继承人死亡后的遗产分配和被继承人的生前扶养问题作出约定。法院认为，只要协议内容不违反法律、法规的强制性规定，就可以认为是当事人之间的合意，理应合法有效。我们认为，通过以上的案例分析，可以发现我国《继承法》存在以下不足：一是没有对继承协议予以定义和认可。实际上，继承协议在我国民众的生活中时有发生，成为民众所采用的一种约定遗产分配和解决养老问题、防止继承纠纷发生的方式。二是也没有对继承协议的具体形式、签订主体和方式、变更及效力等作出规定。这导致法院在认定继承协议的效力时，对继承协议的具体条款、格式是否合法于法无据，这容易造成同案不同判的情况发生。

（九）涉及遗产债务清偿案例的简介与评析

案情简介：2014 年 12 月 22 日马某某向李某借款 3 万元，并出具欠据一张。2015 年 9 月 10 日马某某去世。马某某之女马某 1 系马某某唯一合法继承人，承继了马某某的全部财产。马某某生前贷款购买房屋一套，马某 1 于 2016 年 2 月 15 日提前偿还该房贷款 166684.65 元，并于 2016 年 7 月 8 日将该房屋以 30 万元价格出售。现该房屋已过户到王某某名下。马某某于 2008 年 3 月 17 日购买小型轿车一辆。马某某去世后，马某 1 于 2016 年 4 月 8 日将该车出卖给王某甲，并已更名过户。为此原告李某多次找马某 1 要求其偿还其父亲生前的欠款，被告拒不偿还，原告李某遂诉至法院要求马某 1 偿还其父亲生前的欠款。被告马某 1 辩称房屋出卖款扣除自己垫付偿还贷款部分，剩余部分已经用于偿还朱某某、张某某、徐某的债务，故无剩余遗产偿还李某的欠款。

法院审理后认为：根据我国《继承法》第 33 条的规定，继承遗产应当清偿被继承人依法应当缴纳的税款和债务，缴纳税款和清偿债务以他的遗产实际价值为限。继承人放弃继承的，对被继承人依法应当缴纳的税款和债务可以不负偿还责任。马某 1 作为马某某唯一的继承人，在马某某去世之后，将马某某房屋一套和小型汽车一辆出卖，并均已更名过户。证明马某 1 已经继承了其父马某某的一辆小汽车和一处房产的事实。马某 1 称房屋出卖款扣除自己垫付偿还贷款部分，剩余部分已经用于偿还朱某某、张某某、徐某的债务，但其提供的证据不足以证明朱某某、张某某、徐某三人与在马某某生前彼此之间存在真实有效的债权债务关系，也就不能证明其所继承的遗产已用于清偿被继承人债务的事实，且原告李某否认，故本院对此不予认定。故法院判决，马某 1 应在继承遗产范围内承担马某某生前所欠债务的清偿责任。②

适用法律分析：本案争议焦点是继承人是否应当对被继承人的债务承担清偿责任。我国《继承法》第 33 条："继承遗产应当清偿被继承人依法应当缴纳的税款和债务，缴纳税款和清偿债务以他的遗产实际价值为限……继承人放弃继承的，对被继承人依法应当缴

① 参见中国裁判文书网：（2017）豫×民终×号，《刘某 1、刘某 2 继承纠纷二审民事判决书》，载 http://wenshu.court.gov.cn/content/content? DocID = c056a34b - 56eb - 4609 - 867a - a86c00e79317，访问日期：2018 年 10 月 12 日。限于本章篇幅，作者对原案情内容有酌情删改。

② 参见中国裁判文书网：（2017）吉×民初×号，《马某与马某 1 遗产债务清偿纠纷一审民事判决书》，载 http://wenshu.court.gov.cn/content/content? DocID = e8acbb63 - f8ad - 4bf4 - 9602 - a89e00b29a85，访问日期：2019 年 2 月 9 日。限于本章篇幅，作者对原案情内容有酌情删改。

纳的税款和债务可以不负偿还责任。”在本案中，法院认为继承人接受继承即应在继承的遗产价值范围内清偿被继承人生前所欠债务，具有合理性和法律依据。我们认为，通过上述案例分析，可以发现我国《继承法》在遗产债务清偿中对遗产债权人的保护不足，即没有规定继承人有转移遗产、隐瞒遗产、伪造债务等情形时，继承人应承担强制的无限清偿责任，导致在继承人有主观恶意而转移遗产、隐瞒遗产或伪造债务时，仍然以遗产实际价值为限清偿遗产债务，对遗产债权人而言有失公平。

（十）涉及遗产分割案例的简介与评析

案情简介：王某某与其妻子有四个子女即原告王1、被告王2、王3、案外人王4（已去世，其儿子王5为代位继承人）。原告王1与被告王2、王3系兄妹关系，被告王5为原告王1的侄子。原、被告双方均为本案争议房屋的合法继承人。涉案的房屋登记所有权人为王某某（系原告父亲），属于王某某与其妻子的共同财产。2003年，王某某过世时，没有对其遗产包括本案争议房屋进行分配。2006年5月，原告母亲过世后，原、被告及其他家庭成员于2006年6月10日召开家庭会议，对老人生前全部财产进行分配处理，并将分配处理意见形成《家庭会议纪要》，由参加会议的全体人员签字确认。《家庭会议纪要》中约定将本案争议房屋以9万元的价格出售给原告王1，原告王1在房款未全部付清前不能将该房屋产权过户。同时也对原告王1支付房款的方式、时间等作出了约定。《家庭会议纪要》签订后，双方按纪要约定分配了老人生前存款及债务，原告王1也按纪要约定向被告支付了规定约定金额的房款。现原告王1已按约将房款全部付清。因被告王2、王5拒绝配合、协助原告办理房屋产权过户手续而发生纠纷。原告王1提起诉讼，要求依法确认其享有涉案房产的所有权。被告王2辩称，《家庭会议纪要》没有进行公证，不是正式的房产交易活动，所以该纪要没有法律效力，不受法律保护。此外，原告购买的是涉案房屋的居住权，而非所有权。

法院审理后认为，《家庭会议纪要》是所有继承人及其他家庭成员共同协商形成的，其内容为各方真实的意思表示，并不违反法律的规定。尽管该纪要没有在公证处进行公证，但在其形成后，各方均按纪要约定的内容予以履行，因此，该纪要合法有效。该纪要虽然只约定了将本案争议房屋出售给原告王1，并未明确写明房屋产权的归属，但根据对“出售”二字含义的惯常理解，以及纪要第2条第3款“王1在房款未全部付清前不能将该房屋产权过户”的约定，可以看出原告以9万元的价款购买的是本案争议房屋的所有权，而非被告王2所述的居住权。同时，两个被告在庭审中也未出示有效证据证明原告出资9万元购买的是房屋居住权，而非所有权。因此，法院判决涉案房屋归原告王1所有。①

适用法律分析：本案争议焦点是继承人是共同继承人达成的遗产分割协议是否有效。我国《继承法》第15条规定：“继承人应当本着互谅互让、和睦团结的精神，协商处理继承问题。遗产分割的时间、办法和份额，由继承人协商确定。协商不成的，可以由人民

---

① 参见无讼网：（2010）巴法民初字第×号，《王1诉王2等继承纠纷案》，载 https://www.itslaw.com/detail?judgementId=001e4214-5e97-436f-a847-a848813c45c8&area=1&index=6&sortType=1&count=9&conditions=searchWord%2B%E9%81%97%E4%BA%A7%E5%88%86%E5%89%B2%E6%97%B6%E9%97%B4%2B1%2B%E9%81%97%E4%BA%A7%E5%88%86%E5%89%B2%E6%97%B6%E9%97%B4，访问日期：2018年2月12日。限于本章篇幅，作者对原案情内容有酌情删改。

调解委员会调解或者向人民法院提起诉讼。”可见，继承人可以协商确定遗产分割的时间、办法和份额，即遗产分割的时间、办法和份额等均可由继承人协商确定，这体现了遗产分割自由原则。但我们认为，我国《继承法》关于遗产分割的规定仍存在以下不足：一是立法未规定继承人对遗产分割的自由限制的法律情形（如家庭的共同纪念物、生存配偶和其他特殊法定继承人对遗产中家庭住房的先取权或终生使用权等）。二是未规定遗嘱限制遗产分割的具体年限。

（十一）涉及无人承受遗产案例的简介与评析

案情简介：原告王某于2014年3月26日向被告姜某提供借款3.5万元，借款后被告姜某以各种理由拒绝还款。被告姜某于2017年3月死亡。原告遂诉至法院，请求法院判决以姜某的遗产偿还债务，以维护原告的合法权益。

法院审理后认为，被告姜某已死亡，且目前尚无人继承遗产，无人参加诉讼。此种情况导致本案不能按照诉讼程序进行审理。故法院裁定驳回原告王某的起诉。①

适用法律分析：本案争议焦点是无人承受遗产的债务如何清偿的问题。我国《继承法》第32条是对无人继承的遗产仅有的一条规定，“无人继承又无人受遗赠的遗产，归国家所有；死者生前是集体所有制组织成员的，归所在集体所有制组织所有”。可见，此仅是对无人继承的遗产归属规定，但却对无人继承的遗产之遗产管理人选任、无人继承遗产的债务清偿等未作具体规定，这不利于保障遗产利害关系人的权益，此为立法之不足。我们认为，我国现行《民事诉讼法》第191条规定：“申请认定财产无主，由公民、法人或者其他组织向财产所在地基层人民法院提出。申请书应当写明财产的种类、数量以及要求认定财产无主的根据。”第192条规定：“人民法院受理申请后，经审查核实，应当发出财产认领公告。公告满一年无人认领的，判决认定财产无主，收归国家或者集体所有。”此规定宜借鉴增补为无人承受遗产的公告程序，并规定由承受该财产的主体承担清偿被继承人债务的责任，以维护遗产债权人的合法权益。

第三节　当代中国吉林省民众财产继承观念与遗产处理习惯的特点与原因分析

根据本次调查统计数据情况的汇总分析，吉林省被调查者对前述十一个问题所体现出的财产继承观念与遗产处理习惯之特点与原因分析如下：

一、遗产范围界定之特点与原因分析

（一）遗产的种类之特点与原因分析

关于属于遗产种类的民众观念，统计数据显示的特点是，（1）近八成至九成的被调查者认为住房（90.50%）、汽车（92.33%）、存款（89.67%）和股票（79.83%）属于遗产，此认识与我国《继承法》的规定相一致。（2）近一成至七成的人认为家庭日常生

① 参见中国裁判文书网：（2017）内×民初×号，《王某与姜某一审民事裁定书》，载 http://wenshu.court.gov.cn/content/content? DocID=bc2802e4-bcbb-4d6d-aca4-a85000f99c55，访问日期：2018年10月12日。限于本章篇幅，作者对原案情内容有酌情删改。

活用品（68.00%）、死亡赔偿金（60.17%）、欠款（44.83%）和单位出租给被继承人的午休住房（8.00%）属于遗产，此认识与我国《继承法》的规定不一致。（3）五成以上的人认为以被继承人的姓名注册的邮箱、QQ 账号等（53.67%）属于遗产，对此我国《继承法》无规定（见表 3-4）。

以上特点之原因分析：在吉林省被调查者中，（1）近八成至九成的人认为住房、汽车、存款和股票属于遗产，这与我国《继承法》的规定相一致，其原因可能是受到我国《继承法》相关规定的影响。（2）一成至六成的人认为被继承人的债务、家庭日常生活用品、死亡赔偿金属于遗产，这与我国《继承法》的规定不一致的原因：其一，认为债务属于遗产，可能是受中国几千年盛行的“父债子偿”的传统观念的影响；其二，认为家庭日常生活用品属于遗产，可能是被调查者认为家庭日常生活用品应归家庭共同所有，因而不能成为被继承人的个人财产；其三，认为死亡赔偿金属于遗产，其原因可能是其认为死亡赔偿金是对死者生命的补偿，理应属于死者的财产。但此认识与法律规定不一致，对于死亡赔偿金的性质，根据我国 2004 年《关于审理人身损害赔偿案件适用法律若干问题的解释》第 1 条第 2 款规定：“本条所称‘赔偿权利人’，是指因侵权行为或者其他致害原因直接遭受人身损害的受害人、依法由受害人承担扶养义务的被扶养人以及死亡受害人的近亲属。”第 17 条第 3 款规定：“受害人死亡的，赔偿义务人除应当根据抢救治疗情况赔偿本条第一款规定的相关费用外，还应当赔偿丧葬费、被扶养人生活费、死亡补偿费以及受害人亲属办理丧葬事宜支出的交通费、住宿费和误工损失等其他合理费用。”以上规定中表明，死者的人身损害死亡补偿费是对死亡受害人的近亲属的补偿费，其不属于遗产。（3）五成以上的人认为以被继承人的姓名注册的邮箱、QQ 账号等属于遗产的原因可能是被调查者自己主观感受的认识。

关于遗产种类的立法模式之我国立法，我国《继承法》第 3 条规定：“遗产是公民死亡时遗留的个人合法财产，包括：（一）公民的收入；（二）公民的房屋、储蓄和生活用品；（三）公民的林木、牲畜和家禽；（四）公民的文物、图书资料；（五）法律允许公民所有的生产资料；（六）公民的著作权、专利权中的财产权利；（七）公民的其他合法财产。”1985 年《执行继承法意见》第 3 条和第 4 条规定：“公民可继承的其他合法财产包括有价证券和履行标的为财物的债权等。”“承包人死亡时尚未取得承包收益的，可把死者生前对承包所投入的资金和所付出的劳动及其增值和孳息，由发包单位或者接续承包合同的人合理折价、补偿，其价额作为遗产。”可见，被继承人的债务、以被继承人的姓名注册的邮箱、QQ 账号等是否属于遗产无规定。

从域外立法例看，（1）关于遗产的种类的立法模式有以下几种类型：一是未对遗产范围作专门的规定。例如，法国将继承作为财产转移的一种方式，遗产的种类即财产的范围，可为动产或不动产。[①] 二是对遗产的种类作概括性规定。例如，瑞士规定，遗产包括债权、股权、所有权、其他物权、占有物及债务。[②] 三是对遗产的种类作概括性加排除性规定。例如，日本规定，遗产包括被继承人财产的所有权利义务，但专属于被继承人自身

---

① 参见《法国民法典》第 516 条。

② 参见《瑞士民法典》第 560 条。

的权利义务除外。[①]（2）关于债务是否可作为遗产予以继承可分为三种情形：第一种是将债务排除在遗产之外，如英国和美国的规定。[②]第二种是将债务包含在遗产之中，如法国、瑞士之立法。第三种是债务是否为遗产，因继承人选择不同的继承类型而有所不同。例如，法国规定，当继承人选择全部概括继承或部分概括继承时，遗产范围包括债务；当继承人选择以净资产为限接受继承时，其继承的遗产不包括债务。[③]（3）关于网络邮箱和QQ账号等是否属于遗产，多数国家无规定。[④]

从我国诸继承法学者建议稿看，（1）关于遗产的种类范围的立法模式，"梁稿"和"陈稿"均认为对于遗产范围界定应采取概括式与排除式相结合的立法模式。[⑤]"徐稿"和"王稿"均认为应采用列举式与排除式相合的方式规定遗产的范围。[⑥]（2）关于债务是否可作为遗产，"王稿"规定被继承人享有的债务属于遗产。[⑦]（3）关于互联网中的虚拟财产是否属于遗产，"杨稿"规定互联网中的虚拟财产属于遗产，但涉及被继承人个人信息权、隐私权的互联网络虚拟财产不属于遗产。[⑧]

我们认为，（1）我国《继承法》是在改革开放之初的计划经济条件下制定的，因当时民众财产类型及财产数量较少，采取上述正面列举加概括的方式规定遗产的种类这是符合我国当时国情的。但随着我国市场经济体制的建立，经济规模的扩大，人民拥有私有财产的数量和种类大幅增加，仍采取"正面列举"的立法模式规定遗产的范围有失妥当。[⑨]因为一方面，现代社会的民事财产权利是一个开放的体系，它们会随着社会经济的发展不停地增添新的内容，如果对遗产的正面规定仅为纯粹的列举，就难免会存在立法漏洞，并进而增加法律经常需要被修改、补充的可能性。[⑩]所以，我们认为，遗产范围界定宜采取"正面概括加反面排除"的立法模式。另一方面，与被继承人人身不可分割的财产或是由于法律规定而不能被继承的财产应被排除在遗产范围之外，可以避免不必要的纠纷。因此，关于遗产种类范围的立法模式，上述吉林省被调查者的关于应排除人身性、隐私性财产于遗产范围外的民众观念、日本的立法以及"梁稿"和"陈稿"的观点可供我国立法参考。（2）我国应沿用现行遗产不包括债务的立法规定。因此，关于被继承人的债务是否属于遗产的范围，上述英美的立法及"梁稿"、"陈稿"和"徐稿"的观点可供我国立法参考。（3）以被继承人的姓名注册的邮箱、QQ账号、游戏账号、微博、微信等与被继承人人身密切相关的网络虚拟财产不宜被纳入遗产范围。

---

① 参见《日本民法》第896条。

② 参见陈苇、巍小军：《论我国遗产范围立法的完善》，载《河南财经政法大学学报》2013年第6期，第130~137页。

③ 参见《法国民法典》第768条。

④ 美国特拉华州于2014年通过的《数字访问与数字账号委托访问法》，是全美第一部较为全面的旨在规范虚拟财产继承的法律。参见人民网：特拉华州通过美首部数字遗产法，载 http://legal.people.com.cn/n/2014/0826/c188502-25536930.html，访问日期：2018年12月3日。

⑤ 参见"梁稿"第1941条；"陈稿"第25条。

⑥ 参见"徐稿"第四分编第38~41条；"王稿"第538条。

⑦ 参见"王稿"第538条。

⑧ 参见"杨稿"第7条。

⑨ 参见胡光全：《论遗产的范围》，载《郑州大学学报社会科学报》2015年第6期，第62页。

⑩ 参见陈苇主编：《外国继承法比较与中国民法典继承编制定研究》，北京大学出版社2011年版，第231~232页。

（二）被继承人生前特种赠与财产的归扣之特点与原因分析

关于被继承人生前特种赠与财产归扣的民众观念与民间习惯，统计数据显示的特点是，（1）在被调查者的观念中，持否定观点的占近七成半（74.50%），持肯定观点的占一成半以上（16.00%）（见表3-5）；（2）在被调查者所在地区的习惯是：无归扣习惯的，占六成以上（63.00%），有归扣习惯的，占三成半（35.50%）（见表3-7）。

以上特点之原因分析：七成半以上的吉林省被调查者在观念上不认可归扣制度，且只有三成半的被调查者所在地区有归扣习惯，其原因可能是：（1）我国传统的亲情观念中父母对子女全方位的关爱和给予被视作父母的一项义务。中国家庭的父母在生前往往为子女操办各项事宜，或为子女购房，或资助子女留学，或对子女生活进行不同程度的经济资助。（2）认为被继承人的个人财产权属个人处分的私权利，只要是权利人的自由意志的体现，即应受到尊重，所以被继承人生前特种赠与财产不必归扣。

关于归扣制度之我国立法，我国《继承法》无规定。

在域外立法中，为在子女等特殊共同继承人中公平分配遗产，法国、意大利、德国等多个国家都设立有归扣制度。例如，《法国民法典》规定："任何继承人，即使是有限责任继承人，在参与继承时，均应向其他共同继承人返还其因死者生前赠与而直接或间接受领的全部财产。"①《意大利民法典》规定："参加继承的婚生子女、非婚生子女及其婚生或者非婚生卑亲属和配偶，应当交出被继承人生前直接或者间接赠与自己的一切财产，被继承人免除合算义务的，不在此限。合算义务的免除仅在可处分份额以内有效。"②

从我国诸继承法学者建议稿看，六份学者建议稿均建议增设归扣制度。③ 例如，"王稿"第542条规定，继承开始前，继承人因结婚、分居、营业、超过超常标准的教育、职业培训等事项接受的被继承人生前赠与的财产，应将该赠与的价额纳入被继承的遗产；但是被继承人于赠与时有反对意思表示的除外。赠与的价额依赠与时的价值计算。"陈稿"第27条规定，被继承人的晚辈直系血亲在被继承人生前从其处所获的下列财产利益在遗产分割时应当返还，并计入遗产范围：因结婚、分居、生产经营所受赠与财产；大学本科以上的教育费用；工作期间接受职业教育或培训的费用；储蓄性人寿保险金，但已指定特定受益人的除外。上述应予归扣的财产利益，被继承人生前有免予返还的意思表示的，不予归扣，但该意思表示仅限于不超出其可处分份额。

我们认为，我国《继承法》对归扣制度并无明文规定，但我国民间历来有父母在世时进行"分家析产"的传统，尤其是在广大的农村地区。但现代法上的归扣制度是法律制度对公平以及对死者意愿尊重相结合的产物，也充分体现了继承事务从个人本位向社会本位的转变。④ 因此，为贯彻继承权的平等原则，维护继承人之间的公平，结合吉林省被调查者不认可归扣制度的民众观念和民间习惯，我国立法应谨慎考虑是否设立归扣制度。

---

① 《法国民法典》第843条。

② 《意大利民法典》第737条。

③ 参见"梁稿"第1942条；"王稿"第542条；"徐稿"第四分编第444~459条；"张稿"第64条；"陈稿"第27条；"杨稿"第9条。

④ 参见"王稿"第476页。

二、继承开始的通知和公告之特点与原因分析

（一）继承开始的通知和公告的主体之特点与原因分析

关于继承开始的通知和公告的主体的民间习惯，统计数据显示的特点是，吉林省被调查者所在地区的习惯分别是：（1）由知道被继承人死亡的继承人发出的，占三成以上（33.83%）；（2）由保管遗产的继承人发出的，占七成以上（73.50%）；（3）由知道被继承人死亡的单位、村（居）委会发出的，占五成以上（51.67%）；（4）由处理被继承人死亡事件的机构（如公安交警部门）发出的，占四成以上（42.50%）（见表3-10）。

以上特点之原因分析：在吉林省被调查者所在地区，（1）七成以上的地区的习惯是由保管遗产的继承人通知其他人，其原因可能是在一般家庭中，保管遗产的继承人往往是与被继承人共同居住生活或者是与被继承人联系最紧密的人，由他作为通知和公告的主体能够更及时、有效地开始遗产的分割继承。（2）五成以上的地区的习惯是由知道被继承人死亡的单位、村（居）委会作为继承开始的通知主体，其原因可能是：其一，被继承人的单位、村（居）委会可能较早地接触到被继承人死亡的信息，便于通知；其二，受我国《继承法》第23条的规定的影响。[①]（3）四成以上的地区的习惯是由处理被继承人死亡事件的机构，如公安交警部门作为通知主体，其原因可能是因为当被继承人因事故死亡而身边没有亲属，或者其有继承权的亲属居住分散的情况下，作为公安等国家部门，更能够利用其特殊的公权力快速地查找并通知到继承人。

关于继承开始的通知和公告的主体之我国立法，我国《继承法》第23条规定："继承开始后，知道被继承人死亡的继承人应当及时通知其他继承人和遗嘱执行人。继承人中无人知道被继承人死亡或者知道被继承人死亡而不能通知的，由被继承人生前所在单位或者住所地的居民委员会、村民委员会负责通知。"

在域外立法中，许多国家均对继承开始的通知和公告主体有所规定。例如，日本规定，限定继承人在作出限定继承的表示后5日内，应对所有遗产债权人及受遗赠人，公告已表示限定承认事宜及应在一定期限内申报其请求的内容。[②] 英国规定，遗产在有继承人的情况下，在确认被继承人死亡之后，确定遗产代理人之前，法院有权传召遗嘱所指明的任何遗嘱执行人申请或放弃遗嘱认证，即向可能的遗产代理人作出继承开始的通知。在确定遗产代理人之后，负责继承开始通知的主体是遗产代理人。遗产代理人负责领取被继承人死亡证明书，向继承人发出继承通知。[③]

从我国诸继承法学者建议稿看，均主张扩大继承开始的通知和公告的主体范围。例如，"梁稿"在我国《继承法》第23条的基础上，增加了"其他利害关系人知道继承开始的事实的，可以通知继承人或遗嘱执行人"。[④]"杨稿"规定，继承开始后，由知道被继承人死亡的继承人通知其他继承人和遗嘱执行人。在继承人和遗嘱执行人均不知道被继承

---

① 我国《继承法》第23条规定：继承开始后，知道被继承人死亡的继承人应当及时通知其他继承人和遗嘱执行人。继承人中无人知道被继承人死亡或者知道被继承人死亡而不能通知的，由被继承人生前所在单位或者住所地的居民委员会、村民委员会负责通知。

② 《日本民法典》第927条。

③ 参见陈苇主编：《外国继承法比较与中国民法典继承编制定研究》，北京大学出版社2011年版，第113页。

④ 参见"梁稿"第2001条第2款。

人死亡或无能力通知的情形下，由负责处理被继承人死亡事件的部门或基层组织通知。①

我们认为，我国继承开始的通知之主体范围较窄，此为立法之不足。继承开始后，若未及时通知继承人等遗产利害关系人，继承人等遗产利害关系人就无法及时参与继承，这可能会影响遗产利害关系人的合法权益。在实践中，继承开始的通知主体首先选择继承人最为恰当，在无继承人或继承人无人知晓的情形下，再由居民委员会或村民委员会或其他知晓此事的其他机关或个人进行通知较为妥当。因此，上述吉林省被调查者所在地区扩大继承开始的通知与公告的主体的民间习惯、日本的立法以及我国学者建议稿的观点可供我国立法参考。

(二) 继承开始的通知和公告的方式之特点与原因分析

关于继承开始的通知和公告的方式之民间习惯，统计数据显示的特点是，四成至七成的吉林省被调查者所在地区的习惯是：(1) 使用口头、电话、微信等方式的，占近七成半(74.00%)；(2) 使用书信、告知函等方式的，占四成半以上(46.00%)；(3) 采用在村(居)民委员会公告栏公告方式的，占三成(30.00%)；(4) 使用在报纸、电视、网络等平台上发布被继承人的死亡公告方式的，占二成多(20.67%)；(5) 采用申请人民法院以公告程序进行公告方式的，占近三成(29.83%)(见表3-11)。

以上特点之原因分析：在吉林省被调查者所在地区，(1) 七成半以上地区的习惯是采用口头、电话、微信等方式，其原因可能是这些通信方式更为便捷高效并且准确，能够确保通知及时地被其他继承人接收。(2) 四成半以上地区的习惯是采用信件、告知函等书面通知方式，其原因可能是因为此类书面形式的通知方式较为正式，有利于证据的留存；(3) 二成至三成地区的习惯是采用公告方式，如在报纸、电视、网络等平台上发布被继承人死亡的公告，或采用申请人民法院以公告程序进行公告方式，其原因可能是采公告的方式成本较高，故实践中采用得较少。

关于继承开始的通知和公告的方式之我国立法，我国《继承法》无规定。

从域外立法例看，继承开始的通知和公告的方式形式多样，但以书面通知、在指定的报刊公告较为常见。例如，日本规定，限定承认人须对所有遗产债权人及受遗赠人，公告其已表示限定承认事宜及催告债权人和受遗赠人应在一定期限内申报其请求的内容，且该公告应当在官方报纸上登载。② 美国规定继承开始的通知和公告的方式为普通邮递、在报纸上发布、发送邮件或其他方式递交书面通知。③

从我国诸继承法学者建议稿看，继承开始的通知和公告的方式也不尽相同。例如，"王稿"和"张稿"均建议，在继承人和遗产管理人向人民法院递交遗产清册后，由人民法院以公示催告程序的方式催告债权人申报债权。④ "徐稿"规定，继承开始的通知方式为在遗产所在地的报刊刊登，无此报刊的情形下，在省报刊刊登3次。⑤

我们认为，我国欠缺继承开始的通知和公告的方式，此为立法之不足。上述继承开始的通知和公告方式的吉林省被调查者所在地区的民间习惯、域外立法例和我国学者建议稿

① 参见"杨稿"第70条。

② 参见《日本民法典》第927条。

③ 参见 Uniform Probate Code, S3-309, S3-801.

④ 参见"王稿"第652条；"张稿"第18条。

⑤ 参见"徐稿"第四分编第383条。

的观点可供我国立法参考。

（三）继承开始的通知和公告的期间之特点与原因分析

关于继承开始的通知和公告的期间的民众观念，统计数据显示的特点是，对于发出继承开始的通知的时间，（1）认为应在7日内发出的，合计占近五成（48.50%）；（2）认为应在15日或30日内发出的，合计占五成（50.83%）（见表3-12）。

以上特点之原因分析，近五成的吉林省被调查者认为应在7日内发出继承开始的通知，其原因可能是被调查者希望能及时知道被继承人死亡的事实，以便于顺利开启继承事宜，故继承开始的通知和公告的期间不宜过长。

关于继承开始的通知和公告的期间之我国立法，我国《继承法》第23条仅规定“及时”发出继承开始的通知，并没有具体的期间规定。另外，关于公示催告程序，根据我国现行《民事诉讼法》第219条有关票据被盗、遗失等的公告程序规定，人民法院决定受理申请，应在3日内发出公告，催促利害关系人申报权利，公示催告的期间，由人民法院根据情况决定，但不得少于60日。

从域外立法例看，对继承开始的通知或公告的期间内容分为两部分，一是对于继承开始的通知主体发出通知的期间。例如，日本规定，限定继承人在作出限定继承的表示后5日内对遗产债权人及受遗赠人进行公示催告。① 二是继承开始的通知和公告的催告期间。例如，德国规定，公示催告遗产债权人时，如果继承人为多数继承人时，各共同继承人通过公示催告遗产债权人的期间是6个月。②

从我国诸继承法学者建议稿看，对继承开始的通知和公告的期间意见有所不同。例如，“梁稿”第2007条和“王稿”第652条均规定，继承人和遗产管理人应当于知道继承开始后3个月内向人民法院递交遗产清册，由人民法院以公示催告程序催告债权人申报债权。“杨稿”第81条规定，进入遗产清算程序后，继承人或遗产管理人应当通知已知的债权人，并公告通知可能存在的未知债权人；公告的债权申报期限不得少于3个月。

我们认为，对于继承开始的通知和公告的期间，应该结合我国地域广阔的实际情况，考虑到现实生活中复杂的具体情况，仅在合理期间即可，无须作出明确之规定。

三、遗产管理之特点与原因分析

（一）遗产管理人的确定之特点与原因分析

关于遗产管理人的确定的民间习惯，统计数据显示的特点是，吉林省被调查者所在地区的习惯是：（1）由死者的法定继承人担任的，占八成半（85.50%）；（2）由死者家族中的德高望重者担任的，占近三成半（34.50%）（见表3-13）。

以上特点之原因分析：根据关于遗产管理人确定的民间习惯之理由（见表3-14），在吉林省被调查者所在地区，（1）八成半的地区习惯由继承人来担任遗产管理人，其原因是便于清点和妥善管理遗产，也更希望把自己的期待性财产利益交到自己信任的人手中；（2）近三成半的地区习惯由家族中德高望重的人担任遗产管理人，其原因是遗产继承人之外的人或组织来担任，可以防止遗产被隐藏、转移，有利于保护遗产相关人的合法

① 参见《日本民法典》第927条。

② 参见《德国民法典》第2061条。

权益。

关于遗产管理人的确定之我国立法，我国《继承法》无规定。

从域外立法例看，部分国家规定由法院选任遗产管理人。例如，《法国民法典》第812条规定，在其辖区内开始继承的大审法院，应利害关系人的请求，或者应王国初级检察官的请求，任命一名财产管理人。①《瑞士民法典》第551条规定，被继承人最后住所所在地的主管官厅，为遗产的归属应依职权进行必要的保全处分。②《意大利民法典》第508条规定："在交出遗产的声明登记之后，继承开始地的初审法院法官可以根据继承人、债权人、受遗赠人的申请或者依职权任命一名保佐人，以便由该保佐人根据本法第498条及后条的规定对遗产进行清算。"③

从我国诸继承法学者建议稿看，"梁稿"规定共同继承人未推选遗产管理人的，由全体继承人担任遗产管理人。在遗嘱继承中，如遗嘱中已指定遗嘱执行人，即由遗嘱执行人作为遗产管理人管理遗产。④"王稿"有类似规定，并且还规定，在全部继承人放弃继承权时，由被继承人生前住所地的村民委员会或者居民委员会作为遗产管理人。⑤

我们认为，我国欠缺遗产管理人的产生方式，此为立法之不足。在被继承人死亡后，遗产将在一定期间内可能处于无人管理的状态，甚至有些继承人并不知继承已经开始，确定遗产管理人在此期间对遗产进行管理与保护十分必要。因此，我国立法应明确规定相应的遗产管理人的选任规则，避免引起不必要的纠纷。上述吉林省被调查者所在地区由法定继承人担任遗产管理人的民间习惯、域外立法例和我国学者建议稿的观点可供我国立法参考。

（二）遗产管理人的职责与报酬之特点与原因分析

第一，关于遗产管理人的职责的民众观念，统计数据显示的特点是，有五成至九成的吉林省被调查者认为职责包括：清查遗产，制作遗产清单的，占91.33%；妥善保管遗产的，占91.67%；查明被继承人生前的债权和债务，积极地追讨债权或清偿债务的，占72.17%；可以原告或被告的身份参加因遗产引起的诉讼的，占71.83%；查明被继承人是否留有遗嘱，并且确定遗嘱是否真实合法的，占56.83%；定期制作遗产管理报告，向继承人报告遗产管理的情况的，占61.17%（见表3-15）。

以上特点之原因分析，吉林省被调查者认为遗产管理人的职责具有多样性，其原因可能是遗产管理人的职责事关继承人、遗产债权人等遗产利害关系人的切身利益，只要是有利于遗产保管和分割的事项，都可以是遗产管理人的职责。

第二，关于遗产管理人是否可以请求报酬之民间习惯，统计数据显示的特点是，吉林省被调查者所在地区的习惯是：（1）继承人担任的管理人不可以取得报酬的，占近五成（48.83%）；（2）法院指定担任的管理人可以取得报酬的，占六成半以上（66.00%）；（3）继承人选任的第三人担任的管理人，其中，一律可以取得报酬的，占近四成半（44.67%），是否可以取得报酬由继承人决定的，占三成半以上（36.17%）（见表3-16）。

① 参见《法国民法典》第812条。
② 参见《瑞士民法典》第551条。
③ 参见《意大利民法典》第508条。
④ 参见"梁稿"第2002条。
⑤ 参见"王稿"第549条。

以上特点之原因分析：根据关于遗产管理人是否可以获得报酬的民间习惯之理由(见表3-17)，在吉林省被调查者所在地区，(1) 近五成的地区之习惯是由继承人担任的不可以取得报酬，其原因是遗产管理人与被继承人关系密切且其作为继承人可继承遗产，理应不可获取报酬；(2) 近四成半的地区之习惯是由法院指定的可以取得报酬，其原因是由法院指定的人可能为继承人以外的第三人，其管理遗产付出了相应的劳动和时间，请求相应的报酬是合理的。

关于遗产管理人的职责与报酬之我国立法，我国《继承法》第24条规定："存有遗产的，应当妥善保管遗产，任何人不得侵吞或者争抢。"但并未对遗产管理人是否可报酬有所规定。

从域外立法例看，许多国家均对遗产管理人的职责和报酬有所规定。例如，《德国民法典》规定，遗产管理人有管理遗产并从遗产中清偿遗产债务之义务，遗产管理人在特定条件下才可向继承人移交遗产等义务。此外，遗产管理人可因管理遗产而请求适当的报酬。[①]《法国民法典》第813条规定："无人继承的遗产管理人，有义务首先对遗产进行盘点，以确认遗产的状况：遗产管理人行使属于遗产的权利以及经诉讼途径主张此种权利；针对遗产提出的诉讼请求，管理人得予应诉。管理人对遗产进行管理，并且为保全遗产的权利，负责将遗产中的现金以及由出卖动产或不动产所得之价金存于王家信托局的托管处，同事负责向遗产应当归属的人报名账目。"

从我国诸继承法学者建议稿看，大部分学者建议稿均对遗产管理人的职责与报酬问题有所规定。例如，"梁稿"规定遗产管理人有及时清理被继承人的财产并编制遗产清册的职责。继承人和遗嘱执行人以外的人担任遗产管理人的，有权请求与其执行职务相当的报酬，其报酬权列入继承费用优先受清偿。[②] "王稿"也有类似规定，不同之处在于"王稿"未规定遗产管理人的报酬请求权，但对遗嘱执行人的报酬有所规定，即遗嘱人可以在遗嘱中对遗嘱执行人指定报酬。遗嘱人没有作出上述指定的，遗嘱执行人不得请示报酬。但继承人或受遗赠人自愿支付报酬的除外。[③]

我们认为，我国欠缺遗产管遗产人职责与报酬的规定，此为立法之不足。明确规定遗产管理人的具体职责和报酬请求权，有利于引导遗产管理人更准确、更积极地履行职责。"遗产管理并非听从遗产管理人的任性，而是要遵循相应的遗产管理程序，并要接受法律的规制，以实现国家对个人的责任。而对个人的责任，就是创建严谨且完备的遗产管理制度，确保遗产管理的合法有序，充分维护继承人的权益。"[④] 因此，上述吉林省被调查者对遗产管理人的职责有多样性的民众观念、被调查者所在地区区别不同情况确定是否给予遗产管理人报酬的民间习惯、意大利的立法以及我国学者建议稿的观点可供我国立法参考。

(三) 遗产管理人的损害赔偿责任之特点与原因分析

关于遗产管理人的损害赔偿责任的民间习惯，统计数据显示的特点是，吉林省被调查

---

① 参见《德国民法典》第1985~1987条。

② 参见"梁稿"第2003~2005条。

③ 参见"王稿"第551、639条。

④ 参见王歌雅：《俄罗斯联邦继承法的私权守望与价值追求》，载《俄罗斯中亚东欧研究》2009年第5期，第23~24页。

者所在地区的习惯是：（1）凡有故意或重大过失才承担赔偿责任的，占近七成（69.66%）；（2）无论是故意或重大过失或一般轻过失的，都要承担赔偿责任的，占近三成（29.67%）（见表3-18）。

以上特点之原因分析，近七成的吉林省被调查者所在地区的习惯是遗产管理人凡有故意或重大过失才承担赔偿责任，其原因可能是：遗产管理人往往与继承人具有亲密的联系，因此被调查者对遗产管理人的宽容度也相应较高。

关于遗产管理人的损害赔偿责任之我国立法，我国《继承法》无规定。

从域外立法例看，对遗产管理人的损害赔偿责任的规定有所不同。例如，《法国民法典》规定，受委托的遗产管理人因其受委托的任务履行不力的情况下解除委托时，受托人可能有义务返还其作为报酬受领的款项之全部或一部分，且不影响损害赔偿。[①]《意大利民法典》规定遗产管理人（包括遗产保佐人）在遗产管理过程中因过失（包括轻过失或重过失）造成的损害应承担责任。[②]

从我国诸继承法学者建议稿看，遗产管理人损害赔偿责任范围亦有所不同。例如，“梁稿”认为遗产管理人如因其未尽到遗产管理人的职责而使债权人以及受遗赠人的利益受到损失的，应当负赔偿责任。[③]“王稿”则认为遗产管理人须忠实且谨慎地履行其应尽的义务，因其失职而给遗产债权人造成损害的，其应付相应的赔偿责任。并且，“王稿”认为如果继承人作为遗产管理人，因失职造成损害的，则继承人即应对遗产债务承担无限责任。[④]

我们认为，我国欠缺遗产管理人的损害赔偿责任，此为立法之不足。明确遗产管理人的损害赔偿责任条件，有利于促使遗产管理人严格按照法定程序和法定义务履行职责，防止因遗产管理人的过错导致财产的损失。因此，上述关于遗产管理人因故意或重大过失才承担的损害赔偿责任的吉林省被调查者所在地区的民间习惯、域外立法例和我国学者建议稿的观点可供我国立法参考。

四、法定继承之特点与原因分析

（一）法定继承人的范围与顺序之特点与原因分析

第一，关于法定继承人的范围与顺序的民众观念，统计数据显示的特点是，吉林省被调查者较认可的法定继承范围与顺序为：第一顺序为配偶（94.17%）、父母（54.17%）、子女（57.83%）；第二顺序为孙子女、外孙子女（46.33%），祖父母、外祖父母（45.83%）和兄弟姐妹（39.67%）；第三顺序为侄子女、外甥子女（33.00%），伯叔姑舅姨（30.33%）；第四顺序为堂兄弟姐妹（45.50%）、表兄弟姐妹（15.08%）（见表3-19）。

第二，关于配偶与血亲继承人的顺序，统计数据显示的特点是，吉林省被调查者中，（1）认为配偶应当为固定顺序的，即第一顺序：配偶、子女、父母；第二顺序：兄弟姐妹、祖父母、外祖父母；第三顺序：侄子女、外甥子女；配偶有固定顺序，其属于第一顺位继承人的，占八成半（85.33%）。（2）认为配偶应当为不固定顺序的，即第一顺序为

---

① 参见《法国民法典》第812-5条。

② 参见《意大利民法典》第191、466、531条。

③ 参见“梁稿”第2019条。

④ 参见“王稿”第551条。

子女；第二顺序为父母；第三顺序为兄弟姐妹、祖父母、外祖父母、兄弟姐妹的子女(侄子女、外甥子女为代位继承人)；配偶无固定的继承顺序，可分别与第一、第二（或第三）顺序的法定继承人共同继承的，合计只占近一成半（14.67%）（见表3-20）。

以上特点之原因分析：在吉林省被调查者中，（1）认为应扩大法定继承人的范围，其原因可能是受到家族本位与家财不外传的传统思想的影响，出于避免遗产被收归国家的情形考虑。(2) 占八成半的人认为配偶作为第一顺序的法定继承人，其原因可能是受我国《继承法》规定的影响。

关于法定继承人的范围与顺序之我国立法，我国《继承法》第10条规定，"遗产按照下列顺序继承：第一顺序：配偶、子女、父母。第二顺序：兄弟姐妹、祖父母、外祖父母"。第11、12条规定，法定继承人还包括对公婆、岳父母尽了主要赡养义务的丧偶儿媳、女婿，以及代位继承的孙子女、外孙子女及其晚辈直系血亲。

在域外立法中，对于法定继承人的范围与顺序也各有不同。例如，《法国民法典》规定法定继承人范围包括子女及其直系卑血亲，直系尊血亲，兄弟姐妹或其直系卑血亲，其他六亲等以内的旁系血亲。如果死者生前具有行为能力且享有公民权的，则其十二亲等以内的旁系血亲也享有继承权；而配偶只有在死者没有享有继承权的亲属，或者仅有除兄弟姐妹或者兄弟姐妹的直系卑血亲以外的其他旁系血亲时，才享有继承权。① 为防止遗产因无人继承而归公，有的国家的立法有扩大法定继承人范围的趋势。如《俄罗斯联邦民法典》对法定继承人的范围作了重大修改，已极大地扩大了法定继承人的范围：长辈血亲止于被继承人的曾祖父母和外曾祖父母及表、堂祖父母，表、堂外祖父母的子女，晚辈血亲止于被继承人的表、堂孙子女的子女，此外还包括被继承人的继父、继母以及继承人之外受被继承人扶养的人等。②

从我国诸继承法学者建议稿看，均建议扩大法定继承人的范围并增加法定继承人的顺序，但具体的立法建议有所不同。第一种是将四等亲以内的亲属作为第三顺序。例如，"梁稿"及"王稿"均建议在沿用我国《继承法》第10条的基础上，增加了第三顺序继承人，即"四等亲以内的亲属"。③ 第二种是将法定继承人的范围和顺序扩展到第四顺序。例如，"陈稿"建议继承人之范围和顺序如下：第一顺序为子女及其晚辈直系血亲；第二顺序为父母；第三顺序为兄弟姐妹及其子女；第四顺序为祖父母，包括父系祖父母和母系祖父母；配偶可以和任一顺序的血亲继承人共同继承。④

我们认为，我国《继承法》将法定继承人的范围仅限于三代以内的近亲属，且仅有两个顺序，再加之计划生育政策的实施，容易出现无法定继承人继承遗产的现象，此为我国立法之不足。⑤ 从保护私有财产权，在坚持尽量使遗产不收归国有的指导原则下，扩大继承人范围和顺序，既符合我国传统文化，又能与时俱进充分发挥遗产养老育幼、维护亲属伦理关系的功能。因此，上述吉林省被调查者扩大法定继承人的范围和增加法定顺序的

---

① 参见吴国平：《法定继承人范围与顺序的局限与扩张探究》，载《江南大学学报》2015年第4期，第41页。

② 参见陈苇、冉启玉：《完善我国法定继承人范围及立法顺序的思考》，载《法学论坛》2013年第2期，第55页。

③ 参见"梁稿"第1946；"王稿"第564条。

④ 参见"陈稿"第45条。

⑤ 参见郭明瑞：《民法典编纂中继承法的修订原则》，载《比较法研究》2015年第3期，第90页。

民众观念、域外立法例和我国学者建议稿的观点可供我国立法参考。

（二）配偶与血亲继承人的法定应继份之特点与原因分析

关于配偶与血亲继承人的法定应继份的民众观念，统计数据显示的特点是，在吉林省被调查者中，（1）认为配偶为无固定继承顺序，可参与第一、第二（或第三）顺序且在不同顺序其应继份不同的，合计占五成半以上（56.83%）；（2）认为配偶为固定顺序的继承人，与第一顺序的继承人共同继承并平均分配遗产的，占四成以上（41.50%）（见表3-21）。值得注意的是，前述关于法定继承顺序的调查统计数据可知，认同配偶固定为第一顺序继承人，且与其他第一顺序的继承人平均分配的占八成半（85.33%）；认同配偶不固定顺序可与不同顺序继承人共同继承的，以便于让其他近血亲继承人能够参与继承取得适当的遗产，合计占近一成半（14.67%）（见表3-20）。而关于法定应继份却又有五成半以上的被调查者主张配偶无固定继承顺序。也就是说，在实际分配遗产时，有占五成半以上的被调查者主张配偶无固定继承顺序，其应当与不同顺序的血亲继承人共同继承，且不同顺序其应继份不同，以兼顾保护配偶继承人与血亲继承人的利益。

以上特点之原因分析：在吉林省被调查者中，（1）四成以上的人认为配偶应作为固定顺序即第一顺序的法定继承人，其原因可能是被继承人与配偶之间往往形成了相濡以沫的情感，因此更希望配偶可以多分得自己的财产，安稳度过晚年，认为将配偶与父母、子女放在同一继承顺序比较妥当。（2）五成半以上的人认为配偶作为无固定顺序继承人，以便于让其他近血亲继承人能够参与继承取得适当的遗产，其原因可能是被调查者认为，现在的离婚率居高不下，自己与配偶的感情未必会一直稳定，因此不愿让配偶固定在第一顺序，这可能导致后顺序的血亲继承人不能继承遗产。

关于配偶与血亲继承人的法定应继份之我国立法，我国《继承法》第10条和第13条规定，配偶、子女、父母均为第一顺序，且同一顺序继承人继承遗产的份额，一般应当均等。对生活有特殊困难的缺乏劳动能力的继承人，分配遗产时，应当予以照顾。对被继承人尽了主要扶养义务或者与被继承人共同生活的继承人，分配遗产时，可以多分；有扶养能力和有扶养条件的继承人，不尽扶养义务的，分配遗产时，应当不分或者少分；继承人协商同意的，也可以不均等。

从域外立法例看，对配偶的继承顺序和份额的立法主要有两种类型。第一种是配偶为无固定顺序继承人，可以与不同顺序的血亲继承人共同继承。大陆法系国家中采用较为广泛的是按比例继承，有别于均等继承的方式，根据配偶参与继承顺序的血亲继承人的不同而继承不同比例的遗产份额。[①] 例如，《瑞士民法典》第462条规定，配偶无固定顺序，当配偶与被继承人的直系卑亲属共同继承时，其取得遗产的二分之一；当其与被继承人的父亲、母亲或父母亲的继承人共同继承时，其取得遗产的四分之三；当父系和母系均无继承人时，其继承全部遗产。第二种是配偶为固定顺序继承人。例如，《俄罗斯联邦民法典》第1141、1142条规定，第一顺位法定继承人是被继承人的子女、配偶和父母。同一个顺序的继承人继承的份额均等。

从我国诸继承法学者建议稿看，对配偶的继承顺序和份额同样分为固定顺序和不固定顺序两种类型。例如，"梁稿""徐稿""王稿"和"杨稿"均规定配偶为第一顺位继承

① 陈苇主编：《外国继承法比较与中国民法典继承编制定研究》，北京大学出版社2011年版，第409页。

人，同一顺序继承人，均分遗产。[①] 而“陈稿”和“张稿”均建议配偶作为不固定顺序的继承人，与不同顺序的血亲继承人共同继承，并且配偶与不同顺序的血亲继承人共同继承时，取得不同的份额。[②]

我们认为，虽然有学者主张不应固定配偶的继承顺序，但我国《继承法》中对配偶第一继承顺序的规定经过30多年的实施，已经成为民间的习惯性做法，民众一时之间难以接受将配偶作为无固定顺序继承人。

（三）配偶对遗产中家庭住房的先取权与终生使用权之特点与原因分析

关于配偶是否享有对遗产中家庭住房的先取权与终生使用权的民间习惯，统计数据显示的特点是，在吉林省被调查者所在地区，（1）有此习惯的，占四成半以上（46.17%）；（2）无此习惯的，占五成以上（53.83%）（见表3-22）。

以上特点之原因分析：在吉林省被调查者所在地区，（1）五成以上的地区无此习惯的，其原因可能是考虑到目前房价高昂的现实情况下，房产可能作为遗产中价值最大的遗产，被调查者不希望因为被继承人的配偶而无法分割该房产。（2）五成以上的地区有此习惯的，其原因可能是：其一，家庭住房是被继承人与其配偶生前共同生活场所，双方均对该家庭住房做出过或大或小的贡献，特别是当该家庭住房为夫妻的唯一住房时，如果该住房被共同继承人分割后，生存配偶可能会遭遇无处所居的困境；其二，该家庭住房不仅具有很高的经济价值，也有很高的精神价值。配偶优先取得遗产中的家庭住房，不仅可以保障生存配偶有固定的居所，而且还可以具有一定的精神慰藉。

关于配偶对遗产中家庭住房的先取权与终生使用权之我国立法，我国《继承法》无规定。

从域外立法例看，部分国家对配偶对遗产中家庭住房的先取权与用益物权有所规定。例如，《意大利民法典》规定，有多个继承人的，如果用作居住的房屋和家具的所有权属于被继承人或者属于配偶双方，则房屋的居住权以及使用家具的权利属于配偶。[③] 英国规定：配偶有独立的继承权，配偶对先亡配偶的遗产享有终生的用益权，与子女共同继承时，享有二分之一的用益权，与其他亲属继承时，享有全部用益权。当死者有直系卑亲属，配偶可先取得全部个人物品。[④]

从我国诸继承法学者建议稿看，“王稿”建议设立配偶的法定用益物权，即被继承人的配偶尚生存且无自己的住房的，如果未继承被继承人的房屋，则对遗产中的住房享有用益物权。生存配偶需支付给继承该房屋的继承人不超过市价的租金，具体数额可以由双方协商，协商不成可以提起诉讼。[⑤]“张稿”规定，配偶对遗产中供自己使用的住房和日常生活用品享有先取权。[⑥]“陈稿”规定，生存配偶对遗产中的婚姻住宅和家庭日常生活用品享有先取权。如其继承份额小于该家庭日常生活用品的价值，其也可以选择对该家庭日常生活用品享有终生使用权。生存配偶对遗产中的婚姻住宅享有优先扣除其继承遗产份额

① 参见“梁稿”第1946条；“徐稿”第四分编第495条；“王稿”第564、575条；“杨稿”第57条。
② 参见“陈稿”第45条；“张稿”第28条。
③ 参见《意大利民法典》第540条第2款。
④ 李启欣著译：《外国法制史研究文选》，中国法制出版社2000年版，第232~236页。
⑤ 参见“王稿”第580条。
⑥ 参见“张稿”第32条。

的权利。如其继承份额小于该婚姻住宅的价值，其也可以选择对婚姻住宅享有终生居住权。[①] 此外，也有学者撰写论文提出相似建议。[②]

我们认为，我国欠缺配偶对遗产中家庭住房的先取权与终生使用权，此为立法之不足。无论是从保障生存配偶的基本生活，还是更好地发挥遗产养老育幼的功能，从立法上保障配偶对家庭住房的先取权或用益物权都具有合理性。因此，关于配偶对遗产中家庭住房的先取权与终生使用权的上述吉林省被调查者的民间习惯、意大利和英国的立法以及我国学者建议稿的观点可供我国立法参考。

（四）后顺序特殊法定继承人对遗产中原使用的住房及日常生活用品的终生使用权之特点与原因分析

关于后顺序特殊法定继承人对特殊遗产是否享有使用权的民间习惯，统计数据显示的特点是，（1）在吉林省被调查者所在地区，有此习惯的，占八成以上（81.00%）；无此习惯的，占近二成（19.00%）（见表3-25）。（2）关于后顺序特殊法定继承人对原使用的遗产住房及日常生活用品的使用是否付费，有不需要付费之习惯的，占六成以上（63.83%）；有需要付费之习惯的，占三成半以上（36.17%）（见表3-26）。

以上特点之原因分析，关于后顺序特殊法定继承人对特殊遗产是否享有使用权，八成以上的吉林省被调查者所在地区有此习惯、六成以上的地区有无须付费的习惯，其原因可能是：（1）由于后顺位特殊法定继承人一般为法定继承人的父母（如父母改为第二顺序）、祖父母或外祖父母，从我国的传统道德观念与血脉亲情的考量，应该支持后顺序法定继承人对该特殊遗产享有无偿的终生使用权。（2）在遗产的分配与使用上，出于对家庭成员之间的和睦与相互扶助的重视，也已被多数民众所认同。

关于后顺序特殊法定继承人对特殊遗产的终生使用权之我国立法，我国《继承法》未作规定。

从域外立法例看，个别国家对后顺序特殊法定继承人对特殊遗产享有的使用权有所规定。例如，《德国民法典》第1969条规定，在继承开始后的30日内，继承人有义务向在被继承人死亡时属于被继承人家计并受其扶养的被继承人家属给予扶养费，并许可其使用住宅和家庭用具。

从我国诸继承法学者建议稿看，“张稿”和“陈稿”对此有所规定。例如，“张稿”第33条规定，父母因顺序在后未参加继承的，对遗产中供其个人日常生活使用的住房和其他物品有终生使用权。“陈稿”第48条第2款也有类似规定。

我们认为，我国欠缺后顺序特殊法定继承人对特殊遗产的终生使用权，此为立法之不足。为了更好地弘扬中华民族尊老敬老的传统美德，并充分发挥遗产养老育幼的功能，理应对后顺序特殊法定继承人对特殊遗产的终生使用权作出规定。因此，上述关于后顺序特殊法定继承人对特殊遗产的终生使用权之吉林省被调查者所在地区的民间习惯、德国的立法以及“张稿”和“陈稿”的观点可供我国立法参考。

---

① 参见“陈稿”第48条。

② 参见陈苇、杜江涌：《我国法定继承制度的立法构想》，载《现代法学》2002年第3期，第96~103页。参见吴国平：《法定继承人范围与顺序的立法完善探析》，载《西华师范大学学报（哲学社会科学版）》2011年第6期，第72页。

（五）尽了主要赡养义务的丧偶儿媳或女婿的遗产分配方式之特点与原因分析

关于尽了主要赡养义务的丧偶儿媳或女婿的遗产分配方式的民间习惯，统计数据显示的特点是，吉林省被调查者所在地区的习惯是：（1）其作为第一顺序的法定继承人与被继承人其他子女共同继承并且平均分配遗产的，占六成（60.84%）；（2）其不可与被继承人其他子女共同继承但其可分得适当的遗产的，占三成半以上（37.33%）（见表3-28）。

以上特点之原因分析，六成的吉林省被调查者所在地区的习惯是尽了主要赡养义务的丧偶儿媳或女婿可以作为第一顺序的法定继承人与其他继承人平均分配遗产，其原因可能是：（1）符合权利义务相一致的原则；（2）可以积极引导丧偶儿媳或女婿对公婆或岳父母尽孝，符合权利义务相一致原则。

关于尽了主要赡养义务的丧偶儿媳或女婿的遗产分配之我国立法，我国《继承法》第12条规定，对尽了主要赡养义务的丧偶儿媳对公婆，丧偶女婿对岳父、岳母可作为第一顺序继承人之规定的影响。1985年《执行继承法意见》第29条规定，丧偶儿媳对公婆、丧偶女婿对岳父、岳母，无论其是否再婚，依《继承法》第12条规定作为第一顺序继承人时，不影响其子女代位继承。从《关于〈中华人民共和国继承法〉（草案）的说明》第四部分[①]内容可以看出，继承法作此规定，立法意旨在于通过赋予丧偶儿媳与女婿的继承权来激励其赡养老人。[②] 而我国现行《婚姻法》并未规定丧偶儿媳或女婿有扶养老人的义务。

从域外立法例看，目前未考察到将尽了主要赡养义务的丧偶儿媳或女婿作为第一顺序的法定继承人之规定。

从我国诸继承法学者建议稿看，对是否继续保留“将尽了主要赡养义务的丧偶儿媳或女婿作为第一顺序的法定继承人”之立法的意见有分歧。例如，“杨稿”建议仍将尽了主要赡养义务的丧偶儿媳或女婿作为第一顺序的法定继承人。[③] “王稿”则规定，丧偶儿媳对公婆，丧偶女婿对岳父、岳母尽了主要赡养义务的，没有代位继承人的，作为第一顺位法定继承人参与继承，不论其是否再婚。有代位继承人时，可以按照遗产酌给请求权的规定分得适当遗产。[④]

我们认为，我国立法规定尽了主要赡养义务的儿媳或女婿作为第一顺序法定继承人，此立法有不合理之处。而将对尽了主要赡养义务的丧偶儿媳或者丧偶女婿作为酌分请求权人，既有利于积极引导丧偶儿媳对公、婆或者丧偶女婿对岳父、岳母发扬敬老、养老的传统美德，同时可以避免他们作为第一顺序继承人在无其他法定继承人时有可能独自取得全部遗产，从而更好地保护被继承人的血亲继承人的继承权益。因此，关于尽了主要赡养义务的丧偶儿媳或女婿的遗产分配，上述“王稿”的观点可供我国立法参考。

---

① 《关于〈中华人民共和国继承法〉（草案）的说明》第四部分对“关于扶养老幼”中作了如下说明：“宪法规定‘成年子女有赡养扶助子女的义务’，‘禁止虐待老人’。继承法草案为了贯彻这个精神，从继承权、继承遗产的份额等方面作了规定……第五，丧偶儿媳赡养公、婆直至其死亡，丧偶女婿赡养岳父、岳母直至其死亡，为第一顺序继承人。这些规定，都是为了有利于更好地赡养老人。”

② 参见王蓓：《法定继承人范围改革研究》，载《西南民族大学学报》2010年第5期，第115~116页。

③ 参见“杨稿”第60条。

④ 参见“王稿”第569条。

五、遗嘱继承之特点与原因分析

（一）公证遗嘱与其他形式遗嘱的效力之特点与原因分析

关于公证遗嘱与其他形式遗嘱何者优先发生效力的民众观念，统计数据显示的特点是，在吉林省被调查者中，（1）认为后遗嘱优先于前一遗嘱（包括公证遗嘱）适用的，合计占六成半以上（67.50%）；（2）认为公证遗嘱应当优先适用的，占三成以上（32.50%）（见表3-29）。

以上特点之原因分析：根据关于公证遗嘱与其他形式遗嘱的效力的民众观念的理由（见表3-30），在吉林省被调查者中，（1）六成半以上的人认为后遗嘱优先于前一遗嘱（包括公证遗嘱）适用，其原因是最后作出的遗嘱才是被继承人最后的意思表示，被继承人对自己财产的处分应当享有意思自治的权利；（2）三成以上的人认为公证遗嘱应当优先发生效力，其原因是：其一，公证遗嘱的程序规范，具有较强的公示效力和证明效力；其二，受我国《继承法》相关规定的影响。

关于公证遗嘱与其他形式遗嘱何者优先发生效力之我国立法，我国《继承法》第20条和1985年《执行继承法意见》第42条的规定，立有数份遗嘱且内容相抵触的，以最后的遗嘱为准。但自书、代书、录音、口头遗嘱，不得撤销、变更公证遗嘱。

从域外立法例看，部分国家对于遗嘱的效力有所规定。例如，《瑞士民法典》规定，立遗嘱人未明确撤销先遗嘱，又订立后遗嘱，只要不能肯定新遗嘱为旧遗嘱的补充，新遗嘱代替原遗嘱。对同一物设立两份遗嘱，后遗嘱效力优先于前遗嘱。①《日本民法典》规定，遗嘱人可以随时按遗嘱的方式将其遗嘱全部或部分撤回。前遗嘱与后遗嘱有抵触时，就其抵触部分，视为后遗嘱将前遗嘱撤回。②

从我国诸继承法学者建议稿看，对公正遗嘱的效力及有多份遗嘱的效力标准有所规定。例如，"王稿"规定，遗嘱人立有数份遗嘱的，内容相抵触的，以最后设立的遗嘱为准。遗嘱人立有数份遗嘱，内容相抵触的，有公证遗嘱的，以公证遗嘱为准，无公证遗嘱的，以最后设立的遗嘱为准。③"陈稿"规定，遗嘱人有权变更先前订立的遗嘱，前遗嘱与后遗嘱两者的内容不一致的，以后订立的遗嘱为准。④此外，也有学者认为，在遗嘱形式要件缓和的语境下，遗嘱形式从效力性形式转换到兼顾保护性形式的方向，不同遗嘱形式也就并非认定遗嘱是否无效的终极标准，而仅仅是查清遗嘱人真实意思表示时的一种证明责任分配手段。⑤遗嘱的形式不应成为判断遗嘱有效的唯一标准，赋予公证遗嘱极高的效力不符合现代继承法发展的趋势。

我们认为，公正遗嘱效力优先于其他形式遗嘱适用有失妥当，此为我国立法之不足。而如果法律赋予后遗嘱具有优先适用的效力，可以尊重被继承人处理遗产的真实意愿，有利于维护被继承人的遗嘱自由。因此，关于后遗嘱优先于前一遗嘱适用的上述吉林省被调查者的民众观念、瑞士和日本的立法以及"陈稿"的观点可供我国立法参考。

---

① 参见《瑞士民法典》第509~511条。

② 参见《日本民法典》第1022、1023条。

③ 参见"王稿"第604、605、606条。

④ 参见"陈稿"第38条。

⑤ 参见魏小军：《遗嘱有效要件研究》，中国法制出版社2010年版，第23页。

（二）遗嘱自由的限制——特留份之特点与原因分析

关于遗嘱处分个人财产是否应予以限制的民众观念，统计数据显示的特点是，对于被继承人以遗嘱将个人遗产全部赠给他人的做法，在吉林省被调查者中，（1）认为该行为不适当，即应对遗嘱的自由予以限制的，占七成稍多（71.17%）；（2）认为该行为适当，即不应对遗嘱的自由予以限制的，仅占二成半多（26.33%）（见表3-31）。

以上特点之原因分析，根据关于以遗嘱将个人遗产全部赠给他人之民众观念的理由（见表3-32），六成半的吉林省被调查者认为应对遗嘱的自由予以限制的，一是因为被继承人以遗嘱将其遗产全部赠与他人会造成家庭财产外流，不利于保障被继承人的配偶及其子女的生活；二是因为被继承人以遗嘱将其遗产全部赠与他人不符合风俗习惯，实为常人所难以接受。

关于遗嘱处分个人财产是否应予限制之我国立法，我国《继承法》第16条规定，“公民可以立遗嘱将个人财产指定由法定继承人的一人或数人继承，也可立遗嘱将个人财产赠给国家、集体或者法定继承人以外的人”。第19条规定：“遗嘱应当对缺乏劳动能力又没有生活来源的继承人保留必要的遗产份额。”

从域外立法例看，许多大陆法系国家均要求遗嘱人应当为特定人员留下特留份或者必要的扶养费。例如，《瑞士民法典》第470、471条规定：被继承人有直系卑血亲、父母或配偶为继承人的，其对继承人特留份范围以外的财产有遗嘱处分权。直系卑血亲的特留份各为其法定继承权的四分之三；父母中的任何一方的特留份为其法定继承权的二分之一；尚生存的配偶的特留份为其法定继承权的二分之一。《德国民法典》第2303条规定：“特留份权利人包括被继承人的晚辈直系血亲、父母和配偶，特留份为法定应继份的价额的一半。”

从我国诸继承法学者建议稿看，多数学者建议稿均造成设立特留份制度，只是对特留份制度中的具体规定未形成统一意见。例如，“梁稿”和“王稿”均赞成建立特留份制度，并且认为特留份的份额如下，即“第一顺序法定继承人的特留份为其应继份额的二分之一；第二顺序法定继承人的特留份为其应继份额的三分之一”。[①]“杨稿”亦支持建立特留份制度，其建议被继承人的配偶、晚辈直系血亲、父母享有特留份继承权，特留份额是其法定继承数额的二分之一。[②]

我们认为，我国欠缺特留份制度，此为立法之不足。我国《继承法》中的必留份制度更侧重对与被继承人关系密切的无工作能力又无生活来源的“双无人员”的基本生活保障，而特留份制度是维系一定范围内近亲属的血缘关系和亲情伦理关系，无须满足其他条件即可因身份关系而获得一定份额的遗产。正如我国学者所言，建立特留份制度，既符合公民最朴素的亲情伦理之理念，又与国际立法思想相接轨，体现继承立法的先进性和公平性。[③]因此，关于对遗嘱的自由必须适当地限制的上述吉林省被调查者的民众观念、德国的立法以及我国学者建议稿的观点可供我国立法参考。

（三）夫妻共同遗嘱之特点与原因分析

关于夫妻共同遗嘱的民众观念与民间习惯，统计数据显示的特点是，（1）在吉林省

---

① 参见“梁稿”第1961条；“王稿”第585条。

② 参见“杨稿”第49条。

③ 参见夏吟兰：《特留份制度之伦理价值分析》，载《现代法学》2012年第5期，第41~45页。

被调查者的观念中，持赞成态度的占七成半以上（77.50%），持不赞同态度的占二成以上（22.50%）（见表3-33）；（2）吉林省被调查者所在地区的习惯是：有夫妻共同遗嘱之习惯的，占七成以上（72.50%）；无夫妻共同遗嘱之习惯的，占二成半以上（27.50%）（见表3-35）。

以上特点之原因分析：根据关于夫妻共同遗嘱的民众观念情况之理由（见表3-34），在吉林省被调查者中，（1）七成半以上的人对夫妻共同遗嘱持赞成态度、七成以上的地区有该习惯，其原因是该遗嘱反映了双方的共同意愿，应为双方所遵守；（2）二成以上的人对夫妻共同遗嘱持不赞同态度、二成半以上的地区无该习惯，其原因是该遗嘱无法应对出现的新情况和新问题，限制了双方对自己财产的处分权。

从域外立法例看，对夫妻共同遗嘱制度的立法态度也有所不同。一是持否定态度。例如，《日本民法典》第975条规定，遗嘱不得由两人以上制作成同一证书。二是持肯定态度。例如，《德国民法典》第2265~2272条规定，仅认可夫妻共同遗嘱，并对其形式、效力、撤回等内容进行了具体的规定。

关于夫妻共同遗嘱之我国立法，我国《继承法》无规定。

从我国诸继承法学者建议稿看，对是否应设立夫妻共同遗嘱制度的观点不统一。一是主张设立夫妻共同遗嘱。例如，“杨稿”第37条规定，“夫妻可以设立共同遗嘱，共同遗嘱的效力以配偶一方死亡前婚姻关系存续为前提”。又如，“徐稿”第四分编继承法第60条规定，两人或多人在一个时间订立的遗嘱无效，但夫妻之间的共同遗嘱除外。二是不主张设立夫妻共同遗嘱。例如，“梁稿”“张稿”和“陈稿”均未规定夫妻共同遗嘱。

我们认为，夫妻共同遗嘱是夫妻双方对其财产处分的真实意思表示，又没有其他违反法律强制性规定的情形，理应得到立法的认可。我国《继承法》未规定夫妻共同遗嘱，此为立法之不足。因此，关于赞成夫妻共同遗嘱的上述吉林省被调查者的民众观念与民间习惯、德国的立法和“杨稿”“徐稿”的观点可供我国立法参考。

六、继承和遗赠的接受与放弃之特点与原因分析

（一）继承的接受和放弃的时间之特点与原因分析

关于继承的接受和放弃的时间的民众观念，统计数据显示的特点是，在吉林省被调查者中，（1）认为继承人应遗产处理前作出放弃继承的意思表示的，占六成半以上（67.17%）；（2）认为继承人应在知道继承开始的2个月内作出放弃继承的表示的，仅占三成以上（32.83%）（见表3-36）。

以上特点之原因分析：根据关于继承的接受与放弃的时间与方式的民众观念之理由（见表3-37），在吉林省被调查者中，（1）六成半以上的人认为继承人放弃继承应当在遗产处理前作出放弃继承的意思表示，其原因是这样既不影响其他继承人的利益，又可以保证继承人行使放弃继承的权利。（2）三成以上的人认为继承人放弃继承应在知道继承开始的2个月内作出放弃继承的表示，其原因是有利于及时督促继承人行使权利。

关于继承的接受和放弃的时间之我国立法，我国《继承法》第25条第1款规定：“继承开始后，继承人放弃继承的，应当在遗产处理前，作出放弃继承的表示。没有表示的，视为接受继承。”此外，1985年《执行继承法意见》第47条规定：“继承人放弃继承应当以书面形式向其他继承人表示。用口头方式表示放弃继承，本人承认，或有其它充

分证据证明的，也应当认定其有效。”第 48 条规定：“在诉讼中，继承人向人民法院以口头方式表示放弃继承的，要制作笔录，由放弃继承的人签名。”

从域外立法例看，如《法国民法典》第 804 条规定，继承的抛弃不得适用推定的方式。全部概括继承人或部分概括继承人放弃继承，应当向继承开始地的大审法院书记室提出，才能对抗第三人。《日本民法典》第 915 条明确规定，“继承人须知道自己为继承人开始时起 3 个月内，就继承表示单纯继承、限定继承或放弃。该期间可以根据利害关系人或检察官的请求，由家庭法院予以延长”。

从我国诸继承法学者建议稿看，均对作出放弃继承表示的时间有所规定，只是具体期限和效力有所不同。例如，“梁稿”“王稿”“张稿”和“陈稿”均规定继承人应当在知道继承开始后 2 个月内以书面形式放弃继承；且逾期未表示的，视为接受继承。“杨稿”规定继承人应当自知道或者应当知道继承开始之日起 3 个月内作出是否接受继承的表示。[①]

我们认为，我国《继承法》规定，继承人在遗产处理前均可以作出放弃继承的意思表示。但“遗产处理前”这个时间是不确定的，其不足表现在，一方面容易导致遗产权属不稳定，影响交易安全，另一方面，增加了继承人生老病死等特殊情形产生的概率，容易引发不必要的继承纠纷。因此，大多数国家均规定继承的接受与放弃须在法定期间内作出。所以，上述吉林省被调查者主张继承开始后 2 个月内作出继承的接受与放弃的民众观念、法国的立法例和我国学者建议稿的观点可供我国立法参考。

（二）遗赠的接受与放弃的方式与效力之特点与原因分析

关于遗赠的接受与放弃的方式与效力的民众观念，统计数据显示的特点是，在吉林省被调查者中，（1）认为受遗赠人未作表示应认定为接受遗赠的，占六成半以上（66.83%）；（2）认为受遗赠人未作表示应认定为放弃遗赠的，占三成以上（33.17%）（见表 3-38）。

以上特点之原因分析：关于遗赠的接受与放弃的方式与效力的民众观念之理由（见表 3-39），在吉林省被调查者中，（1）六成半以上的人认为受遗赠人未作表示应该被视为接受该遗赠，其原因是接受遗赠是一种纯获利行为，只有明确作出拒绝或者放弃的意思表示才意味着放弃遗赠，未作表示应当被认为是接受遗赠。正如我国学者所言，依照民法的基本理念，对于财产权益，权利人没有表示放弃的，应当视为接受，而不是放弃。[②]（2）三成以上的人认为受遗赠人未作表示应认定为放弃遗赠，其原因是如果受遗赠人想要接受遗赠，就会作出相应的意思表示，故其未作表示理应是放弃受遗赠。

关于遗赠的接受与放弃的方式与效力之我国立法，我国《继承法》第 25 条第 2 款规定：“受遗赠人应当在知道受遗赠后两个月内，作出接受或者放弃接受遗赠的表示。到期没有表示的，视为放弃接受遗赠。”

从域外立法例看，对于遗赠的接受与放弃的方式与效力的规定分为两种类型。第一种是明示接受。例如，德国规定，继承开始后，遗赠人可以作出接受或拒绝遗赠的表示，但不得附条件或附期限，且未对期间有所规定。[③] 第二种是明示接受与未作表示推定接受。

---

① 参见“杨稿”第 12 条。

② 参见陈苇主编：《改革开放三十年（1978—2008）中国婚姻家庭继承法研究之回顾与展望》，中国政法大学出版社 2010 年版，第 398 页。

③ 参见《德国民法典》第 2180 条。

例如，日本规定，对遗赠的履行负有义务的人及其他利害关系人，可以设定一定的期间，催告受遗赠人应在该期间内作出对遗赠的接受或放弃。如果受遗赠人在该期间内未对遗赠义务人作出意思表示时，视为已接受遗赠。①

从我国诸继承法学者建议稿看，关于接受或放弃遗赠的方式，诸学者立法建议也有所不同。第一种是明示接受、未作表示推定为放弃遗赠。例如，“梁稿”和“王稿”均沿用了继承法规定的接受遗赠的方式，即受遗赠人应在知道受遗赠后2个月内作出接受继承的意思表示，如逾期未作表示，则应视为放弃受遗赠。② 第二种是明示接受、未作表示推定为接受遗赠。例如，“陈稿”和“张稿”规定，受遗赠人未在规定的期间内明确表示放弃遗赠的，视为接受遗赠。③

我们认为，我国对于遗赠的接受与放弃的方式与效力之规定存在不足。采用明示接受与未作表示视为接受遗赠相结合的方式，更有利于保障受遗赠人的利益。因此，上述吉林省被调查者认为受遗赠人未作表示应认定为接受遗赠的民众观念、日本的立法和“张稿”“陈稿”的观点可供我国立法参考。

（三）继承的放弃与债权人的撤销权之特点与原因分析

关于继承的放弃能否被债权人予以撤销的民众观念和民间习惯，统计数据显示的特点是，（1）在吉林省被调查者的观念中，认为可以被撤销的，占近五成（48.17%）；认为不可以被撤销的，占五成以上（51.83%）（见表3-40）。（2）在被调查者所在地区的习惯是：可以被撤销的，占八成以上（82.68%）；不可以被撤销的，占一成半以上（17.32%）（见表3-42）。

以上特点之原因分析：根据关于继承的放弃能否被债权人予以撤销的民众观念之理由（见表3-41），在吉林省被调查者中，（1）五成以上的人认为继承人放弃继承的行为不可以被其债权人撤销、一成半以上的地区有该习惯，其原因是继承人是否放弃继承是其自己的权利和自由，他人无权干涉。（2）近五成的人认为继承人放弃继承的行为可以被其债权人撤销、八成以上的地区有该习惯的，其原因是如果继承人放弃继承会导致债权人的权利受到侵害时，债权人便可行使撤销权以维护自己的利益。

关于继承的放弃能否被债权人予以撤销之我国立法，我国《继承法》无规定。1985年《执行继承法意见》第46条规定：“继承人因放弃继承权，致其不能履行法定义务的，放弃继承权的行为无效。”

从域外立法例看，部分国家的立法赋予了债权人对继承人放弃继承的撤销权或有限代位继承权，如《瑞士民法典》第578条规定，当继承人为逃避债务而抛弃继承权时，如果债务数额超过继承时所得的财产数额，法律赋予债权人和遗产管理人可于6个月内诉请撤销该放弃继承表示的权利，但债务人能够为其债务提供担保的除外。④《法国民法典》第779条规定，当继承人放弃接受遗产或放弃继承损害到他本人的债权人的权利时，债权人得受法院准许，替代他们的债务人并以其名义接受继承。⑤

---

① 参见《日本民法典》第986~989条。

② 参见“梁稿”第2008条第2款；“王稿”第554条第2款。

③ 参见“陈稿”第59条；“张稿”第9条。

④ 参见《瑞士民法典》第578条。

⑤ 参见《法国民法典》第779条。

从我国诸继承法学者建议稿看，关于放弃继承与债权人的撤销权，诸学者建议稿的观点可分为两种。第一种是债权人享有撤销权。例如，“梁稿”和“王稿”均规定，继承人放弃继承损害其债权人利益时，债权人可以在知道或应当知道继承人放弃继承之日起 6 个月内申请人民法院撤销继承人的放弃行为。① 第二种是债权人不享有撤销权。例如，“徐稿”规定，任何人无权撤销被继承人对遗产的抛弃，本人或其法定代理人因胁迫或欺诈作出抛弃的除外。②

我们认为，我国未规定债权人是否可以撤销继承人放弃继承的行为，此为立法之不足。我国实行当然继承主义，即继承开始后，除继承人明确表示放弃外，继承人当然取得遗产，故放弃继承是对既得财产权利的放弃，属于行使撤销权中的“无偿转让财产”的情形，当放弃继承危及债权人债权时，债权人当然可以行使撤销权保障其债权。故从保护债权人的利益出发，对继承权的放弃作出一定的限制是必要的。因此，上述吉林省被调查者认为放弃继承的行为可以被债权人撤销的民众观念、瑞士和法国的立法及“梁稿”和“王稿”的观点可供我国立法参考。

七、继承权的丧失、被继承人的宥恕与代位继承之特点与原因分析

（一）继承权的丧失与被继承人的宥恕之特点与原因分析

关于继承权的丧失与被继承人的宥恕的民众观念，统计数据显示的特点是，对于因欺诈、胁迫行为的继承人丧失继承权的，如获得被继承人谅解其继承权是否可以恢复，在吉林省被调查者中，(1) 认为可以恢复的，占七成半（75.67%）；(2) 认为不可以恢复的，占近二成半（24.33%）（见表 3-43）。

以上特点之原因分析，七成半的吉林省被调查者认为因欺诈、胁迫行为的继承人丧失继承权的，可因被继承人的谅解其继承权恢复的原因可能是：(1) 受到我国传统家庭观念的影响，从维护家庭关系的和睦和家族财产在家庭内部的有序传承的考虑，只要获得被继承人谅解，继承权的丧失后是可以恢复的；(2) 在我国的亲情观念中，长辈对于晚辈尤其是父母对于子女的包容心是极大的，只要晚辈知错能改，长辈就应该原谅他们；(3) 被继承人对其遗产如何分配可自主决定，虽然继承人因不良行为导致继承权的丧失，但只要被继承人选择原谅，就应该尊重被继承人的意愿。

关于继承权的丧失与被继承人的宥恕之我国立法，我国《继承法》未作规定。但 1985 年《执行继承法意见》第 13 条规定：“继承人虐待被继承人情节严重的，或者遗弃被继承人的，如以后确有悔改表现，而且被虐待人、被遗弃人生前又表示宽恕，可不确认其丧失继承权。”可见，我国立法并未规定继承人因欺诈、胁迫行为的继承人丧失继承权的在获得被继承人宽恕后能否恢复继承权。

从域外立法例看，不少国家对继承权的丧失后的恢复作了规定。例如，日本规定：“有特留份的推定继承人虐待、重大侮辱被继承人时，或者推定继承人有其他严重劣迹时，被继承人可以请求法院废除该推定继承人。被继承人可以随时请求法院撤销推定继承

---

① 参见“梁稿”第 2012 条；“王稿”第 562 条。

② 参见“徐稿”第四分编第 340 条。

人的废除。"① 意大利规定，如果被继承人在遗嘱中或者在公证书中明确表示恢复无继承资格人的继承权，则允许其参加继承。无继承资格人未被明确恢复权利的，如果遗嘱人知道其无继承资格的原因，但是依然在遗嘱中对其加以考虑，则允许该人在遗嘱规定的范围内参加继承。②

从我国诸继承法学者建议稿看，对继承权的丧失与宥恕立法建议分为两类：第一类是相对丧失（继承权的丧失可因被继承人的宽恕或原谅而恢复）与绝对丧失（继承权的丧失后不可恢复）相结合。例如，"梁稿"认为除为争夺遗产而杀害其他继承人而丧失继承权不可恢复外，其他丧失继承权的情形中，只要被继承人表示宽恕，即可恢复继承权。③"杨稿"规定，继承人因故意不法杀害被继承人的，或为争夺遗产而杀害其他继承人之外的事由而丧失继承权，如经被继承人事后宽恕，可恢复其继承权。被继承人知道继承人有丧失继承权的事由，仍然在遗嘱中指定其为继承人的，视为宽恕。④ 第二类是只有相对丧失。例如，"陈稿"规定，继承人有丧失继承权的法定情形时，但被继承人在遗嘱或公证书中明确表示宽恕的，不丧失继承权。被继承人知道继承人丧失继承资格的事由后，仍然在遗嘱中对其进行遗嘱处分的，视为宽恕。⑤

我们认为，我国对相对丧失继承权范围的规定过于狭窄，此为立法之不足。无论是在何种法定情形下丧失继承权的（被继承人因此已死亡的除外），如果被继承人表示宽恕的，继承权应予以恢复，一方面，可以保障被继承人的遗嘱自由之权利；另一方面，也可以保护继承人的继承利益，维护社会关系的稳定。因此，关于继承权的丧失与被继承人的宥恕，即对于因欺诈、胁迫行为的继承人丧失继承权的，如获得被继承人谅解其继承权可以恢复的上述吉林省被调查者的民众观念、域外立法例及我国学者建议稿的观点可供我国立法参考。

（二）继承权的丧失与代位继承之特点与原因分析

关于继承权的丧失与代位继承的民众观念，统计数据显示的特点是，对于继承人继承权的丧失的其晚辈直系血亲是否可代位继承，在吉林省被调查者中，（1）认为不可以代位继承的，占七成以上（72.50%）；（2）认为可以代位继承的，占近三成（27.50%）（见表3-44）。

以上特点之原因分析：对于继承人继承权的丧失的其晚辈直系血亲是否可代位继承，在吉林省被调查者中，（1）七成以上的人认为不可代位继承，其原因可能是被调查者受传统观念的影响较大，他们往往认为继承权是具有延续性的，如果一个人被剥夺了继承权，那么就意味着在家族中他所代表的这"一支"都丧失了继承的权利，这也是我国古代宗族观念的另一种体现。（2）近三成的人认为可代位继承，其原因可能是代位继承人

① 《日本民法典》第892、894条。

② 参见《意大利民法典》第466条。

③ 参见"梁稿"第1940条规定："继承人有下列行为之一的，丧失继承权：（一）为争夺遗产而杀害其他继承人的；（二）故意杀害被继承人的，但正当防卫的除外；（三）遗弃被继承人的，或者虐待被继承人情节严重的；（四）伪造、篡改或者销毁遗嘱，情节严重的；（五）以欺诈或者胁迫的手段，迫使或者妨碍被继承人设立、变更或者撤销遗嘱，情节严重的。继承人因前款第（二）、（三）、（四）、（五）种情形丧失继承权，如经被继承人宽恕的，可不确认其丧失继承权。继承权丧失的事由准用于受遗赠权的丧失。"

④ 参见"杨稿"第11条。

⑤ 参见"陈稿"第17条。

本身有继承权，与被代位的继承人是否丧失继承权无直接关系。

关于继承权的丧失与代位继承之我国立法，1985 年《执行继承法意见》第 28 条规定："继承人丧失继承权的，其晚辈直系血亲不得代位继承。如该代位继承人缺乏劳动能力又没有生活来源，或对被继承人尽赡养义务较多的，可适当分给遗产。"

从域外立法例看，关于代位继承权的立法体例分为两种类型：第一种是采取"固有权说"。"固有权说"认为代位人享有继承权是基于自身的权利与地位，与被代位人是否丧失继承权无关。例如，《日本民法典》第 887 条规定，被继承人的子女为继承人，被继承人的子女先于被继承人死亡或符合第 891 条规定（继承人丧失继承权的五条事由）或因废除而丧失继承权时，其子女代位成为继承人。第二种是采取"代位权说"。例如，《俄罗斯联邦民法典》第 1146 条规定，如果法定继承人由被继承人剥夺了继承权，则其后代不得代位继承。

从我国诸继承法学者建议稿看，多数学者建议稿的规定对于代位继承均主张采取"固有权说"。例如，"杨稿"规定，"被继承人的子女先于被继承人死亡、丧失继承权或者放弃继承权的，由被继承人的子女的晚辈直系血亲代位继承。代位继承人只能继承被代位人的法定应继份。代位继承不受辈数的限制，由辈分在先者代位"。[①]"陈稿"第 19 条规定："继承人丧失继承权的，其晚辈直系血亲仍得代位继承，但该继承人不得对其子女继承的遗产享有用益权。"

我们认为，继承人代位继承权是法律赋予继承权而固有的权利。且从现代民法"自己责任原则"考虑，长辈丧失继承权的后果不应波及无辜的晚辈。我国《继承法》规定丧失继承权的晚辈直系血亲不得代位继承，为立法之不足。因此，关于被代位继承人丧失继承权的其子女可代位继承的上述吉林省被调查者的民众观念、域外立法例及"杨稿"和"陈稿"的观点可供我国立法参考。

八、继承协议之特点与原因分析

（一）继承协议的订立主体与方式之特点与原因分析

关于继承协议的订立主体与方式的民众观念和民间习惯，统计数据显示的特点是，在吉林省被调查者中，（1）关于继承协议的订立主体与方式的民众观念，认可继承协议应由被继承人与全体法定继承人共同订立的，占近六成（57.33%）；认可继承协议应由被扶养人与承担约定扶养义务人共同签订的，占二成以上（21.17%）；认可继承协议由继承人之间签订即可，无须被继承人知晓或同意的，占二成以上（21.50%）（见表 3-45）。（2）关于继承协议的民间习惯，被调查者所在地区的习惯是：听说过或经历过签订继承协议的，占五成以上（52.50%）；没有听说或经历过签订继承协议的，占四成半以上（47.50%）（见表 3-46）。

以上特点之原因分析：（1）近六成的吉林省被调查者认可继承协议，其原因可能是受我国"养儿防老"传统观念的影响，认可由全体继承人与被继承人签订扶养协议，可以避免日后产生继承纠纷。（2）五成以上的吉林省被调查者所在地区有听说过或经历过签订继承协议之习惯，其原因可能是目前我国处于社会主义初级阶段，物质条件的缺乏和

① 参见"杨稿"第 17 条。

社会保障的不完善，家庭养老仍是老年人主要的养老模式，故为解决被扶养人养老送终的而签订继承协议的情形时常发生。

关于继承协议之我国立法，对于被继承人与法定继承人之间签订继承协议，我国《继承法》无规定。

从域外立法例看，对继承协议制度的立法可分为两种类型。第一种是认可继承协议。例如，瑞士规定，被继承人年满 18 周岁且具有判断能力可以订立继承协议。[①] 第二种是否定继承协议。例如，法国规定，任何人不得预先放弃未开始的继承，也不得就类似的继承订立条款，即使得到被继承人的同意也不行。[②]

从我国诸继承法学者建议稿看，对继承协议的立法态度有所不同。第一，赞成设立继承协议制度。例如，“张稿”第 54 条规定，被继承人可以与共同继承人订立继承合同，约定由一个或几个继承人承担赡养（扶养）被继承人的义务，被继承人死后，由承担赡养（扶养）义务的继承人按照继承合同继承遗产。合同对赡养（扶养）人继承遗产的部分未作明确约定的，视为继承全部遗产。继承合同应当以书面的形式订阅，并从有效成立时起生效。“杨稿”第 69 条规定，被继承人可以与继承人订立继承协议，由继承人承担比法定扶养义务更高的扶养义务，并继承约定的遗产。第二，不赞成继承协议制度。例如，“梁稿”“王稿”仅规定了遗赠扶养协议制度，未规定继承人与被继承人签订的继承协议。

我们认为，签订继承协议作为继承人与被继承人双方约定，通过对被继承人扶养及遗产分配进行合理安排的一种方式，立法应当予以认可。由于我国《继承法》规定放弃继承只能在继承开始之后，因此，在实践中签订的继承协议往往被认定为无效，不仅违背了被继承人的意思表示，而且依照协议履行了较多扶养义务继承人却不能按照协议取得约定的遗产，有违公平。我国现行立法未规定继承协议，此为立法之不足。因此，上述吉林省被调查者认可继承协议的民众观念和听说过或经历过继承协议的民间习惯、瑞士的立法及“杨稿”和“张稿”的观点可供我国立法参考。

（二）继承协议的变更方式及效力之特点与原因分析

关于继承协议的变更及效力的民众观念，统计数据显示的特点是，在继承协议履行过程中，如扶养人先于被扶养人去世，在吉林省被调查者中，（1）认为在原扶养人的子女有扶养能力的，被扶养人与该子女双方同意的情况下，可由该子女继续履行该继承协议的，即认可代位扶养的，占三成以上（32.10%）；（2）认为原继承协议终止，须签订新的继承协议，由新的扶养人履行扶养义务并继承遗产的，合计占四成以上（42.18%），其中，对于原扶养人超过其扶养义务所支出的费用，认为需要对原扶养人补偿费用的，占三成半（35.29%），认为不需要对原扶养人补偿费用的，占不到一成（6.89%）；（3）认为应由所有法定继承人共同扶养的，即实行法定赡养的，占二成半（25.21%）（见表 3-48）。

以上特点之原因分析：根据关于继承协议的变更方式与效力的民众观念之理由（见表 3-49），在吉林省被调查者中，（1）四成以上的人认为可以允许有条件地代位扶养，该合同继续有效，其原因是这样既可以维持被扶养人的一贯生活方式，也是尊重被扶养人

---

① 参见《瑞士民法典》第 468、494 条。

② 参见《法国民法典》第 1130 条。

的意思自治。(2)六成半以上的人认为承担扶养义务的人先于被继承人死亡该继承协议终止，其原因是继承协议具有人身性质，如继承协议中履行扶养义务一方死亡，则其子女不能当然地代为履行协议。因此，承担扶养义务的人先于被继承人死亡应是继承协议解除的情形。(3)三成半的人认为应对已去世的扶养人支付的超出其扶养义务的部分扶养费予以补偿，其原因是赡养被继承人是所有子女的共同法定义务，根据权利义务相一致的原则，依据继承协议不承担扶养义务的其他继承人，理应对依照继承协议已履行了扶养义务的主体给予适当补偿。(4)二成半的人认为原继承协议终止，故应由法定扶养义务人履行赡养义务，这符合法律规定。

关于继承协议的变更及效力之我国立法，我国《继承法》无规定。

从域外立法例看，在承认继承协议的部分国家立法中，对继承协议的变更及效力有所规定。例如，德国规定，在被继承人有权解除的继承合同中，继承可以在订立继承合同另一方当事人死亡后，以遗嘱废止继承合同中对遗产的处分。[①] 瑞士规定，继承人在被继承人死亡前死亡的，继承协议自然解除。继承人死亡之日，对于处分人在继承协议所获得的利益，死者的继承人可请求利益返还，但继承协议另有约定的除外。[②]

从我国诸继承法学者建议稿看，在赞成设立继承协议制度的学者建议稿中，“张稿”第55条规定，扶养义务人因为死亡或丧失扶养能力而不能继续履行合同义务，被继承人可以解除合同。合同解除后，义务人已经支付的扶养费用应当在共同继承人之间进行结算。“陈稿”第64、65条规定，扶养人先于受扶养人死亡，继承合同自动解除。受扶养人同意接受已经死亡的扶养人之继承人继续承担扶养的义务，继承合同继续履行。继承合同解除时，除合同另有约定外，受扶养人应当对扶养人已经履行的扶养义务适当支付补偿费用。

我们认为，我国立法未规定继承协议的变更方式及效力，此为立法之不足。作为继承协议的一方主体，被继承人可以选择由死亡继承人的子女继续履行继承协议，既是对被继承人意思自治的尊重，也可以不改变被继承人一贯的生活环境和方式，也避免了扶养费用的再次清算。因此，关于继承协议的变更及效力的上述吉林省被调查者的民众观念、瑞士的立法及我国学者建议稿的观点可供我国立法参考。

九、遗产债务清偿之特点与原因分析

(一) 遗产债务清偿责任的类型之特点与原因分析

关于继承人清偿遗产债务责任类型的民众观念，统计数据显示的特点是，对于被继承人的生前债务，在吉林省被调查者中，(1)认为继承人应承担自愿的无限清偿责任的，合计占六成半(65.33%)；(2)认为继承人应对其继承的遗产承担有限清偿责任的，占近八成(79.17%)；(3)认为继承人如有侵害遗产的行为应承担强制的无限清偿责任的，占五成半以上(56.67%)(见表3-50)。

以上特点之原因分析：在吉林省被调查者中，(1)近八成的人认为继承人对遗产债务应承担有限清偿责任，其原因可能是继承本身应当是一种增加财产或者至少是不能减少

① 参见《德国民法典》第2297条。

② 参见《瑞士民法典》第515条。

继承人财产的制度，因此继承人只能在遗产范围内清偿债务。（2）六成半的人认同继承人应对其继承的遗产承担自愿的无限清偿责任，其原因可能是受“父债子偿”的观念的影响，无论该债务是否已经超出被继承人留下的遗产价值范围。（3）五成半以上的人认为继承人应承担强制的无限清偿责任原因可能是，以此作为对继承人恶意的转移、隐瞒遗产而侵害遗产债权人的权利行为的惩罚。

关于继承人的债务清偿责任之我国立法，我国《继承法》第33条规定：“继承遗产应当清偿被继承人依法应当缴纳的税款和债务，缴纳税款和清偿债务以他的遗产实际价值为限。超过遗产实际价值部分，继承人自愿偿还的不在此限。继承人放弃继承的，对被继承人依法应当缴纳的税款和债务可以不负偿还责任。”

从域外立法例看，继承可分为限定责任继承（在遗产价值范围内清偿遗产债务）和无限责任继承（不以遗产价值为限清偿遗产债务）。前者可分为有条件的限定继承和无条件的限定继承；而后者可分为意定的无限责任继承（又称概括继承、单纯继承）与法定的无限继承（又称强制概括继承）。[①] 法国、日本等国家均规定了有条件的限定责任继承和法定的无限责任继承。例如，法国规定，继承人应在法定期限内向法院提交忠实而明确的遗产清册，然后声明限定继承或放弃继承。如果继承人不在法定期限内声明放弃继承或声明限定继承并提交遗产清册，或编制遗产清册不忠实，则须对遗产债务负无限责任。[②] 日本规定，继承人表示限定继承时，应在继承所得财产的限度内清偿被继承人的债务及遗赠。但继承人不在规定的期间内表示接受或放弃继承时，或继承人作出限定继承或放弃继承后，隐匿继承财产的全部或部分，私自消费或者恶意不将其记载于继承财产目录时，须无限制地继承被继承人的权利义务（含债务）。[③]

从我国诸继承法学者建议稿看，对遗产债务清偿责任可分两种类型。第一种是保留我国《继承法》的无条件的限定清偿责任和自愿的无限清偿责任，如“梁稿”第2014条和“王稿”第658条均规定，继承人以其所接受遗产的实际价值为限对遗产债务承担责任。超过遗产实际价值部分，继承人自愿偿还的，不在此限。继承人放弃继承的，对被继承人依法应当缴纳的税款和债务不承担偿还责任。第二种是在我国《继承法》的现行立法基础上，增设有条件的限定清偿责任和有条件的强制无限清偿责任。例如，“杨稿”中规定，继承人在制作遗产清单并公证后，如果有隐匿重要遗产的；在遗产清单中故意漏记重要遗产，或者计入不存在的债务的；处分遗产损害遗产债权人权利的情形时，仍应对全部遗产债务承担责任。[④]

我们认为，我国立法规定无条件的有限责任继承，此为立法之不足。第一，对被继承人遗产债务，是承担有条件的有限清偿责任还是自愿的无限清偿责任，应该给予继承人选择的自由；第二，当继承人有恶意损害遗产债权人权益的行为时，应使其承担无限清偿责任。因此，关于继承人清偿遗产债务责任类型，应设立强制的无限清偿责任的上述吉林省被调查者的民众观念、域外立法例及我国学者建议稿的观点可供我国立法参考。

① 参见陈苇主编：《中国遗产处理制度系统化构建研究》，中国人民公安大学出版社2019年版，第300页。

② 参见《法国民法典》第793~803条。

③ 参见《日本民法典》第921条。

④ 参见“杨稿”第80条。

（二）被继承人丧葬费的支付之特点与原因分析

关于被继承人丧葬费的支付的民间习惯，统计数据显示的特点是，在吉林省被调查者所在地区的习惯是，（1）由全体继承人共同支付的，占五成（50.83%）；（2）从被继承人的遗产中支付的，占近五成（48.67%）（见表 3-52）。

以上特点之原因分析：对于被继承人丧葬费的支付，在吉林省被调查者所在地区，（1）五成的地区习惯是由全体继承人共同支付，其原因可能是受中国传统文化的影响，父母养育子女，子女对父母有生养死葬的义务是天经地义。（2）近五成的地区习惯是从被继承人的遗产中支付，其原因可能是丧葬费用是被继承人的债务，理应从遗产中进行支付。

关于被继承人丧葬费的支付之我国立法，我国《继承法》无规定。

从域外立法例看，对被继承人的丧葬费用的支付分为两种类型。第一种是由继承人支付。例如，德国规定，由继承人负责被继承人的丧葬费用。① 第二种是由被继承人的遗产支付。例如，日本规定，对于因殡葬费用产生的债权者，于债务人的总财产上有先取特权。②

从我国诸继承法学者建议稿看，对丧葬费用的支付观点不一。例如，“王稿”第 651 条规定，被继承人的与其社会地位相称的丧葬费，由继承人负担。但“陈稿”第 68 条规定，合理的丧葬费用属于遗产债务。“杨稿”第 83 条规定，合理的丧葬费由遗产支付。

我们认为，我国立法未规定被继承人丧葬费的支付，此为立法之不足。虽然丧葬费用不是被继承人的债务，但妥善安葬死者是继承的前提，故该费用应与遗产管理等费用一样，由遗产支付。此外，由遗产支付合理的丧葬费用，有利于避免在丧葬事宜上铺张浪费，同时有助于继承人妥善办理被继承人的丧葬事宜。因此，关于被继承人丧葬费从被继承人的遗产中支付的上述吉林省被调查者所在地区的民间习惯、日本的立法及我国学者建议稿的观点可供我国立法参考。

（三）遗产债务的清偿顺序之特点与原因分析

关于遗产债务的清偿顺序的民众观念与民间习惯，统计数据显示的特点是，（1）吉林省被调查者所在地区的遗产债务清偿顺序的习惯是：第一顺序“丧葬费用”（占63.17%）；第二顺序“遗产管理等费用”（占 23.33%）和“欠债”（占 27.17%）；第三顺序“欠付的工资”（占 24.83%）；第四顺序“受被继承人扶养人的生活费”（占21.17%）；第五顺序“税款”（占 11.50%）和“对被继承人扶养较多的人之酌情分配遗产份额”（占 15.83%）；第六顺序“遗赠扶养协议写明遗赠的遗产”（占 17.50%）（见表3-53）。（2）在吉林省被调查者的观念上，遗产债务清偿顺序如下：第一顺序“丧葬费用”（占 51.33%）和“遗赠扶养协议写明遗赠的遗产”（占 14.00%）；第二顺序“欠债”（占 20.00%）和“对被继承人扶养较多的人之酌情分配遗产份额”（占 19.17%）；第三顺序“欠付的工资”（占 18.33%）；第四顺序“受被继承人扶养人的生活费”（占17.00%）；第五顺序“税款”（13.33%）；第六顺序“遗产管理等费用”（占 24.00%）（见表 3-54）。

---

① 参见《德国民法典》第 1968 条。

② 参见《日本民法典》第 306 条。

以上特点之原因分析：(1) 丧葬费用是用于妥善处理被继承人死亡事宜之花费，妥善处理被继承人的丧葬事宜是清偿遗产债务，分割遗产的前提，应当被优先受偿。(2) 欠债和欠付的工资，都是被继承人与一般民事主体发生的债务关系，可能是出于维护社会稳定、保障交易安全的考虑，排在丧葬费用之后进行清偿。(3) 对于受被继承人扶养的生活费、对被继承人扶养较多的人之酌情分配遗产份额、税款和遗赠扶养协议写明遗赠的清偿顺序，可能是无法对这几项债务所代表的价值或意义作出明确判断，因此吉林省被调查者对其的清偿顺序未形成统一意见。

关于遗产债务清偿的顺序之我国立法，我国《继承法》第33条规定，“继承遗产应当清偿被继承人依法应当缴纳的税款和债务，缴纳税款和清偿债务以他的遗产实际价值为限”。

从域外立法例看，第一，部分国家通过多个法条分散地对遗产债务清偿顺序进行了规定，如德国的遗产债务清偿顺序为：遗产管理费、财产目录制作费；有优先权的债务；扶养费；普通债务；特留份；遗赠。[①] 第二，部分国家专门对遗产债务清偿顺序作了具体规定，如俄罗斯规定，遗产债务清偿顺序为：一是继承费用包括因被继承人患病和丧葬而发生的费用、遗产保护和管理费、遗嘱执行费用；二是被继承人的债务；三是必继份；四是遗赠。[②]

从我国诸继承法学者建议稿看，对遗产债务清偿顺序的规定有所不同。例如，“王稿”第650条规定了遗产债务清偿的五种顺序，即按继承费用、遗产税、被继承人生前所欠债务、遗产酌给债务，因特留份扣减权、遗赠等产生的债务顺序进行清偿。“张稿”第20条规定，遗产债务清偿顺序为四顺序：清偿顺序依次为遗产管理费用；被继承人生前扶养的、无劳动能力的人的必要的生活费用；被继承人生前所负债务；遗赠。即使遗产不足以清偿第三顺序的债务，也必须为无劳动能力又无其他生活来源的继承人保留必要的生活费用。

我们认为，我国欠缺遗产债务清偿的顺序，此为立法之不足。遗产债务清偿顺序关系到继承人、遗产债权人等遗产利害关系人的权益保护。因此，关于遗产债务的清偿顺序，上述吉林省被调查者的民众观念与民间习惯、域外立法例及我国学者建议稿的观点可供我国立法参考。

十、遗产分割之特点与原因分析

（一）遗产分割的自由与限制之特点与原因分析

第一，关于遗产分割的自由与限制的民间习惯，统计数据显示的特点是，在吉林省被调查者所在地区的习惯是：(1) 由各继承人共同协商后进行遗产分割的，占六成以上(63.00%)；(2) 只要有继承人要求分割遗产就得进行分割的，占近二成（17.83%)；(3) 当遗嘱禁止分割遗产则不得分割遗产的，占一成半以上（16.50%）（见表3-55）。

以上特点之原因分析：根据关于遗产分割的自由与限制的民间习惯之理由（见表

① 参见陈苇主编：《外国继承法比较与中国民法典继承编制定研究》，北京大学出版社2011年版，第514页。

② 参见《俄罗斯联邦民法典》第1174、1175、1149条。参见陈苇主编：《中国遗产处理制度系统化构建研究》，中国人民公安出版社2019年版，第310页。

3-56)，(1) 六成以上的地区的习惯是由各继承人共同协商后进行遗产分割，其原因是遗产由各继承人共同继承，遗产分割涉及各继承人的利益。(2) 近二成的地区的习惯是继承人要求分割遗产就得进行分割，其原因是尊重继承人的意愿，及时分割遗产。

第二，关于提出遗产分割请求的时间的民间习惯，统计数据显示的特点是，当被继承人死亡后，其子女继承人是否可以向被继承人之配偶（子女之在世的父亲或母亲）提出分割遗产请求，被调查者所在地区的习惯是：(1) 不会提出分割特殊遗产之请求的，占八成（80.70%）；(2) 会提出分割特殊遗产之请求（包括有条件的分割和无条件的分割）的，占近二成（19.29%）（见表 3-57）。

以上特点之原因分析，根据关于提出遗产分割请求时间的民间习惯之理由（见表 3-58)，八成的吉林省被调查者所在地区的习惯是不会提出分割特殊遗产之请求，其原因是被继承人的遗产就应该由其生存配偶全部继承，故其子女不能向母亲提出遗产分割的请求，如果提出会被视作不孝敬老人的表现。

第三，关于被继承人可否立遗嘱限制一定时期内不分割特定遗产的民众观念，统计数据显示的特点是，(1) 关于被继承人可否通过遗嘱限制遗产的分割，主张可以的占近八成（79.97%）；主张不可以的占二成（20.03%）（见表 3-59）。(2) 关于被继承人立遗嘱限制遗产分割之具体期限，认为以 5 年为宜的，占近三成（28.72%）；认为以 10 年为宜的，占近三成（28.38%）；认为以 15 年为宜的，占一成（9.40%）（见表 3-61）。(3) 关于是否遵守被继承人遗嘱中对遗产分割限制，在被调查者所在地区，可以不遵守遗嘱对遗产分割的限制的，占四成半（45.55%）；不可以不遵守被继承人遗嘱限制遗产分割时间约束的，占近五成半（54.45%）（见表 3-62）。

以上特点之原因分析：根据关于遗嘱限制遗产分割的民众观念的理由（见表 3-60)，在吉林省被调查者中，(1) 近八成的人认为被继承人可以通过遗嘱限制遗产的分割，其原因是遗产是被继承人生前的个人财产，被继承人在设立遗嘱时有权决定遗产的分配及其分割。(2) 近三成的人认为被继承人立遗嘱限制遗产分割之具体期限以 5 年为宜，其原因是有利于发挥物的效用及价值，即遗嘱限制分割的时间不能太长。(3) 近五成半的地区习惯有必须遵守被继承人遗嘱限制遗产分割限制的习惯，其原因是遗产本归被继承人所有，必须遵守其在遗嘱中限制遗产分割的规定。

关于遗产分割自由与限制之我国立法，我国《继承法》第 15 条规定，"遗产分割的时间、办法和份额，由继承人协商确定。协商不成的，可以由人民调解委员会调解或者向人民法院提起诉讼"。

在域外立法中，大部分国家均规定继承开始以后可随时请求分割遗产，但同时均作出了一定的限制性规定。例如，《法国民法典》第 815 条规定，任何人均不受强制维持财产共有。继承人可以随时提出遗产分割的要求，但判决或契约另行规定暂缓分割遗产的不在此限。《意大利民法典》第 713 条规定，共同继承人可以随时请求分割遗产。但全体或者部分继承人是未成年人的，遗嘱人可以决定在年龄最小的继承人成年后的 1 年内不得进行遗产分割。遗嘱人还可以决定在遗嘱人死亡后不超过 5 年的期间内不得对遗产或者某些遗产进行分割。

从我国诸继承法学者建议稿看，"梁稿"第 2021 条规定，遗产债务尚未清偿完毕、遗嘱指定在一定期间内不可分割（但该期间不得超过 5 年，超过 5 年的，缩短为 5 年），或者继承人协商同意于一定期间内不可分割的，则不得请求分割遗产，且对特定遗产进行限时分割会严重损害其价值的，人民法院经继承人申请，可以裁判暂缓分割。“王稿”第645条规定，继承开始后，继承人可以随时请求分割遗产，但当遗嘱指定遗产于一定期间内不得分割（但此期间不得超过5年，超过5年的，缩短为5年），或继承人协商同意于一定期限内不分割遗产，或遗产中某一项一经分割会严重损害其价值的，如果继承人对其分割达不成协议，应当整体的分给一个继承人，并有该继承人按照遗产份额对其他继承人进行补偿时除外。

我们认为，我国对遗产分割限制的立法存在不足。为了避免不必要的继承纠纷产生，应对遗产分割的时间、限制、特殊情形下遗产分割等内容作出明确的规定。因此，关于遗产分割的自由予以适当限制的上述吉林省被调查者的民间习惯和民众观念、意大利的立法及我国学者建议稿的观点可供我国立法参考。

（二）遗产分割瑕疵的担保责任之特点与原因分析

关于遗产分割瑕疵的担保责任的民间习惯，统计数据显示的特点是，吉林省被调查者所在地区的习惯是：（1）由共同继承人相互承担的，占四成（40.50%）；（2）由分得瑕疵遗产的继承人自行承担，即继承人间不相互承担遗产分割瑕疵担保责任的，占近六成（58.17%）（见表3-63）。

以上特点之原因分析：在吉林省被调查者所在地区，（1）四成的地区的习惯是由共同继承人相互承担的，其原因可能是出于公平角度考虑，在共同继承人之间，只让一个人承担遗产的瑕疵责任，有失公平；（2）近六成的地区的习惯是由分得瑕疵遗产的继承人自行承担，即继承人间不相互承担遗产分割瑕疵担保责任的，其原因可能是继承人之间都是亲属关系，对于分到瑕疵遗产的继承人来说，会为了维护继承人之间关系的和睦而选择自认倒霉，以避免发生纠纷。

关于遗产分割瑕疵的担保责任之我国立法，我国《继承法》无规定。

从域外立法例看，许多国家都对遗产分割瑕疵的担保责任有所规定。例如，《日本民法典》第911条规定，各共同继承人对其他共同继承人，按其继承份额负与出卖人相同的担保责任。《意大利民法典》第758条规定，共同继承人之间仅应对于遗产分割前的事由发生的纠纷和追夺相互担保；但遗产分割文书明确免除共同继承人之间担保，或者追夺是由于继承人自己过失造成的除外。

从我国诸继承法学者建议稿看，部分学者建议稿均对遗产分割后的瑕疵担保责任进行了规定。例如，“王稿”第648条规定，各继承人应以其所得的遗产份额为限对其他继承人分得的遗产负与出卖人同样的瑕疵担保责任。各继承人对其他继承人分得的债权，就遗产分割时债务人的支付能力，负担保责任。“梁稿”第2025条和“陈稿”第79条对此也有规定。

我们认为，公平原则是民法的基本原则之一，可以保护继承人的利益，防止由于分得遗产的瑕疵而造成在分割遗产后导致实质上的不公平，我国立法欠缺此制度，是立法之不足。因此，上述吉林省被调查者所在地区对遗产分割的瑕疵由共同继承人相互承担的民间习惯、域外立法例和我国学者建议稿的观点可供我国立法参考。

十一、无人承受遗产的处理之特点与原因分析

（一）无人承受遗产的归属之特点与原因分析

关于无人承受遗产的归属主体的民众观念，统计数据显示的特点是，在吉林省被调查者中，（1）主张归属主体为社会公共组织（包括归属于国家、死者生前所在地的国库、死者生前所在地民政部门的社会福利机构和死者生前所在地的居委会）的，占八成（城镇居民 81.50%，农村居民 80.67%）；（2）主张归属主体为自然人（归属于不是继承人的其他亲属）的，占一成半以上（城镇居民 17.17%，农村居民 17.83%）（见表 3-64、表 3-66）。

以上特点之原因分析：根据关于无人承受遗产的归属主体的民众观念之理由（见表 3-65），在吉林省被调查者中，（1）八成的人认为无人承受遗产的归属主体社会公共组织，其原因是：其一，归公有可以便于规范财产秩序，有利于对遗产的清算、管理和利用；其二，受我国《继承法》第 32 条规定的影响。（2）一成半以上的人认为无人承受遗产的归属主体为自然人，其原因是不是继承人的其他亲属与死者有血缘或者其他亲密关系，由其取得遗产理所应当。

关于无人承受遗产的归属主体之我国立法，我国《继承法》第 32 条规定："无人继承又无人受遗赠的遗产，归国家所有；死者生前是集体所有制组织成员的，归所在集体所有制组织所有。"

从域外立法例看，许多国家都对无人承受遗产的归属主体有所规定。例如，《瑞士民法典》第 466 条规定，被继承人无继承人的，其遗产归属于其最后住所地所在地的州，或依州法归属于有权利的乡镇。《日本民法典》第 959 条规定，依据对特别关系人的继承财产分与的规定无法处理的继承财产，归属国库。

从我国诸继承法学者建议稿看，"梁稿"第 2029 条规定，无人承受的遗产，在人民法院指定的遗产管理人依本法规定清偿了遗产债务和继承费用之后仍有剩余的，由遗产管理人移交有关部门上缴国库所有；死者生前是集体所有制组织成员的，移交其所在的集体所有制组织。"陈稿"第 87 条规定，无人承受的遗产，经遗产债务清偿、执行遗赠后有剩余的，遗产管理人经书面请求居民委员会或村民委员会主任并获同意及签字后，遗产管理人可依具体情况将遗产的全部或部分酌情分配给依靠被继承人扶养的人、对被继承人扶养较多的人、与被继承人一同生活的人或其他与被继承人关系密切的人。在无前款规定人员的情形下，遗产管理人应当将剩余的遗产移交国家或者集体组织所有。

我们认为，关于无人承受遗产的归属主体，我国可以保留现行立法之规定。这既符合八成被调查者之"归公的意愿"，也与域外立法例归国家或乡镇的规定相一致。对于无人承受的遗产，应首先考虑是否可以酌情分给依靠被继承人扶养的人、对被继承人扶养较多的人、与被继承人一同生活的人或其他与被继承人关系密切的人，在酌分后剩余的无人承受的遗产，才应归属于国家或集体组织。因此，关于无人承受遗产的归属主体的上述吉林省被调查者的民众观念、瑞士的立法及我国学者建议稿的观点可供我国立法参考。

（二）无人承受遗产的处理之特点与原因分析

1. 无人承受遗产的管理人

关于无人承受遗产管理人的产生方式的民众观念，统计数据显示的特点是，在吉林省

被调查者中，（1）认为由人民法院指定的，占五成以上（53.33%）；（2）认为由死者户籍所在地的居委会或村委会或所在单位指定的，占三成（30.17%）；（3）认为由民政部门指定的，占近一成半（14.67%）（见表 3-67）。

以上特点之原因分析：根据关于无人继承遗产管理人产生方式的民众观念之理由（见表 3-68），在吉林省被调查者中，（1）五成以上的人认为应由人民法院指定无人承受遗产管理人，其原因是由人民法院指定更具有权威性，有利于公平保护相关债权人的利益；（2）三成的人认为由死者户籍所在地的居委会或村委会或所在单位指定无人承受遗产管理人，其原因是有利于对遗产进行清算、管理和利用。

关于无人承受遗产的管理人的产生方式之我国立法，我国《继承法》无规定。

从域外立法例看，许多国家均对无人承受遗产的管理人有所规定。例如，《日本民法典》第 952 条规定，继承人的存在不明确时，家庭法院根据利害关系人或检察官的请求，须为继承财产选任管理人。家庭法院选任继承财产管理人后，须毫不迟缓地予以公告。

从我国诸继承法学者建议稿看，诸学者建议稿对无人承受遗产的管理人产生方式观点不同。例如，“张稿”第 67 条规定，无人承受遗产的遗产管理人由法院指定。“杨稿”规定，继承开始后，有无继承人不明的，或者已知的继承人、受遗赠人丧失、放弃继承权或受遗赠权的，有关人员、部门或基层组织应将情况及时通知民政部门。民政部门在接到通知后，应指定遗产管理人管理遗产。

我们认为，无人承受遗产的管理人的确定，我国《继承法》未作规定，此为立法之不足。因此，关于无人承受遗产管理人的产生方式的上述吉林省被调查者的民众观念、日本的立法以及我国学者建议稿的观点可供我国立法参考。

2. 无人承受遗产的酌分请求权人

关于无人承受的遗产之酌情分配请求主体的民众观念，统计数据显示的特点是，在吉林省被调查者中，有六成至七成的人主张无人承受的遗产的酌分请求权人包括：依靠死者扶养的人占 77.83%；与死者共同生活的人占 62.83%；与死者有密切联系且对其帮助较多的人占 69.67%（见表 3-69）。

以上特点之原因分析：吉林省被调查者认为无人承受遗产的酌分请求权主体较我国《继承法》的规定范围更大，其原因可能是：（1）可以避免无人承受的遗产收归国家所有，能够更好地发挥遗产的扶养功能；（2）依靠死者扶养的人、与死者共同生活的人、与死者关系密切且对其帮助较多的人等，均与被继承人有密切关系，或帮助较多，将遗产酌情分配给他们符合情理。

关于无人承受的遗产之酌情分配请求主体之我国立法，我国《继承法》无规定。但 1985 年《执行继承法意见》第 57 条规定：“遗产因无人继承收归国家或集体所有时，按继承法第十四条规定可以分给遗产的人提出取得遗产的要求，人民法院应视情况适当分给遗产。”

从域外立法例看，部分国家对无人承受遗产的酌分请求权主体有所规定。例如，《日本民法典》第 958-2 条规定，法院认为适当时，可以根据曾与被继承人共同生活的、对被继承人的疗养看护尽力的人及其他与被继承人有特别关系的人之请求，将遗产的全部或部分分配给此人。英国规定，王室可以自由裁量，将遗产给实际上依靠无遗嘱死亡者的人，而不论其是否与无遗嘱死亡者有关系。或者其他无遗嘱死亡者希望供养的人。

从我国诸继承法学者建议稿看，部分学者对无人承受遗产的酌分请求权有所规定。例如，“张稿”第70条规定，无人承受遗产的酌分遗产人为与被继承人共同生活或者精心照顾被继承人的人。

我们认为，我国无人承受的遗产之酌情分配请求主体范围较窄，此为立法之不足。将无人承受的遗产分配给由被继承人扶养的人、对被继承人扶养较多的人、与被继承人一同生活的人或其他与被继承人有密切关系的人等，尽可能地充分发挥遗产养老育幼、维护伦理亲情的作用。因此，上述吉林省被调查者主张扩大无人承受的遗产之酌情分配请求主体的民众观念、日本立法和“张稿”的观点可供我国立法参考。

第四节　当代中国吉林省民众财产继承观念与遗产处理习惯对中国民法典继承编制定的立法启示

以上，我们根据吉林省被调查者的财产继承观念与遗产处理习惯实证调查的统计汇总数据，分析归纳其特点，研究其特点的产生原因，并考察我国司法实践相关案例，分析我国继承法律制度的适用情况，进而结合考察域外立法例和我国诸继承法学者建议稿的观点，总结我国《继承法》相关制度的优点和剖析其不足。以下，我们将以吉林省被调查者的财产继承观念与遗产处理习惯为参考基础，从中国实际出发，借鉴域外立法例和我国诸继承法学者建议稿的有益观点，对我国“民法典继承法编”编纂中相关继承制度的修改完善或予以保留，提出立法建议，以供我国立法机关参考。

一、我国遗产范围界定制度之不足与立法完善建议

（一）我国遗产范围界定制度之不足

关于遗产范围界定制度，我国《继承法》主要存在的不足为：第一，对遗产范围仅有正面列举与概括相结合规定，欠缺反面排除的规定。我国社会经济的发展带来了财产形式的多样化，现行法律中列举的遗产形式的局限性也随之凸显，这导致民众对遗产的种类认识发生偏差。例如，在吉林省被调查者中，近五成至六成的被调查者对被继承人的债务和以被继承人的姓名注册的邮箱、QQ账号等是否属于遗产的认识不一，这可能会引起遗产继承的纠纷（见表3-4）。第二，未规定被继承人生前特种赠与财产归扣制度，不利于遗产在共同继承人之间公平地分配，但近七成半的吉林省被调查者不认同归扣制度，且六成以上的地区无此习惯（见表3-5、表3-7）。

（二）我国遗产范围界定制度之立法完善建议

综上，我们针对我国遗产范围制度的修改完善提出以下建议：

1. 遗产范围界定模式之立法建议

建议应适度延展遗产范围。例如，公民的特许经营权等具有重要财产价值的权利，以及网络虚拟财产这一新型财产也应被纳入遗产范围。

建议补充遗产范围的反面排除的规定。对于遗产的种类，在继续坚持我国《继承法》正面列举与概括相结合规定的基础上，补充反面排除的规定，明确遗产是被继承人死亡时遗留的个人所有的财产。但与被继承人人身性质不可分割的财产和法律规定不得继承的财产，不属于遗产。

2. 被继承人生前特种赠与财产的归扣之立法建议

建议对于是否增设遗产归扣制度应采取谨慎态度。即使为了维护继承公平而设立遗产归扣制度，也应经历本土化的过程。①

二、我国继承开始的通知和公告制度之不足与立法完善建议

（一）我国继承开始的通知和公告制度之不足

关于继承开始的通知和公告制度，我国《继承法》主要存在两个方面的不足：第一，继承开始的通知和公告的主体范围狭窄，不利于及时告知继承权利人以及遗产利害关系人前来参与遗产处理，不利于保障遗产利害关系人的权益。从本次吉林省被调查者所在地区的习惯看，继承开始的通知和公告的主体较我国《继承法》规定的通知主体更广泛（见表3-10）。第二，欠缺继承通知和公告的方式的规定，不利于继承开始的通知主体积极履行义务，容易引发继承纠纷。从本次吉林省被调查者所在地区的习惯看，继承开始的通知和公告方式呈现出多样化（见表3-11）。前述涉及继承开始的通知和公告制度的案例之司法审判实践中，也反映出我国继承开始的通知和公告制度存在此不足。

（二）我国继承开始的通知和公告制度之立法完善建议

综上，我们针对我国继承开始的通知和公告制度的完善提出以下建议：

1. 继承开始的通知和公告的主体之立法建议

建议扩大继承开始后通知主体的范围，一是将受遗赠人、遗产债权人等其他利害关系人纳入通知主体的范围；二是应适当增加相应的政府机构作为继承开始的通知和公告主体。

2. 继承开始的通知和公告的方式之立法建议

建议对通知和公告的方式进一步加以完善细化。例如，可以采用列举方式指明当事人可以采用书信、电话、电报、口信以及公告等形式，但不限于此范围。

3. 继承开始的通知和公告的期间之立法建议

对于继承开始的通知和公告的期间，由于其与被继承人、继承人所处环境与条件的不同而差异较大，所以仅在合理期间即可，建议无须作出明确之规定。

三、我国遗产管理制度之不足与立法完善建议

（一）我国遗产管理制度之不足

关于遗产管理制度，我国《继承法》主要存在以下不足：第一，对遗产管理人的选任没有规定；八成半的吉林省被调查者所在地区有由法定继承人担任遗产管理人的习惯（见表3-13）。第二，对遗产管理人的职责与报酬欠缺的规定；吉林省被调查者认同遗产管理人职责的多样性，对于遗产管理人是否可以请求报酬的习惯各地不一（见表3-15、表3-16）。第三，缺乏遗产管理人的损害赔偿责任等内容。近七成的吉林省被调查者认为遗产管理人只有在中重大过失才承担遗产损害赔偿责任（见表3-18）。前述涉及遗产管理制度的案例之司法审判实践，也反映出我国遗产管理制度存在此不足。

---

① 参见李洪祥：《遗产归扣制度的理论、制度构成及其本土化》，载《现代法学》2012年第5期，第54~62页。

（二）我国遗产管理制度之立法完善建议

综上，我们针对我国遗产管理制度的修改完善提出以下建议：

1. 遗产管理人的产生方式之立法建议

建议增设遗产管理人的产生方式。遗产管理人的选任，宜采取被继承人生前指定或继承人在继承开始后协商推选为主，法定补充为辅的遗产管理人选任制度，即“如果遗嘱中指定了遗产管理人，则应当尊重当事人的意思。如果被继承人没有通过遗嘱指定遗产管理人，则应通过继承人推举或者法院指定的方式确定。同时，在全体继承人都放弃继承时，也应当选择遗产管理人负责清偿债务”。①

2. 遗产管理人的管理职责与报酬之立法建议

建议增设遗产管理人的管理职责和报酬。②

3. 遗产管理人的损害赔偿责任之立法建议

建议增设遗产管理人的损害赔偿责任。建议应根据“过错责任原则”确定遗产管理人是否需承担损害赔偿责任，即遗产管理人因故意或重大过失，未尽遗产管理义务而造成遗产毁损或灭失的，应当承担损害赔偿责任。

四、我国法定继承制度之不足与立法完善建议

（一）我国法定继承制度之不足

关于法定继承制度，我国《继承法》主要存在五个方面的不足：第一，法定继承人范围较窄、顺序较少，容易导致被继承人的遗产无人继承。在吉林省被调查者的观念中，认可的法定继承人的范围更广，法定继承人的顺序更多（见表3-19、表3-20）。第二，配偶为第一顺序的法定继承人，不利于保障配偶及后顺序的血亲继承人的继承权益。第三，未规定配偶对遗产中家庭住房的先取权与终生使用权，不利于保障生存配偶的基本生存权和居住权；四成半以上的吉林省被调查者所在地区有此习惯（见表3-22）。第四，未规定后顺序特殊法定继承人对特殊遗产的终生使用权，不利于后顺序特殊法定继承人的基本生存权和居住权，且八成以上的吉林省被调查者认同后顺序特殊法定继承人对特殊遗产可无偿地享有终生期限的使用权（见表3-25、表3-26）。第五，尽了主要赡养义务的丧偶儿媳（或女婿）作为第一顺序法定继承人，不利于保护其他共同继承人之继承权。前述涉及法定继承制度的案例之司法审判实践中，也反映出我国尽了主要赡养义务的丧偶儿媳或女婿的遗产分配方式存在此不足。

（二）我国法定继承制度之立法完善建议

综上，我们针对我国法定继承制度的修改完善提出以下建议：

1. 法定继承人的范围与顺序之立法建议

由于我国长期实行计划生育政策，而且人们的婚姻、生育观念发生了改变，我国的人口结构与30年前早已不同，法定血亲继承人的数量逐渐减少，这就可能出现被继承人死亡后财产无人继承的现象。若财产最终被收归国有，则与民法保护私人财产所有权的理念

① 参见王利明：《继承法修改的若干问题》，载《社会科学战线》2013年第7期，第181页。

② 具体立法内容参见陈苇主编：《中国遗产处理制度系统化构建研究》，中国人民公安大学出版社2019年版，第158页。

背道而驰，因此需要适当扩大继承人范围和增补顺序。在扩展法定继承人范围和增补顺序时，应考虑与被继承人具有一定经济上和情感上联系、在一定情况下能尽扶养和扶助义务、民间有相互继承遗产习惯的血亲为宜。[①] 我们建议将法定继承人的范围扩大到四亲等内的亲属，并将这些亲属作为第三顺序即可。

2. 生存配偶与血亲继承人的法定应继份之立法建议

建议仍将配偶作为第一顺序继承人且原则上与同顺序的继承人均分遗产规定比较妥当。

3. 配偶对遗产中的家庭住房的先取权与终生使用权之立法建议

建议增加配偶对遗产中的家庭住房的先取权与终生使用权。

4. 后顺序特殊法定继承人对遗产中的家庭住房的先取权与终生使用权之立法建议

建议增加后顺序特殊法定继承人对原使用的遗产住房及生活用品的终生使用权的内容，即祖父母或外祖父母等近亲属因顺序在后未参加继承时，对遗产中的家庭住房和其他物品享有先取权或终生使用权。

5. 尽了主要赡养义务的丧偶儿媳或女婿的遗产分配方式之立法建议

建议不应将尽了主要赡养义务的丧偶儿媳或女婿继续作为第一顺序的法定继承人，但如有代位继承人时，则他们应作为酌分遗产请求权人。

五、我国遗嘱继承制度之不足与立法完善建议

（一）我国遗嘱继承制度的不足

关于遗嘱继承制度，我国《继承法》主要存在三个方面的不足：第一，公证遗嘱具有最高效力，且只能采用公证的形式进行变更，不符合遗嘱继承自由原则。合计六成半以上的吉林省被调查者认为后遗嘱优先于前一遗嘱（包括公证遗嘱）（见表3-29）。前述涉及遗嘱继承制度的案例之司法审判实践，也反映出我国公证遗嘱适用效力之不足。第二，未规定特留份制度，不利于防止遗嘱自由权利的滥用和发挥遗产养老育幼的功能；七成以上的吉林省被调查者认为应对遗嘱处分个人财产的自由予以一定限制（见表3-31）。第三，未规定夫妻共同遗嘱，不利于规范夫妻共同遗嘱行为，容易引发继承纠纷，且七成以上的吉林省被调查者认可夫妻共同设立遗嘱，七成以上的地区有此习惯（见表3-33、表3-35）。

（二）我国遗嘱继承制度之立法完善建议

综上，我们针对我国遗嘱继承制度的修改完善提出以下建议：

1. 公证遗嘱与其他形式遗嘱的效力之立法建议

建议取消关于公证遗嘱效力最高的规定，即当被继承人立有数份不同形式的遗嘱时，遗嘱内容相抵触的，以最后订立的遗嘱为准。

2. 遗嘱自由的限制——特留份之立法建议

建议增设特留份制度，即遗嘱人以遗嘱处分财产，但其应为其晚辈直系血亲、配偶和父母保留特定的遗产份额。

---

① 参见陈苇、冉启玉：《完善我国法定继承人范围和顺序的立法思考》，载《法学论坛》2013年第28期，第54~57页。

3. 夫妻共同遗嘱之立法建议

建议明确规定夫妻共同遗嘱的法律效力，并对其形式、内容等作出具体规定。

六、我国继承和遗赠的接受与放弃制度之不足与立法完善建议

（一）我国继承和遗赠的接受与放弃制度之不足

关于继承和遗赠的接受与放弃制度，我国《继承法》主要存在三方面的不足：第一，未明确规定继承人作出接受或者放弃继承的意思表示的期限。第二，在受遗赠人未作表示的情况下视为放弃受遗赠，不利于保护当事人的合法权利，且六成半以上的吉林省被调查者对遗赠接受的时间和方式的认识与我国现行法律的规定不一致（见表3-37）。前述涉及继承与遗赠的接受与放弃制度的案例之司法审判实践，也反映出继承放弃的方式与效力存在此不足。第三，未明确规定继承人放弃继承时，债权人能否撤销继承人放弃继承的行为，容易引发纠纷。近五成的吉林省被调查者认为债权人可以撤销继承人放弃继承的意思表示（见表3-40）。

（二）我国继承和遗赠的接受与放弃制度之立法完善建议

综上，我们针对我国继承和遗赠的接受与放弃制度的修改完善提出以下建议：

1. 继承的接受与放弃的时间与方式之立法建议

建议明确规定继承人作出接受或者放弃继承的意思表示的期限，从其知道或应当知道继承开始时起算，以便更好地敦促继承人行使自己的权利。

2. 遗赠的接受与放弃的方式与效力之立法建议

建议修改为受遗赠人应当在知道受遗赠后2个月内作出放弃接受遗赠的表示；受遗赠人到期未作明确表示的，视为接受遗赠。

3. 继承的放弃与债权人的撤销权之立法建议

建议增设债权人的撤销权，即继承人放弃继承损害其债权人利益时，债权人可以在知道或应当知道继承人放弃继承之日起6个月内申请人民法院撤销继承人的放弃行为。

七、我国继承权的丧失、被继承人的宥恕与代位继承制度之不足与立法完善建议

（一）我国继承权的丧失、被继承人的宥恕与代位继承制度之不足

关于继承权的丧失、被继承人的宥恕与代位继承制度，我国《继承法》主要存在两方面的不足：第一，我国《继承法》未对继承权丧失后是否可经继承人的宥恕而恢复的法定情形进行规定，虽然1985年《执行继承法意见》对继承权丧失后的恢复有所规定，但内容简略，且其属于司法解释，不便于民众知法守法和用法。七成半的吉林省被调查者认为继承人因欺诈、胁迫行为的继承人丧失继承权的在获得被继承人宽恕后可以恢复继承权（见表3-43）。前述涉及继承权的丧失、被继承人的宥恕与代位继承制度的案例之司法审判实践，也反映出我国继承权的丧失、被继承人的宥恕制度存在此不足。第二，1985年《执行继承法意见》规定继承人丧失继承权的，其晚辈直系血亲不得代位继承，不符合现代民法的“自己责任原则”，近三成的吉林省被调查者认为继承人丧失继承权后其晚辈直系血可以代位继承（见表3-44）。

（二）我国继承权的丧失、被继承人的宥恕与代位继承制度之立法完善建议

综上，我们针对我国继承权的丧失与恢复制度的修改完善提出以下建议：

1. 继承权的丧失与被继承人的宥恕之立法建议

建议适当扩充丧失继承权的法定事由，即将以欺诈或者胁迫的手段，迫使或者妨碍被继承人设立、变更或者撤销遗嘱，情节严重的，列入丧失继承权的法定事由。

2. 继承权的丧失与代位继承之立法建议

建议规定，在继承人因法定事由被剥夺继承权时，其晚辈直系血亲的代位继承权不受影响。

八、我国遗赠扶养协议制度之不足与立法增补建议

（一）我国遗赠扶养协议制度之不足

关于遗赠扶养协议制度，我国《继承法》主要存在的不足为：第一，遗赠扶养协议的主体范围较窄，即遗赠扶养协议签订主体只能是非法定继承人，且未规定继承协议签订主体、变更与效力等内容，这无法满足继承人与被继承人之间订立继承协议的现实需要。近六成的吉林省被调查者认可继承协议且该协议的订立主体应是被继承人与全体继承人，五成以上被调查者所在地区为解决被继承人养老送终而签订继承协议的情形时常发生（见表3-45、表3-46）。并且前述涉及继承协议制度的案例之司法审判实践，也反映出我国继承协议制度之不足。第二，未设立继承协议制度，缺乏对继承协议的变更与效力问题的规定。在继承协议履行过程中，如扶养人先于被扶养人去世，在吉林省被调查者中，三成以上的人认为可以允许有条件的代位扶养，即该合同继续有效；六成半以上的人认为承担扶养义务的人先于被继承人死亡应当是继承协议终止的事由之一；近四成的人认为应签订新的继承协议；六成的人认为应对已去世的扶养人支付的超出其扶养义务的部分扶养费予以补偿（见表3-48）。

（二）我国继承扶养协议制度的立法增补建议

综上，我们针对增设继承扶养协议制度提出以下建议：

1. 继承扶养协议的订立主体与方式之立法建议

建议增设继承扶养协议制度。而继承协议的形式要件，与当事人的利益有密切关系，订立继承协议应当采用书面形式。

2. 继承扶养协议的变更及效力之立法建议

建议规定继承扶养协议的变更及效力。即扶养人先于受扶养人死亡，继承扶养协议自动终止。受扶养人同意接受已经死亡的扶养人之继承人继续承担扶养的义务，继承扶养协议可继续履行。继承扶养协议解除时，除协议另有约定外，受扶养人应当对扶养人已经履行超出其法定的扶养义务的费用给予补偿。

九、我国遗产债务清偿制度之不足与立法完善建议

（一）我国遗产债务清偿制度之不足

关于遗产债务清偿制度，我们《继承法》主要存在三个方面的不足：第一，规定继承属于无条件的限定继承，且未规定遗产债务的清偿的无限清偿责任，不利于保护继承人及遗产债权人的利益。六成半的吉林省被调查者倾向于在保留我国《继承法》无条件的有限清偿责任的基础上，增设强制的无限清偿责任类型（见表3-50）。并且前述涉及遗产债务清偿制度的案例之司法审判实践中，也反映出我国遗产债务清偿责任的类型之不足。

第二，未规定被继承人丧葬费的支付，对此，近五成的吉林省被调查者所在地区的习惯是由遗产支付（见表3-52）。第三，对遗产债务的清偿顺序没有明确规定，不利保障遗产权利人利益的实现。吉林省被调查者在观念上和习惯上，对丧葬费用（第一顺序）、欠债（第二顺序）、欠付的工资（第三顺序）的清偿顺序较为一致（见表3-53、表3-54）。

（二）我国遗产债务清偿制度之立法完善建议

综上，我们针对我国遗产债务清偿制度的修改完善提出以下建议：

1. 遗产债务的清偿责任之立法建议

建议增补有条件的有限清偿责任和有条件的强制无限清偿责任。具体而言，继承人可以自愿选择在法定期间内依法制作遗产清册而承担有限的清偿责任或自愿的无限清偿责任。但在法定期间内不依法制作遗产清册，或对遗产进行了全部或部分处分，或故意未将遗产全部或部分记入遗产清册的，继承人应当承担强制的无限清偿责任。

2. 被继承人丧葬费的支付方式之立法建议

建议规定被继承人的丧葬费用由遗产支付。

3. 遗产债务的清偿顺序之立法建议

建议遗产债务按下列次序进行清偿：（1）继承费用（含丧葬费用和遗产管理费用等）；（2）有优先权的债务；（3）被继承人生前所欠税款及普通债务；（4）遗赠扶养协议之债；（5）特留份之债、遗赠之债、遗产酌给之债。

十、我国遗产分割制度之不足与立法完善建议

（一）我国遗产分割制度之不足

关于遗产分割制度，我国《继承法》主要存在两个方面的不足：第一，虽然有体现遗产分割自由的规定，但是未规定遗产分割的请求时间和限制遗产分割的条件与期间。在吉林省被调查者中，六成以上的人认可由共同继承人协商一致可以对遗产分割的自由进行一定的限制；近八成的人认可被继承人可以立遗嘱限制一定时期内不分割特定遗产，且限制分割的期限以5年为宜（见表3-55、表3-57、表3-62）。前述涉及遗产分割制度的案例之司法审判实践，也反映出我国遗产分割的自由与限制之不足。第二，欠缺遗产分割之共同继承人瑕疵担保责任制度，不利于公平的保护共同继承人的权利，有四成的吉林省被调查者所在地区习惯由共同继承人相互承担遗产分割瑕疵的担保责任（见表3-63）。

（二）我国遗产分割制度之立法完善建议

综上，我们针对我国遗产分割制度的修改完善提出以下建议：

1. 遗产分割的自由与限制之立法建议

建议明确遗产分割的时间，并增设遗嘱可以在一定时间内禁止分割全部或者某些遗产的条款，时间可以限制在5~10年。

2. 遗产分割瑕疵的担保责任之立法建议

建议当存在遗产债务时，对遗产的分割作出限制规定。此外，规定共同继承人之间遗产的瑕疵担保责任，保障继承人的合法权益不被侵害。

十一、我国无人承受遗产的处理制度之不足与立法完善建议

（一）我国无人承受遗产的处理制度之不足

关于无人承受遗产制度，我国《继承法》主要存在两个方面的不足：第一，对无人承受遗产的管理人的产生方式未作规定，不利于无人承受遗产的债权人或其他遗产利害关系人的权利实现。在吉林省被调查者中主张由人民法院指定的占五成以上，主张由死者户籍所在地的居委会或村委会或所在单位指定的占三成（见表3-67）。前述涉及无人承受遗产案例制度的案例之司法审判实践中，也反映出无人承受遗产管理制度的不足。第二，无人承受遗产的酌分遗产人的范围较窄，这不利于保护弱者、对被继承人付出较多人、与被继承人共同生活的人的权益；各有六成至七成的吉林省被调查者主张依靠死者扶养的人、与死者共同生活的人、与死者关系密切且对其帮助较多的人可以酌情分得无人承受的遗产（见表3-69）。

（二）我国无人承受遗产的处理制度之立法完善建议

综上，我们针对我国无人承受遗产制度的修改完善提出以下建议：

1. 无人承受遗产的管理之立法建议

建议对于无人承受遗产的管理人由人民法院指定，因为人民法院在群众心中具有更高的权威性与公信力。并且，该遗产管理人的职责适用普通遗产管理人职责的规定。

2. 无人承受遗产的酌分请求权主体之立法建议

建议扩大无人承受遗产的酌分请求权主体范围，对于无人承受遗产可酌情分配给依靠被继承人扶养的人、对被继承人扶养较多的人、与被继承人一同生活的人或其他与被继承人关系密切的人。

第四章　当代中国上海市民众财产继承观念与遗产处理习惯实证调查研究*

第一节　当代中国上海市民众财产继承观念与遗产处理习惯实证调查概况

一、被调查地区概况

（一）上海市社会经济发展水平情况

2018 年全年实现上海市生产总值（GDP）32679.87 亿元，比上年增长 6.6%。在上海市生产总值中，公有制经济增加值 15896.97 亿元，比上年增长 6.6%；非公有制经济增加值 16782.90 亿元，比上年增长 6.5%。非公有制经济增加值占上海市生产总值的比重为 51.4%。①

（二）上海市人口结构情况

2018 年年末，全市常住人口总数为 2418.33 万。从全省人口性别结构看，男性人口为 1232.38 万人，女性人口为 1185.95 万人，性别比为 103.9：100。② 从全省人口年龄结构看，2018 年上海 60 岁及以上常住人口达到 539.12 万人，上海老龄化率达到 14.3%，在国内主要城市中老龄化程度偏高。③ 2018 年，全市常住人口总数为 2423.78 万。其中，户籍常住人口 1447.57 万人，外来常住人口 976.21 万人。④

（三）上海市城乡人口的年均收入情况

2018 年，全年全市居民人均可支配收入 64183 元，比上年增长 8.8%。其中，城镇常住居民人均可支配收入 68034 元，比上年增长 8.7%；农村常住居民人均可支配收入

* 作者简介：许莉，女，华东政法大学教授；白玉，女，西南政法大学民商法学博士研究生；张叶，女，华东政法大学民商法学硕士研究生；柯婵娟，女，华东政法大学民商法学硕士研究生。

① 中国统计信息网：《上海市 2018 年国民经济和社会发展统计公报》，载 http://www.tjcn.org/tjgb/09sh/35767_6.html，访问日期：2019 年 5 月 23 日。

② 《2018 年上海市国民经济运行情况》，载 http://www.stats-sh.gov.cn/html/xwdt/201801/1001501.html，访问日期：2019 年 5 月 6 日。

③ 中国产业信息：载 http://www.chyxx.com/industry/201805/645507.html，访问日期：2019 年 5 月 6 日。

④ 中国统计信息网：《上海市 2018 年国民经济和社会发展统计公报》，载 http://www.tjcn.org/tjgb/09sh/35767_6.html，访问日期：2019 年 5 月 23 日。

30375 元，比上年增长 9.2%。①

二、实证调查情况简介

2016 年 11 月，西南政法大学陈苇教授主持申报的司法部科研项目“我国遗产处理制度系统化构建研究”被批准立项。为给本项目的理论研究和制度研究提供国情资料，必须调查了解当代中国民众的财产继承观念与遗产处理习惯。由于课题组的人力、物力限制，陈苇教授选择我国十省市包括东北部的吉林省、东部的上海市、北部的河北省、中部的湖北省和江西省、南部的广东省和海南省、东南部的福建省、西南部的重庆市和四川省作为被调查地区，然后联系确定了各省市调查组组长，共同组织开展本项目的子课题“当代中国民众财产继承观念与遗产处理习惯实证调查研究”。本次“当代中国上海市民众财产继承观念与遗产处理习惯实证调查研究”是西南政法大学陈苇教授主持的“当代中国民众财产继承观念与遗产处理习惯实证调查研究”的组成部分之一，由华东政法大学许莉教授担任上海市调查组组长。

（一）调查问卷的设计和学生调查员的召集与培训

2016 年 11 月中旬，陈苇教授组织重庆市课题组成员分工合作，设计制作“当代中国民众财产继承观念与遗产处理习惯实证调查研究”的调查问卷，至同年 12 月中旬完成了调查问卷的设计工作。然后，陈苇教授把调查问卷电子版通过电子邮件发送给参加本次实证调查的十省市调查组组长，以供开展实地调查时十省市被调查地区统一使用。同年 12 月下旬，根据陈苇教授撰写的“当代中国民众财产继承观念与遗产处理习惯社会调查动员会和培训会”说明书，上海市调查组组长许莉教授在华东政法大学召集上海市籍学生 76 名作为调查员，于 2017 年 1 月召开“当代中国上海市民众财产继承观念与遗产处理习惯实证调查动员暨社会调查知识培训会”。会上，许莉教授给每位社会学生调查员发放 6 份调查问卷，针对问卷的问题，逐一讲解调查要点和具体的调查方法，要求被调查对象应当为具有上海本地户籍的本地人，并且被调查者须男女均等，分为老、中、青（61 岁以上、41~60 岁、20~40 岁）三个年龄段，并且最好具有不同的职业背景，并且要求每名学生调查员利用 2017 年的寒假期间各自在家乡开展实地社会调查。

（二）实地社会调查的方式

2017 年 1 月至 2 月的寒假期间，上海市学生调查员们在各自家乡开展实地社会调查。本次调查主要采取学生调查员“入户问卷调查”和“个人访谈”的方式。

一是入户问卷调查。要求调查员在 2017 年的寒假期间回到自己的家乡，对当地的民众进行入户问卷调查。根据本次调查的对象选取要求，每位调查员选取的被调查对象必须符合培训会的条件要求，而且每位被调查者只能填写一份调查问卷。学生调查员入户后首先向被调查者讲解说明本次调查的目的意义和调查问卷填写的问题，采取被调查者自己填写问卷或者学生调查员向被调查者询问后代为填写，这两种方式完成问卷的填写。

二是个人访谈。要求采取“一对一”的个人访谈方式，以收集与遗产继承有关的纠纷或案例。本次实地调查，除填写调查问卷外，还要求辅以“一对一”的个人访谈，收

① 中国统计信息网：《上海市 2018 年国民经济和社会发展统计公报》，载 http://www.tjcn.org/tjgb/09sh/35767_6.html，访问日期：2019 年 5 月 23 日。

集和记录典型的继承纠纷或相关案例的内容。因为调查问卷涉及客观选择与主观理由两部分内容，采取“一对一”的个人访谈方式，可以避免被调查者受到他人的影响，便于更客观深入地了解被调查民众的真实想法。

（三）调查问卷数据的录入、统计汇总、复核与撰写调查研究报告

2017 年 3 月开学后，上海市调查组教师组织统一回收调查问卷和典型案例的访谈记录，然后组织学生统计员对调查问卷进行数据统计工作。本次调查实际发放问卷 396 份，剔除其中的无效问卷后，共收回有效问卷 353 份，有效问卷率为 89.14%。随后，根据有效问卷进行调查数据的录入和统计汇总，再进行统计汇总数据表的复核工作。2017 年 4 月底，完成了《〈当代中国民众财产继承观念与遗产处理习惯实证调查问卷〉上海市被调查民众实证调查统计数据汇总表》的定稿。我们在此需要特别说明，关于各项调查问题之统计人数的合计，凡单选题的人数合计均为 100%，均合计在统计表中；凡多选题的人数合计均超过 100%，故不予进行合计统计。本调查研究就是以此次调查统计数据汇总表为基础资料进行分析和研究而撰写。在此，特向所有参与本次实证调查工作的老师和同学表示衷心感谢！①

2017 年 4 月，陈苇教授拟定了“当代中国民众财产继承观念与遗产处理习惯实证调查研究的写作提纲和写作要求”。2017 年 5 月起，我们根据此写作提纲和写作要求进入参考文献资料的收集和调查报告的写作和修改阶段。本章“当代中国上海市民众财产继承观念与遗产处理习惯实证调查研究”由华东政法大学许莉教授、民商法硕士研究生张叶和柯婵娟共同撰写初稿至第五稿，其间，根据陈苇教授对初稿至第五稿的历次修改意见和中期评审专家意见，对稿件进行了相应的多次修改和补充，最后向课题负责人陈苇教授交稿。2019 年 1 月，陈苇教授继续对上海市调查研究报告进行审阅和修改补充，然后组织重庆市调查组博士生对上海市调查研究报告统一进行了三次修改补充，最终于 2019 年 6 月完成定稿。

三、被调查对象的基本情况

本次调查的对象为上海市常住人口，我们根据 353 份有效问卷，以下对 353 名被调查者的性别、年龄和职业情况统计如下：

（一）被调查者的性别情况

表 4-1　被调查者的性别情况统计

性别	人数	比例
男性	164	46.50%
女性	189	53.50%
合计	353	100%

关于被调查者的性别情况，统计数据显示，在 353 名被调查者中，男性有 164 人（占

① 参与上海市民众财产继承观念与遗产处理习惯的实地调查以及调查数据统计汇总等工作的师生名单，详见“鸣谢”。

46.50%）；女性有 189 人（占 53.50%）。可见，上海市被调查者中，男女性别比例大体平衡。

（二）被调查者的年龄情况

表 4-2　被调查者的年龄情况统计

年龄	人数	比例
20~30 岁	124	35.13%
31~40 岁	47	13.31%
41~50 岁	83	23.51%
51~60 岁	41	11.61%
61~70 岁	29	8.22%
71 岁以上	29	8.22%
合计	353	100%

关于被调查者的年龄情况，统计数据显示，在 353 名被调查者中：青年人（20~40 岁）有 171 人（占 48.44%）；中年人（41~60 岁）有 124 人（占 35.12%）；老年人（61 岁以上）有 58 人（占 16.44%）。可见，从上海市被调查者年龄结构情况看，以中青年人为主，合计占八成以上（83.56%）。

（三）被调查者的职业情况

表 4-3　被调查者的职业情况统计

职业	人数	比例
农民	18	5.10%
工人	18	5.10%
经商	15	4.25%
公务员及企事业单位人员	154	43.63%
其他（打工等不固定职业）	148	41.92%
合计	353	100%

关于被调查者的职业情况，统计数据显示，在 353 名被调查者中，各个职业的分布比例为：职业为“农民”的人数为 18（占 5.10%）；职业为“工人”的人数为 18（占 5.1%）；职业为“经商”的人数为 15（占 4.25%）；职业为“公务员及企事业单位”的人数为 154（占 43.64%）；职业为“其他”的人数为 148（占 41.92%）。可见，本次被调查者包括农民、工人、商人和企事业单位等不同岗位的职业者，能够较为全面地反映出上海市不同群体的民众继承习惯。另外，填写“其他”职业的人数占比超过四成（41.92%），这反映了上海市以服务业为主的第三行业已逐渐成为经济发展的重要力量之一。

综上，本次被调查者的性别比基本持平，老、中、青各年龄段均有，以中青年人居多，合计占八成以上，他们的职业涉及广泛，本次调查数据基本上能够反映不同性别、年龄和职业被调查者的财产继承观念和遗产处理习惯。

第二节　当代中国上海市民众财产继承观念与遗产处理习惯实证调查的数据统计情况

一、遗产范围界定之调查数据统计情况

关于遗产范围界定之调查数据统计，我们主要从遗产的种类和被继承人生前特种赠与财产的归扣，这两个方面进行调查数据的统计情况汇总分析。

（一）遗产的种类

问题【一、（一）】“2016 年 2 月某甲因车祸死亡，经清理某甲个人名下的遗物如下，请问哪些属于某甲的遗产：A. 住房一套；B. 小汽车一辆；C. 家庭日常生活用品若干；D. 存款 10 万元；E. 股票 10 万元；F. 某甲以其姓名注册的邮箱、QQ 账号等；G. 单位出租给某甲的午休住房一间；H. 某甲向公司购货的欠款 5 万元；I. 某甲因交通事故死亡获得 50 万元的赔偿金。（多选）”

表 4-4　属于遗产种类的民众观念情况统计（多选）

选项	人数	比例
A. 住房一套	349	98.90%
B. 小汽车一辆	346	98.00%
C. 家庭日常生活用品若干	209	59.20%
D. 存款 10 万元	341	96.70%
E. 股票 10 万元	321	90.90%
F. 某甲以其姓名注册的邮箱、QQ 账号等	107	30.30%
G. 单位出租给某甲的午休住房一间	25	7.10%
H. 某甲向公司购货的欠款 5 万元	210	59.50%
I. 某甲因交通事故死亡获得 50 万元的赔偿金	250	20.80%

关于属于遗产种类的民众观念，调查统计数据显示，在 353 名被调查者中，（1）选择 A、B、D、E 项，认为房屋（98.90%）、汽车（98.00%）、存款（96.70%）、股票（90.90%）属于遗产的，占九成以上；认为单位出租给某甲的午休住房不属于遗产的，占九成以上（92.90%）①；　（2）选择 C、H、I 项，认为某甲向公司购货的欠款（59.50%）、家庭日常生活用品若干（59.20%）和死亡赔偿金（20.80%）属于遗产的，各占二成至五成以上；（3）选择 F 项，认为某甲以其姓名注册的邮箱、QQ 账号等属于遗

① 认为“单位出租给某甲的午休住房”属于遗产的仅占 7.10%，即有九成以上（92.90%）的被调查者认为其不属于遗产。

产的占三成（30.30%）。

（二）被继承人生前特种赠与财产的归扣

1. 被继承人生前特种赠与财产是否应归入遗产范围的民众观念情况统计

问题【一、（二）1.】“张老汉有三个儿子，在10年前大儿子甲结婚时，张老汉给其资助购买婚房的现金20万元；二儿子乙一直未结婚，但5年前在其开办豆腐坊时，张老汉资助其营业资金10万元。在2年前小儿子丙结婚时，张老汉为其购买一套价值30万元的房屋（产权登记在小儿子丙名下）；2016年1月张老汉去世时遗留个人所有的住房一套和50万元存款。据此，问卷列出了几种可能的遗产供选择：A. 张老汉生前给三个儿子不同资助的财产与死亡时其遗留的住房、存款，均应当合并计算为遗产；B. 张老汉去世时遗留的个人所有的住房和50万元存款，才可以计算为遗产；C. 其他。（单选）”

表4-5　被继承人生前特种赠与财产是否应归入遗产范围的民众观念情况统计（单选）

选项	人数	比例
A. 张老汉生前给三个儿子不同资助的财产与死亡时其遗留的住房、存款，均应当合并计算为遗产	56	16.00%
B. 张老汉去世时遗留的个人所有的住房和50万元存款，才可以计算为遗产	290	82.90%
C. 其他	4	1.10%
合计	350	100%

关于被继承人生前特种赠与财产是否应归入遗产范围的民众观念，调查统计数据显示，在350名被调查者中，（1）选择B项被继承人去世时遗留的个人财产才可算作遗产的，占八成以上（82.90%）；（2）选择A项被继承人生前资助子女的财产与死亡时其遗留的住房、存款，均应当合并计算为遗产的，仅占一成半以上（16.00%）。

2. 归扣遗产价值计算时间的民众观念情况统计

问题【一、（二）2.】“如果上述答案您选A，请问张老汉为小儿子丙买房的价值应该按何时计算？A. 买房时；B. 张老汉去世时；C. 实际分割遗产时；D. 其他。（单选）”

表4-6　归扣遗产的价值计算时间的民众观念情况统计（单选）

选项	人数	比例
A. 买房时	16	28.57%
B. 张老汉去世时	15	26.79%
C. 实际分割遗产时	24	42.86%
D. 其他	1	1.78%
合计	56	100%

关于归扣遗产价值的计算时间之民众观念，调查统计数据显示，在认可归扣制度的56名被调查者中，（1）选择C项应按实际分割时计算的，占四成以上（42.86%）；（2）选择A项应按购置该财产时计算的，占近三成（28.57%）；（3）选择B项应按被继承人去世时计算的，占二成半以上（26.79%）。即认为应按实际分割遗产时计算归扣遗

产价值的占比居第一位。

3. 生前特种赠与财产是否归扣纳入遗产范围的民间习惯情况统计

问题【一、（二）3.】“在您所在的地区，如果发生上述张老汉生前给三个儿子不同资助财产的情况，在继承遗产时这些资助财产是否被合计到遗产范围内？A. 是；B. 不是。（单选）”

表 4-7　生前特种赠与财产是否归扣纳入遗产范围的民间习惯情况统计（单选）

选项	人数	比例
A. 是	78	22.10%
B. 不是	275	77.90%
合计	353	100%

关于生前特种赠与财产是否归扣纳入遗产范围的民间习惯，调查统计数据显示，353名被调查者所在地区的继承习惯是：（1）B 项不是，即没有此归扣习惯的，占近八成（77.90%）；（2）A 项是，即有该归扣习惯的，占二成以上（22.10%）。

4. 生前特种赠与财产不归扣纳入遗产的分配方式之民间习惯与理由情况统计

问题【一、（二）4.】“上一题如果您选择 B 项即这些资助财产不是被合计到遗产范围内，三个儿子是如何分配父亲张老汉的遗产的？A. 平均分配；B. 乙应该适当多分；C. 其他。（单选）理由是什么？”

（1）生前特种赠与财产不归扣纳入遗产的分配方式之民间习惯情况统计。

表 4-8　生前特种赠与财产不归扣纳入遗产的分配方式之民间习惯情况统计（单选）

选项	人数	比例
A. 平均分配	195	70.90%
B. 乙应该适当多分	69	25.10%
C. 其他	11	4.00%
合计	275	100%

关于生前特种赠与财产不归扣纳入遗产情况下的分配方式之民间习惯，调查统计数据显示，在填写该问题的 275 名被调查者所在地区的继承习惯是：（1）A 项有平均分配习惯的，占七成（70.90%）；（2）B 项有乙应该适当多分习惯的，只占二成半（25.10%）。

（2）生前特种赠与财产不归扣纳入遗产分配方式的民间习惯之理由统计。

表 4-9　生前特种赠与财产不归扣纳入遗产情况下分配方式的民间习惯之理由统计

项目	人数	比例
A. 不考虑张老汉生前给三个儿子财产的情况，死后平均分配所留遗产，有利于遗产的分割，可以减少纠纷	121	67.60%
B. 张老汉生前给乙的财产较少，在其死后乙应多分些，可以在共同继承人间公平分配遗产，这体现公平原则	36	20.10%

续表

项目	人数	比例
C. 由三个儿子协商决定	22	12.30%
合计	179	100%

关于生前特种赠与财产不归扣纳入遗产情况下分配方式的民间习惯之理由，有179名被调查者填写了选择理由，（1）认为应平均分配遗产的理由是，A项不考虑张老汉生前给三个儿子财产的情况，死后平均分配所留遗产，有利于遗产分割，可以减少纠纷的，占六成半以上（67.60%）；（2）认为乙应该适当多分的理由是，B项张老汉生前给乙的财产较少，在其死后乙应多分些，可以在共同继承人间公平分配遗产，以体现公平原则的，占二成（20.10%）。

二、继承开始的通知和公告之调查数据统计情况

关于继承开始的通知和公告之调查数据统计，我们主要从继承开始的通知和公告的主体、继承开始的通知和公告的方式、继承开始的通知和公告的期间，这三个方面进行调查数据的统计情况汇总分析。

（一）继承开始的通知和公告的主体

问题【二、（一）】“被继承人死亡后，在您所在地区一般由下列哪些人通知涉及遗产分配的相关人员？A. 知道被继承人死亡的继承人；B. 保管遗产的继承人；C. 知道被继承人死亡的单位、村（居）委会；D. 处理被继承人死亡事件的机构，如公安交警部门；E. 其他。（多选）”

表4-10　继承开始的通知和公告主体的民间习惯情况统计（多选）

选项	人数	比例
A. 知道被继承人死亡的继承人	267	78.50%
B. 保管遗产的继承人	192	56.50%
C. 知道被继承人死亡的单位、村（居）委会	104	30.60%
D. 处理被继承人死亡事件的机构，如公安交警部门	124	36.50%
E. 其他	8	2.40%

关于继承开始的通知和公告主体的民间习惯，调查统计数据显示，填写本问题的340名被调查者所在地区的民间习惯是：（1）A、B两项，由继承人作为主体的，各占五成至七成以上，具体包括：“知道被继承人死亡的继承人”（78.50%）和“保管遗产的继承人”（56.50%）；（2）D项由处理被继承人死亡事件的机构作为主体的，占三成半以上（36.50%）；（3）C项由知道被继承人死亡的单位、村（居）委会作为主体的，占三成（30.60%）。

（二）继承开始的通知和公告的方式

问题【二、（二）】“被继承人死亡后，您所在地区的人们一般采取以下哪些方式通

知涉及遗产处理的相关人员？A. 口头、电话、微信等；B. 信件、告知函等书面通知；C. 在报纸、电视、网络等平台上发布被继承人死亡的公告；D. 在被继承人所在地的村（居）委会公告栏公告；E. 申请人民法院以公告程序进行公告；F. 其他。（多选）”

表 4-11　继承开始的通知和公告方式的民间习惯情况统计（多选）

选项	人数	比例
A. 口头、电话、微信等	264	75. 90%
B. 信件、告知函等书面通知	191	54. 90%
C. 在报纸、电视、网络等平台上发布被继承人死亡的公告	55	15. 80%
D. 在被继承人所在地的村（居）委会公告栏公告	62	17. 80%
E. 申请人民法院以公告程序进行公告	80	23. 00%
F. 其他	6	1. 70%

关于继承开始的通知和公告方式的民间习惯，调查统计数据显示，填写本问题的 348 名被调查者所在地区的民间习惯是：（1）A、B 两项，分别通过口头、电话、微信等通知（75. 90%）和信件、告知函等书面通知（54. 90%）的，各占五成至七成以上；（2）C、D、E 三项，分别由申请人民法院以公告程序进行公告（23. 00%）、在被继承人所在地的村（居）委会公告栏公告（17. 80%）和在报纸、电视、网络等平台上发布被继承人死亡公告（15. 80%）的，各占一成至二成以上。

（三）继承开始的通知和公告的期间

问题【二、（三）】“您认为，通知人应该在被继承人死亡后多少天内发出通知？A. 3 日；B. 7 日；C. 15 日；D. 30 日；E. 其他。（单选）”

表 4-12　继承开始的通知和公告期间的民众观念情况统计（单选）

选项	人数	比例
A. 3 日	100	28. 60%
B. 7 日	97	27. 70%
C. 15 日	79	22. 60%
D. 30 日	56	16. 00%
E. 其他	18	5. 10%
合计	350	100%

关于继承开始的通知和公告期间的民众观念，调查统计数据显示，在填写本问题的 350 名被调查者中，（1）选择 A、B 两项应在 7 日内发出的，占五成半以上（56. 30%）；（2）选择 C 项应在 15 日以内发出的，占二成以上（22. 60%）；（3）选择 D 项应在 30 日以内发出的，仅占一成半以上（16. 00%）。

三、遗产管理之调查数据统计情况

关于遗产管理之调查数据统计，我们主要从遗产管理人的确定、遗产管理人的职责与报酬、遗产管理人的损害赔偿责任，这三个方面进行调查数据的统计情况汇总分析。

（一）遗产管理人的确定

问题【三、（一）】“您所在地区人们处理遗产继承时，一般由谁清点和管理遗产？A. 死者的法定继承人：配偶、子女、父母、兄弟姐妹、子女或外孙子女、祖父母或外祖父母；B. 死者的儿媳或女婿；C. 死者家族中的德高望重者；D. 死者的其他亲戚朋友；E. 死者所在的单位或村/居委会；F. 其他。（多选）理由是什么？”

1. 关于遗产管理人的确定的民间习惯情况统计

（1）遗产管理人的确定的民间习惯情况统计。

表 4-13　关于遗产管理人的确定的民间习惯情况统计（多选）

选项	人数	比例
A. 死者的法定继承人	315	90.00%
B. 死者的儿媳或女婿	50	14.30%
C. 死者家族中的德高望重者	122	34.90%
D. 死者的其他亲戚朋友	33	9.40%
E. 死者所在的单位或村/居委会	60	17.10%
F. 其他	4	1.10%

关于遗产管理人的确定的民间习惯，调查统计数据显示，填写该问题的 350 名被调查者所在地区的继承习惯是：①A 项由死者的法定继承人作为遗产管理人的，占九成（90.00%）；②B、C、D、E 四项，分别由死者的儿媳或女婿（14.30%）、死者家族中的德高望重者（34.90%）、死者的其他亲戚朋友（9.40%）和死者所在的单位或村/居委会（17.10%）作为遗产管理人的，各占一成至三成以上。

（2）法定继承人担任遗产管理人的民间习惯情况统计。

表 4-14　法定继承人担任遗产管理人的民间习惯情况统计（多选）

选项	人数	比例
A. 配偶	166	52.60%
B. 子女	141	44.70%
C. 父母	145	46.00%
D. 兄弟姐妹	50	15.80%
E. 孙子女或外孙子女	30	9.50%
F. 祖父母或外祖父母	31	9.80%

关于法定继承人担任遗产管理人的民间习惯，调查统计数据显示，在填写本题的315名被调查者所在地区的继承习惯是：①A、B、C三项，分别由法定继承人中的配偶（52.60%）、父母（46.00%）和子女（44.70%）担任遗产管理人的，各占四成至五成以上；②D项由兄弟姐妹担任遗产管理人的，占一成半以上（15.80%）；③E、F两项，分别由孙子女或外孙子女（9.50%）和祖父母或外祖父母（9.80%）担任遗产管理人的，各占不到一成。

2. 关于遗产管理人的确定的民间习惯之理由情况统计

表4-15 关于遗产管理人的确定的民间习惯之理由情况统计

项目	人数	比例
A. 遗产管理人一般由继承人担任，便于清点和妥善管理遗产	87	65.90%
B. 遗产管理人一般由遗产继承人之外的人或组织来担任，可以防止遗产被隐藏、转移，有利于保护遗产相关人的合法权益	13	9.80%
C. 交给法院等权威组织处理，具有公信力	10	7.60%
D. 其他	22	16.70%
合计	132	100%

关于遗产管理人的确定的民间习惯之理由，调查统计数据显示，132名被调查者填写了选择理由，（1）遗产管理人由法定继承人承担的理由是，A项这便于清点和妥善管理遗产的，占六成半（65.90%）；（2）遗产管理人由遗产继承人之外的人或组织担任的理由是，B项这可以防止遗产被隐藏、转移，有利于保护遗产相关人合法权益的，占不到一成（9.80%）；（3）还有不到一成（7.60%）的人填写了C项交给法院等权威组织处理，这具有公信力等理由。

（二）遗产管理人的职责与报酬

1. 遗产管理人职责的民众观念情况统计

问题【三、（二）1.】“您认为，遗产管理人的职责有哪些？A. 清查遗产，制作遗产清单；B. 妥善保管遗产；C. 查明被继承人生前的债权和债务，积极地追讨债权或清偿债务；D. 查明被继承人是否留有遗嘱，并且确定遗嘱是否真实合法；E. 可以原告或被告的身份参加因遗产引起的诉讼；F. 定期制作遗产管理报告，向继承人报告遗产管理的情况；G. 其他。（多选）”

表4-16 遗产管理人职责的民众观念情况统计（多选）

选项	人数	比例
A. 清查遗产，制作遗产清单	323	92.30%
B. 妥善保管遗产	329	94.00%
C. 查明被继承人生前的债权和债务，积极地追讨债权或清偿债务	242	69.10%

续表

选项	人数	比例
D. 查明被继承人是否留有遗嘱，并且确定遗嘱是否真实合法	208	59.40%
E. 可以原告或被告的身份参加因遗产引起的诉讼	229	65.40%
F. 定期制作遗产管理报告，向继承人报告遗产管理的情况	170	48.50%
G. 其他	10	2.90%

关于遗产管理人职责的民众观念，调查统计数据显示，在填写本问题的350名被调查者中，选择A、B、C、D、E、F六项，认为遗产管理人的职责包括“清查遗产，制作遗产清单”（92.30%）、“妥善保管遗产”（94.00%）、“查明被继承人生前的债权和债务，积极地追讨债权或清偿债务”（69.10%）、“可以原告或被告的身份参加因遗产引起的诉讼”（65.40%）、“查明被继承人是否留有遗嘱，并且确定遗嘱是否真实合法”（59.40%）、“定期制作遗产管理报告，向继承人报告遗产管理的情况”（48.50%）的，各占四成至九成以上。

2. 遗产管理人是否取得报酬的民间习惯与理由情况统计

问题【三、（二）2.】“您所在地区，负责管理遗产的人是否可以获得报酬？A. 继承人担任遗产管理人的，不能请求给付报酬；B. 法院指定的遗产管理人，有权请求给付报酬；C. 继承人选任的第三人作为遗产管理人，是否给付报酬，应当由继承人决定；D. 继承人选任的第三人作为遗产管理人，一律有权请求给付报酬；E. 其他。（多选）理由是什么？”

（1）遗产管理人是否有权取得报酬的民间习惯情况统计。

表4-17 遗产管理人是否有权取得报酬的民间习惯情况统计（多选）

选项	人数	比例
A. 继承人担任遗产管理人的，不能请求给付报酬	187	53.40%
B. 法院指定的遗产管理人，有权请求给付报酬	182	52.00%
C. 继承人选任的第三人作为遗产管理人，是否给付报酬，应当由继承人决定	162	46.20%
D. 继承人选任的第三人作为遗产管理人，一律有权请求给付报酬	118	33.70%
E. 其他	3	0.90%

关于遗产管理人是否有权取得报酬的民间习惯，调查统计数据显示，填写本问题的350名被调查者所在地区的继承习惯是：①A项继承人担任的遗产管理人，不能请求给付报酬的，占五成以上（53.40%）；②B项法院指定的遗产管理人，有权请求给付报酬的，占五成以上（52.00%）；③C、D两项，继承人选任的第三人作为遗产管理人，其中四成半以上（46.20%）的地区有是否给付报酬应当由继承人决定的习惯；近三成半的地区有

一律有权请求给付报酬的习惯（33.70%）。

（2）遗产管理人是否有权取得报酬的民间习惯之理由情况统计。

表 4-18　遗产管理人是否有权取得报酬的民间习惯之理由情况统计

项目	人数	比例
A. 遗产管理人在多数情况下与被继承人关系密切，具有亲情关系，同时遗产管理人又继承遗产，因此管理遗产不需要报酬	54	29.03%
B. 遗产管理人为管理遗产付出了自己的劳动，占用了自己的时间，应该给予一定的费用	39	20.97%
C. 视情况而定，更能符合实际情况	93	50.00%
合计	186	100%

关于遗产管理人是否有权取得报酬的民间习惯之理由，调查统计数据显示，186 名被调查者填写了选择理由，①认为继承人担任的遗产管理人，不能请求给付报酬的理由是，A 项遗产管理人多数情况下与被继承人关系密切，具有亲情关系，同时遗产管理人又继承遗产，因此管理遗产不需要报酬的，占近三成（29.03%）；②认为法院指定的遗产管理人，有权请求给付报酬的理由是，B 项遗产管理人为管理遗产付出了自己的劳动和时间，应该给予一定费用的，占二成（20.97%）；③认为应区别不同情况确定是否给予遗产管理者报酬的理由是，C 项视情况而定，这更能符合实际情况的，占五成（50.00%）。

（三）遗产管理人的损害赔偿责任

问题【三、（三）】“在您所在地区，负责管理遗产的人对因其过错造成较大的财产损失，是否承担赔偿责任？A. 凡有故意或重大过失的，才承担赔偿责任；B. 无论是故意或重大过失或一般轻过失的，都要承担赔偿责任；C. 其他。（单选）”

表 4-19　遗产管理人的损害赔偿责任之民间习惯情况统计（单选）

选项	人数	比例
A. 凡有故意或重大过失的，才承担赔偿责任	220	62.90%
B. 无论是故意或重大过失或一般轻过失的，都要承担赔偿责任	114	32.60%
C. 其他	16	4.50%
合计	350	100%

关于遗产管理人的损害赔偿责任之民间习惯，调查统计数据显示，填写本问题的 350 名被调查者所在地区的继承习惯是：（1）A 项有故意或重大过失才承担赔偿责任的，占六成以上（62.90%）；（2）B 项无论故意、重大过失或一般轻过失都要承担赔偿责任的，占三成以上（32.60%）。

四、法定继承之调查数据统计情况

关于法定继承之调查数据统计，我们主要从法定继承人的范围与顺序、配偶与血亲继承人的法定应继份、配偶对遗产中家庭住房的先取权和终生使用权、后顺序特殊法定继承人对遗产中原使用的住房及日常生活用品的终生使用权、尽了主要赡养义务的丧偶的儿媳或女婿的遗产分配方式，这五个方面进行调查数据的统计情况汇总分析。

（一）法定继承人的范围与顺序

1. 法定继承人范围与顺序的民众观念情况统计

问题【四（一）1.】“下列亲属，您认为哪些应当作为法定继承人？他们各自的继承顺序如何？请根据您认为适当的先后顺序填写数字：1. 2. 3. ……例如，父母（1）；子女（2）；祖父母、外祖父母（3）。如果您认为应当在同一顺序的人，可以填写相同的数字，如配偶（1）；父母（1）；子女（1）；祖父母、外祖父母（1）。”

配偶（　）	父母（　）	儿子（　）女儿（　）
孙子女（　）外孙子女（　）	祖父母（　）外祖父母（　）	兄弟（　）姐妹（　）
侄子女（　）外甥子女（　）	伯叔姑舅姨（　）	堂兄弟姐妹（　）
表兄弟姐妹（　）	其他亲属（称谓）（　）	其他亲属（称谓）（　）

表 4-20　法定继承人范围与顺序的民众观念情况统计

亲属名称	第一顺序		第二顺序		第三顺序		第四顺序		第四顺序以上	
	人数	比例	人数	比例	人数	比例	人数	比例	人数	比例
配偶	411	89.54%	22	4.79%	6	1.31%	2	0.44%	0	0
父母	312	67.97%	104	22.66%	25	5.45%	3	0.65%	0	0
子	308	67.10%	91	19.83%	41	8.93%	2	0.44%	0	0
女	269	58.61%	90	19.61%	37	8.06%	12	2.61%	0	0
孙子女	6	1.31%	230	50.11%	92	20.04%	30	6.54%	17	3.70%
外孙子女	6	1.31%	222	48.37%	92	20.04%	49	10.68%	21	4.58%
祖父母	6	1.31%	224	48.80%	75	16.34%	34	7.41%	45	9.80%
外祖父母	6	1.31%	217	47.28%	91	19.83%	34	7.41%	44	9.59%
兄弟	0	0	209	45.53%	80	17.43%	54	11.76%	51	11.11%
姐妹	0	0	198	43.14%	80	17.43%	57	12.42%	51	11.11%
侄子女	0	0	25	5.45%	125	27.23%	67	14.60%	84	18.30%
外甥子女	0	0	27	5.88%	122	26.58%	63	13.73%	87	18.95%
伯叔姑	0	0	4	0.87%	127	27.67%	53	11.55%	98	21.35%
舅姨	0	0	4	0.87%	127	27.67%	50	10.89%	98	21.35%
堂兄弟	2	0.44%	2	0.44%	98	21.35%	47	10.24%	113	24.62%
堂姐妹	2	0.44%	2	0.44%	98	21.35%	47	10.24%	113	24.62%
表兄弟	0	0	3	0.65%	97	21.13%	53	11.55%	125	27.23%

续表

亲属名称	第一顺序		第二顺序		第三顺序		第四顺序		第四顺序以上	
	人数	比例	人数	比例	人数	比例	人数	比例	人数	比例
表姐妹	0	0	3	0.65%	97	21.13%	53	11.55%	125	27.23%
其他亲属	0	0	0	0%	0	0%	0	0%	0	0%

关于法定继承人范围与顺序的民众观念，统计数据显示，各以被调查者选择占比最高的顺序作为统计依据，被调查者认可的法定继承人的范围与顺序是：第一顺序为配偶(89.54%)、父母（67.97%）、子（67.10%）；女（58.61%）；第二顺序为孙子女(50.11%)、外孙子女（48.37%）、祖父母（48.80%）、外祖父母（47.28%）、兄弟(45.53%)、姐妹（43.14%）；第三顺序为侄子女（27.23%）、外甥子女（26.58%）、伯叔姑舅姨（27.67%）；第四顺序以上为表兄弟姐妹（27.23%）、堂兄弟姐妹（24.62%）。

2. 配偶与血亲继承人顺序的民众观念情况统计

问题【四、(一) 2.】“以下三种法定继承人的范围和顺序，您认为哪一个更为适当？(单选)”

A	B	C
第一顺序：子女	第一顺序：子女	第一顺序：配偶、子女、父母
第二顺序：父母	第二顺序：父母	第二顺序：兄弟姐妹、祖父母、外祖父母
第三顺序：兄弟姐妹、祖父母、外祖父母 兄弟姐妹的子女（侄子女、外甥子女为代位继承人）	第三顺序：兄弟姐妹、祖父母、外祖父母 兄弟姐妹的子女（侄子女、外甥子女为代位继承人）	第三顺序：侄子女、外甥子女
配偶无固定顺序，能够参加第一顺序、第二顺序、第三顺序的继承。	配偶无固定顺序，能够参第一顺序、第二顺序的继承。	配偶有固定顺序，只能参与第一顺序的继承。

表 4-21 配偶与血亲继承人顺序的民众观念情况统计（单选）

选项	人数	比例
A. 配偶无固定顺序，可以参与第一、第二、第三顺序继承	43	13.48%
B. 配偶无固定顺序，可以参与第一、第二顺序继承	20	6.27%
C. 配偶固定第一顺序	256	80.25%
合计	319	100%

关于配偶与血亲继承人顺序的民众观念，调查统计数据显示，在填写本问题的 319 名被调查者中，(1) 选择 C 项第一继承顺序为配偶、子女、父母，配偶为固定的第一顺序

继承人的，占八成（80.25%）；（2）选择A、B两项第一顺序为子女，第二顺序为父母，第三顺序为兄弟姐妹、祖父母、外祖父母、兄弟姐妹的子女，配偶为无固定继承顺序继承人，可以参与第一、第二（或第三）顺序继承的，合计占近二成（19.75%）。

（二）配偶与血亲继承人的法定应继份

问题【四、（二）】"配偶与血亲继承人共同继承各取得遗产的份额，您认为以下哪一项更为适当？（单选）"

A. 配偶无固定继承顺序	B. 配偶无固定继承顺序	C. 配偶有固定继承顺序	D. 其他
配偶与第一顺序的子女共同继承时，其取得遗产的一半，另一半由子女按人数平均继承	配偶与第一顺序的子女共同继承时，其取得遗产的一半，另一半由子女、按人数平均继承	第一顺序继承人为配偶、子女、父母，共同继承时按人数均分遗产	
配偶与第二顺序的父母共同继承时，其取得遗产的三分之二，另外三分之一由父母平均继承	配偶与第二顺序的父母共同继承时，其取得遗产的三分之二，另外三分之一由父母平均继承	无第一顺序血亲继承人时，配偶继承全部遗产	
配偶与第三顺序的兄弟姐妹、祖父母和外祖父母共同继承时，其取得遗产的四分之三，另外四分之一由兄弟姐妹、祖父母、外祖父母，按人数平均继承	无第一顺序、第二顺序血亲继承人时，配偶继承全部遗产		
无上述三个顺序血亲继承人时，配偶取得全部遗产			

表4-22 配偶与血亲继承人的法定应继份的民众观念情况统计（单选）

选项	人数	比例
A. 配偶无固定继承顺序，参与前三顺序的继承，并取得不同份额；无上述三个顺序血亲继承人时，配偶取得全部遗产	118	36.99%
B. 配偶无固定继承顺序，参与前二顺序的继承，并取得不同份额；无第一顺序、第二顺序血亲继承人时，配偶继承全部遗产	65	20.38%
C. 配偶有固定继承顺序，与第一顺序继承人共同继承并均分遗产	132	41.38%
其他	4	1.25%
合计	319	100%

关于配偶与血亲继承人法定应继份的民众观念，调查统计数据显示，在填写本问题的

319 名被调查者中，(1) 选择 A、B 两项配偶应无固定继承顺序，参与前三顺序或前二顺序继承并取得不同份额的，合计占五成半以上（57.37%）；(2) 选择 C 项配偶应按固定顺序继承并均分遗产的，占四成以上（41.38%）。

（三）配偶对遗产中家庭住房的先取权与终生使用权

1. 配偶对遗产中家庭住房的先取权与终生使用权的民间习惯情况统计

问题【四、(三) 1.】“甲乙是夫妻，育有一子丙。甲因病去世时留下的遗产包括：价值 50 万元住房一套（原由甲乙夫妻共同居住，丙已结婚分家另过）、价值 10 万元小汽车一辆和 20 万元存款。请问：如果上述情况发生在您所在地区，被继承人甲的妻子乙是否可以优先继承这套房屋（配偶优先权）? A. 是；B. 否。(单选)”

表 4-23　配偶对遗产中家庭住房的先取权与终生使用权的民间习惯情况统计（单选）

选项	人数	比例
A. 是	282	88.40%
B. 否	37	11.60%
合计	319	100%

关于配偶对遗产中家庭住房先取权与终生使用权的民间习惯，调查统计数据显示，填写本问题的 319 名被调查者所在地区的继承习惯是：(1) A 项是，即有该习惯的，占近九成（88.40%）；(2) B 项否，即无此习惯的，仅占一成以上（11.60%）。

2. 配偶对遗产中家庭住房的先取权与终生使用权费用的民间情况统计

问题【四、(三) 2.】“如果甲的妻子乙可以优先继承这套房屋，但该住房的价值超过其应当继承的遗产份额 40 万元，在您所在地区是否按照下列情况处理的? A. 乙有权继承该住房，且无须向另一法定继承人丙进行补偿。B. 如果乙有经济补偿能力，则应当向另一法定继承人丙适当进行补偿。C. 其他。(单选) 理由是什么?”

(1) 配偶对遗产中家庭住房的先取与终生使用是否付费的民间习惯情况统计。

表 4-24　配偶对遗产中家庭住房的先取与终生使用是否付费的民间习惯情况统计（单选）

选项	人数	比例
A. 乙有权继承该住房，且无须向其他共同应召继承人丙进行补偿	144	45.14%
B. 如果乙有经济补偿能力，则应当向其他共同应召继承人丙适当进行补偿	169	52.98%
C. 其他	6	1.88%
合计	319	100%

关于配偶对遗产中家庭住房的先取与终生使用是否付费的民间习惯，统计数据显示，填写该题的 319 名被调查者所在地区的继承习惯是：①B 项适当补偿的，占五成以上（52.98%）；②A 项无须进行补偿的，占四成半（45.14%），也就是说，如配偶无经济补

偿能力的，可不予补偿而终生使用此房屋。

（2）配偶对遗产中家庭住房的先取与终生使用是否付费的民间习惯之理由情况统计。

表 4-25 配偶对遗产中家庭住房的先取与终生使用是否付费的民间习惯之理由情况统计

项目	人数	比例
A. 应首先保证乙有居住之所，同时，丙是乙的儿子，将来乙的遗产也会由丙来继承，所以，乙无须向丙进行补偿	144	48.48%
B. 由乙向丙进行补偿，这体现公平精神	112	37.71%
C. 其他的理由	41	13.81%
合计	297	100%

关于配偶对遗产中家庭住房的先取与终生使用是否付费的民间习惯之理由，调查统计数据显示，297 名被调查者填写了选择理由，①认为无须支付费用的理由是，A 项应首先保证乙有居住之所，同时丙是乙的儿子，将来乙的遗产也会由丙来继承，所以乙无须向丙进行补偿的，占近五成（48.48%）；②认为应支付一定费用的理由是，B 项这体现公平精神的，占近四成（37.71%）；③还有一成以上（13.81%）的人填写了 C 项其他理由。

（四）后顺序特殊法定继承人对遗产中原使用的住房及日常生活用品的终生使用权

关于后顺序特殊法定继承人对遗产中原使用的住房及日常生活用品的终生使用权，也可称为后顺序特殊法定继承人对特殊遗产的终生使用权。

1. 后顺序特殊法定继承人对遗产中原使用的住房及日常生活用品的终生使用权的民间习惯情况统计

问题【四、（四）1.】“某甲死亡时留下若干遗产，其中包括一套三室一厅的住房（其中的一间房屋一直由某甲的祖父居住）。由于某甲的祖父属于后顺序继承人而不能参加继承，遗产全部由某甲的第一顺序继承人配偶及其子女等继承。请问：在您所在的地区，如果发生了上述情况，有哪些下列处理方式？某甲的祖父对该供其居住的房屋，是否可以继续居住？A. 是；B. 否。（单选）”

表 4-26 后顺序特殊法定继承人对特殊遗产的终生使用权的民间习惯情况统计（单选）

选项	人数	比例
A. 是	295	92.48%
B. 否	24	7.52%
合计	319	100%

关于后顺序特殊法定继承人对特殊遗产的终生使用权的民间习惯，调查统计数据显示，填写本问题的 319 名被调查者所在地区的继承习惯是：（1）A 项是，即有该习惯的，占九成以上（92.48%）；（2）B 项否，即无该习惯的，仅占不到一成（7.52%）。

2. 后顺序特殊法定继承人对遗产中原使用的住房及日常生活用品的终生使用是否付费的民间习惯情况统计

问题【四、（四）2.】“如果某甲的祖父可以继续居住，是否其可以不交租金？A. 是；B. 否。（单选）”

表 4-27 后顺序特殊继承人对特殊遗产终生使用是否付费的民间习惯情况统计（单选）

选项	人数	比例
A. 是	274	85.89%
B. 否	45	14.11%
合计	319	100%

关于后顺序特殊继承人对特殊遗产终生使用是否付费的民间习惯，调查统计数据显示，填写本问题的 319 名被调查者所在地区的继承习惯是：（1）A 项是，即无须支付租金的，占八成半（85.89%）；（2）B 项否，即要支付租金的占一成以上（14.11%）。

3. 后顺序特殊法定继承人对遗产中原使用的住房及日常生活用品的终生使用权之期限的民间习惯情况统计

问题【四、（四）3.】“如果某甲的祖父可以继续居住，是否可以居住到其死亡时为止？（终生使用权）A. 是；B. 否。（单选）”

表 4-28 后顺序特殊法定继承人对特殊遗产的终生使用权之期限的民间习惯情况统计（单选）

选项	人数	比例
A. 是	272	85.27%
B. 否	47	14.73%
合计	319	100%

关于后顺序特殊法定继承人对特殊遗产的终生使用权之期限的民间习惯，调查统计数据显示，填写本问题的 319 名被调查者所在地区的继承习惯是：（1）A 项是，即有该习惯的占八成半（85.27%）；（2）B 项否，即没有该习惯的占一成以上（14.73%）。

（五）尽了主要赡养义务的丧偶儿媳或女婿的遗产分配方式

问题【四、（五）】“村民某甲，老伴因病早年去世，膝下有两个儿子乙和丙。2003 年乙与丁结婚后与某甲共同生活。2012 年 1 月乙因交通事故死亡，但乙的妻子丁仍然一直照料公公某甲的晚年生活，直至 2015 年 1 月某甲去世。请问：在您所在地区，如发生上述情况，因乙的妻子丁对公公某甲尽了主要赡养义务，如何处理某甲的遗产分配问题 A. 丁可以与某甲的二儿子丙共同继承，并且平均分配遗产；B. 丁不能与某甲的二儿子丙共同继承，但其可分得适当的遗产；C. 其他。（单选）理由是什么？”

1. 尽了主要赡养义务的丧偶儿媳或女婿的遗产分配的民间习惯情况统计

表 4-29 尽了主要赡养义务的丧偶儿媳或女婿的遗产分配的民间习惯情况统计（单选）

<table>
<tr><th colspan="2">选项</th><th>人数</th><th>比例</th></tr>
<tr><td colspan="2">A. 丁可以与某甲的二儿子丙共同继承，并且平均分配遗产</td><td>224</td><td>70.44%</td></tr>
<tr><td colspan="2">B. 丁不能与某甲的二儿子丙共同继承，但其可分得适当的遗产</td><td>84</td><td>26.42%</td></tr>
<tr><td rowspan="2">C. 其他</td><td>C1. 丁可以与某甲的二儿子共同继承，但适当少分</td><td rowspan="2">10</td><td rowspan="2">3.14%</td></tr>
<tr><td>C2. 丁应当多分得遗产</td></tr>
<tr><td colspan="2">合计</td><td>318</td><td>100%</td></tr>
</table>

关于尽了主要赡养义务的丧偶儿媳或女婿的遗产分配之民间习惯，调查统计数据显示，填写本问题的318名被调查者所在地区的继承习惯是：（1）A项其可以与第一顺序继承人共同继承且平均分配遗产的，占七成（70.44%）；（2）B项其不能作为第一顺序继承人，但可以酌情分得遗产的，占二成半以上（26.42%）。

2. 尽了主要赡养义务的丧偶儿媳或女婿的遗产分配的民间习惯之理由情况统计

表 4-30 尽了主要赡养义务的丧偶儿媳或女婿的遗产分配的民间习惯之理由情况统计

项目	人数	比例
A. 根据权利义务相一致、秉持公平的理念可以作为第一顺序继承人	198	62.40%
B. 作为儿媳妇，丁孝敬公公，已经尽了赡养义务，符合中国的孝道文化和道德观念，因此有权作为第一顺序继承人	90	28.20%
C. 虽然丁一直照顾公公的晚年生活，但毕竟不是某甲的子女，与某甲不具有血缘关系，遗产不能给了外人，因此，丁不能继承某甲的遗产	30	9.40%
合计	318	100%

关于尽了主要赡养义务的丧偶儿媳或丧偶女婿的遗产分配的民间习惯之理由，调查统计数据显示，318名被调查者填写了选择理由，（1）认为其可以与第一顺序继承人共同继承的理由分别是，A项根据权利义务相一致、秉持公平的理念其可以作为第一顺序继承人的，占六成以上（62.40%）和B项丁作为儿媳，孝敬公公，已经尽了赡养义务，符合中国的孝道文化和道德观念，因此有权作为第一顺序继承人的，占近三成（28.20%）；（2）认为其不能作为第一顺序继承人，但可以酌情分得遗产的理由是，C项虽然丁一直照顾公公的晚年生活，但毕竟不是某甲的子女，与某甲不具有血缘关系，遗产不能给"外人"的，占不到一成（9.40%）。

五、遗嘱继承之调查数据统计情况

关于遗嘱继承之调查数据统计，我们主要从公证遗嘱与其他形式遗嘱的效力、遗嘱自由的限制——特留份、夫妻共同遗嘱，这三个方面进行调查数据的统计情况汇总分析。

（一）公证遗嘱与其他形式遗嘱的效力

问题【五、（一）】“退休职工甲有一套个人住房，他于2011年2月立了一份遗嘱，写明由其妻子乙一人继承该住房，并将该遗嘱进行了公证。后来，甲改变了主意，他重新写了一份遗嘱，写明其妻子乙和儿子丙共同继承该房屋。2016年3月甲住院病危期间，当着二位医生在现场立下口头遗嘱，指定其个人住房由儿子丙继承，两个小时后其抢救无效死亡。请问，您认为，甲的个人住房应该由谁继承？A. 乙；B. 乙和丙；C. 丙。（单选）理由是什么？”

1. 公证遗嘱与其他形式遗嘱适用效力的民众观念情况统计

表4-31　公证遗嘱与其他形式遗嘱适用效力的民众观念情况统计（单选）

选项	人数	比例
A. 乙（公证遗嘱有效）	113	35.42%
B. 乙和丙（后成立的未公证书面遗嘱有效）	100	31.35%
C. 丙（最后的口头遗嘱有效）	106	33.23%
合计	319	100%

关于公证遗嘱与其他形式遗嘱适用效力的民众观念，调查统计数据显示，在填写本问题的319名被调查者中，（1）选择B、C两项即认为后遗嘱的适用效力优先于前一公证遗嘱的，合计占近六成半（64.58%）；（2）选择A项即认为公证遗嘱适用效力优先的，占三成半（35.42%）。

2. 公证遗嘱与其他形式遗嘱适用效力的民众观念之理由情况统计

表4-32　公证遗嘱与其他形式遗嘱适用效力的民众观念之理由情况统计

项目	人数	比例
A. 口头遗嘱形式灵活，且有证人作证，能够反映被继承人的最后真实意愿	99	31.03%
B. 口头遗嘱形式不固定，很难准确、完全地反映被继承人的真实意愿，且有被篡改或修改的可能性	60	18.81%
C. 书面遗嘱（第二份遗嘱）比较正式，取证容易，且其订立在公证遗嘱之后，反映了被继承人的最后的意愿	63	19.75%
D. 公证遗嘱的程序规范，具有较强的公示效力和证明效力	97	30.41%
合计	319	100%

关于公证遗嘱与其他形式遗嘱适用效力的民众观念之理由，调查统计数据显示，319名被调查者填写了选择理由，（1）认为后遗嘱适用效力优先的理由分别是，A项口头遗嘱形式灵活，且有证人作证，能够反映被继承人最后真实意愿的，占三成以上（31.03%）和C项书面遗嘱（第二份遗嘱）比较正式，取证容易，且其订立在公证遗嘱之后，反映了被继承人最后意愿的，占近二成（19.75%）；（2）认为公证遗嘱适用效力优先的理由是，D项公证遗嘱的程序规范，具有较强的公示效力和证明效力的，占三成（30.41%）；（3）还有不到二成（18.81%）的人填写了B项口头遗嘱形式不固定，很难准确、完全地反映被继承人的真实意愿，且有被篡改或修改等理由。

（二）遗嘱自由的限制——特留份

问题【五、（二）】“甲生前立了一份遗嘱，将自己死后遗留下的财产全部赠给他的一个好朋友乙，而他的配偶和子女不能取得甲的任何遗产。请问：您认为甲的这一做法是否适当？A. 适当；B. 不适当；C. 其他。（单选）理由是什么？”

1. 以遗嘱将个人遗产全部赠给他人的民众观念情况统计

表4-33　以遗嘱将个人遗产全部赠给他人的民众观念情况统计（单选）

选项	人数	比例
A. 适当	110	34.48%
B. 不适当	193	60.50%
C. 其他	16	5.02%
合计	319	100%

关于以遗嘱将个人遗产全部赠给他人的民众观念，调查统计数据显示，在填写本问题的319名被调查者中，对被继承人以遗嘱处分个人财产全部给第三人的行为，（1）选择B项不适当的，占六成（60.50%）；（2）选择A项适当的，占近三成半（34.48%）。

2. 以遗嘱将个人遗产全部赠给他人的民众观念之理由情况统计

表4-34　以遗嘱将个人遗产全部赠给他人的民众观念之理由情况统计

项目	人数	比例
A. 甲对自己的财产，享有自由处分的权利，其他人无权干涉	119	37.30%
B. 造成家庭财产外流，不利于保障甲的配偶及其子女的生活，同时也不符合风俗习惯，为常人所难以接受	200	62.70%
合计	319	100%

关于以遗嘱将个人遗产全部赠给他人的民众观念之理由，调查统计数据显示，319名被调查者填写了选择理由，（1）认为该行为不适当的理由是，B项此种行为会造成家庭财产外流，不利于保障配偶及其子女的生活，同时也不符合风俗习惯，为常人所难以接受的，占六成以上（62.70%）；（2）认为该行为适当的理由是，A项遗嘱人甲对自己的财产，享有自由处分的权利，其他人无权干涉的，占近四成（37.30%）。

（三）夫妻共同遗嘱

所谓共同遗嘱也称合立遗嘱，是指两个或两个以上的遗嘱人共同订立的一份遗嘱，在遗嘱中同时处分共同遗嘱人的各自的或共同的财产。①

1. 夫妻共同遗嘱的民众观念与理由情况统计

问题【五、（三）1.】“甲乙是夫妻，双方在生前共同设立了一份遗嘱，对死后的遗产处理进行安排。甲乙双方在遗嘱中约定，不管谁先去世，另一方都不得改变此遗嘱对遗产的处理安排。请问：您是否认同甲乙夫妻双方共同设立遗嘱的此约定？A. 赞同；B. 不赞同。（单选）理由是什么？”

（1）夫妻共同遗嘱的民众观念情况统计。

表 4-35　夫妻共同遗嘱的民众观念情况统计（单选）

选项	人数	比例
A. 赞同	192	60. 19%
B. 不赞同	127	39. 81%
合计	319	100%

关于夫妻共同遗嘱的民众观念，调查统计数据显示，在填写本问题的 319 名被调查者中，对于夫妻设立共同遗嘱，①选择 A 项赞同的，占六成（60. 19%）；②选择 B 项不赞同的，占近四成（39. 81%）。

（2）夫妻共同遗嘱的民众观念之理由情况统计。

表 4-36　夫妻共同遗嘱的民众观念之理由情况统计

项目	人数	比例
A. 该遗嘱为甲乙双方共同设立，反映了双方的共同意愿，理应为双方所遵守	192	60. 19%
B. 该遗嘱无法应对出现的新情况和新问题，限制了双方对自己财产的处分权	127	39. 81%
合计	319	100%

关于夫妻共同遗嘱的民众观念之理由，调查统计数据显示，319 名被调查者填写了选择理由，①赞同设立夫妻共同遗嘱的理由是，A 项该遗嘱为夫妻双方共同设立，反映了双方的共同意愿，理应为双方所遵守的，占六成（60. 19%）；②不赞同设立夫妻共同遗嘱的理由是，B 项该遗嘱无法应对出现的新情况和新问题，限制了双方对自己财产处分权的，占近四成（39. 81%）。

2. 夫妻共同遗嘱存在的民间习惯情况统计

问题【五、（三）2.】“在您所在地区，有无夫妻共同设立遗嘱的情况发生？A. 有；B. 无。（单选）”

---

① 杨立新：《对修正〈继承法〉十个问题的意见》，载《法律适用》2012 年第 8 期。

表 4-37 夫妻共同遗嘱存在的民间习惯情况统计（单选）

选项	人数	比例
A. 有	56	17.55%
B. 无	263	82.45%
合计	319	100%

关于夫妻共同遗嘱存在的民间习惯，调查统计数据显示，在填写本问题的 319 名被调查者所在地区的民间习惯是：（1）B 项无该习惯的，占八成以上（82.45%）；（2）A 项有该习惯的，占近二成（17.55%）。

六、继承和遗赠的接受与放弃之调查数据统计情况

关于继承和遗赠的接受与放弃之调查数据统计，我们主要从继承的接受与放弃的时间与方式、遗赠的接受与放弃的方式与效力、继承的放弃与债权人的撤销权，这三个方面进行调查数据的统计情况汇总分析。

（一）继承的接受与放弃的时间与方式

问题【六、（一）】“对于继承人放弃继承的时间，您认为下列哪一个更为适当？A. 继承人放弃继承的，应在知道继承开始的 2 个月内作出放弃继承的表示；B. 继承开始后继承人放弃继承的，应当在遗产处理前，作出放弃继承的意思表示。（单选）理由是什么？请问您所在地区的民众是如何接受继承的？”

1. 继承的接受与放弃时间的民众观念及理由情况统计

（1）继承的接受与放弃时间的民众观念情况统计。

表 4-38 继承的接受与放弃时间的民众观念情况统计（单选）

选项	人数	比例
A. 继承人放弃继承的，应在知道继承开始的 2 个月内作出放弃继承的意思表示	125	36.67%
B. 继承开始后继承人放弃继承的，应当在遗产处理前，作出放弃继承的意思表示	216	63.33%
合计	341	100%

关于继承的接受与放弃时间的民众观念，调查统计数据显示，在填写本问题的 341 名被调查者中，①选择 B 项应当在遗产处理前作出意思表示的，占近六成半（63.33%）；②选择 A 项应在知道继承开始的 2 个月内作出意思表示的，占三成半以上（36.67%）。

（2）继承的接受与放弃时间的民众观念之理由情况统计。

表 4-39　继承的接受与放弃时间的民众观念之理由情况统计

项目	人数	比例
A. 需要给继承人一定的考虑时间且 2 个月长短较为合适	98	38.28%
B. 在遗产处理前确定继承权问题，便于遗产的处理，减少后续纠纷	158	61.72%
合计	256	100%

关于继承的接受与放弃时间的民众观念之理由，调查统计数据显示，在填写本问题的 256 名被调查者中，①认为应在遗产处理前作出意思表示的理由是，B 项在遗产处理前确定继承权问题，便于处理遗产，减少后续纠纷的，占六成以上（61.72%）；②认为应在知道继承开始的 2 个月内作出意思表示的理由是，A 项需要给继承人一定的考虑时间且 2 个月长短较为合适的，占近四成（38.28%）。

2. 继承的接受与放弃方式的民间习惯情况统计

表 4-40　继承的接受与放弃方式的民间习惯情况统计（单选）

选项	人数	比例
A. 遗产分割前以书面或口头的方式明确表示拒绝继承	73	73.00%
B. 不予表示，也不参加遗产分割，视为放弃	27	27.00%
合计	100	100%

关于继承的接受与放弃方式的民间习惯，调查统计数据显示，在填写本问题的 100 名被调查者所在地区的继承习惯是：（1）A 项遗产分割前以书面或口头的方式明确表示拒绝继承的，占七成以上（73.00%）；（2）B 项不予表示，也不参加遗产分割视为放弃的，占近三成（27.00%）。

（二）遗赠的接受与放弃的方式与效力

问题【六、（二）】“甲生前设立了一份遗嘱，在甲死后，将一辆小汽车赠给其侄子乙。后来甲去世，乙得知遗嘱的内容后，对此遗赠没有作出任何意思表示，既没有说接受，也没有说放弃。您认为下列哪一项更为适当？A. 乙无权取得该小汽车，乙的行为应该被视为放弃该遗赠；B. 乙有权取得该小汽车，乙的行为应该被视为接受该遗赠。（单选）理由是什么？请问您所在地区的民众是如何接受遗赠的？”

1. 遗赠的接受与放弃的方式与效力的民众观念及理由情况统计

（1）遗赠的接受与放弃的方式与效力的民众观念情况统计。

表 4-41　遗赠的接受与放弃的方式与效力的民众观念情况统计（单选）

选项	人数	比例
A. 乙无权取得该小汽车，乙的行为应该被视为放弃该遗赠	94	27.57%

续表

选项	人数	比例
B. 乙有权取得该小汽车，乙的行为应该被视为接受该遗赠	247	72.43%
合计	341	100%

关于遗赠的接受与放弃的方式与效力的民众观念，调查统计数据显示，在填写本问题的341名被调查者中，①选择B项受遗赠人不作表示应视为接受遗赠的，占七成以上(72.43%)；②选择A项受遗赠人不作表示应视为放弃遗赠的，占近三成（27.57%)。

（2）遗赠的接受与放弃的方式与效力的民众观念之理由情况统计。

表4-42　遗赠的接受与放弃的方式与效力的民众观念之理由情况统计

项目	人数	比例
A. 遗赠是单方行为，遗赠人作出即生效，不需要接受表示	25	28.09%
B. 不作表示可以被认定为接受遗赠，这有利于受遗赠人的利益	16	17.98%
C. 接受遗赠必须明确表示，这是基于此为受遗赠人额外获得的利益，应当主动表示接受，否则视为拒绝利益	40	44.94%
D. 其他	8	8.99%
合计	89	100%

关于赠与的接受与放弃的方式与效力的民众观念之理由，调查统计数据显示，有89名被调查者填写了选择理由，①认为受遗赠人不作表示可以被视为接受遗赠的理由分别是，A项遗赠是单方行为，遗赠人作出即生效，不需要接受表示的，占近三成（28.09%）和B项这有利于受遗赠人利益的，占近二成（17.98%)；②认为受遗赠人不作表示应被视为放弃遗赠的理由是，C项此为受遗赠人额外获得的利益，应当主动表示接受，否则视为拒绝该获益的，占近四成半（44.94%)。

2. 遗赠的接受与放弃的方式与效力的民间习惯情况统计

表4-43　遗赠的接受与放弃的方式与效力的民间习惯情况统计（单选）

选项	人数	比例
A. 乙不作表示视为接受遗赠	44	45.83%
B. 乙接受遗赠必须明示，否则视为放弃受遗赠	52	54.17%
合计	96	100%

关于赠与的接受与放弃的方式与效力的民间习惯，统计数据显示，填写本问题的96名被调查者所在地区的继承习惯是：（1）B项接受遗赠必须明示，否则视为放弃受遗赠的，占近五成半（54.17%)；（2）A项不作表示也可视为接受遗赠的，占四成半（45.83%)。

（三）继承的放弃与债权人的撤销权

问题【六、（三）】“甲为乙的父亲，2015年年底，乙因病住院治疗，医治无效去世，留下遗产5万元及房屋一套。此时甲经营的摩配厂已经负债累累，拖欠工人的工资已有10个月，但他考虑儿媳在其丈夫乙去世后独自抚养年幼的女儿有经济困难，于是主动提出放弃继承儿子乙的遗产。甲的债权人却认为甲不应该放弃继承儿子的遗产，这实际上是逃避债务，侵犯了债权人的利益。为此，甲的债权人起诉至人民法院，要求撤销甲放弃继承儿子乙遗产的行为。您认为下列哪一项更为恰当？A. 甲放弃继承乙遗产的行为，可以被撤销；B. 甲放弃继承乙遗产的行为，不可以被撤销。（单选）请问您所在地区的人们是如何处理此类行为的？理由是什么？”

1. 继承的放弃能否被债权人撤销的民众观念情况统计

表4-44 继承的放弃能否被债权人撤销的民众观念情况统计（单选）

选项	人数	比例
A. 甲放弃继承乙遗产的行为，可以被撤销	159	46.63%
B. 甲放弃继承乙遗产的行为，不可以被撤销	182	53.37%
合计	341	100%

关于继承的放弃能否被债权人撤销的民众观念，调查统计数据显示，在填写本问题的341名被调查者中，（1）选择B项不可以被债权人撤销的，占近五成半（53.37%）；（2）选择A项可以被债权人撤销的，占四成半以上（46.63%）。

2. 继承的放弃能否被债权人撤销的民间习惯及理由情况统计

（1）继承的放弃能否被债权人撤销的民间习惯情况统计。

表4-45 被继承人放弃继承的行为可否被撤销的民间习惯情况统计（单选）

选项	人数	比例
A. 甲放弃继承乙遗产的行为，可以被撤销	46	66.67%
B. 甲放弃继承乙遗产的行为，不可以被撤销	23	33.33%
合计	69	100%

关于继承的放弃能否被债权人撤销的民间习惯，调查统计数据显示，填写本问题的69名被调查者所在地区的民间习惯是：①A项可以被债权人撤销的，占六成半以上（66.67%）；②B项不可以被债权人撤销的，占近三成半（33.33%）。

（2）继承的放弃能否被债权人撤销的民间习惯之理由情况统计。

表4-46 继承的放弃能否被债权人撤销的民间习惯之理由情况统计

项目	人数	比例
A. 可以撤销，保护债权人的利益	16	23.88%
B. 可以撤销，防止恶意逃避债务的情形	28	41.79%

续表

项目	人数	比例
C. 不可以撤销，继承人有权放弃自己的继承权，他人无权任意干涉	23	34.33%
合计	67	100%

关于继承的放弃能否被债权人撤销的民间习惯之理由，调查统计数据显示，在填写本问题的67名被调查者中，①认为债权人可以撤销的理由是A、B两项，要保护债权人的利益或防止恶意逃避债务情形的，合计占六成半（65.67%）；②认为债权人不可以撤销的理由是，C项继承人有权放弃自己的继承权，他人无权任意干涉的，占近三成半(34.33%)。

七、继承权的丧失、被继承人的宥恕与代位继承之调查数据统计情况

关于继承权的丧失、被继承人的宥恕与代位继承之调查数据统计，我们主要从继承权丧失与被继承人宥恕、继承权的丧失与代位继承，这两个方面进行调查数据的统计情况汇总分析。

（一）继承权的丧失与被继承人的宥恕

问题【七、（一）】“某甲如果以欺诈或者胁迫的手段，迫使或者妨碍其父乙设立、变更或者撤销遗嘱，情节较为严重，但其后获得乙的原谅。询问被调查者以下哪种处理更为适当：A. 某甲有资格继承其父遗产；B. 某甲仍然不能继承其父遗产。（单选）理由是什么？在您所在地区，人们是如何处理此类行为的？”

1. 继承权的丧失与被继承人的宥恕的民众观念及理由情况统计

（1）继承权的丧失与被继承人的宥恕的民众观念情况统计。

表4-47　继承权的丧失与被继承人的宥恕的民众观念情况统计（单选）

选项	人数	比例
A. 某甲有资格继承其父遗产	253	72.20%
B. 某甲仍然不能继承其父遗产	97	27.80%
合计	350	100%

关于继承权的丧失与被继承人的宥恕的民众观念，调查统计数据显示，在填写本问题的350名被调查者中，对于继承人因欺诈或者胁迫而丧失继承权，可否因被继承人宥恕而恢复继承权，①选择A项可以恢复的，占七成以上（72.20%）；②选择B项不可以恢复的，占近三成（27.80%）。

（2）继承权的丧失与被继承人的宥恕的民众观念之理由情况统计。

表 4-48 继承权的丧失与被继承人宥恕的民众观念之理由情况统计

项目	人数	比例
A. 某甲的行为使其丧失了继承权，但乙的原谅可以使某甲恢复继承权	87	63.00%
B. 某甲的行为造成恶劣影响，即便得到乙的原谅，也应当丧失继承权	28	20.30%
C. 乙对自己的遗产有自由处分权，他想留给某甲，某甲应该可以继承	23	16.70%
合计	138	100%

关于继承权的丧失与被继承人的宥恕的民众观念之理由，调查统计数据显示，在填写本问题的 138 名被调查者中，①认为继承权可以恢复的理由分别是，A 项甲的行为使其丧失了继承权，但乙的原谅可以使某甲恢复继承权的，占六成以上（63.00%）和 C 项乙对自己的遗产有自由处分权，他想留给某甲，某甲就应该可以继承的，占一成半以上（16.70%）；②认为继承权不可以恢复的理由是，B 项某甲的行为造成恶劣影响，即便得到乙的原谅，也应当丧失继承权的，占二成（20.30%）。

2. 继承权的丧失与被继承人的宥恕的民间习惯情况统计

表 4-49 继承权的丧失与被继承人的宥恕的民间习惯情况统计（单选）

选项	人数	比例
A. 某甲的行为使其丧失了继承权，但乙的原谅可以使某甲恢复继承权	62	73.80%
B. 某甲因欺诈胁迫被继承人而确定丧失继承资格并不可恢复	12	14.20%
C. 由被继承人自行决定	10	12.00%
合计	84	100%

关于继承权的丧失与被继承人的宥恕的民间习惯，调查统计数据显示，填写本问题的 84 名被调查者所在地区的民间习惯是：（1）A 项某甲的行为使其丧失了继承权，但被继承人的原谅可以使某甲恢复继承权的，占近七成半（73.80%）；（2）B 项某甲因欺诈胁迫被继承人而确定地丧失了继承资格并不可恢复的，占近一成半（14.20%）；（3）还有一成以上（12.00%）的人填写了 C 项，某甲的继承权丧失与否，应由被继承人自行决定。

（二）继承权的丧失与代位继承

问题【七、（二）】“村民甲死亡后，其子乙因实施伪造遗嘱的行为导致丧失了对其父甲的继承权，乙的儿子丙能否代父乙去继承祖父甲的遗产？A. 丙能够代父乙继承祖父甲的遗产；B. 丙不能够代父乙继承祖父甲的遗产。（单选）请问：在您所在地区的人们是如何处理此情况的？理由是什么？”

1. 继承权丧失的效力是否及于代位继承人的民众观念情况统计

表 4-50 继承权丧失的效力是否及于代位继承人的民众观念情况统计（单选）

选项	人数	比例
A. 丙能够代父乙继承祖父甲的遗产	156	44.80%
B. 丙不能够代父乙继承祖父甲的遗产	192	55.20%
合计	348	100%

关于继承权丧失的效力是否及于代位继承人的民众观念，调查统计数据显示，在填写本问题的 348 名被调查者中，（1）选择 B 项效力及于代位继承人的，占五成半（55.20%）；（2）选择 A 项效力不能及于代位继承人的，占近四成半（44.80%）。

2. 继承权丧失的效力是否及于代位继承人的民间习惯及理由情况统计

（1）继承权丧失的效力是否及于代位继承人的民间习惯情况统计。

表 4-51 继承权丧失的效力是否及于代位继承人的民间习惯情况统计（单选）

选项	人数	比例
A. 丙可以代父乙继承祖父甲的遗产	43	58.10%
B. 丙不能代父乙继承祖父甲的遗产	31	41.90%
合计	74	100%

关于继承权丧失的效力是否及于代位继承人的民间习惯，调查统计数据显示，填写本问题的 74 名被调查者所在地区的继承习惯是：①A 项效力不及于代位继承人的，占近六成（58.10%）；②B 项效力及于代位继承人的，占四成以上（41.90%）。

（2）继承权丧失的效力是否及于代位继承人的民间习惯之理由情况统计。

表 4-52 继承权丧失的效力是否及于代位继承人的民间习惯之理由情况统计

项目	人数	比例
A. 丙是代替乙继承甲的遗产，而乙已经丧失继承权，丙代位继承的前提丧失，所以丙不能继承甲的遗产	71	55.90%
B. 丙以孙子的身份来继承祖父甲的遗产，有独立的继承权，与乙丧失继承权无关，所以丙可以继承甲的遗产	56	44.10%
合计	127	100%

关于继承权丧失的效力是否及于代位继承人的民间习惯之理由，调查统计数据显示，在填写本问题的 127 名被调查者中，①认为及于代位继承人的理由是，A 项孙子丙是代替父亲乙继承祖父的遗产，而乙已经丧失继承权，丙代位继承的前提丧失，所以丙不能继承祖父的遗产的，占五成半（55.90%）；②认为不及于代位继承人的理由是，B 项丙以孙子

的身份来继承祖父甲的遗产，有独立的继承权，与父亲乙丧失继承权无关，所以丙可以继承祖父遗产的，占近四成半（44.10%）。

八、继承协议之调查数据统计情况

必须说明，本节研究的对象是狭义的继承协议（又称继承扶养协议），是指被继承人与继承人之间，就扶养与继承事项签订的协议。关于继承协议之调查数据统计，我们主要从继承协议的订立主体与方式、继承协议的变更方式及效力，这两个方面进行调查数据的统计情况汇总分析。

（一）继承协议的订立主体与方式

问题【八、（一）】“王某，现年70岁，有长子王一，次女王二，两个子女均已成家且分家另过。王某的老伴因患癌症花费了大量医药费后去世，老夫妻的共同财产现所剩无几，现有郊区的一套住房是王某个人财产。虽然王某退休金不多，但身体没有大病，基本生活还是能够维持的。由于长子王一长期在外地工作，为解决父亲王某的养老送终问题，您认为，如下三种做法哪一做法较为妥当？A. 父亲王某与次女王二，双方协商并签订协议，由次女王二一人承担赡养父亲王某的义务，王某的全部遗产指定由王二继承；B. 父亲王某与子女王一、王二，三人协商并签订协议，由次女王二一人承担赡养父亲王某的义务，王某的全部遗产商定由王二继承，王一放弃对父亲王某遗产的继承权；C. 子女王一与王二，两人协商并签订协议，由次女王二一人承担赡养父亲王某的义务，王某的全部遗产商定由王二继承；王一放弃对父亲王某遗产的继承权。（单选）理由是什么？”

1. 继承协议的订立主体与方式的民众观念情况统计

表4-53　继承协议的订立主体与方式的民众观念情况统计（单选）

选项	人数	比例
A. 父亲王某与次女王二协商一致即可签订协议（第一种方式）	78	24.38%
B. 父亲王某需与全部继承人协商，共同签订协议（第二种方式）	189	59.06%
C. 共同继承人间签订协议即可，无须被继承人知晓或同意（第三种方式）	53	16.56%
合计	320	100%

关于继承协议的订立主体与方式的民众观念，调查统计数据显示，在填写本问题的320名被调查者中，（1）选择B项应由被扶养人与全部继承人共同协商签订的，占近六成（59.06%）；（2）选择A项应由被扶养人与扶养人协商签订的，占近二成半（24.38%）；（3）选择C项由共同继承人间协商签订即可，无须被扶养人知晓或同意的，占一成半以上（16.56%）。

2. 继承协议的订立主体与方式的民众观念之理由情况统计

表 4-54　继承协议的订立主体与方式的民众观念之理由情况统计

项目	人数	比例
A. 继承协议由被扶养人与扶养人协商签订即可，这符合被继承人意愿，有利于老人的晚年生活	23	16.67%
B. 三人协商处理更利于减少纠纷，有利于维护生活的安定	89	64.49%
C. 继承人共同商议赡养问题和遗产分配问题，符合意思自治，不易引起纠纷	26	18.84%
合计	138	100%

关于继承协议的订立主体与方式的民众观念之理由，调查统计数据显示，在填写本问题的138名被调查者中，（1）认为继承协议应由被扶养人与全部继承人共同协商签订的理由是，B项共同协商处理更利于减少纠纷，有利于维护老人生活安定的，占近六成半（64.49%）；（2）认为由共同继承人间协商签订继承协议即可的理由是，C项继承人共同商议赡养问题和遗产分配问题，这符合意思自治，不易引起纠纷的，占近二成（18.84%）；（3）认为继承协议应由被扶养人与扶养人协商签订的理由是，A项这符合被继承人意愿，有利于老人晚年生活的，占一成半以上（16.67%）。

（二）继承协议的变更方式及效力

问题【八、（二）】“王某，现年70岁，有长子王一，次女王二，三子王三，三个子女均已成家且分家另过。王某的老伴因患癌症花费了大量医疗费后去世，现有郊区的一套住房是王某个人财产，市场价约为30万元，王某有少量退休金。王某与王二协商并签订继承协议，由王二主要扶养父亲王某，王某的所有遗产由王二继承。协议签订后，王二全家与父亲王某共同生活了5年后的一天，王二因意外交通事故死亡。王二全家在与王某共同生活的期间已为王某花费生活费、医疗费等扶养费共9万元。为解决王某的养老，您同意下列哪一做法？A. 王二的儿子有继续扶养外祖父王某的能力，王某也愿意与王二的儿子共同生活，应当由王二的儿子继续履行扶养义务，并继承王某的全部遗产；B. 王一、王三共同补偿王二家人6万元扶养费后（另有3万元扶养费属于应当由王二承担的），如果王一与父亲王某签订新的继承协议，并与王某共同生活一直扶养至其去世，就由王一继承王某的全部遗产；C. 对王二已经支付的扶养费不予补偿，如果王一与父亲王某签订新的继承协议，并与王某共同生活一直扶养至其去世，就由王一继承王某的全部遗产；D. 王一、王三共同补偿王二家人6万元扶养费后，由两人共同扶养父亲王某；E. 其他。（单选）理由是什么？”

1. 继承协议的变更方式与效力的民众观念情况统计

表 4-55　继承协议的变更方式与效力的民众观念情况统计（单选）

选项	人数	比例
A. 原扶养人的子女有扶养能力，在双方自愿的情况下，由原扶养人的子女继续扶养被扶养人，并继承全部遗产	137	42. 81%
B. 原签订的继承协议效力终止，补偿原扶养人一定费用后，由某一有扶养能力的法定继承人，在双方自愿的情况下签订新协议，继续扶养被扶养人，并继承遗产	79	24. 69%
C. 原签订的继承协议效力终止，对原扶养人无须补偿，应由某一有扶养能力的法定继承人与被扶养人，在双方自愿的情况下签订新协议，继续扶养被扶养人并继承全部遗产	34	10. 62%
D. 原签订的继承协议效力终止，补偿原扶养人一定费用后，应由有扶养能力的全体法定继承人，共同依法对被扶养人尽扶养义务，并依法定继承取得遗产	62	19. 38%
E. 其他	8	2. 50%
合计	320	100%

关于继承协议的变更方式与效力的民众观念，即在继承协议的履行中，如扶养人先于被扶养人去世，被调查者对于该协议的变更方式与效力的认识，调查统计数据显示，在填写该问题的 320 名被调查者中，（1）选择 A 项，该协议可有条件继续履行，如原扶养人的子女有扶养能力，在原扶养人的子女和被扶养人双方同意的情况下，可由原扶养人的子女继续履行该继承协议的，此即代位扶养的，占四成以上（42. 81%）；（2）选择 B 项和 C 项，该协议效力终止，须签订新的继承协议，由新的扶养人履行扶养义务并继承遗产，合计占三成半（35. 31%），其中，B 项认为需要对原扶养人的继承人补偿超过其扶养义务部分费用的，占近二成半（24. 69%），C 项认为不需要对原扶养人的继承人补偿超过其扶养义务部分费用的，占一成（10. 62%）；（3）选择 D 项，该协议效力终止，应补偿原扶养人的继承人超过其扶养义务部分费用后，由所有法定继承人共同扶养，即实行法定赡养的，占近二成（19. 38%）。可见，上海市被调查者对于代位扶养的认可度最高，占四成以上。

2. 继承协议的变更方式与效力的民众观念之理由情况统计

表 4-56　继承协议的变更方式与效力的民众观念之理由情况统计

项目	人数	比例
A. 继承协议继续有效，有利于维持原扶养人一贯的生活方式，使其安度晚年	45	31. 69%
B. 当事人协商一致进行处理，可以减少纠纷	69	48. 59%

续表

项目	人数	比例
C. 应遵从继承协议的效力，如其效力已终止即无须再进行补偿	17	11.97%
D. 基于公平和诚实信用原则，应补偿原扶养人一定费用	11	7.75%
合计	142	100%

关于继承协议的变更方式与效力的民众观念之理由，调查统计数据显示，在填写该问题的142名被调查者中，(1) 认为继承协议可有条件继续履行的理由是，A项这有利于维持原扶养人一贯的生活方式，使其安度晚年的，占三成以上（31.69%）；(2) 认为对原扶养人应补偿一定费用的理由是，D项基于公平和诚实信用原则，应补偿原扶养人一定费用的，占不到一成（7.75%）；(3) 认为对原扶养人无须进行补偿的理由是，C项应遵从继承协议的效力，如其效力已终止即无须再进行补偿的，占一成以上（11.97%）；(4) 还有近五成（48.59%）的人填写了B项应协商一致进行处理，这可以减少纠纷等理由。

九、遗产债务清偿之调查数据统计情况

关于遗产债务清偿之调查数据统计，我们主要从遗产债务清偿责任的类型、被继承人丧葬费的支付、遗产债务的清偿顺序，这三个方面进行调查数据的统计情况汇总分析。

（一）遗产债务清偿责任的类型

问题【九、(一)】"继承遗产，应当清偿被继承人的债务，您是怎么理解这句话的？A. 对被继承人的生前所有债务，继承人都应当予以偿还；B. 对被继承人的生前所有债务，继承人应先用所有遗产偿还债务，不足部分由继承人个人财产偿还；C. 对被继承人的生前所有债务，继承人只以继承的遗产为限予以偿还；D. 对被继承人的生前所有债务，继承人如果存在转移遗产、隐瞒遗产的情形，则其应当负责以遗产和其个人财产偿还所有的债务。(多选) 在您所在的地区，人们遇到继承人有转移遗产、隐瞒遗产的情况是如何处理的？理由是什么？"

1. 遗产债务清偿责任的类型之民众观念情况统计

表4-57 遗产债务清偿责任的类型之民众观念情况统计（多选）

选项	人数	比例
A. 对被继承人的生前所有债务，继承人都应当予以偿还	106	30.70%
B. 对被继承人的生前所有债务，继承人应先用所有遗产偿还债务，不足部分由继承人以个人财产偿还	127	36.80%
C. 对被继承人的生前所有债务，继承人只以继承的遗产为限予以偿还	211	61.10%

续表

选项	人数	比例
D. 对被继承人的生前所有债务，继承人如果存在转移遗产、隐瞒遗产的情形，则其应当负责以遗产和其个人财产偿还所有的债务	152	44.00%

关于遗产债务清偿责任的类型之民众观念，调查统计数据显示，在填写本问题的345名被调查者中，对于被继承人生前欠下的所有债务，（1）选择A、B两项实行自愿的无限清偿责任的，合计占近七成（67.50%）；（2）选择C项实行有限清偿责任的，占六成以上（61.10%）；（3）选择D项实行强制的无限清偿责任的，占近四成半（44.00%）。

2. 继承人侵害遗产的法律责任之民间习惯及理由情况统计

（1）继承人侵害遗产的法律责任之民间习惯情况统计。

表4-58 继承人侵害遗产的法律责任之民间习惯情况统计（单选）

选项	人数	比例
A. 继承人有转移、隐瞒遗产情况时，继承人仍然只在继承财产的范围内进行清偿	10	29.41%
B. 继承人有转移、隐瞒遗产情况时，对被继承人的生前所有债务，继承人都应当予以偿还	20	58.82%
C. 继承人有转移、隐瞒遗产情况时，对超过遗产偿付限度外的被继承人生前债务，由有转移、隐瞒遗产等行为的继承人予以偿还	4	11.77%
合计	34	100%

关于继承人侵害遗产的法律责任之民间习惯，调查统计数据显示，填写本问题的34名被调查者所在地区的继承习惯是：继承人有转移、隐瞒遗产情况时，①B项对被继承人的生前所有债务，继承人都应当予以偿还的，占近六成（58.82%）；②A项继承人仍然只在继承财产的范围内进行清偿的，占近三成（29.41%）；③C项对超过遗产偿付限度外的被继承人生前债务，由有转移、隐瞒遗产等行为的继承人予以偿还的，占一成以上（11.77%）。

（2）继承人侵害遗产的法律责任的民间习惯之理由情况统计。

表4-59 继承人侵害遗产的法律责任的民间习惯之理由情况统计

项目	人数	比例
A. 目前我国实行限定继承制度，所以继承人只需在遗产范围内对被继承人的债务负责	9	26.47%
B. 为保护债权人的合法权益，所有继承人对上述侵害行为均负有偿还的义务	18	52.94%

续表

项目	人数	比例
C. 有转移、隐瞒遗产等行为的继承人侵害了债权人的合法权益，也仅应该由其承担相应的赔偿责任，与其他继承人无关，符合自己责任原则	7	20.59%
合计	34	100%

关于继承人侵害遗产的法律责任的民间习惯之理由，调查统计数据显示，在填写本问题的34名被调查者中，（1）认为继承人有转移、隐瞒遗产情况时，仍然只在继承财产的范围内进行清偿的理由是，A项我国立法规定如此；（2）认为继承人有转移、隐瞒遗产情况时，所有继承人都应当予以偿还的理由是，B项有利于保护债权人的合法权益的，占五成以上（52.94%）；（3）认为继承人有转移、隐瞒遗产情况时，应仅由有过错行为的继承人予以偿还的理由是，C项这符合自己责任原则的，占二成（20.59%）。

（二）被继承人丧葬费的支付

问题【九、（二）】“在您所在的地区，死者的丧葬费一般是如何支付的？A. 由全体继承人共同支付；B. 从被继承人的遗产中支付；C. 其他。（单选）”

表4-60 被继承人丧葬费支付的民间习惯情况统计（单选）

选项	人数	比例
A. 由全体继承人共同支付	179	51.80%
B. 从被继承人的遗产中支付	149	43.20%
C. 其他	17	5.00%
合计	345	100%

关于被继承人丧葬费支付的民间习惯，调查统计数据显示，填写本问题的345名被调查者所在地区的民间习惯是：（1）A项由全体继承人共同支付的，占五成以上（51.80%）；（2）B项从被继承人的遗产中支付的，占近四成半（43.20%）。

（三）遗产债务的清偿顺序

问题【九、（三）】“在您所在地区，对被继承人死亡后遗留的以下费用，一般是按照哪种先后次序进行清偿的？（1）对民间习惯的处理方式；（2）您认为，按照哪种进行先后次序进行清偿才比较合理。（多选）”

A. 丧葬费用	D. 欠付的工资	G. 对被继承人扶养较多的人之酌情分配遗产份额
B. 遗产管理等费用	E. 受被继承人扶养人的生活费	H. 遗赠扶养协议写明遗赠的遗产
C. 欠债	F. 税款	

1. 遗产债务清偿顺序的民间习惯情况统计

表 4-61　遗产债务清偿顺序的民间习惯情况统计（多选）

费用	第一顺序		第二顺序		第三顺序		第四顺序		第五顺序		第六顺序		第七顺序		第八顺序	
	人数	比例%	人数	比例%	人数	比例%	人数	比例%	人数	比例%	人数	比例%	人数	比例%	人数	比例%
A.	300	65.36	9	1.96	10	2.18	23	5.01	7	1.53	0	0	2	0.44	8	0.44
B.	8	1.74	107	23.31	18	3.92	36	7.84	43	9.37	11	2.40	12	2.61	27	5.88
C.	32	6.90	77	16.78	140	30.50	26	5.66	20	4.36	11	2.40	9	1.96	1	0.22
D.	11	2.40	101	22.00	60	13.07	81	17.65	14	3.05	11	2.40	5	1.09	4	0.87
E.	3	0.65	23	5.01	30	6.54	33	7.19	69	15.03	60	13.07	37	8.06	8	1.74
F.	16	3.49	19	4.14	47	10.24	47	7.19	34	7.41	48	10.46	15	3.27	28	6.10
G.	3	0.65	13	2.83	21	4.58	23	5.01	29	6.32	41	8.93	81	17.65	53	11.55
H.	1	0.22	14	3.05	16	3.49	24	5.23	37	8.06	51	11.11	57	12.42	61	13.29

关于遗产债务清偿顺序的民间习惯，调查统计数据显示，各顺序以被调查者选择占比最高的作为统计依据，在被调查者所在地区，遗产债务应按如下顺序清偿：第一顺序为 A 项“丧葬费用”（65.36%）；第二顺序 B 项“遗产管理等费用”（23.31%）、D 项“欠付的工资”（22.00%）；第三顺序 C 项“欠债”（30.50%）；第四顺序 E 项“受被继承人扶养人的生活费”（15.03%）；第五顺序 F 项“税款”（10.46%）；第六顺序 G 项“对被继承人扶养较多的人之酌情分配遗产份额”（17.65%）；第七顺序 H 项“遗赠扶养协议写明遗赠的遗产”（13.29%）。

2. 遗产债务清偿顺序的民众观念情况统计

表 4-62　遗产债务清偿顺序的民众观念情况统计（多选）

费用	第一顺序		第二顺序		第三顺序		第四顺序		第五顺序		第六顺序		第七顺序		第八顺序	
	人数	比例%	人数	比例%	人数	比例%	人数	比例%	人数	比例%	人数	比例%	人数	比例%	人数	比例%
A.	362	78.87	19	4.14	18	3.92	24	5.23	20	4.36	5	1.09	4	0.87	13	2.83
B.	15	3.27	116	25.27	23	5.01	49	10.68	65	14.16	19	4.14	17	3.7	27	5.88
C.	39	8.5	93	20.26	165	35.95	46	10.02	26	5.66	11	2.40	17	3.70	3	0.65
D.	19	4.14	118	25.71	64	13.94	80	17.43	34	7.41	41	8.93	10	2.18	10	2.18
E.	9	1.96	20	4.36	54	11.76	55	11.98	76	16.56	70	15.25	34	7.41	24	5.23
F.	24	5.23	19	4.14	56	12.20	70	15.25	36	7.84	64	13.94	27	5.88	36	7.84
G.	5	1.09	15	3.27	30	6.54	28	6.10	41	8.93	52	11.33	112	24.40	60	13.07
H.	2	0.44	22	4.79	21	4.58	36	7.84	46	10.02	66	14.38	68	14.31	86	18.74

关于遗产债务清偿顺序的民众观念，调查统计数据显示，各顺序以被调查者选择占比最高的作为统计依据，被调查者认可的遗产债务清偿顺序是：第一顺序为 A 项“丧葬费

用”(78.87%)；第二顺序为B项“遗产管理等费用”(25.27%)、D项“欠付的工资”(25.71%)；第三顺序为C项“欠债”(35.95%)；第四顺序为F项“税款”(15.25%)；第五顺序为E项“受被继承人扶养人的生活费”(16.56%)；第六顺序为G项“对被继承人扶养较多的人之酌情分配遗产份额”(24.40%)；第七顺序为H项“遗赠扶养协议写明遗赠的遗产”(18.74%)。

十、遗产分割之调查数据统计情况

关于遗产分割之调查数据统计，我们主要从遗产分割的自由与限制、遗产分割瑕疵的担保责任，这两个方面进行调查数据的统计情况汇总分析。

(一) 遗产分割的自由与限制

问题【十、(一) 1.】“按您当地的民间习惯，对遗产一般如何开始分割的？A. 由各继承人共同协商后进行分割；B. 只要有继承人要求分割遗产，就得进行分割；C. 对于被继承人以遗嘱禁止分割的遗产，不得进行分割；D. 其他。(多选) 理由是什么？”

1. 遗产分割自由与限制的民间习惯与理由情况统计

(1) 遗产分割自由与限制的民间习惯情况统计。

表4-63 遗产分割自由与限制的民间习惯情况统计（多选）

选项	人数	比例
A. 由各继承人共同协商后进行分割	255	81.21%
B. 只要继承人要求分割遗产，就得进行分割	62	19.75%
C. 对于被继承人以遗嘱禁止分割的遗产，不得进行分割	155	49.36%
D. 其他	7	2.23%

关于遗产分割自由与限制的民间习惯，调查统计数据显示，填写本问题的314名被调查者所在地区的继承习惯是：①A项由各继承人共同协商后进行分割的，占八成以上(81.21%)；②C项遗嘱禁止分割的遗产则不得进行分割的，占近五成(49.36%)；③B项只要继承人要求分割遗产就得进行分割的，仅占不到二成(19.75%)。

(2) 遗产分割自由与限制的民间习惯之理由情况统计。

表4-64 遗产分割自由与限制的民间习惯之理由情况统计

项目	人数	比例
A. 遗产由各继承人共同继承，遗产分割关系各继承人的利益，故应共同协商	134	49.81%
B. 每个继承人享有的继承权受法律保护，同时基于效率原则考虑，故继承开始后，基于继承人的要求就可以分割遗产	27	10.04%
C. 遗产是被继承人遗留的个人财产，被继承人在生前有权通过遗嘱决定遗产的归属和分割	108	40.15%
合计	269	100%

关于遗产分割自由与限制的民间习惯之理由，调查统计数据显示，269名被调查者填写了选择理由，①认为遗产应由各继承人共同协商后分割的理由是，A项遗产由各继承人共同继承，遗产分割关系各继承人的利益，故应共同协商的，占近五成（49.81%）；②认为被继承人遗嘱禁止分割的遗产，不得进行分割的理由是，C项遗产是被继承人遗留的个人财产，被继承人在生前有权通过遗嘱决定遗产的归属和分割的，占四成（40.15%）；③认为只要继承人要求分割遗产，就得进行分割的理由是，B项每个继承人享有的继承权受法律保护，同时这符合效率原则的，仅占一成（10.04%）。

2. 提出遗产分割请求时间的民间习惯与理由情况统计

问题【十、（一）2.】“老王去世时留有一套家庭居住的房屋（价值50万元）、存款20万元以及小汽车一辆（价值10万元）。老王去世时，其配偶和唯一的儿子小王均在世。请问：在您所在的地区，老王去世后，其儿子小王是否会马上向其母亲提出分割遗产的请求？A. 会；B. 不会；C. 会提出分割其他遗产的请求，但对其母正在居住房屋的分割需等其母去世进行；D. 其他。（单选）理由是什么？”

（1）提出遗产分割请求时间的民间习惯情况统计。

表4-65　提出遗产分割请求时间的民间习惯情况统计（单选）

选项	人数	比例
A. 会	41	22.91%
B. 不会	105	58.66%
C. 会提出分割其他遗产的请求，但对其母正在居住房屋的分割需等其母去世后进行	33	18.43%
D. 其他	0	0%
合计	179	100%

关于提出遗产分割请求时间的民间习惯，调查统计数据显示，填写本问题的179名被调查者所在地区的继承习惯是：①B项子女不会提出遗产分割请求的，占近六成（58.66%）；②A项子女会提出遗产分割请求的，占二成以上（22.91%）；③C项子女会提出分割其他遗产，但对其母正在居住房屋的分割需要等其母去世后进行，占近二成（18.43%）。可见，主张对其母正在居住的房屋在其生存期间不予分割的，B、C两项合计占近八成（77.09%）。

（2）提出遗产分割请求时间的民间习惯之理由情况统计。

表4-66　提出遗产分割请求时间的民间习惯之理由情况统计

项目	人数	比例
A. 自被继承人死亡后，遗产就处于所有继承人共有的状态，儿子有权向母亲提出分割遗产	9	19.57%
B. 民间有双亲过世前不分家的传统，父母以及儿子的所有财产被视为家庭财产	29	63.04%

续表

项目	人数	比例
C. 因遗产房屋是其母唯一的住房，分割会直接对目前的生活产生重大影响	8	17.39%
合计	46	100%

关于提出遗产分割请求时间的民间习惯之理由，调查统计数据显示，有46名被调查者填写了选择理由，①认为子女不会提出遗产分割请求的理由是，B项民间有双亲过世前不分家的传统，父母及儿子的所有财产应被视为家庭财产的，占六成以上（63.04%）；②认为子女会提出遗产分割请求的理由是，A项自被继承人死亡后，遗产就处于所有继承人共有的状态，儿子有权向母亲提出分割遗产的，占近二成（19.57%）；③认为子女会提出分割其他遗产，但对其母正在居住的房屋需要等其母去世后进行分割的理由是，C项因遗产房屋是其母唯一的住房，分割会直接对其母目前生活产生重大影响，故不会分割的，占一成半以上（17.39%）。

3. 遗产分割是否受遗嘱限制的民众观念与理由情况统计

（1）遗产分割是否受遗嘱限制的民众观念与理由情况统计。

问题【十、（一）3.（1）】“甲乙是夫妻，育有一子丙。甲系个体工商户，他生前立了一份遗嘱，指定由乙和丙共同继承遗产，但其死后遗产中的商铺和家庭住房在20年内不能进行分割。甲死亡时留下的遗产有：商铺一间（价值100万元）；一套三室一厅的家庭住房（价值50万元）、存款20万元以及小汽车一辆（价值10万元）。您认为，甲是否可以在遗嘱中写明在其死后上述商铺和住房在一定期间内不能进行分割？A. 可以；B. 不可以。（单选）理由是什么？”

①遗产分割是否受遗嘱限制的民众观念情况统计。

表4-67　遗产分割是否受遗嘱限制的民众观念情况统计（单选）

选项	人数	比例
A. 可以	283	91.59%
B. 不可以	26	8.41%
合计	309	100%

关于遗产分割是否受遗嘱限制的民众观念，调查统计数据显示，在填写本问题的309名被调查者中，Ⅰ. 选择A项可以限制的，占九成以上（91.59%）；Ⅱ. 选择B项不可以限制的，仅占不到一成（8.41%）。

②遗产分割是否受遗嘱限制的民众观念之理由情况统计。

表 4-68　遗产分割是否受遗嘱限制的民众观念之理由情况统计

项目	人数	比例
A. 遗产是被继承人生前的个人财产，遗嘱人有自由处分之权利	110	72.85%
B. 遗产属于所有继承人共同共有，禁止分割有可能损害所有继承人的利益	33	21.85%
C. 遗产涉及被继承人生前债务清偿、受其扶养之人利益保护等问题，限制分割过于严苛	8	5.30%
合计	151	100%

关于遗产分割是否受遗嘱限制的民众观念之理由，统计数据显示，有 151 名被调查者填写了选择理由，Ⅰ. 认为可以限制的理由是，A 项遗产是被继承人生前的个人财产，遗嘱人有自由处分之权利的，占七成以上（72.85%）；Ⅱ. 认为不可以限制的理由分别是，B 项遗产属于所有继承人共同共有，禁止分割有可能损害所有继承人利益的，占二成以上（21.85%）和 C 项遗产涉及被继承人生前债务清偿、受其扶养之人利益保护等问题，限制分割过于严苛的，仅占不到一成（5.30%）。

（2）被继承人立遗嘱限制遗产分割的具体期限之民众观念情况统计。

问题【十、（一）3.（2）】“在上题中，如果您选择 A 选项，那么该期限多久合适？A. 5 年；B. 10 年；C. 15 年；D. 等共同居住去世了以后才可以分割；E. 根据社会风俗和法律规定处理；F. 根据共同居住人的意愿，可以随时分割；G. 在法律允许的时间范围内可以分割。（单选）”

表 4-69　被继承人立遗嘱限制遗产分割之具体期限的民众观念情况统计（单选）

选项	人数	比例
A. 5 年	121	48.21%
B. 10 年	79	31.47%
C. 15 年	22	8.76%
D. 等共同居住人去世了以后才可以分割	11	4.38%
E. 根据社会风俗和法律规定处理	15	5.98%
F. 根据共同居住人的意愿，可以随时分割	2	0.80%
G. 在法律允许的时间范围内可以分割	1	0.40%
合计	251	100%

关于被继承人立遗嘱限制遗产分割的具体期限之民众观念，调查统计数据显示，在填写本问题的 251 名被调查者中，①选择 A 项 5 年内的，占近五成（48.21%）；②选择 B 项 10 年内的，占三成以上（31.47%）；③选择 C 项 15 年内的，仅占不到一成（8.76%）。

可见，近五成的被调查者均主张，遗嘱限制遗产分割的期限为 5 年以内。

(3) 继承人协商能否变更遗嘱限制进行的民间习惯及理由情况统计。

问题【十、(一) 3. (3) 】"在您所在地区，如果乙和丙一致同意分割上述财产，那么，他们是否可以不遵守甲的遗嘱在一定期限内禁止分割上述房产的规定而进行分割？A. 可以不遵守遗嘱；B. 不可以不遵守遗嘱。(单选) 理由是什么？"

①继承人协商能否变更遗嘱限制的民间习惯情况统计。

表 4-70 继承人协商能否变更遗嘱限制的民间习惯情况统计（单选）

选项	人数	比例
A. 可以不遵守遗嘱	140	45.40%
B. 不可以不遵守遗嘱	169	54.60%
合计	309	100%

关于继承人协商能否变更遗嘱限制的民间习惯，调查统计数据显示，填写本问题的 309 名被调查者所在地区的继承习惯是：Ⅰ.B 项会尊重遗嘱限制的，占近五成半 (54.60%)；Ⅱ.A 项可以不遵守遗嘱限制的，占四成半（45.40%）。

②继承人协商能否变更遗嘱限制的民间习惯之理由情况统计。

表 4-71 继承人协商能否变更遗嘱限制的民间习惯之理由情况统计

项目	人数	比例
A. 被继承人死亡后，遗产处于所有继承人共有的状态，继承人一致同意可以予以处分	49	39.52%
B. 遗产尽快进行分割有利于析产，会减少不必要的纠纷	20	16.13%
C. 遗嘱是被继承人自由处分其财产的合法有效的协议，继承人应当尊重被继承人生前意愿	55	44.35%
合计	124	100%

关于继承人协商能否变更遗嘱限制的民间习惯之理由，调查统计数据显示，有 124 名被调查者填写了选择理由，Ⅰ. 认为不可以变更遗嘱限制的理由是，C 项遗嘱是被继承人自由处分其财产的合法有效的协议，继承人应当尊重被继承人生前意愿的，占近四成半 (44.35%)；Ⅱ. 认为可以变更遗嘱限制的理由分别是，A 项被继承人死亡后，遗产处于所有继承人共有的状态，继承人一致同意则有权予以处分的，占近四成（39.52%）和 B 项遗产尽快进行分割有利于析产，会减少不必要纠纷的，占一成半以上（16.13%）。

(二) 遗产分割瑕疵的担保责任

问题【十、(二) 】"村民老王于 2016 年 12 月 10 日因病去世，去世时他留下 50 只羊。老王有两个儿子甲和乙，故老王去世后，甲、乙各分得 25 只羊。但在双方分完羊两天之后，乙分得的 25 只羊中就有 2 只暴病死亡，这 2 只羊死亡的原因是在兄弟俩分割前就已经得了羊痘（一种急性传染病）。请问：在您所在地区，如果出现此种情况，这 2 只羊死亡的损失应该由谁承担？A. 由乙自行承担，羊群已分配完毕，乙分到了 2 只病羊，应该自认倒霉；B. 由甲和乙共同承担，甲应再分给乙 1 只羊或按照 1 只羊的价格进行补偿；C. 按 1 只羊的价格进行补偿，但乙承担大部分损失，甲承担小部分损失；D. 其他。（单选）理由是什么？"

表 4-72　遗产分割瑕疵的担保责任之民间习惯情况统计（单选）

选项	人数	比例
A. 由乙自行承担，羊群已分配完毕，乙分到了 2 只病羊，应该自认倒霉	157	50.97%
B. 由甲和乙共同承担，甲应再分给乙 1 只羊或按照 1 只羊的价格进行补偿	106	34.42%
C. 按 1 只羊的价格进行补偿，但乙承担大部分损失，甲承担小部分损失	42	13.64%
D. 其他	3	0.97%
合计	308	100%

关于遗产分割瑕疵担保责任的民间习惯，调查统计数据显示，填写本问题的 308 名被调查者所在地区的继承习惯是：对遗产分割的瑕疵，（1）A 项共同继承人间不会共同承担的，占五成（50.97%）；（2）B、C 两项共同继承人间会共同承担的，合计占近五成（48.06%）。

十一、无人承受遗产之调查数据统计情况

关于无人承受的遗产之调查数据统计，我们主要从无人承受遗产的归属和无人承受遗产的处理，这两个方面进行调查数据的统计情况汇总分析。

（一）无人承受遗产的归属

1. 城镇居民无人承受遗产的归属主体的民众观念与理由情况统计

问题【十一、（一）1.】"甲生前系城镇居民，其生前未婚且无其他继承人，其死后留下部分遗产，属于无人承受的遗产。您认为甲的遗产归属于下列哪一主体更合适？A. 国家；B. 死者生前所在地的国库；C. 死者生前所在地民政部门的社会福利机构；D. 死者生前所在地的居委会；E. 不是继承人的其他亲属；F. 其他（您认为更合适的归属主体）。（单选）理由是什么？"

（1）城镇居民无人承受遗产的归属主体之民众观念情况统计。

表 4-73　城镇居民无人承受遗产的归属主体之民众观念情况统计（单选）

选项	人数	比例
A. 国家	122	35.70%
B. 死者生前所在地的国库	32	9.30%
C. 死者生前所在地民政部门的社会福利机构	52	15.20%

续表

选项	人数	比例
D. 死者生前所在地的居委会	8	2.30%
E. 不是继承人的其他亲属	110	32.20%
F. 其他	18	5.30%
合计	342	100%

关于城镇居民无人承受遗产的归属主体之民众观念，调查统计数据显示，在填写本问题的342名被调查者中，①选择A、B、C、D四项，城镇居民无人承受的遗产应归社会公共组织（国家、死者生前所在地的国库、死者生前所在地民政部门的社会福利机构和死者生前所在地的居委会）的，合计占六成以上（62.50%）；②选择E、F两项，城镇居民无人承受的遗产应归自然人（不是继承人的其他亲属等）的，合计占近四成（37.50%）。

（2）城镇居民无人承受遗产的归属主体的民众观念之理由情况统计。

表4-74　城镇居民无人承受遗产的归属主体的民众观念之理由情况统计

项目	人数	比例
A. 由不是继承人的其他亲属承受较为合理，以维护财产私有	37	40.22%
B. 由社会福利机构承受财产更有意义	13	14.13%
C. 法律规定无人承受的遗产应归国家所有，用于为社会生活提供稳定的外部环境	25	27.17%
D. 由生前对甲照顾较多的人承受更为适宜，体现公平原则	17	18.48%
合计	92	100%

关于城镇居民无人承受遗产的归属主体的民众观念之理由，调查统计数据显示，有92名被调查者填写了选择理由，①选择归属社会公共组织的主要理由分别为，C项法律规定无人承受的遗产应归国家所有，用于为社会生活提供稳定的外部环境的，占近三成（27.17%）和B项由社会福利机构承受财产更有意义的，占近一成半（14.13%）；②选择归属自然人的主要理由分别为，A项由不是继承人的其他亲属承受较为合理，以维护财产私有的，占四成（40.22%）和D项由生前对甲照顾较多的人承受更为适宜，这体现公平原则的，占近二成（18.48%）。

2. 农村居民无人承受人遗产的归属主体的民众观念及理由情况统计

问题【十一、（一）2.】"甲生前系农村居民，其生前未婚且无其他继承人，其死后留下部分遗产，属于无人承受的遗产。您认为甲的遗产归属于下列哪一主体更合适？A. 死者生前所在地的国库；B. 死者生前所在地民政部门的社会福利机构；C. 死者生前所在地的集体经济组织；D. 死者生前所在地的村委会；E. 死者生前所在地的村民小组；F. 不是继承人的其他亲属；G. 其他（您认为更合适的归属主体）。（单选）理由是什么？"

（1）农村居民无人承受遗产的归属主体之民众观念情况统计。

表 4-75　农村居民无人承受遗产的归属主体之民众观念情况统计（单选）

选项	人数	比例
A. 死者生前所在地的国库	67	19.60%
B. 死者生前所在地民政部门的社会福利机构	68	19.88%
C. 死者生前所在地的集体经济组织	40	11.70%
D. 死者生前所在地的村委会	22	6.43%
E. 死者生前所在地的村民小组	17	4.97%
F. 不是继承人的其他亲属	110	32.16%
G. 其他	18	5.26%
合计	342	100%

关于农村居民无人承受遗产的归属主体之民众观念，调查统计数据显示，在填写本问题的 342 名被调查者中，①选择 A、B、C、D、E 五项，农村居民无人承受的遗产应归社会公共组织（国家、死者生前所在地的国库、死者生前所在地民政部门的社会福利机构和死者生前所在地的集体经济组织、村委会或村民小组）的，合计占六成以上（62.58%）；②选择 F、G 两项，农村居民无人承受的遗产应归自然人（不是继承人的其他亲属等）的，合计占近四成（37.42%）。

（2）农村居民无人承受遗产的归属主体的民众观念之理由情况统计。

表 4-76　农村居民无人承受遗产的归属主体的民众观念之理由情况统计

项目	人数	比例
A. 由不是继承人的其他亲属承受较为合理，其是与被继承人关系较为密切的人	30	36.14%
B. 由社会福利机构承受财产更有意义，可以用于福利事业	9	10.84%
C. 法律规定无人承受的遗产归国家所有，国家可以更好地发挥财产效用，为社会生活提供福利	28	33.74%
D. 由生前对甲照顾较多的人承受更为适宜，体现了权利与义务相一致	4	4.82%
E. 应当由村民小组承受，村民小组对甲平时照顾较多，付出了一定的劳动，应有所回报	12	14.46%
合计	83	100%

关于农村居民无人承受遗产归属主体的民众观念之理由，调查统计数据显示，有 83 名被调查者填写了选择理由，（1）选择归属社会公共组织的主要理由分别为，C 项认为法律规定无人承受的遗产归国家所有，国家可以更好地发挥财产效用，为社会生活提供福利的，占三成以上（33.74%）；E 项认为应当由村民小组承受，村民小组对甲平时照顾较

多，付出了一定的劳动应有所回报的，占一成半（14.46%）和B项认为由社会福利机构承受财产更有意义，可以用于福利事业的，占一成（10.84%）；（2）选择归属自然人的主要理由分别为，A项认为由不是继承人的其他亲属承受较为合理，其与被继承人关系较为密切的，占三成半以上（36.14%）和D项认为由生前对甲照顾较多的人承受更为适宜，体现了权利与义务相一致的，仅占不到一成（4.82%）。

（二）无人承受遗产的处理

1. 无人承受遗产管理人产生方式的民众观念与民间习惯情况统计

问题【十一、（二）1.】“对于无人继承遗产的管理人，您认为下列哪一种产生方式更合适？A. 死者户籍所在地的居委会、村委会或所在单位指定遗产管理人；B. 人民法院指定遗产管理人；C. 民政部门指定遗产管理人。（单选）理由是什么？请问：在您所在地区人们一般如何确定无人继承遗产管理人的？”

（1）无人承受遗产管理人的产生方式的民众观念及理由情况统计。

①无人承受遗产管理人的产生方式之民众观念情况统计。

表4-77 无人承受遗产的管理人的产生方式之民众观念情况统计（单选）

选项	人数	比例
A. 死者户籍所在地的居委会、村委会或所在单位指定遗产管理人	131	43.81%
B. 人民法院指定遗产管理人	100	33.44%
C. 民政部门指定遗产管理人	68	22.75%
合计	299	100%

关于无人承受遗产的管理人产生方式的民众观念，调查统计数据显示，在填写该题的299名被调查者中，Ⅰ. 选择B、C两项应由人民法院或民政部门指定产生的，合计占五成半以上（56.19%）；Ⅱ. 选择A项应由居委会、村委会或所在单位指定产生的，占四成以上（43.81%）。

②无人承受遗产的管理人的产生方式的民众观念之理由情况统计。

表4-78 无人承受遗产的管理人的产生方式的民众观念之理由情况统计

项目	人数	比例
A. 由居委会、村委会指定遗产管理人更为方便，居委会、村委会熟悉家庭内部关系而且擅长处理家庭事务	38	42.22%
B. 由法院指定遗产管理人更具有权威性，不容易再产生矛盾	34	37.78%
C. 民政局等行政机关处理不易起纠纷	3	3.33%
D. 由了解家庭情况的人担任更合适，了解家庭情况的人可以根据实际情况选择遗产管理人	15	16.67%
合计	90	100%

关于无人承受遗产的管理人的产生方式的民众观念之理由，调查统计数据显示，在填写了理由的90名被调查者中，Ⅰ.主张由社会公共组织指定的主要理由为A、B、C三项，居委会、村委会熟悉家庭内部关系而且擅长处理家庭事务、法院指定遗产管理人更具有权威性或民政局等行政机关处理不易起纠纷；Ⅱ.主张由自然人指定的主要理由为，D项由了解家庭情况的人担任更合适，了解家庭情况的人可以根据实际情况选择遗产管理人。

（2）无人承受遗产的管理人的产生方式之民间习惯情况统计。

表4-79　无人承受遗产的管理人的产生方式之民间习惯情况统计（单选）

选项	人数	比例
A. 村委会、居委会指定	23	53.49%
B. 法院指定	16	37.21%
C. 民政部门指定	4	9.30%
合计	43	100%

关于无人承受遗产的管理人的产生方式之民间习惯，调查统计数据显示，填写该问题的43名被调查者所在地区的民间习惯是：①A项由村委会、居委会指定产生的，占五成以上（53.49%）；②B、C两项由法院或民政部门指定产生的，占四成半以上（46.51%）。

2. 无人承受遗产酌分请求权主体的民众观念与民间习惯情况统计

问题【十一、（二）2.】“您认为下列哪些人可以酌情分得无人继承的遗产？A. 依靠死者扶养的人；B. 与死者共同生活的人；C. 与死者关系密切且对其帮助较多的人；D. 其他。（多选）请问：在您所在地区人们一般是如何分配此类遗产的？”

（1）无人承受遗产之酌分请求权主体的民众观念情况统计。

表4-80　无人承受遗产的酌分请求权主体的民众观念情况统计（多选）

选项	人数	比例
A. 依靠死者扶养的人	229	66.90%
B. 与死者共同生活的人	188	54.90%
C. 与死者关系密切且对其帮助较多的人	273	79.80%
D. 其他	11	3.20%

关于无人承受遗产之酌分请求权主体的民众观念，调查统计数据显示，在填写了本题的342名被调查者中，选择A、B、C三项，“依靠死者扶养的人”（66.90%）、“与死者共同生活的人”（54.90%）和“与死者关系密切且对其帮助较多的人”（79.80%）可以请求酌情分配无人承受遗产的，各占五成至七成以上。

（2）无人承受遗产之酌分请求权主体的民间习惯情况统计。

表 4-81 无人承受遗产的酌分请求权主体之民间习惯的统计情况（单选）

选项	人数	比例
A. 与死者关系密切且对其帮助较多的人	42	55.26%
B. 和死者共同居住或关系亲近的不是继承人的其他亲属	8	10.53%
C. 国家	6	7.89%
D. 依靠死者扶养的人	13	17.11%
E. 其他	7	9.21%
合计	76	100%

关于无人承受遗产之酌分请求权主体的民间习惯，调查统计数据显示，填写了本问题的 76 名被调查者所在地区的民间习惯是：A、B、D 三项，与死者关系密切且对其帮助较多的人、依靠死者扶养的人、和死者共同居住的人或与死者关系亲近的不是继承人的其他亲属可以酌情分得无人承受遗产的，各占一成至五成。

十二、遗产处理相关案例的简介与评析

（一）涉及遗产范围界定案例的简介与评析

案情简介：原告杨某某系被继承人陆某某之母，被继承人之父于 2000 年 8 月 10 日死亡。被告王某某与原告杨某某是婆媳关系，与被继承人陆某某系夫妻，于 2001 年 1 月 18 日登记结婚。被继承人陆某某于 2012 年 5 月 14 日因工伤死亡。2012 年 7 月 17 日，被告王某某领取了被继承人单位发放的一次性工伤死亡补助金 436200 元、丧葬补助金 25986 元。另外，被告王某某为被继承人办理丧事，购买墓地花费 49723 元。原告杨某某与儿媳王某某因补助金等遗产的分割发生纠纷，起诉至法院。原告杨某某认为，上述工伤死亡补助金应属于遗产由被继承人第一顺序法定继承人继承，即应由其与儿媳平均分割。被告王某某认为上述费用不属于遗产，是事故责任方赔偿给其的精神抚慰性质的费用，应由其所有。

法院审理后认为，公民、法人的合法民事权益受法律保护。被继承人死亡时，其遗留的个人合法财产才属于遗产。而一次性工伤死亡补助金和丧葬费补助金均不属于遗产，而属于对该死者近亲属的补偿费。首先，被告王某某领取的被继承人单位发放的一次性工伤死亡补助金 436200 元，该款应由第一顺位法定继承人双方均分，被告王某某应将领取的上述工伤死亡补助金的一半补偿给原告杨某某。其次，关于系争丧葬补助金，被告王某某领取丧葬补助金 25986 元，但被告为被继承人购买墓穴花费了 49723 元，故法院判决原告酌情补偿支付被告王某某 5000 元。[①]

① 参见中国裁判文书网：（2017）沪×民初×号，《杨某某与王某某法定继承纠纷一审民事判决书》，载 http://wenshu.court.gov.cn/content/content? DocID=e3681a1e-6fc8-4612-b26d-a7fe0167cf4e&KeyWord=（2017）沪×民初×号，访问日期：2019 年 3 月 8 日。限于本章篇幅，作者对原案情内容有酌情删改。

适用法律分析：本案的争议焦点在于工伤死亡补助金是否属于遗产，以及丧葬费应如何支付的问题。我国《继承法》第3条采用概括性加列举的方式明确规定：“遗产是公民死亡时遗留的个人合法财产，包括：（一）公民的收入；（二）公民的房屋、储蓄和生活用品；（三）公民的林木、牲畜和家禽；（四）公民的文物、图书资料；（五）法律允许公民所有的生产资料；（六）公民的著作权、专利权中的财产权利；（七）公民的其他合法财产。”我国《继承法》第4条和1985年《执行继承法意见》第3条还规定，个人承包应得的个人收益、有价证券和履行标的为财物的债权也属于遗产范围。根据我国现行《工伤保险条例》第39条①规定，工伤死亡补助金和丧葬补助金都是相关单位给予死者近亲属及被扶养人的生活补助费及给予死者亲属处理死者后事的一种补助，应当用于补助死者近亲属及被扶养人和支付丧葬费用，而不能作为被继承人死亡时遗留的个人财产，故该款项均不属于遗产范围。对于工伤死亡补助金和丧葬补助金，在司法实践中，工伤死亡补助金一般由死者供养的直系亲属和配偶均分，丧葬补助金在支付完丧葬费用后有剩余的，可在继承人之间参考遗产的分配方式进行分割。因此，人民法院认为原、被告应共同支付被继承人丧葬费用并均分工伤死亡补助金的判决是符合法律规定的。但是，我们认为，由于我国《继承法》欠缺遗产范围的排除规定，导致部分继承人对工伤死亡补助金等财产是否属于遗产存在争议，在司法实践中易引发纠纷，这是我国立法之不足。

（二）涉及继承开始的通知和公告案例的简介与评析

案情简介：被继承人张某芬生育四个子女，分别为李某泉、李某元、李某海和李某菊。2011年下半年被继承人张某芬去世。她去世后，四个子女间因母亲去世其他子女没有通知身在外地的大哥李某泉而发生纠纷，诉至法院。原告李某泉认为，三个弟妹未履行继承开始的通知义务，导致其不能参加吊唁、祭奠等仪式，侵犯了其人格权，并据此要求三人赔偿其精神损害抚慰金12万元。被告李某元、李某海、李某菊均承认在其母亲去世后并未告知大哥李某泉。

法院经审理查明，三被告主张其母生前多次陈述“因李某泉不孝，死后不通知他”，但李某元、李某海、李某菊均未提交证据予以证实。本案中，原告李某泉援引我国《继承法》第23条之规定并据此主张李某元、李某海、李某菊在其母去世后负有通知义务，但该条设定的知道被继承人死亡的继承人对其他继承人的通知义务，其立法本意应当是保障被继承人的所有继承人均享有参与被继承人遗产继承的均等机会，但我国《继承法》并没有规定不及时通知，要承担人格权受到损害的赔偿责任。且李某元、李某海、李某菊亦未有故意隐瞒遗产或者故意阻挠遗产分割的行为。因此依法判决，李某泉主张李某元、李某海、李某菊在其母亲去世后未及时通知他，导致其不能参加吊唁、祭奠等仪式，侵犯

---

① 我国现行《工伤保险条例》第39条：“职工因工死亡，其近亲属按照下列规定从工伤保险基金领取丧葬补助金、供养亲属抚恤金和一次性工亡补助金：（一）丧葬补助金为6个月的统筹地区上年度职工月平均工资；（二）供养亲属抚恤金按照职工本人工资的一定比例发给由因工死亡职工生前提供主要生活来源、无劳动能力的亲属。标准为：配偶每月40%，其他亲属每人每月30%，孤寡老人或者孤儿每人每月在上述标准的基础上增加10%。核定的各供养亲属的抚恤金和不应高于因工死亡职工生前的工资。供养亲属的具体范围由国务院社会保险行政部门规定；（三）一次性工亡补助金标准为上一年度全国城镇居民人均可支配收入的20倍。”

了其人格权，并据此要求三人赔偿其精神损害抚慰金 12 万元的主张，人民法院不予支持。①

适用法律分析：本案涉及继承开始后的通知义务以及不履行通知义务是否应承担相关赔偿责任的问题。我国《继承法》第 23 条规定："继承开始后，知道被继承人死亡的继承人应当及时通知其他继承人和遗嘱执行人。"这表明，知道被继承人死亡的继承人负有继承开始的通知和公告义务。但违反该义务的后果和责任法律并未明确规定，导致知道被继承人死亡的继承人在违反义务时，应当如何处理于法无据。一般认为，该条的立法本意应当是保障被继承人的所有继承人均享有参与被继承人遗产继承的均等机会，因此，如果知道被继承人死亡的继承人没有履行通知和公告义务，从而不正当地获得了超出其原有份额的遗产，损害其他继承人的利益，该继承人应当负返还义务和赔偿责任。本案中，原告起诉要求确认知道被继承人死亡的继承人违反继承开始的通知义务，从而导致其不能参加吊唁、祭奠等仪式，侵犯了其人格权，要求三被告承担精神损害赔偿金的主张，人民法院不予支持。对于继承人的吊唁权或人格权之保护，目前，我国《继承法》对此无规定。由本案可见，我国《继承法》欠缺不履行该通知义务的法律后果之规定，这是其立法之不足。

（三）涉及遗产管理案例的简介与评析

案情简介：陈某某与侯某某在被继承人债务清偿纠纷一案中，原、被告都是陈某芳之子。2009 年 1 月，因房屋拆迁问题，陈某芳与儿子陈某某签署一份《拆迁补偿协议》，约定由母亲陈某芳补偿给儿子陈某某 10 万元拆迁款，在 6 个月内付清。后陈某某多次向其母主张给付该拆迁补偿款，但一直没有被给付。2012 年 7 月 25 日，陈某芳因病去世。原告陈某某认为，母亲生前偏爱儿子侯某某，并且其是陈某芳的遗产管理人，应由其在遗产范围内负责清偿上述债务，并诉至法院。

法院审理后查明，根据《拆迁补偿协议》的约定，陈某芳对原告负有支付拆迁补偿款 10 万元的债务。陈某芳去世后，其债务依法应由其继承人在陈某芳的遗产范围内予以偿还。但被告在纠纷发生后曾与原告签订了一份新的《动迁协议》，承诺由被告侯某某代被继承人陈某芳出售×路房屋后，以所得房款偿还该 10 万元债务。该约定应视为被告承诺作为陈某芳的遗产管理人，为其清偿债务，并不意味着被告对陈某芳的债务承担连带责任。然而，根据所查明的事实，×路房屋早在 2010 年既已被出售，且被告作为陈某芳的代理人从银行领取了 32 万元房款。在被告既未到庭应诉，也未提供相关证据的情况下，审理法院无法确定该笔款项的使用情况，故推定该款项仍在被告侯某某的保管之下，且数额大于陈某芳所负的 10 万元债务。被告在明知×路房屋已被出售的情况下，仍向原告承诺将×路房屋出售后偿还陈某芳的债务，其作为出售×路房屋所得房款的实际保管人，故法院判决由被告负责以该售房款清偿陈某芳对原告所负的 10 万元债务。②

---

① 参见中国裁判文书网：（2016）×01 民终×号，《李某泉与李某元、李某海、李某菊侵权责任纠纷二审民事判决书》，载 http://wenshu. court. gov. cn/content/content? DocID = 4a383ea4 - b915 - 4578 - aa7a - 96ce91f5bf6a&KeyWord =（2016）鲁×民终×号，访问日期：2019 年 3 月 8 日。限于本章篇幅，作者对原案情内容有酌情删改。

② 参见中国裁判文书网：（2012）×民三（民）初字第×号，《陈某某与侯某某遗产债务清偿纠纷一审民事判决书》，载 http://wenshu. court. gov. cn/Index，访问日期：2019 年 3 月 8 日。限于本章篇幅，作者对原案情内容有酌情删改。

适用法律分析：本案的争议焦点在于，侯某某作为被继承人的遗产管理人，应如何承担清偿被继承人生前欠债的责任，以及不尽职履行遗产管理人的职责是否应承担法律责任。根据我国《继承法》第 33 条："继承遗产应当清偿被继承人依法应当缴纳的税款和债务。"本案中，继承人候某某作为实际保存遗产管理人，法院判决由其清偿遗产债务，这是符合法律规定的。目前我国《继承法》没有规定遗产管理人制度。实践中通常由存有遗产的法定继承人对遗产进行管理和处置。根据我国《继承法》第 24 条："存有遗产的人，应当妥善保管遗产，任何人不得侵吞或者争抢。"该遗产管理人应当承担妥善保管遗产、清偿遗产债务和转交或分割遗产的职责。由于我国现行法没有明确规定遗产管理人主体、权利义务及应承担的法律责任，导致实践中遗产管理人隐瞒遗产或逃避债务的情形时有发生。本案中，继承人侯某某作为遗产管理人，法院判定其向原告清偿 10 万元遗产债务，判决合理。但其是否应承担隐匿 30 多万元售房款此侵害遗产行为的法律责任，我国立法没有规定，即我国欠缺较为完善的遗产管理人制度，此为立法之不足。

（四）涉及法定继承案例简介与评析

案情简介：陆某 1、陆某 2、陆某 3、陆某 4、陆某 5 系被继承人曹某珍与配偶陆某鸿的子女。陆某鸿于 1982 年 8 月 6 日去世，曹某珍于 2010 年 11 月 17 日去世，被继承人曹某珍父母均先于被继承人过世多年。曹某珍名下有 x 区 x 路 x 室房屋一套。被继承人曹某珍与配偶陆某鸿曾生育一女陆某某，年幼时由被继承人曹某珍的妹妹收养，后一直随养父母生活。被继承人曹某珍去世后，原告陆某某作为无劳动能力和经济来源人，起诉至法院要求继承争议房屋的份额。

法院审理后认为，公民的合法继承权，受法律保护。继承开始后，按照法定继承办理，有遗嘱的按照遗嘱继承或遗赠办理。自收养关系成立之日起，养父母与养子女之间的权利义务关系，适用法律关于父母子女关系的规定；养子女与生父母及其他近亲属间的权利义务关系，因收养关系的成立而消除。法院依法判决本案被继承人曹某珍生前遗留的遗产房屋，除陆某某被他人收养之外，应由曹某珍的五个子女平均继承。①

适用法律分析：本案涉及法定继承人范围的确定。根据我国现行《婚姻法》第 25、26、27 条规定，父母子女关系可分为以下两大类：一是，自然血亲的父母子女关系；二是，拟制血亲的父母子女关系。本案中，陆某某在其被被继承人的妹妹收养后已形成了法律意义上的养父母子女的关系。根据我国现行《婚姻法》第 26 条规定："养子女和生父母间的权利和义务，因收养关系的成立而消除。"并且，我国现行《收养法》第 23 条规定："养子女与生父母及其他近亲属间的权利义务关系，因收养关系的成立而消除。"由于陆某某与被继承人妹妹的收养关系已经形成而且并未解除，所以其与被继承人由于自然血缘而形成的父母关系已解除。因此，本案原告陆某某并非被继承人的法定继承人。但是，已经形成收养关系的生子女也并非不能够取得生父母的遗产。1985 年《执行继承法意见》第 19 条作出特别规定："被收养人对养父母尽了赡养义务，同时又对生父母扶养较多的，除可依继承法第十条的规定继承养父母的遗产外，还可依继承法第十四条的规定

① 参见裁判文书网：（2015）长×（民）初字第×号，《陆某某与陆某 1 等法定继承纠纷一审民事判决书》，载 http://wenshu.court.gov.cn/content/content?DocID=ed605b3f-1325-4da7-8b74-29414e092492&KeyWord=长×（民）初字第×号，访问日期：2019 年 3 月 8 日。限于本章篇幅，作者对原案情内容有酌情删改。

分得生父母的适当的遗产。”由于本案中陆某某并未事实上赡养被继承人，因此，本案法院将陆某某排除于法定继承人范围之外，并将陆某某排除于酌分遗产请求权主体之外的判决，是符合法律规定的。可见，我国现行《收养法》明确规定收养成立之后对养子女的生父母、养父母的法律效力，有利于减少此类纠纷，这是我国立法的优点。但部分民众对此规定不知晓，还有待加强法律知识的学习，国家对普法宣传工作也应坚持开展。

（五）涉及遗嘱继承案例简介与评析

案情简介：张某甲与李某乙于1972年登记结婚，婚后双方未生育子女。1975年二人即因感情不和分开居住，双方未办理离婚手续但分居后不再往来。李某1、李某2、李某3、李某4、李某5与李某乙是兄弟姐妹关系。2001年，李某乙购买产权房，产权登记在自己名下。2009年6月16日，李某乙在×号×室李某2家立下遗嘱，言明：与张某甲分居20多年，没有子女。现年老多病，全靠兄弟姐妹照顾生活。经慎重考虑，决定将全部财产平均赠与兄弟姐妹，并负责养老送终。遗嘱下方有李某乙签字。该遗嘱由许某某代书，丁某某在场证明，许某某和丁某某均在该遗嘱下方证明人处签字。李某乙过世后，由其兄弟姐妹为其办理后事。五被告自知晓遗嘱起均表示愿意按遗嘱接受李某乙的遗产。李某乙去世后，遗嘱、系争房屋产权证、房屋钥匙等均由五人保管。后原告张某甲在被继承人去世后因遗产继承与五被告李某1、李某2、李某3、李某4、李某5发生纠纷，诉至法院。原告认为李某乙立遗嘱时已年老体弱且神志不清，请求法院认定该遗嘱无效。

法院审理后认为，本案遗嘱有效。首先，原告主张被告立遗嘱时已年老多病且神志不清，该份遗嘱并不是其真实的意思表示，但并未提交相应证据佐证被继承人李某乙存在年老神志不清的事实。并且结合被告五人提交的李某乙年老时确由兄弟姐妹照顾的证据，应认定被继承人李某乙立遗嘱时具备遗嘱能力，并且该遗嘱符合其内心的真实意愿。其次，本案是代书遗嘱，代书人和见证人具备资格，与被继承人李某乙无利害关系，与遗嘱继承人和受遗赠人也均不存在利害关系。最后，本案虽然张某甲否认遗嘱的真实性，但本案遗嘱代书人和见证人均作为证人出庭作证，能确认该遗嘱是李某乙的真实意思表示。综上，人民法院依法判决李某乙于2009年6月16日所立遗嘱有效。①

适用法律分析：本案的争议焦点在于被继承人所立遗嘱是否有效。根据我国《民法总则》第17、18条之规定“十八周岁以上的自然人为成年人”，“成年人为完全民事行为能力人，可以独立实施民事法律行为”。此案中，被继承人虽然身体不好，但是没有证据显示其心智受到影响，因而被继承人为完全民事行为能力人，具有遗嘱能力。另外，根据我国《继承法》第17条规定：“代书遗嘱应当有两个以上见证人在场见证，由其中一人代书，注明年、月、日，并由代书人、其他见证人和遗嘱人签名。”本案中，许某某和丁某某为被继承人的遗嘱见证人，与被继承人仅为朋友关系，与被继承人和其他继承人并无特殊关系和遗产利害关系。因此，人民法院认定该代书遗嘱有效的判决是符合法律规定的。由本案可见，我国《继承法》明确规定代书遗嘱的形式要件，有利于指导当事人依法订立代书遗嘱，这是其立法优点，应予坚持。

① 参见中国裁判文书网：（2015）长×（民）再初字第×号，《张某甲与李某1等继承纠纷再审民事判决书》，载 http://wenshu.court.gov.cn/content/content?DocID=7bf2fac4-807e-4623-b568-265245722a4b&KeyWord=长×（民）再初字第×号，访问日期：2019年3月8日。限于本章篇幅，作者对原案情内容有酌情删改。

（六）涉及继承和遗赠的接受与放弃案例的简介与评析

案情简介：被继承人周某某于2014年3月15日因发癫痫去世。周某某生前育有四个子女，依次为施甲、施乙、施丙、施丁。原告施某某是施乙之子、周某某之孙。周某某名下有×市×区×村×号房屋一套。周某某在去世前几年已有不认人、不认路的症状。2013年3月11日上午，周某某由施乙、施某某先带至×区中心医院急诊内科就诊，就诊记录记载主诉患者近两日反复干咳……检查神志清醒……随后周某某被带至×律师事务所，由该所律师杨某、徐某增见证，由杨某代书，立下遗嘱一份。遗嘱内容为：本人百年之后，本人名下的系争房屋由孙子施某某继承；除上条所述房产外，本人其余财产均按照法律规定继承分配。周某某去世后，各继承人对其遗产依法开始继承，曾多次相互协商系争房屋和存款等遗产应如何分割与分配份额等问题。此期间，施乙与原告施某某均未表示被继承人周某某立有遗嘱这一情况。待一年后系争房屋欲出售时，原告施某某才出具了上述遗嘱。后原告与被告因系争房屋的归属问题发生纠纷，诉至法院。原告施某某请求按照该遗嘱取得遗赠房屋；除施乙外的施甲、施丙、施丁三被告要求系争房屋由四子女各得四分之一。

法院审理后认为，根据规定，继承开始后，按照法定继承办理，有遗嘱的按照遗嘱或者遗赠办理。遗赠的，受遗赠人应当在知道受遗赠后2个月内，作出接受或者放弃遗赠的表示，到期没有表示的，视为放弃受遗赠。本案中，原告不是周某某的应召法定继承人，如果周某某立遗嘱将其财产遗留给原告的，属遗赠。周某某在立遗嘱时已94周岁，在立遗嘱前已有不认人、不认路的症状，其立遗嘱时的民事行为能力存疑。即使周某某有立遗嘱的民事行为能力，但原告没有在法律规定的2个月期限内表示接受遗赠，应当视为其放弃遗赠，审理法院依法判决系争房屋不应按遗赠处理。①

适用法律分析：本案的争议焦点是，原告施某某是否放弃了遗赠。我国《继承法》第25条第2款明确规定："受遗赠人应当在知道受遗赠后两个月内，作出接受或者放弃受遗赠的表示。到期没有表示的，视为放弃接受遗赠。"这意味着在遗赠有效的前提下，受遗赠人若要获得遗赠，必须明确表示接受遗赠，且表示的期限是知道受遗赠后2个月内，否则即视为放弃遗赠。相对于继承的接受，我国法律对遗赠的接受是比较严格的。本案中，审理法院依据我国《继承法》第25条第2款，认定原告没有在知道受遗赠后的2个月内表示接受遗赠，视为其已经放弃接受遗赠的判决，符合我国法律的规定。但是我们认为，此案例反映出我国该方面立法的合理性有待商榷。接受遗赠作为一种纯获利行为。受遗赠人未作表示拒绝遗赠，应当被视为接受遗赠，才有利于保护受遗赠人的利益。

（七）涉及继承权的丧失、被继承人的宥恕与代位继承案例的简介与评析

案情简介：原告计甲系被继承人计某余儿子，被告沈某某系计某余母亲。计某余与妻子蔡某某于1993年4月20日离婚，原告计甲随蔡某某共同生活。本案系争的×区×镇×小区×号楼×室房屋，为计某余、计甲和沈某某按出资比例共同所有。2010年9月3日，计某余因患病死亡。系争房屋被其母沈某某出售，价款为52万元占为己有。后原告计甲与被告沈某某对该售房款的分配问题发生纠纷，因协商未果，原告计甲诉至法院，要求参与

① 参见中国裁判文书网：（2017）沪×民初×号，《施某某与施甲等继承纠纷一审民事判决书》，载 http://wenshu.court.gov.cn/content/content?DocID=e3681a1e-6fc8-4612-b26d-a7fe0167cf4e&KeyWord=沪×民初×号，访问日期：2019年3月8日。限于本章篇幅，作者对原案情内容有酌情删改。

继承并按法定继承份额取得房屋出售金。被告沈某某主张，计甲在父母离婚后一直随其母蔡某某共同生活，在被继承人病重期间从未探望，不尽孝道，应丧失继承权。①

法院审理后认为：原告自计某余与蔡某某离婚后一直随母亲生活，在被继承人病重时其虽然未来看望，但其与计某余仍然是父子关系，并且不具有丧失继承权的法定事由，没有丧失继承权。故判决该涉案房屋的出售款 52 万元，由原告计甲、被告沈某某各得 245080.66 元。

适用法律分析：本案的争议焦点将在于原告计甲是否丧失了继承权的问题。继承权丧失一般是指本来具有继承资格的人因有故意杀害被继承人等某些严重违法犯罪行为，或有严重的不道德行为，被依法剥夺继承人资格不再享有继承遗产的权利。根据我国《继承法》第 7 条之规定："继承人有下列行为之一的，丧失继承权：（一）故意杀害被继承人的；（二）为争夺遗产而杀害其他继承人的；（三）遗弃被继承人的，或者虐待被继承人情节严重的；（四）伪造、篡改或者销毁遗嘱、情节严重的。"遗弃被继承人是指对没有劳动能力又没有生活来源的被继承人有扶养义务而拒不履行扶养义务；而虐待被继承人是指在被继承人生前对其从身体上或精神上进行摧残或者折磨。本案中，虽然原告计甲在父母离婚后一直随母亲生活，在被继承人病重期间并未探望，但是并不具有法律上虐待被继承人的情形。因而，法院审理后判决确定原告计甲与计某余仍然是父子关系，没有丧失继承权，这是符合法律规定的。从本案可见，我国《继承法》明列丧失继承权的法定情形，有利于民众知法守法，有利于法官执法，这是其优点。

（八）涉及继承协议案例的简介与评析

案情简介：史某培和王某宝夫妻共生育原告史某甲、被告史某乙。史某培名下有存款 8 万元。2014 年 4 月 25 日（王某宝死亡后第五天），史某培因病住院治疗，且神志不清；经史某某、黄某某调解，原、被告（原、被告之配偶在场）签订《家庭赡养扶助继承协议书》，约定："照顾父亲，并聘请专业人员费用由史某甲一人负担；父亲的医疗费支出由史某甲负担；百年后的丧事支付由史某甲负担。之后父亲的工资收入和遗产归史某甲所有。"被继承人史某培去世后，两人因遗产继承发生纠纷，原告史某甲因史某乙拒绝履行《家庭赡养扶助继承协议书》，诉至法院。原告史某甲认为应按照签订的《家庭赡养扶助继承协议书》分割遗产；被告史某乙认为以上协议无效，应按照法定继承分割被继承人的遗产，并共同分担生前照顾被继承人的费用。

法院审理后认为，继承开始后，按照法定继承办理；有遗嘱的，按照遗嘱继承或者遗赠办理。该份《家庭赡养扶助继承协议书》真实、合法、有效，是当事人各方的真实意思表示，法院予以确认。根据我国《继承法》第 5 条、第 10 条、第 26 条之规定，判决被继承人史某培遗产应由原告史某甲继承。②

适用法律分析：本案涉及继承人间签订的继承协议是否有效的问题。我国《继承法》

---

① 参见中国裁判文书网：（2011）松×（民）初字第×号，《计甲与沈某某法定继承纠纷一审民事判决书》，载 http://wenshu.court.gov.cn/Index，访问日期：2019 年 3 月 8 日。限于本章篇幅，作者对原案情内容有酌情删改。

② 参见中国裁判文书网：（2015）浦×（民）初字第×号，《史某甲与史某乙继承纠纷一审民事裁定书》，载 http://wenshu.court.gov.cn/list/list/?sorttype=1&number=LWGCRD7U&guid=0bebbae2-d162-7945b7d5-ef19a45c35fa&conditions=searchWord+QWJS+++全文检索：浦×（民）初字第×号，访问日期：2019 年 3 月 8 日。限于本章篇幅，作者对原案情内容有酌情删改。

对遗嘱继承人和受遗赠人的范围皆有限制。遗嘱继承只涉及法定继承人继承顺序和继承份额之变动，而遗赠扶养协议均被限定为是被继承人与法定继承人之外的人签订的以生养死葬和遗赠财产为内容的协议。目前，我国立法并没有规定继承协议制度，学界多认为继承协议是“被继承人与某法定继承人或全体共同继承人就继承权的取得与放弃以及赡养等达成合意的双方法律行为”①，其应该是有效的。本案中，原告与被告在双方自愿的情况下签订了继承协议，且协议签订时，协议双方都具有完全民事行为能力，意思表示真实。民法乃是权利法，法彦有云：法无禁止即自由。该继承协议意思表示真实，也并未违反法律的禁止性规定，从维护当事人意思自治的角度考量，我们认为，从本案的审理结果看，该人民法院的判决是符合情理的，但我国立法欠缺继承协议制度，导致现实生活中，民众对该协议的效力认识不一，有些法院亦不承认继承协议的效力，这是其立法之不足。

（九）涉及遗产债务清偿案例的简介与评析

案情简介：原告吴某某和借款人邵某华是邻居。2014 年 7 月下旬，邵某华为炒股向原告借款人民币 16 万元。后邵某华去世，2015 年 3 月 2 日原告提起诉讼，以邵某华唯一法定继承人其儿子邵某翔为被告的被继承人债务清偿纠纷案，同年 3 月 31 日法院判决邵某翔从其继承财产范围内偿还本案债务。后邵某翔发现其父邵某华有遗嘱的新情况，诉至法院，认为应由邵某华的兄弟邵某甲、邵某乙，即遗产的遗嘱继承人承担上述债务。而被告邵某甲、邵某乙表示对该笔债务并不知情，是原告邵某翔与邻居吴某某恶意编造的债务。

法院审理后查明：本案源于借款人邵某华生前向原告借款 16 万元而产生，该笔借贷关系事实清楚，借条和银行转账记录在时间、金额上可互相印证，佐证了吴某某和邵某华间 16 万元借贷事实的客观存在。因此，不存在邻居吴某某和原告邵某翔串通损害被告利益的事实。两被告是兄长邵某华的房产、积蓄等遗产的唯一继承人，系获益方，也应由其承担清偿被继承人债务的责任。据此，依照我国《合同法》第 60、206、207 条，我国《继承法》第 5、25、33 条之规定，判决被告邵某甲、邵某乙应在其依遗嘱继承被继承人邵某华的遗产范围内向原告邵某翔归还借款人民币 16 万元，由其代为偿还被继承人的生前欠债。②

适用法律分析：本案涉及被继承人遗产债务的清偿问题。我国《继承法》第 5 条规定：“继承开始后，按照法定继承办理；有遗嘱的，按照遗嘱继承或者遗赠办理；有遗赠扶养协议的，按照协议办理。”我国《继承法》第 33 条规定：“继承遗产应当清偿被继承人依法应当缴纳的税款和债务，缴纳税款和清偿债务以他的遗产实际价值为限。超过遗产实际价值部分，继承人自愿偿还的不在此限。继承人放弃继承的，对被继承人依法应当缴纳的税款和债务可以不负偿还责任。”可见，我国采取限定继承的原则，继承人一旦接受继承，就必须以遗产的实际价值为限，清偿被继承人的遗产债务，但对于超出遗产实际价值的债务，不负清偿责任。本案中，两被告邵某甲、邵某乙作为遗嘱继承人，继承了被继

① 刘耀东：《论继承合同制度及其在我国民法典继承编的立法建构》，载《河南财经政法大学学报》2015 年第 6 期。

② 参见裁判文书网：（2016）沪×民初×号，《邵某翔与邵某甲、邵某乙被继承人债务清偿纠纷一审民事判决书》，载 http://wenshu.court.gov.cn/content/content? DocID = 0196c298 - 82af - 4237 - a9e4 - 9c338be72991&KeyWord = (2016)沪×民初×号，访问日期：2019 年 3 月 8 日。限于本章篇幅，作者对原案情内容有酌情删改。

承人全部遗产，依法应当在遗产实际范围内清偿对被继承人的遗产债务。本案法定继承人并未实际继承被继承人遗产，不应对被继承人生前债务承担清偿责任。综上，法院判决被告邵某甲、邵某乙在其继承被继承人遗产范围内向原告邵某翔归还借款是符合法律规定的。由本案可见，我国《继承法》明确规定遗嘱继承优先于法定继承被适用，这有利于明确被继承人的债务之清偿责任人，这是立法的优点。但我国立法欠缺遗产债务的清偿顺序之规定，如遗产债务有多种时，则可能会难以确定何种债务优先受偿，这不利于依法保护遗产债权人的利益，这是其立法之不足。

（十）涉及遗产分割案例的简介与评析

案情简介：刘某1与贺某霞系夫妻关系，婚内生育原告刘某2，系争房屋于1993年12月25日产权登记为刘某1，贺某霞于2001年4月7日死亡。2002年7月，被告刘某1与徐某某登记结婚，婚后一直居住在系争房屋中，2017年7月5日，在未告知儿子刘某2的情况下，刘某1将系争房屋变更登记为刘某1、徐某某共同共有。后原告刘某2与被告刘某1因对房屋的分割发生纠纷，诉至法院。原告刘某2认为，系争房屋为夫妻共同财产，其母去世时，对其母拥有的50%产权份额应由自己和父亲各继承一半。被告刘某1私自变更房屋产权登记的行为，侵害其对系争房屋的继承权，要求依法确认其对系争房屋享有25%产权份额。而被告刘某1认为，刘某2的请求已过诉讼时效。

法院审理后认为，关于继承纠纷诉讼时效，继承开始后，原告在继承开始后，并未作出放弃继承的意思表示，故应当认定为原告接受继承。虽然系争房产在被继承人贺某霞去世后，长期由被告刘某1和第三人徐某某管理和使用，在原告主张分割遗产前，并未产生否认继承权之继承纠纷，故不存在诉讼时效的起算问题。鉴于此，对于被告刘某1和徐某某主张原告提起的继承纠纷超过诉讼时效的主张，不予支持。系争房屋为刘某1、贺某霞的夫妻共同财产，应当先析出一半产权即50%份额为刘某1所有，另50%产权份额为被继承人贺某霞名下的遗产，而2017年7月5日未经原告同意，被告将房屋产权变更登记为刘某1、徐某某共同所有，这侵犯了共同继承人刘某2的遗产继承份额。故法院判决认为刘某1处分其所有及继承的份额部分有效，处分应属原告继承的份额部分无效。①

适用法律分析：本案涉及遗产分割的诉讼时效以及系争房屋如何分割的问题。我国《继承法》第8条规定："继承权纠纷提起诉讼的期限为二年，自继承人知道或者应当知道其权利被侵犯之日起计算。但是，自继承开始之日起超过二十年的，不得再提起诉讼。"原告在贺某霞死亡、继承开始后，并未明确作出放弃继承的意思表示。根据我国《继承法》第25条的规定："继承开始后，继承人放弃继承的，应当在遗产处理前，作出放弃继承的表示。没有表示的，视为接受继承。"首先，继承开始后，即发生了共同继承，并且共同继承人之间从未发生否认继承权的纠纷，故该案刘某2的遗产分割请求没有超过诉讼时效。其次，被继承人贺某霞生前未留有遗嘱，故本案应按照法定继承办理。根据我国《继承法》第26条规定："夫妻在婚姻关系存续期间所得的共同所有的财产，除有约定的以外，如果分割遗产，应当先将共同所有的财产的一半分出为配偶所有，其余的

---

① 参见裁判文书网：（2017）沪×民初×号，《刘某1与刘某2法定继承纠纷一审民事判决书》，载 http://wenshu.court.gov.cn/content/content?DocID=2bd4c3cf-e13e-4d89-b48c-a81f009a536c&KeyWord=（2017）沪×民初×号，访问日期：2019年3月8日。限于本章篇幅，作者对原案情内容有酌情删改。

为被继承人的遗产。”系争房屋为刘某1、贺某霞的夫妻共同财产，依法应当先析出一半产权即50%的份额为刘某1所有，另50%的产权份额为被继承人贺某霞名下的遗产，由刘某1和刘某2共同继承。综上，本案审理法院对遗产分割中诉讼时效和房屋分配的判决，符合法律规定。由本案可见，我国《继承法》明确规定了应从共有财产中析出遗产，这有利于依法确定遗产的范围，这是我国立法的优点。

（十一）涉及无人承受遗产案例的简介与评析

案情简介：被继承人周某1生前工作于×有限公司，该公司和公安户籍资料均证明周某1生前未婚、无子女，独自生活。公安机关证明周某1于2015年2月7日猝死于×村×号房屋。×有限公司还出具证明，称周某1智力低下，公司为解决员工家庭困难，公司同意周某1顶替其母为单位员工，发放最低工资；周某1的后事也由其侄子周某2办理，该公司派人上门慰问周某1时，曾看到周某2在周某1的床前照料。周某1去世后，周某2诉至法院，申请继承周某1的遗产。

法院审理后认为，我国《继承法》第14条规定，对继承人以外的依靠被继承人扶养的缺乏劳动能力又没有生活来源的人，或者继承人以外的对被继承人扶养较多的人，可以分配给他们适当的遗产。但由于周某1有生活来源、周某2并未对周某1提供主要的经济生活来源；同时双方居住地相距较远。周某1最后系被邻居发现多日不见，报警后警方破门而入才发现其已经死亡，申请人、证人和居委会均陈述其已经死亡多日，可见，周某2对周某1的照顾尚未达到在生活上提供主要的经济来源，或在劳务等方面给予主要扶助的程度。依照我国《继承法》第14和32条、1985年《执行继承法意见》第30条、我国现行《民事诉讼法》第192条的规定，判决如下：×区×村房屋为无主财产，收归国家所有；周某1个人住房公积金账户全部余额为无主财产，收归国家所有；周某1名下存款和利息归周某2所有。[①]

适用法律分析：本案的争议焦点在于无人继承的遗产应如何处理的问题。本案中，周某1未婚无子女，父母也先于其死亡，经审理后法院确认其无法定继承人存在，其财产为无人承受的遗产。根据我国《继承法》第32条规定：“无人继承又无人受遗赠的遗产，归国家所有；死者生前是集体所有制组织成员的，归所在的集体所有制组织所有。”本案中，周某2主张应由其继承周某1的遗产，审理法院认为周某2对周某1的照顾尚未达到在生活上提供主要的经济来源，或在劳务等方面给与主要扶助的程度，故不属于酌分遗产的请求权主体，此判决于法有据。但从本案也可以看出，我国无人承受遗产的立法存在某些不足。我们认为，本案中，周某1死亡的后事均由侄子周某2办理，该公司派人上门慰问周某1时，也曾看到周某2在周某1的床前照料。因此，认为×村×号房屋和住房公积金归国家所有，周某2仅能酌情分得周某1存款的判决，未充分考量侄子周某2所尽的照顾义务，不利于保护自然人的私有财产和亲情伦理的维护，酌分遗产的份额偏少。我们认为，我国无人承受遗产的酌分请求权主体范围较窄，这是我国立法之不足。

① 参见中国裁判文书网：（2016）沪×4民×号，《周某2申请认定财产无主特别程序民事判决书》，载http://wenshu.court.gov.cn/content/content?DocID=2a610782-b56c-4421-bcff-a81600e2ef79&KeyWord=（2016）沪×民×号，访问日期：2019年3月8日。限于本章篇幅，作者对原案情内容有酌情删改。

第三节 当代中国上海市民众财产继承观念与遗产处理习惯的特点与原因分析

根据本次调查统计数据情况的汇总分析，我们以下对上海市被调查者对前述十一个问题所体现出的财产继承观念与遗产处理习惯之特点与原因分析如下：

一、遗产范围界定之特点与原因分析

（一）遗产的种类之特点与原因分析

关于属于遗产种类的民众观念，统计数据显示的特点是，在上海市被调查者中，（1）认为房屋（98.90%）、汽车（98.00%）、存款（96.70%）、股票（90.90%）属于遗产的，占九成以上；认为单位出租给某甲的午休住房不属于遗产的，占九成以上（92.90%），此认识与我国现行法规定相一致；（2）认为某甲公司购货的欠款（59.50%）、家庭日常生活用品（59.20%）和死亡赔偿金（20.80%）属于遗产的，各占二成至五成以上，此认识与我国现行法的规定不一致；（3）认为某甲以其姓名注册的邮箱、QQ账号等属于遗产的占三成（30.30%），对此我国现行法无规定（见表4-4）。

以上特点的原因分析，在上海市被调查者中，（1）九成以上的人认为房屋、汽车、存款、股票属于遗产、单位出租给某甲的午休住房不属于遗产，其原因可能是受我国立法的影响。我国现行法采取了列举加概括的方式规定遗产的范围，凡属于个人所有的合法财产都可以作为遗产，说明上海市被调查民众对我国《继承法》中列举的遗产类型较为了解；（2）二成至五成以上的人认为死亡赔偿金、欠款和家庭日常生活用品属于遗产，此认识与我国现行法的规定不一致，其原因可能是：其一，对于死亡赔偿金的性质，根据我国2004年《关于审理人身损害赔偿案件适用法律若干问题的解释》第1条第2款规定："本条所称'赔偿权利人'，是指因侵权行为或者其他致害原因直接遭受人身损害的受害人、依法由受害人承担扶养义务的被扶养人以及死亡受害人的近亲属。"第17条第3款规定："受害人死亡的，赔偿义务人除应当根据抢救治疗情况赔偿本条第一款规定的相关费用外，还应当赔偿丧葬费、被扶养人生活费、死亡补偿费以及受害人亲属办理丧葬事宜支出的交通费、住宿费和误工损失等其他合理费用。"以上规定中表明，死者的人身损害死亡补偿费是对死亡受害人的近亲属的补偿费，其不属于遗产。其二，对于欠债的性质，通说认为我国遗产范围的界定采取"积极财产说"，即不包括消极性质的被调查者的生前欠债。其三，还有近六成的人认为家庭日常生活用品属于遗产，被继承人对这些物品也在使用。但此认识有一定偏差，因为只有其中被继承人享有的份额才属于遗产，但被调查者对此范围的认识不够清楚，而认为全部属于遗产。（3）有三成的人认为邮箱、QQ账号等属于遗产，七成的人认为其不属于遗产，其原因可能是这些物与人身密切相关，如其被他人继承则可能会侵犯被继承人的个人隐私。这表明具有人身性质的物，应排除在遗产范围之外。

关于遗产的种类之我国立法现状，我国《继承法》第3条规定："遗产是公民死亡时遗留的个人合法财产，包括：（一）公民的收入；（二）公民的房屋、储蓄和生活用品；（三）公民的林木、牲畜和家禽；（四）公民的文物、图书资料；（五）法律允许公民所

有的生产资料；（六）公民的著作权、专利权中的财产权利；（七）公民的其他合法财产。”我国《继承法》第4条规定：“个人承包应得的个人收益，依照本法规定继承。个人承包，依照法律允许由继承人继续承包的，按照承包合同办理。”1985年《执行继承法意见》第4条还规定：“承包人死亡时尚未取得承包收益的，可把死者生前对承包所投入的资金和所付出的劳动及其增值和孳息，由发包单位或者接续承包合同的人合理折价、补偿，其价额作为遗产。”

从域外立法例看，《日本民法典》在第896条将遗产概括为“被继承人财产的一切权利、义务，但是，专属于被继承人本人者不在此限”。《葡萄牙民法典》列举了四类属于遗产的财产，并将基于性质或法律规定随主体死亡而消灭的排除在外。①

从我国诸继承法学者建议稿看，“梁稿”认为：“遗产是自然人死亡时遗留的个人合法财产。前款规定的遗产包括自然人因其死亡而获得的未指定受益人的保险金、补偿金、赔偿金以及其他基于该自然人生前行为而应获得的财产利益。下列权利义务不得作为继承的标的：（一）与被继承人人身不可分割的人身权利；（二）与被继承人人身有关的专属性债权债务；（三）法律规定不得继承的其他财产。”② 即“梁稿”采取的是正面列举和概括加反面排除式的立法模式。“陈稿”第25条规定：“遗产是被继承人死亡时遗留的个人所有财产。与被继承人人身不可分割的财产和法律规定不得继承的财产，不属于遗产。”即“陈稿”采取正面概括加反面排除的立法模式。

我们认为，我国遗产范围界定欠缺反面排除的规定，这是其立法之不足。因此，上述建议增加遗产范围反面排除规定的上海市被调查民众的观念、域外立法例和我国学者建议稿的观点，可供我国立法参考。

（二）被继承人生前特种赠与财产的归扣之特点与原因分析

第一，关于被继承人生前特种赠与财产是否应归入遗产范围的民众观念与民间习惯，统计数据显示的特点是，（1）在上海市被调查者的观念上，认为被继承人去世时遗留的个人财产才可算作遗产的，占八成以上（82.90%）；被继承人生前资助子女的财产与死亡时其遗留的住房、存款，均应当合并计算为遗产的，仅占一成半以上（16.00%）（见表4-5）；（2）被调查者所在地区的继承习惯是，没有该归扣习惯的，占近八成（77.90%）；有该归扣习惯的，占二成以上（22.10%）（见表4-7）。

以上特点的原因分析，（1）八成以上的上海市被调查者不认可遗产归扣制度，近八成的该市被调查者所在地区也没有该习惯，其原因可能是受到现行法和传统习惯的影响；（2）还有一成半以上的上海市被调查者认可遗产归扣制度，一成半以上的该市被调查者所在地区有该习惯，其原因可能是认为该制度有利于在共同继承人之间公平分配遗产。

第二，关于生前特种赠与财产不归扣纳入遗产情况下的分配方式之民间习惯，统计数据显示的特点是，在被调查者所在地区，（1）有平均分配习惯的，占七成（70.90%）；（2）有乙应当适当多分习惯的，只占二成半（25.10%）（见表4-9）。

以上特点的原因分析，根据上海市被调查者填写的生前特种赠与财产不归扣纳入遗产情况下分配方式的民间习惯之理由（见表4-9），（1）六成半以上的地区有平均分配遗产

---

① 《葡萄牙民法典》第2025、2069条。

② “梁稿”第1941条。

的习惯，原因是不考虑张老汉生前给三个儿子财产的情况，死后平均分配所留遗产，有利于遗产分割，可以减少纠纷；（2）二成的地区有乙应该适当多分遗产的习惯，原因是张老汉生前给乙的财产较少，在其死后乙应多分些，可以在共同继承人间公平分配遗产，以体现公平原则。

关于遗产归扣制度之我国立法，我国《继承法》对此无规定。

从域外立法例看，《日本民法典》规定，第一，关于归扣的主体，从被继承人处接受遗赠或者因婚姻、收养或作为生计资本而接受赠与的共同继承人为归扣的义务主体，即被继承人的配偶、子女、直系尊亲属及兄弟姐妹均可以成为归扣义务人。而其他共同继承人为归扣权利人。① 第二，关于归扣的标的，自被继承人处接受的遗赠或因婚姻或收养，或作为生计资本而接受的赠与应归扣加入遗产的总额中。② 第三，关于归扣的标的，分为意定免除与法定免除。关于意定免除，被继承人已作出免除归扣的意思表示时，以不违反特留份规定的份额为限。关于法定免除，遗赠或者赠与的价额等于或者超过继承份额的价额时，受遗赠人或者受赠人不得接受其继承份额。③ 第四，关于归扣的方法，采取价值充当。归扣以被继承人在继承开始时持有财产的价额再加上其赠与价额的财产确定。赠与的价额，即便因受赠人的行为致使作为其标的的财产灭失，或者使其价格增减，视为继承开始时的原状未变而确定。④《法国民法典》第843条也明确规定，一切继承人应对其他继承人返还死者生前直接或间接赠与的一切财产。另外《瑞士民法典》和《日本民法典》对此也有规定。⑤

从我国诸继承法学者建议稿看，“梁稿”规定：“继承开始之前，继承人因结婚、分居、营业以及其他事由而从被继承人处获得的赠与的财产应当列入遗产范围，但被继承人生前有相反意思表示的除外。”⑥“王稿”“杨稿”“张稿”和“陈稿”中对此也有规定。⑦

我们认为，我国欠缺遗产归扣制度，这是其立法之不足。因此，上述主张设立遗产归扣制度的上海市被调查民众的观念与习惯、域外立法例和我国学者建议稿的观点，可供我国立法参考。

二、继承开始的通知和公告之特点与原因分析

（一）继承开始的通知和公告的主体之特点与原因分析

关于继承开始的通知和公告主体的民间习惯，统计数据显示的特点是，在上海市被调查者所在地区，（1）由继承人作为主体的，各占五成至七成以上，具体包括：知道被继承人死亡的继承人（78.50%）和保管遗产的继承人（56.50%）；（2）由处理被继承人死亡事件的机构作为主体的，占三成半以上（36.50%）；（3）由知道被继承人死亡的单位、村（居）委会作为主体的，占三成（30.60%）（见表4-10）。可见，上海市被调查民众

① 参见《日本民法典》第887~890条、903条。

② 参见《日本民法典》第903条。

③ 参见《日本民法典》第903条第2、3款。

④ 参见《日本民法典》第903、904条。

⑤ 参见《瑞士民法典》第626条；《日本民法典》第903、904条。

⑥ 参见“梁稿”第1942条。

⑦ 参见“王稿”第542条；“杨稿”第9条；“张稿”第64条；“陈稿”第26~28条。

认可的通知和公告主体范围，要广于我国现行法的规定。

以上特点的原因分析，在上海市被调查者所在地区，（1）五成至七成以上的地区有由继承人作为通知主体的习惯，其原因可能是受我国立法的影响；（2）三成半以上的地区有由处理被继承人死亡事件的机构作为通知主体的习惯，如公安交警部门，其原因可能是认为该通知主体应尽可能广泛，以便及时发出继承开始的通知和公告。

关于继承开始的通知主体之我国立法，我国《继承法》第23条规定："继承开始后，知道被继承人死亡的继承人应当及时通知其他继承人和遗嘱执行人。继承人中无人知道被继承人死亡或者知道被继承人死亡而不能通知的，由被继承人生前所在单位或者住所地的居民委员会、村民委员会负责通知。"2015年《民诉法解释》第55条规定："在诉讼中，一方当事人死亡，需要等待继承人表明是否参加诉讼的，裁定中止诉讼。人民法院应当及时通知继承人作为当事人承担诉讼，被继承人已经进行的诉讼行为对承担诉讼的继承人有效。"

从域外立法例看，大陆法系的许多国家的立法均有规定继承开始的通知与公告的主体，在催告继承和遗赠的接受或放弃、催告债权人、无人继承遗产的处理等相关规定中有所体现。法国、意大利等国均规定继承人和法院是继承开始的通知与公告的主体之一。① 例如，《德国民法典》关于继承开始的通知与公告主体的规定，主要体现在公开申报继承权、对遗产债权人的公示催告方面。② 一是当继承人在适当期间内无法查明的，遗产法院必须确定不存在除国库外的继承人，应公开催告继承权的申报；二是继承人接受继承后，可提出对遗产债权人的公示催告程序的申请。当继承人为多人时，各共同继承人可以公开催告遗产债权人向共同继承人或向遗产法院申报他们的债权。③

从我国诸继承法学者建议稿看，"梁稿"在现行法规定的基础上增加一款，即"其他利害关系人知道继承开始的事实的，也可以通知继承人或遗嘱执行人"。④ "杨稿"在保留我国《继承法》规定的基础上，补充规定处理被继承人死亡事件的部门或基层组织为通知义务人，同时还增加了通知义务人的赔偿责任之规定。⑤

我们认为，我国继承开始的通知和公告主体的范围较窄，这是其立法之不足。因此，上述主张扩大主体范围的上海市被调查民众的习惯、域外立法例和我国学者建议稿的观点，可供我国立法参考。

（二）继承开始的通知和公告的方式之特点与原因分析

关于继承开始的通知和公告方式的民间习惯，统计数据显示的特点是，在上海市被调查者所在地区，（1）分别通过口头、电话、微信等通知（75.90%）和信件、告知函等书面通知（54.90%）的，各占五成至七成以上；（2）分别由申请人民法院以公告程序进行公告（23.00%）、在被继承人所在地的村（居）委会公告栏公告（17.80%）和在报纸、电视、网络等平台上发布被继承人死亡公告（15.80%）的，各占一成至二成以上（见表4-11）。可见，上海市被调查民众所在地区，有关继承开始的通知和公告方式的民间习惯

① 参见《法国民法典》第788、789、792条；《意大利民法典》第481、501、650条。

② 参见陈苇主编：《中国遗产处理制度系统化构建研究》，中国人民公安大学出版社2019年版，第46页。

③ 参见《德国民法典》第1964、2061条。

④ 参见"梁稿"第2001条。

⑤ 参见"杨稿"第70条。

特点较为多样。

以上特点的原因分析，（1）五至七成以上的地区有通过口头、电话或告知函等方式通知的习惯，其原因可能是根据实际需要可选择各种通知方式，包括简便、及时的口头、电话、微信通知和正式的信件、告知函，多种方式便于方便、及时地发出继承开始的通知；（2）一成至二成以上的地区有发布公告的习惯，其原因可能是在继承人有无不明时，公告方式便于寻找相关继承人。

关于继承开始的通知的具体方式之我国立法，我国《继承法》对此无规定，并且也没有设立继承开始的公告制度。

从域外立法例看，大陆法系的德国、瑞士、日本、意大利等国均规定在继承人有无不明时，应发布寻找继承人的公告，催告权利人在一定期限内申明其继承权。① 例如，《意大利民法典》规定，按遗产清单接受继承的继承人，如果知晓债权人和受遗赠人的住所或居所，则申报债权的通知应当用挂号信直接送达，同时，还应当将申报债权的通知刊登在升级法律公报上。②

从我国诸继承法学者建议稿看，“徐稿”第四分编第 383 条规定：“一切遗嘱执行人对继承的开始负通知义务，此等通知应在遗产所在地的报刊上刊登，无此等报刊时在省会的报刊上刊登 3 次。”“王稿”第 662 条规定：“人民法院决定受理申请，应在三日内发生公告，催促继承人、受遗赠人、债权人等其他利害关系人申报、登记。公示催告的期间，由人民法院根据情况决定，但不得少于六十日”。

我们认为，对于是否应具体地规定继承开始的通知和公告方式，由于科技的进步，现代的通知和公告方式更为多元，没有必要以立法采取逐一列举的方式规定。

（三）继承开始的通知和公告的期间之特点与原因分析

关于继承开始的通知和公告期间的民众观念，统计数据显示的特点是，在上海市被调查者中，（1）应在 7 日内发出的，占五成半以上（56.30%）；（2）应在 15 日以内发出的，占二成以上（22.60%）；（3）应在 30 日内发出的，仅占一成半以上（16.00%）（见表 4-12）。

以上特点的原因分析，五成半以上的上海市被调查者认为应在 7 日以内的较短期间发出通知和公告，占比最高，其原因可能是这符合民众实际生活的需要，便于及时地通知相关权利人参加吊唁、参与继承或申报债权等。

关于继承开始的通知和公告期间之我国立法，我国《继承法》对此无规定。但我国现行《民事诉讼法》第 191、192 条对于认定财产无主公告的期间规定为 1 年。

从域外立法例看，大陆法系国家和英美法系国家对于继承开始通知和公告的期间多有规定。③ 例如，《日本民法典》对继承开始通知与公告期间之规定，主要体现在对遗产债权人及受遗赠人的公告与催告、继承人有无不明时的公示催告、对遗赠的接受和放弃的催告等规定之中。第一，对遗产债权人及受遗赠人进行公告与催告的期间。限定承认人在作出限定继承的表示后 5 日内，对遗产债权人及受遗赠人进行公示催告的期间不得少于 2 个

① 参见《日本民法典》第 958 条；《瑞士民法典》第 555 条；《德国民法典》第 1965 条。

② 参见《意大利民法典》第 498 条。

③ 参见陈苇主编：《中国遗产处理制度系统化构建研究》，中国人民公安大学出版社 2019 年版，第 52~53 页。

月；当继承人有无不明时，管理人须及时对所有的遗产债权人及受遗赠人发出应在2个月内申报其请求为内容的公告。第二，催告继承权的公告期间。当继承人有无不明时，家庭法院选任遗产管理人并公告后2个月内，继承人有无仍然不明时，家庭法院根据管理人或检察官的请求，须发出以如果有继承人则应在一定期间内主张权利为内容的公告，此公告期间不能少于6个月。第三，催告受遗赠人作出接受或放弃遗赠的催告期间。交付遗赠义务人（负有履行遗赠义务的人）及其利害关系人，可以催告受遗赠人在指定期间内作出接受或放弃遗赠的表示。① 对公告期间的规定，如德国法规定的公示期间为3个月，瑞士法规定为1年。②

从我国诸继承法学者建议稿看，“王稿”规定继承的公告期间为60日；“杨稿”规定遗产管理人应当在接受指定后10日内发出寻找遗产承受权利人、遗产债权人的公告，公告期限为6个月；“陈稿”和“张稿”规定的公告期限为6个月。③

我们认为，我国《继承法》没有规定继承开始的通知和公告的期间，是其立法之不足。因此，上述主张在较短期间内发出继承开始通知和公告的上海市被调查民众的观念、域外立法例和我国学者建议稿的观点，可供我国立法参考。

三、遗产管理之特点与原因分析

（一）遗产管理人的确定之特点与原因分析

关于遗产管理人的确定的民间习惯，统计数据显示的特点是，在上海市被调查者所在地区，（1）由死者的法定继承人作为遗产管理人的，占九成（90.00%）；（2）分别由死者的儿媳或女婿（14.30%）、死者家族中的德高望重者（34.90%）、死者的其他亲戚朋友（9.40%）和死者所在的单位或村/居委会（17.10%）作为遗产管理人的，各占一成至三成以上（见表4-13）。

以上特点的原因分析，根据上海市被调查者填写的遗产管理人的确定的民间习惯之理由（见表4-15），（1）九成的地区有由法定继承人承担遗产管理人的习惯，其原因是这便于清点和妥善地管理遗产；（2）一成至三成以上的地区有由遗产继承人之外的人或组织（儿媳或女婿、德高望重者、其他亲戚朋友、单位或村/居委会）担任遗产管理人的习惯，其原因是这可以防止遗产被隐藏、转移，有利于保护遗产相关人的合法权益。

关于遗产管理人制度之我国立法，我国《继承法》对此无规定，但存在遗产管理人的概念。如我国《民法总则》第194条将“继承开始后未确定继承人或者遗产管理人”作为诉讼时效中止的原因。2001年《信托法》第39条第2款规定：“受托人职责终止时，其继承人或者遗产管理人、监护人、清算人应当妥善保管信托财产，协助新受托人接管信托事务。”即此规定有遗产管理人的协助义务。我国《继承法》第24条规定：“存有遗产的人，应当妥善保管遗产，任何人不得侵吞或者争抢。”该条仅有存有遗产的人的保管义务。

从域外立法例看，不少国家立法对于确定遗产管理人有所规定。《法国民法典》规

---

① 参见《日本民法典》第927、957、958、987条。

② 参见《德国民法典》第1965条；《瑞士民法典》第555条。

③ 参见“王稿”第662条；“杨稿”第92条；“陈稿”第85条；“张稿”第67条。

定，民事法院院长有权管理遗产，亦有权指定一名共有人作为遗产管理人①；《日本民法典》规定由家庭法院选任管理人②；《德国民法典》规定由遗产法院建立遗产管理，或在被监护人死亡时监护人管理遗产。③ 可见，域外立法例通常由法院选定遗产管理人，或者由继承人互推出一个遗产管理人。

从我国诸继承法学者建议稿看，“梁稿”认为：“继承开始后两个月内，继承人应当举行会议推选遗产管理人。共同继承人未推选遗产管理人的，由全体继承人共同行使遗产管理人的职责。遗嘱中指定有遗嘱执行人的，由遗嘱执行人行使遗产管理人的职责。在下列情况下，经利害关系人申请，人民法院可以指定遗产管理人：（一）遗嘱未指定遗产执行人，继承人对遗产管理人的选任有争议的；（二）没有继承人或者继承人下落不明，而遗嘱中又未指定遗嘱执行人的；（三）遗产债权人有证据证明继承人的行为已经或将要损害其利益的。人民法院在指定遗产管理人之前，经利害关系人的申请，可以对遗产进行必要的处分。”④ 该建议稿充分考虑了各种情形下遗产管理人的选任，综合考虑了继承人利益和被继承人意愿，也适当照顾了利害关系人利益。

我们认为，我国欠缺确定遗产管理人的方式，这是其立法之不足。遗产管理人的选任对于继承人和遗产债权人有重要意义，因此，上述确定遗产管理人范围的上海市被调查民众的习惯、域外立法例和我国学者建议稿的观点，可供我国立法参考。

（二）遗产管理人的职责与报酬之特点与原因分析

第一，关于遗产管理人职责的民众观念，统计数据显示的特点是，在上海市被调查者中，认为遗产管理人的职责包括清查遗产，制作遗产清单（92.30%）、妥善保管遗产（94.00%）、查明被继承人生前的债权和债务，积极地追讨债权或清偿债务（69.10%）、可以原告或被告的身份参加因遗产引起的诉讼（65.40%）、查明被继承人是否留有遗嘱，并且确定遗嘱是否真实合法（59.40%）、定期制作遗产管理报告向继承人报告遗产管理的情况（48.50%）的，各占四成至九成以上（见表4-16）。

以上特点的原因分析，我国《继承法》第24条规定“存有遗产的人，应当妥善保管遗产”，但没有规定遗产管理人的具体职责，但四成至九成以上的上海市被调查者认可的遗产管理人之职责的内容较为广泛，其原因可能是为指导遗产管理人积极履行义务。

关于遗产管理人的职责之我国立法，我国《继承法》对此无规定。

从域外立法例看，《德国民法典》较为概括地规定，遗产管理人需要管理遗产、处理债权和移交继承人。⑤《法国民法典》规定的遗产管理人职责包括：制作遗产清册、追讨遗产债务与公示催告遗产债权人、保全和管理遗产、制订清偿方案和清偿遗产、制作账目、提交与公示管理账目等。⑥

从我国诸继承法学者建议稿看，“梁稿”认为，遗产管理人的职责应当包括妥善保管

① 参见《法国民法典》第815条。
② 参见《日本民法典》第918条。
③ 参见《德国民法典》第1981条。
④ 参见“梁稿”第2002条。
⑤ 参见《德国民法典》第1985、1986条。
⑥ 参见《法国民法典》第789~792、796~810、811-1条。

遗产、编制遗产清册和移转遗产，以及为保存遗产价值进行必要的处分。① “王稿”规定的遗产管理人职责包括：编制遗产清册、管理遗产、将遗产转移给继承人和受遗赠人等。②

我们认为，我国欠缺遗产管理人的具体职责，这是其立法之不足。因此，上述主张明确遗产管理人职责的上海市被调查民众的观念、域外立法例和我国继承法学者建议稿的观点，可供我国立法参考。

第二，关于遗产管理人是否有权取得报酬的民间习惯，统计数据显示的特点是，在被调查者所在地区，（1）继承人担任的遗产管理人，不能请求给付报酬的，占五成以上（53.40%）；（2）法院指定的遗产管理人，有权请求给付报酬的，占五成以上（52.00%）；（3）继承人选任的第三人作为遗产管理人，其中四成半以上（46.20%）的地区有是否给付报酬，应当由继承人决定的习惯；近三成半（33.70%）的地区有一律有权请求给付报酬的习惯（见表 4-17）。

以上特点的原因分析，根据上海市被调查者填写的遗产管理人是否有权取得报酬的民间习惯之理由（见表 4-18），（1）五成以上的地区有继承人担任的遗产管理人不能取得报酬的习惯，其原因是遗产管理人多数情况下与被继承人关系密切，具有亲情关系，同时遗产管理人又继承遗产，因此管理遗产不需要报酬；（2）五成以上的地区有法院指定的遗产管理人有权取得报酬的习惯，其原因是遗产管理人为管理遗产付出了自己的劳动和时间，应该给予一定费用；（3）继承人选任的第三人作为遗产管理人，其中四成半以上的地区有是否给付报酬，应当由继承人决定的习惯；近三成半的地区有一律有权请求给付报酬的习惯，其原因是视情况而定，这更能符合实际情况。

关于遗产管理人是否有权取得报酬之我国立法，我国《继承法》对此无规定。

从域外立法例看，《德国民法典》肯定遗产管理人得因其执行职务而请求相当的报酬③；法国原则上也肯定管理人可以因管理活动取得报酬。④

从我国诸继承法学者建议稿看，“梁稿”认为：“继承人或者遗嘱执行人以外的遗产管理人有权请求与其所执行职务相当的报酬，其报酬列入继承费用优先受清偿。”⑤ “陈稿”规定，非继承人担任遗产管理人的，应支付相应的报酬⑥；“徐稿”规定，遗嘱执行人的报酬由遗嘱确定，遗嘱未确定的，由法院考虑财产量及执行职务的劳动量确定报酬额。⑦

我们认为，我国欠缺遗产管理人之报酬的规定，这是其立法之不足。因此，上述主张区别不同情况确定是否给予遗产管理者报酬的上海市被调查者所在地区的习惯、域外立法例和我国学者建议稿的观点，可供我国立法参考。

（三）遗产管理人的损害赔偿责任之特点与原因分析

关于遗产管理人的损害赔偿责任之民间习惯，统计数据显示的特点是，在上海市被调

---

① 参见梁慧星主编：《中国民法典草案建议稿附理由·继承编》，法律出版社 2013 年版，第 156~159 页。

② 参见“王稿”第 551、553、637 条。

③ 参见《德国民法典》第 1987 条。

④ 参见《法国民法典》第 815 条。

⑤ 参见“梁稿”第 2003 条。

⑥ 参见“陈稿”第 9 条。

⑦ 参见“徐稿”第四分编第 397 条。

查者所在地区，（1）有故意或重大过失才承担赔偿责任的，占六成以上（62.90%）；（2）无论故意、重大过失或一般轻过失都要承担赔偿责任的，占三成以上（32.60%）（见表4-19）。

以上特点的原因分析，在上海市被调查者所在地区，（1）六成以上的地区有遗产管理人有故意或重大过失，才承担赔偿责任的习惯，其原因可能是被调查民众认为该损害赔偿责任更为适度，不至于使遗产管理人背负较为沉重的管理负担。（2）三成以上的地区有无论是故意或重大过失或一般轻过失，都要承担赔偿责任的习惯，其原因可能是需要严格规范遗产管理人的行为，以防止其滥用权利。

关于遗产管理人的损害赔偿责任之我国立法，我国《继承法》对此无规定。

从域外立法例看，《德国民法典》规定，继承人和法院任命的遗产管理人需就其所实施的遗产管理行为向债权人负责，如因其违反申请开始支付不能程序的义务而导致债权人的损失，则应就该损害向债权人负责；遗嘱执行人因其过错违反其所担负的义务的，对因此而发生的损害向继承人和受遗赠人负责。①

从我国诸继承法学者建议稿看，“王稿”“梁稿”和“张稿”均规定，如果遗产管理人违背忠实管理的义务给债权人带来损害时，其须对遗产债权人承担相应的责任；而其所承担的责任应视其执行遗嘱是否有偿而有所不同，如果无偿，则应对其故意或重大过失导致的损失承担责任，如果有偿，则应对其一切过失所导致的损失承担损害赔偿责任。②

我们认为，我国欠缺遗产管理人的损害赔偿责任，这是其立法之不足。因此，上述主张遗产管理人应承担一定损害赔偿责任的上海市被调查者所在地区的习惯，域外立法例和我国学者建议稿的观点，可供我国立法参考。

四、法定继承之特点与原因分析

（一）法定继承人的范围与顺序之特点与原因分析

第一，关于法定继承人范围与顺序的民众观念，统计数据显示的特点是，上海市被调查者认可的法定继承人的范围与顺序是：第一顺序为配偶（89.54%）、父母（67.97%）、子（67.10%）；女（58.61%）；第二顺序为孙子女（50.11%）、外孙子女（48.37%）、祖父母（48.80%）、外祖父母（47.28%）、兄弟（45.53%）、姐妹（43.14%）；第三顺序为侄子女（27.23%）、外甥子女（26.58%）、伯叔姑舅姨（27.67%）；第四顺序以上为表兄弟姐妹（27.23%）、堂兄弟姐妹（24.62%）（见表4-20）。可见，上海市被调查者认可的法定继承人的范围更广、顺序应更多。

第二，关于配偶与血亲继承人顺序的民众观念，统计数据显示的特点是，在被调查者中，（1）第一继承顺序为配偶、子女、父母，配偶为固定的第一顺序继承人的，占八成（80.25%）；（2）第一顺序为子女，第二顺序为父母，第三顺序为兄弟姐妹、祖父母、外祖父母、兄弟姐妹的子女，配偶为无固定继承顺序继承人，可以参与第一、第二（或第三）顺序继承的，合计占近二成（19.75%）（见表4-21）。

以上特点的原因分析，（1）上海市被调查者认可的法定继承人的范围更广、顺序应

---

① 参见《德国民法典》第1978~1980、1985、2219条。

② 参见“王稿”第637条；“梁稿”第1892条；“张稿”第50条。

更多，包括亲属关系比较亲近、密切的伯叔姑舅姨等也应当被纳入法定继承人的范围之中。其原因可能是我国现行法定继承人范围过于狭窄。现行法中，只有六类近亲属被纳入法定继承人的范围之中。孙子女和外孙子女是法定的代位继承人，其在被代位继承人死亡时参与继承。有学者感叹“其有关法定继承范围和方式的规定，客观上形成私人财产只在有限的亲属范围内发生继承的后果，从而缩短了私有财产收归国有的行程。”① 但被调查民众更倾向于遗产应由更多具有血缘关系的旁系血亲继承，如侄子女、外甥子女、伯叔姑舅姨等，以免发生财产无人继承的情况。（2）八成的上海市被调查者认为配偶应为固定的第一顺序继承人，其原因可能是受我国现行法之影响。

关于法定继承人的范围与顺序之我国立法，我国《继承法》第 10 条规定：“遗产按照下列顺序继承：第一顺序：配偶、子女、父母。第二顺序：兄弟姐妹、祖父母、外祖父母。继承开始后，由第一顺序继承人继承，第二顺序继承人不继承。没有第一顺序继承人继承的，由第二顺序继承人继承。”

从域外立法例看，关于法定继承人的范围和顺序，一些国家的立法不尽相同。例如，《德国民法典》规定的法定继承人的范围较宽且顺序也多，包括第一顺序晚辈直系血亲、第二顺序父母及其晚辈直系血亲、第三顺序祖父母外祖父母及其晚辈直系血亲、第四顺序祖父母的父母及其晚辈直系血亲、比上述四个顺序的法定继承人更大的祖先及其晚辈直系血亲②；《法国民法典》将死者的子女及其直系卑血亲、直系尊血亲，旁系血亲及其尚存的配偶纳入法定继承的范围。③ 关于法定继承人的顺序，《法国民法典》规定，第一顺序为子女及其直系晚辈血亲；第二顺序为父母、兄弟姐妹及其直系晚辈血亲；第三顺序为除父母以外的直系长辈血亲；第四顺序为除兄弟姐妹及其直系晚辈血亲以外的六亲等内的旁系血亲；配偶没有固定的继承顺序，其与被继承人的子女或直系晚辈血亲或其父母共同继承。④

从我国诸继承法学者建议稿看，关于法定继承人的范围和顺序，“梁稿”规定：“第一顺序为配偶、子女、父母；第二顺序为兄弟姐妹、祖父母、外祖父母；第三顺序为其他四亲等以内的亲属。”⑤ “张稿”规定：“第一顺序子女及其晚辈直系血亲；第二顺序父母；第三顺序兄弟姐妹及其子女；第四顺序祖父母，包括父系祖父母和母系祖父母。配偶可以和任一顺序的血亲继承人共同继承。”⑥

我们认为，我国法定继承人的范围过于狭窄，这是我国立法之不足。在我国计划生育政策和民众生育观念的改变的影响下，目前家庭规模相较于过去缩小，在一对夫妻加一个独生子女的家庭里，该子女没有兄弟姐妹，在两个独生子女结婚组成的家庭中，没有伯叔姑舅姨，也没有堂兄弟姐妹、表兄弟姐妹。该种情形下，如果仍然沿用现行法定继承范围和顺序之规定，容易导致遗产无人继承，这不利于保护自然人的私人财产所有权。因此，上述主张适当扩大我国法定继承人范围的上海市被调查民众的观念，域外立法例和我国学

① 孙学致：《应修改继承法扩大继承人范围——从溥仪著作权继承之争说起》，载《法学》2008 年第 2 期。
② 参见《德国民法典》第 1924～1930 条。
③ 参见《法国民法典》第 734、735 条。
④ 参见《法国民法典》第 734、756、757 条。
⑤ 参见“梁稿”第 1946 条。
⑥ 参见“张稿”第 28 条。

者建议稿的观点，可供我国立法参考。

（二）配偶与血亲继承人的法定应继份之特点与原因分析

关于配偶与血亲继承人法定应继份的民众观念，统计数据显示的特点是，（1）配偶应无固定继承顺序，参与前三顺序或前二顺序继承并取得不同份额的，合计占五成半以上（57.37%）；（2）配偶应按固定顺序继承并均分遗产的，占四成以上（41.38%）（见表4-22）。

以上特点的原因分析，在上海市被调查者中，（1）五成半以上的人认为，配偶应为无固定顺序继承人，参与前三顺序或前二顺序继承并取得不同份额，这与我国现行法的规定不同。其原因可能是我国配偶固定第一继承顺序的规定存在一定问题，如果第一顺序继承人中，被继承人的父母、子女均已经去世，配偶将继承全部遗产，这会导致被继承人的其他近血亲，如兄弟姐妹、父系祖父母、母系祖父母均不能取得任何遗产。这于情于理均不合，既不利于保护被继承人的血亲继承人之利益，也不利于充分发挥遗产之养老育幼的职能，特别是如果夫妻结婚时间不长而一方死亡时，这种不合理尤为突出。（2）四成以上的人认为，配偶应为固定顺序继承人并均分遗产，其原因可能是受我国现行立法影响。

关于配偶与血亲继承人的法定应继份之我国立法，我国《继承法》第10条和第13条之规定，将配偶固定为第一顺序法定继承人，并且同一顺序继承人继承遗产的份额，一般应当均等。

从域外立法例看，多数国家将配偶作为无固定顺序继承人，与某些顺序或者所有顺序继承人共同继承遗产，其中配偶的遗产的份额与继承顺序成反比。例如，《德国民法典》规定："被继承人的生存配偶作为法定继承人的应继承份额，在与第一顺序的血亲共同继承时，为遗产的四分之一；在与第二顺序的继承人共同继承时，为遗产之半。"①《日本民法典》规定："配偶与子女共同继承遗产时，其遗产份额为二分之一；配偶与直系尊亲属为继承人的时候，配偶的应继份为三分之二；配偶同兄弟姐妹为继承人时，配偶的份额为四分之三。"②

从我国诸继承法学者建议稿看，"梁稿"提出增加了法定继承人的人数，并未对配偶固定作为第一顺序继承人参与法定继承这一规定进行修改。"张稿"认为，配偶作为不固定顺序继承人，可以和任意顺序的血亲继承人共同继承，"配偶与第一顺序血亲继承人共同继承时，各继承人应继份均等；配偶与第二顺序血亲继承人共同继承时，其应继份为二分之一；配偶与第三顺序血亲继承人共同继承时，其应继份为三分之二；配偶与第四顺序血亲继承人共同继承时，其应继份为四分之三；无血亲继承人时，配偶继承全部遗产"。③其主要理由是配偶无固定顺序参与法定继承能够兼顾血亲继承人的保护。

我们认为，我国将配偶作为固定第一顺序法定继承人，此立法存在某些不足。因为，配偶固定在第一顺序参与法定继承时，虽然彰显了配偶与被继承人的亲密关系和性别平等之理念，但也是有可能独自继承所有遗产的。"在婚姻关系稳定性降低的社会环境下，让配偶绝对排斥顺序在后的血亲继承全部遗产，其合理性值得商榷。"④ 而当配偶无固定继

① 参见《德国民法典》第1931条。
② 参见《日本民法典》第900条。
③ 参见"张稿"第28、31条。
④ 张玉敏：《法定继承人范围和顺序的确定》，载《法学》2012年第8期。

承顺序时，后面的其他顺序的血亲继承人能够得到一定遗产的可能性更大，更利于家族和睦。因此，上述主张配偶为无固定继承顺序继承人的上海市被调查民众的观念、域外立法例和“张稿”的观点，可供我国立法参考。

（三）配偶对遗产中家庭住房的先取权与终生使用权之特点与原因分析

第一，关于配偶对遗产中家庭住房的先取权与终生使用权的民间习惯，统计数据显示的特点是，在上海市被调查者所在地区，（1）有该习惯的占近九成（88.40%）；（2）无此习惯的仅占一成以上（11.60%）（见表4-23）。

以上特点的原因分析，在上海市被调查者所在地区，（1）近九成的地区有该继承习惯，其原因可能是为满足生存配偶维持原有婚姻家庭居住条件的现实需要，以期保障生存配偶及其抚养的未成年子女的生存权之实现；（2）还有一成以上的地区没有该习惯，其原因可能是受我国立法之影响。

第二，关于配偶对遗产中家庭住房的先取与终生使用是否付费的民间习惯，统计数据显示的特点是，在上海市被调查者所在地区，（1）适当补偿的占五成以上（52.98%）；（2）无须进行补偿的占四成半（45.14%），也就是说，如配偶无经济补偿能力的，可不予补偿而终生使用此房屋（见表4-24）。

以上特点的原因分析，根据上海市被调查者填写的配偶对遗产中家庭住房的先取与终生使用是否付费的民间习惯之理由（见表4-25），（1）五成以上的地区有支付一定费用的习惯，其原因是这符合法律规定且体现公平精神；（2）四成半的地区有无须支付费用的习惯，其原因是应首先保证乙有居住之所，同时丙是乙的儿子，将来乙的遗产也会由丙来继承，所以乙无须向丙进行补偿的，占近五成（48.48%）。

关于配偶对遗产中家庭住房的先取权与终生使用权之我国立法，我国《继承法》对此无规定。

从域外立法例看，部分国家立法规定了配偶对遗产中家庭住房享有先取权与终生使用权。例如，《瑞士民法典》第612条的规定，首先，生存配偶享有获得遗产中双方居住过的家庭住房及日常生活用品的优先权；其次，一定条件下家庭住房和日常生活用品的所有权可以转化为用益权或居住权。

从我国诸继承法学者建议稿看，关于配偶对遗产中家庭住房的先取权与终生使用权，“王稿”第580条规定：“被继承人的配偶尚生存而没有自己的住房的，如果没有继承继承人遗产中的房屋，则对于遗产中的房屋享有法定的用益物权。生存配偶为此需支付取得房屋所有权的继承人不超过市价的租金。具体租金数额及期限由配偶与房屋所有权人协商。协商不成的，双方均可以提起诉讼。”“徐稿”第四分编第289条规定：“如果用作居所的房屋和家具的所有权属于被继承人或属于配偶双方，则房屋的居住权以及使用家具的权利属于配偶。”

我们认为，在社会保障和福利体系尚未健全的今天，我国欠缺配偶对遗产中家庭住房的先取权与终生使用权，这是其立法之不足。婚姻关系不同于其他的社会关系，夫妻双方相互负有扶助之义务，而此种扶助义务在配偶一方死亡后转化为配偶对遗产分割享有的优先地位具有合理性。因此，上述主张规定该制度的上海市被调查民众的习惯、域外立法例和我国学者建议稿的观点，可供我国立法参考。

（四）后顺序特殊法定继承人对遗产中原使用的住房及日常生活用品的终生使用权之特点与原因分析

第一，关于后顺序特殊法定继承人对特殊遗产的终生使用权的民间习惯，统计数据显示的特点是，在上海市被调查者所在地区，（1）有该习惯的占九成以上（92.48%）；（2）没有该习惯的仅占不到一成（7.52%）（见表4-26）。

以上特点的原因分析，九成以上的上海市被调查者所在地区有该继承习惯，其原因可能是在传统家本位观念下，房屋住宅等财产被视为家族财产供家族共同居住和使用。虽然现在家族观念已经淡化，但是与祖父母和外祖父母共同生活、由孙子女赡养祖父母外祖父母的家庭仍然存在。因此，九成以上的被调查者所在地区仍然有此习惯，以保障他们的居住权。

第二，关于后顺序特殊继承人对特殊遗产终生使用是否付费及其期限的民间习惯，统计数据显示的特点是，在上海市被调查者所在地区，（1）对于费用情况，没有支付租金习惯的地区占八成半（85.89%）（见表4-27）；（2）对于期限情况，有终生使用习惯的地区占八成半（85.27%）（见表4-28）。

以上特点的原因分析，在上海市被调查者所在地区，（1）八成半的地区对此有无须支付租金的习惯，其原因可能是房屋居住对家庭中长辈收取租金会被认为是不孝的，不利于维护家庭关系的和谐；（2）八成半的地区有可以终生使用的习惯，其原因可能是保护后顺序特殊法定继承人居住权之需要，使老人可以安度晚年。

关于后顺序特殊法定继承人对特殊遗产的终生使用权之我国立法，我国《继承法》对此无规定。

从域外立法例看，除俄罗斯法在一定程度上体现了对后顺位继承人先取权的保护外，其他多数国家的先取权主体仍主要是配偶。例如，《俄罗斯联邦民法典》第1168条规定："如果遗产中的住房（房屋、住宅）等不能实物分割，则在遗产分割时，继承开始前居住在该处而且没有其他住房的继承人对于不是住房所有人的其他继承人享有作为其继承份额取得该住房的优先权。"此外，日本等国则采取了配偶无固定顺位继承的法定继承制度，第二顺位以及之后顺位继承人参与继承遗产的可能性更大，它们对配偶以外的其他血亲的继承权的保护力度更大。以祖父母外祖父母为首的后顺位特殊继承人在应召继承时，能够参与居住房屋以及其他生活用品的分割。相较而言，我国采取固定顺位的继承制度，只要被继承人存在第一顺位的继承人，后顺序继承人则无法参与法定继承。

从我国诸继承法学者建议稿看，"张稿"规定，父母因顺序在后未参加继承时，对遗产中供其个人日常生活使用的住房和其他物品有终生使用权①；"陈稿"规定的后顺序特殊法定继承人之范围较宽，其规定依靠被继承人扶养的法定继承人在未参加继承时，对遗产中供其个人日常生活使用的物品和住房享有终生使用权或用益权。②

我们认为，我国欠缺后顺序特殊法定继承人对特殊遗产的终生使用权，这是其立法之不足。而我国现行社会保险和福利还有待提高，家庭和家族仍然是养老育幼责任的主要承担者。一旦作为自己唯一生活保障者的晚辈去世，以祖父母和外祖父母等为代表的后顺序

① 参见"张稿"第33条。

② 参见"陈稿"第48条。

法定继承人的生活问题就是法律和社会必须关注、解决的问题。虽然我国现行《婚姻法》第28条已经规定："……有负担能力的孙子女、外孙子女，对于子女已经死亡或无力赡养的祖父母、外祖父母，有赡养义务。"而且，祖父母和外祖父母也可以依照我国《继承法》第14条[①]以缺乏劳动能力又无生活来源的身份酌分部分遗产。但是，这并不意味着后顺位特殊继承人的利益得到了充分保护，他们依然面对前顺序继承人分割遗产房屋后其可能无家可归的问题。因此，上述主张规定后顺序特殊继承人对特殊遗产终生使用权的上海市被调查民众的习惯、域外立法例和我国学者建议稿的观点，可供我国立法参考。

（五）尽了主要赡养义务的丧偶儿媳或女婿的遗产分配方式之特点与原因分析

关于尽了主要赡养义务的丧偶儿媳或女婿的遗产分配之民间习惯，统计数据显示的特点是，在上海市被调查者所在地区，（1）其可以与第一顺序继承人共同继承且平均分配遗产的，占七成（70.44%）；（2）其不能作为第一顺序继承人，但可以酌情分得遗产的，占二成半以上（26.42%）（见表4-29）。

以上特点的原因分析，根据上海市被调查者填写的尽了主要赡养义务的丧偶儿媳或女婿的遗产分配的民间习惯之理由（见表4-30），（1）七成的地区有其可以与第一顺序继承人共同继承遗产的习惯，其原因是根据权利义务相一致、秉持公平的理念其可以作为第一顺序继承人或丁作为儿媳，孝敬公公，已经尽了赡养义务，符合中国的孝道文化和道德观念，因此有权作为第一顺序继承人；（2）二成半以上的地区有其不能作为第一顺序继承人的习惯，其原因是虽然丁一直照顾公公的晚年生活，但毕竟不是某甲的子女，与某甲不具有血缘关系，遗产不能给"外人"。

关于尽了主要赡养义务的丧偶儿媳或女婿的遗产分配方式之我国立法，我国《继承法》第12条规定："丧偶儿媳对公、婆，丧偶女婿对岳父、岳母，尽了主要赡养义务的，作为第一顺序继承人。"

从域外立法例看，大多数国家的立法一般根据与被继承人血缘关系和亲属关系的远近来决定其参与继承的顺序，而儿媳和女婿为姻亲关系则根本不在传统继承人范围之内。我国将尽赡养义务的丧偶儿媳和女婿纳入法定继承人范围的做法来源于对前苏联民法典之借鉴。苏联是第一个将姻亲关系和扶养关系作为法定继承权取得的基础的国家。1964年开始施行的《苏俄民法典》第532条规定："在死亡人生前扶养不少于一年的无劳动能力的人也为法定继承人。在有其他继承人的情况下，他们与应召继承的其他继承人按同一顺序继承。"[②] 此立法被其他社会主义国家所效仿，如"南斯拉夫将与死者以某种长期结合的形式共同生活的特定类型的人也列入法定继承人的范围"。[③]

从我国诸继承法学者建议稿看，主要分为两种观点：一是，认为尽了主要赡养义务的丧偶儿媳或女婿应该作为第一顺序继承人。例如，"杨稿"规定丧偶儿媳或女婿对公婆或岳父母尽了主要赡养义务的，作为第一顺序继承人[④]；"王稿"规定丧偶儿媳或女婿对公

① 我国《继承法》第14条规定："对继承人以外的依靠被继承人扶养的缺乏劳动能力又没有生活来源的人，或者继承人以外的对被继承人扶养较多的人，可以分配给他们适当的遗产。"

② 参见中国社会科学院法学研究所民法研究室编：《苏俄民法典》，中国社会科学出版社1980年版，第172页。

③ 刘春茂著：《中国民法学·财产继承》，中国人民公安大学出版社1990年版，第134页。

④ 参见"杨稿"第60条。

婆或岳父母尽了主要赡养义务的，没有代位继承人时，作为第一顺序继承人。[①] 二是，尽了主要赡养义务的丧偶儿媳或女婿应作为酌分遗产请求权人。例如，“陈稿”规定偶儿媳或女婿对公婆或岳父母尽了主要赡养义务的，可以酌情分给适当财产。[②]

我们认为，尽管有学者提出将此条删去，取而代之的是将尽了赡养义务的儿媳和女婿纳入可以适当分得遗产的人的范围。[③] 但有学者提出，尽管世界上多数国家和地区未将尽了主要赡养义务的丧偶儿媳和女婿纳入法定继承人的范围，此立法是我国继承立法的特色之一，这是对中华人民共和国成立以来司法实践的总结和发展。[④] 所以，我们赞同维持我国《继承法》第 12 条的规定。

五、遗嘱继承之特点与原因分析

（一）公证遗嘱与其他形式遗嘱的效力之特点与原因分析

关于公证遗嘱与其他形式遗嘱效力的民众观念，统计数据显示的特点是，（1）认为后遗嘱的适用效力优先于前一公证遗嘱的，合计占近六成半（64.58%）；（2）认为公证遗嘱适用效力优先的，占三成半（35.42%）（见表 4-31）。

以上特点的原因分析，根据上海市被调查者填写的公证遗嘱与其他形式遗嘱效力的民众观念之理由（见表 4-32），（1）近六成半的人认为后遗嘱的适用效力优先于前一公证遗嘱，其原因是口头遗嘱形式灵活，且有证人作证，能够反映被继承人最后的真实意愿或书面遗嘱比较正式，取证容易，且其订立在公证遗嘱之后，也能反映被继承人的真实意愿；（2）三成半的人认为公证遗嘱的适用效力优先，其原因是公证遗嘱的程序规范，具有较强的公示效力和证明效力。

关于公证遗嘱与其他形式遗嘱的效力之我国立法，我国《继承法》第 20 条第 3 款规定：“自书、代书、录音、口头遗嘱，不得撤销、变更公证遗嘱。”1985 年《执行继承法意见》第 42 条也规定：“遗嘱人以不同形式立有数份内容相抵触的遗嘱，其中有公证遗嘱的，以最后所立公证遗嘱为准；没有公证遗嘱的，以最后所立的遗嘱为准。”

从域外立法例看，《日本民法典》规定：“之前遗嘱与之后遗嘱相抵触的，就该抵触的部分，视为之后遗嘱撤销之前遗嘱。”[⑤]《瑞士民法典》规定，如果立遗嘱人设立了新遗嘱，则即使该遗嘱未明确废除原遗嘱，也应视为新遗嘱取代了原遗嘱，但能够确定新遗嘱为原遗嘱之补充的除外。[⑥]

从我国诸继承法学者建议稿看，“梁稿”规定：“遗嘱人得以任何一种法定遗嘱形式撤销其在先前依其他法定形式所设立的遗嘱。”[⑦] “杨稿”规定：“立有数份遗嘱，内容相抵触的，以最后的遗嘱为准，前遗嘱抵触部分视为撤回。”[⑧]

---

① 参见“王稿”第 569 条。

② 参见“陈稿”第 50 条。

③ 梁慧星主编：《中国民法典草案建议稿附理由 · 继承编》，法律出版社 2013 年版，第 60~61 页；张玉敏主编：《中国继承法立法建议稿及立法理由》，人民出版社 2006 年版，第 85 页。

④ 何勤华、殷啸虎著：《中华人民共和国民法史》，复旦大学出版社 1999 年版，第 313 页。

⑤ 参见《日本民法典》第 1023 条。

⑥ 参见《瑞士民法典》第 511 条。

⑦ 参见“梁稿”第 1980 条。

⑧ 参见“杨稿”第 33 条。

我们认为，我国立法规定公证遗嘱具有最优先适用的效力，此为我国立法之不足。公证遗嘱相较于其他遗嘱形式，只是设立程序更为严格，经过了国家机关认可，赋予其诉讼过程中推定真实的效力即可。如果赋予公证遗嘱高于其他形式遗嘱遗嘱的效力，会使遗嘱人的遗嘱自由受到限制，遗嘱人只能够通过另设一份公证遗嘱的方法来消灭之前公证遗嘱作出的意思表示，不利于遗嘱人最后真实意思的表达。因此，上述主张后遗嘱适用效力优先于前一公证遗嘱的上海市被调查者的观念，域外立法例和我国学者建议稿的观点，可供我国立法参考。

（二）遗嘱自由的限制——特留份之特点与原因分析

关于以遗嘱将个人遗产全部赠给他人之民众观念，统计数据显示的特点是，对被继承人以遗嘱处分个人财产全部给第三人的行为，（1）认为不适当的占六成（60.50%）；（2）认为适当的占近三成半（34.48%）（见表4-33）。

以上特点的原因分析，根据上海市被调查者填写的以遗嘱将个人遗产全部赠给他人的民众观念之理由（见表4-34），（1）六成的人认为该行为不适当，其原因是此种行为会造成家庭财产外流，不利于保障配偶及其子女的生活，同时也不符合风俗习惯，为常人所难接受；（2）三成半的人认为该行为适当，其原因是遗嘱人甲对自己的财产，享有自由处分的权利，其他人无权干涉。

关于遗嘱自由与限制之我国立法，我国并未规定有特留份制度。我国《继承法》第19条规定："遗嘱应当对缺乏劳动能力又没有生活来源的继承人保留必要的遗产份额。"即我国立法规定了必留份制度，缺乏劳动能力又无生活来源的继承人可以获得必要遗产份额。特留份与必留份制度都对遗嘱自由权的行使进行了限制，但是二者保护的对象有着显著不同。必留份保护的则是存在特定情势的继承人，从各国立法例来看一般包括受被继承人扶养的人、无劳动能力的人等。而特留份则旨在维护以血缘和婚姻为基础的家庭伦理理念，此时限制遗嘱自由的目的是肯定和维护以配偶、子女等为代表的被继承人法定继承人的情感和利益。

从域外立法例看，多数国家设立了特留份制度。例如，《法国民法典》第913条规定："如财产处分时仅留有子女1人，其可以通过生前赠与或遗嘱无偿处分的财产部分不超过其全部财产的二分之一；如处分人留有子女2人，其有权以此种方式无偿处分的财产部分不得超过其全部财产的三分之一；如留有子女3人或3人以上，可以无偿处分的财产不得超过本人所有的财产的四分之一。"[①]《德国民法典》第2303条规定："被继承人的晚辈直系血亲被死因处分排除在继承顺序之外的，该晚辈直系血亲可以向继承人请求特留份。特留份为法定继承份的价额的一半。被继承人的父母或配偶被死因处分排除在继承顺序之外的，享有同样的权利。"

从我国诸继承法学者建议稿看，"梁稿"第1962条规定："第一顺序的法定继承人的特留份为其应继份的二分之一。第二顺序的法定继承人的特留份为其应继份的三分之一。特留份的继承顺序准用法定继承人的继承顺序。""王稿"第585条规定："遗嘱人设立遗嘱时，必须为下列法定继承人预留本法规定的份额。第一顺序法定继承人的特留份为其应继份的二分之一；第二顺序法定继承人的特留份为其应继份的三分之一；除本法有特别规

① 参见《法国民法典》第913条。

定外，特留份权适用本法关于法定继承的规定。”

我们认为，我国立法没有规定特留份制度，是其立法之不足。我国目前只建立了必留份制度，但是随着经济之发展，除了未成年人和残疾人外，实务中符合缺乏劳动能力又无生活来源的人很少，只建立必留份制度难以实现延续近亲扶养义务之功能。而且，特留份的立法宗旨也与必留份略有差异，特留份旨在维系亲情伦理，“根本原因在于对个人意志自由的保护不能突破伦理道德的底线”。[①] 因此，上述主张设立特留份制度的上海市被调查民众的观念，域外立法例和我国学者建议稿的观点，可供我国立法参考。

（三）夫妻共同遗嘱之特点与原因分析

关于夫妻共同遗嘱的民众观念与民间习惯，统计数据显示的特点是，对于夫妻设立共同遗嘱，（1）在上海市被调查者的观念上，表示赞同的，占六成（60.19%），表示不赞同的，占近四成（39.81%）（见表4-35）；（2）被调查者所在地区的继承习惯是：无该习惯的占八成以上（82.45%）；有该习惯的占近二成（17.55%）（见表4-37）。

以上特点的原因分析，根据上海市被调查者填写的夫妻共同遗嘱的民众观念之理由（见表4-36），（1）六成的人赞同设立夫妻共同遗嘱，近二成的地区有该习惯，其原因是该遗嘱为夫妻双方共同设立，反映了双方的共同意愿，理应为双方所遵守；（2）近四成的人不赞同设立夫妻共同遗嘱，八成以上的地区没有该习惯，其原因是该遗嘱无法应对出现的新情况和新问题，限制了双方对各自财产的处分权。

关于夫妻共同遗嘱之我国立法，我国《遗嘱公证细则》一定程度上体现出承认共同遗嘱的效力。我国《遗嘱公证细则》第15条规定：“两个以上的遗嘱人申请办理共同遗嘱公证的，公证处应当引导他们分别设立遗嘱。遗嘱人坚持申请办理共同遗嘱公证的，共同遗嘱中应当明确遗嘱变更、撤销及生效的条件。”

从域外立法例看，一些国家对共同遗嘱的态度大相径庭。德国等国家承认共同遗嘱的合法性。在德国，共同遗嘱只能够由配偶双方做出，未经登记的同居伴侣、兄弟姐妹等不是共同遗嘱的适格行为人。此外，《德国民法典》还规定：“配偶双方已在共同遗嘱中为处分，而由这些处分须认为假如没有配偶另一方的处分，配偶一方就不会为之的，其中一项处分之无效或被撤回，导致另一项处分之不生效力。配偶双方互相使对方受益，或一方向另一方做出的有利于与后者有血统关系或以其他方式与之有亲近关系者的处分，有疑义时，应认为这些处分具有第一款规定的相互关联性。”可见，德国民法不仅承认共同遗嘱的效力，还规定了共同遗嘱关联性处分的效力。对于因另一方配偶处分而为的处分或者互相使对方收益及对配偶一方的给予，在另一方处分无效或者被撤回之时，该处分不产生法律效力。日本等国对共同遗嘱的态度却截然相反，《日本民法典》第975条规定：“遗嘱不得由二名以上的人用同一证书订立。”[②]《法国民法典》第968条也禁止设立共同遗嘱，其规定：“二人或数人不得用同一文书为第三人受益或者以相互处分遗产的名义订立遗嘱。”[③]

从我国诸继承法学者建议稿看，有学者建议将夫妻共同遗嘱入法。例如，“杨稿”第

① 许莉：《我国继承法应增设特留份制度》，载《法学》2012年第8期。

② 参见《日本民法典》第975条。

③ 参见《法国民法典》第968条。

36 条规定："但夫妻双方订立同一遗嘱，符合法律关于遗嘱有效条件要求的，应当认定为有效。共同遗嘱的效力以配偶一方死亡前婚姻关系存续为前提……"①

我们认为，与一般遗嘱相比，共同遗嘱实质上是双方法律行为，而且是共同行为，双方或多方民事主体的意思表示一致且方向相同内容同一。这就意味着，与一般遗嘱可以自主决定变更和撤销不同，共同遗嘱的成立变更和撤销受到了其他共同遗嘱人意志的限制，这不利于保障遗嘱人变更或撤销遗嘱之自由。因此，我国立法对夫妻共同遗嘱不予规定为宜。

六、继承和遗赠的接受与放弃之特点与原因分析

（一）继承的接受与放弃的时间与方式之特点与原因分析

第一，关于继承的接受与放弃时间的民众观念，统计数据显示的特点是，在被调查者中，继承人接受或放弃继承的意思表示，（1）应当在遗产处理前作出的，占近六成半（63.33%）；（2）应在知道继承开始的 2 个月内作出的，占三成半以上（36.67%）（见表 4-38）。

以上特点的原因分析，根据上海市被调查者填写的继承的接受与放弃时间的民众观念之理由（见表 4-39），（1）近六成半的人认为继承人接受或放弃继承应在遗产处理前作出意思表示，原因是在遗产处理前确定继承权问题，便于处理遗产，减少后续纠纷；（2）三成半以上的人认为继承人接受或放弃继承应在知道继承开始的 2 个月内作出意思表示，原因是需要给继承人一定的考虑时间，且 2 个月长短较为合适的。

第二，关于继承的接受与放弃方式的民间习惯，统计数据显示的特点是，在被调查者所在地区，（1）遗产分割前以书面或口头的方式明确表示拒绝继承的，占七成以上（73.00%）；（2）不予表示，也不参加遗产分割视为放弃的，占近三成（27.00%）（见表 4-40）。也就是说，七成以上的被调查者认为放弃继承应以明示方式作出，未作表示的，视为接受继承，此与我国立法相一致。

以上特点的原因分析，在上海市被调查者所在地区，（1）七成以上的地区有通过书面或口头的方式放弃继承的习惯，其原因可能是书面放弃继承更为正式，而口头的方式放弃继承更为简便；（2）近三成的地区有不表示，也不参加遗产分割视为放弃继承的习惯，其原因可能是继承人不参与遗产分割，即通过不参加继承的不作为方式，反映了其放弃继承的内心意愿。

关于继承的接受与放弃的时间与方式之我国立法，我国《继承法》第 25 条第 1 款规定："继承开始后，继承人放弃继承的，应当在遗产处理前，作出放弃继承的表示。没有表示的，视为接受继承。" 1985 年《执行继承法意见》第 47 条规定："继承人放弃继承应当以书面形式向其他继承人表示。用口头方式表示放弃继承，本人承认，或有其他充分证据证明的，也应当认定其有效。"第 49 条规定："继承人放弃继承的意思表示，应当在继承开始后、遗产分割前作出。遗产分割后表示放弃的不再是继承权，而是所有权。"

从域外立法例看，《日本民法典》规定，继承人应自知有为自己继承开始之时起 3 个月以内，为单纯或限定的承认，或者表示放弃，但此期间，因利害关系人或检察官的请

---

① 杨立新著：《继承法修订入典之重点问题》，中国法制出版社 2015 年版，第 256 页。

求，得由家庭法院予以延长，其放弃的方式是将其意旨向家庭法院申述①；《德国民法典》规定，在继承开始时，继承人即可作出接受或放弃的表示，在知悉继承开始后6个星期内可以为拒绝，拒绝的方式是以意思表示向遗产法院表示，不拒绝则视为接受。②

从我国诸继承法学者建议稿看，"梁稿"认为："继承人放弃继承的，应当在知道继承开始后两个月内以书面形式作出放弃继承的意思表示；逾期未表示的，视为接受继承。"③"张稿"认为："自继承人知道自己为应召继承人时起，或者自遗嘱开启时起2个月内，继承人可以声明放弃继承或者以制作遗产清单的方式接受继承（限定继承）。继承人在国外的，上述期限为6个月。"

我们认为，虽然近六成半的上海市被调查者认为，在遗产处理前作出接受或放弃继承的意思表示即可，但是出于尽快确定遗产权利或义务人，以便更好保护当事人利益考量，遗产接受或放弃的时间规定一个具体期限为宜。因此，上述主张明确继承的接受时间的上海市被调查者的观念，域外立法例和我国学者建议稿的观点，可供我国立法参考。至于接受或放弃继承的具体方式，可以不予规定，由继承人根据自身情况自由选择适合的方式即可。

（二）遗赠的接受与放弃的方式与效力之特点与原因分析

关于遗赠的接受与放弃的方式与效力的民众观念与民间习惯，统计数据显示的特点是，（1）在上海市被调查者的观念上，认为受遗赠人不作表示应视为接受遗赠的，占七成以上（72.43%），认为受遗赠人不作表示应视为放弃遗赠的，占近三成（27.57%）（见表4-41）；（2）被调查者所在地区的继承习惯是：接受遗赠必须明示否则视为放弃受遗赠的，占近五成半（54.17%）；不作表示也可视为接受遗赠的，占四成半（45.83%）（见表4-43）。

以上特点的原因分析，根据上海市被调查者填写的遗赠的接受与放弃的方式与效力的民众观念之理由（见表4-42），（1）七成以上的人认为受遗赠人不作表示可以被视为接受遗赠，四成半的地区也有该习惯，其原因是遗赠是单方行为，遗赠人作出即生效，不需要接受表示或这有利于受遗赠人的利益；（2）近三成的人认为受遗赠人不作表示应被视为放弃遗赠，近五成半的地区也有该习惯，其原因是此为受遗赠人额外获得的利益，应当主动表示接受，否则视为拒绝该获益。

关于遗赠的接受与放弃的方式与效力之我国立法，我国《继承法》第25条第2款规定："受遗赠人应当在知道受遗赠后两个月内，作出接受或者放弃受遗赠的表示。到期没有表示的，视为放弃接受遗赠。"

从域外立法例看，《法国民法典》规定，受遗赠人应当提出请求转移遗赠财产或者自愿同意接受转移的遗赠财产；在受遗赠人拒绝受领或丧失受领能力的情况下，遗赠失去效力。④《意大利民法典》规定，遗赠不需要承认而取得，遗赠的标的，在遗嘱人死亡瞬间从遗嘱人移转于受遗赠人。⑤

① 参见《日本民法典》第915、938条。

② 参见《德国民法典》第1943、1944、1945、1946条。

③ 参见"梁稿"第2008条。

④ 参见《法国民法典》第1042、1043条。

⑤ 参见《意大利民法典》第649条。

从我国诸继承法学者建议稿看，“梁稿”规定：“受遗赠人接受遗赠的，应当在知道受遗赠后两个月内作出接受遗赠的意思表示；逾期未表示的，视为放弃受遗赠。”① 此沿用我国现行法的规定。“陈稿”规定：“受遗赠人在遗赠人死亡以后，可表示放弃接受遗赠，放弃的效力溯及至遗赠后1年内作出，1年内未作出的视为接受遗赠。”②

我们认为，我国有关遗赠的接受方式与效力之规定存在不足。因此，上述主张受遗赠人未作出表示应被视为接受遗赠的上海市被调查民众的观念与习惯、域外立法例和我国学者建议稿的观点，可供我国立法参考。

（三）继承的放弃与债权人的撤销权之特点与原因分析

关于继承的放弃能否被债权人撤销的民众观念与民间习惯，统计数据显示的特点是，（1）在上海市被调查者的观念上，认为不可以被债权人撤销的，占近五成半（53.37%）；而认为可以被债权人撤销的，占四成半以上（46.63%）（见表4-44）；（2）被调查者所在地区的继承习惯是：可以被债权人撤销的，占六成半以上（66.67%）；不可以被债权人撤销的，占近三成半（33.33%）（见表4-45）。

以上特点的原因分析，根据上海市被调查者填写的继承的放弃能否被债权人撤销的民间习惯之理由（见表4-46），（1）近五成半的人认为该行为不可以被债权人撤销，近三成半的地区也有该习惯，其原因是继承人有权放弃自己的继承权，他人无权任意干涉；（2）四成半以上的人认为该行为可以被债权人撤销，六成半以上的地区也有该习惯，其原因是要保护债权人的利益或防止恶意逃避债务的情形。

关于继承的放弃与债权人的撤销权之我国立法，我国《继承法》对此无规定。1985年《执行继承法意见》第46条规定：“继承人因放弃继承权，致其不能履行法定义务的，放弃继承权的行为无效。”但这并不是债权人撤销的结果，而是行为本身无效的问题。

从域外立法例看，关于这一问题也存在不同立法模式。《法国民法典》规定，因继承人抛弃继承而受到损害之债权人，得请求法院授权其以债务人之名义，取代债务人之地位接受继承③，即认为继承的放弃具有相对效力，债权人可以撤销。而《德国民法典》对此未作规定，但通说认为继承之抛弃行为不得为债权人撤销权之标的。

从我国诸继承法学者建议稿看，“梁稿”认为：“继承人放弃继承损害其债权人利益的，债权人可以在知道或者应当知道继承人放弃继承之日起六个月内申请人民法院作出放弃继承无效的裁定，但继承人提供充分担保的除外。”④ “王稿”认为：“继承人放弃继承损害其债权人利益的，债权人可以在知道或者应当知道继承人放弃继承之日起六个月内申请人民法院撤销继承人的放弃行为。”⑤

我们认为，我国立法没有规定债权人是否可以撤销继承人放弃继承的行为，这是其立法不足。因此，上述主张债权人享有撤销权的上海市被调查民众的观念与习惯、域外立法例和我国学者建议稿的观点，可供我国立法参考。

---

① 参见“梁稿”第2008条。

② 参见“陈稿”第59条。

③ 参见《法国民法典》第788条。

④ 参见“梁稿”第2012条。

⑤ 参见“王稿”第562条。

七、继承权的丧失、被继承人的宥恕与代位继承之特点与原因分析

（一）继承权的丧失与被继承人的宥恕之特点与原因分析

关于继承权的丧失与被继承人的宥恕的民众观念与民间习惯，统计数据显示的特点是，（1）在上海市被调查者的观念上，对于继承人因欺诈或者胁迫而丧失继承权，可否因被继承人宥恕而恢复继承权，认为可以恢复的，占七成以上（72.20%），而认为不可以恢复的，占近三成（27.80%）（见表4-47）；（2）被调查者所在地区的继承习惯是：某甲的行为使其丧失了继承权，但被继承人的原谅可以使某甲恢复继承权的，占近七成半（73.80%），某甲因欺诈胁迫被继承人而确定丧失继承资格并不可恢复的，占近一成半（14.20%）（见表4-49）。

以上特点的原因分析，根据上海市被调查者填写的继承权的丧失与被继承人的宥恕的民众观念之理由（见表4-48），（1）七成以上的人认为该情况继承权可以恢复，近七成半的地区也有该习惯，其原因是某甲的行为使其丧失了继承权，但乙的原谅可以使某甲恢复继承权或乙对自己的遗产有自由处分权，他想留给某甲，某甲就应该可以继承遗产；（2）近三成的人认为继承权不可以恢复，近一成半的地区也有该习惯，其原因是某甲的行为造成恶劣影响，即便得到乙的原谅，也应当丧失继承权。

关于继承权的丧失与被继承人的宥恕之我国立法，我国《继承法》第7条规定：“继承人有下列行为之一的，丧失继承权：（一）故意杀害被继承人的；（二）为争夺遗产而杀害其他继承人的；（三）遗弃被继承人的，或者虐待被继承人情节严重的；（四）伪造、篡改或者销毁遗嘱，情节严重的。”1985年《执行继承法意见》第13条规定：“继承人虐待被继承人情节严重的，或者遗弃被继承人的，如以后确有悔改表现，而且被虐待人、被遗弃人生前又表示宽恕，可不确认其丧失继承权。”但对于继承人因欺诈、胁迫丧失继承权，获得被继承人宥恕后可否恢复继承权，我国立法没有规定。

从域外立法例看，多规定了继承权的丧失情形，但各国规定继承权丧失的法定事由有所不同。德国法规定继承权的丧失事由有故意或者违法地致被继承人死亡，故意或违法地妨碍被继承人为死因处分或者撤销死因处分，以恶意欺诈或违法地以胁迫促使被继承人为死因处分或者撤销死因处分等。[①] 日本法规定继承权的丧失事由有故意杀害被继承人或先顺位、同顺位继承人，知被继承人被杀害而不告发或者告诉，以欺诈或胁迫妨碍或者使被继承人订立、撤销或者变更关于继承的遗嘱，伪造、变造、破毁或者隐匿被继承人关于继承的遗嘱者。[②]

从我国诸继承法学者建议稿看，“梁稿”建议将遗嘱欺诈或胁迫行为作为继承权相对丧失的情形之一，并认为应当明确除为争夺遗产而杀害其他继承人的，属于继承权的绝对丧失，其余情形均为相对丧失。[③]

我们认为，将遗嘱欺诈或胁迫行为纳入继承权的丧失的法定情形之一，并可以因获得被继承人宥恕而恢复继承权，是存在法理基础和民众基础的。我国立法没有对此作出规

① 参见《德国民法典》第2339条。

② 参见《日本民法典》第891条。

③ 参见“梁稿”第1940条。

定，这是其立法之不足。因此，上述主张该种情形下可以恢复继承权的上海市被调查民众的观念与习惯、域外立法例和我国学者建议稿的观点，可供我国立法参考。

（二）继承权的丧失与代位继承之特点与原因分析

关于继承权丧失的效力是否及于代位继承人的民众观念与民间习惯，统计数据显示的特点是，（1）在上海市被调查者的观念上，认为效力及于代位继承人的，占五成半（55.20%），而认为效力不能及于代位继承人的，占近四成半（44.80%）（见表4-50）；（2）被调查者所在地区的继承习惯是：效力不及于代位继承人的，占近六成（58.10%）；效力及于代位继承人的，占四成以上（41.90%）（见表4-51）。

以上特点的原因分析，根据上海市被调查者填写的继承权丧失的效力是否及于代位继承人的民众观念之理由（见表4-52），（1）五成半的人认为效力及于代位继承人，四成以上的地区也有该习惯，其原因是孙子丙是代替父亲乙继承祖父的遗产，而乙已经丧失继承权，丙代位继承的前提丧失，所以丙不能继承祖父的遗产；（2）近四成半的人认为效力不及于代位继承人，近六成的地区也有该习惯，其原因是丙以孙子的身份来继承祖父的遗产，有独立的继承权，与父亲乙丧失继承权无关，所以丙可以继承祖父的遗产。

关于继承权的丧失与代位继承权之我国立法，1985年《执行继承法意见》第28条规定："继承人丧失继承权的，其晚辈直系血亲不得代位继承。"

从域外立法例看，德国、法国、瑞士、意大利等国家均明确规定，继承人丧失继承权的，其晚辈直系血亲仍有代位继承权，但该继承人丧失对其子女继承遗产的用益权。① 例如，《意大利民法典》第465条规定，丧失继承权的父母，其子女仍可以代位继承遗产，父母不再享有法律赋予的用益权和管理权。

从我国诸继承法学者建议稿看，"梁稿""王稿""杨稿""张稿"和"陈稿"均规定继承人丧失继承权的，不影响其子女代位继承。② 例如，"王稿"第572条规定："被继承人的子女在继承开始前先于或同时与被继承人死亡的或者丧失继承权的，由被继承人子女的直系卑亲属代位继承。"

我们认为，我国立法有关继承权的丧失与代位继承之规定存在不足。考虑"固有权说"能够彰显现代民法之"自己责任原则"，因此，上述主张可以代位继承的上海市被调查民众的观念与习惯、域外立法例和我国学者建议稿的观点，可供我国立法参考。

八、继承协议之特点与原因分析

（一）继承协议的订立主体与方式之特点与原因分析

关于继承协议的订立主体与方式的民众观念，统计数据显示的特点是，（1）认为继承协议应由被扶养人与全部继承人共同协商签订的，占近六成（59.06%）；（2）认为继承协议应由被扶养人与扶养人协商签订的，占近二成半（24.38%）；（3）认为由继承人间协商签订继承协议即可，无须被扶养人知晓或同意的，仅占一成半以上（16.56%）（见表4-53）。

---

① 参见《德国民法典》第1924、2096条；《法国民法典》第728条；《瑞士民法典》第541条；《意大利民法典》第465条。

② 参见"梁稿"第1951条；"王稿"第572条；"杨稿"第17条；"张稿"第13条；"陈稿"第19条。

以上特点的原因分析，根据上海市被调查者填写的继承协议的订立主体与方式的民众观念之理由（见表4-54），（1）近六成的人认为继承协议应由被扶养人与全部继承人共同协商签订，其原因是共同协商处理更利于减少纠纷，有利于维护老人生活的安定；（2）近二成半的人认为继承协议应由被扶养人与扶养人协商签订，其原因是这符合被继承人意愿，有利于老人的晚年生活；（3）占一成半以上的人认为由共同继承人间协商签订继承协议即可，其原因是继承人共同商议赡养问题和遗产分配问题，这符合意思自治，不易引起纠纷。

关于继承协议制度之我国立法，我国《继承法》第31条规定："公民可以与扶养人签订遗赠扶养协议。按照协议，扶养人承担该公民生养死葬的义务，享有受遗赠的权利。公民可以与集体所有制组织签订遗赠扶养协议。按照协议，集体所有制组织承担该公民生养死葬的义务，享有受遗赠的权利。"目前，我国仅规定了遗赠扶养协议，没规定继承协议制度。但两者存在区别：前者的订立主体是被继承人与法定继承人以外的人或组织，后者是被继承人与法定继承人。

从域外立法例看，《德国民法典》明确规定了继承合同制度。① 继承合同的订立主体是有完全行为能力的被继承人，合同另一方当事人则为部分或全部法定继承人。继承合同只能由公证人做成记录，在双方当事人同时在场的情况下订立，此为形式要求。继承合同可以撤销、废止、解除和变更。《瑞士民法典》规定，处分人可以通过继承协议将遗产或遗赠物留给协议另一方或第三人。②

从我国诸继承法学者建议稿看，"张稿"第54条规定："被继承人可以与共同继承人订立继承合同，约定由一个继承人或几个继承人承担赡养（扶养）被继承人的义务，被继承人死亡后，由承担赡养（扶养）义务的继承人按照合同继承遗产。合同对赡养（扶养）人继承遗产的部分未做明确约定的，视为继承全部遗产。""杨稿"第69条规定："被继承人可以与继承人订立继承扶养协议，由继承人承担比法定扶养义务更高的扶养义务，并继承约定的遗产。"

我们认为，我国欠缺继承协议制度，这是其立法之不足，不能满足部分被继承人作为受扶养人想与子女（法定继承人）签订继承协议之需要。因此，上述主张规定该制度的上海市被调查民众的观念、域外立法例和我国学者建议稿的观点，可供我国立法参考。

（二）继承协议的变更方式与效力之特点与原因分析

关于继承协议的变更方式与效力的民众观念，统计数据显示的特点是，（1）认为该协议可有条件继续履行，如原扶养人的子女有扶养能力，在原扶养人的子女和被扶养人双方同意的情况下，可由原扶养人的子女继续履行该继承协议的，此即代位扶养的，占四成以上（42.81%）；（2）认为该协议效力终止，须签订新的继承协议，由新的扶养人履行扶养义务并继承遗产，合计占三成半（35.31%），其中，认为需要对原扶养人的继承人补偿超过其扶养义务部分费用的，占近二成半（24.69%），认为不需要对原扶养人的继承人补偿超过其扶养义务部分费用的，占一成（10.62%）；（3）认为该协议效力终止，应补偿原扶养人的继承人补偿超过其扶养义务部分费用后，由所有法定继承人共同扶养，

① 参见《德国民法典》第2274~2302条。

② 参见《瑞士民法典》第494条。

即实行法定赡养的，占近二成（19.38%）（见表4-55）。

以上特点的原因分析，根据上海市被调查者填写的继承协议的变更方式与效力的民众观念之理由（见表4-56），（1）四成以上的人认为继承协议可有条件继续履行，其原因是这有利于维持原扶养人一贯的生活方式，使其安度晚年；（2）合计近四成半的人认为对原扶养人应补偿一定费用，其原因是基于公平和诚实信用原则；（3）一成的人认为对原扶养人无须进行补偿，其原因是应遵从继承协议的效力，如其效力已终止即无须再进行补偿。

关于继承协议的变更方式及效力之我国立法，我国《继承法》对此无规定。

从域外立法例看，《德国民法典》规定，被继承人可以在订立合同的当事人另一方死亡后，以被继承人有权解除为限，以遗嘱废止合于合同的处分①；《瑞士民法典》规定，继承人或受遗赠人在处分人之前先死亡的，继承协议自然解除。②

从我国诸继承法学者建议稿看，部分建议稿没有规定继承协议变更的具体方式。在已经规定了变更方式的建议稿中，"徐稿"第四分编第516条、"陈稿"第65条规定继承协议中扶养人一方先于被扶养人死亡后合同即可解除③，"陈稿"同时还规定了继承协议解除的效力，即受扶养人应当对扶养人已经履行的扶养义务适当支付补偿费用。④

我们认为，我国欠缺继承协议制度及其变更方式等具体内容，这是其立法之不足。因此，上述主张规定继承协议变更方式的上海市被调查民众的观念、域外立法例和我国学者建议稿的观点，可供我国立法参考。

九、遗产债务清偿之特点与原因分析

（一）遗产债务清偿责任的类型之特点与原因分析

第一，关于遗产债务清偿责任的类型之民众观念，统计数据显示的特点是，（1）主张实行自愿的无限清偿责任的，合计占近七成（67.50%）；（2）主张实行有限清偿责任的，占六成以上（61.10%）；（3）主张实行强制的无限清偿责任的，占近四成半（44.00%）（见表4-57）。

以上特点的原因分析，在上海市被调查者中，其一，近七成的人主张实行自愿的无限清偿责任，其原因可能是我国民间和传统文化中有"父债子偿"的继承观念；其二，六成以上的人主张实行有限清偿责任，其原因可能是受我国立法之影响。其三，近四成半的人主张对有侵害遗产违法行为者应当实行强制的无限清偿责任，其原因可能是有转移、隐瞒遗产等行为的继承人侵害了债权人的合法权益，应对其进行惩戒，以防止侵害遗产行为的发生。

第二，关于继承人侵害遗产的法律责任之民间习惯，统计数据显示的特点是，在被调查者所在地区，继承人有转移、隐瞒遗产情况时，（1）对被继承人的生前所有债务，继承人都应当予以偿还的，占近六成（58.82%）；（2）继承人仍然只在继承财产的范围内进行清偿的，占近三成（29.41%）；（3）对超过遗产偿付限度外的被继承人生前债务，

① 参见《德国民法典》第2297条。
② 参见《瑞士民法典》第515条。
③ 参见"徐稿"第四分编第516条；"陈稿"第65条；"张稿"第55条。
④ 参见"陈稿"第65条。

由有转移、隐瞒遗产等行为的继承人予以偿还的，占一成以上（11.77%）（见表4-58）。

以上特点的原因分析，根据上海市被调查者填写的继承人侵害遗产法律责任的民间习惯之理由（见表4-59），(1) 近六成的地区继承人有转移、隐瞒遗产情况时，有所有继承人都应当予以偿还的习惯，其原因是这利于保护债权人的合法权益；(2) 近三成的地区继承人有转移、隐瞒遗产情况时，有仍然只在继承财产的范围内进行清偿的习惯，其原因是我国立法规定如此；(3) 一成以上的人认为继承人有转移、隐瞒遗产情况时，有由有过错行为的继承人予以偿还的习惯，其原因是这符合自己责任原则。

关于遗产债务清偿责任的类型之我国立法，我国《继承法》第33条规定："继承遗产应当清偿被继承人依法应当缴纳的税款和债务，缴纳税款和清偿债务以他的遗产实际价值为限。超过遗产实际价值部分，继承人自愿偿还的不在此限。"可见，我国《继承法》规定的是无条件的限定清偿责任制度和自愿的无限责任制度。1985年《执行继承法意见》第59条规定："人民法院对故意隐匿、侵吞或争抢遗产的继承人，可以酌情减少其应继承的遗产。"

从域外立法例看，大陆法系不少国家规定的遗产债务的清偿责任都包括两大类型，一是有限清偿责任；二是无限清偿责任，包括自愿的无限清查责任和强制的无限清偿责任。[①] 例如，法国法规定，(1) 有限清偿责任，继承人欲表明其限定承认之取得继承人资格之声明，应向其辖区内的法院书记室作出，继承人得自继承开始之日起3个月内提出声明[②]；(2) 自愿的无限清偿责任，"遗产继承，得为单纯承认，或者为限定承认"[③]；(3) 强制的无限清偿责任，继承人如隐匿属于遗产之财产，或故意并恶意将属于遗产的财产漏记或不计入遗产清册，即丧失享有有限责任继承之权利，应对遗产债务承担无限清偿责任。[④]

从我国诸继承法学者建议稿看，第一，主张设立有限清偿责任、自愿的无限清偿责任和损害赔偿责任的有"梁稿"和"王稿"。例如，"梁稿"第2018条规定，催告期届满后，继承人和遗产管理人应当依据已申报的债权和其他已知债权的数额或比例，以遗产分别偿还，对遗产享有担保物权的债权人可以实行担保物权；第2019条规定，继承人或者遗产管理人违反规定，对遗产债权人和受遗赠人造成损害的，应承担赔偿责任。第二，主张同时设立有条件的有限清偿责任、自愿的无限清偿责任、强制的无限清偿责任及损害赔偿责任的有"陈稿"、"张稿"和"杨稿"。例如，"陈稿"第69条规定："（一）遗产债务的有限清偿责任，对被继承人的债务，继承人自愿选择实行有条件的限定继承且依法制作遗产清册的，仅在遗产的实际价值范围内承担有限清偿责任。（二）遗产债务的无限清偿责任，对被继承人的债务，继承人自愿选择实行无条件概括继承的，如果遗产的实际价值不足以清偿债务的，应当以继承人个人所有的财产承担无限清偿责任。（三）遗产债务的连带清偿责任，对被继承人的债务，共同继承人应当承担连带清偿责任。"第72条第1款规定了遗产管理人和继承人对遗产债权人的损害赔偿责任，"遗产管理人和继承人在任

① 参见陈苇主编：《中国遗产处理制度系统化构建研究》，中国人民公安大学出版社2019年版，第300~304、306~307页。

② 《法国民法典》第782、793~795条。

③ 《法国民法典》第774条。

④ 《法国民法典》第792、801条。

何时间都应当支付遗产债权人提出的合法请求。有下列情形之一的，遗产管理人和继承人应对因其支付行为受到损害的遗产债权之请求人承担个人赔偿责任”。

我们认为，我国欠缺继承人恶意转移遗产、损害其他债权人利益的赔偿责任，这是其立法之不足。因此，上述主张增加强制的遗产债务无限清偿责任的上海市被调查民众的观念、域外立法例和我国学者建议稿的观点，可供我国立法参考。

（二）被继承人丧葬费的支付之特点与原因分析

关于被继承人丧葬费支付的民间习惯，统计数据显示的特点是，在被调查者所在地区，（1）由全体继承人共同支付的，占五成以上（51.80%）；（2）从被继承人的遗产中支付的，占近四成半（43.20%）（见表4-60）。

以上特点的原因分析，在上海市被调查者所在地区，（1）五成以上的地区有继承人共同支付丧葬费的习惯，其原因可能是这符合我国传统的家庭道德，继承人承担丧葬费是对被继承人尽“生养死葬”的义务之要求；（2）还有近四成半的地区有丧葬费由被继承人从遗产中支付的习惯，其原因可能是这符合各共同继承人的利益。

关于被继承人丧葬费的支付方式之我国立法，我国《继承法》对此无规定。

从域外立法例看，对于丧葬费用主要有两种立法例，一是，丧葬费应从遗产中支付。例如，《俄罗斯联邦民法典》第1174条规定，丧葬费应由继承人支付。又如，《德国民法典》第1968条明确规定，被继承人与其社会地位相称的殡葬费用，由继承人负担。

从我国诸继承法学者建议稿看，亦存在两种观点，一是，丧葬费应从遗产中支付。例如，“陈稿”规定，继承费用，包括合理的丧葬费用、制作遗产目录、发布公告继承的通知或公告、清点和保管遗产所必要的费用、遗产分割的费用、执行遗嘱的费用等属于被继承人遗留的个人债务，即遗产债务。[①] 二是，丧葬费应由继承人支付。例如，“王稿”规定，被继承人的、与其社会地位相称的丧葬费用，由继承人负担。[②]

我们认为，结合立法实践需求，充分平衡制度的实践价值和可行性，再决定是否规定死者丧葬费用的支付方式。该问题本质上属于私权事务，法律并不需要面面俱到地规定，应尊重民事主体的自由决定和选择。

（三）遗产债务的清偿顺序之特点与原因分析

关于遗产债务清偿顺序的民间习惯，统计数据显示的特点是，遗产债务应按如下顺序清偿：第一顺序为“丧葬费用”（65.36%）；第二顺序“遗产管理等费用”（23.31%）、“欠付的工资”（22.00%）；第三顺序“欠债”（30.50%）；第四顺序“受被继承人扶养人的生活费”（15.03%）；第五顺序“税款”（10.46%）；第六顺序“对被继承人扶养较多的人之酌情分配遗产份额”（17.65%）；第七顺序“遗赠扶养协议写明遗赠的遗产”（13.29%）（见表4-61）。

以上特点的原因分析，（1）优先清偿丧葬费和遗产管理等费用，其原因可能是二者属于共益性费用，由全体继承人优先清偿，符合公平原则；（2）欠付的工资优先于欠债受到清偿，其原因可能是工资一般为维系家庭生活的必须费用，优先清偿有助于保障职工等群体的基本生存权；（3）受被继承人扶养人的生活费优先于税款受到清偿，其原因可

① 参见“陈稿”第68条。

② 参见“王稿”第651条。

能是认为个人利益应优先于国家利益收到清偿；（4）但对被继承人扶养较多的人之酌情分配遗产份额优先于遗赠扶养协议写明遗赠的遗产受到清偿，该习惯的合理性有待商榷，因为遗赠扶养协议写明遗赠的遗产具有对价性，并且有合法的协议作为法律依据。

关于遗产债务的清偿顺序之我国立法，1985 年《执行继承法意见》第 61 条规定：“继承人中有缺乏劳动能力又没有生活来源的人，即使遗产不足清偿债务，也应为其保留适当遗产……”

从域外立法例看，《俄罗斯联邦民法典》第 1174 条规定，第一顺序补偿被继承人的疾病和丧葬所支出的费用；第二顺序补偿保护遗产和管理遗产所指出的费用；第三顺序补偿与执行遗嘱有关的费用。第 1138 条规定，被遗嘱人责成负有遗赠义务的继承人，应在转移给他的遗产价值范围内扣除他应支付的遗嘱人的债务后执行遗赠。《日本民法典》确立的遗产债务清偿顺序为：特别贡献份额之债；共益费用；享有不动产抵押权之债；一般先取特权之债；除去共益费用之外的其他继承费用；有优先权的债务；普通债务；特留份；遗赠；对特别关系人的继承财产分与。①

从我国诸继承法学者建议稿看，“张稿”认为，遗产债务的清偿顺序为遗产管理费用、被继承人生前扶养的、无劳动能力的人的必要生活费用、被继承人生前所负债务、遗赠。②“杨稿”认为，遗产债务的清偿顺序为遗产管理费用、遗嘱执行费用；被继承人生前所负债务；遗赠扶养协议与继承协议中抚养人取得遗产的权利；受遗赠人取得遗赠的权利。③

我们认为，我国《继承法》没有规定遗产债务的清偿顺序，这是其立法之不足。因此，上述主张明确规定遗产债务清偿顺序的上海市被调查民众的财产继承观念、域外立法例和我国学者建议稿的观点，可供我国立法参考。

十、遗产分割之特点与原因分析

（一）遗产分割的自由与限制之特点与原因分析

第一，关于遗产分割自由与限制的民间习惯，统计数据显示的特点是，在被调查者所在地区，（1）由各继承人共同协商后进行分割的，占八成以上（81.21%）；（2）遗嘱禁止分割的遗产则不得进行分割的，占近五成（49.36%）；（3）只要继承人要求分割遗产就得进行分割的，仅占不到二成（19.75%）（见表 4-63）。

以上特点的原因分析，根据上海市被调查者填写的遗产分割自由与限制的民间习惯之理由（见表 4-64），（1）八成以上的地区有遗产由各继承人共同协商后分割的习惯，其原因是遗产由各继承人共同继承，遗产分割关系各继承人的利益，故应共同协商；（2）近五成的地区有被继承人遗嘱禁止分割的遗产，不得进行分割的习惯，其原因是遗产是被继承人遗留的个人财产，被继承人在生前有权通过遗嘱决定遗产的归属和分割；（3）不到二成的地区有只要继承人要求分割遗产就得进行分割的习惯，其原因是每个继承人享有的继承权受法律保护，同时这符合效率原则的，仅占一成（10.04%）。

---

① 参见姜大伟：《我国遗产债务清偿顺序探析》，载《湖北社会科学》2012 年第 10 期。
② 参见“张稿”第 20 条。
③ 参见“杨稿”第 83 条。

第二，关于提出遗产分割请求时间的民间习惯，统计数据显示的特点是，在上海市被调查者所在地区，（1）子女不会提出遗产分割请求的，占近六成（58.66%）；（2）子女会提出遗产分割请求的，占二成以上（22.91%）；（3）子女会提出分割其他遗产，但对其母正在居住房屋的分割需等其母去世后进行的，占近二成（18.43%）（见表4-65）。

以上特点的原因分析，根据上海市被调查者填写的提出遗产分割请求时间的民间习惯之理由（见表4-66），（1）近六成的地区有子女不会提出遗产分割请求的习惯，其原因是民间有双亲过世前不分家的传统，父母及儿子的所有财产应被视为家庭财产；（2）二成以上的地区有子女会提出遗产分割请求的习惯，其原因是自被继承人死亡后，遗产就处于所有继承人共有的状态，儿子有权向母亲提出分割遗产；（3）近二成的地区有子女会提出分割其他遗产，但对其母正在居住的房屋需要等其母去世后进行分割的习惯，其原因是因该遗产房屋是其母唯一的住房，分割会直接对其母目前的生活产生重大影响，故不会分割。

第三，关于遗产分割是否受遗嘱限制的民众观念，统计数据显示的特点是，在上海市被调查者中，（1）认为可以限制的占九成以上（91.59%）；认为不可以限制的仅占不到一成（8.41%）（见表4-67）；（2）并且近五成（48.21%）的被调查者均主张，遗嘱限制遗产分割的期限为5年以内（见表4-69）。

以上特点的原因分析，根据上海市被调查者填写的遗产分割是否受遗嘱限制的民众观念之理由（见表4-68），（1）九成以上的人认为可以限制，其原因是遗产是被继承人生前的个人财产，遗嘱人有自由处分之权利；（2）近五成的人认为不可以限制，其原因是遗产属于所有继承人共同共有，禁止分割有可能损害所有继承人的利益或遗产涉及被继承人生前债务清偿、受其扶养之人利益保护等问题，限制分割过于严苛。

第四，关于继承人协商能否变更遗嘱限制的民间习惯，统计数据显示的特点是，在上海市被调查者所在地区，（1）会尊重遗嘱限制的，占近五成半（54.60%）；（2）可以不遵守遗嘱限制的，占四成半（45.40%）（见表4-70）。

以上特点的原因分析，根据上海市被调查者填写的继承人协商能否变更遗嘱限制的民间习惯之理由（见表4-71），（1）近五成半的地区有不可以变更遗嘱限制的习惯，其原因是遗嘱是被继承人自由处分其财产的合法有效的协议，继承人应当尊重被继承人生前的意愿；（2）四成半的地区有可以变更遗嘱限制的习惯，其原因是被继承人死亡后，遗产处于所有继承人共有的状态，继承人一致同意则有权予以处分或遗产尽快进行分割有利于析产，会减少不必要的纠纷。

关于遗产分割的自由与限制之我国立法，我国《继承法》第15条第2款规定："遗产分割的时间、办法和份额，由继承人协商确定。协商不成的，可以由人民调解委员会调解或者向人民法院提起诉讼。"第28条规定："遗产分割时，应当保留胎儿的继承份额。胎儿出生时是死体的，保留的份额按照法定继承办理。"

从域外立法例看，《德国民法典》第2042条规定："共同继承人的任何一人可以随时请求分割遗产。"《日本民法典》第907条规定，共同继承人无论何时，都得以协议为遗产的分割，当无法达成协议时，可以请求家庭法院分割。但域外立法例也均对以上遗产分割的自由进行了一定的限制。例如，德国法对遗产分割自由的限制有三类：一是，遗嘱对遗产分割时间的限制；二是，法律对遗产分割时间的限制，包括为保护胎儿利益不得分割；在继承人身份关系确定前不得分割；遗产债务必须先从遗产中予以清除；三是，继承人的协议或请求对遗产分割时间的限制。①

从我国诸继承法学者建议稿看，“梁稿”规定：“继承开始后，继承人可以随时请求分割遗产，但有下列情形之一的除外：（一）遗产债务尚未清偿完毕；（二）遗嘱指定遗产于一定期间内不得分割，但该期间不得超过五年；超过五年的，缩短为五年；（三）继承人协商同意于一定期间内不分割遗产。胎儿未出生的，请求分割遗产时，应当为胎儿保留其应继份。出生后为死胎的，保留份额依照法定继承处理。对特定遗产进行即时分割将会严重损害其价值的，人民法院经继承人申请，可以裁判暂缓分割。”② 另外，“王稿”第645条、“杨稿”第85条、“陈稿”第74条和“张稿”第58条也对遗产分割自由及其限制作出了规定。

我们认为，我国立法有关遗嘱自由之限制条款存在不足。因此，上述主张对遗产分割自由增加限制条款的上海市被调查民众的观念与习惯、域外立法例和我国学者建议稿的观点，可供我国立法参考。

（二）遗产分割瑕疵的担保责任之特点与原因分析

关于遗产分割瑕疵担保责任的民间习惯，统计数据显示的特点是，在上海市被调查者所在地区，对遗产分割的瑕疵，（1）共同继承人间不会共同承担的，占五成（50.97%）；（2）共同继承人间会共同承担的，合计占近五成（48.06%）（见表4-72）。

以上特点的原因分析，在上海市被调查者所在地区，（1）有遗产分割瑕疵担保责任习惯的与没有该习惯的地区人数基本持平，五成的地区有不会共同承担的习惯，其原因可能是受我国现行立法之影响；（2）近五成的地区有会共同承担的习惯，其原因可能是这有利于在继承人间公平地分配遗产。

关于遗产分割瑕疵的担保责任之我国立法，我国《继承法》对此无规定。

从域外立法例看，《日本民法典》第911条规定：“各共同继承人，对于其他共同继承人，与出卖人相同，按照其继承份额负担保责任。”③

从我国诸继承法学者建议稿看，“张稿”建议“继承人以其所得遗产的价值为限，按继承比例对其他继承人因分割所得遗产承担与出卖人相同的瑕疵担保责任”。④“梁稿”建议“遗产分割后，各继承人以其所得遗产份额为限，对其他继承人分得的遗产，承担与出卖人相同的担保责任”。⑤

我们认为，我国欠缺遗产分割瑕疵的担保责任，这是其立法之不足。由于该制度能够保证在共同继承人间公平分配遗产，因此，上述主张规定遗产分割瑕疵担保责任的上海市被调查民众的习惯、域外立法例和我国学者建议稿的观点，可供我国立法参考。

---

① 参见《德国民法典》第2043~2047条。
② 参见“梁稿”第2021条。
③ 参见《日本民法典》第911条。
④ 参见“张稿”第65条。
⑤ 参见“梁稿”第2025条。

十一、无人承受遗产之特点与原因分析

(一) 无人承受遗产的归属之特点与原因分析

第一，关于城镇居民无人承受遗产的归属主体之民众观念，统计数据显示的特点是，在上海市被调查者中，(1) 认为城镇居民无人承受的遗产应归社会公共组织（国家、死者生前所在地的国库、死者生前所在地民政部门的社会福利机构和死者生前所在地的居委会）的，合计占六成以上（62.50%）；(2) 认为城镇居民无人承受的遗产应归自然人（不是继承人的其他亲属等）的，合计占近四成（37.50%）（见表4-73）。

以上特点的原因分析，根据上海市被调查者填写的城镇居民无人承受遗产的归属主体的民众观念之理由（见表4-74），(1) 六成以上的人认为其应归属社会公共组织，其原因是法律规定无人承受的遗产应归国家所有，用于为社会生活提供稳定的外部环境或由社会福利机构承受财产更有意义；(2) 近四成的人认为其应归属自然人，其原因是由不是继承人的其他亲属承受较为合理，以维护自然人的财产私有权或由生前对甲照顾较多的人承受更为适宜，这能体现公平原则。

第二，关于农村居民无人承受遗产的归属主体之民众观念，统计数据显示的特点是，在上海市被调查者中，(1) 认为农村居民无人承受的遗产应归社会公共组织（国家、死者生前所在地的国库、死者生前所在地民政部门的社会福利机构和死者生前所在的集体经济组织、村委会或村民小组）的，合计占六成以上（62.58%）；(2) 农村居民无人承受的遗产应归自然人（不是继承人的其他亲属等）的，合计占近四成（37.42%）（见表4-75）。

以上特点的原因分析，根据上海市被调查者填写的农村居民无人承受遗产归属主体的民众观念之理由，(1) 六成以上的人认为其应归属社会公共组织所有，原因是认为法律规定无人承受的遗产归国家所有，国家可以更好地发挥财产效用，为社会生活提供福利或认为应当由村民小组承受，村民小组对甲平时照顾较多，付出了一定的劳动应有所回报或认为由社会福利机构承受财产更有意义，可以用于福利事业；(2) 近四成的人认为其应归属自然人，原因是认为由不是继承人的其他亲属承受较为合理，其与被继承人关系较为密切或认为由生前对甲照顾较多的人承受更为适宜，这体现了权利与义务相一致。

关于无人承受遗产的归属主体之我国立法，我国《继承法》第32条规定：“无人继承又无人受遗赠的遗产，归国家所有；死者生前是集体所有制组织成员的，归所在集体所有制组织所有。”

从域外立法例看，关于无人承受遗产的归属主体，《德国民法典》第1936条规定：“在继承开始时，被继承人既没有血亲，也没有同性生活伴侣，也没有配偶的，被继承人死亡时所隶属的邦的国库是法定继承人……”《日本民法典》第959条则规定：“没有能按照前条规定处分的财产归属国库。”

从我国诸继承法学者建议稿看，“王稿”规定，对继承人、受遗赠人、债权人的公示催告期间届满，无继承人承认继承时，其遗产于清偿债务并交付遗赠物后，如有剩余，由遗产管理人移交有关部门上缴国库所有；如果死者生前是集体所有制组织成员的，则应移交所在的集体所有制组织并归其所有。①

① “王稿”第666条。

我们认为，鉴于上海市被调查民众的财产继承观念与我国现行法之规定较为一致，应该维持现有立法中无人承受遗产应收归国家或集体经济组织所有的规定。

（二）无人承受遗产的处理之特点与原因分析

第一，关于无人承受遗产管理人产生方式的民众观念，统计数据显示的特点是，（1）认为应由人民法院或民政部门指定产生的，合计占五成半以上（56.19%）；（2）认为应由居委会、村委会或所在单位指定产生的，占四成以上（43.81%）（见表4-77）。

以上特点的原因分析，根据上海市被调查者填写的无人承受遗产的管理人之产生方式的民众观念之理由（见表4-78），（1）五成半以上的人主张由人民法院或民政部门指定产生，原因是法院指定遗产管理人更具有权威性或民政局等行政机关处理不易起纠纷；（2）四成以上的人主张由居委会、村委会或所在单位指定产生，原因是居委会、村委会或所在单位熟悉家庭内部关系而且擅长处理家庭事务。

关于无人承受遗产的管理之我国立法，目前我国缺乏无人承受遗产的管理制度，也没有具体规定遗产管理人的产生方式。

从域外立法例看，《日本民法典》第951~952条规定，继承人有无不明时继承财产为法人，家庭法院因利害关系人或检察官的请求应选任继承财产管理人。

从我国诸继承法学者建议稿看，“张稿”建议：“继承开始后，继承人有无不明的，被继承人居所地的居民委员会、村民委员会或其所在单位，应于继承开始后尽快报告法院。法院在接到报告后，应当按照本法第24条的规定指定遗产管理人，并公示催告继承人和利害关系人于规定期限主张权利。”①

我们认为，我国《继承法》没有规定无人承受遗产管理人的产生方式，是其立法不足。因此，上述主张明确该管理人产生方式的上海市被调查民众的观念、域外立法例和我国学者建议稿的观点，可供我国立法参考。

第二，关于无人承受遗产之酌分请求权主体的民众观念与民间习惯，统计数据显示的特点是，（1）在上海市被调查者的观念上，认为依靠死者扶养的人（66.90%）、与死者共同生活的人（54.90%）和与死者关系密切且帮助较多的人（79.80%）可以请求酌情分配无人承受遗产的，各占五成至七成以上（见表4-80）；（2）被调查者所在地区的继承习惯是：与死者关系密切且对其帮助较多的人、依靠死者扶养的人、与死者共同居住的人或与死者关系亲近的不是继承人的其他亲属可以酌情分得无人承受遗产的，各占一成至五成（见表4-81）。

以上特点的原因分析，上海市被调查民众观念与地区习惯上认可的无人承受遗产酌分请求权主体均较为广泛，其原因可能是认为，依靠死者扶养的人、对死者帮助较多的人等群体生前与死者关系密切，可以酌情分得适当遗产，有利于生前对被继承人进行照顾，也有助于维护家庭伦理亲情。

关于无人承受遗产的酌分请求权主体之我国立法，1985年《执行继承法意见》第57条规定：“遗产因无人继承收归国家或集体组织所有时，按继承法第十四条规定可以分给遗产的人提出取得遗产的要求，人民法院应视情况适当分给遗产。”

从域外立法例看，有国家的立法明确规定对与被继承人有密切关系者可以酌情分配遗

① 参见“张稿”第67条。

产。例如，《日本民法典》第958-3条规定，遗产无人继承时，家庭法院因与被继承人共谋生计者、悉心治疗护养被继承人者及其他与被继承人有特别关系者的请求，可以向其分配清算后剩余财产的全部或一部分。

从我国诸继承法学者建议稿看，“陈稿”第87条规定，无人承受遗产，经清偿债务、执行遗赠后有剩余的，遗产管理人经书面请求居民委员会或村民委员会主任并获同意及签字后，遗产管理人可依情况将遗产的全部或部分酌情分配给依靠被继承人扶养的人、对被继承人扶养较多的人、与被继承人一同生活的人或其他与被继承人有密切关系的人。

我们认为，我国无人承受遗产之酌分请求权主体较窄，这是其立法之不足。因此，上述主张适当扩大无人承受遗产的酌分请求权主体的上海市被调查民众的观念与习惯、域外立法例和我国学者建议稿的观点，可供我国立法参考。

第四节　当代中国上海市民众财产继承观念与遗产处理习惯对中国民法典继承编制定的立法启示

以上，我们针对上海市被调查者的财产继承观念与遗产处理习惯的调查统计的汇总数据，分析归纳其特点，研究其特点的产生原因，考察和分析我国司法实践的相关案例，研究我国继承法律制度的适用情况，进而结合考察域外立法例和我国诸继承法学者建议稿的观点，剖析我国《继承法》相关制度存在的优点与不足。以下，我们将以上海市被调查者的财产继承观念与遗产处理习惯为参考基础，借鉴域外立法例和我国诸继承法学者建议稿的有益观点，对我国“民法典继承法编”编纂中相关继承制度的修改完善或予以保留，提出立法建议，以供我国立法机关参考。

一、我国遗产范围界定制度之不足与立法完善建议

（一）我国遗产范围界定制度之不足

有关遗产的范围，我国立法的主要问题表现为以下两方面：第一，欠缺遗产的排除式规定。有关遗产的范围，二成至五成的上海市被调查者认为欠款、家庭日常生活用品、死亡赔偿金、个人邮箱和QQ号等属于遗产（见表4-4）。前述涉及遗产范围界定案例之司法审判实践，也反映出我国欠缺此反面排除规定之不足。第二，我国《继承法》中没有被继承人生前特种赠与财产的归扣制度，不利于在共同继承人间公平地分配遗产。

（二）我国遗产范围界定制度之立法完善建议

针对以上立法之不足，我们提出以下两方面立法完善建议：

1. 遗产范围界定模式之立法建议

建议立法中明确排除不得作为遗产的财产范围，与被继承人人身不可分割的人身权利不属于遗产。[①]

2. 被继承人生前特种赠与财产的归扣之立法建议

从上海市被调查民众的财产继承观念来看，对此制度的民意接受度较低，但我们建议，我国立法应该增加遗产归扣制度，其有助于在共同继承人间公平地分配遗产。

---

① 参见“梁稿”第1941条。

二、我国继承开始的通知和公告制度之不足与立法完善建议

（一）我国继承开始的通知和公告制度之不足

关于继承开始的通知和公告制度，我国目前立法主要存在以下两方面不足：第一，上海市被调查民众认可的继承开始的通知主体范围要广于我国现行立法的规定，有近八成的被调查者认为通知和公告义务的主体除我国《继承法》的现有规定外，还应当包括处理被继承人死亡事件的机构，如公安交警部门（见表4-10）。并且欠缺义务主体不履行通知和公告义务的法律责任。前述涉及继承开始的通知与公告案例之司法审判实践，也反映出我国此立法之不足。第二，欠缺继承开始的通知和公告期间，不利于及时发出继承开始的通知与公告。五成半以上的上海市被调查者认为应在 7 日内发出继承开始的通知和公告（见表 4-12）。

（二）我国继承开始的通知和公告制度之立法完善建议

针对以上立法之不足，我们提出以下两方面立法完善建议：

1. 继承开始的通知和公告主体之立法建议

建议明确继承开始的通知和公告的主体，除我国《继承法》的现有规定外，还应当包括处理被继承人死亡事件的机构，如公安交警部门。

如果上述主体不履行法定通知或公告义务造成遗产损失的，应当承担相应的损害赔偿责任。

2. 继承开始的通知和公告方式及期间之立法建议

关于继承开始的通知和公告的方式，调查结果表明各种方式均有一定的采用，建议立法不予规定，由习惯调整即可。而继承开始的通知和公告的期间，义务主体应在 7 日以内发出继承开始的通知和公告。

三、我国遗产管理制度之不足与立法完善建议

（一）我国遗产管理制度之不足

我国《继承法》尚无系统的遗产管理制度，仅在该法第 16 条和第 24 条以及 1985 年《执行继承法意见》第 44 条中原则性地规定了遗嘱执行和遗产保管的部分内容，但缺乏对遗产管理人的资格、产生、职责、法律责任、管理费用和报酬、遗产管理终止原因的规定。关于遗产管理人范围的确定，九成的上海市被调查者所在地区，有由死者的法定继承人作为遗产管理人的习惯（见表4-13）；关于遗产管理人职责，四成至九成以上的上海市被调查者认为遗产管理人的职责应包括清查遗产，制作遗产清单、妥善保管遗产、查明被继承人生前的债权和债务，积极地追讨债权或清偿债务等（见表4-16）。前述涉及遗产管理案例之司法审判实践，也反映出我国遗产管理制度存在遗产管理人职责不明之不足。

（二）我国遗产管理制度之立法完善建议

针对以上立法之不足，我们提出以下三方面立法完善建议：

1. 遗产管理人的确定之立法建议

遗产管理人一般由死者的法定继承人担任。如果法定继承人协商不成，可诉请人民法院指定。

2. 遗产管理人的职责与报酬之立法建议

建议规定如下：遗产管理人的职责包含清查遗产，制作遗产清单；妥善保管遗产；查明被继承人生前的债权和债务，积极地追讨债权或清偿债务；查明被继承人是否留有遗嘱，并且确定遗嘱是否真实合法；可以原告或被告的身份参加因遗产引起的诉讼。

遗产管理人由继承人担任的，不得取得报酬；由继承人以外的人担任的，可以取得报酬。

3. 遗产管理人的损害赔偿责任之立法建议

建议规定遗产管理人和继承人对因其故意或重大过失行为造成的遗产损害，应当承担损害赔偿责任。

四、我国法定继承制度之不足与立法完善建议

（一）我国法定继承制度之不足

关于法定继承制度，我国立法主要存在以下三方面问题：第一，我国法定继承人的范围较小，且仅有两个顺位，易造成较多无人继承遗产的情形，不利于维护自然人个人的财产权益。上海市被调查者认可的法定继承人的范围和顺序为：第一顺序为配偶、父母、子女；第二顺序为孙子女外孙子女、祖父母外祖父母、兄弟姐妹；第三顺序为侄子女外甥子女、伯叔姑舅姨。而表兄弟姐妹、堂兄弟姐妹只能排在第四顺序以上（见表 4-20）。第二，我国配偶作为固定顺位参与继承存在某些不合理性。关于配偶的继承顺序与份额，在上海市被调查者中，尽管其观念上八成的人认可配偶应作为第一顺序继承人参与继承，但涉及具体的继承份额时，五成半以上的人更赞同配偶作为无固定顺序继承人（见表 4-21、表 4-22）。第三，欠缺配偶和后顺位特殊继承人对特殊遗产的先取权和终生使用权，不能满足配偶或后顺位特殊继承人对遗产房屋居住等现实需要。九成左右的上海市被调查者人认可配偶和后顺序特殊继承人对特殊遗产享有先取权和终生使用权（见表 4-23、表 4-26）。

（二）我国法定继承制度之立法完善建议

针对以上立法之不足，我们提出以下五方面立法完善建议：

1. 法定继承人的范围和顺序之立法建议

建议扩大法定继承人的范围，对法定继承人的顺序进行补充，以减少遗产无人继承的情况。

2. 配偶与血亲继承人的法定应继份之立法建议

建议配偶应作为无固定顺序继承人，根据其所在顺位不同继承不同遗产份额。具体还应结合其他省市被调查者的观念与习惯，进一步对立法进行完善。

3. 配偶与后顺序特殊法定继承人对遗产中家庭住房的先取权与终生使用权之立法建议

关于配偶对遗产中家庭住房的先取权与终生使用权，以及后顺序特殊法定继承人对原使用的遗产住房及日常生活用品的终生使用权，都存在一定的习惯和民众观念基础，但现行法并无明确规定，我国立法对此制度应予增设，相信民众会有一定的接受度。

4. 尽了主要赡养义务的丧偶儿媳或女婿的遗产分配方式之立法建议

从尊重被调查民众的财产继承观念与遗产处理习惯考量，建议维持现行法中尽了主要

赡养义务的丧偶儿媳或女婿第一顺序法定继承人身份及遗产分配方式。

五、我国遗嘱继承制度之不足与立法完善建议

（一）我国遗嘱继承制度之不足

关于遗嘱继承，我国立法存在的不足，主要表现以下两方面：第一，对公证遗嘱与其他形式遗嘱的适用效力规定不足。相较于其他形式遗嘱，我国公正遗嘱具有优先适用的效力，一定程度上妨害了被继承人真实意思的表达。关于公证遗嘱与其他形式遗嘱适用效力的民众观念，认为后遗嘱的适用效力优先于前一公证遗嘱的上海市被调查者，合计占近六成半（见表4-31）。第二，我国目前并没有特留份制度，不能起到较好地防止被继承人滥用遗嘱权利的目的对于遗嘱的效力。而认为以遗嘱将个人遗产全部赠给他人的行为不适当，即赞成设立特留份制度的上海市被调查者，占六成（见表4-33）。

（二）我国遗嘱继承制度之立法完善建议

针对以上立法之不足，我们提出以下三方面立法完善建议：

1. 公证遗嘱与其他形式遗嘱的效力之立法建议

建议结合其他省市被调查民众的财产继承观念与遗产处理习惯，充分平衡制度的实践价值和可行性，再予调整，以最后成立的合法遗嘱的适用效力为准更为适宜。

2. 遗嘱自由的限制——特留份之立法建议

建议结合其他省市被调查者的财产继承观念与遗产处理习惯，充分平衡制度的实践价值和可行性，增设特留份制度。

3. 夫妻共同遗嘱之立法建议

夫妻共同遗嘱作为契约，可能无法应对出现的新情况和新问题，限制了双方对自己财产的处分权。建议结合其他地区被调查者观念和习惯，充分平衡制度的实践价值和可行性，再予确定，暂不建议规定夫妻共同遗嘱制度。

六、我国继承和遗赠的接受与放弃制度之不足与立法完善建议

（一）我国继承和遗赠的接受与放弃制度之不足

关于继承和遗赠的接受与放弃，我国立法存在的不足为：第一，我国继承的接受或放弃的时间过于宽泛，不利于尽快确定遗产的相关权利人和义务人，以实现遗产的分割。关于继承的接受与放弃的时间与方式的民众观念，认为应当在遗产处理前作出放弃继承的意思表示的，上海市被调查者占近六成半，同时也有三成半以上的被调查者认为应当在继承开始的2个月内作出放弃继承表示（见表4-38）。第二，我国对于遗赠的接受方式的规定不尽合理。关于遗赠的接受与放弃的时间与方式，超过七成以上的上海市被调查者认为，受遗赠人不作表示的可以被视为接受遗赠（见表4-41）。前述涉及继承和遗赠的接受与放弃案例之司法审判实践，也反映出我国有关遗赠的接受方式之规定存在不足。

（二）我国继承和遗赠的接受与放弃制度之立法完善建议

针对以上立法之不足，我们提出以下三方面立法完善建议：

1. 继承的接受与放弃的时间与方式之立法建议

从及时确定遗产权利义务人，便于开始遗产分割的角度考量，立法应进一步明确继承接受或放弃的时间，以2个月内为宜。

关于继承的接受与放弃的方式，建议无须作出规定，将1985年《执行继承法意见》第47条的规定上升为立法即可："继承人放弃继承应当以书面形式向其他继承人表示。用口头方式表示放弃继承，本人承认，或有其它充分证据证明的，也应当认定其有效。"

2. 遗赠的接受与放弃的方式与效力之立法建议

建议修改我国《继承法》中遗赠的接受必须明示的规定，改为受遗赠人放弃遗赠的意思表示在知道或应该知道受遗赠2个月内作出，逾期未作出的视为接受遗赠。

3. 继承的放弃与债权人的撤销权之立法建议

建议应在一定条件下赋予债权人以撤销权，即继承人放弃继承损害到债权人利益的，债权人可以在知道或者应当知道继承人放弃之日起6个月内申请人民法院撤销继承人的放弃行为。

七、我国继承权的丧失、被继承人的宥恕与代位继承制度之不足与立法完善建议

（一）我国继承权的丧失、被继承人的宥恕与代位继承制度之不足

关于继承权的丧失与恢复的法定情形，我国立法表现出的不足，主要表现为对丧失继承权法定事由的规定不够充分。关于继承权丧失与被继承人宥恕，认为继承人因欺诈、胁迫丧失继承权，获得被继承人宥恕后仍可以恢复继承权的上海市被调查者，占七成以上（见表4-47）。

（二）我国继承权的丧失、被继承人的宥恕与代位继承制度之立法完善建议

针对以上立法之不足，我们提出以下两方面立法完善建议：

1. 继承权的丧失与被继承人的宥恕之立法建议

建议将"以欺诈、或者胁迫的手段，迫使或者妨碍被继承人设立、变更或者撤销遗嘱的"作为丧失继承权的第五种情形，且属于相对丧失，可以通过继承人的原谅而恢复。需要说明的是，不需要以"情节严重"为限定。"情节严重"作为弹性标准，对法院的审判实践提出了较高的要求，对当事人规范性和指引性也不够彻底。而且现行司法解释将"情节严重"限定为"侵害了缺乏劳动能力又无生活来源的继承人的利益，并造成其生活困难的"，过于狭窄，限制了继承权丧失制度的打击范围，不利于继承秩序的维护。

2. 继承权的丧失与代位继承权之立法建议

建议立法保留现有规定。尽管上述域外立法例和我国继承法学者建议稿中，"固有权说"占主导地位，但是考虑到遵从上海市被调查民众的财产继承观念以及我国的立法传统，建议仍沿用"代表权说"为宜。

八、我国遗赠扶养协议制度之不足与立法增补建议

（一）我国遗赠扶养协议制度之不足

我国目前立法并没有规定继承扶养协议制度，只有遗赠扶养协议制度。但是在现实生活中，由于赡养老年人的现实需要，已经表现出了迫切地对继承扶养协议制度的需求。关于继承扶养协议的订立主体与方式，认为被继承人需与全部继承人协商，共同签订协议的上海市被调查者占近六成（见表4-53）。前述涉及继承协议案例之司法审判实践，也反映出我国此制度之不足。

（二）我国继承扶养协议制度之立法增补建议

针对以上立法之不足，我们提出以下两方面立法完善建议：

1. 继承扶养协议的订立主体与方式之立法建议

建议在我国已有遗赠扶养协议概念的基础上，为与遗赠扶养协议相区分，继承扶养协议应是被继承人与继承人间签订的扶养协议。从合同的内容看，基于“当事人意思自治”原则，只要不违反法律强行性规定，当事人双方可以自由约定合同中的权利义务，即合同内容由被继承人与相对人的合意决定。

就订立的方式而言，其与遗赠扶养协议具有相似性，应以书面形式定立。

2. 继承扶养协议的变更及效力之立法建议

扶养义务人死亡后，如果该义务人的子女有扶养能力，且与受扶养人协商双方均同意的，可由原扶养义务人的子女继续履行扶养义务，并继承受扶养人的全部遗产。

九、我国遗产债务清偿制度之不足与立法完善建议

（一）我国遗产债务清偿制度之不足

关于遗产债务清偿制度，我国立法主要存在以下问题：第一，我国实行无条件的限定继承制度，没有规定继承人恶意转移遗产、损害其他债权人利益的赔偿责任。关于遗产债务清偿责任的类型，在上海市被调查者中，主张实行自愿的无限清偿责任的，合计占近七成；主张实行有限清偿责任的，占六成以上；主张实行强制的无限清偿责任的，占近四成半（44.00%）（见表4-57）。第二，对于遗产债务清偿的顺序，目前我国《继承法》尚无规定。在上海市被调查者所在地区，遗产债务按如下顺序清偿：第一顺序为丧葬费用；第二顺序遗产管理等费用、欠付的工资；第三顺序欠债；第四顺序受被继承人扶养人的生活费；第五顺序税款；第六顺序对被继承人扶养较多的人之酌情分配遗产份额；第七顺序遗赠扶养协议写明遗赠的遗产（见表4-62）。前述涉及遗产债务清偿案例之司法审判实践，也反映出我国此立法之不足。

（二）我国遗产债务清偿制度之立法完善建议

针对以上立法之不足，我们提出以下三方面立法完善建议：

1. 遗产债务的范围之立法建议

建议保留现行立法，上海市被调查者对现行的限定继承制度接受度较高。

建议规定继承人或遗产管理人违反其管理职责，对遗产债权人或者受遗赠人造成损害的，应当承担赔偿责任。

2. 被继承人丧葬费的支付之立法建议

建议立法结合实践需求，充分平衡制度的实践价值和可行性，再决定是否规定死者丧葬费用的支付方式。该问题本质上属于私权事务，法律并不需要对此作出规定。除非实践中有大量相关的纠纷产生，需要法律进行引导，否则立法应尊重民事主体的自由决定和选择。

3. 遗产债务清偿顺序之立法建议

建议立法应明确遗产债务清偿的顺序或者确定遗产债务清偿顺序的原则，以减少实务中的分歧及可能的纠纷；在具体顺序上，建议立法结合其他省市被调查者观念与习惯，充分平衡继承人利益和第三人利益。此外，无论是上海市被调查民众的观念与习惯，均是丧

葬费用和遗产管理费用应当优先于税款、欠付工资受支付，我国立法应予以参考。

十、我国遗产分割制度之不足与立法完善建议

（一）我国遗产分割制度之不足

关于遗产分割制度，我国立法存在以下不足：第一，我国遗产分割自由的限制规定，存在不足。关于被继承人可否立遗嘱限制遗产分割，九成以上的上海市被调查者认为可以限制（见表4-67）。第二，欠缺共同继承人对遗产分割瑕疵的担保责任。上海市被调查者所在地区的习惯并未表现出明显倾向性，认可遗产分割瑕疵的担保责任与不认可的人数基本持平，均占五成左右（见表4-72）。

（二）我国遗产分割制度之立法完善建议

针对以上立法之不足，我们提出以下两方面立法完善建议：

1. 遗产分割的自由与限制之立法建议

建议对于遗产分割开始的时间，尊重继承人的意见，以协商约定的时间为准。对生存配偶居住的遗产房屋，在其生存期间暂不分割。尊重限制分割遗产的遗嘱的效力，但需要对其进行一个合理的期限限制，既尊重遗嘱自由，又不妨碍物尽其用，同时照顾继承人利益。

2. 遗产分割瑕疵的担保责任之立法建议

建议规定共同继承人之间对遗产分割瑕疵的担保责任，具体应包括三方面内容：一是对遗产分割瑕疵的担保责任；二是对遗产被追夺的担保责任；三是对债权的担保责任。

十一、我国无人承受遗产制度之不足与立法完善建议

（一）我国无人承受遗产制度之不足

关于无人承受遗产的处理，我国立法的不足主要表现为：第一，缺少无人承受遗产的管理制度，不利于对无人承受的遗产进行有序处理。关于无人承受遗产管理人产生方式，在上海市被调查者中，主张由人民法院或民政部门指定产生的，合计占五成半以上；主张由居委会、村委会或所在单位指定产生的，占四成以上（见表4-77）。第二，我国无人承受遗产的酌分请求权主体过窄。在上海市被调查者中，认为依靠死者扶养的人、与死者共同生活的人和与死者关系密切且对其帮助较多的人可以请求酌情分得无人承受遗产的，占五至近八成（见表4-80）。前述涉及无人承受遗产案例之司法审判实践，也反映出我国无人承受遗产的酌分请求权主体较窄之不足。法律应该从保护公民私有财产权和实现遗产的扶养功能出发，使以上与被继承人关系密切的人可以适当分得遗产。

（二）我国无人承受遗产制度之立法完善建议

针对以上立法之不足，我们提出以下两方面立法完善建议：

1. 无人承受遗产的归属主体与酌分请求权主体之立法建议

从遵从上海市被调查民众的财产继承观念考量，无人承受遗产应归国家或集体经济组织所有，即维持我国现有立法的规定。

2. 无人承受遗产的管理之立法建议

在继承人有无不明或无继承人时，为避免遗产的损失，应明确规定遗产管理人的产生、职责等内容的完整遗产管理制度。

建议将与被继承人关系密切的其他非法定继承人作为无人承受的酌分请求权主体。

第五章　当代中国河北省民众财产继承观念与遗产处理习惯实证调查研究*

第一节　当代中国河北省民众财产继承观念与遗产处理习惯实证调查概况

一、被调查地区概况

（一）河北省社会经济发展水平情况

2018 年全省生产总值实现 36010.3 亿元，同比增长 6.60%。其中，第一产业增加值 3338.0 亿元，同比增长 3.00%；第二产业增加值 16040.1 亿元，同比增长 4.30%；第三产业增加值 16632.2 亿元，同比增长 9.80%。①

（二）河北省人口结构情况

2018 年年末河北省常住总人口 7556.30 万人。其中，城镇常住人口 4264.02 万人，占总人口比重（常住人口城镇化率）为 56.43%，户籍人口城镇化率为 39.89%。② 2017 年河北省 0~14 岁人口（人口抽样调查）为 11152 人，占比 17.96%；15~64 岁人口（人口抽样调查）为 43608 人，占比 70.24%；65 岁及以上人口（人口抽样调查）为 7326 人，占比 11.80%。③

（三）河北省城乡人口的年均收入情况

2018 年全省居民人均可支配收入为 23446 元，同比增长 9.10%。城镇居民人均可支配收入 32997 元，比上年增长 8.00%；农村居民人均可支配收入 14031 元，增长 8.90%。城镇居民人均消费支出 22127 元，同比增长 7.40%；农村居民人均消费支出 11383 元，增

* 作者简介：罗杰，女，法学博士，燕山大学文法学院副教授；贺海燕，女，西南政法大学民商法学院 2017 级博士研究生；尹鸽，女，燕山大学硕士研究生。

① 参见《河北省 2018 年国民经济和社会发展统计公报》，载 http://tjj.hebei.gov.cn/hetj/tjgbtg/101548813276747.html，访问日期：2019 年 6 月 20 日。

② 参见《河北省 2018 年国民经济和社会发展统计公报》，载 http://tjj.hebei.gov.cn/hetj/tjgbtg/101548813276747.html，访问日期：2019 年 6 月 20 日。

③ 必须说明，在国家统计局官网，河北省人口统计情况最新数据仍为 2017 年的。河北省人口抽样调查总数 62086 人。数据来自国家统计局：http://data.stats.gov.cn/easyquery.htm? cn = E0103&zb = A030801® = 130000&sj = 2017，访问日期：2019 年 2 月 15 日。

长 8.00%。[①]

二、实证调查情况简介

2016 年 11 月，西南政法大学陈苇教授主持申报的司法部科研项目“我国遗产处理制度系统化构建研究”被批准立项。为了给本项目的理论研究和制度研究提供国情资料，必须调查了解当代中国民众的财产继承观念与遗产处理习惯。考虑到课题组人力、物力的限制，陈苇教授选择我国十省市包括东北部的吉林省、东部的上海市、北部的河北省、中部的湖北省和江西省、南部的广东省和海南省、东南部的福建省、西南部的重庆市和四川省作为被调查地点，然后联系确定了各省市调查组组长共同组织开展本项目的子课题“当代中国民众财产继承观念与遗产处理习惯实证调查研究”。本次“当代中国河北省民众财产继承观念与遗产处理习惯实证调查研究”是“当代中国民众财产继承观念与遗产处理习惯实证调查研究”的组成部分之一。河北省调查组组长为燕山大学文法学院罗杰副教授。

（一）调查问卷的设计和学生调查员的召集与培训

2016 年 11 月中旬，陈苇教授组织重庆市课题组成员分工合作，设计制作“当代中国民众财产继承观念与遗产处理习惯实证调查研究”的调查问卷，至同年 12 月中旬完成了调查问卷的设计工作。然后，陈苇教授把调查问卷通过电子邮件发送给参与本次实证调查的十省市调查组组长，以供开展实地调查时十省市被调查地区统一使用。同年 12 月下旬，根据陈苇教授撰写的“当代中国民众财产继承观念与遗产处理习惯社会调查动员和培训会”的说明书，河北省调查组组长罗杰副教授负责召集、遴选河北省籍的学生调查员 125 名，然后组织召开“当代中国河北省民众财产继承观念与遗产处理习惯实证调查动员暨社会调查知识培训会”。在会上，罗杰副教授给每位学生调查员发放了 6 份调查问卷，针对问卷的问题，逐一讲解调查要点和具体的调查方法，要求被调查者应当具有河北省户籍，且必须是男女各 3 名，分为老、中、青（61 岁以上、41～60 岁、20～40 岁）三个年龄段，并且要求每名学生调查员利用 2017 年的寒假期间各自在家乡开展实地社会调查。

（二）实地社会调查的方式

2017 年 1 月至 2 月的寒假期间，河北省籍的学生调查员们回到各自家乡开展实地社会调查。本次调查主要采取学生调查员“入户问卷调查”和“个人访谈”的方式。

一是入户问卷调查。学生调查员在 2017 年的寒假期间回到自己的家乡，对当地的民众进行入户问卷调查。每位被调查对象必须符合培训会说明的条件要求，而且其只能填写一份调查问卷。学生调查员入户后首先向被调查者讲解说明本次调查的目的意义和调查问卷填写的相关问题，采取被调查者自己填写问卷或者学生调查员向被调查者询问后代为填写，这两种方式完成问卷的填写。

二是个人访谈。要求采取“一对一”的个人访谈方式，以收集与遗产继承有关的纠纷或案例。本次实地调查，除填写调查问卷外，还要求辅以“一对一”的个人访谈，收集和记录典型的继承纠纷或相关案例的内容。因为，调查问卷涉及客观选择与主观理由两

① 参见《河北省 2018 年国民经济和社会发展统计公报》，载 http://tjj.hebei.gov.cn/hetj/tjgbtg/101548813276747.html，访问日期：2019 年 6 月 20 日。

部分内容，采取“一对一”的个人访谈方式，可以避免被调查者受到他人的影响，以便能够较为客观深入地了解被调查民众的真实想法。

（三）调查问卷数据的录入、统计汇总、复核与撰写调查研究报告

2017 年 3 月开学后，本调查组统一回收调查问卷与典型案例的访谈记录，然后组织学生统计员进行数据统计工作。本次实地调查实际发放问卷 750 份，剔除无效问卷后，共计回收有效问卷 703 份，有效问卷率为 94.00%。随后，根据有效问卷进行调查数据的录入、制作统计汇总表，并且进行统计汇总数据的复核。2017 年 4 月底完成《〈当代中国民众财产继承观念与遗产处理习惯实证调查问卷〉河北省民众实证调查统计数据汇总表》的定稿。我们在此需要特别说明，关于各项调查问题之统计人数的合计，凡单选题的人数合计均为 100%，均合计在统计表中；凡多选题的人数合计均超过 100%，故不予进行合计的统计。本调查研究报告的撰写就是以此次调查统计数据汇总表作为基础资料进行分析和研究而成。在此，特向所有参与此次调查活动的老师和同学表示衷心感谢！①

2017 年 4 月陈苇教授拟定了“当代中国民众财产继承观念与遗产处理习惯实证调查研究的写作提纲和写作要求”。2017 年 5 月起，我们根据此写作提纲和写作要求，进入参考文献资料的收集和调查报告的写作阶段。本章“当代中国河北省民众财产继承观念与遗产处理习惯实证调查研究”由罗杰副教授和法学研究生尹鸽同学共同撰写初稿至第四稿，其间，根据陈苇教授对初稿至第四稿的历次修改意见和中期评审专家意见，对稿件进行了相应的多次修改和补充，最后向课题负责人陈苇教授交稿。2019 年 1 月，陈苇教授对河北省调查研究报告继续进行审阅和修改补充，然后组织重庆市调查组博士生对该调查研究报告统一进行了三次修改补充，最终于 2019 年 6 月完成定稿。

三、被调查对象的基本情况

本次被调查对象均为河北省常住人口，我们对 703 名的被调查者的性别、年龄和职业情况进行了如下统计：

（一）被调查者的性别情况

表 5-1　被调查者的性别情况统计

性别	人数	比例
男	340	48.36%
女	363	51.64%
合计	703	100%

关于被调查者的性别，调查统计数据显示，在 703 名被调查者中，男性有 340 人（占 48.36%）；女性有 363 人（占 51.64%）。可见，被调查者性别比例大体持平。

① 参与河北省民众财产继承观念与遗产处理习惯的实地调查以及调查数据统计汇总等工作的师生名单，详见“鸣谢”。

（二）被调查者的年龄情况

表 5-2 被调查者的年龄情况统计

年龄	人数	比例
20~30	158	22.48%
31~40	106	15.08%
41~50	130	18.49%
51~60	112	15.93%
61~70	114	16.22%
≥71	83	11.81%
合计	703	100%

关于被调查者的年龄，调查统计数据显示，在 703 名被调查者中，20~40 岁青年人占三成半以上（37.56%）、41~60 岁的中年人占近三成半（34.42%），60 岁以上的老年人，合计占近三成（28.03%）。即本次被调查者以中青年为主体，合计占七成稍多（71.98%）。

（三）被调查者的职业情况

表 5-3 被调查者的职业状况情况统计

职业	人数	比例
农民	157	22.33%
工人	68	9.67%
经商	57	8.11%
公务员、企事业单位职工	160	22.76%
其他（打工等不固定职业）	261	37.13%
合计	703	100%

关于被调查者的职业，调查统计数据显示，在 703 名被调查者中，农民和工人合计占三成稍多（32%）；公务员和企事业单位职工合计占二成稍多（22.76%）；经商只占近一成（8.11%）；其他职业的占比三成半稍多（37.13%）。

综上，本次被调查者的性别比例大体持平，老、中、青各年龄段的均有，但以中青年为主体，且他们的职业涉及广泛，本次调查数据基本上能够反映不同性别、年龄和职业的被调查者的意愿。

第二节 当代中国河北省民众财产继承观念与遗产处理习惯实证调查的数据统计情况

一、遗产范围界定之调查数据统计情况

关于遗产范围界定之调查数据统计，我们主要从遗产的种类和被继承人生前特种赠与财产的归扣，这两个方面进行调查数据的统计情况汇总分析。

（一）遗产的种类

问题【一、（一）】“2016年2月某甲因车祸死亡，经清理某甲个人名下的遗物，您认为，以下哪些属于某甲的遗产：A. 住房一套；B. 小汽车一辆；C. 家庭日常生活用品若干；D. 存款10万元；E. 股票10万元；F. 某甲以其姓名注册的邮箱、QQ账号等；G. 单位出租给某甲的午休住房一间；H. 某甲向某公司购货的欠款5万元；I. 某甲因交通事故死亡获得50万元赔偿金。（单选）”

表5-4 属于遗产种类的民众观念情况统计（单选）

选项	遗产	
	人数	比例
A. 住房一套	693	98.58%
B. 小汽车一辆	666	94.74%
C. 家庭日常生活用品若干	469	66.71%
D. 存款10万元	677	96.30%
E. 股票10万元	572	81.37%
F. 某甲以其姓名注册的邮箱、QQ账号等	184	26.17%
G. 单位出租给某甲的午休住房一间	63	8.96%
H. 某甲向某公司购货的欠款5万元	318	45.23%
I. 某甲因交通事故死亡获得50万元赔偿金	479	68.14%

关于属于遗产种类的民众观念，统计数据显示，在703名被调查者中，（1）有八成至九成以上的人认为A项住房（98.58%）、B项汽车（94.74%）、D项存款（96.30%）和E项股票（81.37%）属于遗产；（2）一成至七成多的人认为C项家庭日常生活用品（66.71%）、H项债务（45.23%）、I项交通事故死亡赔偿金（68.14%）、G项单位出租房（8.96%）属于遗产；（3）有近二成半的人认为F项以被继承人的姓名注册的邮箱和QQ账号等（26.17%）属于遗产。

（二）被继承人生前特种赠与财产的归扣

1. 被继承人生前特种赠与财产是否归入遗产范围的民众观念情况统计

问题【一、（二）1.】“张老汉有三个儿子，在10年前大儿子甲结婚时，张老汉给其

资助购买婚房的现金 20 万元；二儿子乙一直未结婚，但 5 年前在其开办豆腐坊时，张老汉资助其营业资金 10 万元；在 2 年前小儿子丙结婚时，张老汉为其购买一套价值 30 万元的房屋（产权登记在小儿子丙名下）。2016 年 1 月张老汉去世时遗留有个人所有的住房一套和 50 万元存款。您认为，上述哪些财产应当计算入遗产：A. 张老汉生前给三个儿子不同资助的财产与死亡时遗留的住房、存款，均应当合并计算为遗产；B. 张老汉去世时遗留的个人所有的住房和 50 万元存款，才可以计算为遗产；C. 其他。（单选）”

表 5-5 被继承人生前资助的财产是否应归入遗产范围的民众观念情况统计（单选）

选项	人数	比例
A. 张老汉生前给三个儿子不同资助的财产与死亡时遗留的住房、存款，均应当合并计算为遗产	100	14.22%
B. 张老汉去世时遗留的个人所有的住房和 50 万元存款，才可以计算为遗产	603	85.78%
C. 其他	0	0
合计	703	100%

关于被继承人生前特种赠与财产是否归入遗产范围的民众观念，调查统计数据显示，在 703 名被调查者中，（1）选择 B 项即持否定观点的，占八成半（85.78%），（2）选择 A 项即持肯定观点的，只占近一成半（14.22%）。

2. 归扣遗产价值计算时间的民众观念情况统计

问题【一、（二）2.】“如果上述答案您选 A，请问张老汉为小儿子丙买房的价值应该按何时计算？A. 买房时；B. 张老汉去世时；C. 实际分割遗产时；D. 其他。（单选）”

表 5-6 归扣遗产价值计算时间的民众观念情况统计（单选）

选项	人数	比例
A. 买房时	41	41.00%
B. 张老汉去世时	22	22.00%
C. 实际分割遗产时	37	37.00%
D. 其他	0	0
合计	100	100%

关于归扣遗产价值计算时间的民众观念，调查统计数据显示，在填写该问题的 100 名被调查者中，根据其占比高低排序如下：（1）选择 A 项认为应以赠与时为准的，占四成稍多（41.00%）；（2）选择 C 项认为应以分割遗产时为准的，占三成半稍多（37.00%）；（3）选择 B 项认为以继承开始时为准的，占二成稍多（22.00%）。即认为应以分割遗产时计算归扣遗产价值的占比居于第一位。

3. 生前特种赠与财产是否归入遗产范围的民间习惯情况统计

问题【一、（二）3.】“在您所在地区，如果发生上述张老汉生前给三个儿子不同资助财产的情况，在继承遗产时这些资助财产是否被合计到遗产范围内？A. 是；B. 不是。（单选）”

表 5-7　生前特种赠与财产是否归入遗产范围的民间习惯情况统计（单选）

选项	人数	比例
A. 是	146	20.77%
B. 不是	557	79.23%
合计	703	100%

关于生前特种赠与财产是否归入遗产范围的民间习惯，调查统计数据显示，703 名被调查者所在地区的习惯是：（1）B 项不是，即无归扣习惯的，占近八成（79.23%）；（2）A 项是，即有归扣习惯的，占二成（20.77%）。

4. 生前特种赠与财产不归扣纳入遗产情况下的分配方式之民间习惯情况统计

问题【一、（二）4.】“如果您选择 B 项即这些资产不是被合计到遗产范围内，三个儿子是如何分配父亲张老汉的遗产的？①按遗嘱分配或由被继承人自由意志决定；②尽赡养义务多分或按资助成分比例分配；③其他（大儿子多分）。（单选）”

（1）生前特种赠与财产不归入遗产情况下的遗产分配方式之民间习惯情况统计。

表 5-8　生前特种赠与财产不归入遗产情况下的遗产分配方式之民间习惯情况统计（单选）

选项	人数	比例
A. 按遗嘱分配或由被继承人自由意志决定	6	26.09%
B. 尽赡养义务多分或按资助成分比例分配	2	8.70%
C. 其他（大儿子多分）	15	65.22%
合计	23	100%

关于被继承人生前特种赠与财产不归入遗产情况下的分配方式之民间习惯，调查统计数据显示，填写该问题的 23 名被调查者所在地区的习惯是：①C 项大儿子可以多分的，占六成半（65.22%），这反映出至今部分地区仍然存有“长子继承”的传统习惯；②A 项按遗嘱分配或由被继承人决定的，占二成半稍多（26.09%）；③B 项尽赡养义务者多分或按资助成分比例分配的，占不到一成（8.70%）。

二、继承开始的通知和公告之调查数据统计情况

关于继承开始的通知和公告之调查数据统计，我们主要从继承开始的通知和公告的主体、继承开始的通知和公告的方式、继承开始的通知和公告的期间，这三个方面进行调查数据的统计情况汇总分析。

（一）继承开始的通知和公告的主体

问题【二、（一）】“被继承人死亡后，在您所在地区一般由下列哪些人通知涉及遗产分配的相关人员？A. 知道被继承人死亡的继承人；B. 保管遗产的继承人；C. 知道被

继承人死亡的单位、村（居）委会；D. 处理被继承人死亡事件的机构，如公安交警部门；E. 其他。（多选）”

表 5-9 继承开始的通知和公告的主体之民间习惯情况统计（多选）

选项		人数	比例
A. 知道被继承人死亡的继承人		436	62.02%
B. 保管遗产的继承人		385	54.77%
C. 知道被继承人死亡的单位、村（居）委会		298	42.39%
D. 处理被继承人死亡事件的机构，如公安交警部门		238	33.85%
E. 其他	E1. 审理继承案件的人民法院	3	0.43%
	E2. 朋友、亲戚或保管人	7	1%

关于继承开始的通知和公告的主体的民间习惯，调查统计数据显示，703 名被调查者填写的所在地区的习惯分别是：（1）A 项知道被继承人死亡的继承人的，占六成稍多（62.02%）；（2）B 项保管遗产的继承人的，占近五成半（54.77%）；（3）C 项知道被继承人死亡的单位、村（居）委会的，占四成稍多（42.39%）；（4）D 项处理被继承人死亡事件的机构（如公安交警部门）的，占近三成半（33.85%）。

（二）继承开始的通知和公告的方式

问题【二、（二）】“被继承人死亡后，您所在地区的人们一般采取以下哪些方式通知涉及遗产处理的相关人员：A. 口头、电话、微信等；B. 信件、告知函等书面通知；C. 在报纸、电视、网络等平台上发布被继承人死亡的公告；D. 在被继承人所在地的村（居）委会公告栏公告；E. 申请人民法院以公告程序进行公告；F. 其他。（多选）”

表 5-10 继承开始的通知和公告的方式民间习惯情况统计（多选）

选项	人数	比例
A. 口头、电话、微信等	544	77.38%
B. 信件、告知函等书面通知	340	48.36%
C. 在报纸、电视、网络等平台上发布被继承人死亡的公告	113	16.07%
D. 在被继承人所在地的村（居）委会公告栏公告	189	26.88%
E. 申请人民法院以公告程序进行公告	209	29.73%
F. 其他	29	4.13%

关于继承开始的通知和公告的方式的民间习惯，调查统计数据显示，703 名被调查者填写的所在地区的习惯是：（1）A 项使用口头、电话、微信等方式的，占近八成（77.38%）；（2）B 项使用书信、告知函等方式的，占近五成（48.36%）；（3）E 项采用申请人民法院以公告程序进行公告方式的，占近三成（29.73%）；（4）D 项采用在村（居）民委员会公告栏公告方式的，占二成半稍多（26.88%）；（5）C 项使用在报纸、电

视、网络等平台上发布被继承人的死亡公告方式的，占一成半稍多（16.07%）。

（三）继承开始的通知和公告的期间

问题【二、（三）】“您认为，通知人应在被继承人死亡后几日内发出通知：A.3 日；B.7 日；C.15 日；D.30 日；E. 其他。（单选）”

表 5-11　继承开始的通知和公告的期间的民众观念情况统计（单选）

选项		人数	比例
A.3 日		304	43.24%
B.7 日		190	27.03%
C.15 日		82	11.66%
D.30 日		82	11.66%
E. 其他	E1. 立即	30	4.27%
	E2. 当天	15	2.13%
合计		703	100%

关于继承开始的通知和公告的期间的民众观念，调查统计数据显示，在 703 名被调查者中，对于被继承人死亡后发出继承开始的通知的时间，（1）选择 A 项、B 项和 E 项，认为应在 7 日内发出的，合计占七成半稍多（76.67%）；（2）选择 C 项和 D 项，认为应在 15 日或 30 日内发出的，合计占二成半（23.32%）。

三、遗产管理之调查数据统计情况

关于遗产管理之调查数据统计，我们主要从遗产管理人的确定、遗产管理人的职责与报酬、遗产管理人的损害赔偿责任，这三个方面进行调查数据的统计情况汇总分析。

（一）遗产管理人的确定

1. 关于遗产管理人的确定的民间习惯情况统计

问题【三、（一）】“您所在地区人们处理遗产继承时，一般是由谁清点和管理遗产？A. 死者的法定继承人：配偶、子女、父母、兄弟姐妹、孙子女或外孙子女、祖父母或外祖父母；B. 死者的儿媳或女婿；C. 死者家族中的德高望重者；D. 死者的其他亲戚朋友；E. 死者所在的单位或村/居委会；F. 其他。（多选）其理由是什么？”

表 5-12　关于遗产管理人的确定的民间习惯情况统计（多选）

选项	人数	比例
A. 死者的法定继承人：配偶、子女、父母、兄弟姐妹、孙子女或外孙子女、祖父母或外祖父母	629	89.47%

续表

选项		人数	比例
A 项分项计算	A1. 配偶	615	87.48%
	A2. 子女	602	85.63%
	A3. 父母	561	79.8%
	A4. 兄弟姐妹	385	54.77%
	A5. 孙子女和外孙子女	292	41.54%
	A6. 祖父母和外祖父母	281	39.97%
B. 死者的儿媳或女婿		117	16.64%
C. 死者家族中的德高望重者		338	48.08%
D. 死者的其他亲戚朋友		103	14.65%
E. 死者所在的单位或村/居委会		221	31.44%
F. 其他		13	1.85%
F. 其他分开计算	F1. 律师	1	0.14%
	F2. 与死者亲近的人	3	0.43%

关于遗产管理人的确定的民间习惯，调查统计数据显示，703 名被调查者填写的所在地区的习惯排在前两位的是：（1）A 项由死者的法定继承人担任的，占近九成（89.47%）；（2）C 项由死者家族中的德高望重者担任的，占近五成（48.08%）。

2. 关于遗产管理人的确定的民间习惯之理由情况统计

表 5-13　关于遗产管理人的确定的民间习惯之理由情况统计

项目	人数	比例
A. 遗产管理人一般由法定继承人来担任，便于清点和妥善管理遗产	91	81.25%
B. 遗产管理人一般由法定继承人之外的人或组织来担任，可以防止遗产被隐藏、转移，有利于保护遗产相关人的合法权益	18	16.07%
C. 其他（符合风俗习惯和民众认知）	3	2.68%
合计	112	100%

关于遗产管理人确定的民间习惯之理由，调查统计数据显示，在填写该理由的 112 名被调查者的所在地区，（1）由法定继承人担任遗产管理人的理由是，A 项便于清点和妥善管理遗产的，占八成稍多（81.25%）；（2）由法定继承人之外的人或组织来担任的理由是，B 项可以防止遗产被隐藏、转移，有利于保护遗产相关人的合法权益的，占一成半稍多（16.07%）。

（二）遗产管理人的职责与报酬

1. 遗产管理人职责的民众观念情况统计

问题【三、（二）1.】“您认为，遗产人管理的职责有哪些？A. 清查遗产，制作遗产清单；B. 妥善保管遗产；C. 查明被继承人生前的债权和债务，积极地追讨债权或清偿债务；D. 查明被继承人是否留有遗嘱，并且确定遗嘱是否真实合法；E. 可以原告或被告的身份参加因遗产引起的诉讼；F. 定期制作遗产管理报告，向继承人报告遗产管理的情况；G. 其他。（多选）”

表 5-14　遗产管理人的管理职责的民众观念情况统计（多选）

选项		人数	比例
A. 清查遗产，制作遗产清单		648	92.18%
B. 妥善保管遗产		660	93.88%
C. 查明被继承人生前的债权和债务，积极地追讨债权或清偿债务		502	71.41%
D. 查明被继承人是否留有遗嘱，并且确定遗嘱是否真实合法		338	48.08%
E. 可以原告或被告的身份参加因遗产引起的诉讼		457	65.01%
F. 定期制作遗产管理报告，向继承人报告遗产管理的情况		398	56.61%
G. 其他		7	1%
G. 其他	G1. 法律规范与习惯	5	0.71%
	G2. 协商	2	0.28%

关于对遗产管理人职责的民众观念，调查统计数据显示，在 703 名被调查者中，占四成至九成的人认为其职责包括：（1）A 项清查遗产，制作遗产清单的，占 92.18%；（2）B项妥善保管遗产的，占 93.88%；（3）C 项查明被继承人生前的债权和债务，积极地追讨债权或清偿债务的，占 71.41%；（4）E 项可以原告或被告的身份参加因遗产引起的诉讼的，占 65.01%；（5）F 项定期制作遗产管理报告，向继承人报告遗产管理的情况的，占 56.61%；（6）D 项查明被继承人是否留有遗嘱，并且确定遗嘱是否真实合法的，占 48.08%。

2. 遗产管理人是否取得报酬的民间习惯情况统计

问题【三、（二）2.】“您所在地区，负责管理遗产的人是否可以获得报酬？A. 继承人担任遗产管理人的，不能请求给付报酬；B. 法院指定的遗产管理人，有权请求给付报酬；C. 继承人选任的第三人作为遗产管理人，是否给付报酬，应当由继承人决定；D. 继承人选任的第三人作为遗产管理人，一律有权请求给付报酬；E. 其他。（多选）”

表 5-15　遗产管理人是否可以取得报酬的民间习惯情况统计（多选）

选项	人数	比例
A. 继承人担任遗产管理人的，不能请求给付报酬	343	48.79%

续表

选项	人数	比例
B. 法院指定的遗产管理人，有权请求给付报酬	394	56.05%
C. 继承人选任的第三人作为遗产管理人，是否给付报酬，应当由继承人决定	281	39.97%
D. 继承人选任的第三人作为遗产管理人，一律有权请求给付报酬	245	34.85%
E. 其他	23	3.27%

关于遗产管理人是否可以取得报酬的民间习惯，调查统计数据显示，703 名被调查者填写的所在地区的习惯是：（1）A 项继承人担任的遗产管理人不可以取得报酬的，占近五成（48.79%）；（2）B 项法院指定担任的遗产管理人可以取得报酬的，占五成半稍多（56.05%）；（3）继承人选任的第三人担任的遗产管理人，其中，C 项是否可以取得报酬由继承人决定的，占近四成（39.97%）；D 项一律有权请求给付报酬的，占近三成半（34.85%）。

（三）遗产管理人的损害赔偿责任

问题【三、（三）】“在您所在地区，负责管理遗产的人对因其过错造成的较大财产损失，是否承担赔偿责任？A. 凡有故意或重大过失的，才承担赔偿责任；B. 无论是故意或重大过失或一般轻过失的，都要承担赔偿责任；C. 其他。（单选）”

表 5-16 遗产管理人是否承担赔偿责任的民间习惯情况统计（单选）

<table>
<tr><th colspan="2">选项</th><th>人数</th><th>比例</th></tr>
<tr><td colspan="2">A. 凡有故意或重大过失的，才承担赔偿责任</td><td>370</td><td>52.63%</td></tr>
<tr><td colspan="2">B. 无论是故意或重大过失或一般轻过失的，都要承担赔偿责任</td><td>300</td><td>42.67%</td></tr>
<tr><td colspan="2">C. 其他</td><td>33</td><td>4.69%</td></tr>
<tr><td rowspan="3">C. 其他</td><td>C1. 根据当事人要求</td><td>5</td><td>0.71%</td></tr>
<tr><td>C2. 有偿管理才予以赔偿</td><td>12</td><td>1.70%</td></tr>
<tr><td>C3. 是否赔偿依据习惯</td><td>16</td><td>2.28%</td></tr>
<tr><td colspan="2">合计</td><td>703</td><td>100%</td></tr>
</table>

关于遗产管理人是否承担赔偿责任的民间习惯，调查统计数据显示，703 名被调查者填写的所在地区的习惯是：（1）A 项凡有故意或重大过失才承担赔偿责任的，占五成稍多（52.63%）；（2）B 项无论是故意或重大过失或一般轻过失的都要承担赔偿责任的，占四成稍多（42.67%）。

四、法定继承之调查数据统计情况

关于法定继承之调查数据统计，我们主要从法定继承人的范围和顺序、配偶与血亲继承人的法定应继份、配偶对遗产中家庭住房的先取权和终生使用权、后顺序特殊法定继承人对遗产中原使用的住房及日常生活用品的终生使用权、尽了主要赡养义务的丧偶儿媳或女婿的遗产分配方式，这五个方面进行调查数据的统计情况汇总分析。

（一）法定继承人的范围与顺序

1. 法定继承人范围与顺序的民众观念的情况统计

问题【四、（一）1.】“下列亲属，您认为哪些应当作为法定继承人？他们各自的继承顺序如何？请根据您认为适当的先后顺序填写数字：1.2.3.……例如，父母（1）；子女（2）；祖父母、外祖父母（3）。如果您认为应当在同一顺序的人，可以填写相同的数字，如配偶（1）；父母（1）；子女（1）；祖父母、外祖父母（1）。”

配偶（ ）	父母（ ）	儿子（ ）女儿（ ）
孙子女（ ）外孙子女（ ）	祖父母（ ）外祖父母（ ）	兄弟（ ）姐妹（ ）
侄子女（ ）外甥子女（ ）	伯叔姑舅姨（ ）	堂兄弟姐妹（ ）
表兄弟姐妹（ ）	其他亲属（称谓）（ ）	其他亲属（称谓）（ ）

表 5-17 法定继承人的范围与顺序的民众观念情况统计（多选）

亲属名称	第一顺序		第二顺序		第三顺序		第四顺序		第四顺序以上	
	人数	比例%	人数	比例%	人数	比例%	人数	比例%	人数	比例%
配偶	647	92.03	31	4.41	8	1.14	6	0.85	1	0.14
父母	480	68.28	141	20.06	54	7.68	13	1.85	1	0.14
子	485	68.99	140	19.91	68	9.67	1	0.14	0	0
女	438	62.30	154	21.91	72	10.24	15	2.13	0	0
孙子女	20	2.84	351	49.93	140	19.91	64	9.10	44	6.26
外孙子女	16	2.28	297	42.25	149	21.19	73	10.38	57	8.11
祖父母	24	3.41	331	47.08	124	17.64	60	8.53	67	9.53
外祖父母	21	2.99	297	42.25	134	19.06	63	8.96	75	10.67
兄弟	11	1.56	318	45.23	147	20.91	65	9.25	84	11.95
姐妹	12	1.71	307	43.67	143	20.34	67	9.53	79	11.24
侄子女	10	1.42	13	1.85	233	33.14	100	14.22	133	18.92
外甥子女	12	1.71	13	1.85	224	31.86	93	13.23	144	20.48
伯叔姑	11	1.56	15	2.13	222	31.58	93	13.23	141	20.06
舅姨	10	1.42	15	2.13	222	31.58	93	13.23	141	20.06
堂兄弟	10	1.42	5	0.71	197	28.02	107	15.22	150	21.34

续表

亲属名称	第一顺序		第二顺序		第三顺序		第四顺序		第四顺序以上	
	人数	比例%	人数	比例%	人数	比例%	人数	比例%	人数	比例%
堂姐妹	10	1.42	5	0.71	197	28.02	107	15.22	150	21.34
表兄弟	22	3.13	9	1.28	129	18.35	129	17.78	175	24.89
表姐妹	22	3.13	9	1.28	129	18.35	125	17.78	175	24.89

关于法定继承人的范围与顺序的民众观念，各顺序以被调查者选择占比最高的作为统计依据，703 名被调查者较认可的法定继承范围与顺序为：（1）第一顺序为配偶(92.03%)、父母（68.28%）、儿子（68.99%）、女儿（62.30%）；（2）第二顺序为孙子女（49.93%）、外孙子女（42.25%），祖父母（47.08%）、外祖父母（42.25%）和兄弟(45.23%)、姐妹（43.67%）；（3）第三顺序的为侄子女（33.14%）、外甥子女(31.86%)、堂兄弟姐妹（28.02%）、伯叔姑舅姨（31.58%）；（4）第四顺序以上为表兄弟姐妹（24.89%）。

2. 配偶与血亲继承人顺序的民众观念的情况统计

问题【四、(一) 2.】“以下三种法定继承人的范围和顺序，您认为哪一个更为适当？(单选)”

A	B	C
第一顺序：子女	第一顺序：子女	第一顺序：配偶、子女、父母
第二顺序：父母	第二顺序：父母	第二顺序：兄弟姐妹、祖父母、外祖父母
第三顺序：兄弟姐妹、祖父母、外祖父母 兄弟姐妹的子女（侄子女、外甥子女为代位继承人）	第三顺序：兄弟姐妹、祖父母、外祖父母 兄弟姐妹的子女（侄子女、外甥子女为代位继承人）	第三顺序：侄子女、外甥子女
配偶无固定顺序，能够参与第一顺序、第二顺序、第三个顺序的继承	配偶无固定顺序，能够参与第一顺序、第二顺序的继承	配偶有固定顺序，只能参与第一顺序的继承

表 5-18 配偶与血亲继承人顺序的民众观念情况统计（单选）

选项	人数	比例
A. 配偶无固定顺序，可以参与第一、第二、第三顺序继承	76	10.81%
B. 配偶无固定顺序，可以参与第一、第二顺序继承	56	7.97%
C. 配偶与子女、父母同为第一顺序，共同继承	571	81.22%
合计	703	100%

关于配偶与血亲继承人顺序的民众观念，调查统计数据显示，在703名被调查者中，(1) 选择C项顺序为第一顺序：配偶、子女、父母；第二顺序：兄弟姐妹、祖父母外祖父母；第三顺序：侄子女、外甥子女；配偶有固定顺序，其属于第一顺位继承人的，占八成稍多（81.22%）。(2) 选择A、B两项顺序为：第一顺序为子女；第二顺序为父母；第三顺序为兄弟姐妹、祖父母、外祖父母、兄弟姐妹的子女（侄子女、外甥子女为代位继承人）；配偶无固定的继承顺序，可分别与第一、第二（或第三）顺序的法定继承人共同继承的，合计只占近二成（18.78%）。

（二）配偶与血亲继承人的法定应继份

问题【四、（二）】“配偶与血亲继承人共同继承各取得遗产的份额，您认为以下哪一项更为适当？（单选）”

A. 生存配偶无固定继承顺序	B. 生存配偶无固定继承顺序	C. 生存配偶有固定继承顺序	D. 其他（您认为适当的生存配偶继承份额）
生存配偶与第一顺序的子女共同继承时，其取得遗产的一半。另一半由子女按人数平均继承	生存配偶与第一顺序的子女共同继承时，其取得遗产的一半，另一半由子女按人数平均继承	第一顺序继承人为配偶、子女、父母，共同继承时按人数均分遗产	
生存配偶与第二顺序的父母共同继承时，其取得遗产的三分之二。另外三分之一由父母平均继承	生存配偶与第二顺序的父母共同继承时，其取得遗产的三分之二，另外三分之一由父母平均继承	无第一顺序血亲继承人时，生存配偶继承全部遗产	
生存配偶与第三顺序的兄弟姐妹、祖父母和外祖父母共同继承时，其取得遗产的四分之三。另外四分之一由兄弟姐妹、祖父母、外祖父，按人数平均继承	无第一、第二顺序血亲继承人时，生存配偶继承全部遗产		
无上述三个顺序血亲继承人时，生存配偶取得全部遗产			

表5-19 配偶与血亲继承人的法定应继份的民众观念的情况统计（单选）

选项	人数	比例
A. 配偶无固定继承顺序，参与前三顺序的继承并取得不同份额；无上述三个顺序血亲继承人时，配偶取得全部遗产	204	29.02%
B. 配偶无固定继承顺序，参与前二顺序的继承并取得不同份额；无第一、第二顺序血亲继承人时，配偶继承全部遗产	120	17.07%

续表

<table>
<tr><th colspan="2">选项</th><th>人数</th><th>比例</th></tr>
<tr><td colspan="2">C. 配偶有固定继承顺序并均分遗产，与第一顺序继承人共同继承</td><td>364</td><td>51.78%</td></tr>
<tr><td rowspan="2">D. 其他</td><td>D1 配偶是否对遗产有贡献</td><td rowspan="2">15</td><td rowspan="2">2.13%</td></tr>
<tr><td>D2 平均分配</td></tr>
<tr><td colspan="2">合计</td><td>703</td><td>100%</td></tr>
</table>

关于配偶与血亲继承人的法定应继份的民众观念，调查统计数据显示，在703名被调查者中，(1) 选择A项和B项，配偶为无固定继承顺序，可参与第一、第二（或第三）顺序且在不同顺序其应继份不同的，合计占四成半稍多（46.09%）；(2) 选择C项，配偶为固定顺序的继承人，与第一顺序的继承人共同继承并平均分配遗产的，占五成稍多（51.78%）。

（三）配偶对遗产中家庭住房的先取权与终生使用权

1. 配偶对遗产中家庭住房的先取权与终生使用权的民间习惯情况统计

问题【四、(三) 1.】“甲乙是夫妻，育有一子丙。甲因病去世时留下的遗产包括价值50万元住房一套（原由甲乙夫妻共同居住，丙已结婚分家另过）、价值10万元小汽车一辆和20万元存款。如果上述情况发生在您所在地区，被继承人甲的妻子乙是否可以优先继承这套房屋（配偶先取权）？A. 是；B. 否。（单选）”

表5-20　配偶对遗产中家庭住房的先取权与终生使用权的民间习惯情况统计（单选）

选项	人数	比例
A. 是	604	85.92%
B. 否	99	14.08%
合计	703	100%

关于配偶对遗产中家庭住房的先取权与终生使用权之民间习惯，调查统计数据显示，703名被调查者填写的所在地区的习惯是：（1）A项是，即有此习惯的，占八成半（85.92%）；(2) B项否，即无此习惯的，仅占近一成半（14.08%）。

2. 配偶对遗产中家庭住房的先取或终生使用是否付费的民间习惯情况统计

问题【四、(三) 2.】“如果甲的妻子乙可以优先继承这套房屋，但该住房的价值超过其应当继承的遗产份额40万元，在您所在地区是否按照下列情况处理的？A. 乙有权继承该住房，且无须向另一法定继承人丙进行补偿；B. 如果乙有经济补偿能力，则应当向另一法定继承人丙适当进行补偿；C. 其他。（单选）”

表 5-21 配偶对遗产中家庭住房的先取或终生使用是否付费的民间习惯情况统计（单选）

选项	人数	比例
A. 乙有权继承该住房，且无须向其他共同应召继承人丙进行补偿	36	12.72%
B. 如果乙有经济补偿能力，则应当向其他共同应召继承人丙适当进行补偿	116	40.99%
C. 其他（基于公序良俗决定是否补偿）	131	46.29%
合计	283	100%

关于配偶对遗产中家庭住房的先取或终生使用是否付费之民间习惯，调查统计数据显示，填写该问题的283名被调查者所在地区的习惯是：（1）C项根据公序良俗决定配偶是否补偿的，占四成半稍多（46.29%）；（2）B项如果配偶有经济补偿能力则需要补偿费用的，占四成（占40.99%）；（3）A项配偶无须补偿的，占一成稍多（12.72%）。

（四）后顺序特殊法定继承人对遗产中原使用的住房及日常生活用品的终生使用权

后顺序特殊法定继承人对遗产中原使用的住房及日常生活用品的终生使用权，也可称为后顺序特殊法定继承人对特殊遗产的终生使用权。

1. 后顺序特殊法定继承人对遗产中原使用的住房及日常生活用品的终生使用权的民间习惯情况统计

问题【四、（四）1.】“某甲死亡时留下若干遗产，其中包括一套三室一厅的住房（其中的一间房屋一直由某甲的祖父居住）。由于某甲的祖父属于后顺序继承人而不能参加继承，遗产全部由某甲的第一顺序继承人配偶及其子女等继承。请问：在您所在地区，如果发生了上述情况，有哪些下列处理方式？某甲的祖父对该供其居住的房屋，是否可以继续居住？A. 是；B. 否。（单选）”

表 5-22 后顺序特殊法定继承人对特殊遗产的终生使用权之民间习惯情况统计（单选）

选项	人数	比例
A. 是	633	91.47%
B. 否	59	8.53%
合计	692	100%

关于后顺序特殊法定继承人对特殊遗产的终生使用权之民间习惯，调查统计数据显示，填写该问题的692名被调查者所在地区的习惯是：（1）A项是，即有此习惯的，占九成稍多（91.47%）；（2）B项否，即无此习惯的，占不到一成（8.53%）。

2. 后顺序特殊法定继承人对遗产中原使用的住房及日常生活用品的终生使用是否付费的民间习惯情况统计

问题【四、（四）2.】“如果某甲的祖父可以继续居住，是否其可以不交租金？（单选）”

表 5-23　后顺序特殊法定继承人对特殊遗产的终生使用是否付费的民间习惯情况统计（单选）

选项	人数	比例
A. 是	535	78.22%
B. 否	149	21.78%
合计	684	100%

关于后顺序特殊法定继承人对特殊遗产的终生使用是否付费的民间习惯，调查统计数据显示，填写该问题的684名被调查者所在地区的习惯是：（1）A项是，即无须支付费用的，占近八成（78.22%）；（2）B项否，即需要支付费用的，占二成稍多（21.78%）。

3. 后顺序特殊法定继承人对遗产中原使用的住房及日常生活用品的终生使用权之期限的民间习惯情况统计

问题【四、（四）3.】“如果某甲的祖父可以继续居住，是否可以居住到其死亡时为止（终生使用权）。（单选）”

表 5-24　后顺序特殊法定继承人对特殊遗产的终生使用权之期限的民间习惯情况统计（单选）

选项	人数	比例
A. 是	562	81.45%
B. 否	128	18.55%
合计	690	100%

关于后顺序特殊法定继承人对特殊遗产的终生使用权之期限的民间习惯，调查统计数据显示，填写该问题的690名被调查者所在地区的习惯是：（1）A项是，即有此习惯的，占八成稍多（81.45%）；（2）B项否，即无此习惯的，仅占近二成（18.55%）。

（五）尽了主要赡养义务的丧偶儿媳或女婿的遗产分配方式

问题【四、（五）】“村民某甲，老伴因病早年去世，膝下有两个儿子乙和丙。2003年乙与丁结婚后与某甲共同生活。2012年1月乙因交通事故死亡，但乙的妻子丁仍然一直照料公公某甲的晚年生活，直至2015年1月某甲去世。请问：在您所在地区，如发生上述情况，因乙的妻子丁对公公某甲尽了主要赡养义务，如何处理某甲的遗产分配问题？A. 丁可以与某甲的二儿子丙共同继承，并且平均分配遗产；B. 丁不能与某甲的二儿子丙共同继承，但其可分得适当的遗产；C. 其他。（单选）其理由是什么？”

1. 尽了主要赡养义务的丧偶儿媳或女婿的遗产分配的民间习惯的情况统计

表 5-25　尽了主要赡养义务的丧偶儿媳或女婿的遗产分配的民间习惯情况统计（单选）

选项	人数	比例
A. 丁可以与某甲的二儿子丙共同继承，并且平均分配遗产	491	69.84%
B. 丁不能与某甲的二儿子丙共同继承，但其可分得适当的遗产	181	25.75%

续表

选项		人数	比例
C. 其他	C1. 丙和丁共同继承，且丁可多分	13	1.85%
	C2. 获得全部	18	2.56%
合计		703	100%

关于尽了主要赡养义务的丧偶儿媳或女婿的遗产分配的民间习惯，调查统计数据显示，703名被调查者所在地区的习惯是：（1）A项其与被继承人其他子女共同继承并且平均分配遗产的，占近七成（69.84%）；（2）B项其不可与被继承人其他子女共同继承但其可分得适当遗产的，仅占二成半（25.75%）。

2. 尽了主要赡养义务的丧偶儿媳或女婿的遗产分配方式的民间习惯的理由情况统计

表5-26　尽了主要赡养义务的丧偶儿媳或女婿的遗产分配方式民间习惯的理由情况统计

项目		数量	比例
A. 作为儿媳妇，丁孝敬公公，已经尽了赡养义务，符合中国的孝道文化和道德观念，因此有权继承遗产		197	72.69%
B. 虽然丁一直照顾公公的晚年生活，但毕竟不是某甲的子女，与某甲不具有血缘关系，遗产不能给了外人，因此，不能继承某甲的遗产		17	6.27%
C. 其他	C1. 根据法律规定，丁有权继承	11	4.06%
	C2. 根据公平原则，丁可继承	46	16.97%
合计		271	100%

关于尽了主要赡养义务的丧偶儿媳或女婿的遗产分配方式的民间习惯的理由，在填写该理由的271名被调查者中，（1）其可以作为第一顺位继承人继承遗产的习惯之理由是，A项和C项出于我国传统孝道文化与道德观念、符合法律规定和公平原则的，合计占比九成稍多（93.73%）；（2）其不能继承公公的遗产的习惯之理由是，B项认为其与被继承人无血缘关系，遗产不能给外人的，占比不到一成（6.27%）。

五、遗嘱继承之调查数据统计情况

关于遗嘱继承之调查数据统计，我们主要从公证遗嘱与其他形式遗嘱的效力、遗嘱自由的限制——特留份、夫妻共同遗嘱，这三个方面进行调查数据的统计情况汇总分析。

（一）公证遗嘱与其他形式遗嘱的效力

问题【五、（一）】“退休职工甲有一套个人住房，他于2011年2月立了一份遗嘱，写明由其妻子乙一人继承该住房，并将该遗嘱进行了公证。后来，甲改变了主意，他重新写了一份遗嘱，写明由其妻子乙和儿子丙共同继承该房屋。2016年3月甲住院病危期间，当着二位医生在现场立下口头遗嘱，指定其个人住房由儿子丙继承，两个小时后其抢救无效死亡。请问：您认为，甲的个人住房应该由谁继承？A. 乙；B. 乙和丙；C. 丙。（单选）其理由是什么？”

1. 公证遗嘱与其他形式遗嘱的适用效力的民众观念情况统计

表 5-27 公证遗嘱与其他形式遗嘱的适用效力的民众观念情况统计（单选）

选项	人数	比例
A. 乙（公证遗嘱有效）	244	34.71%
B. 乙和丙（后成立的未公证书面遗嘱有效）	212	30.16%
C. 丙（最后的口头遗嘱有效）	247	35.14%
合计	703	100%

关于公证遗嘱与其他形式遗嘱的适用效力的民众观念，调查统计数据显示，在703名被调查者中，（1）选择B项和C项后遗嘱优先于前一遗嘱（包括公证遗嘱）适用的，合计占六成半（65.30%）；（2）选择A项公证遗嘱应当优先适用的，占近三成半（34.71%）。

2. 公证遗嘱与其他形式遗嘱的适用效力的民众观念的理由情况统计

表 5-28 公证遗嘱与其他形式遗嘱的适用效力的民众观念的理由情况统计

项目	人数	比例
A. 公证遗嘱的程序规范，具有较强的公示效力和证明效力	215	52.31%
B. 书面遗嘱（第二份遗嘱）比较正式，取证容易，且其订立在公证遗嘱之后，反映了被继承人的最后意愿	50	12.17%
C. 口头遗嘱形式灵活，且有证人作证，能够反映被继承人的最后真实意愿	146	35.52%
D. 口头遗嘱形式不固定，很难准确、完全地反映被继承人的真实意愿，且有被篡改或修改的可能性	0	0.00%
合计	411	100%

关于公证遗嘱与其他形式遗嘱的适用效力的民众观念的理由，调查统计数据显示，在填写该理由的411名被调查者中，（1）认为公证遗嘱当优先适用的理由是，A项公证遗嘱程序规范，具有较强的公示公信力和证明效力的，占五成稍多（52.31%）；（2）认为后遗嘱应当优先于前遗嘱（包括公证遗嘱）适用理由是，B项和C项后遗嘱更能反映遗嘱人最后真实意愿的，合计占四成半稍多（47.69%）。

（二）遗嘱自由的限制——特留份

问题【五、（二）】“甲生前立了一份遗嘱，将自己死后遗留下的财产全部赠给他的一个好朋友乙，而他的配偶和子女不能取得甲的任何遗产。请问：您认为甲的这一做法是否适当？A. 适当；B. 不适当；C. 其他。（单选）”

以遗嘱将个人遗产全部赠给他人之民众观念的情况统计如下：

表 5-29　以遗嘱将个人遗产全部赠给他人之民众观念的情况统计（单选）

选项	人数	比例
A. 适当	223	31.72%
B. 不适当	461	65.58%
C. 其他	19	2.70%
合计	703	100%

对于以遗嘱将个人遗产全部赠给他人之民众观念，调查统计数据显示，在 703 名被调查者中，（1）选择 B 项该行为不适当，即应对遗嘱的自由予以限制的，占六成半（65.58%）；（2）选择 A 项该行为适当，即不应对遗嘱的自由予以限制的，占三成稍多（31.72%）

（三）夫妻共同遗嘱

1. 夫妻共同遗嘱的民众观念情况统计

问题【五、（三）1.】“甲乙是夫妻，双方在生前共同设立一份遗嘱，对死后的遗产处理进行安排。甲乙双方在遗嘱中约定，不管谁先去世，另一方都不得改变此遗嘱对遗产的处理安排。您是否认同甲乙夫妻双方共同设立遗嘱的此约定？A. 赞同；B. 不赞同。（单选）”

表 5-30　夫妻共同遗嘱的民众观念情况统计（单选）

选项	人数	比例
A. 赞同	534	75.96%
B. 不赞同	169	24.04%
合计	703	100%

关于夫妻共同遗嘱的民众观念，调查统计数据显示，在 703 名被调查者中，（1）选择 A 项持赞成态度的，占七成半（75.96%）；（2）选择 B 项持不赞同态度的，占近二成半（24.04%）。

2. 夫妻共同遗嘱的民间习惯情况统计

问题【五、（三）2.】“在您所在地区，有无夫妻共同设立遗嘱的情况发生？A. 有；B. 无。（单选）”

表 5-31　夫妻共同遗嘱的民间习惯情况统计（单选）

选项	人数	比例
A. 有	160	22.76%
B. 无	543	77.24%
合计	703	100%

关于夫妻共同遗嘱的民间习惯，调查统计数据显示，703 名被调查者填写的所在地区的习惯是：（1）A 项有该习惯的，仅占二成稍多（22.76%）；（2）B 项无该习惯的，占七成半稍多（77.24%）。

六、继承和遗赠的接受与放弃之调查数据统计情况

关于继承和遗赠的接受与放弃之调查数据统计，我们主要从继承的接受与放弃的时间与方式、遗赠的接受与放弃的方式与效力、继承的放弃与债权人的撤销权，这三个方面进行调查数据的统计情况汇总分析。

（一）继承的接受与放弃的时间与方式

问题【六、（一）】“继承人放弃继承的时间，您认为下列哪一个更为适当？A. 继承人放弃继承的，应在知道继承开始的 2 个月内作出放弃继承的表示；B. 继承开始后继承人放弃继承的，应当在遗产处理前，作出放弃继承的意思表示。（单选）其理由是什么？请问您所在地区的人们是如何处理此类行为的？”

1. 继承的接受与放弃的时间的民众观念情况统计

表 5-32　继承的接受与放弃的时间的民众观念情况统计（单选）

选项	人数	比例
A. 继承人放弃继承的，应在知道继承开始的 2 个月内作出放弃继承的意思表示	273	38.83%
B. 继承开始后继承人放弃继承的，应当在遗产处理前，作出放弃继承的意思表示	430	61.17%
合计	703	100%

关于继承的接受与放弃的时间的民众观念，调查统计数据显示，在 703 名被调查者中，（1）选择 B 项继承人应在遗产处理前作出放弃继承意思表示的，占六成稍多（61.17%）；（2）选择 A 项继承人应在知道继承开始的 2 个月内作出放弃继承意思表示的，占近四成（38.83%）。

2. 继承的接受与放弃的方式的民间习惯情况统计

表 5-33　继承的接受与放弃的方式的民间习惯情况统计（单选）

选项	人数	比例
A. 书面表示放弃	43	18.38%
B. 口头表示放弃	64	27.35%
C. 继承人作出明确表示	114	48.72%
D. 按照实际情况	13	5.56%
合计	234	100%

关于继承的接受与放弃的时间与方式的民间习惯，调查统计数据显示，填写该问题的

234 名被调查者所在地区的习惯是：(1) 前三项，应当以明确表示（包括书面和口头等方式）作出的，合计占近九成半（94.44%）；(2) D 项，按照实际情况的，占比仅有半成（5.56%）。

3. 继承的接受与放弃的时间的民众观念之理由情况统计

表 5-34 继承的接受与放弃的时间的民众观念之理由情况统计

项目	人数	比例
A. 2 个月的时间较为合适，可以让继承人有一定的时间去考虑是否放弃继承权，同时，又可以督促继承人积极行使权利，或符合公序良俗	130	50.78%
B. 在遗产处理前，继承人就可以放弃继承权，这样既不影响其他继承人的利益，又可以保证继承人行使放弃继承的权利，符合法律规定	126	49.22%
合计	256	100%

关于继承人放弃继承的时间的民众观念之理由，调查统计数据显示，在填写该理由的 256 名被调查者中，(1) 认为继承开始的 2 个月内作出放弃继承较为合适的理由是，A 项可以让继承人有一定的时间去考虑是否放弃继承权，同时又可以督促继承人积极行使权利，而且符合公序良俗，占五成（50.78%）；(2) 认为在遗产处理前继承人就可以放弃继承权的理由是，B 项这样既不影响其他继承人的利益，又可以保证继承人行使放弃继承的权利，而且符合法律规定，占近五成（49.22%）。

（二）遗赠的接受与放弃的方式与效力

1. 遗赠的接受与放弃的方式与效力的民众观念情况统计

问题【六、(二)】“甲生前设立了一份遗嘱，其内容为：在甲死后，将一辆小汽车赠给其侄子乙。后来甲去世，乙得知遗嘱的内容后，对此遗赠没有作出任何意思表示，既没有说接受，也没有说放弃。您认为下列哪一项更为适当？A. 乙无权取得该小汽车，乙的行为应该被视为放弃该遗赠；B. 乙有权取得该小汽车，乙的行为应该被视为接受该遗赠。(单选) 其理由是什么？请问您所在地区的人们是如何处理此类行为的？”

表 5-35 遗赠的接受与放弃的方式与效力的民众观念情况统计（单选）

选项	人数	比例
A. 乙无权取得该小汽车，乙的行为应该被视为放弃该遗赠	245	34.85%
B. 乙有权取得该小汽车，乙的行为应该被视为接受该遗赠	458	65.15%
合计	703	100%

关于遗赠的接受与放弃的方式与效力的民众观念，调查统计数据显示，在 703 名被调查者中，(1) 选择 B 项受遗赠人未作表示应认定为接受遗赠的，占六成半（65.15%）；(2) 选择 A 项受遗赠人未作表示应认定为放弃遗赠的，占近三成半（34.85%）。

2. 遗赠的接受与放弃的方式与效力的民间习惯情况统计

表 5-36　遗赠的接受与放弃的方式与效力的民间习惯情况统计（单选）

选项	人数	比例
A. 作出明确的表示	127	48.66%
B. 默认接受	59	22.61%
C. 依据法律	8	3.07%
D. 订立书面协议	29	11.11%
E. 征得继承人的同意	15	5.75%
F. 依据被继承人的遗嘱	23	8.81%
合计	261	100%

关于遗赠的接受与放弃的方式与效力的民间习惯，调查统计数据显示，填写该问题的261名被调查者所在地区的习惯是：（1）A项、C项、D项和E项，接受遗赠必须以明示方式，而受遗赠人未作表示推定为放弃遗赠的，合计占近七成（68.58%）；（2）B项和F项，受遗赠人未作表示推定为接受遗产的，合计占三成稍多（31.42%）。

3. 遗赠的接受与放弃的方式与效力的民间习惯之理由情况统计

表 5-37　遗赠的接受与放弃的方式与效力的民间习惯之理由情况统计

项目	人数	比例
A. 接受遗赠毕竟是一种纯获利行为，乙不表示，就应该视为接受，如其不接受，那他早就作出不接受的表示了	72	44.44%
B. 乙有权选择是否接受甲的遗赠，如乙没有表示，就应该视为放弃遗赠，这与现行法规定一致	90	55.56%
合计	162	100%

关于遗赠的接受与放弃的方式与效力的民间习惯之理由，调查统计数据显示，在填写该理由的162名被调查者中，（1）受遗赠人未作表示则理应视为放弃接受遗赠的理由是，B项与现行法规定一致的，占五成半（55.56%）；（2）受遗赠人未作表示应推定为接受遗赠的理由是，A项接受遗赠是一种纯获利行为的，占近四成半（44.44%）。

（三）继承的放弃与债权人的撤销权

1. 继承的放弃能否被债权人撤销的民众观念情况统计

问题【六、（三）】“甲为乙的父亲，2015年年底，乙因病住院治疗，医治无效去世，留下遗产5万元及房屋一套。此时甲经营的摩配厂已经负债累累，拖欠工人的工资已有10个月，但他考虑儿媳在其丈夫乙去世后个人抚养年幼的女儿有经济困难，于是主动提出放弃继承儿子乙的遗产。甲的债权人却认为甲不应放弃继承儿子的遗产，这实际上是逃避债务，侵犯了债权人利益。为此，甲的债权人起诉至法院，要求撤销甲放弃继承儿子乙遗产的行为。您认为下列哪一项更为适当？A. 甲放弃继承乙遗产的行为，可以被撤销；B. 甲放弃继承乙遗产的行为，不可以被撤销。（单选）其理由是什么？请问您所在地区的人们是如何处理此类行为的？”

表 5-38 继承的放弃行为能否被债权人撤销的民众观念情况统计（单选）

选项	人数	比例
A. 甲放弃继承乙遗产的行为，可以被撤销	326	46.37%
B. 甲放弃继承乙遗产的行为，不可以被撤销	377	53.63%
合计	703	100%

关于继承的放弃行为能否被债权人撤销的民众观念，调查统计数据显示，在 703 名被调查者中，（1）选择 B 项不可以被撤销的，占五成稍多（53.63%）；（2）选择 A 项可以被撤销的，占四成半稍多（46.37%）。

2. 继承的放弃能否被债权人撤销的民间习惯情况统计

表 5-39 继承的放弃能否被债权人撤销的民间习惯情况统计（单选）

选项	人数	比例
A. 可以撤销	40	31.50%
B. 不可撤销	37	29.13%
C. 依据法律规定，诉至法院	11	8.66%
D. 尊重个人自由意志	28	22.05%
E. 保护弱势群体	11	8.66%
合计	127	100%

关于继承人放弃的行为能否被债权人撤销的民间习惯，调查统计数据显示，填写该问题的 127 名被调查者所在地区的习惯是：（1）A 项、C 项和 E 项，可以被撤销的，占近五成（48.82%）；（2）B 项和 D 项，不可以被撤销的，占五成稍多（51.18%）。

3. 继承的放弃能否被债权人撤销的民众观念的理由情况统计

表 5-40 继承的放弃能否被债权人撤销的民众观念的理由情况统计

项目	人数	比例
A. 不可以被撤销，有利于照顾儿媳及其孙女的生活，她们是弱势群体，理应获得优先照顾	124	52.10%
B. 可以被撤销，甲的债权人利益需要被保护	114	47.90%
合计	238	100%

关于继承的放弃能否被债权人撤销的民众观念之理由，调查统计数据显示，在填写该

理由的238名被调查者中，（1）认为不可以被撤销的理由是，A项应当兼顾被继承人照顾的其他近亲属的利益的，占五成稍多（52.10%）的；（2）认为可以被债权人撤销的理由是，B项继承人的债权人利益需要被保护的，占四成半稍多（47.90%）。

七、继承权的丧失、被继承人的宥恕与代位继承的调查数据统计情况

关于继承权的丧失、被继承人的宥恕与代位继承之调查数据统计，我们主要从继承权的丧失与被继承人的宥恕、继承权的丧失与代位继承，这两个方面进行调查数据的统计情况汇总分析。

（一）继承权的丧失与被继承人的宥恕

问题【七、（一）】“某甲如果以欺诈或者胁迫的手段，迫使或者妨碍其父乙设立、变更或者撤销遗嘱，情节较为严重，但后来其获得乙的原谅。您认为以下哪一种处理更为适当？A. 某甲有资格继承其父遗产；B. 某甲仍然不能继承其父遗产。（单选）在您所在地区，人们是如何处理此类行为的？”

1. 继承权的丧失与被继承人的宥恕的民众观念与民间习惯情况统计

表5-41 继承权的丧失与被继承人的宥恕的民众观念之情况统计（单选）

选项	人数	比例
A. 某甲有资格继承其父遗产	484	70.04%
B. 某甲依然不能继承其父遗产	207	29.96%
合计	691	100%

关于继承权的丧失与被继承人的宥恕的民众观念，即因欺诈、胁迫行为丧失继承权的，如获得被继承人谅解其继承权是否可以恢复，调查统计数据显示，在填写该问题的691名被调查者中，（1）选择A项可以恢复的，占七成（70.04%），（2）选择B项不可以恢复的，占近三成（29.96%）。

2. 继承权的丧失与被继承人的宥恕的民间习惯情况统计

表5-42 继承权的丧失与被继承人的宥恕的民间习惯情况统计（单选）

选项	人数	比例
A. 可以继承	51	31.88%
B. 不可以继承	34	21.25%
C. 共同协商	37	23.13%
D. 由被继承人决定	38	23.75%
合计	160	100%

关于继承权的丧失与被继承人的宥恕的民间习惯，调查统计数据显示，在填写该问题的160名被调查所在地区的习惯是：（1）A项、C项和D项，可以恢复的，合计占近八成（78.75%）；（2）B项不可以恢复的，占二成稍多（21.25%）。

（二）继承权的丧失与代位继承

问题【七、（二）】“村民甲死亡后，其子乙因实施伪造遗嘱的行为导致丧失了对其父甲的遗产继承权，乙的儿子丙能否代父乙去继承祖父甲的遗产，您认为以下哪一种处理更为适当？A. 丙能够代父乙继承祖父甲遗产；B. 丙不能代父乙继承祖父甲遗产。（单选）请问：在您所在地区的人们是如何处理此类情况的？”

1. 继承权的丧失的效力是否及于代位继承人的民众观念情况统计

表 5-43　继承权的丧失的效力是否及于代位继承人的民众观念之情况统计（单选）

选项	人数	比例
A. 丙能够代父乙继承祖父甲的遗产	312	45.88%
B. 丙不能代父乙继承祖父甲的遗产	368	54.12%
合计	680	100%

关于继承权的丧失的效力是否及于代位继承人的民众观念，调查统计数据显示，在填写该问题的680名被调查者中，（1）选择B项认为不可以代位继承的，占近五成半（54.12%）；（2）选择A项认为可以代位继承的，占四成半（45.88%）。

2. 继承权的丧失的效力是否及于代位继承人的民间习惯情况统计

表 5-44　继承权的丧失的效力是否及于代位继承人的民间习惯情况统计（单选）

选项	人数	比例
A. 丙可继承遗产	70	76.09%
B. 丙或甲的配偶继承	7	7.61%
C. 根据风俗习惯	10	10.87%
D. 诉至法院	5	5.43%
合计	92	100%

关于继承权的丧失的效力是否及于代位继承人的民间习惯，调查统计数据显示，填写该问题的92名被调查者所在地区的习惯是：（1）A项和B项，可以代位继承的，占八成稍多（83.70%）；（2）D项应诉至法院，即不可以代位继承的，占不到一成（5.43%）。

八、继承协议之调查数据统计情况

必须说明，本节研究的对象是狭义的继承协议（又称继承扶养协议）。关于继承协议之调查数据统计，我们主要从继承协议的订立主体与方式、继承协议的变更方式及效力，这两个方面进行调查数据的统计情况汇总分析。

（一）继承协议的订立主体与方式

1. 继承协议的订立主体与方式的民众观念情况统计

问题【八、（一）1.】“王某，现年70岁，有长子王一，次女王二，两子女均已成家且分家另过。王某的老伴因患癌症花费了大量医药费后去世，老夫妻的共同财产现所剩无儿，现有郊区的一套住房是王某个人财产。虽然王某退休金不多，但身体没有大病，基本生活还是能够维持的。由于长子王一长期在外地工作，为解决父亲王某的养老送终问题，您认为，如下三种做法哪种较为妥当？A. 父亲王某与次女王二，双方协商并签订协议，由次女王二一人承担赡养父亲王某的义务，王某的全部遗产指定由王二继承；B. 父亲王某与子女王一、王二，三人协商并签订协议，由次女王二一人承担赡养父亲王某的义务，王某的全部遗产商定由王二继承，王一放弃对父亲王某遗产的继承权；C. 子女王一与王二，两人协商并签订协议，由次女王二一人承担赡养父亲王某的义务，王某的全部遗产商定由王二继承，王一放弃对父亲王某遗产的继承权。（单选）”

表 5-45　继承协议的订立主体与方式的民众观念情况统计（单选）

选项	人数	比例
A. 父亲王某与次女王二协商一致即可签订协议（第一种方式）	90	12.80%
B. 父亲王某需与全部继承人协商，共同签订协议（第二种方式）	507	72.12%
C. 共同继承人间签订协议即可，无须被继承人知晓或同意（第三种方式）	106	15.08%
合计	703	100%

关于继承协议的订立主体与方式的民众观念，调查统计数据显示，在 703 名被调查者中，（1）选择 B 项由被继承人与全体法定继承人共同订立的，占七成稍多（72.12%）；（2）选择 C 项由共同继承人之间签订而无须被继承人知晓或同意的，占一成半（15.08%）；　（3）选择 A 项由被扶养人与扶养义务人共同签订的，占一成稍多（12.80%）。

2. 继承协议的民间习惯情况统计

问题【八、（一）2.】“您过去是否听说或者经历过以上类似的情况？A. 听说过或经历过；B. 从没听说或经历过以上情况。（单选）在听说过或经历过签订继承协议的人中，听说过或经历过的方式是哪一种？A. 第一种方式；B. 第二种方式；C. 第三种方式。（单选）”

（1）关于继承协议的民间习惯情况统计。

表 5-46　继承协议的民间习惯情况统计（单选）

选项	人数	比例
A. 听说过或经历过	399	56.76%
B. 从没听说或经历过以上情况	304	43.24%
合计	703	100%

关于继承协议的民间习惯，调查统计数据显示，在 703 名被调查者填写的所在地区的

习惯是：①A 项即听说过或经历过的，占五成半稍多（56.76%）；②B 项没有听说或经历过的，占四成稍多（43.24%）。

（2）关于听说过或经历过签订继承协议的方式的民间习惯情况统计。

表 5-47 听说过或经历过签订继承协议的方式的民间习惯情况统计（单选）

选项	人数	比例
A. 第一种方式	72	18.05%
B. 第二种方式	230	57.64%
C. 第三种方式	97	24.31%
合计	399	100%

关于听说过或经历过签订继承协议的方式之民间习惯，调查统计数据显示，填写该问题的 399 名被调查者所在地区的习惯是：①B 项由被继承人与全体法定继承人共同订立的，占五成半稍多（57.64%）；②C 项由继承人之间签订的，占近二成半（24.31%）；③A项由被扶养人与扶养义务人共同签订的，占近二成（18.05%）。

（二）继承协议的变更方式及效力

问题【八、（二）】“王某，现年 70 岁，有长子王一，次女王二，三子王三，三个子女均已成家且分家另过。王某的老伴因患癌症花费了大量医药费后去世，现有郊区的一套住房是王某个人财产，市场价约为 30 万元，王某有少量退休金。王某与王二协商并签订继承协议，由王二主要扶养父亲王某，王某的所有遗产由王二继承。协议签订后，王二全家与父亲王某共同生活了五年后的一天，王二因意外交通事故死亡。王二全家在与王某共同生活的期间已为王某花费生活费、医疗费等扶养费共 9 万元。为解决王某的养老，您同意下列哪些做法？A. 王二的儿子有继续扶养外祖父王某的能力，王某也愿意与王二的儿子共同生活，应当由王二的儿子继续履行扶养义务，并继承王某的全部遗产；B. 王一、王三共同补偿王二家人 6 万元扶养费后（另有 3 万元扶养费属于应当由王二承担的），如果王一与父亲王某签订新的继承协议，并与王某共同生活一直扶养至其去世，就由王一继承王某的全部遗产；C. 对王二已经支付的扶养费不予补偿，如果王一与父亲王某签订新的继承协议，并与王某共同生活一直扶养至其去世，就由王一继承王某的全部遗产；D. 王一、王三共同补偿王二家人 6 万元扶养费后，由两人共同扶养父亲王某；E. 其他。（单选）”

表 5-48 继承协议的变更方式及效力的民众观念情况统计（单选）

选项	人数	比例
A. 原扶养人的子女有扶养能力的，在双方自愿的情况下，由原扶养人的子女继续扶养被扶养人，并继承全部遗产	281	39.97%
B. 原签订的继承协议效力终止，补偿原扶养人一定费用后，由某一有扶养能力的法定继承人，在双方自愿的情况下签订新继承协议，继续扶养被扶养人，并继承全部遗产	202	28.73%

续表

选项		人数	比例
C. 原签订的继承协议效力终止，对原扶养人无须补偿，应由某一有扶养能力的法定继承人与被扶养人，在双方自愿的情况下签订新继承协议，继续扶养被扶养人并继承全部遗产		55	7.82%
D. 原签订的继承协议效力终止，补偿原扶养人一定费用后，应由有扶养能力的全体法定继承人，共同依法对被扶养人尽扶养义务，并依法定继承取得遗产		153	21.76%
E. 其他	E1. 三人共同继承	8	1.14%
	E2. 王一与王二合意情况下支持 A	4	0.57%
合计		703	100%

关于继承协议的变更方式及效力的民众观念，即在继承协议的履行中，如扶养人先于被扶养人去世，被调查者对于该协议的变更方式与效力的认识，调查统计数据显示，在703名被调查者中，(1) 选择A项，认为该协议可有条件继续履行发生效力，如原扶养人的子女有扶养能力的，在原扶养人的子女和被扶养人双方同意的情况下，可由原扶养人的子女继续履行该继承协议的，此即代位扶养的，占近四成（39.97%）；(2) 选择B项和C项，认为该协议终止，须签订新的继承协议，由新的扶养人履行扶养义务并继承遗产的，合计占三成半稍多（36.55%），其中，B项认为需要对原扶养人的继承人补偿超过其扶养义务部分费用的，占近三成（28.73%），C项认为不需要对原扶养人的继承人补偿超过其扶养义务部分费用的，占不到一成（7.82%）；(3) 选择D项，认为该协议终止，应补偿原扶养人的继承人超过其扶养义务部分费用后，由所有法定继承人共同扶养的，即实行法定赡养的，占二成稍多（21.76%）。可见，河北省被调查者对于代位扶养的认可度最高，占近四成。

九、遗产债务清偿之调查数据统计情况

关于遗产债务清偿之调查数据统计，我们主要从遗产债务清偿责任的类型、被继承人丧葬费的支付、遗产债务的清偿顺序，这三个方面进行调查数据的统计情况汇总分析。

（一）遗产债务清偿责任的类型

问题【九、（一）】“继承遗产，应当清偿被继承人的债务，您是怎么理解这句话的？A. 对被继承人的生前所有债务，继承人都应当予以偿还；B. 对被继承人的生前所有债务，继承人应先用所有遗产偿还债务，不足部分由继承人个人财产偿还；C. 对被继承人的生前所有债务，继承人只以继承的遗产为限予以偿还；D. 对被继承人的生前所有债务，继承人如果存在转移遗产、隐瞒遗产的情形，则其应当负责以遗产和其个人财产偿还所有的债务。在您所在的地区，人们遇到继承人有转移遗产、隐瞒遗产的情况时，一般是如何处理的？为什么？（多选）”

表 5-49 继承人遗产债务清偿责任类型的民众观念情况统计（多选）

选项	人数	比例
A. 对被继承人的生前所有债务，继承人都应当予以偿还	260	36.98%
B. 对被继承人的生前所有债务，继承人应先用所有遗产偿还债务，不足部分由继承人以个人财产偿还	255	36.27%
C. 对被继承人的生前所有债务，继承人只以继承的遗产为限予以偿还	325	46.23%
D. 对被继承人的生前所有债务，继承人如果存在转移遗产、隐瞒遗产的情形，则其应当负责以遗产和其个人财产偿还所有的债务	297	42.25%

关于继承人遗产债务清偿责任类型的民众观念，调查统计数据显示，在填写该问题的被调查者中，(1) 选择 A 项和 B 项，认为继承人应承担自愿的无限清偿责任的，合计占七成稍多（73.25%）；(2) 选择 C 项，认为继承人应以继承的遗产承担有限清偿责任的，占四成半稍多（46.23%）；(3) 选择 D 项，认为继承人如有侵害遗产的行为应承担强制的无限清偿责任的，占四成稍多（42.25%）。

（二）被继承人丧葬费的支付

问题【九、(二)】“在您所在地区，死者的丧葬费一般是如何支付的？A. 由全体继承人共同支付；B. 从被继承人的遗产中支付；C. 其他。(单选)”

表 5-50 被继承人丧葬费支付的民间习惯情况统计（单选）

选项		人数	比例
A. 由全体继承人共同支付		456	64.86%
B. 从被继承人的遗产中支付		198	28.17%
C. 其他	C1. 由儿子全部支付	7	1%
	C2. 依照风俗习惯	42	5.97%
合计		703	100%

关于被继承人丧葬费的支付的民间习惯，调查统计数据显示，703 名被调查者填写的所在地区的习惯是：(1) A 项由全体继承人共同支付的，占近六成半（64.86%）；(2) B 项从被继承人的遗产中支付的，占近三成（28.17%）。

（三）遗产债务的清偿顺序

问题【九、(三)】“在您所在地区，对被继承人死亡后遗留的以下费用，一般是按照下列表格中哪种先后次序进行清偿的？”(多选)

A. 丧葬费用	D. 欠付的工资	G. 对被继承人扶养较多的人之酌情分配遗产份额
B. 遗产管理等费用	E. 受被继承人扶养人的生活费	H. 遗赠扶养协议写明遗赠的遗产
C. 欠债	F. 税款	

1. 遗产债务清偿顺序的民间习惯情况统计

表 5-51　遗产债务清偿顺序的民间习惯情况统计（多选）

费用	第一顺序		第二顺序		第三顺序		第四顺序		第五顺序		第六顺序		第七顺序		第八顺序	
	人数	比例%	人数	比例%	人数	比例%	人数	比例%	人数	比例%	人数	比例%	人数	比例%	人数	比例%
A.	406	57.8	47	6.7	38	5.4	25	3.6	13	1.8	4	0.6	8	1.1	16	2.3
B.	24	3.4	187	26.6	80	11.4	49	7.0	48	6.8	30	4.3	15	2.1	17	2.4
C.	44	6.3	167	23.8	144	20.5	88	12.5	40	5.7	24	3.4	14	2.0	6	0.9
D.	29	4.1	66	9.4	107	15.2	70	10	50	7.1	47	6.7	20	2.8	12	1.7
E.	14	2.0	30	4.3	66	9.4	84	11.9	90	12.8	75	10.7	36	5.1	19	2.7
F.	37	5.3	38	5.4	42	6.0	66	9.4	51	7.3	50	7.1	37	5.3	49	7.0
G.	22	3.1	34	4.8	43	6.1	42	6.0	51	7.3	59	8.4	97	13.8	64	9.1
H.	17	2.4	23	3.3	40	5.7	56	8.0	49	7.0	49	7.0	73	10.4	79	11.2

关于遗产债务清偿顺序的民间习惯，各顺序以被调查者选择占比最高的作为统计依据，703 名被调查者填写的所在地区的遗产债务清偿顺序的习惯是：第一顺序“A. 丧葬费用”（占 57.8%）；第二顺序“B. 遗产管理等费用”（占 26.6%）和“C. 欠债”（占 23.8%）；第三顺序“D. 欠付的工资”（占 15.2%）；第四顺序“F. 税款”（占 9.4%）；第五顺序“E. 受被继承人扶养人的生活费”（占 12.8%）；第六顺序“G. 对被继承人扶养较多的人之酌情分配遗产份额”（占 13.8%）；第七顺序“H. 遗赠扶养协议写明遗赠的遗产”（占 11.2%）。

2. 遗产债务清偿顺序的民众观念情况统计

表 5-52　遗产债务清偿顺序的民众观念情况统计（多选）

费用	第一顺序		第二顺序		第三顺序		第四顺序		第五顺序		第六顺序		第七顺序		第八顺序	
	人数	比例%	人数	比例%	人数	比例%	人数	比例%	人数	比例%	人数	比例%	人数	比例%	人数	比例%
A.	366	52.1	57	8.1	38	5.4	29	4.1	23	3.3	17	2.4	14	2.0	5	0.7
B.	32	4.6	186	26.5	80	11.4	67	9.5	50	7.1	31	4.4	15	2.1	6	0.9
C.	64	9.1	142	20.2	149	21.2	75	10.7	36	5.1	19	2.7	21	3.0	10	1.4
D.	24	3.4	67	9.5	94	13.4	90	12.8	56	8.0	50	7.1	26	3.7	20	2.8

续表

费用	第一顺序		第二顺序		第三顺序		第四顺序		第五顺序		第六顺序		第七顺序		第八顺序	
	人数	比例%	人数	比例%	人数	比例%	人数	比例%	人数	比例%	人数	比例%	人数	比例%	人数	比例%
E.	22	3.1	30	4.3	69	9.8	77	11.0	101	14.4	68	9.7	39	5.5	19	2.7
F.	43	6.1	43	6.1	62	8.8	63	9.0	45	6.4	45	6.4	40	5.7	70	10.0
G.	15	2.1	25	3.6	46	6.5	45	6.4	68	9.7	60	8.5	103	14.7	58	8.3
H.	30	4.3	27	3.8	35	5.0	61	8.7	52	7.4	63	9.0	71	10.1	74	10.5

关于遗产债务清偿顺序的民众观念，各顺序以被调查者选择占比最高作为统计依据，703名被调查者观念中的遗产债务清偿顺序如下：第一顺序“A. 丧葬费用”（占52.10%）；第二顺序“B. 遗产管理等费用”（占26.50%）；第三顺序“C. 欠债”（占21.20%）和“D. 欠付的工资”（占13.40%）；第四顺序“E. 受被继承人扶养人的生活费”（占14.4%）；第五顺序“G. 对被继承人扶养较多的人之酌情分配遗产份额”（占14.70%）；第六顺序“H. 遗赠扶养协议写明遗赠的遗产”（占10.50%）和“F. 税款”（占10.00%）。

十、遗产分割之调查数据统计情况

关于遗产分割之调查数据统计，我们主要从遗产分割的自由与限制、遗产分割瑕疵的担保责任，这两个方面进行调查数据的统计情况汇总分析。

（一）遗产分割的自由与限制

问题【十、（一）1.】“按您当地的民间习惯，对遗产一般何时开始分割？A. 由各继承人共同协商后进行分割；B. 只要有继承人要求分割遗产，就得进行分割；C. 对于被继承人以遗嘱禁止分割的遗产，不得进行分割；D. 其他。（多选）其理由是什么？”

1. 遗产分割自由与限制的民间习惯与理由情况统计

（1）遗产分割自由与限制的民间习惯情况统计。

表5-53 遗产分割的自由与限制民间习惯的情况统计（多选）

选项	人数	比例
A. 由各继承人共同协商后进行分割	590	83.93%
B. 只要有继承人要求分割遗产，就得进行分割	146	20.77%
C. 对于被继承人以遗嘱禁止分割的遗产，不得进行分割	338	48.08%
D. 其他	13	1.85%

关于遗产分割的自由与限制的民间习惯，调查统计数据显示，703名被调查者填写的所在地区的习惯是：①A项由各继承人共同协商后进行遗产分割的，占八成稍多（83.93%）；②C项当被继承人以遗嘱禁止则不得分割遗产的，占近五成（48.08%）；③B项只要有继承人要求分割遗产就得进行分割的，占二成（20.77%）。

（2）遗产分割的自由与限制的民间习惯的理由情况统计。

表 5-53　遗产分割的自由与限制的民间习惯的理由情况统计

项目	人数	比例
A. 遗产由各继承人共同继承，遗产分割涉及各继承人的利益，故遗产的分割应共同协商	109	49.32%
B. 每个继承人享有的继承权受法律保护，同时基于效率原则考虑，故继承开始后，基于继承人的要求就可以分割遗产	20	9.05%
C. 遗产是被继承人死亡时遗留下来的个人财产，当然有权通过遗嘱决定遗产的归属和分割	92	41.63%
合计	221	100%

关于遗产分割的自由与限制的民间习惯的理由，调查统计数据显示，在填写该理由的221名被调查者所在地区，①遗产的分割应当由各遗产继承人共同协商的理由是，A项遗产由各继承人共同继承，遗产分割涉及各继承人的利益，占近五成（49.32%）；②遗嘱人有权通过遗嘱禁止分割遗产的理由是，C项遗产是被继承人死亡时遗留下来的个人财产，其有权自由处分包括一定期限内禁止分割的，占四成稍多（41.63%）；③继承开始后基于继承人的要求就可以分割遗产的理由是，B项每个继承人享有的继承权受法律保护，同时基于效率原则考虑的，占比近一成（9.05%）。

2. 提出遗产分割请求时间的民间习惯与理由情况统计

问题【十、（一）2.】“老王死亡时留有一套家庭居住的房屋（价值50万元）、存款20万元以及小汽车一辆（价值10万元）。老王去世时，其配偶和唯一的儿子小王均在世。请问：如果在您所在的地区，老王死亡后，其儿子小王是否会马上向其母亲提出分割遗产的请求？A. 会；B. 不会；C. 会提出分割其他遗产的请求，但对其母正在居住房屋的分割需等其母去世后进行；D. 其他。（单选）其理由是什么？”

（1）提出遗产分割请求时间的民间习惯情况统计。

表 5-55　提出遗产分割请求时间的民间习惯情况统计（单选）

选项	人数	比例
A. 会	70	9.96%
B. 不会	544	77.38%
C. 会提出分割其他遗产的请求，但对其母正在居住房屋的分割需等其母去世后进行	74	10.53%
D. 其他	15	2.13%
合计	703	100%

关于提出遗产分割请求时间的民间习惯，即当被继承人死亡后，其子女继承人是否可以向其母亲（被继承人的生存配偶）提出分割遗产请求，调查统计数据显示，703名被调

查者填写的所在地区的习惯是：①A 项会提出遗产分割请求的，占不到一成（9.96%）；②B 项不会提出遗产分割请求的，占七成半稍多（77.38%）；③C 项会提出分割其他遗产，但对其母正在居住房屋的分割需等其母去世后进行的，占一成（10.53%）。可见，B 项和 C 项，即主张对其母正在居住房屋在其生存期间不予分割的，合计占近九成（87.91%）。

（2）提出遗产分割请求时间的民间习惯的理由情况统计。

表 5-56　提出遗产分割请求时间的民间习惯的理由情况统计

项目		人数	比例
A. 遗产是由小王及其母亲共同继承，继承开始后，小王有权根据法律规定提出遗产分割的请求，并且有利于防止日后发生不必要的纠纷		9	3.02%
B. 根据当地观念，小王的父亲的遗产就应该由其母亲全部继承，故小王不能向其母亲提出遗产分割的请求，如果提出，会被视作不孝敬老人的表现		86	28.86%
C. 体现孝敬老人，保证老人的晚年生活，小王可以提出分割其他遗产，但对其母正在居住房屋的分割需等其母去世后进行		145	48.66%
D. 其他	D1. 基于本人的继承权可以分割	46	15.44%
	D2. 根据当事人意愿	12	4.03%
合计		298	100%

关于提出遗产分割请求时间的民间习惯的理由，即当被继承人死亡后，关于其子女可否与母亲提出分割遗产的理由，调查统计数据显示，在填写该理由的 298 名被调查者所在地区，①有可以提出遗产分割之习惯的，其中，其一，可无条件提出遗产分割的理由是，A 项和 D 项基于本人的继承权可以分割、根据当事人意愿、符合法律的，合计占二成稍多（22.49%）；其二，可有条件地提出遗产分割，即其子女不可以提出分割母亲正在居住的房屋但可提出分割其他遗产的理由是，C 项体现孝敬老人，保证老人的晚年生活，但对其母正在居住房屋的分割需等其母去世后进行的，占近五成（48.66%）。②有不可以提出遗产分割之习惯的理由是，B 项根据当地观念，被继承人的遗产就应该由其生存配偶全部继承，故其子女不能向母亲提出遗产分割的请求，如果提出，会被视作不孝敬老人的表现的，占近三成（28.86%）。

3. 遗嘱可否限制遗产分割的民众观念与理由情况

（1）遗嘱可否限制遗产分割的民众观念情况统计。

问题【十、（一）3.（1）】“甲乙是夫妻，育有一子丙。甲生前立了一份遗嘱，指定由乙和丙共同继承遗产。甲死亡时留下一套家庭住房（价值 50 万元）、存款 20 万元以及小汽车一辆（价值 10 万元）。您认为，甲是否可以在遗嘱中写明在其死后上述房屋在一定期间内不能分割？A. 可以；B. 不可以。（单选）其理由是什么？”

表 5-57　遗嘱可否限制遗产分割的民众观念之情况统计（单选）

选项	人数	比例
A. 可以	552	85. 32%
B. 不可以	95	14. 68%
合计	647	100%

关于遗嘱可否限制遗产分割的民众观念，调查统计数据显示，在填写该问题的 647 名被调查者中，①选择 A 项可以的，占八成半（85. 32%）；②选择 B 项不可以的，占近一成半（14. 68%）。

（2）遗嘱限制遗产分割之具体期限的民众观念情况统计。

问题【十、（一）3.（2）】“在上题中，如果您选择 A 项，那么该期限多久合适？A. 5 年；B. 10 年；C. 15 年；D. 其他。（单选）”

表 5-58　遗嘱限制遗产分割之具体期限的民众观念情况统计（单选）

<table>
<tr><th colspan="2">选项</th><th colspan="2">人数</th><th colspan="2">比例</th></tr>
<tr><td colspan="2">A. 5 年</td><td colspan="2">232</td><td colspan="2">35. 20%</td></tr>
<tr><td colspan="2">B. 10 年</td><td colspan="2">175</td><td colspan="2">26. 56%</td></tr>
<tr><td colspan="2">C. 15 年</td><td colspan="2">68</td><td colspan="2">10. 32%</td></tr>
<tr><td rowspan="4">D. 其他</td><td>D1. 母亲死后</td><td rowspan="4">184</td><td>42</td><td rowspan="4">27. 92%</td><td>6. 37%</td></tr>
<tr><td>D2. 子女成年后</td><td>7</td><td>1. 06%</td></tr>
<tr><td>D3. 期限应由甲确定</td><td>25</td><td>3. 79%</td></tr>
<tr><td>D4. 适当期限</td><td>110</td><td>16. 69%</td></tr>
<tr><td colspan="2">合计</td><td colspan="2">659</td><td colspan="2">100%</td></tr>
</table>

关于遗嘱限制遗产分割的具体期限的民众观念，调查统计数据显示，在填写该问题的 659 名被调查者中，①选择 A 项 5 年之内的，占三成半（35. 20%）；选择 D 项其他的，合计占近三成（27. 92%）；②选择 B 项 10 年之内的，占二成半稍多（26. 56%）；③选择 C 项 15 年之内的，占一成（10. 32%）。

（3）继承人协商能否变更遗嘱限制的民间习惯情况统计。

问题【十、（一）3.（3）】“在您所在地区，如果乙和丙一致同意分割上诉财产，那么，他们是否可以不遵守甲的遗嘱在一定期间内禁止分割该房屋的规定而进行分割？A. 可以不遵守遗嘱；B. 不可以不遵守遗嘱。（单选）”

表 5-59 继承人协商能否变更遗嘱限制的民间习惯情况统计（单选）

选项	人数	比例
A. 可以不遵守遗嘱	354	50.36%
B. 不可以不遵守遗嘱	349	49.64%
合计	703	100%

关于继承人协商能否变更遗嘱限制的民间习惯，对于遗嘱对遗产分割的限制是否可以不遵守，调查统计数据显示，703 名被调查者填写的所在地区的习惯是：（1）A 项可以不遵守的，占五成（50.36%）；（2）B 项不可以不遵守的，占近五成（49.64%）。

（二）遗产分割瑕疵的担保责任

问题【十、（二）】“村民老王于 2016 年 12 月 10 日因病去世，死亡时他留下 50 只羊。老王有两个儿子甲和乙，故老王死后，甲乙各分得 25 只羊。但在双方分完羊两天之后，乙分得的 25 只羊就有 2 只暴病死亡，这 2 只羊死亡的原因是在兄弟分割之前就得了羊痘（一种急性传染病）。请问，在您所在地区，如果出现此种情况，这 2 只羊死亡的损失应该由谁承担？A. 由乙自行承担，羊群已分配完毕，乙分到了 2 只病羊，应该自认倒霉；B. 由甲和乙共同承担，甲应再分给乙 1 只羊或按 1 只羊的价格进行补偿；C. 按 1 只羊的价格进行补偿，但乙承担大部分损失，甲承担小部分损失；D. 其他。（单选）其理由是什么？”

1. 遗产分割瑕疵的担保责任的民间习惯情况统计

表 5-60 遗产分割瑕疵的担保责任的民间习惯之情况统计（单选）

选项	人数	比例
A. 由乙自行承担，羊群已分配完毕，乙分到了 2 只病羊，应该自认倒霉	345	49.08%
B. 由甲和乙共同承担，甲应再分给乙 1 只羊或按 1 只羊的价格进行补偿	223	31.72%
C. 按 1 只羊的价格进行补偿，但乙承担大部分损失，甲承担小部分损失	88	12.52%
D. 其他	47	6.68%
合计	703	100%

关于遗产分割瑕疵担保责任的民间习惯，调查统计数据显示，703 名被调查者所在地区的习惯是：①A 项由分得瑕疵遗产的继承人自行承担，即继承人间不相互承担遗产分割瑕疵担保责任的，占近五成（49.08%）；②B 项和 C 项由共同继承人相互承担的，合计近四成半（44.24%）。

2. 遗产分割瑕疵的担保责任的民间习惯之理由情况统计

表 5-61　遗产分割瑕疵的担保责任的民间习惯之理由情况统计（单选）

项目	人数	比例
A. 乙分得的 25 只羊是随机分配的，事先甲乙两人都不知道，因此，对于 2 只病羊的损失，与甲无关，只能由乙自己承担	29	14.65%
B. 50 只羊是由甲和乙共同继承的，对于 2 只病羊的损失也应该由甲和乙共同承担；如果让乙一个人承担，则有悖公平原则	157	79.80%
C. 其他（依照法律规定）	11	5.56%
合计	198	100%

关于遗产分割瑕疵的担保责任的民间习惯之理由，调查统计数据显示，在填写该理由的 198 名被调查者中，（1）有由共同继承人相互承担的习惯之理由是，A 项如果让分得瑕疵遗产的继承人一个人承担有悖公平原则的，占近一成半（14.65%）；（2）有由分得瑕疵遗产的继承人自行承担，即继承人之间不相互承担遗产分割瑕疵担保责任的习惯之理由是，B 项被继承人分得瑕疵遗产是随机分配的，事先所有继承人都不知晓，因此只能由分得瑕疵遗产的继承人自行承担责任的，占近八成（79.80%）。

十一、无人承受遗产之调查数据统计情况

关于无人承受遗产之调查数据统计，我们主要从无人承受遗产归属和无人承受遗产的处理，这两个方面进行调查数据的统计情况汇总分析。

（一）无人承受遗产的归属

1. 城镇居民无人承受遗产的归属主体的民众观念与理由情况

问题【十一、（一）1.】“甲生前系城镇居民，其生前终生未婚且无其他继承人，其死后留下部分遗产，属于无人继承的遗产，您认为甲的遗产应当归属下列哪一主体更合适？A. 国家；B. 死者生前所在地的国库；C. 死者生前所在地民政部门的社会福利机构；D. 死者生前所在地的居委会；E. 不是继承人的其他亲属；F. 其他。（单选）其理由是什么？”

（1）城镇居民无人承受遗产的归属主体的民众观念之情况统计。

表 5-62　城镇居民无人承受遗产的归属主体的民众观念之情况统计（单选）

选项	人数	比例
A. 国家	233	33.14%
B. 死者生前所在地的国库	50	7.11%
C. 死者生前所在地民政部门的社会福利机构	146	20.77%
D. 死者生前所在地的居委会	70	9.96%
E. 不是继承人的其他亲属	168	23.90%

续表

选项		人数		比例	
F. 其他	F1. 谁赡养谁继承	36	19	5.12%	2.70%
	F2. 关系密切的人		17		2.42%
合计		703		100%	

关于城镇居民无人承受遗产的归属主体的民众观念，调查统计数据显示，在703名被调查者中，①选择A、B、C、D四个选项，即主张归属主体为社会公共组织（包括归属于国家、死者生前所在地的国库、死者生前所在地民政部门的社会福利机构和死者生前所在地的居委会）的，合计占七成稍多（70.98%）；②选择E项，即主张归属主体为自然人（归属于不是继承人的其他亲属）的，占二成稍多（23.90%）。

（2）城镇居民无人承受遗产的归属主体的民众观念之理由情况统计。

表5-63 城镇居民无人承受遗产的归属主体的民众观念之理由情况统计

项目	人数	比例
A. 甲的遗产没有人继承，为规范财产秩序，甲的遗产只能归国家所有，同时，这也与部分国家的做法相一致	58	20.79%
B. 甲的遗产归甲生前所在地的国库，有利于对遗产的清算、管理和利用	20	7.17%
C. 甲的其他亲属是与甲有一定亲属关系且有较密切联系的人，甲的遗产归其他亲戚所有，符合情理	63	22.58%
D. 回报社会	99	35.48%
E. 依照法律规定	18	6.45%
F. 有效避免纠纷，维护社会和谐	21	7.53%
合计	279	100%

关于城镇居民无人承受遗产的归属主体的民众观念之理由，调查统计数据显示，在填写该理由的279名被调查者中，①主张归属主体为社会公共组织，主要理由包括其一，归国家（或国库）的理由是，A项可以规范财产秩序，也与部分国家的做法相一致，或B项和E项符合法律规定的，合计占近三成半（34.41%）；其二，归民政部门的社会福利机构的理由是，D项捐赠给慈善机构做公益利于回报社会的，占三成半（35.48%）。②主张归属主体为自然人的理由是，C项归不是继承人的其他亲戚所有符合情理的，占二成稍多（22.58%）。

2. 农村居民无人承受遗产的归属主体的民众观念与理由情况

问题【十一、（一）2.】“甲生前系农村居民，其生前未婚且无其他继承人，其死后留下部分遗产，属于无人继承的遗产，您认为甲的遗产归属下列哪一主体更合适？A. 死者生前所在地的国库；B. 死者生前所在地民政部门的社会福利机构；C. 死者生前所在的集体经济组织；D. 死者生前所在的村委会；E. 死者生前所在的村民小组；F. 不是继承人的其他亲属；G. 其他。（单选）”

表 5-64 农村居民无人承受遗产的归属主体的民众观念之情况统计（单选）

选项	人数	比例
A. 死者生前所在地的国库	110	16. 59%
B. 死者生前所在地民政部门的社会福利机构	109	16. 44%
C. 死者生前所在的集体经济组织	54	8. 14%
D. 死者生前所在的村委会	146	22. 02%
E. 死者生前所在的村民小组	41	6. 18%
F. 不是继承人的其他亲属	181	27. 30%
G. 其他（尽了赡养义务的人）	22	3. 32%
合计	663	100%

关于农村居民承受遗产的归属主体，调查统计数据显示，在填写该问题的 663 名被调查者中，（1）选择 A、B、C、D、E 项，即归属主体为社会公共组织（包括归属于国家、死者生前所在地的国库、死者生前所在地民政部门的社会福利机构和死者生前所在的集体经济组织、村委会或村民小组）的，合计占近七成（69. 38%）；（2）选择 F 项和 G 项不是继承人的其他亲属和尽了赡养义务的人，即主张归属主体为自然人的，占三成（30. 62%）。

（二）无人承受遗产的处理

1. 无人承受遗产管理人的产生方式的民众观念情况统计

问题【十一、（二）1.】“对于无人继承遗产的管理人，您认为下列哪一种产生方式更合适？A. 死者户籍所在地的居委会或村委会或所在单位指定遗产管理人；B. 人民法院指定遗产管理人；C. 民政部门指定遗产管理人。（单选）”

表 5-65 无人承受遗产管理人的产生方式的民众观念情况统计（单选）

选项	人数	比例
A. 死者户籍所在地的居委会或村委会或所在单位指定遗产管理人	377	53. 63%
B. 人民法院指定遗产管理人	218	31. 01%
C. 民政部门指定遗产管理人	108	15. 36%
合计	703	100%

关于无人承受遗产管理人的产生方式的民众观念，调查统计数据显示，在 703 名被调查者中，（1）选择 A 项由死者户籍所在地的居委会或村委会或所在单位指定的，占五成稍多（53. 63%）；（2）选择 B 项由人民法院指定的，占三成稍多（31. 01%）；（3）选择

C 项由民政部门指定的，占一成半（15.36%）。

2. 无人承受遗产的酌分请求权主体的民众观念情况统计

问题【十一、（二）2.】“您认为下列哪些人可以酌情分得无人继承的遗产？A. 依靠死者扶养的人；B. 与死者共同生活的人；C. 与死者有密切联系且对其帮助较多的人；D. 其他。（多选）”

表 5-66 无人承受的遗产之酌分请求权主体的民众观念情况统计（多选）

选项	人数	比例
A. 依靠死者扶养的人	481	68.42%
B. 与死者共同生活的人	436	62.02%
C. 与死者关系密切且对其帮助较多的人	545	77.52%
D. 其他（填写您认为其他适当人选表）	13	1.85%

关于无人承受遗产的酌分请求权主体的民众观念，调查统计数据显示，在 703 名被调查者中，分别占六成至七成半多的人认为无人承受的遗产的酌分请求权人包括：A 项依靠死者扶养的人，占 68.42%；B 项与死者共同生活的人，占 62.02%；C 项与死者关系密切且对其帮助较多的人，占 77.52%。

十二、遗产处理相关案例的简介与评析

（一）涉及遗产范围界定案例的简介与评析

案情简介：原审原告（上诉人）付某自 56 岁起（2005 年）与张某龙一起生活，未办理结婚登记。张某甲、张某乙、张某丙系张某龙子女（三者均系原审被告，被上诉人）。2011 年 11 月 6 日，张某龙出具涉案房屋产权变更证明，将其购买的某村住宅楼（涉案房屋）产权归为张某任所有。2012 年 9 月 7 日，被继承人张某龙由刘某华律师代书遗嘱，由张某疆、石某荣见证，遗嘱主要内容为：一、张某龙于 2011 年购买的某村住宅楼（涉案房屋）归付某所有，首付款是遗嘱人与付某的共同财产，由付某负责偿还以陈某义名义从某信用社所贷的 5 万元贷款；二、遗嘱人应得的退休金和国家给付的抚恤金、补助金偿还陈某义垫付的医药费、伙食费，如有剩余全部归付某所有。某司法鉴定意见书鉴定为，张某龙 2012 年 9 月 7 日遗嘱中的签字与 2011 年 11 月 6 日楼房产权变更证明中的签字为同一人书写。原被告双方因遗产分割事宜产生纠纷，原告付某遂诉至法院，请求确认张某龙擅自将房屋产权变更为张某任的行为无效，且张某龙的抚恤金、补助金系其应得的合法财产，其本人有权对抚恤金、补助金的分配进行处分。被告辩称，订立遗嘱时，涉案房产的所有权已经发生变更，不能依遗嘱来确认其财产的所有权；抚恤金不属于遗产。

一审法院审理后认定，遗嘱人张某龙于 2012 年 9 月 7 日订立遗嘱，遗嘱分为两部分，第一部分涉及其 2011 年首付 73880 元购买的涉案房屋，张某龙于 2011 年 11 月 6 日出具楼房产权变更证明，将该房屋产权变更为张某任所有，且该房屋已经交付张某任。楼房产权变更证明的内容与张某龙的遗嘱内容相矛盾，故原告依据遗嘱对该房屋主张所有权，本

院不予支持。遗嘱第二部分涉及抚恤金的分配，因抚恤金是在遗嘱人去世后根据国家政策对其法定继承人、其生前扶养的人给予的经济上的抚恤，不属于张某龙死亡时遗留的个人合法财产，张某龙无权处分，故张某龙遗嘱第二部分无效。故一审法院判决：张某龙于2012年9月7日所立遗嘱内容无效。

判决后，原告付某不服提出上诉。二审法院审理查明的事实与一审法院查明的事实一致。二审法院判决驳回上诉，维持原判。①

法律适用分析：本案关于遗产范围的争议焦点，即已变更产权的房屋和抚恤金是否属于被继承人的遗产。根据我国《继承法》第3条规定，被继承人死亡时遗留的具有个人所有权的房屋属于遗产。遗产具有四个特性，即时间特定性、财产性、专属性、限定性。时间特定性即遗产为继承人死亡时所遗留的财产。财产性包括被继承人所遗留的财产权利与财产义务。专属性即遗产为被继承人的个人财产。限定性为遗产必须是能依照我国《继承法》转移给他人的一定财产。② 但是，由于本案中的房屋已经变更了产权，房屋已经不属于被继承人的个人所有财产，所以依据遗产的专属性，本案中的房屋不属于遗产范围。抚恤金是对死者家属的抚慰和经济补偿，不属于被继承人遗留的个人合法财产，所以依据遗产的专属性，其也不属于被继承人的遗产。二审法院对于这两项争议焦点的处理于法有据、合情合理。

通过上述案例，可见我国《继承法》之遗产范围立法的优点与不足。我国《继承法》之遗产范围立法的一个特点即采取列举式与概括式相结合的立法模式，此种立法模式的优点有二：第一，列举式使遗产范围一目了然，方便民众查询和了解。第二，随着时代的发展，遗产的类型越来越多，概括式的规定可以避免依据新出现的遗产类型反复更改立法，有效保证立法的稳定性。同时，该遗产范围立法的不足有二：第一，遗产的特性突出不明显，欠缺反面排除性规定，很多民众在查阅相关立法时，只会注意到所列举的遗产范围，对遗产的性质关注、了解较少。第二，随着时代的发展，新的遗产类型增加，对于某些极具争议性的财产，立法应明确其是否属于遗产。

（二）涉及继承开始的通知和公告案例的简介与评析

案例简介：原告种某甲、种某乙、种某丙、种某丁，被告王某、种某戊。被继承人种某已与被告王某于某年某月登记结婚，双方均系再婚。结婚时被继承人种某已的长子种某甲、长女种某乙、次子种某丙已成年，次女种某丁在中学读书。被告王某与前夫的之女种某戊在上小学。被告王某在种某已病重期间，时常关心伺候。但有一天王某生病了去看病，回家后发现原告四人把种某已接走了，事前也没有跟王某商量。1999年12月20日，种某已去世时，王某没在家，四原告也没通知被告，被告连种某已最后一面也没见到，四原告就把种某已安葬了。原告种某甲又把老家中的生活用品及所有财产全部拉走。被继承人种某已去世时，留有遗产：某村房屋一处。种某已于1998年10月21日立有遗嘱一份，言明："待我过世后，家中房产及财产属于我的，不得由王某继承，而由子女种某甲、种某乙、种某丙、种某丁继承。"四原告要求将父亲种某已名下的位于某村的房屋变更到四

① 参见中国裁判文书网，（2014）沧民终字第×号，《付某诉张某甲等遗嘱继承纠纷二审民事判决书》，载 http://wenshu.court.gov.cn/content/content?DocID=7940239a-387b-4960-8d3c-87b10f93bf61，访问日期2018年11月5日。限于本章篇幅，作者对原案情内容有酌情删改。

② 参见陈苇：《婚姻家庭继承法学案例教程（第三版）》，群众出版社2017年版，第154页。

原告名下，多次遭到两被告阻挠，两被告要求村里将房产登记在其名下。为此，四原告为了保护自己的合法权益，请求法院依法判决原告的父亲种某已的遗产房屋归原告所有，要求两个被告停止侵占遗产。被告王某、种某戊辩称：涉案遗嘱是假的，因为原告就是想把被告王某赶出家门，将一切房产、财产归他们所有。即便遗嘱是被继承人种某已写的，被告认为房屋是种某已与王某的共同财产，种某已的遗嘱只能处分他个人部分。根据我国《继承法》第19条规定，遗嘱应当对缺乏劳动能力又没有生活来源的继承人保留必要的遗产份额。遗嘱取消缺乏劳动能力又没有生活来源的继承人继承权的无效。而被告王某是法定继承人，符合我国《继承法》第19条规定。所以请求法院给予公正、合理判决。

法院审理后查明，原告种某甲、种某乙、种某丙、种某丁同意在将该诉争之房产确权归其共同所有的前提下，被告王某可居住该房屋至其去世，并给付其经济补偿2000元。被告王某每月享有遗属补助及农村养老补助，共约600元。

法院审理后认为：被继承人于1998年10月21日自己书写的遗嘱符合自书遗嘱的构成要件，其内容没有违反法律禁止性规定，遗嘱所称之房产即原、被告诉争之房产。被告虽对遗嘱的真实性存有异议，但未能提交相关证据证明其主张，且该遗嘱是被继承人所书写，应予采信。现原告种某甲、种某乙、种某丙、种某丁要求按遗嘱继承诉争之房产并无不妥，应予支持。二被告要求按照法定继承分割该房屋各六分之一，本院不予支持。被告王某每月有经济来源，且四原告同意被告王某在诉争之房屋中居住至去世，并给付部分经济补偿，足以满足其基本生活所需，符合我国《继承法》相关规定，但补偿以3000元为宜。二被告要求原告种某甲返还其拉走的属于被继承人种某已与被告王某的共同财产，其提交的证据，原告不予认可，且被告未提交其他证据予以佐证，对其主张，本院不予支持。故法院判决，第一，涉案房屋所有权归原告种某甲、种某乙、种某丙、种某丁共同共有；被告王某可在该房屋居住至去世。第二，被告原告种某甲、种某乙、种某丙、种某丁于本判决生效后7日内给付被告王某经济补偿3000元。①

法律适用分析：本案涉及继承开始的通知，本案中，四原告未将被继承人种某已去世的消息通知王某，即未向王某发出继承开始的通知。本案中，双方当事人未针对继承开始的通知举证质证，法院的判决也未涉及此问题。

通过上述案例，我们认为我国继承开始的通知与公告之立法存在不足。继承开始的通知涉及每一位继承人的权利，如果有继承人恶意不通知其他继承人被继承人死亡的事实，则会对其他继承人造成不利的影响。例如，在本案中，被告人王某未接到继承开始的通知，致使王某没有见到被继承人最后一面，对王某造成了情感上的伤害。此外，继承开始的通知可以召集全体共同继承人分割遗产，本案中，被告诉称："原告种某甲把老家中的生活用品及所有财产全部拉走"，也是原告种某甲未通知被告王某继承开始并转移部分遗产所导致的纠纷。我国《继承法》未规定继承开始通知和公告的具体期限，亦未规定在一定期间内知道被继承人死亡的继承人不通知其他继承人所应承担的不利后果，易造成继承过程中继承人之间的相互猜忌与遗产分割纠纷。

---

① 参见中国裁判文书网，(2016) 冀×民初×号，《种某甲、种某乙等与种某戌、王某遗嘱继承纠纷一审民事判决书》，载 http://wenshu. court. gov. cn/content/content? DocID=df70036a-036f-448e-a319-c2994e57e0eb，访问日期：2018年11月5日。限于本章篇幅，作者对原案情内容有酌情删改。

（三）涉及遗产管理案例的简介与评析

案例简介：2008 年 5 月 30 日，借款人栗某与某县农村信用联社股份有限公司签订抵押借款合同，借款 35 万元，借款期限自 2008 年 5 月 30 日至 2010 年 5 月 30 日。2009 年 11 月 26 日，栗某因车祸去世。栗某遗留个人所有的一套住房。栗某的法定继承人有母亲姚某和女儿高某。2011 年 10 月 17 日，某县农村信用联社股份有限公司作为原告诉至法院，请求被告姚某和高某归还栗某生前的借款本金及利息。被告姚某和高某出庭时答辩认为，她们没有偿还栗某生前所欠的借款本金及利息的义务。

一审法院审理后认为，栗某向某县农村信用联社股份有限公司借款共计 35 万元。栗某于 2009 年 11 月 26 日死亡，其遗留的个人所有的一套住房为其遗产。栗某的法定继承人有母亲姚某和女儿高某，且二人均未表示放弃继承。根据我国《继承法》第 33 条规定："继承遗产应当清偿被继承人依法应当缴纳的税款和债务，缴纳税款和清偿债务以他的遗产实际价值为限。超过遗产实际价值部分，继承人自愿偿还的不在此限。"因此，被告姚某和高某作为栗某的法定继承人，应当作为该遗产的管理人，依法以继承栗某遗产的实际价值为限承担清偿被继承人债务的责任。某县农村信用联社股份有限公司对于栗某的债权向其法定继承人姚某和高某主张清偿，应予支持。故一审法院判决，被告姚某和高某在其所继承的遗产的实际价值范围内承担清偿被继承人债务的责任。被告姚某和高某对该判决不服，遂向二审法院提起上诉。

二审法院审理后认为，二审法院查明的事实与一审查明的事实一致，且一审法院适用法律正确。二审法院遂判决驳回上诉，维持原判。①

法律适用分析：本案的涉及的法律问题有如下两点：第一，遗产管理人选任与职责问题。我国《继承法》第 24 条规定："存有遗产的人，应当妥善保管遗产，任何人不得侵吞或者争抢。"我们认为，由于我国立法对遗产管理人的选任方式及其职责并未作出规定，本案法院从实际出发，指定栗某的法定继承人被告姚某和高某作为遗产管理人，由她们在继承遗产的范围内承担被继承人的债务清偿责任，具有合理性。但通过上述案例，反映出遗产管理人制度的缺失可能导致难以保障其他遗产利害关系人的权益，这表明我国遗产管理制度立法的不足。第二，遗产债务的清偿顺序问题。我国《物权法》第 195 条规定："债务人不履行到期债务或者发生当事人约定的实现抵押权的情形，抵押权人可以与抵押人协议以抵押财产折价或者以拍卖、变卖该抵押财产所得的价款优先受偿。"第 198 条规定："抵押财产折价或者拍卖、变卖后，其价款超过债权数额的部分归抵押人所有，不足部分由债务人清偿。"但我国《继承法》仅在第 33 条规定："继承遗产应当清偿被继承人依法应当缴纳的税款和债务，缴纳税款和清偿债务以他的遗产实际价值为限。超过遗产实际价值部分，继承人自愿偿还的不在此限。"由于我国《继承法》对于遗产债务的清偿顺序没有作出具体规定，这导致有部分民众不知道被继承人的抵押债务应当就抵押财产优先受偿。我们认为，对于本案被继承人的抵押债务，依法首先应以抵押财产优先偿还，对抵押财产不足清偿的部分，才由继承人在继承的其他遗产的实际价值范围内进行清偿。

---

① 参见中国裁判文书网，（2017）冀×民终×号，《某县农村信用联社股份有限公司、姚某金融借款合同纠纷二审民事判决书》，载 http://wenshu. court. gov. cn/content/content? DocID=f0f3f0a4-e16a-4a0a-9256-a839001003ee，访问日期：2018 年 11 月 5 日。限于本章篇幅，作者对原案情内容有酌情删改。

因此，该案例法院的判决未予明确应当以遗产中的抵押财产优先清偿被继承人的抵押债务，此为其不妥之处。同时该案也反映出，我国《继承法》未对遗产债务清偿顺序作出具体规定，不利于减少遗产处理纠纷，既不利于引导民众学法守法用法，也不利于指导法官释法、执法，故此为立法之不足。

（四）涉及法定继承案例的简介与评析

案例简介：本案原告杨某某，被告贾某甲、贾某乙、贾某丙、贾某丁、赵某甲、赵某乙。被继承人贾某华于2013年农历十月初九因病去世，生前与原告杨某某系夫妻关系。贾某华与前妻李某更生的三子二女即长子贾某甲、次子贾某乙、三子贾某丙、长女贾某荣、次女贾某丁。贾某荣于2014年7月2日因病去世，贾某荣的丈夫赵某甲、儿子赵某乙参加本案诉讼。被继承人贾某华去世后，其他被告不让原告杨某某参与继承，认为该继母不能参与分割遗产。现原告杨某某孤苦无依，无房居住，也无任何财产。原告杨某某多次找村委会及某村镇信访办调解，均未果，遂诉至法院。请求将其与贾某华的夫妻共同财产中的一半分给原告后，剩余的一半属于贾某华的遗产，由原告和被告共同继承。被告贾某甲、贾某乙、贾某丙、贾某丁、赵某甲、赵某乙辩称，原告诉讼请求不符合事实，没有任何法律依据和事实证据。因此，请求法院依法驳回原告的诉讼请求。

法院审理后认为，本案中，被继承人贾某华生前在某信用社的存款5000元属于与原告杨某某共同所有的财产，因此，应将其中的一半分出为原告杨某某所有，其余的为被继承人贾某华的遗产。因原告杨某某是生活有特殊困难又缺乏劳动能力、对被继承人贾某华尽了主要扶养义务又与被继承人贾某华共同生活的继承人，因此，分配遗产时应当多分。继承开始后，被继承人贾某华的长女贾某荣没有表示放弃继承，并于2014年7月2日因病去世，其继承遗产的权利转移给贾某荣的合法继承人赵某甲、赵某乙。因此，赵某甲、赵某乙只能继承贾某荣有权继承的遗产份额。故法院判决如下：第一，被继承人贾某华生前在某信用社的存款5000元原告杨某某分得4000元，其余1000元被告贾某甲、贾某乙、贾某丙、贾某丁各分得200元，被告赵某甲和赵某乙共分得200元；第二，被继承人贾某华生前在某信用社的存款5000元的全部利息归原告杨某某所有。①

法律适用评析：本案的争议焦点即法定继承人的范围及顺序。根据我国《继承法》第10条规定："遗产按照下列顺序继承：第一顺序：配偶、子女、父母。第二顺序：兄弟姐妹、祖父母、外祖父母。继承开始后，由第一顺序继承人继承，第二顺序继承人不继承。没有第一顺序继承人继承的，由第二顺序继承人继承。"我国《继承法》第13条规定："同一顺序继承人继承遗产的份额，一般应当均等。对生活有特殊困难的缺乏劳动能力的继承人，分配遗产时，应当予以照顾。对被继承人尽了主要扶养义务或者与被继承人共同生活的继承人，分配遗产时，可以多分。有扶养能力和有扶养条件的继承人，不尽扶养义务的，分配遗产时，应当不分或者少分。继承人协商同意的，也可以不均等。"本案中，法院依照法定继承人的范围和顺序、代位继承、继承人的应继份的相关规定进行遗产分割，并判决支持生活有特殊困难又缺乏劳动能力、对被继承人尽了主要扶养义务又与被

① 参见中国裁判文书网，（2014）宁民初字第×号，《杨某某与贾某甲、贾某乙、贾某丙、贾某丁、赵某甲、赵某乙、第三人张某某继承纠纷一审民事判决书》，载 http://wenshu.court.gov.cn/content/content? DocID=e9f6b4a1-1688-4c83-813a-6749ceb247d9，访问日期：2018年11月5日。限于本章篇幅，作者对原案情内容有酌情删改。

继承人贾某华共同生活的继承人多分遗产。笔者认为，此判决极具说理性，适用法律正确。

通过上述案例，我们认为我国法定继承立法有以下优点。我国《继承法》之法定继承立法的优点有二：第一，确认配偶（包括再婚配偶）与子女作为第一顺序继承人并规定其应继份。原则上同一顺位的继承人应平均分配遗产，但是对于对生活有特殊困难的缺乏劳动能力的继承人、对被继承人尽了主要扶养义务或者与被继承人共同生活的继承人、有扶养能力和有扶养条件但却不尽扶养义务的继承人区别对待。此种做法坚持了公平公正原则，又照顾了弱者的利益。第二，确立了代位继承权，使先于被继承人死亡的子女继承人的继承份额由其子女代位继承，保障了该死亡子女继承人后代的继承权益。

（五）涉及遗嘱继承案例的简介与评析

案情简介：原告毛某甲、毛某乙、毛某丁与被告毛某丙系兄妹，毛某国、吴某琴夫妻系原、被告的父母，一共生育三女一子，长女毛某甲、长子毛某乙、次女毛某丙、三女毛某丁。

2007年9月28日父亲毛某国去世，后吴某琴自书遗嘱，内容为："我叫吴某琴，女，现年93岁，1917年生，汉族，我本人年岁已高为避免我百年之后子女间因继承问题发生争执，我与已故老伴毛某国生前商量，谁养我谁继承涉案房产。他去世后一直由儿子养我，根据老半遗愿决定把涉案房产由儿子毛某乙继承，特立此据。2009年9月9日，立遗嘱人吴某琴。见证人刘某、薛某2010年4月24日见证。"2012年3月11日母亲吴某琴去世。毛某国与吴某琴于1974年在某镇有平房3间（涉案房产）。后毛某乙与毛某丙因遗产分割事宜产生纠纷。原告毛某乙遂诉至法院，请求法院判决其依遗嘱继承吴某琴的遗产，毛某甲、毛某丁请求按法定继承其父亲毛某国的遗产。被告毛某丙辩称：吴某琴的遗嘱不符合法律规定，应当依法认定无效。

一审法院审理后认为，2009年9月9日吴某琴立遗嘱，涉案房产由儿子毛某乙继承，而且原告毛某乙称遗嘱系母亲吴某琴亲笔书写。对吴某琴处分属于自己部分财产的遗嘱，应认定为有效，即涉案房产吴某琴拥有的二分之一产权归原告毛某乙继承。吴某琴处分丈夫毛某国遗产的部分遗嘱，应认定为无效，涉案房产毛某国拥有的二分之一产权（遗产）应由吴某琴、原告毛某乙、毛某甲、毛某丁、被告毛某丙共同继承。原告毛某乙请求按遗嘱继承部分支持。但根据本案实际情况，2007年9月28日原、被告父亲毛某国去世前，被告毛某丙对其父、母尽了较多的赡养义务，在分配遗产时，应予考虑适当多分。

一审判决后，毛某丙不服提出上诉。二审法院查明的事实与原审法院判决认定的事实相一致。遂二审法院判决驳回上诉，维持原判。①

法律适用分析：本案的争议焦点之一为被继承人所立遗嘱是否有效。首先，我们要确定被继承人所立遗嘱为何种形式的遗嘱，我国《继承法》第17条规定："自书遗嘱由遗嘱人亲笔书写，签名，注明年、月、日。"本案中，被继承人亲自书写遗嘱且留下了签名，注明了年、月、日，所以应当认定被继承人所立遗嘱为自书遗嘱。即使其遗嘱中有两

---

① 参见中国裁判文书网，（2014）唐民一终字第×号，《毛某甲、毛某丙等与毛某乙继承纠纷二审民事判决书》，http：//wenshu. court. gov. cn/content/content？DocID＝06fb69d3-cbc5-49d4-aa33-3a1237704ffe，访问日期：2018年11月5日。限于本章篇幅，作者对原案情内容有酌情删改。

位见证人，但并非代书遗嘱。其次，我国《继承法》第22条规定："无行为能力人或者限制行为能力人所立的遗嘱无效。遗嘱必须表示遗嘱人的真实意思，受胁迫、欺骗所立的遗嘱无效。伪造的遗嘱无效。遗嘱被篡改的，篡改的内容无效。"本案中被继承人虽事已高且体弱多病，但并未有证据证明其为无民事行为能力人或限制行为能力人，并且没有证据证明遗嘱是伪造的、是被篡改的或在受胁迫、欺诈情形下做出的，所以被继承人所立遗嘱不存在无效的情形。再次，我们需确定遗嘱是否全部有效。1985年《执行继承法意见》第38条规定："遗嘱人以遗嘱处分了属于国家、集体或他人所有的财产，遗嘱的这部分，应认定无效。"本案中，被继承人只对涉案房屋享有二分之一的所有权，所以其处分另外二分之一所有权的遗嘱内容应为无效，被继承人对涉案房屋所享有的二分之一所有权依照遗嘱处分。原告毛某乙请求按遗嘱继承部分法院予以支持，因原、被告四人均为第一顺序法定继承人有权依法继承涉案房屋中遗嘱无效部分涉及的遗产。最后，根据本案实际情况，2007年9月28日原、被告父亲毛某国去世前，被告毛某丙对其父、母尽了较多的赡养义务，在分配遗产时，应予考虑适当多分。

通过上述案例及分析，我们认为我国遗嘱继承立法优点有二：第一，明确规定不同形式遗嘱的成立条件，使法律工作者和民众可以更好的区分遗嘱形式。第二，明确规定遗嘱无效的四种情形，这便于法官和民众识别不同情形遗嘱的效力。

（六）涉及继承和遗赠的接受与放弃案例的简介与评析

案情简介：原告张某甲与被告张某乙、张某丙、张某丁系同母异父兄弟姐妹。原告张某甲之母郭某兰在原告二周岁时带原告改嫁张某艳。张某艳与郭某兰结婚后又生育一男二女，分别是被告张某乙、张某丙、张某丁，其后原、被告与被继承人郭某兰、张某艳一起生活。坐落于某村房产系原、被告父母的夫妻共同财产。原、被告之母郭某兰于1998年1月29日去世，其父于2005年6月23日去世，生前无遗嘱及遗赠扶养协议。被继承人郭某兰去世3年后，2001年原告搬离唐山，原、被告之间亦无联系。2005年7月7日，某号公证书的主要内容为：被继承人（张某艳、郭某兰）的上述遗产（坐落于某村房产平正房4间）应由其配偶、子女、父母共同继承。因被继承人父母均先于被继承人死亡，被继承人的长女张某丙、次女张某丁均声明自愿放弃继承权，故被继承人的上述遗产由其儿子张某乙继承。某政府某号宅基地使用证登记土地使用权人为张某乙。此公证书中无原告张某甲放弃或接受遗产的意思表示。被告张某乙称公证时，村委会出具证明，证明中表述为现下一儿两女，未提张某甲。后原、被告双方对遗产分割事宜产生纠纷，且未能协议一致。原告遂诉至法院，请求依法继承张某艳、郭某兰涉案房产的50%份额。被告张某乙辩称，张某甲已放弃继承，故无权参与遗产分割。

法院审理后认为，继承开始后，继承人放弃继承的，应当在遗产处理前，作出放弃继承的表示。没有表示的，视为接受继承。本案中，原告自二周岁开始随母亲与被继承人张某艳一起生活，与张某艳已经形成继父与继子间的抚养教育关系，故原告张某甲作为有抚养教育关系的继子，有权继承被继承人张某艳、郭某兰的遗产。在处理被继承人张某艳、郭某兰的遗产时，原告未表示放弃继承，应视为接受继承。被告张某丙、张某丁明确表示放弃继承。故此涉案房产应由原告张某甲、被告张某乙继承。考虑被告张某乙在其赡养被继承人张某艳时尽了主要扶养义务，在分配遗产时，应予以多分。因此，依据我国《继承法》第10条、第13条、第25条之规定，法院判决如下：涉案房产由原告张某甲、被告张某乙共有，原告张某甲占上述房产的20%份额、被告张某乙占80%份额。①

法律适用分析：本案的争议焦点为放弃继承的方式。首先，我国《继承法》第25条规定："继承开始后，继承人放弃继承的，应当在遗产处理前，作出放弃继承的表示。没有表示的，视为接受继承。"由此可知，继承权的放弃必须明示作出，未明确表示放弃继承的，视为接受继承。原告张某甲虽离家多年且不与家人联系，但其并未明确表示自己放弃继承遗产，未明确表明放弃遗产的，视为接受遗产。所以原告并未放弃继承，其有权继承遗产。因此，法院的判决于法有据。

通过上述案例，我们认为，我国继承的接受和放弃的立法优点，即继承权的放弃采明示放弃之方式有利于保障继承人的继承权。例如，上述案例，原告虽常年不与家人联系，但是其从未表明放弃继承，所以其有权继承遗产。此外，明示放弃之立法规定还有利于保护没有被通知继承开始的继承人的继承权。例如，继承人失踪多年后返回家中，但遗产已经分割完毕；被继承人的非婚生子女于遗产分割后主张自己的继承权；继承开始通知者故意不通知继承人，导致继承人未参与遗产分割等情形。但其中也突显我国《继承法》立法的不足，即继承权的放弃期间不明确，因为继承开始后到遗产处理前的这段时间可长可短；且如果继承开始后长期不对遗产进行处理，容易导致遗产的归属具有不确定性，容易引发继承纠纷。

（七）涉及继承权的丧失、被继承人的宥恕与代位继承的案例简介与评析

案例简介：被告刘某（母亲）、杨某（父亲）系杨甲的父母。原告李某是杨甲的妻子。2011年12月9日，原告李某的丈夫杨甲上班途中与郭某涛驾驶的重型半挂车发生交通事故，杨甲受伤后被送往医院抢救。2012年3月8日，在某市交警大队的主持下达成赔偿协议，由肇事者郭某涛一方赔偿杨甲医药费、误工费、护理费、住院伙食补助费、车损费、伤残费、伤残护理费等相关费用共计89万元，被告刘某将此款领取。杨甲于2012年4月23日死亡，未留遗嘱。杨甲的第一顺序继承人为妻子李某、母亲刘某、父亲杨某，共计三人。此后，原被告因遗产分割事宜产生纠纷。原告李某遂诉至法院，要求继承杨甲用于医疗费等后的剩余的赔偿款的三分之一。被告刘某和杨某未出庭参加辩答。

一审法院审理后认为，本案原告李某之夫杨甲因交通事故获得赔偿89万元，根据我国现行《婚姻法》第18条的规定，夫妻一方因身体受到伤害获得的医疗费、残疾人生活补助费等费用，为夫妻一方的财产。因此杨甲获得的赔偿款属杨甲个人财产，杨甲去世后成为杨甲的遗产应当由继承人依法继承。赔偿款支付相关医疗等费用后剩余305706元，此款应当依法分割。杨甲的第一顺序继承人为李某、刘某、杨某三人，现剩余赔偿款由被告刘某持有，故应当由被告刘某给付原告李某相应份额。原告认可被告在救治杨甲过程中，支出医疗费52万元、丧葬费2万元、住宿饮食及护理费等费用3万元。庭审中，原告又认可被告支出14294元。故法院依法判决：原告李某继承杨甲遗产305706元中的9万元，由被告刘某给付原告李某，于本判决生效后10日内履行完毕。

一审法院宣判后，刘某、杨某不服，向本院提起上诉。其主要上诉理由是被上诉人李

① 参见中国裁判文书网，（2015）北民初字第×号，《张某甲与张某乙、张某丙等继承纠纷一审民事判决书》，载 http://wenshu.court.gov.cn/content/content?DocID=9f9b2589-667f-46e5-90bb-ce2a28b56ea7，访问日期：2019年2月20日。限于本章篇幅，作者对原案情内容有酌情删改。

某丧失继承权，不具有继承人资格。杨甲发生交通事故后，其妻李某遗弃杨甲，对杨某甲病情不理不问，至今不能说明杨甲发生交通事故时怀胎，到出生时几乎足月的孩子是被人流，还是出生后被抛弃，被上诉人没有尽到妻子应尽的义务。

二审法院审理后认为，我国《继承法》第7条规定：继承人有下列行为之一的，丧失继承权：（一）故意杀害被继承人的；（二）为争夺遗产杀害其他继承人的；（三）遗弃被继承人的，或者虐待被继承人情节严重的；（四）伪造、篡改或者销毁遗嘱，情节严重的。本案被上诉人李某并没有发生丧失继承权的法定情形，其作为死者杨甲的合法继承人，有权继承杨甲的遗产。上诉人刘某、杨某主张被上诉人李某在杨甲发生交通事故后遗弃杨甲，丧失了继承权，不具有继承人资格，因其未提供充分证据予以证实，依法不予支持。故二审法院判决，驳回上诉，维持原判。①

法律适用分析：本案的争议焦点是被上诉人李某是否丧失继承权。本案中，上诉人指出被上诉人李某在被继承人杨甲发生交通事故后，遗弃被继承人，对其病情不理不问，所以上诉人李某丧失继承权。法院认为，二上诉人未提供充分证据予以证实被上诉人遗弃被继承人，所以被继承人不存在我国《继承法》第7条规定的遗弃或虐待被继承人情节严重的情形，对上诉人主张的被上诉人丧失继承权不予支持。

通过上述案例，我们认为我国继承权丧失立法有以下优点及不足。首先，立法规定了继承人当然丧失继承的具体法定事由。第一，我国《继承法》规定的四种法定事由都是影响十分恶劣，对继承人或被继承人权益损害较大的情形。明确列举丧失继承权的四种法定情形，有利于民众和法律工作者了解相关法律知识，缩小具体案件中法官的自由裁量权。第二，法定继承权的丧失为当然丧失，不用经过诉讼程序认定。此种程序性规定可以避免不必要的诉累。其次，立法的不足是继承权的恢复未被规定在我国《继承法》中，而是被规定在1985年《执行继承法意见》中，不便于民众查阅知晓和守法用法。最后，继承人以欺诈、胁迫手段妨碍被继承人订立、修改遗嘱且情节严重的行为未被规定为丧失继承权的行为，但是此行为对于继承人或被继承人的权益的伤害不低于伪造、篡改或者销毁遗嘱，情节严重的行为。

（八）涉及继承协议案例的简介与评析

案例简介：上诉人（原审原告）隋1、陈1（二人系夫妻）。被上诉人（原审被告）隋2。李某（1917年出生，1975年死亡，无遗嘱）与杜某（2011年11月29日去世）系夫妻，二人无子女。李某1与李某系亲姐妹，隋1和隋2是李某1所生子女。

1988年，杜某申请在杜某宅院内建房做厨房，被批准建南房4间，当时的建房施工许可证载明：原有北房4间，家庭成员为杜某（66岁，户主）、隋1（27岁，养女）、陈1（27岁，女婿）、陈某（1岁，外孙子）。

1990年5月20日，杜某（被扶养人）与隋1（扶养人）签订《遗赠扶养优扶孤老协议书》，该协议书载明："扶养人系被扶养人养女；扶养人的义务为帮助被扶养人领取国家发给定期抚恤和补助金，照顾好被扶养人的日常生活，被扶养人有病时协助就医，被扶

① 参见中国裁判文书网，（2014）沧民终字第×号，《刘某与李某法定继承纠纷二审民事判决书》，载 http://wenshu.court.gov.cn/content/content?DocID=4f484247-f18c-4362-a8aa-189117bf01ca，访问日期：2019年2月20日。限于本章篇幅，作者对原案情内容有酌情删改。

养人死亡后妥善处理好后事，并向有关部门报告；被扶养人的主要财产为房屋10间，在被扶养人健在时归被扶养人所有使用，但不得任意处理、变卖或馈赠他人，被扶养人死亡后其全部财产归扶养人所有，同时有权领取被扶养人的丧葬补助费，本协议自签字之日起生效。”杜某、隋1及村民委员会负责人白某在协议上签字，某村村民委员会在该协议上加盖公章。隋1自出生后不久即在涉案房屋居住，后隋1、陈1和陈某与杜某共同生活，于2000年搬走。后隋2搬入杜某宅院与杜某共同生活，至杜某去世。

2011年8月10日，杜某由佟某代书订立遗嘱一份，内容为：“我今年89岁，现在精神状况良好，由于年事已高，可能发生意外，故立此遗嘱，表示我对自己财产在我去世之后的处理意愿。我名下房产（涉案房产）现由隋2改建，由隋2对我进行赡养，在我去世后，房产和我名下的全部存款由隋2继承，以上是我的真实意思表示。”佟某在代书人、证明人处签字，谢×在证明人处签字。

原被告因遗产分配事宜产生纠纷，遂隋1、陈1作为原告向一审法院起诉请求：依法分割涉案房产的10间房屋，全部判归隋1、陈1所有并居住使用。隋2辩称，隋1是杜某的养女，即杜某法定继承人，根据我国《继承法》规定，《遗赠抚养优扶孤老协议书》不是法律上的遗赠扶养协议，应为无效。

一审法院认为：根据我国《继承法》第5条规定：“继承开始后，按照法定继承办理；有遗嘱的，按照遗嘱继承或者遗赠办理；有遗赠扶养协议的，按照协议办理。”本案中，首先，隋1与杜某于1990年5月20日签订的《遗赠扶养优扶孤老协议书》，系双方的真实意思表示，且不违反法律、行政法规的强制性规定，应系合法有效。因隋1与杜某形成事实上的养父女关系，故隋1系杜某的法定继承人，故上述《遗赠扶养优扶孤老协议书》实为附义务的遗嘱继承。

杜某于2011年8月10日订立的遗嘱，符合法定的形式要件和实质要件，系杜某的真实意思表示，亦系合法有效，因隋2非杜某的法定继承人，故上述遗嘱实为附义务的遗赠。因上述遗嘱系在上述《遗赠扶养优扶孤老协议书》之后订立，故杜某对其财产的处理意见应以上述遗嘱为准。因此，隋1依据上述《遗赠扶养优扶孤老协议书》主张杜某在涉案房屋中的财产权益并要求居住使用房屋，无事实和法律依据，法院不予支持。遂一审法院判决：驳回原告隋1、陈1的全部诉讼请求。原告隋1、陈1不服一审判决，遂提出上诉。

二审法院认为，一审判决认定事实清楚，适用法律正确，应予维持。遂二审法院判决，驳回上诉，维持原判。①

法律适用评析：本案的争议焦点为该《遗赠扶养优扶孤老协议书》与后一遗嘱的法律性质及效力。首先，我国《继承法》第31条规定：“公民可以与扶养人签订遗赠扶养协议。按照协议，扶养人承担该公民生养死葬的义务，享有受遗赠的权利。”可见，我国仅规定了遗赠扶养协议制度，且承担扶养义务的扶养人法定继承人以外的其他人，而未规定被继承人与法定继承人之间签订的继承协议。其次，我国《继承法》第21条规定：

① 参见中国裁判文书网，（2016）京×民终×号，《陈1等与隋2分家析产纠纷二审民事判决书》，载 http://wenshu.court.gov.cn/content/content? DocID=e9b91717-6dca-467e-99d8-ff3fe1d87d02，访问日期：2019年2月20日。限于本章篇幅，作者对原案情内容有酌情删改。

“遗嘱继承或者遗赠附有义务的，继承人或者受遗赠人应当履行义务。没有正当理由不履行义务的，经有关单位或者个人请求，人民法院可以取消他接受遗产的权利。”1985年《执行继承法意见》第56条规定：“扶养人或集体组织与公民订有遗赠扶养协议，扶养人或集体组织无正当理由不履行，致协议解除的，不能享有受遗赠的权利，其支付的供养费用一般不予补偿；遗赠人无正当理由不履行，致协议解除的，则应偿还扶养人或集体组织已支付的供养费用。”但法院认为，本案例中的《遗赠扶养优扶孤老协议书》并非遗赠扶养协议，而是附义务的遗嘱继承，且认可后遗嘱优先生效，有其不妥之处。因为上述案例中的《遗赠扶养优扶孤老协议书》，实质上是继承协议，且法院认定后遗嘱优先生效而直接否定该协议效力，导致尽了约定扶养义务的扶养人未获得应有的补偿，有失公平。

通过上述案例，我们认为我国遗赠扶养协议立法有以下的优点及不足。首先，我国立法的优点即立法允许被继承人与继承人之外的签订遗赠扶养协议，双方互相权利、互负义务，这有利于保障被继承人老有所养，也是对被继承人处理其财产意愿的尊重。其次，我国遗赠扶养协议立法的不足有两点：第一，遗赠扶养协议的签订主体为被继承人与继承人之外的人，制度的适用范围太窄，不能适用于调整被继承人与其法定继承人间签订的继承协议。此规定不合理。第二，欠缺继承协议制度，导致此类案件中继承协议的处理于法无据，未能保护扶养人应得的财产权益。

（九）涉及遗产债务清偿案例的简介与评析

案例简介：上诉人（原审被告）马某1（马某的孙子）。被上诉人（原审原告）马某、王某（马某1的爷爷和奶奶）。原告马某、王某夫妇系被继承人马甲的父母，被告马某1系被继承人马甲之子。2010年6月17日马甲与宋某离婚，婚生子马某1跟随宋某一起生活。2013年10月23日，原告马某与马甲签订了《房屋买卖合同》，马某将一套房产（涉案房屋，76平方米）转让给马甲并办理过户登记。但马甲生前一直未支付该房购房款47.2万元，原告夫妇一直生活居住在该房屋内。2014年12月4日马甲死亡，马甲生前无遗嘱。2015年1月8日经公证，原、被告分割了马甲的遗产银行存款24902.2元。2017年4月25日，本院主持双方调解时均认可，诉争房屋价值15000元/平方米。原、被告因房产分割事宜发生纠纷。原告马某、王某遂诉至法院，请求法院依法认定原告与被继承人马甲之间存在遗留债务47.2万元的事实，并应由被告在遗产范围内偿还该债务并依法分割遗产。被告马某1辩称，被继承人马甲不存在遗留债务47.2万元的事实，且原告隐匿被继承人遗产，应当少分得遗产份额。

一审法院审理后认为，本案诉争的房产是被继承人马甲的遗产，马甲生前未立遗嘱，其遗产应由法定继承人原告马某、王某、被告马某1共同继承，每人继承三分之一的份额。被继承人马甲生前一直未支付该房购房款47.2万元，属遗产债务，应从遗产中扣除。被告主张原告隐匿被继承人遗产，应当少分得遗产份额，但未能提供充分证据证明原告隐匿遗产的事实，且不符合少分遗产的法定情形，本院不能采信。因此，依照我国《继承法》第10条、第13条的规定，一审法院判决如下：被继承人马甲名下涉案房产归原告马某、王某所有，原告马某、王某付给被告马某1遗产222667元。

马某1不服一审判决，遂提起上诉。二审期间，当事人未提交新证据，且二审认定的事实与原审认定的事实一致。二审法院审理后认为，原判认定事实清楚，应用法律正确。

遂二审法院判决驳回上诉，维持原判。[①]

法律适用评析：本案的争议焦点为47.2万元购房款是否属于被继承人遗留的债务，是否由遗产予以偿还。我国《继承法》第33条规定："继承遗产应当清偿被继承人依法应当缴纳的税款和债务，缴纳税款和清偿债务以他的遗产实际价值为限。超过遗产实际价值部分，继承人自愿偿还的不在此限。"可知，被继承人生前所欠债务属于遗产债务，应在遗产分割先行清偿。法院对于此项争议焦点的处理于法有据、公平公正。

通过上述案例及分析，我们认为我国《继承法》之遗产债务清偿立法有以下优点与不足。首先，我国立法的优点是规定了遗产债务清偿制度，可以引导民众对遗产债务在遗产分割前优先受偿，有效保护遗产债权人的利益。其次，我国《继承法》之遗产债务清偿立法的不足有二：第一，我国遗产债务大体包括：酌给遗产债务；必要的遗产份额；被继承人生前所欠的税款和债务；遗赠债务；继承费用[②]。上述遗产债务规定零散，加大了民众查阅遗产债务法律规定的难度。第二，我国《继承法》未规定遗产债务的清偿顺序，只能通过相关法条的规定推定何种遗产债务优先受偿，加大了法律工作者和民众适用法律的难度，也不能体现个人与社会之间的利益平衡，不利于保护各方当事人利益。[③]

（十）涉及遗产分割纠纷案例的简介与评析

案例简介：原告宋某乙与被告宋某甲系同胞兄妹，被继承人宋某系宋某乙与宋某甲的父亲，于2004年2月24日去世，被继承人米某系原告宋某乙与被告宋某甲的母亲，于2011年9月4日去世。被继承人宋某、米某父母均已去世多年。被继承人宋某于生前在某村申请宅基地两块，分别为6号宅基地和13号宅基地，上述两处房产均由被告宋某甲及其子女居住。后因原告宋某乙要求继承被继承人宋某、米某所遗留房产与被告宋某甲协商未果。原告宋某乙于2013年7月诉至法院，原告宋某乙请求依法继承被继承人宋某、米某遗产。但被告宋某甲辩称，被继承人宋某、米某所遗留房屋为其翻建、新建，并非被继承人的遗产；且被继承人宋某、米某生前表示将所有房产赠与被告宋某甲，故原告无权分割遗产。

一审法院审理后认为，位于6号宅基地和13号宅基地所建房屋及门楼，系被继承人宋某、米某的夫妻共同财产。原告宋某乙与被告宋某甲均为本案的第一顺序继承人，对被继承人宋某、米某所留遗产均享有法定继承权，原告宋某乙请求继承被继承人宋某、米某遗产的诉讼请求，法院予以支持。根据我国《继承法》第29条"遗产分割应当有利于生产和生活需要，不损害遗产的效用"的规定，原告宋某乙结婚后，于1970年便从某村搬走，被告宋某甲及其子女与被继承人宋某、米某在某村居住，被告宋某甲两个儿子亦在某村结婚并在被继承人宋某、米某所遗留两处房产中居住数年，现原告宋某乙与被告宋某甲因继承遗产发生纠纷并诉至法院，将位于6号宅基地和13号宅基地两处房屋各分割一半由被告宋某甲、原告宋某乙分别继承，显然不利于被告宋某甲、原告宋某乙生产和生活，故将6号和13号两处房屋分别由原告宋某乙与被告宋某甲各继承一处，较为妥当，亦有

---

① 参见中国裁判文书网，（2017）冀×民×号，《马某1、王某继承纠纷民事判决书》，载 http://wenshu.court.gov.cn/content/content? DocID=fd28f1e7-2044-4bdb-9bbd-a82a001056c5，访问日期：2018年11月5日。限于本章篇幅，作者对原案情内容有酌情删改。

② 陈苇主编：《外国继承法比较与中国民法典继承编制定研究》，北京大学出版社2011年版，第553页。

③ 陈苇、宋豫主编：《中国大陆与港、澳、台继承法比较研究》，群众出版社2007年版，第427页。

利于被告宋某甲、原告宋某乙生活。遂一审法院判决如下：一、6 号宅基地上所建房屋及门楼由原告宋某乙继承所有；二、13 号宅基地上所建房屋及门楼由被告宋某甲继承所有。

一审法院宣判后，原审被告即上诉人宋某甲不服，提起上诉。二审法院查明的事实与一审法院认定的事实一致。遂二审法院判决驳回上诉，维持原判。①

法律适用评析：本案的争议焦点为涉案房屋遗产的分割。我国《继承法》第 29 条规定："遗产分割应当有利于生产和生活需要，不损害遗产的效用。不宜分割的遗产，可以采取折价、适当补偿或者共有等方法处理。"本案中的宋某乙结婚后，于 1970 年从某村搬走，宋某甲及其子女与被继承人宋某、米某在某村居住，宋某甲两个儿子也在某村结婚并于被继承人宋某、米某所遗留两处房产中居住数年，若 6 号房屋和 13 号房屋各分割一半由宋某甲、宋某乙分别继承，明显不利于宋某甲、宋某乙生产和生活，所以法院依据我国《继承法》第 29 条的规定 6 号宅基地和 13 号宅基地两处房屋分别判给宋某乙与宋某甲各继承一处的做法合理合法，且有利于双方的生活需要。

通过上述案例及分析，我们认为我国《继承法》之遗产分割立法有以下优点与不足。首先，我国《继承法》之遗产分割立法的优点即规定了遗产分割应有利于生产生活需要，不得损害遗产价值，这有利于保障实现遗产价值的最大化，也有利于方便继承人的生活生产需要。其次，立法的不足即未对遗产分割的时间作限制性规定，这不利于特殊情况下遗产价值的充分发挥，也不利于继承纠纷中证据的保存和提取。

（十一）涉及无人承受遗产案例的简介与评析

案情简介：柴某达系某村村民，于 1995 年去世。柴某达生前在柴屯村有住房一处；柴某达有一子二女：儿子柴甲、长女柴乙、次女柴丙。原告柴某清系柴甲的儿子、柴某达的孙子。柴某达去世后，其子女均声明放弃对柴某达遗产的继承，并约定柴某达的所有遗产都由原告柴某清继承。被告柴某通、柴某森系父子关系。二被告未经原告柴某清同意，将房屋拆除，拆下的砖块、檩条以及宅基地上的树木、宅基地等占有。原告列出了占用物品的清单，清单上列明财产的价值，根据该清单，给原告造成的直接经济损失为 12 万元。原被告双方因遗产事宜产生纠纷。遂原告向法院提起诉讼，请求依法判决由其继承祖父柴某达的遗产，两被告柴某通、柴某森共同赔偿经济损失 12 万元，并互负连带责任。被告柴某通、柴某森均未参加答辩。

法院审理后认为，原告的祖父柴某达去世后，其遗产应由第一顺序继承人继承，原告系柴某达的孙子，并非法定继承人。我国《继承法》第 10 条规定"遗产按照下列顺序继承：第一顺序：配偶、子女、父母。第二顺序：兄弟姐妹、祖父母、外祖父母。继承开始后，由第一顺序继承人继承，第二顺序继承人不继承。没有第一顺序继承人的，由第二顺序继承人继承……"根据该项规定，在第一顺序继承人生存的情况下，虽第一顺序继承人声明放弃继承权，但原告仍不具有对柴某达遗产的代位继承权。我国《继承法》第 32 条规定："无人继承又无人受遗赠的遗产，归国家所有；死者生前是集体所有制组织成员的，归所在集体所有制组织所有。"柴某达的子女声明放弃继承柴某达的遗产，从而导致

① 参见中国裁判文书网：（2014）邯市民一终字第×号，《宋某乙与宋某甲继承纠纷二审民事判决书》，载 http://wenshu.court.gov.cn/content/content? DocID=c9b3a0a3-45be-48cc-819b-76b81ab41aa9，访问日期：2019 年 4 月 28 日。限于本章篇幅，作者对原案情内容有酌情删改。

无法定继承人继承柴某达的遗产。而柴某达的子女放弃对柴某达遗产继承后，也同时失去了对柴某达遗产的处分权利。因此，原告继承死者柴某达的继承遗产请求无法律依据。原告柴某清诉称二被告拆除柴某清所继承其祖父柴某达房屋，占有其所继承财产，所举证据不足以证实其主张成立，且原告所举证据显示其所主张的财产中有他人的份额，这与其主张之间存在矛盾，并不能证实其所"继承"的财产被二被告所侵害。综上所述，原告要求二被告共同赔偿原告经济损失 12 万元的主张，不能成立。故法院判决，驳回原告的诉讼请求。①

法律适用评析：本案的争议焦点之一为被继承人柴某达的遗产是否为无人承受的遗产。我国《继承法》第 32 条规定："无人继承又无人受遗赠的遗产，归国家所有；死者生前是集体所有制组织成员的，归所在集体所有制组织所有。"何为遗产无人继承又无人受遗赠，我国《继承法》以及 1985 年《执行继承法意见》都未作出明确规定。我国《继承法》第 10 条规定："遗产按照下列顺序继承：第一顺序：配偶、子女、父母；第二顺序：兄弟姐妹、祖父母、外祖父母。继承开始后，由第一顺序继承人继承，第二顺序继承人不继承。没有第一顺序继承人继承的，由第二顺序继承人继承。"此条款指出只有第一顺位没有继承人的，第二顺位继承人才可以继承，并没有规定第一顺位继承人全部放弃继承的，如何处理。此案中法院认为第一顺位继承人全部放弃继承的，遗产则无人继承，应属于无人承受的遗产。我们认为，该法院的此认识不符合法律的规定。因为只有第一顺位、第二顺位继承人全部放弃继承遗产的，遗产才属于无人承受的遗产，本案中第一顺位继承人全部放弃继承的，应由第二顺位继承人继承遗产，如有第二顺序继承人，则不属于无人承受的遗产。

通过上述案例，我们认为我国无人承受遗产立法有以下不足。第一，我国无人承受遗产立法，欠缺无人继承与无人受遗赠的具体情形规定。我国只是将无人承受的遗产概括表述为"遗产无人继承又无人受遗赠"，对于何为无人继承与无人受遗赠并未作具体规定，这就导致在这一问题上形成不同的认知。例如，上述案例，法院审理认为，第一顺位继承人存在但都放弃继承的，其在没有通知或公告查找第二顺序继承人的情况下，就认定该遗产为无人承受的遗产，这并不符合法律规定的本意。因为，第一顺位继承人全部放弃继承的，应由表示接受继承的第二顺位继承人继承遗产。第二，对于放弃继承之无人继承遗产欠缺管理制度，这可能导致遗产损害的发生。此外，在第一顺位继承人放弃继承后，其代位继承人可否代位继承遗产，根据我国 1985 年《执行继承法意见》第 28 条规定："继承人丧失继承权的，其晚辈直系血亲不得代位继承。"第 51 条规定："放弃继承的效力，追溯到继承开始的时间。"即我国对于被代位继承人放弃继承的不允许代位继承，这导致不能保障代位继承人的继承权益，此为我国代位继承立法之不足。

① 参见中国裁判文书网，（2016）冀×民初×号，《柴某清与柴某通、柴某森财产损害赔偿纠纷一审民事判决书》，载 http://wenshu.court.gov.cn/content/content? DocID=4995f350-b21a-4a19-a3e1-9424aff51571，访问日期：2018 年 11 月 5 日。限于本章篇幅，作者对原案情内容有酌情删改。

第三节 当代中国河北省民众财产继承观念与遗产处理习惯的特点与原因分析

根据本次调查统计数据的汇总分析，河北省被调查者对前述十一个问题所体现出的财产继承观念与遗产处理习惯之特点与原因分析如下：

一、遗产的范围之特点与原因分析

（一）遗产的种类之特点与原因分析

关于属于遗产种类的民众观念，统计数据显示的特点是，（1）有八成至九成以上的河北省被调查者认为住房（98.58%）、汽车（94.74%）、存款（96.30%）和股票（81.37%）属于遗产，此认识符合我国《继承法》的规定。（2）一成至近七成的人认为家庭日常生活用品（66.71%）、债务（45.23%）、交通事故死亡赔偿金（68.14%）、单位出租房（8.96%）属于遗产，此认识与我国《继承法》的规定不一致。（3）有近二成半的人认为以被继承人的姓名注册的邮箱和QQ账号等（26.17%）属于遗产，对此我国《继承法》无规定（见表5-4）。

以上特点之原因分析：在河北省被调查者中，（1）有八成至九成以上的人认为住房、汽车、存款等传统财产属于遗产，其原因可能是受我国立法的影响。（2）近七成的人认为死亡赔偿金属于遗产，其原因可能是其认为死亡赔偿金是对死者生命的补偿，理应属于死者的财产。但此认识与法律规定不一致，对于死亡赔偿金的性质，根据我国2004年《关于审理人身损害赔偿案件适用法律若干问题的解释》第1条第2款规定："本条所称'赔偿权利人'，是指因侵权行为或者其他致害原因直接遭受人身损害的受害人、依法由受害人承担扶养义务的被扶养人以及死亡受害人的近亲属。"第17条第3款规定："受害人死亡的，赔偿义务人除应当根据抢救治疗情况赔偿本条第一款规定的相关费用外，还应当赔偿丧葬费、被扶养人生活费、死亡补偿费以及受害人亲属办理丧葬事宜支出的交通费、住宿费和误工损失等其他合理费用。"以上规定中表明，死者的人身损害死亡补偿费是对死亡受害人的近亲属的补偿费，其不属于遗产。（3）有六成半稍多的人认为家庭日常生活用品属于遗产，其原因可能是被继承人也在使用，所以应当属于其遗产。但此认识有误，因为"家庭日常生活用品"中只有属于被继承人的份额部分，才属于遗产。（4）有四成半的人认为债务属于遗产，与现行法的规定不一致，其原因可能是受我国"父债子偿"的传统观念的影响。（5）二成半稍多的人认为以被继承人的姓名注册的邮箱和QQ账号等是遗产，其原因可能是认为将其排除在遗产范围之外，不利于继承人或受遗赠人在感情上的延续；反之，有七成以上的人认为该邮箱和QQ账号等不属于遗产，其原因可能是认为这些特殊遗物具有人身性，不能作为遗产继承。可见，我国立法对于遗产的范围欠缺排除性规定，是民众对某些遗产认识不一致的原因。

关于遗产的种类之我国立法，我国《继承法》第3条规定："遗产是公民死亡时遗留的个人合法财产，包括：（一）公民的收入；（二）公民的房屋、储蓄和生活用品；（三）公民的林木、牲畜和家禽；（四）公民的文物、图书资料；（五）法律允许公民所有的生产资料；（六）公民的著作权、专利权中的财产权利；（七）公民的其他合法财产。"1985

年《执行继承法意见》第3条和第4条规定："公民可继承的其他合法财产包括有价证券和履行标的为财物的债权等。承包人死亡时尚未取得承包收益的，可把死者生前对承包所投入的资金和所付出的劳动及其增值和孳息，由发包单位或者接续承包合同的人合理折价、补偿，其价额作为遗产。"

从域外立法例看，瑞士对遗产范围作了一般性规定，即遗产包括债权、所有权、其他物权、股份、占有物。① 日本规定，遗产包括处被继承人人身专属性权利义务之外的一切财产性权利义务。但具有被继承人本人人身专属性的，不在此限。② 意大利的遗产范围为被继承人所有的权利义务，但因被继承人死亡而消灭的权利义务除外。③ 俄罗斯规定，遗产包括继承开始之日属于被继承人的物和其他财产，包括财产权利和义务。遗产不包括与被继承人的人身不可分割地联系在一起的权利和义务，其中包括领取赡养金的权利、因公民生命或健康受到损害而取得赔偿的权利，以及依据本法典或其他法律不允许通过继承移转的权利和义务。遗产不包括人身非财产权和其他非物质利益。④

从我国诸继承法学者建议稿看，关于遗产范围的规定采用的立法模式不同。例如，"梁稿"规定，遗产是自然人死亡时遗留的个人合法财产，包括自然人因其死亡而获得的未指定受益人的保险金、补偿金、赔偿金以及其他基于该自然人生前行为而应获得的财产利益。下列权利义务不得作为继承的标的：与被继承人人身不可分割的人身权利；与被继承人人身有关的专属性债权债务；法律规定不得继承的其他财产。⑤ "王稿"规定，因自然人死亡获得的保险赔偿金、补偿金、赔偿金等属于遗产，但法律另有规定的除外。⑥ "张稿"规定，遗产为被继承人的全部财产权利、义务和责任，但是专属于被继承人自身以及因继承开始而消灭的除外。⑦

我们认为，我国立法欠缺遗产种类的排除性规定，此为立法之不足。对遗产的种类即其范围界定，随着经济的发展，遗产的类型会继续增多，所以不宜采取列举的方式规定具体的遗产范围，而应该采用概括性规定并辅之反面排除的立法模式，规定遗产是被继承人死亡时所享有的权利义务，但专属于被继承人的除外。因此，上述河北省被调查者关于应排除人身性、隐私性财产于遗产范围外的民众观念、对遗产范围反面排除的域外立法例和我国学者建议稿的观点可供我国立法参考。

（二）被继承人生前特种赠与财产的归扣之特点与原因分析

关于被继承人生前特种赠与财产是否应归入遗产的民众观念与民间习惯，统计数据显示的特点是，（1）在被调查者的观念上，持否定观点的占八成半（85.78%），持肯定观点的占近一成半（14.22%）（见表5-5）；（2）在被调查者所在地区的习惯是：不归入遗产的，占近八成（79.23%），归入遗产的，占二成（20.77%）（见表5-7）。

以上特点之原因分析：在河北省被调查者中，八成多的人在观念上不认可归扣制度，

---

① 参见《瑞士民法典》第560条。
② 参见《日本民法典》第896条。
③ 参见《意大利民法典》第490条第1款。
④ 参见《俄罗斯联邦民法典》第1112条。
⑤ 参见"梁稿"第1941条。
⑥ 参见"王稿"第538条。
⑦ 参见"张稿"第9条第2款。

且被调查者所在地区有归扣习惯较少，其原因可能是，（1）被继承人生前对继承人的赠与应受法律保护，不能因为被继承人死亡，就将赠与特定继承人的财产收回而纳入遗产范围。（2）被继承人因继承人结婚、教育、分家等进行的财产处分是在情理之中，其真实的处分财产意愿应该被尊重。

关于归扣制度之我国立法，我国《继承法》无规定。

从域外立法例看，《法国民法典》规定，任何继承人在参与继承时，应对其他继承人返还死者生前赠与的全部财产，除死者在赠与时已明确此种财产为应继份之外的先取利益或免除返还，继承人不得保留死者赠与的财产。此外，还规定了免予归扣的财产范围。[①]《意大利民法典》规定，参加继承的婚生子女、非婚生子女及其婚生或者非婚生卑亲属和配偶，应将被继承人生前直接或间接赠与自己的一切财产交出，使之参加财产合算；但被继承人免除合算义务的除外。此外，还对配偶的合算范围、对卑亲属或配偶的赠与、对继承人尊亲属的赠与、其他财产的合算、无须合算的费用等内容作了规定。[②]

从我国诸继承法学者建议稿看，关于是否增设归扣制度学者们意见不统一。“梁稿”规定，继承开始之前，继承人因结婚、分居、营业以及其他事由而从被继承人处获得的赠与的财产应当列入遗产范围，但被继承人生前有相反意思表示的除外。前款规定的赠与数额应在遗产分割时从该继承人的应继份中扣除。赠与的具体数额应依赠与当时的价值计算。[③]“王稿”有类似规定。[④]“陈稿”规定，被继承人的晚辈直系血亲在被继承人生前从其处所获的下列财产利益在遗产分割时应当返还，并计入遗产范围：因结婚、分居、生产经营所受赠与财产；大学本科以上的教育费用；工作期间接受职业教育或培训的费用；储蓄性人寿保险金，但已指定特定受益人的除外。上述应予归扣的财产利益，被继承人生前有免予返还的意思表示的，不予归扣，但该意思表示仅限于不超出其可处分份额。[⑤]“张稿”第 64 条和“杨稿”第 9 条也对制度作了规定。

我们认为，我国立法未规定归扣制度，此为立法之不足。关于被继承人生前特种赠与财产的归扣，上述域外立法例和我国学者建议稿的观点可供我国立法参考。因为我国社会生活中实际存在被继承人对特殊法定继承人给与特种赠与财产的情形，如果不设立遗产归扣制度，就只能由道德调整，无法保障在共同继承人中公平分配遗产。现阶段许多国家都规定了遗产归扣制度，我国如不规定此制度，可能会对涉外继承纠纷造成很大的困扰。[⑥]

二、继承开始的通知和公告之特点与原因分析

（一）继承开始的通知和公告的主体之特点与原因分析

关于继承开始的通知和公告的主体的民间习惯，统计数据显示的特点是，三成至六成的河北省被调查者所在地区的习惯分别是：（1）知道被继承人死亡的继承人的，占六成稍多（62.02%）；（2）保管遗产的继承人的，占近五成半（54.77%）；（3）知道被继承

① 参见《法国民法典》第 843、852、853、854、855 条。
② 参见《意大利民法典》第 737~742、770 条。
③ 参见“梁稿”第 1942 条。
④ 参见“王稿”第 542 条。
⑤ 参见“陈稿”第 27 条。
⑥ 参见陈苇主编：《外国继承法比较与中国民法典继承编制定研究》，北京大学出版社 2011 年版，第 258 页。

人死亡的单位、村（居）委会的，占四成稍多（42.39%）；（4）处理被继承人死亡事件的机构（如公安交警部门）的，占近三成半（33.85%）（见表5-9）。

以上特点之原因分析：在河北省被调查者所在地区的习惯中，继承开始的通知和公告主体范围比我国《继承法》规定的更广，其原因可能是：（1）继承人最先知道被继承人死亡的可能性最大，由其作为继承开始的通知主体也最为合理。（2）如果没有继承人、继承人无法通知，则应由被继承人死亡地的居民委员会或村民委员会通知，因为被继承人死亡地的居民委员会和村民委员会与民众的关系比较密切，民众对其也比较信任。

关于继承开始的通知和公告的主体之我国立法，我国《继承法》第23条的规定，继承开始后，知道被继承人死亡的继承人应当及时通知其他继承人和遗嘱执行人。继承人中无人知道被继承人死亡或者知道被继承人死亡而不能通知的，由被继承人生前所在单位或者住所地的居民委员会、村民委员会负责通知。

从域外立法例看，部分国家规定了继承开始的通知和公告的主体，包括继承人、相关职能的行政机关等。例如，德国规定，继承人接受继承后，可提出对遗产债权人的公示催告程序的申请。当继承人为多人时，各共同继承人可以公开催告遗产债权人向共同继承人或向遗产法院申报他们的债权。[①] 日本规定，限定继承人在作出限定继承的表示后5日内，应对所有遗产债权人及受遗赠人，公告已表示限定承认事宜及应在一定期限内申报其请求的内容。[②]

从我国诸继承法学者建议稿看，关于继承开始的通知和公告的主体，“王稿”规定，继承开始后，知道被继承人死亡的继承人应通过适当方式通知其他继承人，继承人中无人知道或知道后无法通知的，由被继承人生前所在的单位或住所地的居民委员会、村民委员会通知。[③]“梁稿”除有类似规定外，还规定，其他利害关系人知道继承开始的事实的，也可以通知继承人或遗嘱执行人。[④]“陈稿”规定，知道被继承人死亡的继承人为继承开始通知的义务人，无继承人知道被继承人死亡，或知道被继承人死亡的继承人无民事行为能力，由被继承人死亡地的居民委员会、村民委员作会为继承开始通知的义务人。被继承人死亡后，继承开始通知的义务人应当通知继承人、遗嘱执行人、受遗赠人、遗嘱保管人、遗产债权人等利害关系人。[⑤]

我们认为，我国继承开始的通知和公告之主体范围较窄，此为立法之不足。在规定继承开始的通知和公告的主体时，最重要的是符合中国国情，一要考虑最早知道被继承人死亡消息的主体，二要考虑该主体与被继承人之间的关系，首先与被继承人关系越密切的主体，越适合做继承开始的通知主体。其次是居民委员会、村民委员会，再次是死者生前所在单位。这既符合我国《继承法》的规定，在现实中的操作性也比较强。考虑到继承人可能在外地死亡，所以我们认为应适当扩大通知主体范围。上述河北省被调查者所在地区扩大继承开始的通知和公告的主体的民间习惯、域外立法例和我国学者建议稿的观点可供我国立法参考。

---

① 参见《德国民法典》第2061条.

② 参见《日本民法典》第927条。

③ 参见“王稿”547条。

④ 参见“梁稿”第2001条。

⑤ 参见“陈稿”第5条。

（二）继承开始的通知和公告的方式之特点与原因分析

关于继承开始的通知和公告的方式的民间习惯，统计数据显示的特点是，一成至七成的河北省被调查者所在地区的习惯是：（1）使用口头、电话、微信等方式的，占近八成（77.38%）；（2）使用书信、告知函等方式的，占近五成（48.36%）；（3）采用申请人民法院以公告程序进行公告方式的，占近三成（29.73%）；（4）采用在村（居）民委员会公告栏公告方式的，占二成半稍多（26.88%）；（5）使用在报纸、电视、网络等平台上发布被继承人的死亡公告方式的，占一成半稍多（16.07%）（见表5-10）。

以上特点之原因分析，在河北省被调查者所在地区，（1）近八成的地区习惯采用口头、电话、微信等方式发出继承开始的通知，其原因可能是现阶段电子技术迅速发展，QQ、微博、微信等社交通信工具因其具有的快捷、经济和普及优势，不被民众用于继承开始的通知活动中；（2）仅有二成至三成的地区选择报纸、公告方式，其原因可能是这些方式不便捷、效率低、成本较高。

关于继承开始的通知和公告的方式之我国立法，我国《继承法》无规定。

从域外立法例看，继承开始的通知和公告的方式较为多样。例如，《法国民法典》规定，继承人以净资产为限接受继承时应向大审法院做出声明，该声明应进行登记并在国内进行公示，且声明可以经电子途径公示。①《日本民法典》规定，限定承认人须对所有遗产债权人及受遗赠人，公告其已表示限定承认事宜及催告债权人和受遗赠人应在一定期限内申报其请求的内容，且该公告应当在官方报纸上登载。②

从我国诸继承法学者建议稿看，关于继承开始的通知和公告的方式意见不统一。"王稿"规定，继承人和遗产管理人向人民法院递交遗产清册，由人民法院以公示催告程序催告债权人申报债权。③"徐稿"规定，继承开始的通知方式为在遗产所在地的报刊刊登，无此报刊的情形下，在省报刊刊登3次。④

我们认为，对于继承开始的通知和公告的方式，不必拘泥于形式，只要有利于群众、方便解决问题即可。⑤

（三）继承开始的通知和公告的期间之特点与原因分析

关于继承开始的通知和公告的期间的民众观念，统计数据显示的特点是，对于被继承人死亡后发出继承开始的通知的时间，（1）认为应在7日内发出的，合计占七成（70.27%）；（2）认为应在15日或30日内发出的，合计占二成稍多（23.32%）（见表5-11）。

以上特点之原因分析：在河北省被调查者中，（1）七成的人认为应7日内发出继承的通知，其原因可能是：继承开始与被继承人死亡对于被继承人来说是件十分重要的事情，所以继承开始的通知和公告期间不宜太长。（2）二成稍多的人认为应在15日或30内发出继承的通知，其原因可能是：继承开始和被继承人死亡的通知固然很重要，但是考虑到交通不便、通信闭塞、筹备相关事宜等各方面因素，继承开始的通知和公告期间也不宜过短。

---

① 参见《法国民法典》第771条。

② 参见《日本民法典》第927条。

③ 参见"王稿"第547条。

④ 参见"徐稿"第四分编第48条。

⑤ 陈苇主编：《外国继承法比较与中国民法典继承编制定研究》，北京大学出版社2011年版，第122、131页。

关于继承开始的通知和公告的期间之我国立法，我国《继承法》第23条仅规定“及时”发出继承开始的通知，并没有具体的期间规定。另外，关于公示催告程序，根据我国现行《民事诉讼法》第219条有关票据被盗、遗失的公告程序规定，人民法院决定受理申请，应在3日内发出公告，催促利害关系人申报权利，公示催告的期间，由人民法院根据情况决定，但不得少于60日。

从域外立法例看，关于继承开始的通知和公告的期间有所不同。例如，法国规定，当继承人向继承开始所在辖区的大审法院做出以净资产为限接受继承的声明后，该声明应在国内进行公示催告债权人申报债权，其期间为15个月。[①] 德国遗产法院应在规定的期间内公开催告申报继承权，公告期间最多为6个月；公示催告遗产债权人时，如果继承人为多数继承人时，各共同继承人通过公示催告遗产债权人的期间是6个月。[②]

从我国诸继承法学者建议稿看，关于继承开始的通知和公告的期间，“杨稿”规定，进行遗产清算程序后，继承人或遗产管理人应当通知已知的债权人，并公告通知可能存在的未知债权人，债权申报期不得少于3个月。[③] “陈稿”第70条规定，继承开始通知的主体，应当书面通知或发布通知与公告，继承人、遗嘱执行人、受遗赠人、遗嘱保管人、遗产债权人等利害关系人，应在2个月的期限内申报权利或履行义务。

我们认为，对于继承的开始一般都会及时发出通知。因此，我国立法无须作出具体进一步规定。

三、遗产管理之特点与原因分析

（一）遗产管理人的确定之特点与原因分析

关于遗产管理人的确定的民间习惯，统计数据显示的特点是，河北省被调查者所在地区的习惯排在前两位的是：（1）由死者的法定继承人担任的占近九成（89.47%）；（2）由死者家族中的德高望重者担任的占近五成（48.08%）（见表5-12）。

以上特点之原因分析：根据关于遗产管理人的确定的民间习惯之理由（见表5-13），在河北省被调查者所在地区，（1）近九成的地区有由法定继承人担任遗产管理人的习惯，其原因是便于清点和妥善管理遗产；（2）近五成的地区有由法定继承人之外的人或组织来担任的习惯，其原因是可以防止遗产被隐藏、转移，有利于保护遗产相关人的合法权益。

关于遗产管理人的确定之我国立法，我国《继承法》无规定。但1985年《执行继承法意见》第44条规定：“人民法院在审理继承案件时，如果知道有继承人而无法通知的，分割遗产时，要保留其应继承的遗产，并确定该遗产的保管人或保管单位。”

从域外立法例看，《德国民法典》规定：第一，遗产法院可以命令为成为继承人的人选任一个保佐人（遗产保佐人）。第二，权利人在裁判上主张对遗产的请求权，申请法院选任遗产保佐人的，遗产法院必须选任遗产保佐人。[④]《日本民法典》规定了关于废除推定继承人的裁定确定前、继承人为数人时、请求财产分离之后继承财产以及无继承人时的

---

① 参见《法国民法典》第792条。

② 参见《德国民法典》第1965、2061条；《德国民事诉讼法》第994条。

③ 参见“杨稿”第70条。

④ 参见《德国民法典》第1959、1960、1961条。

遗产管理，遗产管理人由家庭法院选任。① 《意大利民法典》规定，遗产管理的权利属于被指定的替补人、对被附条件指定的继承人享有增添权的某一个或者数个其他共同继承人。未指定替补人或者没有享有增添权的人的，遗产管理的权利为被推定可能接受遗产的法定继承人。有正当理由的，司法机构也可以采取其他适宜的措施。继承人为胎儿的，遗产管理人为胎儿的父亲，父亲不在的，遗产管理人为母亲。②

从我国诸继承法学者建议稿看，关于遗产管理人，"王稿"和"陈稿"认为，遗嘱指定了遗产管理人的，由遗嘱指定的人担任遗产管理人，遗嘱未指定的，由所有继承人协商确定，协商不成的，可由人民法院指定。③ "梁稿"和"杨稿"规定，遗嘱指定了遗产管理人或遗嘱执行人的，由其担任遗产管理人，无遗嘱执行人的，由继承人协商选任遗产管理人。继承人对遗产管理人选任有争议的，由有完全民事行为能力的法定继承人共同担任遗产管理人。特定情况下可由人民法院指定遗产管理人。④

我们认为，我国立法未规定遗产管理人的产生方式，此为立法之不足。上述河北省被调查者所在地区由法定继承人担任遗产管理人的民间习惯、域外立法例和我国学者建议稿的观点可供我国立法参考。因为其规定了遗产管理人产生的顺序，即遗嘱有规定的，应尊重被继承人的真实意愿，依据遗嘱规定选任遗产管理人；遗嘱没有规定，由继承人协商产生；协商不成的可由人民法院指定。因为继承人协商不成的情况下，各继承人之间肯定存在某些观点和利益冲突，如果由所有继承人共同担任遗产管理人，不利于遗产的顺利分割和处分。

（二）遗产管理人的职责与报酬之特点与原因分析

第一，关于遗产管理人的管理职责的民众观念，统计数据显示的特点是，四成至九成的河北省被调查者认为其职责包括：清查遗产，制作遗产清单的，占 92.18%；妥善保管遗产的，占 93.88%；查明被继承人生前的债权和债务，积极地追讨债权或清偿债务的，占 71.41%；可以原告或被告的身份参加因遗产引起的诉讼的，占 65.01%；查明被继承人是否留有遗嘱，并且确定遗嘱是否真实合法的，占 48.08%；定期制作遗产管理报告，向继承人报告遗产管理的情况的，占 56.61%（见表 5-14）。

以上特点之原因分析：河北省被调查者认为遗产管理人的职责有多样性，其原因可能是：遗产管理人相对于遗产保管人责任更大，其需履行保管遗产、制作财产清单、发布继承开始的通知或公告，参与涉及遗产的诉讼等都是遗产管理人应履行的职责，以保障遗产顺利分割并无后续纠纷。

第二，关于遗产管理人的报酬的民间习惯，统计数据显示的特点是，在河北省被调查者所在地区的习惯是：（1）继承人担任的管理人不可以取得报酬的，占近五成（48.79%）；（2）法院指定担任的管理人可以取得报酬的，占五成半稍多（56.05%）；（3）继承人选任的第三人担任的管理人，是否可以取得报酬由继承人决定的，占近四成

① 参见《日本民法典》第 895、936、943、952 条。继承人为数人的，家庭法院应当从继承人中选任继承财产管理人。当继承人情况不明的，或失踪人的财产管理人，家庭法院应当根据利害关系人或检察官的请示，选任继承财产管理人。

② 参见《意大利民法典》第 642、643、528 条。

③ 参见"王稿"第 549 条；"陈稿"第 7 条。

④ 参见"杨稿"第 72 条；"梁稿"第 2002 条。

(39.97%)；一律可以取得报酬的，占近三成半（34.85%）（见表5-15）。

以上特点之原因分析：河北省超过六成半的被调查者所在地区有法院指定担任的管理人可以获得报酬的习惯，其原因是遗产管理人管理遗产付出了劳动，应该获得相应的报酬。

关于遗产管理人的职责与报酬之我国立法，我国《继承法》第24条规定，存有遗产的人应妥善保管遗产，任何人不得侵吞、窃取。此条规定了遗产存有人的积极作为义务即妥善保管遗产和消极不作为义务即不得侵吞窃取财产，但对于遗产管理人是否可取得报酬我国《继承法》未规定。

从域外立法例看，《德国民法典》规定，第一，遗产管理人的职责包括：管理遗产，清偿遗产债务，遗产管理人向遗产债务人负责，准用继承人对原管理的责任、费用的偿还；遗产债务的清偿、申请开始支付不能程序的相关规定。此外，遗产管理人在特定条件下才可向继承人移交遗产。第二，遗产管理人可因管理遗产而请求适当的报酬。[①]《意大利民法典》规定，遗产管理人与遗产保佐人的权利和义务包括：编制并且执行遗产清单；作为原告提起相关的诉讼，作为被告参加与遗产有关的诉讼；管理遗产；将遗产中的现金或者出售动产或不动产所得的现金存放在初审法院法官指定的邮局或者信贷银行，并且报告管理账目；此外保佐人在获得初审法院法官的准许之后，可以开始对遗产债务和遗赠进行清偿；有权取得遗产的人可以保管、监管及临时管理遗产，遗产中有不宜保存的或者需要支付高额保管费才能保存的财产的，可以请求司法机构准许将其出售。[②]

从我国诸继承法学者建议稿看，关于遗产管理人的职责与报酬，“陈稿”规定，其一，遗产管理人的权利与义务包括以下七项：收集遗产，编制财产清册；在遗产管理期间忠实且谨慎地保护和管理遗产；发出继承公告，催促相关债权人和债务人，申报遗产债权和债务；向继承人报告管理账目；清偿各种由遗产负担的费用、债务和税款；将剩余财产分配给继承人；负责与待继承遗产有关的起诉和应诉。其二，遗产管理人在特定条件下享有报酬请求权，非继承人担任遗产管理人的，应给付相应的报酬，其报酬从遗产内支付，遗产不足时，由接受继承的继承人负担。[③]“杨稿”对遗产管理人的职责与报酬也有具体的规定。[④]

我们认为，我国立法欠缺遗产管理人的职责与报酬，此为立法之不足。上述河北省被调查者遗产管理人的职责有多样性的民众观念、区别不同情况确定是否给予遗产管理人报酬的民间习惯、域外立法例、“陈稿”和“杨稿”的观点可供我国立法参考。因为明确规定遗产管理人的权利和义务，明确了遗产管理人的报酬请求权，有利于更好地保护遗产管理人的权益。

（三）遗产管理人的损害赔偿责任之特点与原因分析

关于遗产管理人的损害赔偿责任的民间习惯，统计数据显示的特点是，在河北省被调查者中，(1) 凡有故意或重大过失才承担赔偿责任的，占五成以上（52.63%）；(2) 无论是故意或重大过失或一般轻过失的都要承担赔偿责任的，占四成稍多（42.67%）（见

① 参见《德国民法典》第1985~1987条。

② 参见《意大利民法典》第529~531、644条。

③ 参见“陈稿”第8、9条。

④ 参见“杨稿”第74、83条。

表 5-16）。

以上特点之原因分析，五成以上河北省被调查者所在地区的习惯是遗产管理人有故意或重大过失才承担赔偿责任的，其原因可能是，遗产管理人有偿管理与无偿管理的注意义务不同，遗产管理人有偿管理的，不论其是否存在故意、重大过失都应赔偿；遗产管理人无偿管理的，只有在故意或重大过失的情况下才承担损害赔偿责任。

关于遗产管理人的损害赔偿责任之我国立法，我国《继承法》无规定。

从域外立法例看，《法国民法典》规定，因受托人对其受委托的任务履行的很不好的情况下解除委托时，受托人可能有义务返还其作为报酬受领的款项之全部或一部分，且不影响损害赔偿。①《意大利民法典》规定，在遗产管理中，享有遗产清单利益的继承人在管理遗产中存在重大过失的才承担责任。②

从我国诸继承法学者建议稿看，关于遗产管理人的损害赔偿责任，"梁稿"规定，因继承人和遗产管理人过失而支出的费用不属于继承费用，由负有过失的继承人和遗产管理人承担。③"王稿"规定，遗产管理人须忠实、谨慎履行上述职责，遗产管理人的不当行为给遗产债权人造成损害的，遗产债权人有权要求遗产管理人承担民事责任，遗产管理人是继承人的，继承人对遗产债务承担无限责任。遗产管理人的行为已经或将要危害继承人、遗产债权人的利益的，其可以申请人民法院更换遗产管理人。④"陈稿"规定，遗产管理人因故意或过失未尽遗产管理义务，致使遗产毁损或灭失的，应当承担损害赔偿责任。⑤

我们认为，我国立法未规定遗产管理人的损害赔偿责任，此为立法之不足。上述河北省被调查者所在地区有遗产管理人在故意或重大过失才承担赔偿责任的民间习惯、意大利的立法和我国学者建议稿的观点可供我国立法参考。

四、法定继承之特点与原因分析

（一）法定继承人的范围与顺序之特点与原因分析

第一，关于法定继承人的范围与顺序的民众观念，统计数据显示的特点是，河北省被调查者较认可的法定继承范围为：第一顺序为配偶（92.03%）、父母（68.28%）、儿子（68.99%）、女儿（62.30%）；第二顺序为孙子女（49.93%）、外孙子女（42.25%），祖父母（47.08%）、外祖父母（42.25%）和兄弟（45.23%）、姐妹（43.67%）；第三顺序的为侄子女（33.14%）、外甥子女（31.86%）、堂兄弟姐妹（28.02%）、伯叔姑舅姨（31.58%）；第四顺序以上为表兄弟姐妹（24.89%）（见表 5-17）。

第二，关于配偶与血亲继承人的顺序的民众观念，在河北省被调查者中，（1）认为配偶应当为固定顺序的，即第一顺序：配偶、子女、父母；第二顺序：兄弟姐妹、祖父母外祖父母；第三顺序：侄子女、外甥子女；配偶有固定顺序，其属于第一顺位继承人的，占八成稍多（81.22%）；（2）认为配偶应当为不固定顺序的，即第一顺序为子女，第二

---

① 参见《法国民法典》第 812-5 条第 2 款。
② 参见《意大利民法典》第 491 条。
③ 参见"梁稿"第 2019 条。
④ 参见"王稿"第 551、552、650 条。
⑤ 参见"陈稿"第 10 条。

顺序为父母，第三顺序为兄弟姐妹、祖父母、外祖父母、兄弟姐妹的子女（侄子女、外甥子女为代位继承人），配偶无固定的继承顺序，可分别与第一、第二（或第三）顺序的法定继承人共同继承的，合计占近二成（18.78%）（见表5-18）。

以上特点之原因分析：(1) 河北省被调查者认为应扩大法定继承人的范围、增加法定继承人的顺序，其原因可能是：其一，被调查者是按照亲属关系的远近对继承顺序进行排序，可以较好地顾及所有与被继承人有血缘关系的继承人的利益，继续保持以婚姻关系、血缘关系为基础确定法定继承人的传统，让更多遗产留在血亲继承人内部。其二，扩大法定继承人的范围和顺序，有利于更好地发挥遗产养老育幼的功能。(2) 关于配偶与血亲继承人的顺序，在河北省被调查者中，其一，八成稍多的人认为配偶应当为固定顺序的，其原因可能是基于配偶间的亲密关系，且受我国立法影响。其二，近二成的人认为配偶应当为无固定顺序的，其原因可能是考虑兼顾保护配偶与血亲继承人的继承利益。

关于法定继承人的范围和顺序之我国立法，我国《继承法》第10条规定，配偶、父母、子女为第一顺位继承人，兄弟姐妹、祖父母、外祖父母为第二顺位继承人。继承开始后，由第一顺位继承人继承，第二顺位继承人不继承。没有第一顺位继承人的，由第二顺位继承人继承。第11、12条分别规定："被继承人的子女先于被继承人死亡的，由被继承人的子女的晚辈直系血亲代位继承。代位继承人一般只能继承他的父亲或者母亲有权继承的遗产份额。""丧偶儿媳对公、婆，丧偶女婿对岳父、岳母，尽了主要赡养义务的，作为第一顺序继承人。"

从域外立法例看，《法国民法典》规定的法定继承人之范围和顺序如下：第一顺序为子女及其直系卑血亲；第二顺序为父母、兄弟姐妹及其直系卑亲；第三顺序为父母之外的直系尊血亲；第四顺序为除兄弟姐妹及其直系卑亲以外的其他六亲等内的旁系亲属；配偶无固定的继承顺序，其与被继承人的子女及其直系卑血亲或父母共同继承。[①]《瑞士民法典》规定的法定继承人之范围和顺序如下：第一顺序为被继承人的子女及其直系卑亲属；第二顺序为被继承人的父母及其直系卑亲属；第三顺序为被继承人的祖辈父母及其直系卑亲属；配偶无固定的继承顺序，参与第一、第二、第三顺序的继承。[②]

从我国诸继承法学者建议稿看，关于法定继承人的范围和顺序，"梁稿"和"王稿"均规定第一顺序为配偶、子女、父母；第二顺序为兄弟姐妹、祖父母、外祖父母；第三顺序为其他四亲等以内的亲属。[③]"张稿"和"陈稿"规定的继承人之范围和顺序如下：第一顺序为子女及其晚辈直系血亲；第二顺序为父母；第三顺序为兄弟姐妹及其子女；第四顺序为祖父母，包括父系祖父母和母系祖父母；配偶可以和任一顺序或前三顺序的血亲继承人共同继承。[④]

我们认为，我国立法规定的法定继承人的范围较窄、顺序较少，此为立法之不足。将子女及其直系晚辈血亲直接规定为第一顺序的法定继承人，且无亲等限制，这可以保证家产不外流；将配偶作为无固定顺序的法定继承人，可以与不同顺序的法定继承人共同继承，可以较好地保障配偶和血亲之间的继承利益。因此，上述河北省被调查者扩大法定继

① 参见《法国民法典》第734、756、757-1、757-2、757-3条。

② 参见《瑞士民法典》第457~460条。

③ 参见"梁稿"第1946条；"王稿"第564条。

④ 参见"张稿"第28条；"陈稿"第45条。

承人范围和增加法定继承顺序的民众观念、法国和瑞士的立法以及“张稿”和“陈稿”的观点可供我国立法参考。

（二）配偶与血亲继承人的法定应继份之特点与原因分析

关于配偶与血亲继承人的法定应继份的民众观念，统计数据显示的特点是，在河北省被调查者中，（1）认为配偶为无固定继承顺序，可参与第一、第二（或第三）顺序且在不同顺序其应继份不同的，合计占四成半稍多（46.09%）；（2）认为配偶为固定顺序的继承人，与第一顺序的继承人共同继承并平均分配遗产的，占五成稍多（51.78%）（见表5-19）。

以上特点之原因分析：在河北省被调查者中，（1）五成稍多的人认为配偶应为固定顺序的继承人，与第一顺序的继承人共同继承并平均分配遗产的，其原因可能是：其一，配偶是产生一切血缘关系的根本起点，其继承利益也应得到足够的重视。其二，将配偶作为第一顺序的法定继承人，可以较好地保障配偶的继承利益。其三，受我国《继承法》规定的影响。（2）四成半稍多的人认为配偶应不固定顺序且在不同顺序其应继份不同，其原因可能是兼顾保护血亲继承人与配偶的继承权益。

关于配偶与血亲继承人的法定应继份之我国立法，我国《继承法》第10条和第13条规定，配偶、子女、父母均为第一顺序，且同一顺序继承人继承遗产的份额，一般应当均等。对生活有特殊困难的缺乏劳动能力的继承人，分配遗产时，应当予以照顾。对被继承人尽了主要扶养义务或者与被继承人共同生活的继承人，分配遗产时，可以多分；有扶养能力和有扶养条件的继承人，不尽扶养义务的，分配遗产时，应当不分或者少分；继承人协商同意的，也可以不均等。

从域外立法例看，《德国民法典》规定，配偶为无固定顺序继承人，配偶的应继份如下：与第一顺位继承人共同继承时，配偶继承遗产的四分之一；与第二顺位继承人或祖父母、外祖父母一起继承时，配偶继承遗产的二分之一；在没有第一顺位直系血亲或第二顺位直系血亲，又无祖父母、外祖父母的，生存配偶得到全部遗产。①《瑞士民法典》规定，配偶无固定顺序，参与第一、第二、第三顺位的继承。配偶与第一顺位继承人共同继承时，取得遗产的二分之一，与第二顺位继承人共同继承时，取得遗产的四分之三。父系或母系均无继承人的，配偶取得全部遗产。②《意大利民法典》规定，配偶为无固定顺序继承人，配偶的应继份如下：配偶与子女的共同继承的，如果子女只有一人，则配偶有权取得遗产的二分之一，子女有多人的，配偶取得遗产的三分之一；配偶与直系尊亲属、兄弟姐妹共同继承的，配偶可取得遗产的三分之二；在没有子女、直系尊亲属、兄弟姐妹参加继承的情形下，配偶继承全部遗产。③

从我国诸继承法学者建议稿看，关于配偶与血亲继承人的法定继承顺序和应继份，“梁稿”和“王稿”规定，配偶与父母、子女均为第一顺序的继承人。同一顺序的继承人按人数平均继承，但法律另有规定的除外。④“张稿”规定，配偶与第一顺序血亲继承人共同继承时，各继承人应继份均等；配偶与第二顺序血亲继承人共同继承时，其应继份为

① 参见《德国民法典》第1931条。
② 参见《瑞士民法典》第462条。
③ 参见《意大利民法典》第581~583条。
④ 参见“梁稿”第1955、1956条；“王稿”第564、575、576、579条。

遗产的二分之一；配偶与第三顺序血亲继承人共同继承时，其应继份为遗产的三分之二；配偶与第四顺序血亲继承人共同继承时，其应继份为遗产的四分之三；无血亲继承人时，配偶继承全部遗产。①

我们认为，我国立法将配偶作为第一顺序的法定继承人，不能平衡配偶与血亲继承人的继承利益，此为立法之不足。关于配偶为无固定顺序且在不同顺序其应继份不同，上述河北省被调查者的民众观念、域外立法例和“张稿”的观点可供我国立法参考。首先，配偶为无固定顺序法定继承人可以避免同一顺位继承人过多时导致配偶的继承份额过小。其次，配偶为无固定顺序法定继承人可以避免同一顺位只有配偶一人时，造成被继承人遗产外流。

（三）配偶对遗产中家庭住房的先取权与终生使用权之特点与原因分析

关于配偶对遗产中家庭住房的先取权与终生使用权的民间习惯，统计数据显示的特点是，被调查者所在地区的习惯是：（1）有此习惯的，占八成半（占85.92%）；（2）无此习惯的，仅占近一成半（14.08%）（见表5-20）。

以上特点之原因分析：近八成的河北省被调查者有配偶对遗产中家庭住房享有的先取权与终生使用权的习惯，其原因可能是：（1）房屋是被继承人与其配偶生前共同居住的地方，其不仅具有很高的经济价值，也有很高的精神价值，即房屋是被继承人配偶情感的寄托，被继承人的配偶可以在二人曾经共同生活的地方继续生活，也是对在世人心理的慰藉。（2）配偶对于房屋有先取权可以保障被继承人配偶有固定的居所，免遭因遗产分割而遭遇老无所居的困境。

关于配偶对遗产中家庭住房的先取权与终生使用权之我国立法，我国《继承法》无规定。

从域外立法例看，《法国民法典》规定，有继承权的健在的配偶实际占有原属于夫妻双方的或者全部属于遗产的住房作为主要住宅，该健在配偶对此住房享有居住权，对住房内的设施及包括遗产在内的家具享有使用权，直到死亡，但被继承人作了相反意思表示的除外。②《俄罗斯联邦民法典》规定，至继承开始之日，与被继承人共同生活的继承人在遗产分割时享有作为其继承份额取得家居用品及日常生活用品的优先权。遗产中的住房（房屋、住宅）等不能实物分割的，则在遗产分割时，继承开始前居住在该处而且没有其他住房的继承人对于不是住房所有人的其他继承人享有作为其继承份额取得该住房的优先权。③

从我国诸继承法学者建议稿看，“王稿”规定，被继承人的配偶尚生存且无自己的住房的，如果未继承被继承人的房屋，则对遗产中的住房享有用益物权。生存配偶需支付给继承该房屋的继承人不超过市价的租金，具体数额可以由双方协商，协商不成可以提起诉讼。④“陈稿”规定，生存配偶对遗产中的婚姻住宅和家庭日常生活用品享有先取权。如其继承份额小于该家庭日常生活用品的价值，其也可以选择对该家庭日常生活用品享有终生使用权。生存配偶对遗产中的婚姻住宅享有优先扣除其继承遗产份额的权利。如其继承

① 参见“张稿”第31条。

② 参见《法国民法典》第764条。

③ 参见《俄罗斯联邦民法典》第1168、1169条。

④ 参见“王稿”第580条。

份额小于该婚姻住宅的价值，其也可以选择对婚姻住宅享有终生居住权。[①]

我们认为，我国立法未规定配偶对遗产中家庭住房的先取权与终生使用权，此为立法之不足。关于配偶对遗产中家庭住房的先取权与终生使用权，上述河北省被调查者所在地区的民间习惯、法国的立法和“陈稿”的观点可供我国立法参考。因为赋予配偶对遗产中家庭住房的先取权与终生使用权，可以保障生存配偶的基本生活，且不会损害到其他继承人的继承权益。

（四）后顺序特殊法定继承人对遗产中原使用的住房及日常生活用品的终生使用权之特点与原因分析

（1）关于后顺序特殊法定继承人对特殊遗产的终生使用权的民间习惯，统计数据显示的特点是，在河北省被调查者所在地区：有此习惯的，占九成稍多（91.47%）；无此习惯的，占不到一成（8.53%）（见表5-22）。（2）关于后顺序特殊法定继承人对特殊遗产的终生使用是否付费的民间习惯，被调查者所在地区的习惯是：无须付费的，占近八成（78.22%）；需要付费的，占二成稍多（21.78%）（见表5-23）。

以上特点之原因分析：九成的河北省被调查者所在地区，有后顺序特殊法定继承人对特殊遗产的终生使用权的习惯、近八成的地区无须付费，其原因可能是：后顺位特殊法定继承人一般为法定继承人的父母、祖父母或外祖父母，基于亲情、照顾弱者或公序良俗等因素可享有该权利且无须付费，有利于保障其安度晚年。

关于后顺位特殊法定继承人对特殊遗产的终生使用权之我国立法，我国《继承法》未规定。

从域外立法例看，《德国民法典》规定，在继承开始后的30日内，继承人有义务向在被继承人死亡时属于被继承人家计并受其扶养的被继承人家属给予扶养费，并许可其使用住宅和家庭用具。[②]

从我国诸继承法学者建议稿看，“张稿”规定，父母因顺序在后未参加继承的，对遗产中供其个人日常生活使用的住房和其他物品有终生使用权。[③]“陈稿”规定，依靠被继承人扶养的无遗嘱继承人没有参加继承的，对遗产中供其个人日常生活适用的物品和住房享有终生的适用权、用益权。[④]

我们认为，我国立法未规定后顺序特殊法定继承人对特殊遗产的终生使用权，此为立法之不足。关于后顺序特殊法定继承人对特殊遗产的终生使用权，上述河北省被调查者所在地区的民间习惯、域外立法例以及“张稿”和“陈稿”的观点可供我国立法参考。

（五）尽了主要赡养义务的丧偶儿媳或女婿的遗产分配方式之特点与原因分析

关于尽了主要赡养义务的丧偶儿媳或女婿的遗产分配方式的民间习惯，统计数据显示的特点是，河北省被调查者所在地区的习惯是：（1）其作为第一顺序的继承人与被继承人其他子女共同继承并且平均分配遗产的，占近七成（69.84%）；（2）其不能作为法定继承人与被继承人其他子女共同继承，但其可分得适当的遗产的，占二成半（25.75%）

---

① 参见“陈稿”第48条第1款。

② 参见《德国民法典》第1969条。

③ 参见“张稿”第33条。

④ 参见“陈稿”第48条第2款。

（见表 5-25）。

以上特点之原因分析，根据关于尽了主要赡养义务的丧偶儿媳和丧偶女婿的遗产分配的民间习惯的理由（见表 5-26），在河北省被调查者所在地区，（1）有近七成的地区有其可以作为第一顺位继承人继承遗产的习惯，其原因是出于我国传统孝道文化与道德观念、符合法律规定和公平原则；（2）有二成半的地区有其不可与被继承人其他子女共同继承，但可分得适当的遗产习惯，其原因是其与被继承人无血缘关系，遗产不能给外人。

关于尽了主要赡养义务的儿媳或女婿的遗产分配方式之我国立法，我国《继承法》第 12 条规定："丧偶儿媳对公、婆，丧偶女婿对岳父、岳母，尽了主要赡养义务的，作为第一顺序继承人。"1985 年《执行继承法意见》第 29、30 条规定："丧偶儿媳对公婆、丧偶女婿对岳父、岳母，无论其是否再婚，依继承法第十二条规定作为第一顺序继承人时，不影响其子女代位继承。对被继承人生活提供了主要经济来源，或在劳务等方面给予了主要扶助的，应当认定其尽了主要赡养义务或主要扶养义务。"

从域外立法例看，法国、德国、瑞士、日本、意大利、俄罗斯均未规定尽了主要赡养义务的丧偶儿媳或女婿可以作为第一顺位法定继承人。

从我国诸继承法学者建议稿看，关于尽了主要赡养义务的丧偶儿媳或女婿的遗产分配，"王稿"规定，丧偶儿媳对公、婆，丧偶女婿对岳父、岳母尽了主要赡养义务的，没有代位继承人的，作为第一顺位法定继承人参与继承，不论其是否再婚。有代位继承人时，可以按照遗产酌分请求权的规定分得适当遗产。[①]"陈稿"规定，对公、婆或岳父、母尽了主要赡养义务的丧偶儿媳或丧偶女婿为酌分遗产请求权人。[②]

我们认为，我国立法规定尽了主要赡养义务的丧偶儿媳或女婿作为第一顺序法定继承人，此立法有不合理之处。因为，如果无第一顺序法定继承人，丧偶儿媳或女婿作为第一顺位法定继承人会导致全部遗产外流。所以，尽了主要赡养义务的丧偶儿媳或女婿不宜作为第一顺位法定继承人，但应酌情分给其遗产，立法可以吸收司法解释关于酌情分得的具体遗产份额。首先，保障丧偶儿媳或女婿得到与其所尽赡养义务相当的遗产份额，可体现权利与义务相一致。其次，赋予丧偶儿媳或女婿酌分遗产请求权，可以激励丧偶儿媳或女婿积极照顾、赡养老人。因此，关于尽了主要赡养义务的丧偶儿媳或女婿其可分得适当的遗产的上述河北省被调查者所在地区民间习惯和"陈稿"的观点可供我国立法参考。

五、遗嘱继承之特点与原因分析

（一）公证遗嘱与其他形式遗嘱的效力之特点与原因分析

关于公证遗嘱与其他形式遗嘱的适用效力的民众观念，统计数据显示的特点是，在河北省被调查者中，（1）认为后遗嘱优先于前一遗嘱包括公证遗嘱适用的，合计占六成半（65.30%）；（2）认为公证遗嘱应当优先适用的，占近三成半（34.71%）（见表 5-27）。

以上特点之原因分析：根据关于公证遗嘱与其他形式遗嘱的适用效力的民众观念的理由（见表 5-28），在河北省被调查者中，（1）六成半的人认为公证遗嘱当优先适用，其原因是公证遗嘱程序规范，具有较强的公示公信力和证明效力；（2）三成半的人认为后

① 参见"王稿"第 569 条。
② 参见"陈稿"第 50 条。

遗嘱应当优先于公证遗嘱适用，其原因是后遗嘱更能反映遗嘱人最后真实意愿。

关于公证遗嘱与其他形式遗嘱的适用效力之我国立法，我国《继承法》第20条明确规定："遗嘱人可以撤销、变更自己所立的遗嘱。立有数份遗嘱，内容相抵触的，以最后的遗嘱为准。自书、代书、录音、口头遗嘱，不得撤销、变更公证遗嘱。"1985年《执行继承法意见》第42条规定："遗嘱人以不同形式立有数份内容抵触的遗嘱，其中有公证遗嘱的，以最后所立公证遗嘱为准；没有公证遗嘱的，以最后所立的遗嘱为准。"

从域外立法例看，《德国民法典》规定，后遗嘱与前遗嘱相抵触的，前遗嘱中抵触部分因后遗嘱而失效。后遗嘱被撤回，原遗嘱视为未被废止过，继续有效。①《瑞士民法典》规定，立遗嘱人未明确撤销先遗嘱，又订立后遗嘱，只要不能肯定新遗嘱为旧遗嘱的补充，新遗嘱代替原遗嘱。对同一物设立两份遗嘱，后遗嘱效力优先于前遗嘱。②《日本民法典》规定，前遗嘱与后遗嘱有抵触时，就其抵触部分，视为后遗嘱将前遗嘱撤回。前项规定准用于遗嘱与遗嘱订立之后的生前处分或其他法律行为相抵触的情形。③

从我国诸继承法学者建议稿看，关于遗嘱的适用效力，"梁稿"和"张稿"均规定，遗嘱人立有数份遗嘱，且内容相抵触的，以最后的遗嘱为准。④"王稿"规定，遗嘱人立有数份遗嘱的，内容相抵触的，以最后设立的遗嘱为准。遗嘱人立有数份遗嘱，内容相抵触的，有公证遗嘱的，以公证遗嘱为准，无公证遗嘱的，以最后设立的遗嘱为准。⑤"陈稿"规定，遗嘱人有权变更先前订立的遗嘱，前遗嘱与后遗嘱两者的内容不一致的，以后订立的遗嘱为准。遗嘱人立有数份遗嘱，且内容互相抵触的，以最后的遗嘱为准，先前的遗嘱视为被撤回。⑥

我们认为，我国规定公证遗嘱比其他形式的遗嘱具有优先适用的效力，此为立法之不足。关于后遗嘱优先于前一遗嘱适用的上述河北省被调查者的民众观念、域外立法例以及"梁稿""张稿"和"陈稿"的观点可供我国立法参考。

（二）遗嘱自由的限制——特留份之特点与原因分析

关于遗嘱处分个人财产是否应予限制的民众观念，统计数据显示的特点是，在河北省被调查者中，（1）认为应对遗嘱的自由予以限制的，占六成半（65.58%）；（2）认为不应对遗嘱的自由予以限制的，占三成稍多（31.72%）（见表5-29）。

以上特点之原因分析，六成半的河北省被调查者认为应对遗嘱处分个人财产的自由予以限制，其原因可能是遗产具有扶养功能，被继承人将其全部遗产赠与法定继承人之外的人，不利于遗产对扶养家庭成员价值的发挥，也不符合人之常情。

关于遗嘱处分个人财产是否应予限制之我国立法，我国《继承法》第16条规定，"公民可以立遗嘱将个人财产指定由法定继承人的一人或数人继承，也可立遗嘱将个人财产赠给国家、集体或者法定继承人以外的人"。第19条规定："遗嘱应当对缺乏劳动能力又没有生活来源的继承人保留必要的遗产份额。"此外，1985年《执行继承法意见》第

---

① 参见《德国民法典》第2253、2254、2255、2256、2258条。
② 参见《瑞士民法典》第509~511条。
③ 参见《日本民法典》第1022、1023、983条。
④ 参见"梁稿"第1966、1980、1981条；"张稿"第42条。
⑤ 参见"王稿"第604、605、606条。
⑥ 参见"陈稿"第38条。

37 条规定："遗嘱人未保留缺乏劳动能力又没有生活来源的继承人的遗产份额，遗产处理时，应当为该继承人留下必要的遗产，所剩余的部分，才可参照遗嘱确定的分配原则处理。"

从域外立法例看，关于特留份制度，《法国民法典》规定，特留份主体包括子女、直系尊血亲和配偶，在不同情形下各特留份主体享有的特留份额有所不同。①《德国民法典》规定，被继承人的晚辈直系血亲、父母或配偶因死因处分而被排除于继承之外的，其可以向继承人请求特留份。特留份为法定应继份的价额的二分之一。②《瑞士民法典》规定：第一，享有特留份的主体包括直系卑亲属、父母、配偶或登记同性伴侣。第二，特留份的份额。特留份按下列方式处理：直系卑亲属的特留份，为其法定继承份额的四分之三；父亲或母亲的特留份，为其法定继承份额的二分之一；生存的配偶或登记同性伴侣的特留份，为其法定继承份额的二分之一。此外，还规定了特留份的剥夺。③

从我国诸继承法学者建议稿看，"梁稿"规定，特留份继承人为第一顺序、第二顺序法定继承人。第一顺序法定继承人的特留份为其应继份的二分之一；第二顺序法定继承人的特留份为其应继份的三分之一。④"王稿"有类似规定。⑤"陈稿"规定，晚辈直系血亲作为特留份权利人的，以亲等近者为先。配偶、晚辈直系血亲、父母的特留份额为在法定继承时各自法定应继份的二分之一。若遗嘱处分侵害了特留份的，特留份权利人可以请求扣减至特留份所需的份额。特留份权利人丧失继承权的，其特留份请求权即丧失。⑥"杨稿"规定，被继承人的配偶、晚辈直系血亲、父母享有特留份继承权。其特留份额是其法定继承数额的二分之一。此外，还规定了不受特留份限制的情形。⑦

我们认为，我国立法未规定特留份制度，此为立法之不足。因为被继承人的配偶、晚辈直系血亲、父母与被继承人关系最为密切，只需赋予他们特留份请求权，而不必赋予第二顺位法定继承人特留份请求权。因此，对遗嘱的自由予以限制，上述河北省被调查者的民众观念、德国的立法以及"杨稿"和"陈稿"的观点可供我国立法参考。

（三）夫妻共同遗嘱之特点与原因分析

关于夫妻共同遗嘱的民众观念和民间习惯，统计数据显示的特点是，（1）在河北省被调查者的观念中，持肯定态度的占七成半（75.96%），持不赞同态度的占近二成半（24.04%）（见表 5-30）。（2）被调查者所在地区的习惯是：有夫妻共同遗嘱的仅占二成稍多（22.76%）；无夫妻共同遗嘱的占七成半稍多（77.24%）（见表 5-31）。

以上特点之原因分析：在河北省被调查者中，（1）七成半的人认可夫妻共同遗嘱、二成多的地区有该习惯，其原因可能是夫妻共同遗嘱是基于夫妻双方真实意思表示成立

---

① 参见《法国民法典》第 913、914、914-1、916 条。

② 参见《德国民法典》第 2303、2305、2317、2333~2338 条。

③ 参见《瑞士民法典》第 470~471、473、477~479、522、533 条。

④ 参见"梁稿"第 1961~1964 条。

⑤ 参见"王稿"第 585、586、587 条。

⑥ 参见"陈稿"第 32 条。

⑦ 不受特留份限制的情形：（1）特留份继承人丧失继承权的；（2）被继承人与扶养人签订遗赠扶养协议，使特留份继承人无须承担扶养义务的；（3）有扶养能力和有扶养条件的特留份继承人，不尽扶养义务的；（4）特留份继承人对被继承人或其近亲属有严重违背伦理或犯罪行为的；（5）特留份继承人依遗嘱继承而取得相当于特留份的遗产的。"杨稿"第 49、50 条。

的，夫妻双方对于各自的遗产享有处分权，夫妻共同遗嘱是夫妻双方处分自己遗产的合理方式，其既符合双方真实意愿，又不违反法律的相关规定。（2）近二成半的人不赞同夫妻共同遗嘱、七成半的地区无该习惯，其原因可能是该遗嘱无法应对出现的新情况和新问题，限制了双方对各自财产的处分权。

关于夫妻的共同遗嘱之我国立法，我国《继承法》无规定。

从域外立法例看，《法国民法典》否认二人或二人以上以同一文书，为第三人利益或相互处分遗产的名义订立遗嘱的效力。[①]《德国民法典》规定，配偶在共同遗嘱中作出的处分，一方处分不生效或被撤销，另一方处分也无效。共同遗嘱中，相互依存处分中的一方撤回的，在配偶双方生前依照继承合同的规定处理，在另一方生前，一方不得以新的死因行为单独废除其处分。配偶一方死亡时，撤回权归于消灭，但生存配偶拒绝向其给予标的，可以废除其处分，在接受赠与后，生存配偶也有废止的权利。[②]

从我国诸继承法学者建议稿看，关于夫妻共同遗嘱，“杨稿”规定：夫妻可以设立共同遗嘱，共同遗嘱的效力以配偶一方死亡前婚姻关系存续为前提。在共同遗嘱中，夫妻互相指定对方为继承人的，自配偶一方死亡时生效。配偶一方撤回指定的，另一方的指定也失效。夫妻可以通过共同遗嘱共同指定遗嘱继承人或受遗赠人。[③]“王稿”规定，两人以上不得订立同一遗嘱。[④]

我们认为，我国立法未规定夫妻共同遗嘱，此为立法之不足。关于承认夫妻共同遗嘱的效力的上述河北省被调查者的民众观念、德国的立法以及“杨稿”的观点可供我国立法参考。因为夫妻有权共同处理其共同财产，且夫妻共同遗嘱是夫妻通过真实意思表示达成的，所以应肯定夫妻共同遗嘱的效力。

六、继承和遗赠的接受与放弃之特点与原因分析

（一）继承的接受与放弃的时间与方式之特点与原因分析

关于继承的接受与放弃的时间与方式的民众观念与民间习惯，统计数据显示的特点是，（1）关于继承的接受与放弃的时间，在河北省被调查者中，认为继承人放弃继承应遗产处理前作出意思表示的，占六成稍多（61.17%）；认为继承人放弃继承应在知道继承开始的2个月内作出表示的，占近四成（38.83%）（见表5-32）。（2）关于继承的接受与放弃的方式，被调查者所在地区的习惯是，以明确表示（包括书面和口头等方式）作出的，合计占近九成（94.44%）（见表5-33）。

以上特点之原因分析：根据关于继承人放弃继承的时间的民众观念之理由，统计数据显示（见表5-34），在河北省被调查者中，（1）近四成的人认为继承开始的2个月内作出放弃继承较为合适，其原因是可以让继承人有一定的时间去考虑是否放弃继承权，同时又可以督促继承人积极行使权利，而且符合公序良俗；（2）六成稍多的人认为遗产处理前继承人都可以放弃继承权，其原因是这样既不影响其他继承人的利益，又可以保证继承人行使放弃继承的权利，而且符合法律规定。

---

① 参见《法国民法典》第968条。
② 参见《德国民法典》第2269~2271条。
③ 参见“杨稿”第37条。
④ 参见“王稿”第597条。

关于继承的接受与放弃的时间与方式之我国立法，我国《继承法》第25条第1款的规定："继承开始后，继承人放弃继承的，应当在遗产处理前，做出放弃继承的表示。没有表示的，视为接受继承。"1985年《执行继承法意见》第47条规定："继承人放弃继承应当以书面形式向其他继承人表示。用口头方式表示放弃继承，本人承认，或有其它充分证据证明的，也应当认定其有效。"第48条规定："在诉讼中，继承人向人民法院以口头方式表示放弃继承的，要制作笔录，由放弃继承的人签名。"第49条规定："继承人放弃继承的意思表示，应当在继承开始后、遗产分割前作出。遗产分割后表示放弃的不再是继承权，而是所有权。"

从域外立法例看，对于接受和放弃继承的时间和方式，《德国民法典》规定，遗产的拒绝只能在6个星期内作出，自继承人知悉财产的归属和有资格做继承人起算。被继承人仅在国外有最后住所，或在期间起算时，继承人在国外居留时，期间为6个月。①《瑞士民法典》规定，放弃继承的期限为3个月，自法定继承人知道被继承人死亡时计算，但其能证明其是后来知道的，不在此限。②《日本民法典》规定，继承人自其知道继承开始之日起3个月内，须就继承表示单纯或限定的承认，或者放弃。但此期间，可以根据利害关系人或检察官的请求，由家庭法院予以延长。要放弃继承的人，须将其意思向家庭法院申述。③

从我国诸继承法学者建议稿看，关于接受和放弃继承的时间与方式，"梁稿"规定，继承人放弃继承的，应当在知道继承开始后2个月内以书面形式作出放弃继承的意思表示；逾期未表示的，视为接受继承。④"王稿"有类似规定。⑤"徐稿"规定，在被继承人死亡后一切分配都可以被抛弃。一切继承人可以依利害关系人的请求作出抛弃或接受继承的意思表示，表示应在请求之日起40日内作出。对于继承人失踪、财产处于远地或者其他重大事由，法院可以延期，但不得超过1年。⑥

我们认为，关于接受和放弃继承的时间与方式，我国放弃继承的期限过长且方式未作具体规定，此为立法之不足。这极易导致财产关系不稳定，不利于督促继承人及时行使自己的继承选择权，也不利于遗产的保护、遗产债务的清偿以及遗产的分割，因此，上述河北省被调查者主张继承开始后2个月内作出继承的接受与放弃的民众观念、相关域外立法例和我国学者建议稿的观点可供我国立法参考。

（二）遗赠的接受与放弃的方式与效力之特点与原因分析

关于遗赠的接受与放弃的方式与效力的民众观念，统计数据显示的特点是，在河北省被调查者中，（1）认为受遗赠人未作表示应认定为接受遗赠的，占六成半（65.15%）；（2）认为受遗赠人的未作表示应认定为放弃遗赠的，占近三成半（34.85%）（见表5-35）。

以上特点之原因分析，在河北省被调查者中，（1）六成半的人认为受遗赠人未作表示应认定为接受遗赠的，其原因可能是接受遗赠是一种纯获利的行为，未表示放弃受遗赠

---

① 参见《德国民法典》第1944、1945、1946、1947条。

② 参见《瑞士民法典》第567、568、576、570条。

③ 参见《日本民法典》第915、916、938条。

④ 参见"梁稿"第2008、2012条。

⑤ 参见"王稿"第554条。

⑥ 参见"徐稿"第四分编第319、320、323、337、338条。

的，应该就是接受遗赠；（2）近三成半的人认为受遗赠人未作表示应推定为接受遗赠，其原因可能是与现行法规定一致。

关于遗赠的接受与放弃的方式与效力之我国立法，我国《继承法》第25条第2款的规定，受遗赠人应当在知道受遗赠后2个月内，作出接受或者放弃受遗赠的表示。到期没有表示的，视为放弃受遗赠。

从域外立法例看，《日本民法典》规定，在遗嘱人死亡以后，受遗赠人可以随时放弃遗赠。对遗赠的履行负有义务的人及其他利害关系人，可以设定相当期间，催告受遗赠人应在该期间内作出对遗赠的承认或放弃。如果受遗赠人在该期间内，未对遗赠义务表示其意思时，视为已承认其遗赠。① 《意大利民法典》规定，遗赠可以不经过接受程序而直接取得，放弃遗赠的情况除外。任何利害关系人可以请求司法机构为受遗赠人确定一个行使放弃遗赠权利的期限，期限届满后，受遗赠人未作出任何表示的，丧失放弃遗赠的权利。②

从我国诸继承法学者建议稿看，"王稿"规定，受遗赠人应在知道或应当知道受遗赠后2个月内，作出接受或放弃受遗赠的意思表示。到期未表示的，视为放弃受遗赠。③ "张稿"规定，受遗赠人可以自遗嘱开启时起2个月内，向继承人或遗产管理人表示接受或者放弃继承。受赠人未明确表示放弃遗赠的，视为接受遗赠。④ "陈稿"第59条和"杨稿"第12条对此均有所规定。

我们认为，我国立法对于遗赠的接受与放弃的方式与效力之规定存在不足。上述河北省被调查者认为受遗赠人未作表示应认定为接受遗赠的民众观念、日本的立法和"张稿"的观点可供我国立法参考。因为在固定期限内受遗赠人未作出接受或放弃遗赠的意思表示的，视为接受遗赠，这有利于保护受遗赠人的权益，保障被继承人处分自身遗产真实意愿的实现。

（三）继承的放弃与债权人撤销权之特点与原因分析

关于债权人是否可以撤销继承人放弃继承的行为的民众观念与民间习惯，统计数据显示的特点是，（1）在河北省被调查者的观念中，认为不可以被撤销的，占五成稍多（53.63%）；持认为可以被撤销的，占四成半稍多（46.37%）（见表5-38）。（2）被调查者所在地区的习惯是：不可以被撤销的，占五成稍多（51.18%）；可以被撤销的，占近五成（48.82%）（见表5-39）。

以上特点之原因分析：根据关于继承的放弃能否被债权人撤销的民众观念之理由（见表5-40），在河北省被调查者中，（1）五成稍多的人认为不可以被撤销、五成稍多的地区有不可以被撤销的习惯，其原因是应当兼顾被继承人照顾的其近亲属的利益；（2）四成半稍多的人认为可以被债权人撤销、近五成的地区有可以被撤销的习惯，其原因是继承人的债权人利益需要被保护。

关于继承的放弃与债权人的撤销权之我国立法，我国《继承法》未规定。

从域外立法例看，关于继承人放弃继承权的行为能否被债权人撤销有两种立法例。第

① 参见《日本民法典》第986~989条。

② 参见《意大利民法典》第649~650条。

③ 参见"王稿"第554条。

④ 参见"张稿"第9条第3款。

一种“否定说”，如法国、德国和日本立法例。第二种“肯定说”，允许债权人在债权额度内撤销。例如，《瑞士民法典》规定，债务超过继承财产的继承人，以妨害债权人的利益为目的而抛弃继承权时，债权人可以在6个月内提起撤销抛弃继承权之诉，债权得到担保的除外。①《意大利民法典》规定，放弃继承损害债权人利益的，该债权人可以为了用遗产进行清偿，请求准许以放弃继承的人的名义和顺序接受遗产，但是以满足债权额为限。②

从我国诸继承法学者建议稿看，“梁稿”和“王稿”均规定，继承人放弃继承损害债权人利益的，债权人可以在知道或应当知道继承人放弃继承之日起6个月内申请人民法院撤销继承人的放弃继承行为。③“杨稿”规定，接受或者放弃继承的意思表示不得撤销。但因欺诈、胁迫、乘人之危或重大误解而作出的，或遗产分配前，经济状况严重恶化的除外。撤销应当自知道或应当知道可撤销事由之日起3个月内提出。④

我们认为，我国立法未规定债权人是否可以撤销继承人放弃继承的行为，此为立法之不足。但放弃继承的行为不可被债权人撤销。因为，首先，如允许债权人向法院申请撤销放弃继承行为，实际上就是变相地强迫继承人接受继承，这与现代继承法人格独立、意志自由的立法精神显然是背道而驰的。其次，在交易发生之时，债权人作为一个理性的经济人，只会考虑债务人当时的财力与信用状况，而不会去考虑债务人将来可能因为继承而获得财产的状况。撤销权的目的是维持债务人现有的责任财产，防止其不当减少，并非在于积极增加责任财产，增强债务人的清偿能力。放弃继承人对于遗产是自始未得，而非得后又放弃，所以，债务人拒绝因继承而取得的财产利益之行为不能成为债权人撤销权标的。⑤因此，上述河北省被调查者认为放弃继承的行为不能被债权人撤销的民众观念、法国、德国和日本的立法以及“杨稿”的观点可供我国立法参考。

七、继承权的丧失、被继承人的宥恕与代位继承之特点与原因分析

（一）继承权的丧失与被继承人的宥恕之特点与原因分析

关于继承权的丧失与被继承人的宥恕的民众观念与民间习惯，统计数据显示的特点是，关于因欺诈、胁迫行为的继承人丧失继承权的，在得到被继承人谅解的情况下其继承权是否可以恢复，（1）在河北省被调查者的观念中，认为可以恢复的，占七成（70.04%）；认为不可以恢复的，占近三成（29.96%）（见表5-41）。（2）被调查者所在地区的习惯是：有可以恢复习惯的，合计占近八成（78.75%），有不可以恢复习惯的，占二成稍多（21.25%）（见表5-42）。

以上特点之原因分析，在河北省被调查者中，七成的人认为因欺诈、胁迫行为的继承人丧失继承权的可因被继承人的原谅而恢复、近八成的地区有此习惯，其原因可能是遗产属于被继承人，其有权依据自己的真实意愿处分遗产，其他法定继承人应充分尊重被继承

① 参见《瑞士民法典》第578条。

② 参见《意大利民法典》第524条。

③ 参见“梁稿”第2012条；“王稿”第562条。

④ 参见“杨稿”第14条。

⑤ 参见陈苇、王巍：《论放弃继承行为不能成为债权人撤销权的标的》，载《甘肃社会科学》2015年第5期，第162~166页。

人的真实意愿。

关于继承权的丧失与被继承人的宥恕之我国立法，我国《继承法》第7条中规定："继承人有下列行为之一的，丧失继承权：（一）故意杀害被继承人的；（二）为争夺遗产而杀害其他继承人的；（三）遗弃被继承人的，或者虐待被继承人情节严重的；（四）伪造、篡改或者销毁遗嘱，情节严重的。"1985年《执行继承法意见》第13条规定："继承人虐待被继承人情节严重的，或者遗弃被继承人的，如以后确有悔改表现，而且被虐待人、被遗弃人生前又表示宽恕，可不确认其丧失继承权。"

从域外立法例看，关于继承权的丧失与被继承人的宥恕，《法国民法典》规定，被继承人在知道被继承人丧失继承权的事实之后，仍通过遗嘱的形式表明继承保留行为人继承权的，或仍对行为人全部或部分概括赠与，行为人仍可继承遗产。[①]《瑞士民法典》规定，丧失继承资格的继承人可因被继承人的宽恕而重新取得遗产。[②]《意大利民法典》规定，被继承人在遗嘱中或者在公证书中明确表示恢复无继承资格人的继承权的，则允许其参加继承。无继承资格人未被明确恢复权利，但遗嘱人知道其无继承资格的原因，仍在遗嘱中对其加以考虑，则允许该人在遗嘱规定的范围内参加继承。[③]

从我国诸继承法学者建议稿看，"杨稿""王稿""梁稿""陈稿""张稿"均认为继承人因遗弃或虐待被继承人情节严重的；伪造、篡改、销毁、隐匿遗嘱；以欺诈、胁迫手段迫使或妨碍被继承人设立、变更或者撤销遗嘱，可因被继承人的宽恕而恢复继承权。对于继承人故意杀害被继承人或其他继承人的，"杨稿""王稿""梁稿"认为故意杀害被继承人、为争夺遗产而杀害其他继承人，导致丧失继承权的，不能因被继承人事后宽恕而恢复其继承权。[④]"陈稿"和"张稿"规定，继承人的继承权可因被继承人的原谅而恢复，不论其因何种原因而丧失继承权。[⑤]

我们认为，我国对相对丧失继承权范围的规定过于狭窄，此为立法之不足。关于继承权的丧失与被继承人的宥恕，即对于因欺诈、胁迫行为的继承人丧失继承权的，如获得被继承人谅解，上述河北省被调查者认为其继承权可以恢复的民众观念、意大利的立法以及"陈稿"和"张稿"的观点可供我国立法参考。因为遗产是被继承人的个人财产，只要其原谅继承人，其就可以依据自己的真实意愿将遗产分配给曾丧失继承权的继承人。这有利于继承人改过自新，给被继承人重新改过的机会，也有利于促进家庭关系和睦，化解家庭矛盾及纠纷。

（二）继承权的丧失与代位继承之特点与原因分析

关于继承人丧失继承权的其晚辈直系血亲能否代位继承的民众观念与民间习惯，统计数据显示的特点是，（1）在被调查者的观念中，认为代位继承人可以继承的，占四成半（45.88%）；认为代位继承人不可以继承的，占近五成半（54.12%）（见表5-43）；（2）被调查者所在地区的习惯是：可以代位继承的，占八成稍多（83.70%）；不可以代位继承的，占不到一成（5.43%）（见表5-44）。

① 参见《法国民法典》第728条。

② 参见《瑞士民法典》第540条。

③ 参见《意大利民法典》第466条。

④ 参见"杨稿"第11条；"王稿"第532、533条；"梁稿"第1940条。

⑤ 参见"陈稿"第17条第2款；"张稿"第6条第2、3款。

以上特点之原因分析，在河北省被调查者中，近五成半的人认为继承人丧失继承权的其子女不可代位继承、不到一成的地区有此习惯，其原因可能是子女的代位继承权来源于被代位继承人的有效继承权和应继份，如果被代位继承人失去了继承资格，其就没有了应继份，继承人的晚辈直系血亲代位继承也理所应当受到影响。

关于继承权的丧失与代位继承之我国立法，根据1985年《执行继承法意见》第28条规定，继承人丧失继承权的，其晚辈直系血亲不得代位继承。如该代位继承人缺乏劳动能力又没有生活来源，或对被继承人尽赡养义务较多的，可适当分给遗产。

从域外立法例看，关于继承权的丧失与代位继承，《法国民法典》规定，无继承资格的人的子女不因无继承资格人的过错而被排除继承权，不论是本身参与继承还是代位继承。无继承资格的人在任何情况下都不得对此种继承的遗产享有法律规定的父母对子女财产本来享有的用益权。[①]《日本民法典》规定被继承人的子女因废除而丧失其继承权时，由被继承人的子女代袭为继承人。但并非被继承人的直系卑亲属的人，不在此限。[②]《意大利民法典》规定，继承人丧失继承权的，不影响其卑亲属的代位继承权。[③]

从我国诸继承法学者建议稿看，“梁稿”和“王稿”均规定，被继承人的子女在继承开始前死亡或者丧失继承权时，由被继承人子女的直系卑亲属代位继承。[④]“陈稿”规定，继承人丧失继承权的不影响其晚辈直系血亲的代位继承权，但丧失继承权的继承人不得对其子女代位继承的遗产享有用益权。“杨稿”规定，被继承人的子女先于被继承人死亡、丧失继承权或者放弃继承权的，由被继承人的子女的晚辈直系血亲代位继承。[⑤]

我们认为，我国立法规定被代位继承人丧失继承权的其子女不可代位继承，此为立法之不足。在继承权丧失的情形下，晚辈直系血亲的代位继承权不因被代位人丧失继承权而丧失，首先，有效保障丧失继承权人子女的继承利益；其次，禁止丧失继承权的继承人对子女代位继承的遗产享有用益权，可以对丧失继承权的继承人起到惩罚作用，避免丧失继承权的继承人因子女的代位继承而享有遗产利益。因此，关于继承人丧失继承权的其子女可代位继承，上述河北省被调查者的民众观念与民间习惯、域外立法例和我国学者建议稿的观点可供我国立法参考。

八、继承协议之特点与原因分析

（一）继承协议的订立主体与方式之特点与原因分析

关于继承协议的订立主体与方式的民众观念与民间习惯，统计数据显示的特点是，（1）对于继承协议的订立，由被继承人与全体法定继承人共同订立的，占七成稍多（72.12%）；由继承人之间签订即可，无须被继承人知晓或同意的，占一成半（15.08%）；由被扶养人与扶养义务人共同签订的，占一成稍多（12.80%）（见表5-45）。（2）关于继承协议的民间习惯，河北省被调查者所在地区的习惯是：听说过或经历过签订继承协议的，占五成半稍多（56.76%）；没有听说或经历过签订继承协议的，占四成

① 参见《法国民法典》第729-1条。

② 参见《日本民法典》第887条。

③ 参见《意大利民法典》第468条。

④ 参见“梁稿”第1951条；“王稿”第572、573条。

⑤ 参见“杨稿”第17条。

稍多（43.24%）（见表5-46）。（3）关于听说过或经历过签订继承协议的方式的民间习惯，被调查者所在地区的习惯是：继承协议的订立，由被扶养人与扶养义务人共同签订的，占近二成（18.05%）；由被继承人与全体法定继承人共同订立的，占五成半稍多（57.64%）；由继承人之间签订的，占近二成半（24.31%）（见表5-47）。

以上特点之原因分析：在河北省被调查者中，（1）七成稍多的人认为继承协议由被继承人与全体法定继承人共同订立，五成半稍多的地区有该习惯，其原因可能是：其一，签订协议一方必须是被继承人，被继承人是被扶养人，双方可以自愿协商决定如何分配扶养和继承的遗产问题；其二，签订协议的另一方应为所有继承人，其主要是为了使所有继承人都知悉相关事宜，避免以后继承人之间产生纠纷。（2）五成稍多的被调查者所在地区的习惯是签订继承协议的情形时常发生，其原因可能是被继承人养老的实际需要，通过签订协议使扶养人取得遗产而促使取其履行对被扶养人养老送终的义务。

关于继承协议之我国立法，我国《继承法》无规定。但我国《继承法》第31条规定："公民可以与扶养人签订遗赠扶养协议。按照协议，扶养人承担该公民生养死葬的义务，享有受遗赠的权利。公民可以与集体所有制组织签订遗赠扶养协议。按照协议，集体所有制组织承担该公民生养死葬的义务，享有受遗赠的权利。"即此立法将法定继承人排除在遗赠扶养协议之外，而继承协议的主体的一方当事人是法定继承人。

从域外立法例看，《法国民法典》对继承协议持否定态度，即任何人不得预先放弃未开始的继承，也不得就类似的继承订立条款，即使得到被继承人的同意也不行。[①]《德国民法典》对继承协议持肯定态度，被继承人须亲自订立合同。只有完全行为能力人才能订立继承合同。配偶一方为限制行为能力人，也可以作为被继承人与其配偶订立继承合同，在此情形下，限制行为能力一方应得到法定代理人的同意，法定代理人为监护人的，应得到监护法院批准。此规定准用于订婚人。[②]《瑞士民法典》规定，被继承人成年，才能订立继承协议。被继承人可以通过继承协议使另一方或第三人取得遗产或遗赠，继承协议签订后，被继承人仍享有处分其财产的自由。[③]

从我国诸继承法学者建议稿看，"王稿"规定，扶养人可以与被扶养人采用书面形式订立遗赠扶养协议，此处的签订主体包括法定继承人。[④]"陈稿"规定，自然人、法人和其他组织，可以与被继承人签订继承合同。继承合同的当事人必须具有完全民事行为能力。订立合同时必须双方意思表示真实。合同的内容不得违反法律和社会公共利益。继承合同的订立，必须采取书面形式，应当有两名以上无利害关系的见证人在场或进行公证。[⑤]"张稿"第54条和"杨稿"第69条对此亦有规定。

我们认为，我国立法未规定继承协议，此为立法之不足。因此，认可继承协议的上述河北省被调查者的民众观念、瑞士的立法以及"张稿"和"陈稿"的观点可供我国立法参考。因为允许被继承人与继承人等签订继承协议，可以充分保障被继承人处分自己遗产，以利用遗产养老的真实意思的实现。

---

① 参见《法国民法典》第1130条。

② 参见《德国民法典》第2274、2275条。

③ 参见《瑞士民法典》第468、494条。

④ 参见"王稿"第642条。

⑤ 参见"陈稿"第61、62条。

（二）继承协议的变更方式及效力之特点与原因分析

关于继承协议的变更方式及效力的民众观念，统计数据显示的特点是，在继承协议履行过程中，如扶养人先于被扶养人去世，在河北省被调查者中，（1）认可在原扶养人的子女和被扶养人双方同意的情况下，其子女有扶养能力的，可由其子女继续履行该继承协议的，即认可代位扶养的，占近四成（39.97%）；（2）认可须签订新的继承协议，由新的扶养人履行扶养义务并继承遗产的，合计占三成半稍多（36.55%），其中，认为需要对原扶养人补偿费用的，占近三成（28.73%），认为不需要对原扶养人补偿费用的，占不到一成（7.82%）；（3）认可由所有法定继承人共同扶养的，实行法定赡养的，占二成稍多（21.76%）（见表5-48）。

以上特点之原因分析：在河北省被调查者中，（1）近四成的人认可代位扶养，其原因可能是：签订继承协议的继承人死亡后，被继承人有决定是否继续履行继承协议的权利，继承协议虽然具有人身性，被继承人对于继承人有更多的信任，但继承人死后，被继承人愿意变更继承协议的主体，使继承协议继续有效的，继承协议不因继承人的死亡而必然终止。（2）三成半稍多的人认为应签订新的继承协议，其原因可能是受扶养人死亡后该协议即终止。如果被扶养人不愿意接受死亡扶养人的子女继续履行继承协议，被扶养人也可以与其他继承人另行签订继承协议，应该尊重被扶养人的意思表示。

关于继承协议的变更方式及效力之我国立法，我国《继承法》无规定。

从域外立法例看，在承认继承协议的国家立法中，《德国民法典》规定，以被继承人有权解除为限，被继承人可以在订立合同另一方当事人死亡后，以遗嘱废止合同中对遗产的处分。[①]《瑞士民法典》规定，继承人在被继承人死亡前死亡的，继承合同自动失效。被继承人在继承人死亡时，对于因继承合同所得的利益，应返还给死者的继承人，另有约定的除外。[②]

从我国诸继承法学者建议稿看，“王稿”规定，关于遗赠扶养协议，本法未作规定的，参照《合同法》。[③]“徐稿”规定，继承人在被继承人死亡前死亡的，继承合同自动失效。被继承人在继承人死亡时，对于因继承合同所得的利益，应返还给死者的继承人，另有约定的除外。[④]“张稿”规定，扶养义务人不按约定履行扶养义务，或者因为死亡或丧失扶养能力而不能继续履行合同义务，被继承人可以解除合同，合同解除后，义务人已经支付的扶养费用应当在共同继承人之间进行结算。[⑤]“陈稿”规定，扶养人先于受扶养人死亡，继承合同自动解除。受扶养人同意接受已经死亡的扶养人之继承人继续承担扶养的义务，继承合同继续履行。[⑥]

我们认为，我国立法未规定继承协议的变更方式及效力，此为立法之不足。因此，上述河北省被调查者关于继承协议的变更方式及效力的民众观念、瑞士的立法和我国学者建议稿的观点可供我国立法参考。必须说明，对于履行扶养义务的继承人先于被继承人死亡

① 参见《德国民法典》第2297条。
② 参见《瑞士民法典》第515条。
③ 参见“王稿”第644条。
④ 参见“徐稿”第四分编第516条。
⑤ 参见“张稿”第55条。
⑥ 参见“陈稿”第64条。

的，继承协议是否继续有效应取决于两个因素，首先，死亡继承人是否有成年子女或在世配偶，其成年子女或在世配偶是否有扶养被继承人的意愿和能力。其次，在死亡继承人成年子女或在世配偶有代替死亡继承人扶养被继承人的愿望和能力时，要考虑被继承人的真实意愿，因为继承协议具有很强的人身性，被继承人之所以选定继承人可能是因为继承人有某些别人不具有的特质，被继承人对继承人十分信任。只有被继承人同意由其他人代替死亡继承人继续履行继承协议时，继承协议才能继续履行。

九、遗产债务清偿之特点与原因分析

（一）遗产债务清偿责任的类型之特点与原因分析

关于继承人的遗产债务清偿责任的类型的民众观念，统计数据显示的特点是，对于遗产债务，在河北省被调查者中，（1）认为继承人应承担自愿的无限清偿责任的，合计占七成稍多（73.25%）；（2）认为继承人应以继承的遗产承担有限清偿责任的，占四成半稍多（46.23%）；（3）认为继承人如有侵害遗产的行为应承担强制的无限清偿责任的，占四成稍多（42.25%）（见表5-49）。

以上特点之原因分析：在河北省被调查者中，（1）七成稍多的人认为继承人应承担自愿的无限清偿责任，其原因可能是受“父债子偿”传统观念的长期影响。（2）四成半稍多的人认为继承人应以继承的遗产承担有限清偿责任，其原因可能是受我国《继承法》规定的影响。（3）四成稍多的人认为如有侵害遗产的行为应承担强制的无限清偿责任，其原因可能是当继承人存在转移、隐瞒财产等侵害遗产行为时，应以遗产和个人财产偿还所有债务，以发挥对继承人的教育引导和惩罚作用。

关于继承人的遗产债务清偿责任的类型之我国立法，我国《继承法》第33条规定：“继承遗产应当清偿被继承人依法应当缴纳的税款和债务，缴纳税款和清偿债务以他的遗产实际价值为限。超过遗产实际价值部分，继承人自愿偿还的不在此限。继承人放弃继承的，对被继承人依法应当缴纳的税款和债务可以不负偿还责任。”

从域外立法例看，《法国民法典》规定，无条件接受继承的全部概括继承人或者部分概括继承人，对遗产的债务与负担负无限责任。以净资产为限接受继承的继承人，仅有义务按照其受领的财产的价值限度清偿遗产的债务。但是当继承人隐匿属于遗产的财产或权利，或者隐瞒存在某一共同继承人，视其为无条件接受继承，即使其已经作出任何放弃继承或者按净资产接受继承的表示，亦同，且不妨碍给予损害赔偿，并且不得对其隐匿或隐瞒的财产或权利主张任何份额。[①] 日本规定，继承人表示限定继承时，应在继承所得财产的限度内清偿被继承人的债务及遗赠。但继承人不在规定的期间内表示接受或放弃继承时，或继承人作出限定继承或放弃继承后，隐匿继承财产的全部或部分，私自消费或者恶意不将其记载于继承财产目录时，须无限制地继承被继承人的权利义务（含债务）。[②]

从我国诸继承法学者建议稿看，“梁稿”规定，继承人以其所接受遗产的实际价值为限对遗产债务承担责任。超过遗产实际价值部分，继承人自愿偿还的不在此限。继承人放

① 参见《法国民法典》第785、791条。
② 参见《日本民法典》第921条。

弃继承的，对被继承人依法应当缴纳的税款和债务不负偿还责任。[①] “张稿” 第 16 条规定，应召继承人可在继承开始后或知道自己为应召继承人后 2 个月内，向法院声明以继承财产的价值为限，承担清偿被继承人债务的责任，并提交忠实准确的遗产清单。但继承人在遗产清单中故意漏记重要遗产，或记入不存在的债务的，擅自对遗产为保存遗产所不必要的处分时，视为单纯继承人，对被继承人的债务承担无限责任，而且不得放弃继承。

我们认为，我国立法规定无条件的有限责任继承，此为立法之不足。确定继承人对遗产债务清偿应承担的责任，应当平衡继承人与遗产债权人的双方利益，继承人不应承担无条件的有限清偿责任，特别是在其有分割遗产利益的不良行为时，理应承担强制的无限清偿责任。因此，关于继承人清偿遗产债务责任和类型，上述河北省被调查者的民众观念、法国和日本的立法以及“张稿” 的观点可供我国立法参考。

（二）被继承人丧葬费的支付之特点与原因分析

关于被继承人丧葬费支付的民间习惯，统计数据显示的特点是，（1）由全体继承人共同支付的，占近六成半（64.86%）；（2）从被继承人的遗产中支付的，占近三成（28.17%）（见表 5-50）。

以上特点之原因分析：近六成半的河北省被调查者所在地区有由全体继承人共同承担被继承人的丧葬费的习惯，其原因可能是受传统道德的影响，即为父母支付丧葬费是为人子女应尽的义务。

关于被继承人丧葬费支付之我国立法，我国《继承法》无规定。

从域外立法例看，《德国民法典》规定，继承人负责被继承人的丧葬费用。[②]《瑞士民法典》规定，在计算被继承人可处分的财产状况时，应先扣除被继承人的债务、丧葬费、封印及财产清单制作费用，和家庭成员一个月的生活费。[③]《俄罗斯联邦民法典》规定，被继承人死亡前患病所发生的费用、丧葬费（包括被继承人墓地的必要费用）、遗产的保护和管理费用以及与遗嘱的执行有关的费用，用遗产进行偿付，但以遗产的价值为限。[④]

从我国诸继承法学者建议稿看，“王稿” 规定，被继承人的、与其社会地位相称的丧葬费，由继承人负担。[⑤]“陈稿” 规定，合理的丧葬费用属于遗产债务。[⑥]“杨稿” 规定，合理的丧葬费由遗产支付。[⑦]

我们认为，我国立法未规定被继承人丧葬费的支付，此为立法之不足。父母将儿女养育成人，花费了很多心血，儿女应该负担父母的丧葬费，不论其分得的遗产多少或有无。因此，上述河北省被调查者所在地区被继承人丧葬费由继承人共同支付的民间习惯、德国的立法和“王稿” 的观点可供我国立法参考。

（三）遗产债务的清偿顺序之特点与原因分析

关于遗产债务的清偿顺序的民众观念与民间习惯，统计数据显示的特点是，（1）被

---

① 参见“梁稿” 第 2014 条。

② 参见《德国民法典》第 1968 条。

③ 参见《瑞士民法典》第 474 条。

④ 参见《俄罗斯联邦民法典》第 1174 条第 1、3 款。

⑤ 参见“王稿” 第 651 条。

⑥ 参见“陈稿” 第 68 条。

⑦ 参见“杨稿” 第 83 条。

调查者所在地区的遗产债务清偿顺序的习惯是：第一顺序“丧葬费用”（占57.80%）；第二顺序“遗产管理等费用”（占26.60%）和“欠款”（占23.80%）；第三顺序“欠付的工资”（占15.2%）；第四顺序“税款”（占9.40%）；第五顺序“受被继承人扶养人的生活费”（占12.80%）；第六顺序“对被继承人扶养较多的人之酌情分配遗产份额”（占13.80%）；第七顺序“遗赠扶养协议写明遗赠的遗产”（占11.20%）（见表5-51）。（2）被调查者观念中的遗产债务清偿顺序如下：第一顺序“丧葬费用”（占52.10%）；第二顺序“遗产管理等费用”（占26.50%）；第三顺序“欠债”（占21.20%）和“欠付的工资”（占13.40%）；第四顺序“受被继承人扶养人的生活费”（占14.40%）；第五顺序“对被继承人扶养较多的人之酌情分配遗产份额”（占14.70%）；第六顺序“遗赠扶养协议写明遗赠的遗产”（占10.50%）和“税款”（占10.00%）（见表5-52）。

以上特点之原因分析：（1）继承费用的开支或者属于遗产本身的耗费，或者属于公益费用，所以应列为第一清偿顺序，优先在遗产中扣除。[①]（2）丧葬费应由继承人支付，不应为遗产债务而由遗产支付。（3）欠付的工资涉及劳动者的报酬是否能及时给付，关系劳动者的基本生活保障，排在第三顺序有其合理性。（4）受被继承人扶养人的生活费、对被继承人扶养较多的人之酌情分配遗产份额和遗赠扶养协议写明遗赠的遗产都排在遗产债务清偿的后三位，其原因可能是这些遗产之债务并非法定义务，因此只能在遗产清偿完债务后有剩余时才可支付。

关于遗产债务清偿的顺序之我国立法，我国《继承法》第33条规定：“继承遗产应当清偿被继承人依法应当缴纳的税款和债务，缴纳税款和清偿债务以他的遗产实际价值为限。”

从域外立法例看，《日本民法典》规定，因下列各项原因产生的债权者，于债务人的总财产上有先取特权：一共益费用；二受雇人的报酬；三殡葬费用；四日用品的供给。[②]根据《俄罗斯联邦民法典》规定[③]，遗产债务的清偿顺序如下：一是继承费用包括因被继承人患病和丧葬而发生的费用、遗产保护和管理费、遗嘱执行费用；二是被继承人的债务；三是必继份；四是遗赠。[④]

从我国诸继承法学者建议稿看，对于遗产债务清偿的顺序，“王稿”“杨稿”规定，按下列顺序清偿：第一，继承费用；第二，税；第三，被继承人生前所欠债务；第四，因继承开始而产生的债务。[⑤]“陈稿”规定，遗产债务按下列顺序清偿：继承费用；有优先权的债务；必留份、确为维持生存所需要的酌给遗产；劳动工资等债务；死者生前所欠的税款及第二、第三顺序以外的普通债务；遗赠扶养协议之债；特留份之债；遗赠之债。[⑥]“张稿”规定，遗产债务按下列顺序清偿：遗产管理费用；被继承人生前扶养的、无劳动能力的人的必要的生活费用；被继承人生前所负债务；遗赠。[⑦]

---

① 参见陈苇主编：《外国继承法比较与中国民法典继承编制定研究》，北京大学出版社2011年版，第562、563页。

② 参见《日本民法典》第306条。

③ 参见《俄罗斯联邦民法典》第1174、1175、1149条。

④ 参见陈苇主编：《中国遗产处理制度系统化构建研究》，中国人民公安大学出版社2019年版，第310页。

⑤ 参见“王稿”第650条；“杨稿”第83条。

⑥ 参见“陈稿”第71条。

⑦ 参见“张稿”第20条。

我们认为，我国立法未规定遗产债务清偿的顺序，此为立法之不足。关于遗产债务的清偿顺序，上述河北省被调查者的民众观念与民间习惯、域外立法例和“陈稿”的观点可供我国立法参考。首先，优先权的债务放在普通债权之前有合理性，如果有优先权的债权不能优先受偿，不仅会损害债权人的利益，更会扰乱市场交易秩序。其次，第二顺序之后的遗产债务清偿顺序都是按照遗产对接受遗产人的重要性排列的，将更需要得到遗产的主体放在前面。最后，遗产债务清偿顺序规定的更为具体、清晰，有利于避免遗产债务纠纷。

十、遗产分割之特点与原因分析

（一）遗产分割的自由与限制之特点与原因分析

第一，关于遗产分割自由与限制的民间习惯，统计数据显示的特点是，在河北省被调查者中，（1）由各继承人共同协商后进行遗产分割的，占八成稍多（83.93%）；（2）当遗嘱禁止分割遗产则不得分割遗产的，占近五成（48.08%）；（3）只要有继承人要求分割遗产就得进行分割的，占二成（20.77%）（见表5-53）。

以上特点之原因分析：根据关于遗产分割自由与限制的民间习惯的理由，统计数据显示（见表5-54），在河北省被调查者所在地区，（1）有近八成半的地区有遗产的分割应当由各遗产继承人共同协商的习惯，其原因是遗产由各继承人共同继承，遗产分割涉及各继承人的利益；（2）有近五成的地区有遗嘱人有权通过遗嘱禁止分割遗产的习惯，其原因是遗产是被继承人死亡时遗留下来的个人财产，其有权自由处分包括一定期限内禁止分割；（3）有二成的地区有继承开始后基于继承人的要求就可以分割遗产的习惯，其原因是每个继承人享有的继承权受法律保护，同时基于效率原则考虑。

第二，关于提出遗产分割请求的时间的民众观念，统计数据显示的特点是，当被继承人死亡后，其子女继承人是否可以向其母亲（被继承人的生存配偶）提出分割遗产请求，被调查者所在地区的习惯是：（1）会提出遗产分割请求的，占不到一成（9.96%）；（2）对其母正在居住房屋在其生存期间不予分割的，合计占近九成（87.91%）（见表5-55）。

以上特点之原因分析：根据关于提出遗产分割请求时间的民间习惯的理由，即当被继承人死亡后，关于其子女可否向母亲提出分割遗产的理由（见表5-56），在河北省被调查者所在地区，（1）有近九成的地区有不可以提出遗产分割之习惯，其原因是根据当地观念，被继承人的遗产就应该由其生存配偶全部继承，故其子女不能向母亲提出遗产分割的请求，如果提出，会被视作不孝敬老人的表现；（2）有近一成的地区有可以提出遗产分割遗产之习惯的，其一，可无条件提出遗产分割的，其原因是基于本人的继承权可以分割、根据当事人意愿、符合法律；其二，可有条件地提出遗产分割，即其子女不可以提出分割母亲正在居住的房屋但可提出分割其他遗产的习惯，其原因是体现孝敬老人，保证老人的晚年生活，但对其母正在居住房屋的分割需等其母去世后进行。

第三，关于遗嘱对遗产分割的限制的民众观念，统计数据显示的特点是，（1）在河北省被调查者中，主张可以的，占八成半（85.32%）；主张不可以的，只占近一成半（14.68%）（见表5-57）。（2）关于遗嘱限制遗产分割之具体期限的民众观念，认为5年之内的，占三成半（35.20%）；认为10年之内的，占二成半稍多（26.56%）（见表5-58）。

以上特点之原因分析：在河北省被调查者中，（1）八成半的人主张遗嘱可以对遗产分割进行限制，其原因可能是遗产是被继承人生前的财产，其有权利通过遗嘱决定遗产的分割时间，应当尊重被继承人的真实意愿；（2）三成半的人认为遗嘱限制遗产分割的期限以5年内为宜，其原因可能是有利于发挥遗产的价值。

关于遗产分割自由与限制之我国立法，我国《继承法》第15条规定："遗产分割的时间、办法和份额，由继承人协商确定。协商不成的，可以由人民调解委员会调解或向人民法院提起诉讼。"

从域外立法例看，对于遗产的分割，如《瑞士民法典》规定，共同继承人可随时请求分割遗产，但依契约或法律规定有共有义务的除外。对遗产中某一物的分割将会严重损害其价值的，法官应继承人中一人的要求，可以暂缓遗产的分割。对于有即将出生的胎儿时，考虑到胎儿的利益，分割推迟至其出生时。①《意大利民法典》规定，共同继承人可以随时请求分割遗产，全体或者部分继承人是未成年人的，遗嘱人可以决定在年龄最小的继承人成年后的1年内不得进行遗产分割。遗嘱人还可以决定在遗嘱人死亡后不超过5年的期间内不得对遗产或者某些遗产进行分割。在上述两种情况下，根据一名或者数名共同继承人的请求的，司法机构可以因重大事由准许立即分割遗产，或者在遗嘱人确定的最低期间之后分割遗产。②

从我国诸继承法学者建议稿看，关于遗产的分割，"杨稿"规定，继承开始后，继承人可以随时请求分割遗产。有以下情形的，遗产不得分割：共同继承人约定不得分割的；遗嘱禁止分割的，但是禁止分割的期限不得超过5年，超过5年的，缩短为5年；遗产被债权人申请禁止分割保全的；依遗产性质不得分割的；依法律规定禁止分割的。③"陈稿"规定，遗产分割的时间、办法和份额，被继承人有遗嘱的，依照遗嘱，无遗嘱、遗嘱无效或遗嘱未规定的，由共同继承人协商确定，协商不成的，可请求人民调解委员会调解或者向人民法院提起诉讼。④

我们认为，我国对遗产分割限制的立法存在不足。对遗产分割的限制，首先，应依据被继承人的遗嘱，无遗嘱或遗嘱未规定的情况下，由继承人共同协商，这充分保障了被继承人处分自己财产的真实意愿的实现。其次，对被继承人所设的禁止分割的期间设置了一定的时间限制，可以保障遗产在固定年限后得以分割。最后，应当设立遗产被债权人申请禁止分割保全的、依遗产性质不得分割的、依法律规定禁止分割的三种禁止分割遗产的情形。因此，上述河北省被调查者对遗产分割的自由予以限制的民众观念及民间习惯、域外立法例和"杨稿"的观点可供我国立法参考。

（二）遗产分割瑕疵的担保责任之特点与原因分析

关于遗产分割瑕疵的担保责任的民间习惯，统计数据显示的特点是，河北省被调查者所在地区的习惯是：（1）由分得瑕疵遗产的继承人自行承担，即继承人间不相互承担遗产分割瑕疵担保责任的，占近五成（49.08%）；（2）由共同继承人相互承担的，合计近四成半（44.24%）（见表5-60）。

以上特点之原因分析，根据关于遗产分割瑕疵的担保责任的民间习惯之理由（见表

① 参见《瑞士民法典》第604、605条。
② 参见《意大利民法典》第713条。
③ 参见"杨稿"第85条。
④ 参见"陈稿"第73条。

5-61），在河北省被调查者所在地区，（1）近五成的地区有由共同继承人相互承担的习惯，其原因是如果让分得瑕疵遗产的继承人一个人承担有悖公平原则；（2）近四成半的地区有由分得瑕疵遗产的继承人自行承担，即继承人间不相互承担遗产分割瑕疵担保责任的习惯，其原因是被继承人分得瑕疵遗产是随机分配的，事先所有继承人都不知晓，因此只能由分得瑕疵遗产的继承人自行承担责任。

关于遗产分割瑕疵的担保责任之我国立法，我国《继承法》无规定。

从域外立法例看，《法国民法典》规定，每一共同继承人均按照其继承遗产的比例，对其他共同继承人因继承遗产被追夺受到的损失负偿还责任。如共有继承人之一无支付能力，由被担保人或其他有清偿能力的被继承人分担。[①]《德国民法典》规定，共同关系废止时，共同标的被分给共同继承人中的一人的，因权利瑕疵或物的瑕疵，其余共同关系人中的每一个人必须以出卖人相同的方式对其应由部分提供担保。[②]《瑞士民法典》规定，共同继承人在遗产分割后，对遗产互负买方、卖方义务。分割时，对归属于各自的债权的成立，继承人之间互为担保，在算定的债权额内，对债务人的支付能力与普通保证人相同的义务。[③]

从我国诸继承法学者建议稿看，“梁稿”和“王稿”规定，遗产分割后，各继承人以其所得的遗产份额为限，对其他继承人分得的遗产，负与出卖人同样的担保责任。受遗赠人所接受的遗产为种类物的，有权要求继承人承担前款规定的责任。各继承人对其他继承人分得的债权，就遗产分割时债务人的支付能力，负担保责任。[④]“徐稿”规定，其份额的半数以上已遭受损害的人，有权以显失公平为由撤销分割。[⑤]“陈稿”规定：“各共同继承人以其所得的遗产份额为限，对其他共同继承人分得的遗产，承担与出卖人相同的担保责任”。[⑥]

我们认为，我国立法未规定遗产分割瑕疵的担保责任，此为立法之不足。上述河北省被调查者所在地区对遗产分割的瑕疵由共同继承人相互承担的民间习惯、德国的立法和“陈稿”的观点可供我国立法参考。因为，共同继承人应对分得遗产具有权利瑕疵或物的瑕疵的继承人承担瑕疵担保责任，此规定不仅可以保护分得瑕疵债权继承人的继承利益，还可以保护分得物的瑕疵继承人的继承利益。

十一、无人承受遗产之特点与原因分析

（一）无人承受遗产的归属之特点与原因分析

关于无人承受遗产的归属主体的民众观念，统计数据显示的特点是，在河北省被调查者中，（1）主张归属主体为社会公共组织（包括归属于国家、死者生前所在地的国库、死者生前所在地民政部门的社会福利机构和死者生前所在地的居委会）的，合计各占七成左右（城镇居民 70.98%，农村居民 69.38%）；（2）主张归属主体为自然人（归属于

---

① 参见《法国民法典》第 885 条。

② 参见《德国民法典》第 757 条。

③ 参见《瑞士民法典》第 637 条。

④ 参见“梁稿”第 2025、2026 条；“王稿”第 648 条。

⑤ 参见“徐稿”第四分编第 438 条。

⑥ 参见“陈稿”第 79 条第 2 款。

不是继承人的其他亲属）的，各占二成至三成（城镇居民 23.90%，农村居民 30.62%）（见表 5-62、表 5-64）。

以上特点之原因分析：根据关于城镇居民无人承受遗产的归属主体的民众观念之理由（见表 5-63），在河北省被调查者中，（1）七成的人主张归属主体为社会公共组织，其原因包括：其一，归国家（或国库）的，其原因是可以规范财产秩序，也与部分国家的做法相一致，符合法律规定；其二，归民政部门的社会福利机构的，其原因是捐赠给慈善机构做公益有利于回报社会。（2）二成稍多的人主张归属主体为自然人，其原因是归不是继承人的其他亲戚所有，符合情理。

关于无人承受遗产的归属主体之我国立法，我国《继承法》第 32 条规定："无人继承又无人受遗赠的遗产，归国家所有；死者生前是集体所有制组织成员的，归所在集体所有制组织所有。"

从域外立法例看，《法国民法典》规定，无人继承的遗产，由国家取得。①《德国民法典》规定，继承人不在于情况适当的期间以内被查明的，遗产法院必须确定，不存在除国库以外的继承人。②《瑞士民法典》规定，被继承人无继承人的，其遗产归属于其最后住所地所在地的州，或依州法归属于有权利的乡镇。③《日本民法典》规定，依据对特别关系人的继承财产分与的规定无法处分的继承财产，归属国库。④

从我国诸继承法学者建议稿看，关于无人承受的遗产，"杨稿""王稿""梁稿"规定，无人继承遗产归国家所有，死者生前是集体所有制组织成员的，归所在集体所有制组织所有。"徐稿"规定，无人继承遗产归国家所有。"张稿"和"陈稿"规定，无人承受的遗产，应先考虑是否可以酌情分给依靠被继承人扶养的人、对被继承人扶养较多的人、与被继承人一同生活的人或其他与被继承人关系密切的人，之后在考虑上缴国库或归集体组织。⑤

我们认为，关于无人承受遗产的归属主体，上述瑞士的立法和"陈稿""张稿"的观点可供我国立法参考。因为对于依靠被继承人扶养的人、对被继承人扶养较多的人、与被继承人一同生活的人或其他与被继承人有密切关系的人，他们并不属于被继承人的法定继承人，所以他们无权分得遗产，但考虑到其与被继承人的关系，分给他们适当的遗产既符合生活常理，也有利于保护弱者，发挥遗产的扶养价值。

（二）无人承受遗产的处理之特点与原因分析

第一，关于无人承受遗产的管理人的民众观念，统计数据显示的特点是，在河北省被调查者中，（1）主张由死者户籍所在地的居委会或村委会或所在单位指定的，占五成稍多（53.63%）；（2）主张由人民法院指定的，占三成稍多（31.01%）；主张由民政部门指定的，占一成半（15.36%）（见表 5-65）。

以上特点之原因分析：五成稍多的河北省被调查者认为无人继承遗产的管理人应由居

① 参见《法国民法典》第 724 条。

② 参见《德国民法典》第 1964 条。

③ 参见《瑞士民法典》第 466 条。

④ 参见《日本民法典》第 959 条。

⑤ 参见"杨稿"第 93 条；"王稿"第 666 条；"梁稿"第 2029 条；"徐稿"第四分编第 498 条；"张稿"第 70 条；"陈稿"第 87 条。

委会、村委会担任，其原因可能是居民委员会、村民委员会或其生前所在的单位最了解当地情况。

关于无人承受遗产的管理人的产生方式之我国立法，我国《继承法》无规定。

从域外立法例看，《法国民法典》规定，对于无人继承的遗产，继承开始地在其管辖区内的大审法院，应利害关系人或王国初级检察官的请求，任命一名财产管理人。①《德国民法典》规定，遗产法院是无人继承遗产的管理人。②《日本民法典》规定，家庭法院根据利害关系人或检察官的请求，须为继承财产选任管理人。③

从我国诸继承法学者建议稿看，"王稿"规定，继承开始时，有无继承人不明时，由村委会或居委会作为遗产管理人。④"张稿"规定，无人承受遗产的遗产管理人由法院指定。⑤"陈稿"规定，无人承受遗产的管理人为被继承人住所地的居民委员会、村民委员会成员。⑥"杨稿"规定，继承开始后，有无继承人不明的，或者已知的继承人、受遗赠人丧失、放弃继承权或受遗赠权的，有关人员、部门或基层组织应将情况及时通知民政部门。民政部门在接到通知后，应指定遗产管理人管理遗产。⑦

我们认为，我国立法未规定无人承受遗产管理人的产生方式，此为立法之不足。关于无人承受遗产管理人的产生方式，上述河北省被调查者的民众观念、"王稿"和"陈稿"的观念可供我国立法参考。因为我国地域广阔，人口众多，由专门的机构或法院管理无人继承的遗产成本太大。我们应结合中国实际情况，利用现有资源。在我国，居民委员会、村民委员会作为基层自治组织，经常处理基层民众的事情，对于被继承人的生前情况了解的比较全面，处理被继承人遗产较为得心应手，其处理办法也更符合当地习惯，更容易被周围民众或被继承人亲属所信服。

第二，关于无人承受遗产的酌分请求权主体的民众观念，统计数据显示的特点是，分别占六成至七成半多的被调查者认为无人承受的遗产的酌分请求权人包括：依靠死者扶养的人，占68.42%；与死者共同生活的人，占62.02%；与死者关系密切且对其帮助较多的人，占77.52%（见表5-66）。

以上特点之原因分析，六成至七成半的河北省被调查者认为靠死者扶养的人、与死者共同生活的人、与死者关系密切且对死者帮助较多的人可以酌分无人的继承遗产，其原因可能是为了更好地保障弱者利益。

关于无人承受遗产的酌分请求权主体之我国立法，根据我国《继承法》第14条规定⑧，1985年《执行继承法意见》第57条规定，遗产因无人继承收归国家或集体组织所有时，按《继承法》第14条规定可以分给遗产的人提出取得遗产的要求，人民法院应当视情况适当分给遗产。即我国无人承受遗产的酌分请求权主体被限定在继承人以外的依靠

---

① 参见《法国民法典》第812条。

② 参见《德国民法典》第1960条。

③ 参见《日本民法典》第952、957、954条。

④ 参见"王稿"第661条。

⑤ 参见"张稿"第67条第2款。

⑥ 参见"陈稿"第83、84条。

⑦ 参见"杨稿"第91条。

⑧ 我国《继承法》第14条：对继承人以外的依靠被继承人扶养的缺乏劳动能力又没有生活来源的人，或者继承人以外的对被继承人扶养较多的人，可以分给他们适当的遗产。

被继承人扶养的缺乏劳动能力又没有生活来源的人、继承人以外的对被继承人扶养较多的这两类人中。

从域外立法例看，对于无人承受遗产的酌分情况，日本规定可以将无人承受的遗产给予和被继承人共同生活的、为被继承人治疗和护理做出贡献的人以及其他与被继承人有特别关系的人。英国规定，王室可以自由裁量，将遗产给实际上依靠无遗嘱死亡者的人，不论其是否和无遗嘱死亡者有关系，或者其他无遗嘱死亡者希望供养的人。①

从我国诸继承法学者建议稿看，“杨稿”“陈稿”“张稿”均规定了无人承受遗产的酌分遗产人。其中“杨稿”未具体说明酌分遗产人的范围，“张稿”规定酌分遗产人为与被继承人共同生活或者精心照顾被继承人的人，“陈稿”则规定酌分遗产人为依靠被继承人扶养的人、对被继承人扶养较多的人、与被继承人一同生活的人或其他与被继承人有密切关系的人。②

我们认为，上述河北省被调查者主张扩大无人承受的遗产之酌情分配请求主体的民众观念、日本的立法和“陈稿”的观点可供我国立法参考。因为，首先，依靠被继承人扶养的人作为酌分遗产人，可以照顾弱者，发挥遗产的扶养价值。其次，对被继承人扶养较多的人作为酌分遗产人，可以使对被继承人扶养较多的人得到回报。最后，与被继承人一同生活的人或其他与被继承人有密切关系的人作为酌分遗产人符合生活常理。

第四节　当代中国河北省民众财产继承观念与遗产处理习惯对中国民法典继承编制定的立法启示

以上，我们根据河北省被调查者的财产继承观念与遗产处理习惯实证调查的统计汇总数据，分析归纳其特点，研究其特点的产生原因，并考察我国司法实践的相关案例，分析我国继承法律制度的适用情况，进而结合考察域外立法例和我国诸继承法学者建议稿的观点，总结我国《继承法》相关制度存在的优点和剖析其不足。以下，我们将以河北省被调查者的财产继承观念与遗产处理习惯为参考基础，从中国实际出发，借鉴域外立法例和我国诸继承法学者建议稿的有益观点，对我国“民法典继承法编”编纂中相关继承制度的修改完善或予以保留，提出立法建议，以供我国立法机关参考。

一、我国遗产范围界定制度之不足与立法完善建议

（一）我国遗产范围界定制度之不足

关于遗产范围制度，我国《继承法》存在的不足有以下两方面：第一，对遗产种类的范围界定，欠缺反面排除的规定，致使河北省被调查民众对死亡赔偿金、欠债、个人邮箱等是否属于遗产的认识不一。例如，一成至七成多的被调查者认为家庭日常生活用品、债务、交通事故死亡赔偿金、单位出租房、以被继承人的姓名注册的邮箱和QQ账号等属于遗产（见表5-4）。并且前述涉及遗产范围界定制度的案例之司法审判实践中也反映出我国遗产范围界定欠缺反面排除之不足。第二，未规定被继承人生前特种赠与财产的归扣

① 陈苇主编：《外国继承法比较与中国民法典继承编制定研究》，北京大学出版社2011年版，第669页。

② 参见“杨稿”第94条；“陈稿”第87条；“张稿”第70条。

制度，这不利于公平地在共同继承人间分配遗产，也不利于全球化背景下对涉外继承人继承权益的保护。

（二）我国遗产范围界定制度之立法完善建议

综上，我们针对我国遗产范围界定制度提出以下修改完善建议：

1. 遗产范围界定模式之立法建议

建议补充规定死亡赔偿金不属于遗产，并对虚拟财产进行界定后纳入遗产范围。第一，是否将死亡赔偿金纳入遗产范围，应首先解决死亡赔偿金在法律上的性质问题，在其他立法未明确指出死亡赔偿金的性质之前，不宜将死亡赔偿金纳入遗产范围，以避免同案不同判的情况。第二，进一步扩大遗产的范围，将虚拟财产明确其具体内涵后纳入遗产范围，同时加大法制宣传力度，这既有利于消除继承法领域长期存在的只有实物财产为遗产的传统观念，也有利于实现遗产经济价值与精神价值同等重要。

2. 被继承人生前特种赠与财产归扣之立法建议

建议增设被继承人生前特种赠与财产的归扣制度。但考虑到我国民众的继承观念和继承习惯，建议不宜对遗产归扣作开放性规定，明确哪些财产属于应归扣的财产。这样既符合广大人民群众的继承观念，又可以引领人们慢慢接触遗产归扣制度。

二、我国继承开始的通知和公告制度之不足与立法完善建议

（一）我国继承开始的通知和公告制度之不足

关于继承开始的通知和公告制度，我国《继承法》存在的不足是继承开始的通知和公告主体范围狭窄，可能会导致继承权利人以及遗产利害关系人等无法及时获知继承开始的信息；河北省被调查者认为继承开始的通知和公告的主体范围较我国《继承法》更广（见表 5-9）。前述涉及继承开始的通知和公告制度的案例之司法审判实践中也反映出我国继承开始的通知和公告制度存在此不足。

（二）我国继承开始的通知和公告制度之立法完善建议

建议扩大继承开始的通知和公告的主体范围，即明确规定继承通知的主体包括：知道被继承人死亡的继承人、遗产管理人、遗嘱执行人、受遗赠人、被继承人生前所在单位、住所地居民委员会或村民委员会、死亡地居民委员会或村民委员会。对于继承开始的通知方式，可以不作具体详细规定，只规定通过适当方式通知即可。但应当增补规定不履行通知义务造成继承人损害之赔偿责任。

三、我国遗产管理制度之不足与立法完善建议

（一）我国遗产管理制度之不足

关于遗产管理制度，我国《继承法》存在的三个方面的不足：第一，未规定遗产管理人的产生方式，致使被继承人死亡后如何确定遗产管理人于法无据；近五成至九成的河北省被调查者所在地区的习惯是由法定继承人和家族中的德高望重者担任（见表 5-12）。第二，未具体规定遗产管理人的职责和报酬，这不利于遗产管理人积极履行职责，也不利于遗产管理人劳动权益的保护；河北省被调查者认为遗产管理人的职责具有多样性，对于是否应给予遗产管理人报酬的民间习惯不一（见表 5-15）。第三，未规定遗产管理人的损害赔偿责任，这易导致遗产管理人不认真管理遗产、逃避损害赔偿，损害继承人或债权人

的合法权益；占五成稍多的河北省被调查者认为遗产管理人在有故意或重大过错时应承担损害赔偿责任（见表5-16）。前述涉及遗产管理制度的案例之司法审判实践中也反映出我国遗产管理制度存在此不足。

（二）我国遗产管理制度之立法完善建议

综上，我们针对我国遗产管理制度提出以下修改完善建议：

1. 遗产管理人确定之立法建议

建议对于遗产管理人的选任，分三种情形：第一，有遗嘱执行人的由遗嘱执行人管理遗产。第二，无遗嘱执行人的由所有继承人推选。第三，推选不出或推选出的遗嘱执行人侵害继承人或其他利害关系人利益的，由人民法院指定。无行为能力或限制行为能力的监护人是其所获遗产的管理主体。

2. 遗产管理人的管理职责与报酬之立法建议

增设遗产管理人的职责，具体包括：清点遗产，编制遗产清册；发出继承的通知；向继承人报告管理账目；清偿遗产债务；分配遗产；参与遗产有关的诉讼活动。除了上述职责，应赋予遗产管求权，报酬请求权优先从遗产中支付。

3. 遗产管理人的损害赔偿责任之立法建议

建议对于遗产管理人的损害赔偿责任作区别规定。遗产管理人为无偿管理的，只有在其存在故意或重大过失的情形下，其才承担损害赔偿责任；遗产管理人为有偿管理的，不论其存在故意、重大过失或一般过失，都应当承担损害赔偿责任。

四、我国法定继承制度之不足与立法完善建议

（一）我国法定继承制度之不足

关于法定继承制度，我国《继承法》存在以下五个方面的不足：第一，法定继承人的范围较窄、顺序较少；河北省被调查者认为的法定继承人范围比我国《继承法》规定的更广、顺序更多（见表5-17、表5-18）。第二，将配偶规定为第一顺位法定继承人，这可能导致继承人为配偶一人时，被继承人的财产外流出家庭；四成半稍多的河北省被调查者认为配偶无固定继承顺序，可参与第一、第二（或第三）顺序且在不同顺序其应继份不同（见表5-19）。第三，未规定配偶对遗产中的家庭住房的先取权与终生使用权，这不利于保障生存配偶一方的基本生活水平，易导致老年生存配偶一方老无所居；八成半稍多的河北省被调查者地区的习惯是配偶可享有对遗产中家庭住房的先取权与终生使用权（见表5-20）。第四，未规定后顺序特殊法定继承人对特殊遗产的终生使用权，此易导致特殊后顺位特殊法定继承人老无所居、老无所养；九成稍多的河北省被调查者地区的习惯是后顺序特殊法定继承人对特殊遗产享有终生使用权（见表5-22、表5-23）。第五，将对公、婆或岳父、岳母尽了主要赡养义务的丧偶儿媳或女婿作为第一顺位法定继承人存有不合理之处，在第一顺位法定继承人只有丧偶儿媳或女婿时，易造成被继承人财产外流出家庭。

（二）我国法定继承制度的完善立法的建议

综上，我们针对我国法定继承制度提出以下修改完善建议：

1. 法定继承人的范围和顺序之立法建议

建议扩大法定继承人的范围、增加法定继承人的顺序如下：第一顺序为子女及其晚辈直系血亲；第二顺序为父母、兄弟姐妹及其子女；第三顺序为祖父母和外祖父母；第四顺

序为伯叔姑舅姨、堂兄弟姐妹、表兄弟姐妹等四亲等以内的其他直系或者旁系血亲。配偶作为无固定顺序的继承人，其可以与前任一顺序的继承顺序共同继承，且与不同顺序的继承人继承时其法定应继份有所不同。

2. 配偶与血亲继承人的法定应继份之立法建议

建议规定配偶为无固定继承顺序继承人，当配偶与第一顺位继承人共同继承时，取得遗产的二分之一；当配偶与第二顺位继承人共同继承时，取得遗产的三分之二；当配偶与第三顺位继承人共同继承时，取得遗产的四分之三；无第一、第二、第三顺位继承人时，由配偶继承全部遗产。

3. 配偶对遗产中的家庭住房的先取权与终生使用权之立法建议

建议增设配偶对遗产中的家庭住房的先取权与终生使用权。生存配偶对房屋即房屋内日常生活用品的居住权和使用权延续至死亡时止。对于继承份额小于这些财产的价值时，生存配偶有义务按照超过部分对遗产进行补偿。继承份额大于这些财产的价值时，生存配偶在现有遗产中受领不足的部分。这样就可以充分保障生存配偶原来的生活方式及基本生活水平。

4. 后顺序特殊法定继承人对遗产中原使用的住房及日常生活用品的终生使用权之立法建议

建议增设后顺位特殊法定继承人对原使用的遗产住房及日常生活用品享有终生使用权，有利于保障后顺位特殊法定继承人“老有所居、老有所养”，使其免于因被继承人死亡而流离失所或改变长期的生活习惯。

5. 尽了主要赡养义务的丧偶儿媳或女婿的遗产分配方式之立法建议

建议将尽了主要赡养义务的丧偶儿媳或女婿作为第一顺位法定继承人继承遗产改为酌情分得遗产，并规定酌情分得遗产的最低限度。这样既可以避免财产全部外流的风险，也可以激励丧偶儿媳或女婿主动赡养老人，又可以保障丧偶儿媳或女婿的财产权益。

五、我国遗嘱继承制度之不足与立法完善建议

（一）我国遗嘱继承制度之不足

关于遗嘱继承制度，我国《继承法》存在以下三个方面的不足：第一，赋予公证遗嘱优先适用的效力不合理，其可能导致危急时刻被继承人后立遗嘱无效，使遗产处分不符合被继承人最后的真实意愿；六成半的河北省被调查者认为后遗嘱优先于前一遗嘱包括公证遗嘱适用（见表5-27）。第二，未规定特留份制度，在被继承人通过遗嘱将自己所有的遗产赠与继承人之外的人时，不利于保护继承人的继承利益；六成半的河北省被调查者认为应对遗嘱的自由予以限制，即认同设立“特留份”制度（见表5-29）。第三，未规定夫妻共同遗嘱，致使现实生活中存在的夫妻共同遗嘱的效力难以认定；七成半的河北省被调查者对夫妻设立共同遗嘱予以认可，但在实践中出现夫妻共同设立遗嘱的情况比较少，仅占二成稍多（见表5-30、表5-31）。

（二）我国遗嘱继承制度之立法完善建议

综上，我们针对我国遗嘱继承和遗赠制度提出以下修改完善建议：

1. 公证遗嘱与其他形式遗嘱的效力之立法建议

建议任何法定形式的遗嘱都可以通过后遗嘱被撤销，不赋予公证遗嘱优先适用的效

力。后遗嘱可以使前遗嘱与之抵触的部分无效。

2. 遗嘱自由的限制——特留份之立法建议

建议增设特留份制度。明确规定特留份请求权人的范围、特留份的具体份额、特留份丧失与恢复的法定情形以及特留份扣减权等。

3. 夫妻共同遗嘱之立法建议

建议增设夫妻共同遗嘱。承认夫妻共同遗嘱的效力，可以保障遗产依据被继承人真实意愿分割。

六、我国继承和遗赠的接受与放弃制度之不足与立法完善建议

（一）我国继承和遗赠的接受与放弃制度之不足

关于继承和遗赠的接受与放弃制度，我国《继承法》存在以下三个方面的不足：第一，未明确规定具体的放弃继承的期间，这不利于继承人积极行使接受或放弃继承的权利，致使继承法律关系长期处于不确定的状态。近四成的河北省被调查者认为继承开始的2个月内作出放弃继承较为合适（见表5-33）。前述涉及继承和遗赠的接受与放弃制度的案例之司法审判实践中也反映出我国继承接受及放弃的时间与方式之不足。第二，对放弃遗赠的推定规定不合理，此规定不利于保护受遗赠人的财产权益，也不利于被继承人处分遗产的真实意愿的实现；六成半的河北省被调查者认为受遗赠人在知道受遗赠后未作出任何意思表示的应视为接受遗赠（见表5-35）。第三，未规定放弃继承的效力，致使被调查者对于债权人是否有权申请撤销被继承人放弃继承的行为观点不一；五成稍多的河北省被调查者认为继承人放弃继承的行为不可以被债权人撤销（见表5-38）。

（二）我国继承和遗赠的接受与放弃制度之立法完善建议

综上，我们针对我国继承和遗赠的接受与放弃制度提出以下修改完善建议：

1. 继承的接受与放弃的时间与方式之立法建议

继承人放弃继承须在知道或应当知道继承开始之日起2个月内以书面形式向其他继承人作出放弃继承意思表示。

2. 遗赠的接受与放弃的方式与效力之立法建议

建议规定受遗赠人应在知道或应当知道受遗赠之日起2个月内，作出接受或放弃受遗赠的意思表示；到期未表示的，视为接受遗赠。接受遗赠的意思表示可向遗产管理人、遗嘱执行人、继承人以书面形式作出。

3. 继承的放弃与债权人的撤销权之立法建议

建议规定放弃继承的行为不可以被债权人撤销，即任何人无权撤销放弃继承的行为，但是继承人因欺诈、胁迫放弃继承的除外。

七、我国继承权的丧失、被继承人的宥恕与代位继承制度之不足与立法完善建议

（一）我国继承权的丧失、被继承人的宥恕与代位继承制度之不足

关于继承权的丧失、被继承人的宥恕与代位继承制度，我国《继承法》存在以下两个方面的不足：第一，继承权丧失的法定情形规定仍有不足，其中对于采用欺诈或胁迫行为妨碍被继承人设立、变更或者撤销遗嘱而继承权丧失后如获得被继承人的原谅是否可以恢复，尚无规定。七成的河北省被调查者认为因欺诈、胁迫行为的继承人丧失继承权的可

因被继承人的原谅而恢复（见表5-41）。并且前述涉及继承权的丧失、被继承人的宥恕与代位继承制度的案例之司法审判实践中也反映出我国继承权的丧失、被继承人的宥恕制度存在不足。第二，1985年《执行继承法意见》规定继承人丧失继承权的，其晚辈直系血亲不得代位继承，不符合现代民法的“自己责任原则”。近五成半的河北省被调查者认为继承人丧失继承权后他的晚辈直系血亲不可以代位继承（见表5-43）。

（二）我国继承权的丧失、被继承人的宥恕与代位继承制度之立法完善建议

综上，我们针对我国继承权的丧失、被继承人的宥恕与代位继承制度提出以下修改完善建议：

1. 继承权的丧失与被继承人的宥恕之立法建议

继承人丧失继承权的情形应包括：一是为争夺遗产而杀害其他继承人的；二是故意杀害被继承人的，但正当防卫的除外；三是遗弃被继承人的，或者虐待被继承人情节严重的；四是伪造、篡改或者销毁遗嘱，情节严重的；五是以欺诈或者胁迫的手段，迫使或者妨碍被继承人设立、变更或者撤销遗嘱，情节严重的。继承人有前款规定的情形之一，如确有悔改表现，经被继承人宥恕的，可恢复继承权。被继承人知道继承人有丧失继承权的事由，仍然在遗嘱中指定其为继承人的，视为宥恕。

2. 继承权的丧失与代位继承之立法建议

晚辈直系血亲不因被代位继承人丧失继承权而丧失代位继承权，但该被代位继承人在任何情况下对其子女代位继承取得的遗产都不享有用益权。

八、我国遗赠扶养协议制度之不足与立法增补建议

（一）我国遗赠扶养协议制度之不足

关于遗赠扶养协议制度，我国《继承法》存在的不足为只规定了遗赠扶养协议，但遗赠扶养协议的主体限于公民与扶养人、集体经济组织，签订主体太狭窄，且未规定继承协议制度，无法满足被扶养人与继承人之间协商扶养与遗产继承事宜的现实需要。七成稍多的河北省被调查者认可继承协议且该协议的订立主体应是被继承人与全体继承人，为解决被继承人养老送终而签订继承协议的情形时常发生，占五成稍多的地区（见表5-45、表5-46）。并且前述涉及继承协议制度的案例之司法审判实践中也反映出我国欠缺继承协议制度之不足。在河北省被调查者中，近四成的人认为可以允许有条件地代位扶养，合计近六成的人认为扶养义务人死亡是继承协议终止的情形之一，合计三成半稍多的人认为应签订新的继承协议，合计近五成的人认为需要对超过原扶养人法定义务的支出予以经济补偿（见表5-48）。

（二）我国继承扶养协议制度的立法增补建议

综上，我们针对我国继承扶养协议制度提出以下修改完善建议：

1. 继承扶养协议的订立主体与方式之立法建议

将遗赠扶养协议更名为继承扶养协议，扩大继承扶养协议的主体范围，法定继承人、其他自然人、法人、其他社会组织都可以成为继承扶养协议的主体。继承扶养协议一方主体必须是被继承人。因为继承扶养协议约定的是双方主体之间的权利义务，所以一般情况下只需要被继承人的相对方签订继承扶养协议即可。如果担心发生不必要的纠纷，也可以由不享有权利承担义务的继承人自愿共同签订继承协议，因为继承协议应尊重当事人意思

自治。

2. 继承扶养协议的变更方式及效力之立法建议

扶养人先于被扶养人死亡的，其继承扶养协议效力应视情况而定。如果死亡扶养人的配偶或成年子女有扶养被继承人的意愿和能力，且被继承人愿意其代替扶养人继续履行继承协议的，继承扶养协议继续有效。如果扶养人无成年子女或在世配偶，或者被继承人不同意更换继承扶养协议主体的，继承扶养协议终止。被扶养人在扶养人死亡时，对于因继承扶养协议所得的利益，应返还给已死亡扶养人的继承人，但另有约定的除外。

九、我国遗产债务清偿制度之不足与立法完善建议

（一）我国遗产债务清偿制度之不足

关于遗产债务清偿制度，我国《继承法》存在以下三个方面的不足：第一，对遗产债务清偿责任的类型的规定不够全面，无法平衡地保障继承人和遗产债权人等多方的利益；河北省被调查者认为在保留我国《继承法》现有的有限清偿责任和自愿的无限清偿责任的基础上，增设有条件的有限清偿责任和强制的无限清偿责任（见表5-49）。第二，未明确丧葬费由谁承担，致使该类型案件在司法实践缺乏裁判依据；近六成半的河北省被调查者所在地区的习惯是由全体继承人共同承担被继承人的丧葬费用（见表5-50）。第三，未规定遗产债务的清偿顺序，这不利于遗产债务的顺利偿还，也不利于保障特殊债权的优先实现。本次调查中，不论在河北省被调查者的习惯上还是在观念上，丧葬费用、遗产管理和欠付的工资等费用都排在遗产债务清偿顺序的前三位；受被继承人扶养人的生活费、对被继承人扶养较多的人之酌情分配遗产份额和遗赠扶养协议写明遗赠的遗产都排在后三位（见表5-51、表5-52）。前述涉及遗产债务清偿制度的案例和遗产管理制度的案例之司法审判实践中也反映出我国遗产债务清偿顺序制度之不足。

（二）我国遗产债务清偿制度之立法完善建议

综上，我们针对我国遗产债务清偿制度提出以下修改完善建议：

1. 遗产债务清偿责任的类型之立法建议

明确遗产债务清偿责任的类型，增补有条件的有限清偿责任和强制的无限清偿责任。具体而言，继承人可以自愿选择实行有条件的限定继承或无条件概括继承。但继承人在法定期间内不依法制作遗产清册、或对遗产进行了全部或部分处分、或故意未将遗产全部或部分记入遗产清册的，继承人应当承担强制的无限清偿责任。

2. 被继承人丧葬费支付之立法建议

丧葬费用应由全体继承人承担被继承人的与其社会地位、当地生活水平相符的丧葬费用。对于被继承人生前指示要风光办理的，超出部分由遗产支付。对于某个或某几个继承人决定风光办理的，超出合理范围的丧葬费由主张风光办理的继承人负担。

3. 遗产债务的清偿顺序之立法建议

建议遗产债务依下列顺序清偿：（1）继承费用；（2）有优先权的债务；（3）必留份以及为维持生存所需的酌分遗产；（4）欠付的工资；（5）死者生前所欠普通债务及税款；（6）遗赠扶养协议之债；（7）特留份之债；（8）遗赠之债。

十、我国遗产分割制度之不足与立法完善建议

（一）我国遗产分割制度之不足

关于遗产分割制度，我国《继承法》存在以下两个方面的不足：第一，未规定遗产分割的时间及禁止分割遗产的情况，这不利于继承人协商分割遗产与遗嘱禁止分割遗产矛盾的解决，易造成遗产分割纠纷。八成稍多的河北省被调查者认可对遗产分割的自由应有一定限制，且被继承人有权通过遗嘱限制遗产的分割时间，七成半稍多的河北省被调查者认为不会在被继承人去世后立即对生存配偶居住的遗产房屋提出分割要求；八成半的河北省被调查者认为被继承人有权通过遗嘱限制遗产的分割时间，且该期限以5年内为宜（见表5-53、表5-55、表5-57、表5-58）。前述涉及遗产分割制度的案例之司法审判实践中也反映出我国遗产分割的限制制度之不足。第二，未规定继承人的瑕疵担保责任，这不利于对分到瑕疵遗产的共同继承人之共同继承权益的保护；近四成半的河北省的被调查者所在地区的习惯是由共同继承人相互承担遗产分割的瑕疵担保责任（见表5-60）。

（二）我国遗产分割制度之立法完善建议

综上，我们针对我国遗产分割制度提出以下修改完善建议：

1. 遗产分割的自由与限制之立法建议

建议明确遗产分割的自由与限制。首先，继承开始后，继承人可以随请求分割遗产。其次，遗产分割自由的限制主要包括三种情况：第一，遗嘱限制。对于被继承人在遗嘱中规定了遗产分割时间的，应按遗嘱规定的时间分割遗产，但应对遗嘱禁止遗产分割的时间应作限制一定期限的规定。第二，继承人协商限制。继承人可以对遗产的分割时间作一致性规定，可以暂缓遗产分割时间，可以不分割遗产，前提是不违反法律的强制性规定，不侵害第三人利益，不违反公序良俗。第三，法定限制。为了保障继承人和遗产债权人的利益，使物的效用充分发挥，有必要通过法律明确限制遗产的分割时间。

2. 遗产分割瑕疵的担保责任之立法建议

遗产分割后，各继承人以其所得的遗产份额为限，对其他继承人分得的遗产，负与出卖人同等的瑕疵担保责任。对于以债权为标的物的遗产分割，各继承人就遗产分割时债务人的偿付能力负担保责任。如某一个或几个继承人缺乏承担担保责任的能力，由其他继承人负连带责任。

十一、我国无人承受遗产之不足与立法完善建议

（一）我国无人承受遗产制度之不足

关于无人承受遗产制度，我国《继承法》存在以下两个方面的不足：第一，未规定无人承受遗产的遗产管理人的选任，易导致无人承受遗产长时间无人管理，造成遗产价值的流失。五成稍多的河北省被调查者认为无人承受遗产的管理人由死者户籍所在地的居委会、村委会或所在单位指定（见表5-65）。前述涉及无人承受遗产案例制度的案例之司法审判实践中也反映出我国无人承受遗产管理制度的不足。第二，规定无人承受遗产的酌分遗产人范围较窄，限于依靠被继承人扶养的缺乏劳动能力又没有生活来源的人、继承人以外的对被继承人扶养较多的这两类人，这不利于保护对被继承人付出较多的人、与被继承人共同生活的人的财产权益，也不符合生活常理。有六成至七成半多的河北省被调查者认

为与死者关系密切且对死者帮助较多的人、依靠死者扶养的人与和死者共同生活的人均可作为无人承受遗产的酌分请求权人（见表5-66）。

（二）我国无人承受遗产制度之立法完善建议

综上，我们针对我国无人承受遗产制度提出以下修改完善建议：

1. 无人继承遗产管理人的选任之立法建议

在继承开始后，对无人承受的遗产，由被继承人户籍所在地的居民委员会、村民委员会担任遗产管理人，村民委员会、居民委员会可以指定其内部成员中的一人或几人管理遗产。被继承人不在户籍地的，由被继承人最后住所地或主要遗产所在地居委会或村委会担任遗产管理人。

2. 无人承受遗产的酌分请求权主体之立法建议

增设无人承受遗产的酌分制度，即对于无人承受的遗产，归国家所有；死者生前是集体所有制组织成员的，归所在集体所有制组织所有。但由死者扶养的人、与死者共同生活的人、与死者关系密切且对死者帮助较多的人可以请求酌分无人的继承遗产。无人承受的遗产处理完毕后，有继承人或概括受遗赠人出现的，自继承开始后5年内，可以请求国家或者集体所有制组织归还相应遗产。

第六章　当代中国湖北省民众财产继承观念与遗产处理习惯实证调查研究*

第一节　当代中国湖北省民众财产继承观念与遗产处理习惯实证调查概况

一、被调查地区概况

（一）湖北省社会经济发展水平情况

2018 年全省完成生产总值 39366.55 亿元，同比增长 7.8%。其中，第一产业完成增加值 3547.51 亿元，同比增长 2.9%；第二产业完成增加值 17088.95 亿元，同比增长 6.8%；第三产业完成增加值 18730.09 亿元，同比增长 9.9%。[①]

（二）湖北省人口结构情况

2018 年年末全省常住人口 5917 万人，其中，从全省城乡人口结构看，城镇 3567.95 万人，乡村 2349.05 万人。城镇化率达到 60.3%。[②] 从全省人口性别结构看，2017 年湖北男性人口为 2996.76 万人，占总人口的 50.78%；女性为 2905.24 万人，占总人口的 49.22%。男女性别比以为女性为 103.15：100。从全省人口年龄结构看，截至 2017 年年底，全省常住人口达到 5902 万，其中 60 岁及以上人口 1107.85 万，占总人口的 18.77%，高出全国平均水平 1.47 个百分点。[③]

（三）湖北省城乡人口的年均收入情况

2018 年湖北省城镇常住居民人均可支配收入 34455 元，增长 8.00%；湖北省农村常住居民人均可支配收入 14978 元，增长 8.40%。[④]

---

* 作者简介：孟令志，女，法学硕士，中南财经政法大学副教授、硕士生导师；白玉，西南政法大学民商法学 2017 级博士研究生；贾艳艳、李想、元雨，中南财经政法大学民商法 2016 级硕士研究生；彭锦、王传印，中南财经政法大学 2016 级法律硕士研究生。

① 中国统计信息网：《湖北省 2018 年国民经济和社会发展统计公报》，载 http://www.tjcn.org/tjgb/17hb/35799_2.html，访问时间：2019 年 5 月 23 日。

② 中国统计信息网：《湖北省 2018 年国民经济和社会发展统计公报》，载 http://www.tjcn.org/tjgb/17hb/35799_2.html，访问时间：2019 年 5 月 23 日。

③ 湖北新闻：《2017 年湖北省人口老龄化形势报告出炉》，载 http://wh.bendibao.com/news/2018328/91698.shtm，访问时间：2019 年 7 月 13 日。

④ 中国统计信息网：《湖北省 2018 年国民经济和社会发展统计公报》，载 http://www.tjcn.org/tjgb/17hb/35799_2.html，访问时间：2019 年 5 月 23 日。

二、实证调查情况简介

2016年11月，西南政法大学陈苇教授主持申报的司法部科研项目“我国遗产处理制度系统化构建研究”被批准立项。为给本项目的理论研究和制度研究提供国情资料，必须调查了解当代中国民众的财产继承观念与遗产处理习惯。由于课题组的人力、物力限制，陈苇教授选择我国十省市包括东北部的吉林省、东部的上海市、北部的河北省、中部的湖北省和江西省、南部的广东省和海南省、东南部的福建省、西南部的重庆市和四川省作为被调查地区，然后联系确定了各省市调查组组长，共同组织开展本项目的子课题“当代中国民众财产继承观念与遗产处理习惯实证调查研究”。本次“当代中国湖北省民众财产继承观念与遗产处理习惯实证调查研究”是西南政法大学陈苇教授主持的“当代中国民众财产继承观念与遗产处理习惯实证调查研究”的组成部分之一，由中南财经政法大学孟令志副教授担任湖北省调查组组长。

（一）调查问卷的设计和学生调查员的召集与培训

2016年11月中旬，陈苇教授组织重庆市课题组成员分工合作，设计制作“当代中国民众财产继承观念与遗产处理习惯实证调查”的调查问卷，至同年12月中旬完成了调查问卷的设计工作。然后，陈苇教授把该调查问卷电子版通过邮件发送给参加本次实证调查的十省市调查组组长，以供开展实地调查时十省市被调查地区统一使用。同年12月下旬，根据陈苇教授撰写的“当代中国民众财产继承观念与遗产处理习惯社会调查动员会和培训会”说明书，在中南财经政法大学法学院的大力支持下，我们在该法学院民商法系的学生中召集了126名湖北籍学生志愿者，担任学生调查员。为使每位学生调查员了解本次调查的目的和具体要求，我们分五次对126名湖北籍学生调查员召开“当代中国湖北省民众财产继承观念与遗产处理习惯实证调查动员暨社会调查知识培训会”，会上给参加培训的学生每人发放6份调查问卷，针对问卷的问题，逐一讲解调查要点和具体的调查方法，要求被调查者须男女均等，分为老、中、青（61岁以上、41~60岁、20~40岁）三个年龄段，并且最好具有不同的职业背景，并且要求每名学生调查员利用2017年的寒假期间各自在家乡开展实地社会调查。

（二）实地社会调查的方式

2017年1月至2月的寒假期间，湖北省学生调查员们在各自家乡开展实地社会调查。本次调查主要采取学生调查员“入户问卷调查”和“个人访谈”的方式。

一是入户问卷调查。学生调查员在2017年的寒假期间回到自己的家乡，对当地的民众进行入户问卷调查。每位被调查对象必须符合动员会的条件要求，而且其只能填写一份调查问卷。学生调查员入户后首先向被调查者讲解说明本次调查的目的意义和调查问卷填写的相关问题，采取被调查者自己填写问卷或者学生调查员向被调查者询问后代其填写这两种方式完成问卷的填写。

二是个人访谈。要求采取“一对一”的个人访谈方式，以收集与遗产继承有关的纠纷或案例。本次实地调查，除填写调查问卷外，还要求辅以“一对一”的个人访谈，收集和记录典型的继承纠纷或相关案例的内容。因为，调查问卷涉及客观选择与主观理由两部分内容，采取“一对一”的个人访谈方式，可以避免被调查者受到他人的影响，便于客观深入地了解被调查民众的真实想法。

（三）调查问卷数据的录入、统计汇总、复核与撰写调查研究报告

2017 年 3 月开学后，湖北省调查组教师组织统一回收调查问卷与典型案例的访谈记录，然后组织学生统计员对调查问卷进行数据统计工作。学生调查员本次实地调查实际发放调查问卷 672 份，剔除无效问卷后，收回有效问卷为 659 份，有效问卷率达 98.07%。随后，根据有效问卷进行调查数据的录入、制作统计汇总表，并且进行统计汇总数据的复核。孟令志副教授组织 13 位研究生，采取人工统计的方式进行数据录入统计，经过对统计数据汇总表的三次认真复核，于 2017 年 4 月底，完成了《〈当代中国民众财产继承观念与遗产处理习惯实证调查问卷〉湖北省民众实证调查统计数据汇总表》的定稿。我们在此需要特别说明，关于各项调查问题之统计人数的合计，凡单选题的人数合计均为 100%，均合计在统计表中；凡多选题的人数合计均超过 100%，故不予进行合计的统计。本调查研究就是以此次调查统计数据汇总表为基础资料进行分析和研究而撰写。在此，特向所有参与此次调查活动的老师和同学表示衷心感谢！①

2017 年 4 月陈苇教授拟定了“当代中国民众财产继承观念与遗产处理习惯实证调查研究的写作提纲和写作要求”。2017 年 5 月起，我们根据此写作提纲和写作要求进入参考文献资料的收集和调查报告的写作和修改阶段。本章“当代中国湖北省民众财产继承观念与遗产处理习惯实证调查研究”由中南财经政法大学孟令志副教授与贾艳艳、李想、王传印、元雨、彭锦硕士研究生共同撰写初稿至第五稿，其间，根据陈苇教授对初稿至第五稿的历次修改意见和中期评审专家意见，对稿件进行了相应的多次修改和补充，最后向课题负责人陈苇教授交稿。2019 年 1 月，陈苇教授继续对湖北省调查研究报告进行审阅和修改补充，然后组织重庆市调查组博士生对湖北省调查研究报告统一进行了三次修改补充，最终于 2019 年 6 月完成定稿。

三、被调查对象的基本情况

本次调查的对象为湖北省常住人口，我们根据 659 份有效问卷，以下对 659 名被调查者的性别、年龄和职业情况统计如下：

（一）被调查者的性别情况

表 6-1　被调查者的性别情况统计

性别	人数	比例
男	333	50.53%
女	326	49.47%
合计	659	100%

关于被调查者的性别情况，调查统计数据显示，659 位被调查者中，男性有 333 人（占 50.53%）；女性有 326 人（占 49.47%）。男女两性的比例大体平衡。

① 参与湖北省民众财产继承观念和遗产处理习惯的实地调查以及调查数据统计汇总等工作的师生名单，详见“鸣谢”。

（二）被调查者的年龄情况

表 6-2　被调查者的年龄情况统计

年龄	人数	比例
20~30 岁	190	28.83%
31~40 岁	113	17.15%
41~50 岁	151	22.91%
51~60 岁	73	11.08%
61~70 岁	74	11.23%
71 岁以上	58	8.80%
合计	659	100%

关于被调查者的年龄情况，调查统计数据显示，659 位被调查者中，青年人（20~40 岁）有 303 人（占 45.98%）；中年人（41~60 岁）有 224 人（占 33.99%）；老年人（61 岁以上）有 132 人（占 20.03%）。可见，在被调查者中，青年人最多占四成半，其次是中年人占三成以上，而老年被调查者相对较少，只占二成。即被调查者以中青年为主体，合计占近八成（79.97%）。

（三）被调查者的职业情况

表 6-3　被调查者的职业情况统计

职业	人数	比例
农民	99	15.02%
工人	47	7.13%
经商	52	7.89%
公务员及企事业单位人员	177	26.86%
其他职业（打工等不固定职业）	284	43.10%
合计	659	100%

关于被调查者的职业情况，调查统计数据显示，659 位被调查者中，职业为农民的有 99 人（占 15.02%）；工人有 47 人（占 7.13%）；经商的有 52 人（占 7.89%）；公务员及企事业单位人员有 177 人（占 26.86%）；其他职业（打工等不固定职业）有 284 人（占 43.10%）。

综上，本次被调查者的性别比基本持平，老、中、青各年龄段的均有，以中青年为主体占近八成，他们的职业涉及广泛，基本上能够反映不同性别、年龄和职业被调查者的财产继承观念和遗产处理习惯。

第二节　当代中国湖北省民众财产继承观念与遗产处理习惯实证调查的数据统计情况

一、遗产范围界定之调查数据统计情况

关于遗产范围界定之调查数据统计，我们主要从遗产的种类和被继承人生前特种赠与财产的归扣，这两个方面进行调查数据的统计情况汇总分析。

（一）遗产的种类

问题【一、（一）】“2016 年 2 月某甲因车祸死亡，经清理某甲个人名下的遗物如下，请问哪些属于某甲的遗产：A. 住房一套；B. 小汽车一辆；C. 家庭日常生活用品若干；D. 存款 10 万元；E. 股票 10 万元；F. 某甲以其姓名注册的邮箱、QQ 账号等；G. 单位出租给某甲的午休住房一间；H. 某甲向某公司购货的欠款 5 万元；I. 某甲因交通事故死亡获得 50 万元的赔偿金。（多选）”

表 6-4　属于遗产种类的民众观念情况统计（多选）

选项	人数	比例
A. 住房一套	648	98. 33%
B. 小汽车一辆	626	94. 99%
C. 家庭日常生活用品若干	434	65. 86%
D. 存款 10 万元	623	94. 54%
E. 股票 10 万元	558	84. 67%
F. 某甲以其姓名注册的邮箱、QQ 账号等	211	32. 02%
G. 单位出租给某甲的午休住房一间	78	11. 84%
H. 某甲向某公司购货的欠款 5 万元	378	57. 36%
I. 某甲因交通事故死亡获得 50 万元赔偿金	467	70. 86%

关于属于遗产种类的民众观念，统计数据显示，在被调查者中，（1）选择 A、B、D、E、G 项，有八成至九成以上的人认为“住房”（98. 33%）、“小汽车”（94. 99%）、“存款”（94. 54%）、“股票”（84. 67%）属于遗产；认为“单位出租给某甲的午休住房”不属于遗产的，占近九成（88. 16%）①；（2）选择 C、H、I 两项，有五成至七成以上的人认为“家庭日常生活用品若干”（65. 86%）、“欠债”（57. 36%）和“交通事故死亡赔偿金”（70. 86%）属于遗产；（3）有三成以上（32. 02%）的人认为 F 项“某甲以其姓名注册的邮箱、QQ 账号等”属于遗产。

① 认为“单位出租给某甲的午休住房”属于遗产的仅占 11. 84%，即有近九成（88. 16%）的被调查者认为其不属于遗产。

（二）被继承人生前特种赠与财产的归扣

1. 被继承人生前特种赠与财产是否应归入遗产范围的民众观念情况统计

问题【一、（二）1.】“张老汉有三个儿子，在10年前大儿子甲结婚时，张老汉给其资助购买婚房的现金20万元；二儿子乙一直未结婚，但5年前在其开办豆腐坊时，张老汉资助其营业资金10万元。在2年前小儿子丙结婚时，张老汉为其购买一套价值30万元的房屋（产权登记在小儿子丙名下）；2016年1月张老汉去世时遗留有个人所有的住房一套和50万元存款。据此，问卷列出了几种可能的遗产供选择：A. 张老汉生前给三个儿子不同资助的财产与死亡时其遗留的住房、存款，均应当合并计算为遗产；B. 张老汉去世时遗留的个人所有的住房和50万元存款，才可以计算为遗产；C. 其他。（单选）”

表6-5 被继承人生前特种赠与财产是否应归入遗产范围的民众观念情况统计（单选）

选项	人数	比例
A. 张老汉生前给三个儿子不同资助的财产与死亡时其遗留的住房、存款，均应当合并计算为遗产	158	23.98%
B. 张老汉去世时遗留的个人所有的住房和50万元存款，才可以计算为遗产	488	74.05%
C. 其他	13	1.97%
合计	659	100%

关于被继承人生前特种赠与财产是否应归入遗产范围的民众观念，调查统计数据显示，在659名被调查者中，（1）选择B项被继承人去世时遗留的个人财产财才可算作遗产，不包括被继承人生前对子女的特种赠与财产的，占近七成半（74.05%）；（2）选择A项被继承人生前资助子女的财产与死亡时其遗留的住房、存款，均应当合并计算为遗产的，占二成以上（23.98%）。

2. 归扣遗产价值计算时间的民众观念情况统计

问题【一、（二）2.】“如果上述答案您选A，请问张老汉为小儿子丙买房的价值应该按何时计算？A. 买房时；B. 张老汉去世时；C. 实际分割遗产时；D. 其他。（单选）”

表6-6 归扣遗产的价值计算时间的民众观念情况统计（单选）

选项	人数	比例
A. 买房时	51	32.28%
B. 张老汉去世时	32	20.25%
C. 实际分割遗产时	75	47.47%
D. 其他	0	0
合计	158	100%

关于归扣遗产价值的计算时间的民众观念，调查统计数据显示，在回答该问题的158名被调查者中，（1）选择C项应按实际分割遗产时计算的，占近五成（47.47%）；（2）选择A项应按购置该财产时计算的，占三成以上（32.28%）；（3）选择B项应按被继承人去世时计算的，占二成（20.25%）。即认为应按实际分割遗产时计算归扣遗产价值的占比居第一位。

3. 生前特种赠与财产是否归扣纳入遗产范围的民间习惯情况统计

问题【一、（二）3.】“在您所在的地区，如果发生上述张老汉生前给三个儿子不同资助财产的情况，在继承遗产时这些资助财产是否被合计到遗产范围内？A. 是；B. 不是。（单选）”

表6-7　生前特种赠与财产是否归扣纳入遗产范围的民间习惯情况统计（单选）

选项	人数	比例
A. 是	188	28.79%
B. 不是	465	71.21%
合计	653	100%

关于生前特种赠与财产是否归扣纳入遗产范围的民间习惯，调查统计数据显示，回答该问题的653名被调查者所在地区的继承习惯是：（1）B项不是，即没有归扣习惯的占七成以上（71.21%）；（2）A项是，即有归扣习惯的占近三成（28.79%）。

4. 生前特种赠与财产不归扣纳入遗产情况下的分配方式之民间习惯与理由情况统计

问题【一、（二）4.】“上一题如果您选择B项即这些资助财产不是被合计到遗产范围内，三个儿子是如何分配父亲张老汉的遗产的？A. 平均分配；B. 乙应该适当多分；C. 其他。（单选）理由是什么？”

（1）生前特种赠与财产不归扣纳入遗产的分配方式之民间习惯情况统计。

表6-8　生前特种赠与财产不归扣纳入遗产的分配方式之民间习惯情况统计（单选）

选项	人数	比例
A. 平均分配	270	58.06%
B. 乙应当适当多分	163	35.06%
C. 其他	32	6.88%
合计	465	100%

关于被继承人生前对子女特种赠与财产不归扣纳入遗产的分配方式的民间习惯，调查统计数据显示，填写该问题的465名被调查者所在地区的继承习惯是：①A项平均分配的，占近六成（58.06%）；②B项乙应当适当多分的，占三成半（35.06%）。

（2）生前特种赠与财产不归扣纳入遗产的分配方式的民间习惯之理由情况统计。

表 6-9　生前特种赠与财产不归扣纳入遗产的分配方式民间习惯之理由情况统计

项目	理由	人数	比例
A. 平均分配	死后平均分配所留遗产，有利于遗产的分割	111	43.53%
B. 乙应当适当多分	因为张老汉生前给乙的财产较少，在其死后乙应多分些，这体现公平原则	98	38.43%
	没结婚的多分点	5	1.96%
C. 其他	遗嘱决定	8	3.14%
	风俗习惯	5	1.96%
	赡养情况	10	3.92%
	继承人经济情况	10	3.92%
	协商解决	8	3.14%
合计		255	100%

关于生前特种赠与财产不归扣纳入遗产的分配方式之理由，调查统计数据显示，在填写理由的255名被调查者中，①A项平均分配的理由是，死后平均分配所留遗产，有利于遗产分割的，占四成以上（43.53%）；②B项乙应当适当多分的理由是，张老汉生前给乙的财产较少，在其死后乙应多分些，这体现公平原则或没结婚的继承人应多分些的，合计占四成（40.39%）；③还有不到一成的人认为应根据遗嘱决定（3.14%）、继承人经济情况（3.92%）决定或协商解决（3.14%）等。

二、继承开始的通知和公告之调查数据统计情况

关于继承开始的通知和公告之调查数据统计，我们主要从继承开始的通知和公告的主体、继承开始的通知和公告的方式、继承开始的通知和公告的期间，这三个方面进行调查数据的统计情况汇总分析。

（一）继承开始的通知和公告的主体

问题【二、（一）】“被继承人死亡后，在您所在地区一般由下列哪些人通知涉及遗产分配的相关人员？A. 知道被继承人死亡的继承人；B. 保管遗产的继承人；C. 知道被继承人死亡的单位、村（居）委会；D. 处理被继承人死亡事件的机构，如公安交警部门；E. 其他。（多选）”

表 6-10　继承开始的通知和公告主体的民间习惯情况统计（多选）

选项	人数	比例
A. 知道被继承人死亡的继承人	472	71.62%
B. 保管遗产的继承人	432	65.55%
C. 知道被继承人死亡的单位、村（居）委会	312	47.34%

续表

选项	人数	比例
D. 处理被继承人死亡事件的机构，如公安交警部门	250	37.94%
E. 其他	25	3.79%

关于继承开始的通知和公告主体的民间习惯，调查统计数据显示，被调查者所在地区的民间习惯是：（1）A、B 两项由继承人作为主体的，各占六成至七成以上，具体包括：知道被继承人死亡的继承人（71.62%）和保管遗产的继承人（65.55%）；（2）C 项由知道被继承人死亡的单位、村（居）委会作为主体的，占近五成（47.34%）；（3）D 项由处理被继承人死亡事件的机构作为主体的，占近四成（37.94%）。

（二）继承开始的通知和公告的方式

问题【二、（二）】“被继承人死亡后，您所在地区的人们一般采取以下哪些方式通知涉及遗产处理的相关人员？A. 口头、电话、微信等方式通知；B. 信件、告知函等书面通知；C. 在报纸、电视、网络等平台上发布被继承人死亡的公告；D. 在被继承人所在地的村（居）委会公告栏公告；E. 申请人民法院以公告程序进行公告；F. 其他。（多选）”

表 6-11 继承开始的通知和公告方式的民间习惯情况统计（多选）

选项	人数	比例
A. 口头、电话、微信等方式通知	438	66.46%
B. 信件、告知函等书面通知	359	54.48%
C. 在报纸、电视、网络等平台上发布被继承人死亡的公告	169	25.64%
D. 在被继承人所在地的村（居）委会公告栏公告	379	57.51%
E. 申请人民法院以公告程序进行公告	196	29.74%
F. 其他	23	3.49%

关于继承开始的通知和公告方式的民间习惯，调查统计数据显示，被调查者所在地区的民间习惯是：（1）A、B 两项，分别由口头、电话、微信等通知（66.46%）和信件、告知函等书面通知（54.48%）的，各占五成至六成以上；（2）C、D、E 三项，分别在报纸、电视、网络等平台上发布被继承人死亡的公告（25.64%）、在被继承人所在地的村（居）委会公告栏公告（57.51%）和申请人民法院以公告程序进行公告（29.74%）的，各占二成至五成以上。

（三）继承开始的通知和公告的期间

问题【二、（三）】“您认为，通知人应该在被继承人死亡后多少天内发出通知？A. 3 日；B. 7 日；C. 15 日；D. 30 日；E. 其他。（单选）”

表 6-12　继承开始的通知和公告期间的民众观念情况统计（单选）

选项	人数	比例
A. 3 日	229	34.75%
B. 7 日	189	28.68%
C. 15 日	115	17.45%
D. 30 日	101	15.33%
E. 其他	25	3.79%
合计	659	100%

关于继承开始的通知和公告期间的民众观念，调查统计数据显示，在 659 名被调查者中，（1）选择 A、B 两项应在 7 日以内发出的，合计占六成以上（63.43%）；（2）选择 C 项应在 15 日以内发出的，占近二成（17.45%）；（3）选择 D 项应在 30 日以内发出的，仅占一成半（15.33%）。

三、遗产管理之调查数据统计情况

关于遗产管理之调查数据统计，我们主要从遗产管理人的确定、遗产管理人的职责与报酬、遗产管理人的损害赔偿责任，这三个方面进行调查数据的统计情况汇总分析。

（一）遗产管理人的确定

问题【三、（一）】“您所在地区人们处理遗产继承时，一般由谁清点和管理遗产？A. 死者的法定继承人：配偶、子女、父母、兄弟姐妹、孙子女或外孙子女、祖父母或外祖父母；B. 死者的儿媳或女婿；C. 死者家族中的德高望重者；D. 死者的其他亲戚朋友；E. 死者所在的单位或村/居委会；F. 其他。（多选）理由是什么？”

1. 关于遗产管理人的确定的民间习惯情况统计

（1）遗产管理人的确定的民间习惯情况统计。

表 6-13　遗产管理人的确定的民间习惯情况统计（多选）

选项	人数	比例
A. 死者的法定继承人	583	88.47%
B. 死者的儿媳或女婿	182	27.62%
C. 死者家族中的德高望重者	293	44.46%
D. 死者的其他亲戚朋友	127	19.27%
E. 死者所在的单位或村/居委会	210	31.87%
F. 其他	26	3.95%

关于遗产管理人的确定的民间习惯，调查统计数据显示，被调查者所在地区的民间习惯是：①A 项由死者的法定继承人作为遗产管理人的，占近九成（88.47%）；②B、C、

D、E 四项，分别由死者的儿媳或女婿（27.62%）、死者家族中的德高望重者（44.46%）、死者的其他亲戚朋友（19.27%）和死者所在的单位或村/居委会（31.87%）作为遗产管理人的，各占近二成至四成以上。

（2）法定继承人担任遗产管理人的民间习惯情况统计。

表 6-14　法定继承人担任遗产管理人的民间习惯情况统计（多选）

选项	人数	比例
A. 配偶	380	65.18%
B. 子女	370	63.46%
C. 父母	347	59.52%
D. 兄弟姐妹	221	37.91%
E. 孙子女或者外孙子女	120	20.58%
F. 祖父母或者外祖父母	92	15.78%

关于法定继承人担任遗产管理人的民间习惯，调查统计数据显示，回答该问题的 583 名被调查者所在地区的民间习惯是：①A、B、C 三项，分别由配偶（65.18%）、子女（63.46%）、父母（59.52%）担任遗产管理人的，各占近六成至六成以上；②D、E、F 三项，分别由兄弟姐妹（37.91%）、孙子女或者外孙子女（20.58%）、祖父母或者外祖父母（15.78%）担任遗产管理人的，各占一成半至三成以上。

2. 关于遗产管理人的确定的民间习惯之理由情况统计

表 6-15　遗产管理人的确定的民间习惯之理由情况统计

项目	人数	比例
A. 由遗产继承人来担任，便于清点和妥善管理遗产	132	60.27%
B. 由遗产继承人之外的人或组织来担任，可以防止遗产被隐藏、转移，有利于保护遗产相关人的合法权益	52	23.74%
C. 可以自由选择管理人	10	4.57%
D. 风俗习惯	6	2.74%
E. 德高望重的亲戚，可以使人信服	19	8.68%
合计	219	100%

关于遗产管理人的确定的民间习惯之理由，调查统计数据显示，219 名被调查者填写了选择理由，（1）认为应由遗产继承人来担任管理人的理由是，A 项便于清点和妥善管理遗产的，占六成（60.27%）；（2）认为应由遗产继承人之外的人或组织来担任管理人的理由是，B 项防止遗产被隐藏、转移，这有利于保护遗产相关人合法权益的，占二成以上（23.74%）；（3）还有不到一成的人填写了 E 项由德高望重的亲戚担任遗产管理人，可以使人信服（8.68%）或 D 项根据风俗习惯处理（2.74%）等。

(二) 遗产管理人的职责与报酬

1. 遗产管理人职责的民众观念情况统计

问题【三、(二)1.】"您认为，遗产管理人的管理职责有哪些？A. 清查遗产，制作遗产清单；B. 妥善保管遗产；C. 查明被继承人生前的债权和债务，积极地追讨债权或清偿债务；D. 查明被继承人是否留有遗嘱，并且确定遗嘱是否真实合法；E. 可以原告或被告的身份参加因遗产引起的诉讼；F. 定期制作遗产管理报告，向继承人报告遗产管理的情况；G. 其他。(多选)"

表 6-16　遗产管理人职责的民众观念情况统计（多选）

选项	人数	比例
A. 清查遗产，制作遗产清单	605	91.81%
B. 妥善保管遗产	620	94.08%
C. 查明被继承人生前的债权和债务，积极地追讨债权或清偿债务	483	73.29%
D. 查明被继承人是否留有遗嘱，并且确定遗嘱是否真实合法	353	53.57%
E. 可以原告或被告的身份参加因遗产引起的诉讼	429	65.10%
F. 定期制作遗产管理报告，向继承人报告遗产管理的情况	390	59.18%
G. 其他	25	3.79%

关于遗产管理人职责的民众观念，调查统计数据显示，在被调查者中，选择 A、B、C、D、E、F 六项，遗产管理人的职责包括"清查遗产，制作遗产清单"（91.81%）、"妥善保管遗产"（94.08%）、"查明被继承人生前的债权和债务，积极地追讨债权或清偿债务"（73.29%）、"查明被继承人是否留有遗嘱，并且确定遗嘱是否真实合法"（53.57%）、"可以原告或被告的身份参加因遗产引起的诉讼"（65.10%）和"定期制作遗产管理报告，向继承人报告遗产管理的情况"（59.18%）的，各占五成至九成以上。

2. 遗产管理人是否有权取得报酬的民间习惯与理由情况统计

问题【三、(二)2.】"您所在地区，负责管理遗产的人是否可以获得报酬？A. 继承人担任遗产管理人的，不能请求给付报酬；B. 法院指定的遗产管理人，有权请求给付报酬；C. 继承人选任的第三人作为遗产管理人，是否给付报酬，应当由继承人决定；D. 继承人选任的第三人作为遗产管理人，一律有权请求给付报酬；E. 其他。(多选) 理由是什么？"

(1) 遗产管理人是否有权取得报酬的民间习惯情况统计。

表 6-17　遗产管理人是否有权取得报酬的民间习惯情况统计（多选）

选项	人数	比例
A. 继承人担任遗产管理人的，不能请求给付报酬	331	50.23%
B. 法院指定的遗产管理人，有权请求给付报酬	356	54.02%

续表

选项	人数	比例
C. 继承人选任的第三人作为遗产管理人，是否给付报酬，应当由继承人决定	336	50.97%
D. 继承人选任的第三人作为遗产管理人，一律有权请求给付报酬	236	35.81%
E. 其他	26	3.94%

关于遗产管理人是否有权取得报酬的民间习惯，调查统计数据显示，被调查者所在地区的民间习惯是：①A 项继承人担任的遗产管理人，五成（50.23%）的地区有管理人不能请求给付报酬的习惯；②B 项法院指定的遗产管理人，近五成半（54.02%）的地区有可以请求给付报酬的习惯；③C、D 两项继承人选任的第三人作为遗产管理人，其中，五成（50.98%）的地区有是否给付报酬应当由继承人决定的习惯；三成半（35.81%）的地区有一律有权请求给付报酬的习惯。

（2）遗产管理人是否有权取得报酬的民间习惯之理由情况统计。

表 6-18　遗产管理人是否有权取得报酬的民间习惯之理由情况统计

项目	人数	比例
A. 遗产管理人多数情况下与被继承人关系密切，具有亲情关系，同时，遗产管理人又继承遗产，因此，管理遗产不需要报酬	86	44.33%
B. 遗产管理人为管理遗产付出了自己的劳动，占用了自己的时间，应该给予一定的费用	98	50.52%
C. 视情况而定，更能符合实际情况	10	5.15%
合计	194	100%

关于遗产管理人是否有权取得报酬的民间习惯之理由，调查统计数据显示，有 194 名被调查者填写了选择理由，①认为其有权取得报酬的理由是，B 项遗产管理人为管理遗产付出了自己的劳动和时间，应该给予一定费用的，占五成（50.52%）；②认为其无权取得报酬的理由是，A 项遗产管理人多数情况下与被继承人关系密切，具有亲情关系，同时，遗产管理人又继承遗产，因此管理遗产不需要报酬的，占近四成半（44.33%）；③还有不到一成（5.15%）的人填写了视情况而定，这更能符合实际情况等理由。

（三）遗产管理人的损害赔偿责任

问题【三、（三）】“在您所在地区，负责管理遗产的人对因其过错造成较大的财产损失，是否承担赔偿责任？A. 凡有故意或重大过失的，才承担损害赔偿责任；B. 无论是故意或重大过失或一般轻过失的，都要承担损害赔偿责任；C. 其他。（单选）”

表 6-19 遗产管理人的损害赔偿责任之民间习惯情况统计（单选）

选项	人数	比例
A. 凡有故意或重大过失的，才承担损害赔偿责任	363	55.67%
B. 无论是故意或重大过失或一般轻过失的，都要承担损害赔偿责任	276	42.34%
C. 其他	13	1.99%
合计	652	100%

关于遗产管理人的损害赔偿责任之民间习惯，调查统计数据显示，回答该问题652名被调查者所在地区的民间习惯是：（1）A 项有故意或重大过失，才承担损害赔偿责任的，占五成半（55.67%）；（2）B 项无论有故意、重大过失或一般轻过失，都要承担损害赔偿责任的，占四成以上（42.34%）。

四、法定继承之调查数据统计情况

关于法定继承之调查数据统计，我们主要从法定继承人的范围和顺序、配偶与血亲继承人的法定应继份、配偶对遗产中家庭住房的先取权和终生使用权、后顺序特殊法定继承人对遗产中原使用的住房及日常生活用品的终生使用权、尽了主要赡养义务的丧偶儿媳或女婿的遗产分配方式，这五个方面进行调查数据的统计情况汇总分析。

（一）法定继承人的范围与顺序

1. 法定继承人范围与顺序的民众观念情况统计

问题【四、（一）1.】“下列亲属，您认为哪些应当作为法定继承人？他们各自的继承顺序如何？请根据您认为适当的先后顺序填写数字：1.2.3.……例如，父母（1）；子女（2）；祖父母、外祖父母（3）。如果您认为应当在同一顺序的人，可以填写相同的数字。例如，配偶（1）；父母（1）；子女（1）；祖父母、外祖父母（1）。”

配偶（ ）	父母（ ）	儿子（ ）女儿（ ）
孙子女（ ）外孙子女（ ）	祖父母（ ）外祖父母（ ）	兄弟（ ）姐妹（ ）
侄子女（ ）外甥子女（ ）	伯叔姑舅姨（ ）	堂兄弟姐妹（ ）
表兄弟姐妹（ ）	其他亲属（称谓）（ ）	其他亲属（称谓）（ ）

表 6-20 法定继承人范围与顺序民众观念情况统计（多选）

亲属名称	第一顺序		第二顺序		第三顺序		第四顺序		第四顺序以上	
	人数	比例	人数	比例	人数	比例	人数	比例	人数	比例
配偶	601	91.20%	33	5.01%	13	1.97%	1	0.15%	1	0.15%
父母	432	65.55%	163	24.73%	50	7.59%	14	2.12%	0	0.00%
子	484	73.44%	114	17.30%	41	6.22%	3	0.46%	0	0.00%

续表

亲属名称	第一顺序		第二顺序		第三顺序		第四顺序		第四顺序以上	
	人数	比例	人数	比例	人数	比例	人数	比例	人数	比例
女	451	68.44%	122	18.51%	43	6.53%	17	2.58%	2	0.30%
孙子女	23	3.49%	323	49.01%	136	20.64%	64	9.71%	33	5.01%
外孙子女	20	3.03%	285	43.25%	139	21.09%	69	10.47%	52	7.89%
祖父母	14	2.12%	312	47.34%	133	20.18%	54	8.19%	54	8.19%
外祖父母	11	1.67%	270	40.97%	149	22.61%	60	9.10%	57	8.65%
兄弟	12	1.82%	308	46.74%	131	19.88%	59	8.95%	72	10.93%
姐妹	11	1.67%	293	44.46%	130	19.73%	62	9.41%	72	10.93%
侄子女	0	0.00%	27	4.10%	207	31.41%	93	14.11%	73	11.08%
外甥子女	0	0.00%	26	3.95%	212	32.17%	95	14.42%	98	14.87%
伯叔姑	0	0.00%	18	2.73%	298	45.22%	96	14.57%	101	15.33%
舅姨	0	0.00%	17	2.58%	186	28.22%	93	14.11%	103	15.63%
堂兄弟	0	0.00%	26	3.95%	185	28.07%	90	13.66%	110	16.69%
堂姐妹	0	0.00%	25	3.79%	183	27.77%	88	13.35%	110	16.69%
表兄弟	0	0.00%	20	3.03%	129	19.58%	115	17.45%	120	18.21%
表姐妹	0	0.00%	19	2.88%	127	19.27%	115	17.45%	118	17.91%

关于法定继承人范围与顺序的民众观念，各以被调查者选择占比最高的顺序作为统计依据，调查统计数据显示，被调查者认可的法定继承人的范围与顺序是：第一顺序为配偶（91.20%）、父母（65.55%）、子（73.44%）、女（68.44%）；第二顺序为孙子女（49.01%）、外孙子女（43.25%）、祖父母（47.34%）、外祖父母（40.97%）、兄弟（46.74%）、姐妹（44.46%）；第三顺序为侄子女（31.41%）、外甥子女（32.17%）、伯叔姑（45.22%）、舅姨（28.22%）、堂兄弟（28.07%）、堂姐妹（27.77%）、表兄弟（19.58%）、表姐妹（19.27%）。

2. 配偶与血亲继承人顺序的民众观念情况统计

问题【四、（一）2.】“以下三种法定继承人的范围和顺序，您认为哪一个更为适当？（单选）”

A	B	C
第一顺序：子女	第一顺序：子女	第一顺序：配偶、子女、父母
第二顺序：父母	第二顺序：父母	第二顺序：兄弟姐妹、祖父母、外祖父母

续表

A	B	C
第三顺序：兄弟姐妹、祖父母、外祖父母 兄弟姐妹的子女（侄子女、外甥子女为代位继承人）	第三顺序：兄弟姐妹、祖父母、外祖父母 兄弟姐妹的子女（侄子女、外甥子女为代位继承人）	第三顺序：侄子女、外甥子女
配偶无固定顺序，能够参加第一顺序、第二顺序、第三个顺序的继承	配偶无固定顺序，能够参第一顺序、第二顺序的继承	配偶有固定顺序，只能参与第一顺序的继承

表6-21　配偶与血亲继承人顺序的民众观念情况统计（单选）

选项	人数	比例
A. 配偶无固定顺序，可以参与第一、第二、第三顺序继承	96	14.77%
B. 配偶无固定顺序，可以参与第一、第二顺序继承	90	13.85%
C. 配偶固定第一顺序	464	71.38%
合计	650	100%

关于配偶与血亲继承人顺序的民众观念，调查统计数据显示，在填写本问题的650名被调查者中，（1）选择C项第一继承顺序为配偶、子女、父母，配偶为固定的第一顺序继承人的，占七成以上（71.38%）；（2）选择A、B两项第一顺序为子女，第二顺序为父母，第三顺序为兄弟姐妹、祖父母、外祖父母、兄弟姐妹的子女，配偶为无固定继承顺序继承人，可以参与第一、第二（或第三）顺序继承的，合计占近三成（28.62%）。

（二）配偶与血亲继承人的法定应继份

问题【四、（二）】“配偶与血亲继承人共同继承各取得遗产的份额，您认为以下哪一项更为适当？（单选）”

A. 配偶无固定继承顺序	B. 配偶无固定继承顺序	C. 配偶有固定继承顺序	D. 其他
配偶与第一顺序的子女共同继承时，其取得遗产的一半。另一半由子女按人数平均继承	配偶与第一顺序的子女共同继承时，其取得遗产的一半，另一半由子女按人数平均继承	第一顺序继承人为配偶、子女、父母，共同继承时按人数均分遗产	
配偶与第二顺序的父母共同继承时，其取得遗产的三分之二。另外三分之一由父母平均继承	配偶与第二顺序的父母共同继承时，其取得遗产的三分之二，另外三分之一由父母平均继承	无第一顺序血亲继承人时，配偶继承全部遗产	

续表

A. 配偶无固定继承顺序	B. 配偶无固定继承顺序	C. 配偶有固定继承顺序	D. 其他
配偶与第三顺序的兄弟姐妹、祖父母和外祖父母共同继承时，其取得遗产的四分之三。另外四分之一由兄弟姐妹、祖父母、外祖父母，按人数平均继承	无第一、第二顺序血亲继承人时，配偶继承全部遗产		
无上述三个顺序血亲继承人时，配偶取得全部遗产			

表 6-22　配偶与血亲继承人的法定应继份的民众观念情况统计（单选）

选项	人数	比例
A. 配偶无固定继承顺序，参与前三顺序继承，并取得不同份额；无上述三个顺序血亲继承人时，配偶取得全部遗产	234	36.00%
B. 配偶无固定继承顺序，参与前二顺序继承，并取得不同份额；无第一、第二顺序血亲继承人时，配偶继承全部遗产	121	18.62%
C. 配偶有固定继承顺序，与第一顺序继承人共同继承并均分遗产	290	44.62%
D. 其他	5	0.76%
合计	650	100%

关于配偶与血亲继承人法定应继份的民众观念，调查统计数据显示，在回答该问题的650名被调查者中，（1）选择A、B两项配偶应无固定继承顺序的，参与前三顺序或前二顺序继承并取得不同份额的，合计占五成以上（54.62%）；（2）选择C项配偶应有固定继承顺序，与第一顺序继承人共同继承并均分遗产的，占近四成半（44.62%）。

（三）配偶对遗产中家庭住房的先取权与终生使用权

1. 配偶对遗产中家庭住房的先取权与终生使用权的民间习惯情况统计

问题【四、（三）1.】"甲乙是夫妻，育有一子丙。甲因病去世时留下的遗产包括价值50万元住房一套（原由甲乙夫妻共同居住，丙已结婚分家另过）、价值10万元小汽车一辆和20万元存款。请问：如果上述情况发生在您所在地区，被继承人甲的妻子乙是否可以优先继承这套房屋（配偶优先权）？A. 是；B. 否。（单选）"

表 6-23　配偶对遗产中家庭住房的先取权与终生使用权的民间习惯情况统计（单选）

选项	人数	比例
A. 是	570	87.29%
B. 否	83	12.71%

续表

选项	人数	比例
合计	653	100%

关于配偶对遗产中家庭住房的先取权与终生使用权的民间习惯，调查统计数据显示，回答该问题的653名被调查者所在地区的继承习惯是：（1）A项是，即有该习惯的，占近九成（87.29%）；（2）B项否，即无此习惯的，占一成以上（12.71%）。

2. 配偶对遗产中家庭住房的先取与终生使用是否付费的民间习惯及理由情况统计

问题【四、（三）2.】“如果甲的妻子乙可以优先继承这套房屋，但该住房的价值超过其应当继承的遗产份额40万元，在您所在地区是否按照下列情况处理的？A. 乙有权继承该住房，且无须向另一法定继承人丙进行补偿。B. 如果乙有经济补偿能力，则应当向另一法定继承人丙适当进行补偿。C. 其他。（单选）理由是什么？”

（1）配偶对遗产中家庭住房的先取与终生使用是否付费的民间习惯情况统计。

表6-24　配偶对遗产中家庭住房的先取与终生使用是否付费的民间习惯情况统计（单选）

选项	人数	比例
A. 乙有权继承该住房，且无须向其他共同应召继承人丙进行补偿	246	37.33%
B. 如果乙有经济补偿能力，则应当向其他共同应召继承人丙适当进行补偿	357	54.17%
C. 其他	56	8.50%
合计	659	100%

关于配偶对遗产中家庭住房的先取与终生使用是否付费的民间习惯，调查统计数据显示，659名被调查者所在地区的继承习惯是：①B项适当补偿的，占近五成半（54.17%）；②A项无须进行补偿的，占近四成（37.33%），也就是说，如配偶无经济补偿能力的，可不予补偿而终生使用此房屋。

（2）配偶对遗产中家庭住房的先取与终生使用是否付费的民间习惯之理由情况统计。

表6-25　配偶对遗产中家庭住房的先取与终生使用是否付费的民间习惯之理由情况统计

项目	人数	百分比
A. 首先保证乙有居住之所，同时，丙是乙的儿子，将来乙的遗产也会由丙来继承，所以，乙无须向丙进行补偿	92	40.89%
B. 由乙向丙进行补偿，这体现公平精神	110	48.89%
C. 丙成家后无须住房	9	4.00%
D. 配偶优先继承	6	2.67%

续表

项目	人数	百分比
E. 风俗习惯	8	3.56%
合计	225	100%

关于配偶对遗产中家庭住房的先取与终生使用是否付费的民间习惯之理由，调查统计数据显示，填写理由的225名被调查者中，①认为乙应当向丙进行补偿的理由是，B项这体现公平精神的，占近五成（48.89%）；②认为乙无须向丙进行补偿的理由是，A项应首先保证配偶乙有居住之所，同时丙是乙的儿子，将来乙的遗产也会由丙来继承，所以无须补偿的，占四成（40.89%）；③还有不到一成的人填写了D项配偶应优先继承（2.67%）或E项依风俗习惯处理（3.56%）等理由。

（四）后顺序特殊法定继承人对遗产中原使用的住房及日常生活用品的终生使用权

关于后顺序特殊法定继承人对遗产中原使用的住房及日常生活用品的终生使用权，也可称为后顺序特殊法定继承人对特殊遗产的终生使用权。

1. 后顺序特殊法定继承人对遗产中原使用的住房及日常生活用品的终生使用权之民间习惯情况统计

问题【四、（四）1.】“某甲死亡时留下若干遗产，其中包括一套三室一厅的住房（其中的一间房屋一直由某甲的祖父居住）。由于某甲的祖父属于后顺序继承人而不能参加继承，遗产全部由某甲的第一顺序继承人配偶及其子女等继承。请问：在您所在的地区，如果发生了上述情况，有哪些下列处理方式？某甲的祖父对该供其居住的房屋，是否可以继续居住？A. 是；B. 否。（单选）”

表6-26 后顺序特殊法定继承人对特殊遗产的终生使用权之民间习惯情况统计（单选）

选项	人数	比例
A. 是	603	92.63%
B. 否	48	7.37%
合计	651	100%

关于后顺序特殊法定继承人对特殊遗产的终生使用权之民间习惯，调查统计数据显示，回答该问题的651名被调查者所在地区的继承习惯是：（1）A项是，即有该习惯的，占九成以上（92.63%）；（2）B项否，即无该习惯的，仅占不到一成（7.37%）。

2. 后顺序特殊法定继承人对遗产中原使用的住房及日常生活用品的终生使用是否付费的民间习惯情况统计

问题【四、（四）2.】“如果某甲的祖父可以继续居住，是否其可以不交租金？A. 是；B. 否。（单选）”

表 6-27　后顺序特殊法定继承人对特殊遗产的终生使用是否付费的民间习惯情况统计（单选）

选项	人数	比例
A. 是	501	80.68%
B. 否	120	19.32%
合计	621	100%

关于后顺序特殊法定继承人对特殊遗产的终生使用是否付费的民间习惯，调查统计数据显示，回答该问题的621名被调查者所在地区的民间习惯是：（1）A 项是，即无须支付租金的占八成（80.68%）；（2）B 项否，即要支付租金的占近二成（19.32%）。

3. 后顺序特殊法定继承人对遗产中原使用的住房及日常生活用品的终生使用权之期限的民间习惯情况统计

问题【四、（四）3.】“如果某甲的祖父可以继续居住，是否可以居住到其死亡时为止（终生使用权）A. 是；B. 否。（单选）”

表 6-28　后顺序特殊法定继承人对特殊遗产的终生使用权之期限的民间习惯情况统计（单选）

选项	人数	比例
A. 是	528	82.76%
B. 否	110	17.24%
合计	638	100%

关于后顺序特殊法定继承人对特殊遗产的终生使用权之期限的民间习惯，调查统计数据显示，回答该问题的638名被调查者所在地区的继承习惯是：（1）A 项是，即有无偿终生使用习惯占八成以上（82.76%）；（2）B 项否，即没有无偿终生使用习惯的仅占近二成（17.24%）。

（五）尽了主要赡养义务的丧偶儿媳或女婿的遗产分配方式

问题【四、（五）】“村民某甲，老伴因病早年去世，膝下有两个儿子乙和丙。2003年乙与丁结婚后与某甲共同生活。2012年1月乙因交通事故死亡，但乙的妻子丁仍然一直照料公公某甲的晚年生活，直至2015年1月某甲去世。请问：在您所在地区，如发生上述情况，因乙的妻子丁对公公某甲尽了主要赡养义务，如何处理某甲的遗产分配问题？A. 丁可以与某甲的二儿子丙共同继承，并且平均分配遗产；B. 丁不能与某甲的二儿子丙共同继承，但其可分得适当的遗产；C. 其他。（单选）理由是什么？”

1. 尽了主要赡养义务的丧偶儿媳或女婿的遗产分配的民间习惯情况统计

表 6-29　尽了主要赡养义务的丧偶儿媳或女婿的遗产分配方式之民间习惯情况统计（单选）

选项	人数	比例
A. 丁可以与某甲的二儿子丙共同继承，并且平均分配遗产	418	64.01%

续表

选项	人数	比例
B. 丁不能与某甲的二儿子丙共同继承，但其可分得适当的遗产	213	32.62%
C. 其他	22	3.37%
合计	653	100%

关于尽了主要赡养义务的丧偶儿媳或女婿的遗产分配方式之民间习惯，调查统计数据显示，回答该问题的653名被调查者所在地区的继承习惯是：（1）A项其可以与第一顺序继承人共同继承且平均分配遗产的，占近六成半（64.01%）；（2）B项其不能作为第一顺序继承人，但可以酌情分得遗产的，占三成以上（32.62%）。

2. 尽了主要赡养义务的丧偶儿媳或女婿的遗产分配的民间习惯之理由情况统计

表6-30 尽了主要赡养义务的丧偶儿媳或女婿的遗产分配的民间习惯之理由情况统计

项目	人数	比例
A. 作为儿媳妇，丁孝敬公公，已经尽了赡养义务，符合中国的孝道文化和道德观念，因此有权继承遗产	173	67.05%
B. 丁一直照顾公公的晚年生活，但毕竟不是某甲的子女，与某甲不具有血缘关系，遗产不能给了外人，因此不能继承某甲的遗产	50	19.38%
C. 儿媳与儿子有同等继承权	7	2.71%
D. 丁可以代替乙继承	4	1.55%
E. 按照所尽义务确定	14	5.43%
F. 公序良俗	10	3.88%
合计	258	100%

关于尽了主要赡养义务的丧偶儿媳或女婿的遗产分配的民间习惯之理由情况，调查统计数据显示，258名被调查者填写了选择理由，（1）认为其可以与第一顺序继承人共同继承且平均分配遗产的理由是，A项丁作为儿媳妇孝敬公公，已经尽了赡养义务，符合中国的孝道文化和道德观念，因此有权继承遗产的，占近七成（67.05%）；（2）认为其不能作为第一顺序继承人的理由是，B项儿媳妇丁一直照顾公公的晚年生活，但毕竟不是某甲的子女，与某甲不具有血缘关系，遗产不能给了"外人"，因此不能继承某甲遗产的，占二成（19.38%）；（3）还有不到一成的人填写了E项按照所尽义务确定（5.43%）或F项依公序良俗处理（3.88%）等理由。

五、遗嘱继承之调查数据统计情况

关于遗嘱继承之调查数据统计，我们主要从公证遗嘱与其他形式遗嘱的效力、遗嘱自由的限制——特留份、夫妻共同遗嘱，这三个方面进行调查数据的统计情况汇总分析。

（一）公证遗嘱与其他形式遗嘱的效力

问题【五、（一）】“退休职工甲有一套个人住房，他于2011年2月立了一份遗嘱，写明由其妻子乙一人继承该住房，并将该遗嘱进行了公证。后来，甲改变了主意，他重新写了一份遗嘱，写明其妻子乙和儿子丙共同继承该房屋。2016年3月甲住院病危期间，当着二位医生在现场立下口头遗嘱，指定其个人住房由儿子丙继承，两个小时后其抢救无效死亡。请问，您认为，甲的个人住房应该由谁继承？A. 乙；B. 乙和丙；C. 丙。（单选）理由是什么？”

1. 公证遗嘱与其他形式遗嘱适用效力的民众观念情况统计

表 6-31　公证遗嘱与其他形式遗嘱适用效力的民众观念情况统计（单选）

选项	人数	比例
A. 乙（公证遗嘱有效）	179	27.33%
B. 乙和丙（后成立的未公证书面遗嘱有效）	227	34.66%
C. 丙（最后的口头遗嘱有效）	249	38.01%
合计	655	100%

关于公证遗嘱与其他形式遗嘱适用效力的民众观念，调查统计数据显示，在回答该问题的655名被调查者中，（1）选择B、C两项后遗嘱的适用效力优先于前一公证遗嘱的，合计占七成以上（72.67%）；（2）而选择A项公证遗嘱效力适用优先的，占近三成（27.33%）。

2. 公证遗嘱与其他形式遗嘱适用效力的民众观念之理由情况统计

表 6-32　公证遗嘱与其他形式遗嘱适用效力的民众观念之理由情况统计

项目	人数	比例
A. 公证遗嘱的程序规范，具有较强的公示效力和证明效力	88	30.56%
B. 书面遗嘱比较正式，取证容易，且其订立在公证遗嘱之后，反映了被继承人最后的意愿	50	17.36%
C. 口头遗嘱形式灵活，且有证人作证，能够反映被继承人最后的真实意愿	55	19.10%
D. 口头遗嘱形式不固定，很难准确、完全地反映被继承人的真实意愿，且有被篡改或修改的可能性	28	9.72%
E. 尊重死者意愿	67	23.26%
合计	288	100%

关于公证遗嘱与其他形式遗嘱适用效力的民众观念之理由，调查统计数据显示，有288名被调查者填写了选择理由，（1）认为公证遗嘱适用效力优先的理由是，A项公证遗

嘱的程序规范，具有较强的公示效力和证明效力的，占三成（30.56%）；（2）认为后遗嘱适用效力优先的理由是B、C两项，书面遗嘱比较正式，取证容易或口头遗嘱形式灵活，且有证人作证，二者均能够反映被继承人最后真实意愿的，合计占三成半以上（36.46%）；（3）还有一成至二成左右的人填写了E项尊重死者意愿（23.26%）或D项口头遗嘱形式不固定且有被篡改或修改的可能（9.72%）等理由。

（二）遗嘱自由的限制——特留份

问题【五、（二）】“甲生前立了一份遗嘱，将自己死后遗留下的财产全部赠给他的一个好朋友乙，而他的配偶和子女不能取得甲的任何遗产。请问：您认为甲的这一做法是否适当？A. 适当；B. 不适当；C. 其他。（单选）理由是什么？”

1. 以遗嘱将个人遗产全部赠给他人的民众观念情况统计

表6-33　以遗嘱将个人遗产全部赠给他人的民众观念情况统计（单选）

选项	人数	比例
A. 适当	183	28.02%
B. 不适当	448	68.61%
C. 其他	22	3.37%
合计	653	100%

关于以遗嘱将个人遗产全部赠给他人的民众观念，调查统计数据显示，在回答该问题的653名被调查者中，对被继承人以遗嘱处分个人财产全部赠给第三人的行为，（1）选择B项不适当的，占近七成（68.61%）；（2）选择A项适当的，占近三成（28.02%）。

2. 以遗嘱将个人财产全部赠给他人的民众观念之理由情况统计

表6-34　以遗嘱将个人财产全部赠给他人的民众观念之理由情况统计

项目	人数	比例
A. 遗嘱人对自己的财产享有自由处分的权利，他人无权干涉	92	31.51%
B. 将遗产全部赠与他人会造成家庭财产外流，不利于保障配偶及子女的生活，同时也不符合风俗习惯，为常人所难以接受	173	59.25%
C. 具体情况具体分析	3	1.02%
D. 为配偶、子女留一部分	24	8.22%
合计	292	100%

关于以遗嘱将个人财产全部赠给他人的民众观念之理由，调查统计数据显示，有292名被调查者填写了选择理由，对被继承人以遗嘱处分个人财产全部赠给第三人的行为，（1）认为不适当的理由是B、D两项，将遗产全部赠与他人会造成家庭财产外流，不利于保障配偶及子女的生活，同时也不符合风俗习惯，为常人所难以接受或为配偶、子女留一部分遗产的，合计占六成半以上（67.47%）；（2）认为适当的理由是，A项遗嘱人对自己的财产享有自由处分的权利，他人无权干涉的，占三成以上（31.51%）。

（三）夫妻共同遗嘱

1. 夫妻共同遗嘱的民众观念与理由情况统计

问题【五、（三）1.】“甲乙是夫妻，双方在生前共同设立一份遗嘱，对死后的遗产处理进行安排。甲乙双方在遗嘱中约定，不管谁先去世，另一方都不得改变此遗嘱对遗产的处理安排。请问：您是否认同甲乙夫妻双方共同设立遗嘱的此约定？A. 赞同；B. 不赞同。（单选）理由是什么？”

（1）夫妻共同遗嘱的民众观念情况统计。

表 6-35　夫妻共同遗嘱的民众观念情况统计（单选）

选项	人数	比例
A. 赞成	500	76.45%
B. 不赞成	154	23.55%
合计	654	100%

关于夫妻共同遗嘱的民众观念，调查统计数据显示，在回答该问题的 654 名被调查者中，对于夫妻设立共同遗嘱，①选择 A 项赞成的，占七成半以上（76.45%）；②选择 B 项不赞成的，占二成以上（23.55%）。

（2）夫妻共同遗嘱的民众观念之理由情况统计。

表 6-36　夫妻共同遗嘱的民众观念之理由情况统计（单选）

项目	人数	比例
A. 共同遗嘱为双方共同设立，反映了双方的共同意愿，理应为双方所遵守	193	75.98%
B. 共同遗嘱无法应对出现的新情况和新问题，限制了双方对自己财产的处分权	52	20.47%
C. 共同遗嘱有利于为子女保留一定的遗产份额	4	1.58%
D. 共同遗嘱的设立可以避免纠纷	5	1.97%
合计	254	100%

关于夫妻共同遗嘱的民众观念之理由，有 254 名被调查者填写了选择理由，①赞同设立夫妻共同遗嘱的理由是 A、C、D 三项，共同遗嘱为双方共同设立，反映了双方的共同意愿，理应为双方所遵守、共同遗嘱有利于为子女保留一定的遗产份额或可以避免纠纷的，合计占近八成（79.53%）；②不赞同设立夫妻共同遗嘱的理由是，B 项共同遗嘱无法应对出现的新情况和新问题，限制了双方对自己财产处分权的，占二成（20.47%）。

2. 夫妻共同遗嘱存在的民间习惯情况统计

问题【五、（三）2.】“在您所在地区，有无夫妻共同设立遗嘱的情况发生？A. 有；B. 无。（单选）”

表 6-37　夫妻共同遗嘱存在的民间习惯情况统计（单选）

选项	人数	比例
A. 有	123	30.07%
B. 无	286	69.93%
合计	409	100%

关于夫妻共同遗嘱存在与否的民间习惯，调查统计数据显示，回答该问题的 409 名被调查者所在地区的继承习惯是：（1）B 项无该习惯的，占近七成（69.93%）；（2）A 项有该习惯的，占三成（30.07%）。

六、继承和遗赠的接受与放弃之调查数据统计情况

关于继承和遗赠的接受与放弃之调查数据统计，我们主要从继承的接受与放弃的时间与方式、遗赠的接受与放弃的方式与效力、继承的放弃与债权人的撤销权，这三个方面进行调查数据的统计情况汇总分析。

（一）继承的接受与放弃的时间与方式

问题【六、（一）】“对于继承人放弃继承的时间，您认为下列哪一个更为适当？A. 继承人放弃继承的，应在知道继承开始的 2 个月内作出放弃继承的表示；B. 继承开始后继承人放弃继承的，应当在遗产处理前，作出放弃继承的意思表示。（单选）理由是什么？请问：在您所在地区的人们是如何确定继承人放弃继承的？”

1. 继承的接受与放弃的时间之民众观念及理由情况统计

（1）继承的接受与放弃的时间之民众观念情况统计。

表 6-38　继承的接受与放弃的时间之民众观念情况统计（单选）

选项	人数	比例
A. 继承人放弃继承的，应在知道继承开始的 2 个月内作出放弃继承的表示	184	28.22%
B. 继承开始后继承人放弃继承的，应当在遗产处理前，作出放弃继承的意思表示	468	71.78%
合计	652	100%

关于继承的接受与放弃的时间之民众观念，调查统计数据显示，在回答该问题的 652 名被调查者中，继承人接受或放弃继承的意思表示，①选择 B 项应当在遗产处理前作出的，占七成以上（71.78%）；②选择 A 项应在知道继承开始的 2 个月内作出的，占近三成（28.22%）。

（2）继承的接受与放弃时间的民众观念之理由情况统计。

表 6-39　继承的接受与放弃时间的民众观念之理由情况统计

项目	人数	比例
A. 2个月的时间较为合适，可以让继承人有一定的时间去考虑是否放弃继承权，同时，又可以督促继承人积极行使权利	26	24.76%
B. 在遗产处理前，继承人都可以放弃继承权，这样既不影响其他继承人的利益，又可以保证继承人行使放弃继承的权利	76	72.38%
C. 其他	3	2.86%
合计	105	100%

关于继承的接受与放弃时间的民众观念之理由，调查统计数据显示，有105名被调查者填写了选择理由，①认为在遗产处理前，继承人都可以放弃继承权的理由是，B项这样既不影响其他继承人的利益，又可以保证继承人行使放弃继承权利的，占七成以上（72.38%）；②认为应在知道继承开始的2个月内作出意思表示的理由是，A项2个月的时间较为合适，可以让继承人有一定的时间去考虑是否放弃继承权，同时，又可以督促继承人积极行使权利的，占近二成半（24.76%）。

2. 继承的接受与放弃的方式之民间习惯情况统计

表 6-40　继承的接受与放弃的方式之民间习惯情况统计（单选）

选项	人数	比例
A. 书面表示	53	46.09%
B. 公证处公证	6	5.21%
C. 继承人无须作任何表示	56	48.70%
合计	115	100%

关于继承的接受与放弃的方式之民间习惯，调查统计数据显示，填写该问题的115名被调查者所在地区的民间习惯是：（1）A、B两项通过书面或公证处公证表示接受继承的，合计占五成以上（51.30%）；（2）C项继承人接受继承无须作任何表示的，占近五成（48.70%）。

（二）遗赠的接受与放弃的方式与效力

问题【六、（二）】“甲生前设立一份遗嘱，其内容为：在甲死后，将一辆小汽车赠给其侄子乙。后来甲去世，乙得知遗嘱的内容后，对此遗赠没有作出任何意思表示，既没有说接受，也没有说放弃。您认为下列哪一项更为适当？A. 乙无权取得该小汽车，乙的行为应该被视为放弃该遗赠；B. 乙有权取得该小汽车，乙的行为应该被视为接受该遗赠。（单选）理由是什么？”

1. 遗赠的接受与放弃的方式与效力之民众观念情况统计

表 6-41 遗赠的接受与放弃的方式与效力之民众观念情况统计（单选）

选项	人数	比例
A. 乙无权取得该小汽车，乙的行为应该被视为放弃该遗赠	207	31.94%
B. 乙有权取得该小汽车，乙的行为应该被视为接受该遗赠	441	68.06%
合计	648	100%

关于遗赠的接受与放弃的方式与效力之民众观念，调查统计数据显示，在回答该问题的 648 名被调查者，（1）选择 A 项受遗赠人未作表示应视为放弃遗赠的，占三成以上（31.94%）；（2）选择 B 项受遗赠人未作表示应视为接受遗赠的，占近七成（68.06%）。

2. 遗赠的接受与放弃的方式与效力的民众观念之理由情况统计

表 6-42 遗赠的接受与放弃的方式与效力的民众观念之理由情况统计

项目	人数	比例
A. 接受遗赠是一种纯获利行为，乙不表示，就应该视为接受	99	41.42%
B. 乙有权选择是否接受甲的遗赠，如乙没有表示，就应该视为放弃遗赠，这也体现了对乙人格的尊重	57	23.85%
C. 接受应当面表示	50	20.92%
D. 出具申明	23	9.62%
E. 遵循死者意愿	10	4.19%
合计	239	100%

关于遗赠的接受与放弃的方式与效力的民众观念之理由，调查统计数据显示，239 名被调查者填写了选择理由，（1）认为受遗赠人未作表示应视为接受遗赠的理由是 A、E 两项，接受遗赠是一种纯获利行为，乙不表示，就应该视为接受或这也符合死者意愿的，合计占四成半（45.61%）；（2）受遗赠人未作表示应视为放弃遗赠的理由是 B、C 两项，乙有权选择是否接受甲的遗赠，如乙没有表示，就应该视为放弃遗赠，这也体现了对乙人格的尊重或接受遗赠应当面表示的，合计占近四成半（44.77%）。

（三）继承的放弃与债权人的撤销权

问题【六、（三）】“甲为乙的父亲，2015 年年底，乙因病住院治疗，医治无效去世，留下遗产 5 万元及房屋一套。此时甲经营的摩配厂已经负债累累，拖欠工人的工资已有 10 个月，但他考虑儿媳在其丈夫乙去世后独自抚养年幼的女儿有经济困难，于是主动提出放弃继承儿子乙的遗产。甲的债权人却认为甲不应该放弃继承儿子的遗产，这实际上是逃避债务，侵犯了债权人的利益。为此，甲的债权人起诉至人民法院，要求撤销甲放弃继承儿子乙遗产的行为。您认为下列哪一项更为恰当？A. 甲放弃继承乙遗产的行为，可以被撤销；B. 甲放弃继承乙遗产的行为，不可以被撤销。（单选）理由是什么？”

1. 继承的放弃能否被债权人撤销的民众观念情况统计

表 6-43　继承的放弃能否被债权人撤销的民众观念情况统计（单选）

选项	人数	比例
A. 甲放弃继承乙遗产的行为，可以被撤销	284	43.76%
B. 甲放弃继承乙遗产的行为，不可以被撤销	365	56.24%
合计	649	100%

关于继承的放弃能否被债权人撤销的民众观念，调查统计数据显示，在回答该问题的649名被调查者，对于继承人放弃继承的行为，（1）选择B项不可以被撤销的，占五成半以上（56.24%）；（2）选择A项可以被撤销的，占四成以上（43.76%）。

2. 继承的放弃能否被债权人撤销的民众观念之理由情况统计

表 6-44　继承的放弃能否被债权人撤销的民众观念之理由情况统计

项目	人数	比例
A. 不可以被撤销，因为这有利于照顾儿媳及其孙女的生活，她们是弱势群体，理应获得优先照顾	78	37.86%
B. 可以被撤销，因为甲的债权人利益也需要被考虑	93	45.15%
C. 遵循甲的意愿	22	10.68%
D. 允许撤销部分，考虑债权人利益	3	1.46%
E. 不可以撤销，放弃继承是继承人的自由	10	4.85%
合计	206	100%

关于继承的放弃能否被债权人撤销的民众观念之理由，调查统计数据显示，206名被调查者填写了选择理由，（1）不可以被债权人撤销的理由是A、C、E三项，这有利于照顾儿媳及其孙女的生活，她们是弱势群体，理应获得优先照顾或应遵循甲的意愿、放弃继承是继承人的自由的，合计占五成以上（53.39%）；（2）可以被债权人撤销的理由是B、D两项，甲的债权人利益也需要被考虑，这有利于保护债权人利益的，合计占四成半以上（46.61%）。

七、继承权的丧失、被继承人的宥恕与代位继承之调查数据统计情况

关于继承权的丧失、被继承人的宥恕与代位继承之调查数据统计，我们主要从继承权丧失与被继承人的宥恕、继承权的丧失与代位继承，这两个方面进行调查数据的统计情况汇总分析。

（一）继承权的丧失与被继承人的宥恕

问题【七、（一）】“某甲如果以欺诈或者胁迫的手段，迫使或者妨碍其父乙设立、变更或者撤销遗嘱，情节较为严重，但其后获得乙的原谅。并询问以下哪种处理更为适当：A. 某甲有资格继承其父遗产；B. 某甲仍然不能继承其父遗产。（单选）理由是

什么？”

1. 继承权的丧失与被继承人的宥恕的民众观念情况统计

表 6-45　继承权的丧失与被继承人的宥恕的民众观念情况统计（单选）

选项	人数	比例
A. 某甲有资格继承其父遗产	477	73.27%
B. 某甲仍然不能继承其父遗产	174	26.73%
合计	651	100%

关于继承权的丧失与被继承人的宥恕的民众观念，调查统计数据显示，在回答该问题的651名被调查者中，对于继承人因欺诈或者胁迫而丧失继承权，可否因被继承人的宥恕而恢复继承权，（1）选择A项可以恢复的，占七成以上（73.27%）；（2）选择B项不可以恢复的，占二成半以上（26.73%）。

2. 继承权的丧失与被继承人的宥恕的民众观念之理由情况统计

表 6-46　继承权的丧失与被继承人的宥恕的民众观念之理由情况统计

项目	人数	比例
A. 乙有权处分自己的遗产，如果乙已经原谅了某甲，则可以恢复某甲的继承权	176	72.13%
B. 某甲的行为造成恶劣影响，导致其丧失继承权，即使乙原谅了某甲，也不能恢复某甲的继承权	47	19.26%
C. 某甲丧失继承权，因为不能让别有用心的人有继承权	7	2.87%
D. 某甲有继承权，因为应当尊重其父亲的最后决定	14	5.74%
合计	244	100%

关于继承权的丧失与被继承人的宥恕的民众观念之理由，调查统计数据显示，244名被调查者填写了选择理由，（1）认为可以恢复继承权的理由是A、D两项，乙有权处分自己的遗产，如果乙已经原谅了某甲，则可以恢复某甲的继承权或应当尊重父亲乙的最后决定，合计占近八成（占77.87%）；（2）认为不可以恢复继承权的理由是B、C两项，某甲的行为造成恶劣影响，导致其丧失继承权，即使乙原谅了某甲，也不能恢复某甲的继承权或不能让别有用心的人有继承权，合计占二成以上（占22.13%）。

（二）继承权的丧失与代位继承

问题【七、（二）】“村民甲死亡后，其子乙因实施伪造遗嘱的行为导致丧失了对其父甲的继承权，乙的儿子丙能否代父乙去继承祖父甲的遗产？A. 丙能够代父乙继承祖父甲遗产；B. 丙不能代父乙继承祖父甲遗产。（单选）理由是什么？”

1. 继承权丧失的效力是否及于代位继承人的民众观念情况统计

表 6-47 继承权丧失的效力是否及于代位继承人的民众观念情况统计（单选）

选项	人数	比例
A. 丙能够代父乙继承祖父甲的遗产	296	46.18%
B. 丙不能代父乙继承祖父甲的遗产	345	53.82%
合计	641	100%

关于继承权丧失的效力是否及于代位继承人的民众观念，调查统计数据显示，在回答该问题的641名被调查者中，（1）选择B项及于代位继承人的，占近五成半（53.82%）；（2）选择A项不及于代位继承人的，占四成半以上（46.18%）。

2. 继承权丧失的效力是否及于代位继承人的民众观念之理由情况统计

表 6-48 继承权丧失的效力是否及于代位继承人的民众观念之理由情况统计

项目	人数	比例
A. 丙作为独立的民事主体，可以孙子的身份来继承祖父甲的遗产，与乙丧失继承权没有关系	107	47.98%
B. 乙已经丧失继承权，导致丙代替乙继承的前提丧失，所以丙不能代替乙继承甲的遗产	106	47.53%
C. 伪造遗嘱等不正当手段，不受法律保护	3	1.35%
D. 丙的继承顺序靠后，不得代位	6	2.69%
E. 谁负责养老，谁继承	1	0.45%
合计	223	100%

关于继承权丧失的效力是否及于代位继承人的民众观念之理由，调查统计数据显示，223名被调查者填写了选择理由，（1）认为继承权丧失的效力不及于代位继承人的理由是，A项丙作为独立的民事主体，可以孙子的身份来继承祖父甲的遗产，与乙丧失继承权没有关系的，占近五成（47.98%）；（2）认为继承权丧失的效力及于代位继承人的理由是B、C、D三项，乙已经丧失继承权，导致丙代替乙继承的前提丧失、伪造遗嘱等不正当手段，不受法律保护或丙的继承顺序靠后，不得代位的，合计占五成以上（51.57%）。

八、继承协议之调查数据统计情况

必须说明，本节研究的对象是狭义的继承协议（又称继承扶养协议），是被继承人与继承人之间，就扶养与继承事项签订的协议。关于继承协议之调查数据统计，我们主要从继承协议的订立主体与方式、继承协议的变更方式及效力，这两个方面进行调查数据的统计情况汇总分析。

（一）继承协议的订立主体与方式

问题【八、（一）】“王某，现年70岁，有长子王一，次女王二，两个子女均已成家且分家另过。王某的老伴因患癌症花费了大量医药费后去世，老夫妻的共同财产现所剩无几，现有郊区的一套住房是王某个人财产。虽然王某退休金不多，但身体没有大病，基本生活还是能够维持的。由于长子王一长期在外地工作，为解决父亲王某的养老送终问题，您认为，如下三种做法哪一做法较为妥当？A. 父亲王某与次女王二，双方协商并签订协议，由次女王二一人承担赡养父亲王某的义务，王某的全部遗产指定由王二继承；B. 父亲王某与子女王一、王二，三人协商并签订协议，由次女王二一人承担赡养父亲王某的义务，王某的全部遗产商定由王二继承；王一放弃对父亲王某遗产的继承权；C. 子女王一与王二，两人协商并签订协议，由次女王二一人承担赡养父亲王某的义务，王某的全部遗产商定由王二继承；王一放弃对父亲王某遗产的继承权（单选）。"

表 6-49　继承协议的订立主体与方式的民众观念情况统计（单选）

选项	人数	比例
A. 父亲王某与次女王二协商一致即可签订协议（第一种方式）	156	24.19%
B. 父亲王某需与全部继承人协商，共同签订协议（第二种方式）	411	63.72%
C. 共同继承人间签订协议即可，无须被继承人知晓或同意（第三种方式）	78	12.09%
合计	645	100%

关于继承协议的订立主体与方式的民众观念，调查统计数据显示，在填写该问题的645名被调查者中，（1）选择B项应由被扶养人与全部继承人共同协商签订的，占六成以上（63.72%）；（2）选择A项应由被扶养人与扶养人协商签订的，占近二成半（24.19%）；（3）选择C项共同继承人间协商签订即可而无须被扶养人知晓或同意的，占一成以上（12.09%）。

（二）继承协议的变更方式及效力

问题【八、（二）】"王某，现年70岁，有长子王一，次女王二，三子王三，三个子女均已成家且分家另过。王某的老伴因患癌症花费了大量医疗费后去世，现有郊区的一套住房是王某个人财产，市场价约为30万元，王某有少量退休金。王某与王二协商并签订继承协议，由王二主要扶养父亲王某，王某的所有遗产由王二继承。协议签订后，王二全家与父亲王某共同生活了5年后的一天，王二因意外交通事故死亡。王二全家在与王某共同生活的期间已为王某花费生活费、医疗费等扶养费共9万元。为解决王某的养老，您同意下列哪一做法？A. 王二的儿子有继续扶养外祖父王某的能力，王某也愿意与王二的儿子共同生活，应当由王二的儿子继续履行扶养义务，并继承王某的全部遗产；B. 王一、王三共同补偿王二家人6万元扶养费后（另有3万元扶养费属于应当由王二承担的），如果王一与父亲王某签订新的继承协议，并与王某共同生活一直扶养至其去世，就由王一继承王某的全部遗产；C. 对王二已经支付的扶养费不予补偿，如果王一与父亲王某签订新的继承协议，并与王某共同生活一直扶养至其去世，就由王一继承王某的全部遗产；D. 王一、王三共同补偿王二家人6万元扶养费后，由两人共同扶养父亲王某；E. 其他。（单选）理由是什么？"

1. 继承协议的变更方式及效力的民众观念情况统计

表 6-50 继承协议的变更方式及效力的民众观念情况统计（单选）

选项	人数	比例
A. 原扶养人的子女有扶养能力的，在双方自愿的情况下，由原扶养人的子女继续扶养被扶养人，并继承全部遗产	295	45.74%
B. 原签订的继承协议效力终止，补偿原扶养人一定费用后，由某一有扶养能力的法定继承人，在双方自愿的情况下签订新继承协议，继续扶养被扶养人，并继承全部遗产	193	29.92%
C. 原签订的继承协议效力终止，对原扶养人无须补偿，应由某一有扶养能力的法定继承人与被扶养人，在双方自愿的情况下签订新继承协议，继续扶养被扶养人并继承全部遗产	48	7.44%
D. 原签订的继承协议效力终止，补偿原扶养人一定费用后，应由有扶养能力的全体法定继承人，共同依法对被扶养人尽扶养义务，并依法定继承取得遗产	103	15.97%
E. 其他	6	0.93%
合计	645	100%

关于继承协议的变更方式与效力的民众观念，即在继承协议的履行中，如扶养人先于被扶养人去世，被调查者对于该协议的变更方式与效力的认识，调查统计数据显示，在645名被调查者中，（1）选择A项，该协议可有条件继续履行，如原扶养人的子女有扶养能力的，在原扶养人的子女和被扶养人双方同意的情况下，可由原扶养人的子女继续履行该继承协议的，此即代位扶养的，占四成半（45.74%）；（2）选择B项和C项，该协议终止，须签订新的继承协议，由新的扶养人履行扶养义务并继承遗产的，合计占近四成（37.36%），其中，B项需要对原扶养人的继承人补偿超过其扶养义务部分费用的，占近三成（29.92%），C项不需要对原扶养人的继承人补偿超过其扶养义务部分费用的，占不到一成（7.44%）；（3）选择D项，该协议终止，应补偿原扶养人的继承人超过其扶养义务部分费用后，由所有法定继承人共同扶养的，即实行法定赡养的，占一成半（15.97%）。可见，湖北省被调查者对于代位扶养的认可度最高，占四成半。

2. 继承协议的变更方式及效力的民众观念之理由情况统计

表 6-51 继承协议的变更方式及效力的民众观念之理由情况统计

项目	人数	比例
A. 由王二的儿子继续扶养王某，使继承协议继续履行，有利于维持被扶养人一贯的生活方式，使其安度晚年	295	46.17%
B. 赡养王某是其子女的法定义务，由于法律规定扶养义务人应平等承担赡养义务，王一、王三应当补偿王二家人6万元	296	46.32%

续表

项目	人数	比例
C. 原签订的继承协议效力终止，故依据协议对原扶养人的家人无须补偿	48	7.51%
合计	639	100%

关于继承协议的变更方式及效力的民众观念之理由，调查统计数据显示，在填写该问题的639名被调查者中，（1）认为该协议可有条件继续履行的理由是，A项由王二的儿子继续扶养王某，使继承协议继续履行，有利于维持被扶养人一贯的生活方式，使其安度晚年的，占四成半以上（46.17%）；（2）认为补偿原扶养人家人一定费用的理由是，B项赡养王某是其子女的法定义务，由于法律规定扶养义务人应平等承担赡养义务，故王一、王三应当补偿王二家人6万元的，占四成半以上（46.32%）；（3）认为对原扶养人家人无须补偿的理由是，C项原签订的继承协议效力终止，故依据协议对原扶养人的家人无须补偿的，仅占不到一成（7.51%）。

九、遗产债务清偿之调查数据统计情况

关于遗产债务清偿之调查数据统计，我们主要从遗产债务清偿责任的类型、被继承人丧葬费的支付、遗产债务的清偿顺序，这三个方面进行调查数据的统计情况汇总分析。

（一）遗产债务清偿责任的类型

问题【九、（一）】"继承遗产，应当清偿被继承人的债务，您是怎么理解这句话的？A. 对被继承人的生前所有债务，继承人都应当予以偿还；B. 对被继承人的生前所有债务，继承人应先用所有遗产偿还债务，不足部分由继承人个人财产偿还；C. 对被继承人的生前所有债务，继承人只以继承的遗产为限予以偿还；D. 对被继承人的生前所有债务，继承人如果存在转移遗产、隐瞒遗产的情形，则其应当负责以遗产和其个人财产偿还所有的债务。（多选）在您所在的地区，人们遇到继承人有转移遗产、隐瞒遗产的情况是如何处理的？"

1. 遗产债务清偿责任的类型之民众观念情况统计

表6-52 继承人清偿遗产债务责任的类型之民众观念情况统计（多选）

选项	人数	比例
A. 对被继承人的生前所有债务，继承人都应当予以偿还	204	31.29%
B. 对被继承人的生前所有债务，继承人应先用所有遗产偿还债务，不足部分由继承人以个人财产偿还	232	35.58%
C. 对被继承人的生前所有债务，继承人只以继承的遗产为限予以偿还	314	48.16%
D. 对被继承人的生前所有债务，继承人如果存在转移遗产、隐瞒遗产的情形，则其应当负责以遗产和其个人财产偿还所有的债务	282	43.25%

关于遗产债务清偿责任的类型之民众观念，调查统计数据显示，在被调查者中，对于被继承人生前欠下的所有债务，（1）选择A、B两项实行自愿的无限清偿责任的，合计占六成半以上（66.87%）；（2）选择C项实行有限清偿责任的，占近五成（48.16%）；（3）选择D项实行强制的无限清偿责任的，占四成以上（43.25%）。

2. 继承人侵害遗产的法律责任之民间习惯情况统计

表6-53　继承人侵害遗产的法律责任之民间习惯情况统计（单选）

选项	人数	比例
A. 由法院处理	17	25.00%
B. 继承人应承担清偿所有债务的责任	21	30.88%
C. 对有转移、隐瞒遗产的继承人应当少分或不分	16	23.53%
D. 应当返还转移部分	10	14.71%
E. 遗产应该重新分配	4	5.88%
合计	68	100%

关于继承人侵害遗产的法律责任之民间习惯，调查统计数据显示，回答该问题68名被调查者所在地区的民间习惯是：（1）B项继承人应承担清偿所有债务责任的，占三成（30.88%）；（2）C项转移、隐瞒遗产的继承人会少分或不分遗产的，占二成以上（23.53%）；（3）D、E两项会返还转移部分（14.71%）或遗产会重新分配（5.88%）的，各占一成左右；（4）还有二成半（25.00%）的地区有交给法院处理的习惯。

（二）被继承人丧葬费的支付

问题【九、（二）】“在您所在的地区，死者的丧葬费用一般是如何支付的？A. 由全体继承人共同支付；B. 从被继承人的遗产中支付；C. 其他。（单选）”

表6-54　被继承人丧葬费支付的民间习惯情况统计（单选）

选项	人数	比例
A. 由全体继承人共同支付	345	57.21%
B. 从被继承人的遗产中支付	233	38.64%
C. 其他	25	4.15%
合计	603	100%

关于被继承人丧葬费支付的民间习惯，调查统计数据显示，回答该问题的603名被调查者所在地区的民间习惯是：（1）A项由全体继承人共同支付的，占近六成（57.21%）；（2）B项从被继承人的遗产中支付的，占近四成（38.64%）。

（三）遗产债务的清偿顺序

问题【九、（三）】“在您所在地区，对被继承人死亡后遗留的以下费用，一般是按照哪种先后次序进行清偿的？（多选）”

A. 丧葬费用	D. 欠付的工资	G. 对被继承人扶养较多的人之酌情分配遗产份额
B. 遗产管理等费用	E. 受被继承人扶养人的生活费	H. 遗赠扶养协议写明遗赠的遗产
C. 欠债	F. 税款	

表 6-55 遗产债务清偿顺序的民间习惯情况统计（多选）

选项	第一顺序		第二顺序		第三顺序		第四顺序		第五顺序		第六顺序		第七顺序		第八顺序	
	人数	比例%	人数	比例%	人数	比例%	人数	比例%	人数	比例%	人数	比例%	人数	比例%	人数	比例%
A.	364	55.83	26	3.99	19	2.91	38	5.83	21	3.22	7	1.07	7	1.07	9	1.38
B.	12	1.84	137	21.01	38	5.83	65	9.97	84	12.88	45	6.90	23	3.53	24	3.68
C.	45	6.9	146	22.39	168	25.77	66	10.12	33	5.06	8	1.23	16	2.45	7	1.07
D.	23	3.53	145	22.24	137	21.01	105	16.10	25	3.83	18	2.76	10	1.53	6	0.92
E.	6	0.92	21	3.22	44	6.74	71	10.89	90	13.8	80	12.27	63	9.66	32	4.91
F.	41	6.29	39	5.98	63	9.66	55	8.44	65	9.97	46	7.06	17	2.61	48	7.36
G.	9	1.38	18	2.76	20	3.07	31	4.75	60	9.20	87	13.34	111	17.02	89	13.65
H.	7	1.07	9	1.38	25	3.83	29	4.45	43	6.60	87	13.34	101	15.49	87	13.34

关于遗产债务清偿顺序的民间习惯，统计数据显示，各顺序以被调查者选择占比最高的作为统计依据，在被调查者所在地区，遗产债务按如下顺序清偿：第一顺序为 A 项“丧葬费用”（55.83%）；第二顺序为 B 项“遗产管理等费用”（21.01%）、D 项“欠付的工资”（22.24%）；第三顺序为 C 项“欠债”（25.77%）；第四顺序为 E 项“受被继承人扶养人的生活费”（13.8%）、F 项“税款”（9.97%）；第五顺序为 G 项“对被继承人扶养较多的人之酌情分配遗产份额”（17.02%）、H 项“遗赠扶养协议写明遗赠的遗产”（15.49%）。

十、遗产分割之调查数据统计情况

关于遗产分割之调查数据统计，我们主要从遗产分割的自由与限制、遗产分割瑕疵的担保责任，这两个方面进行调查数据的统计情况汇总分析。

（一）遗产分割的自由与限制

问题【十、（一）1.】“按您当地的民间习惯，对遗产一般如何开始分割的？A. 由各继承人共同协商后进行分割；B. 只要有继承人要求分割遗产，就得进行分割；C. 对于被继承人以遗嘱禁止分割的遗产，不得进行分割；D. 其他。（多选）理由是什么？”

1. 遗产分割自由与限制的民间习惯及理由情况统计

（1）遗产分割自由与限制的民间习惯情况统计。

表 6-56 遗产分割自由与限制的民间习惯情况统计（多选）

选项	人数	比例
A. 由各继承人共同协商后进行分割	572	86.80%
B. 只要有继承人要求分割遗产，就得进行分割	126	19.12%
C. 对于被继承人以遗嘱禁止分割的遗产，不得进行分割	461	69.95%
D. 其他	12	1.82%

关于遗产分割自由与限制的民间习惯，调查统计数据显示，被调查者所在地区的继承习惯是：①A 项共同协商后分割遗产的，占八成半以上（86.80%）；②C 项遗嘱禁止分割则不得分割的，占近七成（69.95%）；③B 项只要有继承人要求分割遗产就得进行分割的，占不到二成（19.12%）。

（2）遗产分割自由与限制的民间习惯之理由情况统计。

表 6-57 遗产分割自由与限制的民间习惯之理由情况统计

项目	人数	比例
A. 遗产由各继承人共同所有，遗产分割关系各继承人的共同利益，故遗产的分割由各遗产继承人共同协商	139	59.40%
B. 每个继承人享有的继承权受法律保护，同时基于效率原则考虑，故继承开始后，基于继承人的要求就可以分割遗产	40	17.09%
C. 遗产是被继承人遗留的个人财产，其当然有权通过遗嘱决定遗产的归属和分割	45	19.23%
D. 应从风俗习惯	10	4.28%
合计	234	100%

关于遗产分割自由与限制的民间习惯之理由，调查统计数据显示，234 名被调查者填写了选择理由，①遗产应由各继承人共同协商后进行分割的理由是，A 项遗产由各继承人共同所有，遗产分割关系各继承人的共同利益，故遗产的分割由各遗产继承人共同协商的，占近六成（59.40%）；②遗嘱禁止分割的遗产则不得分割的理由是，C 项遗产是被继承人遗留的个人财产，其当然有权通过遗嘱决定遗产归属和分割的，占近二成（19.23%）；③只要有继承人要求分割遗产就得进行分割的理由是，B 项每个继承人享有的继承权受法律保护，同时基于效率原则考虑，故继承开始后，基于继承人的要求就可以分割遗产的，占一成半以上（17.09%）。

2. 提出遗产分割请求时间的民间习惯及理由情况统计

问题【十、（一）2.】“老王死时留有一套家庭居住的房屋（价值 50 万元）、存款 20 万元以及小汽车一辆（价值 10 万元）。老王去世时，其配偶和唯一的儿子小王均在世。

请问：在您所在的地区，老王去世后，其儿子小王是否会马上向其母亲提出分割遗产的请求？A. 会；B. 不会；C. 会提出分割其他遗产的请求，但对其母正在居住的房屋的分割需等其母去世后进行；D. 其他。（单选）理由是什么？”

（1）提出遗产分割请求时间的民间习惯情况统计。

表 6-58　提出遗产分割请求时间的民间习惯情况统计（单选）

选项	人数	比例
A. 会	49	7.60%
B. 不会	485	75.19%
C. 会提出分割其他遗产的请求，但对其母正在居住的房屋的分割需等其母去世后进行	104	16.12%
D. 其他	7	1.09%
合计	645	100%

关于提出遗产分割请求时间的民间习惯，调查统计数据显示，回答该问题的 645 名被调查者所在地区的继承习惯是：①B 项子女不会提出遗产分割请求的，占近七成半（75.19%）；②C 项子女会提出分割其他遗产，但对其母正在居住的房屋的分割需要等其母去世后进行的，占一成半稍多（16.12%）；③仅有不到一成（7.60%）的极少数地区有子女会马上向其母亲提出分割遗产的习惯。可见，主张对其母正在居住的房屋在其生存期间不予分割的，B、C 两项合计占九成以上（91.31%）。

（2）提出遗产分割请求时间的民间习惯之理由情况统计。

表 6-59　提出遗产分割请求时间的民间习惯之理由情况统计

项目	人数	比例
A. 遗产是由小王及其母亲共同继承，继承开始后，小王有权根据法律规定提出遗产分割的请求，并且有利于防止日后发生不必要的纠纷	8	4.47%
B. 根据当地观念，小王的父亲去世遗留下的财产就应该由其母亲全部继承	79	44.13%
C. 体现孝敬老人，保证老人的晚年生活，小王可以提出分割其他遗产，但对其母正在居住房屋的分割需等其母去世后进行	88	49.16%
D. 其他	4	2.24%
合计	179	100%

关于提出遗产分割请求时间的民间习惯之理由，调查统计数据显示，179 名被调查者填写了选择理由，①认为子女不会提出遗产分割请求的理由是，B 项根据当地观念，小王的父亲去世遗留下的财产就应该由其母亲全部继承的，占近四成半（44.13%）；②认为子女会提出分割其他遗产，但对其母正在居住的房屋需要等其母去世后进行分割的理由

是，C 项孝敬老人，这有助于保证老人的晚年生活的，占近五成（49.16%）；③认为子女会马上向其母亲提出分割遗产的理由是，A 项遗产是由小王及其母亲共同继承，继承开始后，小王有权根据法律规定提出遗产分割的请求，并且有利于防止日后发生不必要的纠纷的，仅占不到一成（4.47%）。

3. 遗嘱可否限制遗产分割的民众观念情况统计

（1）遗嘱可否限制遗产分割的民众观念情况统计。

问题【十、（一）3.（1）】“甲乙是夫妻，育有一子丙。甲系个体工商户，他生前立了一份遗嘱，指定由乙和丙共同继承遗产，但其死后遗产中的商铺门面房和家庭住房在20 年内不能进行分割。甲死亡时留下的遗产有：商铺门面房一间（价值 100 万元）；一套三室一厅的家庭住房（价值 50 万元）、存款 20 万元以及小汽车一辆（价值 10 万元）。您认为，甲是否可以在遗嘱中写明在其死后上述商铺门面房和住房在一定期间内不能进行分割？A. 可以；B. 不可以。（单选）”

表 6-60　遗嘱可否限制遗产分割的民众观念情况统计（单选）

选项	人数	比例
A. 可以	538	83.02%
B. 不可以	110	16.98%
合计	648	100%

关于遗嘱可否限制遗产分割的民众观念，调查统计数据显示，在回答该问题的 648 名被调查者中，①选择 A 项可以限制的，占八成以上（83.02%）；②选择 B 项不可以限制的，占一成半以上（16.98%）。

（2）遗嘱限制遗产分割之具体期限的民众观念情况统计。

问题【十、（一）3.（2）】“在上题中，如果您选择 A 选项，那么该期限多久合适？A. 5 年；B. 10 年；C. 15 年；D. 其他。（单选）”

表 6-61　遗嘱限制遗产分割之具体期限的民众观念情况统计（单选）

选项	人数	比例
A. 5 年	185	34.39%
B. 10 年	148	27.51%
C. 15 年	67	12.45%
D. 其他	138	25.65%
合计	538	100%

关于遗嘱限制遗产分割之具体期限的民众观念，调查统计数据显示，在填写该问题的538 名被调查者中，①选择 A 项 5 年内的，占近三成半（34.39%）；②选择 B 项 10 年内的，占近三成（27.51%）；③选择 C 项 15 年内的，仅占一成以上（12.45%）。

（3）继承人协商能否变更遗嘱限制的民间习惯及理由情况统计。

问题【十、（一）3.（3）】“在您所在地区，如果乙和丙一致同意分割上述财产，那么，他们是否可以不遵守甲的遗嘱在一定期限内禁止分割上述房产的规定而进行分割？A. 可以不遵守遗嘱；B. 不可以不遵守遗嘱。（单选）理由是什么？”

①继承人协商能否变更遗嘱限制的民间习惯情况统计。

表 6-62　继承人协商能否变更遗嘱限制的民间习惯情况统计（单选）

选项	人数	比例
A. 可以不遵守遗嘱	313	50.57%
B. 不可以不遵守遗嘱	306	49.43%
合计	619	100%

关于继承人协商能否变更遗嘱限制的民间习惯，调查统计数据显示，填写该问题的 619 名被调查者所在地区的民间习惯是：Ⅰ.B 项会遵守遗嘱限制的，占近五成（49.43%）；Ⅱ.A 项可以不遵守遗嘱限制的，占五成（50.57%）。

②继承人协商能否变更遗嘱限制的民间习惯之理由情况统计。

表 6-63　继承人协商能否变更遗嘱限制的民间习惯之理由情况统计

项目	人数	比例
A. 乙和丙共同继承这些遗产，共同享有所有权，二人当然有权决定分割这些遗产，同时也有利于发挥物的效用价值	8	4.47%
B. 乙和丙根据甲设立的遗嘱享有继承权，对于遗产的分割问题，也应该依据遗嘱	79	44.13%
C. 遗嘱不当，继承人才可变更	88	49.16%
D. 遗产属于夫妻共有	4	2.24%
合计	179	100%

关于继承人协商能否变更遗嘱限制的民间习惯之理由，调查统计数据显示，230 名被调查者填写选择理由，Ⅰ. 认为继承人协商不可以变更遗嘱限制的理由是，B 项乙和丙根据甲设立的遗嘱享有继承权，对于遗产的分割问题，也应该依据遗嘱的，占近四成半（44.13%）；Ⅱ. 认为继承人协商可以变更遗嘱限制的理由是，A 项乙和丙共同继承这些遗产，共同享有所有权，二人当然有权决定分割这些遗产，同时也有利于发挥物之效用价值的，仅占不到一成（4.47%）；Ⅲ. 还有近五成（49.16%）的人填写了 C 项只有遗嘱不当时继承人才可变更等理由。

（二）遗产分割瑕疵的担保责任

问题【十、（二）】“村民老王于 2016 年 12 月 10 日因病去世，死亡时他留下有 50 只羊。老王有两个儿子甲和乙，故老王死后，甲、乙各分得 25 只羊。但在双方分完羊两天之后，乙分得的 25 只羊中就有 2 只暴病死亡，这 2 只羊死亡的原因是在兄弟俩分割前就已经得了羊痘（一种急性传染病）。请问：在您所在地区，如果出现此种情况时，这 2 只羊死亡的损失应该由谁承担？A. 由乙自行承担，羊群已分配完毕，乙分到了 2 只病羊，应该自认倒霉；B. 由甲和乙共同承担，甲应再分给乙 1 只羊或按照 1 只羊的价格进行补偿；C. 按 1 只羊的价格进行补偿，但乙承担大部分损失，甲承担小部分损失；D. 其他。（单选）理由是什么？"

1. 遗产分割瑕疵的担保责任的民间习惯情况统计

表 6-64 遗产分割瑕疵担保责任的民间习惯情况统计（单选）

选项	人数	比例
A. 由乙自行承担，羊群已分配完毕，乙分到了 2 只病羊，应该自认倒霉	250	41.32%
B. 由甲和乙共同承担，甲应再分给乙 1 只羊或按照 1 只羊的价格进行补偿	248	40.99%
C. 按 1 只羊的价格进行补偿，但乙承担大部分损失，甲承担小部分损失	104	17.19%
D. 其他	3	0.50%
合计	605	100%

关于遗产分割瑕疵担保责任的民间习惯，调查统计数据显示，填写该问题的 605 名被调查者所在地区的继承习惯是：（1）对遗产分割的瑕疵，B、C 两项共同继承人共同承担的，合计占近六成（58.18%）；（2）A 项由"乙自行承担"，即共同继承人间不会共同承担的，占四成以上（41.32%）。

2. 遗产分割瑕疵的担保责任的民间习惯之理由情况统计

表 6-65 遗产分割瑕疵的担保责任的民间习惯之理由情况统计

项目	人数	比例
A. 乙分得的 25 只羊是随机分配的，事先甲乙两人都不知道，因此，对于 2 只病羊的损失与甲无关，应由乙自己承担	103	49.76%
B. 50 只羊是由甲和乙共同继承的，对于 2 只病羊的损失也应该由甲和乙共同承担；如果让乙一个人承担，则有悖公平原则	94	45.41%
C. 遗产分割应促进家庭和谐	3	1.45%
D. 尽量兼顾双方利益	7	3.38%
合计	207	100%

关于遗产分割瑕疵担保责任的民间习惯之理由，调查统计数据显示，207 名被调查者填写了选择理由，（1）认为共同继承人间无须互担遗产瑕疵担保责任的理由是，A 项乙分得的 25 只羊是随机分配的，事先甲乙两人都不知道，因此，对于 2 只病羊的损失与甲无关，应由乙自己承担的，占近五成（49.76%）；（2）认为共同继承人间应互担遗产瑕

疵担保责任的理由是，B 项 50 只羊是由甲和乙共同继承的，对于 2 只病羊的损失也应该由甲和乙共同承担；如果让乙一个人承担，则有悖公平原则的，占四成半（45.41%）；（3）还有不到一成的人填写了 C 项遗产分割应促进家庭和谐（1.45%）或 D 项尽量兼顾双方利益（3.38%）等理由。

十一、无人承受遗产之调查数据统计情况

关于无人承受遗产之调查数据统计，我们主要从无人承受遗产归属和无人承受遗产的处理，这两个方面进行调查数据的统计情况汇总分析。

（一）无人承受遗产的归属

1. 城镇居民无人承受遗产的归属主体的民众观念与理由情况

问题【十一、（一）1.】“甲生前系城镇居民，其生前终身未婚且无其他继承人，其死后留下部分遗产，属于无人承受的遗产。您认为甲的遗产应当归属于下列哪一主体更合适？A. 国家；B. 死者生前所在地的国库；C. 死者生前所在地民政部门的社会福利机构；D. 死者生前所在地的居委会；E. 不是继承人的其他亲属；F. 其他（您认为更合适的归属主体）。（单选）理由是什么？”

（1）城镇居民无人承受遗产的归属主体的民众观念情况统计。

表 6-66　城镇居民无人承受遗产的归属主体的民众观念情况统计（单选）

选项	人数	比例
A. 国家	206	31.26%
B. 死者生前所在地的国库	70	10.62%
C. 死者生前所在地民政部门的社会福利机构	157	23.82%
D. 死者生前所在地的居委会	45	6.83%
E. 不是继承人的其他亲属	166	25.19%
F. 其他	15	2.28%
合计	659	100%

关于城镇居民无人承受遗产的归属主体的民众观念，调查统计数据显示，在 659 名被调查者中，①选择 A、B、C、D 四项，城镇居民无人继承遗产应收归社会公共组织（包括国家、死者生前所在地的国库、死者生前所在地民政部门的社会福利机构和死者生前所在地的居委会）的，合计占七成以上（72.53%）；②选择 E、F 两项，城镇居民无人继承遗产应归自然人（不是继承人的其他亲属等），合计占近三成（27.47%）。

（2）城镇居民无人承受遗产的归属主体的民众观念之理由情况统计。

表 6-67　城镇居民无人承受遗产的归属主体的民众观念之理由情况统计

项目	人数	比例
A. 为规范财产秩序，甲的遗产应归国家所有，同时，这也与部分国家的做法相一致	83	39.90%
B. 甲的遗产归甲生前所在地的国库，有利于对遗产的清算、管理和利用	19	9.13%
C. 甲的其他亲属是与甲有较密切联系的人，甲的遗产归其他亲戚所有，符合情理	62	29.81%
D. 归属福利机构，以更好造福社会	38	18.27%
E. 谁为其养老送终就应该归谁	6	2.90%
合计	208	100%

关于城镇居民无人承受遗产的归属主体的民众观念之理由，调查统计数据显示，208名被调查者填写了选择理由，①认为其应归社会公共组织的主要理由是，A 项甲的遗产应归国家所有可以规范财产秩序，同时这也与部分国家的做法相一致的，占近四成（39.90%）；B 项甲的遗产归甲生前所在地的国库，有利于对遗产的清算、管理和利用的，占不到一成（9.13%）；D 项归属福利机构，以更好造福社会的，占近二成（18.27%）。②认为其应归自然人所有的主要理由是，C 项甲的其他亲属是与甲有较密切联系的人，甲的遗产归其他亲戚所有，这符合情理的，占近三成（29.81%）。

2. 农村居民无人承受遗产的归属主体的民众观念及理由情况统计

问题【十一、（一）2.】“甲生前系农村居民，其生前未婚且无其他继承人，其死后留下部分遗产，属于无人承受的遗产。您认为甲的遗产归属于下列哪一主体更合适？A. 死者生前所在地的国库；B. 死者生前所在地民政部门的社会福利机构；C. 死者生前所在的集体经济组织；D. 死者生前所在的村委会；E. 死者生前所在的村民小组；F. 不是继承人的其他亲属；G. 其他（您认为更合适的归属主体）。（单选）理由是什么？”

（1）农村居民无人承受遗产的归属主体的民众观念情况统计。

表 6-68　农村居民无人承受遗产的归属主体的民众观念情况统计（单选）

选项	人数	比例
A. 死者生前所在地的国库	131	19.88%
B. 死者生前所在地民政部门的社会福利机构	131	19.88%
C. 死者生前所在的集体经济组织	55	8.35%
D. 死者生前所在地的村委会	104	15.78%
E. 死者生前所在的村民小组	32	4.86%

续表

选项	人数	比例
F. 不是继承人的其他亲属	176	26.71%
G. 其他	30	4.54%
合计	659	100%

关于农村居民无人承受遗产的归属主体的民众观念，调查统计数据显示，在659名被调查者中，①选择A、B、C、D、E五项，农村居民无人继承遗产应收归社会公共组织(包括国家、死者生前所在地的国库、死者生前所在地民政部门的社会福利机构和死者生前所在的集体经济组织、村委会或村民小组）的，合计占近七成（68.75%)；②选择F、G两项，农村居民无人继承遗产应归自然人（不是继承人的其他亲属等）的，合计占三成以上（31.25%)。

(2）农村居民无人承受遗产的归属主体的民众观念之理由情况统计。

表6-69 农村居民无人承受遗产的归属主体的民众观念之理由情况统计

项目	人数	比例
A. 甲的遗产归甲生前所在地的集体经济组织，有利于对遗产的清算、管理和利用	49	31.41%
B. 甲的其他亲属是与甲有较密切联系的人，甲的遗产归其他亲戚所有，符合情理	58	37.18%
C. 归属福利机构，可以更好造福社会	30	19.23%
D. 国家更好利用	6	3.85%
E. 公平处理	11	7.05%
F. 应尊重习俗	2	1.28%
合计	156	100%

关于农村居民无人承受遗产的归属主体的民众观念之理由，调查统计数据显示，156名被调查者填写了选择理由，①认为应归社会公共组织的主要理由是，A项甲的遗产归甲生前所在地的集体经济组织，这有利于对遗产的清算、管理和利用的，占三成以上(31.41%)；C项归属福利机构，可以更好造福社会的，占近二成（19.23%)；D项国家更好利用的占不到一成（3.85%)。②认为应归自然人所有的主要理由是，B项甲的其他亲属是与甲有较密切联系的人，甲的遗产归其他亲戚所有，这符合情理的占近四成(37.18%)。

(二）无人承受遗产的处理

1. 无人承受遗产管理人产生方式的民众观念与民间习惯情况统计

问题【十一、(二）1.】“对于无人继承遗产的管理人，您认为下列哪一种产生方式更合适？A. 死者户籍所在地的居委会或村委会或所在单位指定遗产管理人；B. 人民法院指定遗产管理人；C. 民政部门指定遗产管理人。（单选）理由是什么？请问：在您所在地区人们一般如何确定无人继承遗产的管理人？”

（1）无人承受遗产管理人的产生方式的民众观念及理由情况统计。

①无人承受遗产管理人的产生方式的民众观念情况统计。

表 6-70 无人承受遗产的管理人之产生方式的民众观念情况统计（单选）

选项	人数	比例
A. 死者户籍所在地的居委会/村委会或所在单位指定遗产管理人	343	52.77%
B. 人民法院指定遗产管理人	232	35.69%
C. 民政部门指定遗产管理人	75	11.54%
合计	650	100%

关于无人承受遗产管理人的产生方式之民众观念，调查统计数据显示，填写该题的 650 名被调查者中，Ⅰ. 选择 A 项应由居委会、村委会或所在单位指定的，占五成以上（52.77%）；Ⅱ. 选择 B、C 两项应由人民法院或民政部门指定的，合计占近五成（47.23%）。

②无人承受遗产管理人的产生方式的民众观念之理由情况统计。

表 6-71 无人承受遗产管理人的产生方式的民众观念之理由情况统计

项目	人数	比例
A. 死者户籍所在地的居委会或村委会或所在单位对死者及其遗产的情况比较清楚，由其指定遗产管理人，有利于对遗产进行清算、管理和利用	92	54.76%
B. 人民法院通过法定程序，对遗产进行清算和管理，由其指定遗产管理人，有利于公平保护相关债权人的利益	64	38.10%
C. 人民法院办案压力大，可能无暇顾及遗产管理人的指定	10	5.95%
D. 由老人指定，有威望	2	1.19%
合计	168	100%

关于无人承受遗产管理人的产生方式的民众观念之理由，调查统计数据显示，168 名被调查者填写了选择理由，Ⅰ. 认为应由居委会或村委会或所在单位指定的原因是，A 项上述主体对死者及其遗产的情况比较清楚，由其指定遗产管理人，这有利于对遗产进行清算、管理和利用的，占近五成半（54.76%）；Ⅱ. 认为应由人民法院指定的理由是，B 项人民法院通过法定程序，对遗产进行清算和管理，由其指定遗产管理人，这有利于公平保护相关债权人利益的，占近四成（38.10%）；Ⅲ. 还有不到一成的人填写了 C 项人民法院办案压力大，可能无暇顾及遗产管理人的指定（5.95%）或 D 项由家中老人指定更有威望（1.19%）等理由。

（2）无人承受遗产管理人的产生方式的民间习惯情况统计。

表 6-72 无人继承遗产的管理人产生方式的民间习惯情况统计（单选）

选项	人数	比例
A. 人民法院指定	17	26.56%
B. 村委会或居委会指定	27	42.19%
C. 民政部门指定	16	25.00%
D. 单位指定	4	6.25%
合计	64	100%

关于无人承受遗产管理人的产生方式的民间习惯，调查统计数据显示，填写该问题的64名被调查者所在地区的民间习惯是：①A、C两项由人民法院或民政部门指定的，合计占五成以上（51.56%）；②B、D两项由村委会、居委会或单位指定的，合计占近五成（48.44%）。

2. 无人承受遗产的酌分请求权主体的民众观念与民间习惯情况统计

问题【十一、（二）2.】“您认为下列哪些人可以酌情分得无人继承的遗产？A. 依靠死者扶养的人；B. 与死者共同生活的人；C. 与死者有密切联系且对其帮助较多的人；D. 其他。（多选）请问：在您所在地区人们一般是如何分配此类遗产的？”

（1）无人承受遗产的酌分请求权主体的民众观念情况统计。

表 6-73 无人承受遗产的酌分请求权主体的民众观念情况统计（多选）

选项	人数	比例
A. 依靠死者扶养的人	461	71.70%
B. 与死者共同生活的人	386	60.03%
C. 与死者关系密切且对其帮助较多的人	467	72.63%
D. 其他	21	3.27%

关于无人承受遗产的酌分请求权主体的民众观念，调查统计数据显示，在被调查者中，选择A、B、C三项，依靠死者扶养的人（71.70%）、与死者共同生活的人（60.03%）和与死者关系密切且对其帮助较多的人（72.63%）均可以成为无人承受遗产的酌分请求权主体的，各占六成至七成以上。

（2）无人承受遗产的酌分请求权主体的民间习惯情况统计。

表 6-74 无人承受遗产的酌分请求权主体的民间习惯情况统计（单选）

选项	人数	比例
A. 交给法院处理	5	5.55%
B. 与死者共同生活的人	18	20.00%

续表

选项	人数	比例
C. 照顾过死者的人	37	41.11%
D. 对死者有帮助的人	15	16.67%
E. 不是继承人的其他亲属	15	16.67%
合计	90	100%

关于无人承受遗产的酌分请求权主体的民间习惯，调查统计数据显示，填写该问题的90名被调查者所在地区的民间习惯是：①B、C、D、E四项，与死者共同生活的人（20.00%）、照顾过死者的人（41.11%）、对死者有帮助的人（16.67%）和不是继承人的其他亲属（16.67%）可以请求酌分无人承受遗产的，各占一成至四成以上；②还有不到一成（5.55%）的地区，该种情况下有交给法院处理的习惯。

十二、遗产处理相关案例的简介与评析

（一）涉及遗产范围界定案例的简介与评析

案情简介：被继承人史某晖生前与×人寿×公司签订保险单，生效日期为2011年1月5日。该保单的保险责任中，关于身故保险金第2款的约定为："本合同生效之日起1年后，被保险人非因意外伤害导致身故，我们按本合同的保险金额向身故保险金受益人给付非意外身故保险金，本合同终止。"保险合同的原投保人与被保险人均是史某晖，史某晖已于2012年6月27日将该保险的投保人变更为母亲田某丽，由其继续为其投保，被保险人仍然是史某辉，且通知了保险人并办理了投保人变更手续。史某晖于2013年4月21日因意外身故，保险单保险金额为315000元。原告田某丽与被告史某晖的子女史某华、史某岚因保险金的分割发生纠纷，诉至法院。原告田某丽认为，自2012年6月27日起，由其为儿子史某晖投保，该保险金应属于其个人财产。被告史某华、史某岚认为，其父的保险金应属于遗产，由法定继承人共同继承。

一审法院审理后认为，我国现行《保险法》第42条规定："被保险人死亡后，有下列情形之一的，保险金作为被保险人的遗产，由保险人依照《中华人民共和国继承法》的规定履行给付保险金的义务：（一）没有指定受益人，或者受益人指定不明无法确定的。"由此可见，适用《保险法》第42条规定的"保险金作为被保险人的遗产"的前提条件是享有保险金请求权的人无法确定的情形。史某晖投保时在保单受益人处填写"法定"，因法律并未规定"法定受益人"，故应视为未明确指定受益人。因此，依法判决意外身故保险金315000元应作为被保险人（史某晖）的遗产，由原被告三人共同继承。①后原告田某丽不服一审判决，提起上述。二审和再审人民法院认为，一审法院认定事实清楚，适用法律正确，依法维持原判。

① 参见中国裁判文书网：(2015) 晋×第×号，《再审申请人史某华、史某岚与被申请人田某丽继承纠纷再审审查民事裁定书》，载 http://wenshu.court.gov.cn/content/content?DocID=742846be-f1e9-4600-8e9c-76fee36f7cff&KeyWord=(2015)晋×第×号，访问日期：2019年3月8日。限于本章篇幅，作者对原案情内容有酌情删改。

适用法律分析：本案的争议焦点在于，保险金 315000 元是属于被保险人即本案被继承人史某晖的遗产，还是投保人田某丽的财产。被继承人史某晖投保时在保单受益人处填写“法定”，因法律并未规定“法定受益人”，故应视为未明确指定受益人。根据前述我国《保险法》第 42 条的规定，被保险人史某晖死亡后，没有指定受益人，或者受益人指定不明无法确定的，保险金作为被保险人史某晖的遗产。我们认为，本案审理法院关于意外身故保险金应作为被保险人（史某晖）遗产的判决是符合法律规定的。关于遗产范围的界定，我国 1985 年《继承法》对其进行了列举和概括式结合的立法，改革开放 40 多年来，一些新型财产是否属于遗产，我国民众的认识还不充分。此案由于涉及保险金，需要在我国《保险法》中查找遗产界定的相关依据，这也在一定程度上导致民众对遗产范围的界定认识不明，容易导致纠纷，这是我国立法之不足。

（二）涉及继承开始的通知和公告案例的简介与评析

案情简介：史某林与高某琴系夫妻关系，二人育有子女四人，长子史某田，长女史某芬，次女史某芳，三女史某玲。史某林与高某琴分别于 2011 年 9 月 12 日、2010 年 3 月 22 日病亡，二人生前遗留房屋一处，坐落于×市×区。2013 年 2 月 16 日，长子史某田没有通知其他两位继承人史某芬、史某玲，并隐瞒有其他继承人事实的情况下出售房屋，史某芳表示了放弃继承权。后史某田、史某芬、史某玲三人因房屋售房款的分配问题发生纠纷，诉至法院。原告史某芬、史某玲认为，该遗产房屋三人均有权继承，被告史某田作为房屋的实际管理人，负有继承开始的通知义务而不作为，侵害了两人的继承权。

法院审理后认为，继承开始后有遗嘱的按遗嘱继承，没有遗嘱的按法定继承处理。本案史某林与高某琴、育有四子女，史某田、史某芬、史某芳、史某玲。其中，史某芳明确表示放弃继承权，因此，该遗产房屋应由史某田、史某芬、史某玲三子女平均继承。本案中被告史某田作为房屋的实际掌管人，没有通知其他继承人，谎称史某林只有二名子女，其中一人放弃继承权而出售了该房屋，侵害了其他继承人的合法权益。法院依法判决史某田应偿还史某芬、史某玲对应房屋继承份额的售房款。①

适用法律分析：本案涉及继承人在继承开始后没有通知其他继承人，并侵害其他继承人合法权益的问题。本案史某芳放弃继承权，长子史某田在没有通知其他继承人的情况下隐瞒还有其他继承人的事实，私自对遗产房屋进行处分。我国《继承法》第 23 条规定：“继承开始后，知道被继承人死亡的继承人应当及时通知其他继承人和遗嘱执行人。”可见，继承开始的通知是我国《继承法》明确规定的一项义务，负有通知义务的继承人或单位、组织都应当积极履行。审理法院认为，史某田没有积极履行继承开始的通知义务，侵害了其他继承人的合法权利，故判决其应返还两位原告继承份额的售房款，这是符合法律规定的。但是，审理法院也仅判决被告返还相应继承份额的售房款，没有判决其承担恶意转移财产的损害赔偿责任。我国欠缺继承人或遗产管理人未履行通知义务造成其他继承人损失的法律责任，这是其立法之不足。

（三）涉及遗产管理案例的简介与评析

案情简介：解某生生前系×市×厂职工，任财务部会计。2015 年 4 月 20 日解某生在上

---

① 参见中国裁判文书网：（2016）黑×行初×号，《史某田与史某芬、史某玲房屋纠纷一审民事判决书》，载 http://wenshu. court. gov. cn/content/content? DocID=b7e82faf-9103-4407-8ef3-bb6514941e7d&KeyWord=（2016）黑×行初×号，访问日期：2019 年 3 月 8 日。限于本章篇幅，作者对原案情内容有酌情删改。

班时间被同事发现头部碰伤，被送往医院救治无效死亡。李某、解某1、解某2、刘某系解某生法定继承人。2015年11月25日×公司委托会计师事务所有限公司对解某生负责×公司的账簿凭证进行审计，会计师事务所审查认为，解某生负责×公司会计和出纳工作期间，未入账银行资金净流出125000元；未记账的收取现金597400元；重复支付运费24283.3元；四笔业务凭证付款金额与原始单据不符，总计凭证比原始单据多付3004.9元。原告×公司认为，被继承人解某生生前恶意给×公司造成了上述损失，后以被告李某、解某1、解某2、刘某作为解某生的遗产管理人，应负责清偿被继承人生前债务为由诉至法院。被告李某、解某1、解某2、刘某认为，不存在上述债务，他们也没有义务负责偿还。

一审法院审理后查明，2015年4月解某生死亡后，×公司未委托第三方将解某生负责工作期间的所有账簿凭证进行封存，且委托会计师事务所审核的时间是在解某生死亡6个多月后，×公司无法证明其提供账簿凭证的真实性和全面性，且该会计师事务所有限公司审计的结论不能证明案涉款项损失系由解某生本人原因造成。故×公司提供的证据不足以证实其主张的损失系由解某生造成，其应承担举证不能的法律后果。故×公司的上述损失不属于被继承人的生前债务，对其主张被告李某、解某1、解某2、刘某作为解某生的遗产管理人，负责清偿被继承人生前债务的请求，不予支持。后原告×公司不服一审判决提起上述。二审和再审法院均认为，一审法院认定事实清楚，适用法律正确，依法维持原判。①

适用法律分析：解某生生前在×公司从事财务工作，解某生因伤离开工作岗位到医院救治后死亡，其间，该公司未在第一时间封存解某生经手账目，而是在解某生死亡半年多后委托会计师事务所有限公司出具资金审核报告，存在着较大时间跨度，并且该公司以审核报告为据主张其损失，与该损失系解某生本人所致之间缺乏直接因果关系和排他的唯一性。故李某、解某1、解某2、刘某虽然是解某生财产的继承人和遗产管理人，但并没有向×公司偿还债务的责任。目前，我国并没有明确规定遗产管理人制度。我国《继承法》第24条规定："存有遗产的人，应当妥善保管遗产，任何人不得侵吞或者争抢。"本案×公司提供的证据不足以证实其主张的损失系由解某生造成，故不能认定被继承人解某生对×公司存在欠债，也不能要求其继承人李某、解某1、解某2、刘某作为解某生的遗产管理人，承担偿还债务的责任。因此，人民法院的判决是符合法律规定的。我国欠缺遗产管理制度，在司法实践中，法院指定遗产管理人欠缺法律依据，这是其立法之不足。

（四）涉及法定继承案例的简介与评析

案情简介：原告李×1、李×2系被继承人李×3的子女。1995年3月，被告杨×通过欺骗方式取得结婚登记，后该结婚证经人民法院审理后撤销，其与李×3的婚姻关系自始无效，双方为同居关系。2013年被继承人李×3去世，李×1、李×2和杨×因遗产房屋的分配产生纠纷，诉至法院。原告李×1、李×2认为，涉案房屋是李×3所在单位分配的房改房，带有一定的国家政策及特定人身身份属性，而被告杨×为农业人口，不具备享受房改福利

① 参见中国裁判文书网：（2018）冀×申×号，《×公司、李某等债务清偿纠纷再审审查与审判监督民事裁定书》，载 http://wenshu.court.gov.cn/content/content? DocID=8dd4913c-bbeb-4c60-8d4f-a92200114750&KeyWord=（2018）冀×申×号，访问日期：2019年3月8日。限于本章篇幅，作者对原案情内容有酌情删改。

政策的身份。被告杨×认为，涉案房屋为其与李×3 同居期间共同购得的房屋，其享有部分房屋所有权。

一审法院审理后认为，李×1、李×2 作为李×3 的子女，是李×3 遗产的法定继承人；因杨×与李×3 的婚姻关系经人民法院生效判决确认为无效，故其不是李×3 的法定继承人。杨×、李×3 非婚同居 10 余年，涉案房屋是双方同居期间所购，房屋所有权证亦于此间取得。李×1、李×2 主张涉案房屋均系李×3 的个人财产，但未能提供充分有效的证据予以证明，故法院判决该房屋应属杨×与李×3 双方共同共有。虽然杨×不是李×3 的法定继承人，但其对涉案房屋享有二分之一的产权。后李×1、李×2 因不服一审判决，提起上述。二审和再审法院均认为，一审法院认定事实清楚，适用法律正确，依法维持原判。①

适用法律分析：本案涉及法定继承中分家析产以及涉案房屋的分配问题。首先，杨×与李×3 的婚姻关系，经人民法院生效判决确认为无效。因此，二人共同生活的 10 余年应当被认定为是非婚同居关系，即被告杨×不是李×3 的合法配偶和法定继承人，对李×3 的遗产不享有法定继承权。其次，被告杨×虽然不是李×3 的法定继承人，但涉案房屋是双方同居期间所购，并且再审申请人的证据不能充分表明涉案房屋为李×3 的个人财产。因此该房屋应属杨×与李×3 双方共同共有。根据 1989 年《关于人民法院审理未办结婚登记而以夫妻名义同居生活案件的若干意见》第 10 条："解除非法同居关系时，同居生活期间双方共同所得的收入和购置的财产，按一般共有财产处理。"和我国《继承法》第 26 条："夫妻在婚姻关系存续期间所得的共同所有的财产，除有约定的以外，如果分割遗产，应当先将共同所有的财产的一半分出为配偶所有，其余的为被继承人的遗产。遗产在家庭共有财产之中的，遗产分割时，应当先分出他人的财产。"应当将此同居期间购买的共同财产先析产，然后将其中的一半作为李×3 的遗产。二审和再审人民法院认为，一审人民法院结合案件的实际情况判令各方按份享有涉案房屋，并无不当。我们认为，审理法院的判决符合法律规定。本案中，应先析出杨×二分之一的房屋产权，其余二分之一的房屋产权作为李×3 的遗产，由李×1、李×2 按照法定继承平均分割。

（五）涉及遗嘱继承案例的简介与评析

案情简介：原、被告系兄弟关系，被继承人李某某系双方之母。李某某与李某勤共育有五名子女，分别为原、被告五人。1987 年 7 月，李某勤去世。2006 年 7 月 24 日，李某某去世。因遗产继承问题，五名子女发生纠纷并诉至法院。原告李×1、李×2、李×3、李×4 认为李某某所立遗嘱并非本人签字，该遗嘱无效系被告李×5 伪造，请求依法定继承分割被继承人李某某的遗产；被告李×5 主张，被继承人李某某于 2004 年 1 月 20 日立有遗嘱，并交给自己保管，被继承人的遗产应按遗嘱继承处理。

法院审理后查明，原告提交多份被继承人李某某年轻时的签名，主张遗嘱中的笔迹及书写习惯与被继承人生前不同。但审理法院认为作为一个 81 岁高龄的老人，其书写方法相比十几年前有所变化亦属常人可以理解的范畴。原告并未提供充分的证据使本院确信该遗嘱并非李某某书写，也没有申请进行笔记鉴定。故对原告主张不予采纳。被继承人李某

① 参见中国裁判文书网：（2014）高×字第×号，《李×1 等法定继承纠纷申诉、申请民事裁定书》，载 http://wenshu.court.gov.cn/content/content? DocID=ec5ab317-3f16-4347-a751-752a345646f9&KeyWord=（2014）高×第×号，访问日期：2019 年 3 月 8 日。限于本章篇幅，作者对原案情内容有酌情删改。

某于2004年1月20日所立遗嘱，由其本人签名，并注有日期，形式上符合自书遗嘱的法律要求，内容亦不违反法律、行政法规的强制性规定，应为合法有效。李某某立有遗嘱，本案不存在法定继承问题，依法判决按照遗嘱继承处理。①

适用法律分析：本案涉及被继承人所立遗嘱是否有效、遗产应按法定继承还是遗嘱继承处理的问题。2004年1月20日，李某某立下遗嘱一份，载明其遗产房屋和存款由李×5继承，其他任何人不得干涉。虽然原告对该份遗嘱的真实性不予认可，并提交了多份李某某于20世纪八九十年代的书信签名等材料，欲以此证明遗嘱中的笔迹及书写习惯与李某某的笔迹及书写习惯不同，但又没有申请笔记鉴定，可见原告并未提供充分的证据证明该遗嘱并非李某某书写。被继承人李某某所立遗嘱，由其本人签名，并注有日期，形式上符合自书遗嘱的法律规定，内容亦不违反法律、行政法规的强制性规定，应为合法有效。我们认为，本案审理法院的判决是符合法律规定的。公民可以立遗嘱将个人财产指定由法定继承人的一人或者数人继承。继承开始后，按法定继承办理；有遗嘱的，按照遗嘱继承或遗赠办理。

（六）涉及继承和遗赠的接受与放弃案例的简介与评析

案情简介：被继承人赵某忱死亡后，其遗产由儿子赵某经管理。其间，赵某英、洛某雄明确表示放弃继承被继承人遗产。但是其后发现，赵某经隐匿了《平安帖》等大部分古董字画，价值较大。后因遗产继承发生纠纷，原告赵某英、洛某雄诉至法院，要求被告赵某经返还隐匿财产并依法分割。被告赵某经认为，赵某英、洛某雄二人已明确表示放弃被继承人遗产，因此这些后发现的古董字画也一并因放弃继承而丧失继承该部分遗产的权利。

一审法院审理后认为，本案遗产清单中不包括本案讼争的《平安帖》等遗产。赵某经隐匿了较大数量的财产占为已有。因赵某经隐匿遗产，使其他法定继承人只知道当时现存的遗产状况，导致他们作出错误的决定而放弃继承。因此，赵某英、洛某雄二人现主张他们并没有对《平安帖》等古董字画的继承权予以放弃，法院依法判决对赵某经的主张不予支持。② 后被告赵某经不服一审判决，提起上述。二审和再审法院经审理后认为，一审法院认定事实清楚，适用法律正确，依法维持原判。

适用法律分析：本案涉及继承人赵某英、洛某雄是否已经放弃继承的问题。根据我国《继承法》第25条规定，继承开始后，继承人放弃继承的，应当在遗产处理前，作出放弃继承的表示。没有表示的，视为接受继承。因之前赵某经隐匿财产，使其他共同法定继承人只知道当时现存的遗产，并导致其他两位共同继承人错误地作出放弃该遗产继承的意思表示。根据我国《民法通则》第58条的规定，一方以欺诈、胁迫的手段或者乘人之危，使对方在违背真实意思的情况下所为的民事行为无效。所以，不能认为赵某英、洛某雄已经表示放弃对《平安帖》等古董字画的继承权。我们认为，再审人民法院根据我国

① 参见中国裁判文书网：（2012）西×第×号，《李×2等与李×5继承纠纷一审民事判决书》，载 http://wenshu.court.gov.cn/content/content?DocID=66dface2-66d9-44af-bbd3-32712ad688cc&KeyWord=(2012)西×第×号，访问日期：2019年3月8日。限于本章篇幅，作者对原案情内容有酌情删改。

② 参见中国裁判文书网：（2015）民×第×号，《赵某英、洛某雄与赵某经法定继承纠纷申请再审民事裁定书》，载 http://wenshu.court.gov.cn/content/content?DocID=8f55e913-c6f0-4cf3-b246-63ef49226510&KeyWord=(2015)民×第×号，访问日期：2019年3月8日。限于本章篇幅，作者对原案情内容有酌情删改。

法律，结合一审、二审查明的事实，认定赵某英、洛某雄没有放弃继承的判决是符合法律规定的。

（七）涉及继承权的丧失、被继承人的宥恕与代位继承案例的简介与评析

案情简介：刘某莲育有五个儿子，杨某丙、杨某乙、杨某甲、杨某求、杨某告。被继承人刘某莲去世后，杨某甲提交遗嘱一份，记载："吾年岁正高，在病重之际，只三子杨某甲尽心尽力照顾我，我去世后，愿将我应得的房产、财产，全部由三子杨某甲继承。立嘱人：刘某莲（签字、捺印）；见证人：刘某（签字）、赵某（签字）。2006 年 8 月 26 日代书人：刘某之。"被继承人刘某莲去世后，五个儿子因遗产继承问题产生纠纷，诉至法院。原告杨某丙、杨某乙、杨某求、杨某告认为，三子杨某甲提交的该份遗嘱系伪造故其应当丧失继承权，被继承人遗产应按照法定继承处理。被告杨某甲认为，该份遗嘱真实合法，被继承人遗产应按遗嘱继承处理，其不存在伪造遗嘱因而丧失继承权的行为。

一审法院审理后查明，针对该份遗嘱是否属于伪造，而杨某甲应否丧失继承权的问题。一是，从遗嘱的代书人看，代书人刘某之否认该遗嘱的内容与其代书的内容一致，杨某甲又不能提供刘某之的代书手写原件与之对照。虽代书人刘某之认可对遗嘱签过字，但并不认可在杨某甲提交的 2006 年 8 月 26 日遗嘱上签字。二是，杨某甲对于遗嘱打印的过程陈述自相矛盾又与另外二证人的陈述亦不一致。三是，从两位见证人看，见证人刘某、赵某在一审调查笔录中均称记不清楚遗嘱的内容，刘某在一审出庭时又认可该遗嘱内容，赵某则未出庭作证。因此两见证人亦不能证明该遗嘱内容是被继承人刘某莲的真实意思表示。综上，一审法院认为，对杨某甲不能认定其有伪造遗嘱的行为，但杨某甲未提供充分证据证明该遗嘱的真实性，判决本案被继承人遗产应按法定继承处理。后被告杨某甲不服一审判决，提起上诉。二审和再审法院审理后认为，一审法院认定事实清楚，适用法律正确，一审法院未采信其提供的 2006 年 8 月 26 日遗嘱并无不当，依法维持原判。①

适用法律分析：该案涉及杨某甲提供的遗嘱是否属于伪造而丧失继承权的问题。首先，对于该代书遗嘱是否有效，审理法院从以下几个方面予以判定：一是从遗嘱的代书人看，代书人刘某之否认该遗嘱的内容与其代书的内容一致；二是杨某甲对于遗嘱打印的过程陈述与另外二证人的陈述亦不一致；三是从两位见证人看，见证人刘某、赵某两人在一审调查笔录中均称记不清楚遗嘱内容。综上，审理法院认定该代书遗嘱无效。其次，对于杨某甲是否因伪造遗嘱而丧失继承权的问题，根据我国《继承法》第 7 条规定："继承人有下列行为之一的，丧失继承权：（一）故意杀害被继承人的；（二）为争夺遗产而杀害其他继承人的；（三）遗弃被继承人的，或者虐待被继承人情节严重的；（四）伪造、篡改或者销毁遗嘱，情节严重的。"审理法院认为，杨某甲的行为并不属于伪造遗嘱情节严重的行为，对于原告主张杨某甲应丧失继承权的请求不予支持。我们认为，该代书遗嘱无效的认定有待商榷。该代书遗嘱有立嘱人刘某莲的签字和捺印，有见证人刘某、赵某的签字，有代书人刘某之的签字。可见，该代书遗嘱符合法律要求。之所以对代书遗嘱的效力产生疑问，在于代书人刘某之否认该遗嘱的内容与其代书的内容一致；见证人刘某、赵某

---

① 参见中国裁判文书网：（2013）鲁×字第×号，《杨某甲、杨某乙等继承纠纷再审民事判决书》，载 http://wenshu.court.gov.cn/content/content? DocID=dc99bc50-64bb-4cda-8668-1a0b39e037f0&KeyWord=（2013）鲁×第×号，访问日期：2019 年 3 月 8 日。限于本章篇幅，作者对原案情内容有酌情删改。

在一审调查笔录中均称记不清楚遗嘱内容。因此该遗嘱被法院认定为无效。然而，遗嘱是否可因代书人和见证人的当时不尽职或事后记不清内容而不产生效力，有待商榷。

（八）涉及继承协议案例的简介与评析

案情简介：吴某亮与袁某珍系夫妻，两人婚后生育六个子女，即吴某1、吴某2、吴某3、吴某4、吴某5、吴某6。2009年7月22日袁某珍去世，2015年5月27日吴某亮去世。吴某亮生前于2001年购买位于×路×栋×号房屋一套，产权为夫妻共同所有。2002年7月，袁某珍和吴某亮生前因年纪较大，需要人照顾，经子女间协商并取得两位老人同意后，当事人间签订协议，决定由原告吴某4负责照顾两位老人生活，待父母去世后由其继承×路×栋×号房屋。在母亲袁某珍去世后，吴某4又照顾父亲吴某亮直至其去世，其间其他兄弟姐妹或给钱或买东西有时前来看望父母。2014年6月9日，被继承人吴某亮由他人代书立下遗嘱一份，将上述房屋赠与吴某4。2015年9月28日，继承人间因遗产继承问题发生纠纷，原告吴某4向法院起诉要求按2002年7月签订的继承协议处理遗产，由原告继承系争遗产房屋；被告吴某1、吴某2、吴某3、吴某5、吴某6则认为该份继承协议无效。

法院审理后查明，位于×路×栋×号房屋的所有权人登记为吴某亮，但该房屋购买于吴某亮与袁某珍的婚姻关系存续期间，应为吴某亮与袁某珍的夫妻共同财产，吴某亮与袁某珍应各享有一半的所有权。2009年7月22日妻子袁某珍去世，该房屋继承发生，因袁某珍并未留下遗嘱，故袁某珍死亡后应按法定继承对涉案房屋中属于其个人所有的产权份额予以继承，法定继承人为丈夫吴某亮及其六名子女吴某1、吴某2、吴某3、吴某4、吴某5、吴某6。2014年6月9日被继承人吴某亮请魏某某代书遗嘱，该遗嘱真实、合法，法院予以确认。故法院判决认定吴某亮将其个人所有的涉案房屋之产权份额产权赠与吴某4的行为合法有效。而对于之前袁某珍、吴某亮夫妻二人同意，各继承人共同签订的继承协议的效力不予承认。①

适用法律分析：本案涉及当事人间签订的继承协议是否有效以及涉案房屋如何分配的问题。关于涉案房屋的归属，共有两项分割依据，一是，在7年前经子女间协商并经两位老人同意后，当事人间签订的继承协议；二是，2014年6月9日，被继承人吴某亮由他人代书立下遗嘱，将上述房屋赠与吴某4。目前我国立法仅规定了遗赠扶养协议，且主体须为不是法定继承人的扶养人和集体所有制组织。对于被扶养人与法定继承人间签订的继承协议是否有效，我国立法并未规定。本案人民法院根据吴某亮生前所立的有效代书遗嘱，认定吴某亮将其个人享有的涉案房屋的产权赠与吴某4的行为合法有效，但并没有承认继承人间签订的继承协议的效力。我们认为，法院的判决符合我国现行法律规定，但其不承认继承协议效力的合理性有待商榷。在2002年7月，由于袁某珍和吴某亮因年纪较大需要人照顾，经与其子女间协商并取得两位老人同意后，当事人间已经签订了一份继承协议，决定由原告吴某4负责照顾两位老人生活，两位老人去世后由其继承系争房屋。虽然我国立法没有认可该种继承协议的效力，但根据权利与义务相一致原则和平等自愿原

① 参见中国裁判文书网：（2015）鄂×民初字第×号，《吴某4与吴某1等继承纠纷一案一审民事判决书》，载http://wenshu.court.gov.cn/content/content?DocID=7b9d9521-92cb-4193-8d1b-a9e34b13e887&KeyWord=(2015)鄂×民初字第×号，访问日期：2019年3月8日。限于本章篇幅，作者对原案情内容有酌情删改。

则，受扶养人与法定继承人间签订的继承协议并未被法律所禁止。而本案根据被继承人吴某亮生前所立的有效代书遗嘱为依据，对其享有个人所有权的涉案房屋份额，由吴某4依遗嘱继承。对于袁某珍享有的产权房屋却是按法定继承由所有的法定继承人共同继承，即否认了继承协议的效力。这在一定程度上损害了继承人吴某4的财产权益。我们认为，我国欠缺继承协议制度，不能满足部分受扶养人意欲与法定继承人签订继承协议之需要，这是我国立法之不足。

（九）涉及遗产债务清偿案例的简介与评析

案情简介：2014年1月28日，朱某斌向原告兰某威出具了内容为“今借兰某威现金肆拾万元整。按月息2%计”的借条一份。2014年12月26日，朱某斌因病去世。朱某斌遗产由其儿子朱某海继承，但遗产份额不足以清偿上述欠债。后因遗产债务清偿问题发生纠纷，原告兰某威诉至法院。原告兰某威提出，2014年4月，朱某斌与他人签订了房屋买卖合同，以21万元出售房屋，朱某斌与唯一继承人朱某海存在恶意逃避债务的嫌疑，应由朱某海承担全部遗产债务。被告朱某海认为，其并未取得上述购房款，其没有责任承担全部遗产债务。

法院审理后查明，被继承人朱某斌生前在2014年4月出售房屋一套，但没有证据显示该笔售房款已交给朱某海，并且朱某海表示其并未接受该笔售房款。根据我国《继承法》第33条规定：“继承遗产应当清偿被继承人依法应当缴纳的税款和债务，缴纳税款和清偿债务以他的遗产实际价值为限。”本案中，虽然被继承人遗产不足以清偿遗产债务，但并没有充分证据显示继承人朱某海存在恶意逃避债务，转移遗产的行为，因此法院判决朱某海对遗产不足以偿还的欠债不承担清偿责任。①

适用法律分析：本案涉及被继承人遗产债务的清偿问题。根据我国《继承法》第33条规定：“继承遗产应当清偿被继承人依法应当缴纳的税款和债务，缴纳税款和清偿债务以他的遗产实际价值为限。”本案被继承人的遗产不足以清偿遗产债务，但并没有充分证据显示继承人朱某海存在恶意逃避债务，转移遗产的行为，因此审理法院认定朱某海仅以遗产的实际价值清偿被继承人的债务，对遗产不足以清偿的欠债不承担清偿责任的判决是正确的。但是我们认为，我国立法对于继承人隐匿、转移遗产而侵害债权人利益的行为，是否应承担相应的赔偿责任没有规定，这是其立法之不足。

（十）涉及遗产分割案例的简介与评析

案情简介：丁某与张某福育有张某甲、张某乙、张某丙、张某丁四个子女。原告孙某与被告张某甲结婚，2009年5月22日，原告孙某与被告张某甲经法院调解离婚。张某福于2010年7月2日死亡。原告孙某与被告张某甲因遗产房屋的分割问题产生纠纷，诉至法院。原告孙某主张，按原告六分之一的比例分割位于×市×区×镇的三层房屋。被告张某甲、丁某等主张，案涉房屋系祖屋，由被告张某甲的父亲张某福及兄弟姐妹共同出资所建，与前妻孙某无关。

法院审理后查明，涉案房屋于2000年拆除老屋后建造第一至二层，当时未办理建房

① 参见中国裁判文书网：（2016）鄂×民初×号，《兰某威与朱某海民间借贷纠纷一审民事判决书》，载 http://wenshu.court.gov.cn/content/content? DocID=c4aa7661-67dd-4a8f-ba18-a7a601391560&KeyWord=(2016)鄂×民初×号，访问日期：2019年3月8日。限于本章篇幅，作者对原案情内容有酌情删改。

审批手续，花费约10万余元。2006年，张某福作为户主申请农村私房加层审批，审批表中载明张某福户的家庭人口为5人，原房占地面积110平方米，原房层次2.5层，申请层次3层，总建筑面积330平方米。5人具体指张某福、丁某、张某甲、孙某、张某丁，镇人民政府予以同意。2010~2011年，诉争房屋加盖第三层，花费约11万元，原告未出资。2000年建造涉案房屋第一至二层时，原告孙某与张某甲以经营饭店所得出资，故涉案房屋应属张某福、丁某、张某甲、孙某、张某丁的家庭共同财产。由此法院依法判决，酌情确定原告对涉案房屋的第一至三层享有八分之一的份额。①

适用法律分析：本案涉及被继承人张某福去世后，遗产房屋如何分割的问题。因原告与被告张某甲现已离婚，共有关系终止，原告要求分割共同财产的诉请，人民法院予以了支持。根据我国《继承法》第26条第2款："遗产在家庭共有财产之中的，遗产分割时，应当先分出他人的财产。"和1993年《最高人民法院关于人民法院审理离婚案件处理财产分割问题的若干具体意见》第8条规定："夫妻共同财产，原则上均等分割。根据生产、生活的实际需要和财产的来源等情况，具体处理时也可以有所差别。属于个人专用的物品，一般归个人所有。"据此精神，对共有财产的分割，有协议的，按协议处理；没有协议的，应当根据等分原则，并且考虑共有人对共有财产的贡献大小，适当照顾共有人生产、生活的实际需要等情况进行处理，人民法院酌情确定原告对案涉房屋的第一至三层享有八分之一的份额。

我们认为，人民法院的判决是符合法律规定的。首先，审理法院准确把握了原告孙某与被告张某甲婚姻关系存续时间与涉案房屋建造时间之间的关系。2009年5月22日，原告孙某与被告张某甲经法院调解离婚。而涉案房屋2000年建造第一至二层，2010~2011年，诉争房屋加盖第三层，花费约11万元，原告未出资。根据对涉案房屋的出资、出力情况，应认定孙某对涉案房屋享有一定份额，但因第三层房屋的建造是在其与张某甲离婚之后，因此原告主张对涉案房屋第一至三层享有六分之一份额的主张不能予以支持。其次，人民法院根据法律规定，对共有财产的分割，有协议的，按协议处理；没有协议的，应当根据等分原则，并且考虑共有人对共有财产的贡献大小，适当照顾共有人生产、生活的实际需要等情况进行处理，因此酌情确定原告对涉案房屋的第一至三层享有八分之一的份额是符合法律规定的。

（十一）*涉及无人承受遗产案例的简介与评析*

案情简介：投保人李某家，1983年2月5日出生，于2013年11月23日、2013年11月27日与×人寿公司签订了二份合同，分别为×健康终身寿险（分红型）、×保险合同，合同受益人为李某家，身故受益人为李某洪（其父）。2016年1月5日20时许，李某家在×市×区×镇一山坡触电身亡，经刑事现场勘查，排除他杀可能。李某家生前无配偶、无子女、无兄弟姐妹，父母、祖父母、外祖父母均已死亡。原告×村委会向本院提出诉讼请求，判令被告×人寿公司向原告支付被保险人李某家享有的保险金10万元。被告×人寿公司认为原告主体不适格。

---

① 参见中国裁判文书网：（2013）杭×民初字第×号，《孙某与丁某、张某甲等分家析产纠纷一审民事判决书》，载 http://wenshu.court.gov.cn/content/content?DocID=258fc23c-09dc-4651-bcec-e5257c5eb738&KeyWord=(2013)杭×民初字第×号，访问日期：2019年3月8日。限于本章篇幅，作者对原案情内容有酌情删改。

法院审理后认为，投保人李某家所投保的保险，保险金指定的身故受益人为其父亲李某洪，没有其他受益人。李某洪已先于投保人死亡，保险金应当作为李某家的遗产，按照法定继承办理。李某家死亡后，无第一顺序、第二顺序继承人，按照我国《继承法》第32条之规定："无人继承又无人受遗赠的遗产，归国家所有；死者生前是集体所有制组织成员的，归所在集体所有制组织所有。"李某家生前所在的集体所有制组织即本案原告有权主张被告依照保险合同支付保险金。法院判决被告×人寿保险有限公司支付原告10万元。①

适用法律分析：本案争议焦点为无人继承遗产如何处理及原告主体是否适格的问题。首先，投保人李某家所投保的保险，保险金指定的身故受益人为其父亲李某洪，没有其他受益人。李某洪已先于投保人死亡，保险金应当作为李某家的遗产，按照法定继承办理。其次，李某家死亡后，无第一顺序、第二顺序继承人，按照我国《继承法》第32条之规定，"无人继承又无人受遗赠的遗产，归国家所有；死者生前是集体所有制组织成员的，归所在集体所有制组织所有"，因此，李某家生前所在的集体所有制组织即本案原告有权主张被告依照保险合同支付保险金。人民法院判决认定李某家所投保的保险应为其遗产，并认定×市×镇×村民委员会具有原告的主体资格，该判决符合法律规定。

第三节 当代中国湖北省民众财产继承观念与遗产处理习惯的特点与原因分析

根据本次调查统计数据的汇总分析，湖北省被调查者对前述十一个问题所体现出的财产继承观念与遗产处理习惯之特点与原因分析如下：

一、遗产范围界定之特点与原因分析

（一）遗产的种类之特点与原因分析

关于遗产种类的民众观念，统计数据显示的特点是，在被调查者中，（1）有八成至九成以上的人认为住房（98.33%）、小汽车（94.99%）、存款（94.54%）、股票（84.67%）属于遗产；认为单位出租给某甲的午休住房不属于遗产的，占近九成（88.16%），此认识与我国现行法的规定相一致；（2）有五成至七成以上的人认为家庭日常生活用品（65.86%）、欠债（57.36%）和交通事故死亡赔偿金（70.86%）属于遗产，此认识与现行法的规定有冲突；（3）有三成以上（32.02%）的人认为"某甲以其姓名注册的邮箱、QQ账号等"属于遗产，对此我国法律目前无规定（见表6-4）。

以上特点的原因分析，在湖北省被调查者中，（1）有八成至九成的人对我国现行法明确列举的住房、小汽车、存款等属于遗产有较清晰的认识，其原因可能是受我国有立法之影响。（2）有五成至七成的人认为家庭日常生活用品、欠款和死亡赔偿金等属于遗产，但此认识与法律规定不一致，其原因可能是：其一，对于家庭日常生活用品属于遗产，被

① 参见中国裁判文书网：(2016) 鄂×民初×号，《×村委会与×人寿保险有限公司人身保险合同纠纷一审民事判决书》，载 http://wenshu.court.gov.cn/content/content?DocID=f848b632-c7e9-4b53-b583-c539a57bc728&KeyWord=(2016)鄂×民初×号，访问日期：2019年3月8日。限于本章篇幅，作者对原案情内容有酌情删改。

继承人对这些物品也在使用。但此认识有一定偏差，因为只有其中被继承人享有的份额才属于遗产，但被调查者对此范围的认识不够清楚，而认为全部属于遗产。其二，对于欠债的性质，通说认为我国遗产范围的界定采取“积极财产说”，即不包括消极性质的被调查者的生前欠债。其三，对于死亡赔偿金的性质，根据我国2004年《关于审理人身损害赔偿案件适用法律若干问题的解释》第1条第2款规定：“本条所称‘赔偿权利人’，是指因侵权行为或者其他致害原因直接遭受人身损害的受害人、依法由受害人承担扶养义务的被扶养人以及死亡受害人的近亲属。”第17条第3款规定：“受害人死亡的，赔偿义务人除应当根据抢救治疗情况赔偿本条第一款规定的相关费用外，还应当赔偿丧葬费、被扶养人生活费、死亡补偿费以及受害人亲属办理丧葬事宜支出的交通费、住宿费和误工损失等其他合理费用。”以上规定中表明，死者的人身损害死亡补偿费是对死亡受害人的近亲属的补偿费，其不属于遗产。（3）有三成以上的被调查者认邮箱、QQ账号等属于遗产，近七成的被调查者认为其不属于遗产，其原因可能是邮箱、QQ账号等与人身密切相关，如其被作为遗产继承可能会侵犯被继承人的个人隐私。

关于遗产的种类之我国立法，我国《继承法》第3条规定：“遗产是公民死亡时遗留的个人合法财产，包括：（一）公民的收入；（二）公民的房屋、储蓄和生活用品；（三）公民的林木、牲畜和家禽；（四）公民的文物、图书资料；（五）法律允许公民所有的生产资料；（六）公民的著作权、专利权中的财产权利；（七）公民的其他合法财产。”1985年《执行继承法意见》第3条规定，公民的其他合法财产包括有价证券和履行标的为财物的债权等。

从域外立法例看，《德国民法典》未列举遗产的范围，而是在第1922条表述为“财产（遗产）总体”。《日本民法典》在第896条将遗产概括为“被继承人财产的一切权利、义务，但是，专属于被继承人本人者不在此限”。

从我国诸继承法学者建议稿看，“梁稿”认为，“遗产是自然人死亡时遗留的个人合法财产。前款规定的遗产包括自然人因其死亡而获得的未指定受益人的保险金、补偿金、赔偿金以及其他基于该自然人生前行为而应获得的财产利益。下列权利义务不得作为继承的标的：（一）与被继承人人身不可分割的人身权利；（二）与被继承人人身有关的专属性债权债务；（三）法律规定不得继承的其他财产”。[①] 可见，“梁稿”采取的是正面概括加反面排除式的立法模式。

我们认为，我国对遗产范围的界定缺少反面排除规定，这是其立法之不足。确定遗产范围，是判断遗产归属、进行遗产分配的前提和基础。[②] 因此，上述建议增加反面排除规定的湖北省被调查民众的观念、域外立法例和我国学者建议稿的观点，可供我国立法参考。

（二）被继承人生前特种赠与财产的归扣之特点与原因分析

关于被继承人生前特种赠与财产是否应扣入遗产范围的民众观念与民间习惯，统计数据显示的特点是，（1）在被调查者的观念上，认为被继承人去世时遗留的个人财产才可

---

① 参见“梁稿”第1941条。

② 参见陈苇、魏小军：《论我国遗产范围立法的完善》，载陈苇主编：《中国继承法修改热点难点问题研究》，群众出版社2013年版，第345页。

算作遗产，不包括被继承人生前对子女的特种赠与财产的，占近七成半（74.05%），而认为被继承人生前资助子女的财产与死亡时其遗留的住房、存款，均应当合并计算为遗产的，占二成以上（23.98%）（见表6-5）；（2）被调查者所在地区的继承习惯是：没有该习惯的占七成以上（71.21%），而有该习惯的占近三成（28.79%）（见表6-7）。

以上特点的原因分析，根据湖北省被调查者填写的生前特种赠与财产不归扣纳入遗产的分配方式民间习惯之理由（见表6-9），（1）近七成半的人认为被继承人去世时遗留的个人财产才可算作遗产，七成以上的地区也有该习惯，其原因是死后平均分配所留遗产，有利于遗产的分割；（2）二成以上的人认为被继承人生前资助子女的财产，均应当合并计算为遗产，近三成的地区也有该习惯，其原因是张老汉生前给乙的财产较少，在其死后乙应多分些，这体现公平原则。

关于遗产归扣制度之我国立法，我国《继承法》对此无规定。

从域外立法例看，一些国家在继承法中规定了遗产归扣制度。例如，《德国民法典》第2050条规定，被继承人的直系卑亲属接受被继承人生前财产赠与的，应当在遗产分割时予以扣除。关于归扣遗产价值计算时间，域外相关立法中，主要有三种立法例：一是以遗产分割时为准，如法国；二以继承开始时为准，如瑞士；三以赠与时为准，如德国。[①]

从我国诸继承法学者建议稿看，对于是否设立遗产归扣制度，我国学界有不同的观点。我国有很多学者主张建立遗产归扣制度，如李洪祥、陈苇等学者。支持遗产归扣理论的学者很多人认为其最大的制度价值就在于平衡继承人之间的利益分配，维护彼此间的公平和平等。[②] 比如，在现实生活中，成年的兄姐在成家立业之时往往得到父母的大额特种赠与，此后，若父亲或母亲死亡，如果无归扣制度，未成年的弟妹在继承时显然处于不利地位。而归扣制度将兄妹所得的大额赠与加入遗产总额中计算分配，因此对于未成年的弟妹才公平。[③] 同时，也有很多反对建立归扣制度的学者[④]，理由主要包括：一是，与现有制度相冲突，与赠与制度相冲突，归扣制度使一般受赠人可获得受赠物而与被继承人关系更近的继承人却要承担受赠物被归扣的忧虑，同时归扣制度否定了赠与的后果，违反了《合同法》；与所有权制度相冲突，归扣将特种赠与视为对继承人的预付，影响了受赠的继承人处分该财产的权利，影响了交易安全和稳定。[⑤] 二是，与《继承法》遗产范围的规定相冲突，归扣的对象属于被继承人生前已处分的财产，不在遗产的范围内。[⑥] 但我国也有学者指出，待归扣的财产实际上属于“不完全遗产”，除被继承人表示免于归扣的外，其被依法归扣计入遗产总额后，就属于遗产的组成部分。[⑦]

---

① 参见《法国民法典》第860条；《瑞士民法典》第630条；《德国民法典》第2055条。

② 参见李洪祥：《遗产归扣制度的理论、制度构成及其本土化》，载《现代法学》2012年第5期；陈苇、杜志红：《我国设立归扣制度的基础与制度构建研究》，载《政法论坛》2013年第2期；张华贵：《财产归扣制度研究》，载《现代法学》2006年第4期；张平华、刘耀东：《遗产分割中归扣法律制度研究》，载《法学论坛》2009年第1期。

③ 参见梁分：《从儿童最大利益原则看〈继承法〉的修改与完善》，载《兰州大学学报（社会科学版）》2010年第5期，第143页。

④ 参见王翔：《对我国应否建立归扣制度的商榷》，载《石河子大学学报（哲学社会科学版）》2007年第6期；沈星：《也谈归扣制度——兼论我国是否应当引入归扣制度》，载《法学论坛》2008年第1期。

⑤ 董欣：《归扣制度适用问题浅析》，载《中国商界》2009年第12期，第311页。

⑥ 沈星：《也谈归扣制度——兼论我国是否应当引入归扣制度》，载《法学论坛》2008年第1期，第150~152页。

⑦ 参见陈苇主编：《外国继承法比较与中国民法典继承编制定研究》，北京大学出版社2011年版，第233、234页。

我们认为，我国欠缺遗产归扣制度，不利于在继承人间公平地分配遗产，这是其立法之不足。遗产归扣制度将父母生前已经分配给某些子女这种大额资助等特殊财产视为该子女应继份的预付，在遗产分割时将该特种赠与财产计人遗产总额，具有保障在子女共同继承人中公平地分配父母的遗产之功能。虽然以上湖北省近七成半的被调查者不认可遗产归扣制度，但此制度具有在共同继承人中公平分配遗产的功能。因此，上述有关遗产归扣制度的湖北省被调查民众的观念与习惯、域外立法例和我国学者建议稿的观点，可供我国立法参考。

二、继承开始的通知和公告之特点与原因分析

（一）继承开始的通知和公告的主体之特点与原因分析

关于继承开始的通知和公告主体的民间习惯，统计数据显示的特点是，在被调查者所在地区，（1）由继承人作为主体的，各占六成至七成以上，具体包括：知道被继承人死亡的继承人（71.62%）和保管遗产的继承人（65.55%）；（2）由知道被继承人死亡的单位、村（居）委会作为主体的，占近五成（47.34%）；（3）由处理被继承人死亡事件的机构作为主体的，占近四成（37.94%）（见表6-10）。

以上特点的原因分析，六成至七成的湖北省被调查民众认可的继承开始的通知和公告主体较为广泛，其原因可能是基于我国立法的规定和现实生活的需要。只有把继承开始的通知或公告尽快发出后，遗产利害关系人才能及时前来参与遗产处理。多种主体通知，有利于及时发出继承开始的通知或公告，符合实际生活的需要。

关于继承开始的通知和公告主体之我国立法，我国《继承法》第23条规定："继承开始后，知道被继承人死亡的继承人应当及时通知其他继承人和遗嘱执行人。继承人中无人知道被继承人死亡或者知道被继承人死亡而不能通知的，由被继承人生前所在单位或者住所地的居民委员会、村民委员会负责通知。"可见，湖北省被调查民众的继承习惯与我国立法有较高的一致性，但民众认可的通知义务主体范围略广于我国现行立法的规定。

从域外立法例看，大陆法系的许多国家均有规定继承开始的通知主体。例如，《法国民法典》规定，继承人得声明以净资产为限取得继承权，此声明得向大审法院作出且须在国内公示，并在2个月内提交遗产清单给法院，并采取与声明相同的方式公示。继承开始后4个月期限届满时，继承人未表示接受或放弃继承的，可以由遗产债权人、共同继承人、后一顺序的其他继承人或者国家采取行动，以司法文书催告继承人作出决定。① 可见，在法国共同继承人、遗产债权人等均为通知和催告主体。

从我国诸继承法学者建议稿看，"杨稿"认为，应在我国《继承法》规定的基础上，增加处理被继承人死亡事件的部门或基层组织为通知义务人。②"梁稿"认为，应在我国《继承法》规定的基础上，增加其他利害关系人作为通知义务人。③

我们认为，继承开始的通知和公告主体应该限制范围，在立法技术上采取明确列举方式是正确的。保管遗产的人应当属于《继承法》第23条规定的知道被继承人死亡的继承

① 参见《法国民法典》第788、189、792条。
② 参见"杨稿"第70条。
③ 参见"梁稿"第2001条。

人，其属于通知主体。至于处理被继承人死亡事件的机构，如公安交警部门等是否可以作为继承开始的通知和公告的发布主体。综上，我们认为，公安交警部门承担通知的义务，并不是继承法为其设立的，而是公法。通知受害人家属（继承人）前来处理死者相关事务，本来就是他们的职责所在，但不属于继承法通知继承开始的义务。

（二）继承开始的通知和公告的方式之特点与原因分析

关于继承开始的通知和公告方式的民间习惯，统计数据显示的特点是，在被调查者所在地区，（1）分别由口头、电话、微信等方式通知（66.46%）和信件、告知函等书面通知（54.48%）的，各占五成至六成以上；（2）分别在报纸、电视、网络等平台上发布被继承人死亡的公告（25.64%）、在被继承人所在地的村（居）委会公告栏公告（57.51%）和申请人民法院以公告程序进行公告（29.74%）的，各占二成至五成以上（见表6-11）。

以上特点的原因分析，在湖北省被调查者所在地区，（1）五成至六成以上的地区有口头、电话、微信等较为快捷、方便的方式发出通知的习惯，其原因可能是随着手机、微信等聊天软件的普及，民众希望继承开始的通知方式能够更便捷、快速、准确的传达到被通知人处。（2）二成至五成以上的地区有发布公告的习惯，其原因可能是认为公告是继承人不明时的必然选择，但随着新兴科技的发展，可以在电视、网络等平台上发布被继承人死亡的公告，便于更大范围内民众知晓该公告。

关于继承开始的通知发出的方式之我国立法，我国《继承法》及司法解释对此无规定。并且，我国《继承法》也没有设立继承开始的公告制度。

从域外立法例看，大陆法系的德国、瑞士、日本等国均规定在继承人有无不明时，应发布寻找继承人的公告，催告权利人在一定期限内申明其继承权。例如，《法国民法典》关于继承开始的通知与公告之方式的规定，主要体现在催告继承人接受或者放弃继承、无人继承遗产的管理方面的规定之中。第一，催告继承人作出接受或放弃继承的选择时，采用的方式是书面催告（司法外文书催告）。第二，继承人以净资产为限接受继承时应向大审法院作出声明，该声明应进行登记并在国内进行公示，且声明可以经电子途径公示。第三，在申请无人继承遗产的管理时，法院作出的对无人继承的遗产实行管理的裁定应当公示。①

从我国诸继承法学者建议稿看，关于继承开始的通知和公告方式，“梁稿”主要体现在对遗产债权的公告的规定中，即继承人和遗产管理人应当于知道继承开始后3个月内向人民法院递交遗产清册，由人民法院依公示催告程序催促债权人申报债权。② 即由继承人或遗产管理人等以递交遗产清册给法院，请求法院发出公示催告的方式。“张稿”对继承开始的通知与公告的方式的规定，在催告债权人、继承人有无不明时的公告中有所体现。③

我们认为，对于继承开始的通知和公告方式，我国立法没有必要予以明确规定，原因在于，随着科技水平的提高，通信方式在不断增多，法律的滞后性有可能限制了通知的方

① 《法国民法典》第771、788、809-1条。

② “梁稿”第2017条。

③ “张稿”第3、24、45、67条。

式的灵活和自由。

（三）继承开始的通知和公告的期间之特点与原因分析

关于继承开始的通知和公告期间的民众观念，统计数据显示的特点是，在被调查者中，（1）认为应在7日以内发出的，合计占六成以上（63.43%）；（2）认为应在15日以内发出的，占近二成（17.45%）；（3）认为应在30日以内发出的，仅占一成半（15.33%）（见表6-12）。

以上特点的原因分析，六成以上的湖北省被调查民众认为，应在7日内的较短期间发出继承开始的通知和公告，其原因可能是希望尽快发出继承开始的通知和公告，以通知相关权利人参与继承或申报债权债务。

关于继承开始的通知和公告的期间之我国立法，我国《继承法》第23条仅规定“及时”发出继承开始的通知，并没有明确规定继承开始的通知期间。另外，对于票据被盗、遗失或灭失的公示催告程序，我国现行《民事诉讼法》第219条规定，人民法院决定受理申请，应在3日内发出公告，催促利害关系人申报权利。公示催告的期间，由人民法院根据情况决定，但不得少于60日。

从域外立法例看，对于继承开始的公示催告期间，《日本民法典》规定，（1）限定承认人在作出限定继承的表示后5日内，对遗产债权人及受遗赠人进行公示催告的期间不得少于2个月。（2）当继承人有无不明时，管理人须及时对所有的遗产债权人及受遗赠人发出应在2个月内申报其请求为内容的公告，此公告期间不能少于6个月。[①]

从我国诸继承法学者建议稿看，关于无人承受遗产的公示催告程序，“王稿”第662条规定：“人民法院决定受理申请，应在3日内发出公告，催促继承人、受遗赠人、债权人等其他利害关系人申报、登记。公示催告的期间，由人民法院根据情况决定，但不得少于六十日。”“张稿”第67条规定：“继承开始后，继承人有无不明的，被继承人居所地的居民委员会、村民委员会或其所在单位，应于继承开始后尽快报告法院。法院在接到报告后应当按照本法第24条的规定指定遗产管理人，并公示催告继承人和利害关系人于规定期限内主张权利。前款公告期限不得少于6个月。”

我们认为，我国欠缺继承开始的通知和公告期间之规定，这是其立法之不足。因此，上述主张在7日内发出继承开始通知和公告的湖北省被调查民众的观念、域外立法例和我国学者建议稿的观点，可供我国立法参考。

三、遗产管理之特点与原因分析

（一）遗产管理人的确定之特点与原因分析

关于遗产管理人的确定的民间习惯，统计数据显示的特点是，在被调查者所在地区，（1）由死者的法定继承人作为遗产管理人的，占近九成（88.47%）；（2）分别由死者的儿媳或女婿（27.62%）、死者家族中的德高望重者（44.46%）、死者的其他亲戚朋友（19.27%）和死者所在的单位或村/居委会（31.87%）作为遗产管理人的，各占近二成至四成以上（见表6-13）。

以上特点的原因分析，根据湖北省被调查者填写的遗产管理人的确定的民间习惯之理

---

① 《日本民法典》第927、957、958、987条。

由（见表6-15），（1）近九成的地区有由法定继承人担任管理人的习惯，其原因是便于清点和妥善管理遗产；（2）近二成至四成以上的地区有由法定继承人之外的人（死者家族中的德高望重者、其他亲戚朋友等）或组织（死者所在的单位或村/居委会）担任管理人的习惯，其原因是防止遗产被隐藏、转移，这有利于保护遗产相关人合法权益。

关于遗产管理人制度之我国立法，我国《继承法》第16条规定："公民可以依照本法规定立遗嘱处分个人财产，并可以指定遗嘱执行人。公民可以立遗嘱将个人财产指定由法定继承人的一人或者数人继承。公民可以立遗嘱将个人财产赠给国家、集体或者法定继承人以外的人。"第24条规定："存有遗产的人，应当妥善保管遗产，任何人不得侵吞或者争抢。"可见，我国现行立法没有设立系统的遗产管理人制度。

从域外立法例看，《德国民法典》规定，如有被继承人的指定，由遗嘱执行人担任遗产管理人。没有遗嘱执行人的，继承人如无因管理人般对遗产享有权利和负担义务，多个继承人则共同享有管理遗产的权利。此外，遗产法院可根据继承人或遗产债权人的申请，发布遗产管理命令，指定遗产管理人管理遗产，在继承人不明或不能肯定其是否已接受遗产的情况下，依法为待继承遗产选任遗产管理人。①

从我国诸继承法学者建议稿看，"梁稿"认为，遗产管理人的产生分为以下四种情况：其一，有遗嘱执行人的，则遗嘱执行人担任遗产管理人；其二，继承人担任，继承开始后2个月内继承人没有放弃继承的，由其自己或者选任其他人履行遗产管理职责，多个继承人没有选任遗产管理人的，其得共同履行管理职责；其三，法院指定，法院在特殊情况下依据利害关系人的申请指定遗产管理人，如没有遗嘱执行人且继承人选任遗产管理人有异议，或没有遗嘱执行人且继承人有无不明或继承人不在的，或遗产债权人证实其权益受到继承人的损害或有损害危险的；其四，村（居）委会担任，有遗嘱但没有遗嘱执行人和法定继承人承担执行遗嘱职责的，死者生前所在单位或者继承开始地的村（居）委会应承担遗产管理的职责。② 另外，"王稿""张稿"等学者建议稿对此也有规定。③

我们认为，我国欠缺遗产管理人的产生方式之规定，这是其立法之不足。因此，上述主张明确遗产管理人产生方式的湖北省被调查民众的习惯、域外立法例和我国学者建议稿的观点，可供我国立法参考。

（二）遗产管理人的职责与报酬之特点与原因分析

第一，关于遗产管理人职责的民众观念，统计数据显示的特点是，在被调查者中，认为遗产管理人的职责包括清查遗产，制作遗产清单（91.81%）；妥善保管遗产（94.08%）；查明被继承人生前的债权和债务，积极地追讨债权或清偿债务（73.29%）；可以原告或被告的身份参加因遗产引起的诉讼（65.10%）；查明被继承人是否留有遗嘱，并且确定遗嘱是否真实合法（53.57%）；定期制作遗产管理报告，向继承人报告遗产管理的情况（59.18%）的，各占五成至九成以上（见表6-16）。

以上特点的原因分析，五成至九成以上的湖北省被调查民众认为遗产管理人应承担较为广泛的管理职责，其原因可能是这有利于引导遗产管理人依法履行职责，有利于平等地

① 参见《德国民法典》第1959~1961、1981、2032、2038、2197、2205条。

② 参见"梁稿"第2002条。

③ 参见"王稿"第549条；"张稿"第45条。

保护继承人和遗产债权人的利益。

第二，关于遗产管理人是否有权取得报酬的民间习惯，统计数据显示的特点是，在被调查者所在地区，（1）继承人担任的遗产管理人，五成（50.23%）的地区有管理人不能请求给付报酬的习惯；（2）法院指定的遗产管理人，近五成半（54.02%）的地区有可以请求给付报酬的习惯；（3）继承人选任的第三人作为遗产管理人，其中，五成（50.97%）的地区有是否给付报酬应当由继承人决定的习惯，三成半（35.81%）的地区有一律有权请求给付报酬的习惯（见表6-17）。

以上特点的原因分析，根据湖北省被调查者填写的遗产管理人是否有权取得报酬的民间习惯之理由（见表6-18），（1）五成的地区有继承人担任遗产管理人不能取得报酬的习惯，其原因是遗产管理人多数情况下与被继承人关系密切，具有亲情关系，同时，遗产管理人又继承遗产，因此管理遗产不需要报酬；（2）近五成半的地区有法院指定的遗产管理人可以请求给付报酬的习惯，其原因是遗产管理人为管理遗产付出了自己的劳动和时间，应该给予一定费用；（3）继承人选任的第三人作为遗产管理人，其中五成的地区有是否给付报酬应当由继承人决定的习惯，三成半的地区有一律有权请求给付报酬的习惯，其原因是视情况而定，这更能符合实际情况。

关于遗产管理人的职责和报酬之我国立法，我国《继承法》缺乏系统、完善的遗产管理制度，亦没有规定遗产管理人的职责和报酬等内容。

从域外立法例看，关于遗产管理人的职责和报酬，大陆法系不少国家都有规定。例如，关于遗产管理人的职责，《瑞士民法典》规定其职责主要有：其一，制作财产清单，将继承财产及债务分项列记，对财物应逐个标明估价；其二，结算被继承人的日常业务；其三，公示催告被继承人的债务人、债权人以及担保权利人在规定的期限内申报债权及债务；其四，清偿被继承人的债务，交付遗赠；其五，根据被继承人的指示或依法分割遗产。此外，当遗产归属国家时，可依职权催告债权人提出债权。接受遗产的州或市镇公共政治团体仅在其从遗产的限度内对遗产的债务负责。[①] 关于遗产管理人的报酬，该法典规定遗嘱执行人为管理执行遗产任务付出的劳务，有获得相当报酬的权利。[②]

从我国诸继承法学者建议稿看，关于遗产管理人的职责和报酬，“梁稿”认为，遗产管理人的职责包括清理和保管遗产；制作遗产清册；公示催告债权人并清偿债务；交付剩余遗产。[③]“陈稿”“王稿”“张稿”对遗产管理人的职责也均有规定。[④] 关于遗产管理人的报酬，“梁稿”规定，继承人或遗嘱执行人以外的遗产管理人有权请求与其所执行职务相当的报酬，且该报酬有优先受偿权；遗嘱执行人的报酬由遗嘱人指定，没有指定的，其不得请求报酬，但继承人或受遗赠人自愿支付的除外。[⑤]“徐稿”“王稿”对遗产管理人的报酬也有规定。[⑥]

我们认为，我国欠缺遗产管理人的职责和报酬之规定，这是其立法不足。因此，以上

---

① 参见《瑞士民法典》第581~582、585、595~596条。

② 参见《瑞士民法典》第517、584条。

③ 参见“梁稿”第2004、2005条。

④ 参见“陈稿”第8条；第2004、2005条；“王稿”第636、652、653条；“张稿”第49条。

⑤ “梁稿”第1995、2003条。

⑥ 参见“徐稿”第一分编第292条；第四分编第397条；“王稿”第639条。

有关遗产管理人的职责和应依据该管理人的不同产生方式而确定是否给付报酬的湖北省被调查民众的观念与习惯、域外立法例和我国学者建议稿的观点，可供我国立法参考。

（三）遗产管理人的损害赔偿责任之特点与原因分析

关于遗产管理人的损害赔偿责任之民间习惯，统计数据显示的特点是，在被调查者所在地区，（1）有故意或重大过失，才承担损害赔偿责任的，占五成半（55.67%）；（2）无论有故意、重大过失或一般轻过失，都要承担损害赔偿责任的，占四成以上（42.34%）（见表6-19）。

以上特点的原因分析，在湖北省被调查者所在地区，（1）五成半的地区有故意或重大过失，才承担损害赔偿责任的习惯，其原因可能是遗产管理人需要承担的职责较多，而且继承人担任遗产管理人还可能没有报酬，为使有关主体能够勇于担任遗产管理人的职责，没有必要规定过重的损害赔偿责任；（2）四成以上的地区有无论有故意、重大过失或一般轻过失，都要承担损害赔偿责任的习惯，其原因可能是对违法行为的惩罚，并且严格损害赔偿责任可以预防侵害遗产违法行为的发生。

关于遗产管理人的损害赔偿责任之我国立法，我国《继承法》对此无规定。

从域外立法例看，《德国民法典》规定，在遗产支付不能或负债过度的情况下，遗产管理人没有申请遗产支付不能程序的，对因此而发生的损害向债权人承担责任。继承人在编制遗产清册时有法定不当行为的，对遗产债务的清偿承担无限责任。[①]《日本民法典》规定，遗产管理人怠于实施公告或催告，或者违反法律的规定不当清偿的，对因此所产生的损害负赔偿责任。继承人处分继承财产的全部或部分，或在限期内作出限定继承或放弃继承后，隐匿继承财产全部或部分，私自消费或恶意不将其记载于继承财产目录的，视为继承人已作出单纯承认。[②]

从我国诸继承法学者建议稿看，“王稿”认为，遗产管理人的法律责任为遗产管理人在遗产管理过程中没有恰当地行使管理职责或违反遗产债权公告和债务清偿规定的，应对由此造成的遗产权利人的损失承担赔偿责任，如遗产管理人是继承人的则应承担无限责任。遗嘱执行人因故意或重大过失，使遗产权利人的利益受损，其应对损害后果担负赔偿责任。如遗嘱是有偿执行的，则无论是各种程度的过错，都应赔偿所有的损害。[③]“陈稿”第10条规定，遗产管理人因故意或过失未尽遗产管理义务，从而造成遗产毁损或灭失的，应当承担损害赔偿责任。

我们认为，我国欠缺遗产管理人的损害赔偿责任，这是其立法之不足。因此，以上湖北省被调查民众的习惯、域外立法例和我国学者建议稿的观点，可供我国立法参考。

四、法定继承的特点与原因分析

（一）法定继承人的范围与顺序之特点与原因分析

第一，关于法定继承人范围和顺序的民众观念，统计数据显示的特点是，被调查者认可的法定继承人的范围和顺序是：第一顺序为配偶（91.20%）、父母（65.55%）、子

① 《德国民法典》第1985、2005条。

② 《日本民法典》第921、934条。

③ “王稿”第654条。

(73.44%)、女(68.44%);第二顺序为孙子女(49.01%)、外孙子女(43.25%)、祖父母(47.34%)、外祖父母(40.97%)、兄弟(46.74%)、姐妹(44.46%);第三顺序为侄子女(31.41%)、外甥子女(32.17%)、伯叔姑(45.22%)、舅姨(28.22%)、堂兄弟(28.07%)、堂姐妹(27.77%)、表兄弟(19.58%)、表姐妹(19.27%)(见表6-20)。

第二,关于配偶与血亲继承人顺序的民众观念,统计数据显示的特点是,在被调查者中,(1)选择C项第一继承顺序为配偶、子女、父母,配偶为固定的第一顺序继承人的,占七成以上(71.38%);(2)选择A、B两项第一顺序为子女,第二顺序为父母,第三顺序为兄弟姐妹、祖父母、外祖父母、兄弟姐妹的子女,配偶为无固定继承顺序继承人,可以参与第一、第二(或第三)顺序继承的,合计占近三成(28.62%)(见表6-21)。

以上特点的原因分析,(1)湖北省被调查民众较认可的法定继承人的范围广于我国立法、顺序也多于现行法之规定,其原因可能是目前我国家庭结构小型化,而且独生子女家庭中没有兄弟姐妹。在此情况下,如果仅仅依据我国《继承法》规定的法定继承人范围和顺序,可能有被继承人死亡后遗产无人继承的情况出现,不利于实现财产在家庭内部传承。(2)七成以上的人主张第一继承顺序为配偶、子女、父母,配偶为固定的第一顺序继承人,其原因可能是受我国现行立法之影响;近三成的人主张第一顺序为子女,第二顺序为父母,第三顺序为兄弟姐妹、祖父母、外祖父母、兄弟姐妹的子女,配偶为无固定继承顺序继承人,可以参与第一、第二(或第三)顺序继承,其原因可能是配偶作为无固定顺序继承人,更有助于兼顾各继承人的利益,防止特殊情况下配偶一人取得全部遗产。

关于法定继承人的范围与顺序之我国立法,我国《继承法》第10条规定,遗产按照下列顺序继承:第一顺序:配偶、子女、父母。第二顺序:兄弟姐妹、祖父母、外祖父母。继承开始后,由第一顺序继承人继承,第二顺序继承人不继承。没有第一顺序继承人继承的,由第二顺序继承人继承。我国《继承法》第13条规定,同一顺序继承人继承遗产的份额,一般应当均等。对生活有特殊困难的缺乏劳动能力的继承人,分配遗产时,应当予以照顾。对被继承人尽了主要扶养义务或者与被继承人共同生活的继承人,分配遗产时,可以多分。有扶养能力和有扶养条件的继承人,不尽扶养义务的,分配遗产时,应当不分或者少分。继承人协商同意的,也可以不均等。

从域外立法例看,《法国民法典》规定,第一顺序为子女及其直系晚辈血亲;第二顺序为父母、兄弟姐妹及其直系晚辈血亲;第三顺序为除父母以外的直系长辈血亲;第四顺序为除兄弟姐妹及其直系晚辈血亲以外的六亲等内的旁系血亲;配偶没有固定的继承顺序,其与被继承人的子女或直系晚辈血亲或其父母共同继承。①

从我国诸继承法学者建议稿看,"梁稿"第1946条规定的法定继承人范围和顺序如下:第一顺序为配偶、子女、父母;第二顺序为兄弟姐妹、祖父母、外祖父母;第三顺序为其他四亲等以内的亲属。"陈稿"第45条规定的继承人之范围和顺序如下:第一顺序为子女及其晚辈直系血亲;第二顺序为父母;第三顺序为兄弟姐妹及其子女;第四顺序为祖父母,包括父系祖父母和母系祖父母;配偶可以和任一顺序的血亲继承人共同继承。

我们认为,我国《继承法》将父母和子女一并列为第一顺序法定继承人,其指导思

---

① 《法国民法典》第734、756、757条。

想是死后扶养，即死者生前应当赡养父母、抚养子女，在死亡后，其财产应当继续发挥该作用。但一般来说，人们希望将财产留给子女并通过他们在自己的直系卑亲属中传递下去。若父母继承财产，该财产可能部分甚至全部归属于死者的兄弟姐妹以及他们的直系卑亲属。在有子女的情况下，人们一般不愿个人财产落入旁系血亲手中。本次调查数据也显示，父母在第一顺序的选择率较配偶、子女更低一些。如配偶为 91. 20%；子为 73. 44%；女为 68. 44%；父母为 65. 55%。因此，父母在继承顺序中的安排值得再行考虑。另外，不宜将侄子女、外甥子女、伯叔姑舅姨、表兄弟姐妹、堂兄弟姐妹列入法定继承人之中。

（二）配偶与血亲继承人的法定应继份之特点与原因分析

关于配偶与血亲继承人法定应继份的民众观念，统计数据显示的特点是，在被调查者中，（1）认为配偶应无固定继承顺序的，合计占五成以上（54. 62%），且在不同顺序其应继份不同；（2）认为配偶应有固定继承顺序，与第一顺序继承人共同继承的，占近四成半（44. 62%）（见表 6-22）。

以上特点的原因分析，在湖北省被调查者中，（1）五成以上的人主张配偶无固定继承顺序，认为配偶应当与不同顺序的血亲继承人共同继承且在不同的继承顺序取得不同的遗产份额，其原因可能是采取现有固定继承顺位的立法，若无父母、子女的情况下，遗产将由配偶一人继承，易造成财产外流出死者的家庭；（2）近四成半的人主张配偶应按固定顺序继承，其原因可能是受我国立法之影响。

关于配偶与血亲继承人的法定应继份之我国立法，根据我国《继承法》第 10、13 条的规定，配偶是第一顺序继承人，并且同一顺序继承人继承遗产的份额，一般应当均等。

从域外立法例看，《德国民法典》规定，关于配偶的应继份，配偶与第一顺序继承人共同继承时，其应继份为遗产的四分之一；与第二顺序继承人或者与父（母）系祖父母共同继承时，其应继份为遗产的二分之一。如果既没有第一、第二顺序继承人，也没有父系祖父母、母系祖父母，配偶获得全部遗产。[①]

从我国诸继承法学者建议稿看，"梁稿"认为，应增加法定继承人的人数，但未对配偶作为固定顺序继承人这一规定进行修改。[②] 而"张稿"第 28 条和"陈稿"第 45 条分别规定配偶无固定继承顺序，配偶可与相应顺序的血亲继承人共同继承遗产，且配偶参与不同顺序与血亲继承人共同继承时，其应继份有所不同。

我们认为，尽管在配偶与血亲继承人法定应继份的民众观念统计中，五成以上的被调查者认为配偶应为无固定顺序继承人，但在配偶与血亲继承人顺序的民众观念统计中，认为配偶应该固定在第一继承顺序的被调查者占七成以上（见表 6-21），从尊重湖北省被调查民众的意愿出发，维持我国《继承法》中固定顺位的规定更适宜。配偶与不同顺序继承人共同继承时的份额，也应按我国《继承法》第 13 条的规定，原则上均等分配，特殊情况下可以多分、少分或不分。

（三）配偶对遗产中家庭住房的先取权与终生使用权之特点与原因分析

第一，关于配偶对遗产中家庭住房的先取权与终生使用权的民间习惯，统计数据显示的特点是，在被调查者所在地区，有该习惯的占近九成（87. 29%）（见表 6-23）。

---

① 参见《德国民法典》第 1931 条。

② 参见"梁稿"第 1946 条。

以上特点的原因分析，近九成的湖北省被调查民众对于配偶对遗产中家庭住房的先取权与终生使用权予以认可，其原因可能是保护生存配偶的居住权，有利于老年人老有所居，体现中华民族的孝道文明。

第二，关于配偶对遗产中家庭住房的先取与终生使用是否付费的民间习惯，统计数据显示的特点是，在被调查者所在地区，（1）适当补偿的，占近五成半（54.17%）；（2）无须进行补偿的，占近四成（37.33%）（见表6-24）。

以上特点的原因分析，根据湖北省被调查者填写的配偶对遗产中家庭住房的先取与终生使用是否付费的民间习惯之理由（见表6-25），（1）近五成半的地区有适当补偿的习惯，其原因是这体现公平精神；（2）近四成的地区有无须进行补偿的习惯，其原因是应首先保证配偶乙有居住之所，同时丙是乙的儿子，将来乙的遗产也会由丙来继承，所以无须补偿。

关于配偶对遗产中家庭住房的先取权与终生使用权及其费用支付情况之我国立法，我国《继承法》对此无规定。

从域外立法例看，多有配偶对遗产中家庭住房的先取权或终生使用权的规定。例如，《法国民法典》第763条规定，配偶一方死亡后，享有继承权的健在配偶可以在1年内当然无偿的使用该住房及住房内属于遗产的动产。第764条规定，配偶一方死亡后，有继承权的健在配偶实际占有原属于夫妻双方或属于死者的住宅作为主要住宅时，对该住宅享有居住权，对住宅内的家具享有使用权，直至本人死亡。第765条规定，居住权与使用权的价值，健在配偶可以从配偶继承的遗产价值中扣减：如果居住权和使用权的价值低于健在配偶应当继承的遗产价值的，其有权从现存遗产中受领不足之部分；如果居住权和使用权的价值高于健在配偶应当继承的遗产价值的，有义务根据超出的部分对遗产给予补偿。

从我国诸继承法学者建议稿看，“王稿”第580条规定：“被继承人的配偶尚生存而没有自己的住房的，如果没有继承被继承人遗产中的房屋，则对于遗产中的房屋享有法定的用益物权。生存配偶为此需支付取得房屋所有权的继承人不超过市价的租金。具体租金数额及期限由配偶与房屋所有权人协商。协商不成的，双方均可以提起诉讼。”

我们认为，目前我国立法并没有规定配偶对遗产中家庭住房的先取权与终生使用权，但是近九成的湖北省被调查者所在地区都有该处理遗产的习惯。域外比较法上的上述规定体现了对配偶的一种倾斜保护。但我们考虑到我国配偶与其他继承人原则上平均分割遗产的立法传统，对该制度不予规定为宜。

（四）后顺序特殊法定继承人对遗产中原使用的住房及日常生活用品的终生使用权之特点与原因分析

第一，关于后顺序特殊法定继承人对特殊遗产的终生使用权之民间习惯，统计数据显示的特点是，在被调查者所在地区，（1）有该习惯的占九成以上（92.63%）；（2）而无该习惯的仅占不到一成（7.37%）（见表6-26）。

第二，关于后顺序特殊法定继承人对特殊遗产的终生使用是否付费及使用期限的民间习惯，统计数据显示的特点是，在被调查者所在地区，（1）无须支付租金的占八成（80.68%），要支付租金的占近二成（19.32%）（见表6-27）；（2）可以无偿终生使用的占八成以上（82.76%），不可无偿终生使用的仅占近二成（17.24%）（见表6-28）。

以上特点的原因分析，在湖北省被调查者所在地区，（1）九成以上的地区有后顺序特殊继承人对特殊遗产终生使用权的习惯，其原因可能是从保护后顺位特殊继承人的居住权考量；(2) 对于后顺序特殊法定继承人对特殊遗产的终生使用是否付费，八成的地区该情况有无须支付租金的习惯，其原因可能是这符合我国尊老敬老的传统美德；(3) 对于后顺序特殊法定继承人对特殊遗产的终生使用权之期限，八成以上的地区有可以终生使用权的习惯，其原因可能是保护后顺序特殊继承人居住权之需要。

关于后顺序特殊法定继承人对特殊遗产的终生使用权之我国立法，我国《继承法》对此无规定。

从域外立法例看，多有关于配偶对遗产中家庭住房的先取权与终生使用权的规定，并且有些国家规定后顺序特殊法定继承人具有该方面的权利。例如，《俄罗斯联邦民法典》第 1168 条第 3 款："如果遗产中的住房（房屋、住宅）等不能实物分割，则在遗产分割时，继承开始前居住在该处而且没有其他住房的继承人对于不是住房所有人的其他继承人享有作为其继承份额取得该住房的优先权。"

从我国诸继承法学者建议稿看，"张稿"第 33 条规定："父母因顺序在后未参加继承时，对遗产中供个人日常生活使用的住房和其他物品有终生使用权。"并且，我国有学者也主张，"关于特殊法定继承人对住房及家庭生活用品的终生使用权，依靠被继承人扶养的父母、父系祖父母或母系祖父母在未参加继承时，对遗产中原供其使用的住房和家庭生活用品享有终生使用权"。[①]

我们认为，后顺序特殊法定继承人对特殊遗产的终生使用权在我国《继承法》中并无规定，也非法定物权。此概念所要表达的核心内容，其实是遗产法定分配与老年人正常生活保障这两者应如何协调。无论从我国传统道德还是从婚姻家庭继承法的规定来看，民众一般都不会无视老人的晚年生活安排问题，故立法无须一刀切地予以规定，以避免可能会越俎代庖，或造成更多矛盾冲突，因此立法对此不予规定为宜。

（五）尽了主要赡养义务的丧偶儿媳或女婿的遗产分配方式之特点与原因分析

关于尽了主要赡养义务的丧偶儿媳或女婿的遗产分配之民间习惯，统计数据显示的特点是，在被调查者所在地区，(1) 其可以与第一顺序继承人共同继承且平均分配遗产的，占近六成半（64.01%）；(2) 其不能作为第一顺序继承人，但可以酌情分得遗产的，占三成以上（32.62%）（见表 6-29）。

以上特点的原因分析，根据湖北省被调查者填写的尽了主要赡养义务的丧偶儿媳或女婿的遗产分配的民间习惯之理由（见表 6-30），(1) 近六成半的人认为其可以与第一顺序继承人共同继承且平均分配遗产，其原因是丁作为儿媳妇孝敬公公，已经尽了赡养义务，符合中国的孝道文化和道德观念，因此有权作为第一顺序继承人继承遗产；(2) 三成以上的人认为其不能作为第一顺序继承人，其原因是虽然媳妇丁一直照顾公公的晚年生活，但毕竟不是某甲的子女，与某甲不具有血缘关系，遗产不能给了"外人"，因此不能继承某甲的遗产。

关于尽了主要赡养义务的丧偶儿媳或女婿的遗产分配方式之我国立法，我国《继承法》第 12 条规定："丧偶儿媳对公、婆，丧偶女婿对岳父、岳母，尽了主要赡养义务的，作为第一顺序继承人。"

---

① 陈苇、董思远：《民法典编纂视野下法定继承制度的反思与重构》，载《河北法学》2017 年第 7 期，第 19 页。

从域外立法例看，虽然各国对于亲属关系的范围规定不尽相同，但姻亲一般不包含在内。但苏联立法对此有所规定，1964年开始施行的《苏俄民法典》第532条规定："在死亡人生前扶养不少于一年的无劳动能力的人也为法定继承人。在有其他继承人的情况下，他们与应召继承的其他继承人按同一顺序继承。"①

从我国诸继承法学者建议稿看，"杨稿"第60条规定，丧偶儿媳（或女婿）对公婆（或岳父母）尽了主要赡养义务的，作为第一顺序继承人。"王稿"第569条规定丧偶儿媳（或女婿）对公婆（或岳父母）尽了主要赡养义务的，没有代位继承人时，作为第一顺序继承人。"梁稿""徐稿""张稿""陈稿"未规定尽了主要赡养义务的丧偶的儿媳或女婿为第一顺序继承人，而是主张根据他们尽赡养义务情况，可以酌情分给适当财产。②

我们认为，从调查统计数据结果来看，近六成半的湖北省被调查民众所在地区有尽了主要赡养义务的丧偶儿媳或女婿可以作为法定继承人的习惯，即他们的习惯与我国《继承法》的规定是相契合的。特别是在人口老龄化日益严重的情况下，老人的扶养将越发成为不容忽视的问题，社会化的扶养不可能一步到位，就必须借助于家庭内部的照顾。对此，维持我国现行法规定为宜。

五、遗嘱继承之特点与原因分析

（一）公证遗嘱与其他形式遗嘱的效力之特点与原因分析

关于公证遗嘱与其他形式遗嘱适用效力的民众观念，统计数据显示的特点是，在被调查者中，（1）认为后遗嘱的适用效力优先于前一公证遗嘱的，合计占七成以上（72.67%）；（2）认为公证遗嘱的适用效力优先的，占近三成（27.33%）（见表6-31）。

以上特点的原因分析，根据湖北省被调查者填写的公证遗嘱与其他形式遗嘱适用效力的民众观念之理由（见表6-32），七成以上的人认为后遗嘱的适用效力优先，其原因是书面遗嘱比较正式，取证容易或口头遗嘱形式灵活，且有证人作证，二者均能够反映被继承人最后的真实意愿；近三成的人认为公证遗嘱适用效力优先，其原因是公证遗嘱的程序规范，具有较强的公示效力和证明效力。

关于公证遗嘱与其他形式遗嘱的效力之我国立法，我国《继承法》第20条规定："遗嘱人可以撤销、变更自己所立的遗嘱。立有数份遗嘱，内容相抵触的，以最后的遗嘱为准。自书、代书、录音、口头遗嘱，不得撤销、变更公证遗嘱。"1985年《执行继承法意见》第42条规定："遗嘱人以不同形式立有数份内容相抵触的遗嘱，其中有公证遗嘱的，以最后所立公证遗嘱为准；没有公证遗嘱的，以最后所立的遗嘱为准。"

从域外立法例看，不少国家规定后遗嘱的适用效力优先于前遗嘱。如《瑞士民法典》第511条规定，如被继承人未明确废除原遗嘱而又重新订立新遗嘱，只要不能肯定新遗嘱为原遗嘱的补充，应视新遗嘱为原遗嘱的替代。同样，被继承人对同一物有两个遗嘱，如前后有抵触，后者代替前者。《日本民法典》第1022~1023条规定，遗嘱人可以以遗嘱的方式，随时撤销其遗嘱的全部或一部分。前遗嘱与后遗嘱抵触时，关于抵触的部分，视为以后遗嘱撤销前遗嘱。

---

① 参见中国社会科学院法学研究所民法研究室编：《苏俄民法典》，中国社会科学出版社1980年版，第172页。

② 参见"梁稿"第1957条；"徐稿"第四分编第497条；"张稿"第61条；"陈稿"第50条。

从我国诸继承法学者建议稿看，多数主张后遗嘱的适用效力优先于前遗嘱。如“杨稿”第33条规定，遗嘱人可以另立遗嘱明确表示撤回变更自己以前所立的遗嘱，遗嘱人故意销毁遗嘱的，视为撤回。设立遗嘱后，遗嘱人实施与遗嘱内容相反的行为，视为对遗嘱相关内容的撤回。立有数份遗嘱，内容相抵触的，以最后的遗嘱为准，前遗嘱抵触部分视为撤回。“张稿”第42条和“陈稿”第38条对此也有规定。

尽管湖北省七成以上的被调查者认为后遗嘱的适用效力应优先于前遗嘱，且域外立法例和我国部分学者建议稿也持此观点。但我们认为，关于遗嘱的适用效力，应该维持公证遗嘱适用效力最高的规定，除公证遗嘱适用效力最高外，其他遗嘱应按照设立的先后顺序确定遗嘱的效力，以维持立法的一贯性。

（二）遗嘱自由的限制——特留份之特点与原因分析

关于以遗嘱将个人财产全部赠给他人的民众观念，统计数据显示的特点是，在被调查者中，对被继承人以遗嘱处分个人财产全部给第三人的行为，（1）认为不适当的，占近七成（68.61%）；（2）认为适当的，占近三成（28.02%）（见表6-33）。

以上特点的原因分析，根据湖北省被调查者填写的以遗嘱将个人财产全部赠给他人的民众观念之理由（见表6-34），对被继承人以遗嘱处分个人财产全部给第三人的行为，（1）近七成的人认为该行为不适当，其原因是将遗产全部赠与他人会造成家庭财产外流，不利于保障配偶及子女的生活，同时也不符合风俗习惯，为常人所难以接受或为配偶、为子女留一部分遗产；（2）近三成的人认为该行为适当，其原因是遗嘱人对自己的财产享有自由处分的权利，他人无权干涉。

关于遗嘱自由的限制之我国立法，我国《继承法》第19条规定：“遗嘱应当对缺乏劳动能力又没有生活来源的继承人保留必要的遗产份额。”1985年《执行继承法意见》第37条规定：“遗嘱人未保留缺乏劳动能力又没有生活来源的继承人的遗产份额，遗产处理时，应当为该继承人留下必要的遗产，所剩余的部分，才可参照遗嘱确定的分配原则处理。”

从域外立法例看，《德国民法典》第2303条规定：“被继承人的晚辈直系血亲被死因处分排除在继承顺序之外的，该晚辈直系血亲可以向继承人请求特留份。特留份为法定继承份的价额的一半。被继承人的父母或配偶被死因处分排除在继承顺序之外的，享有同样的权利。”

从我国诸继承法学者建议稿看，“王稿”第585条规定：“遗嘱人设立遗嘱时，必须为下列法定继承人预留本法规定的份额。第一顺序法定继承人的特留份为其应继份的二分之一；第二顺序法定继承人的特留份为其应继份的三分之一；除本法有特别规定外，特留份权适用本法关于法定继承的规定。”“梁稿”和“杨稿”等学者建议稿也有类似规定。[①]可见，我国继承法学者建议稿中，多赞成设立特留份制度。

我们认为，遗嘱自由过度会导致权利的滥用，阻碍遗产扶养功能的发挥。我国《继承法》仅规定了必留份制度，只有缺乏劳动能力又无生活来源的继承人可以获得必要遗产份额，但没有特留份制度，这是我国立法之不足。因此，以上主张设立特留份制度的湖北省被调查民众的观念、域外立法例和我国学者建议稿的观点，可供我国立法参考。

① 参见“梁稿”第1962条；“杨稿”第49条。

（三）夫妻共同遗嘱之特点与原因分析

关于夫妻间能否设立共同遗嘱的民众观念与民间习惯，统计数据显示的特点是，（1）在被调查者的观念上，对于夫妻设立共同遗嘱，赞成的占七成半以上（76.45%），不赞成的占二成以上（23.55%）（见表6-35）；（2）被调查者所在地区的继承习惯是：无该习惯的占近七成（69.93%），而有该习惯的占三成（30.07%）（见表6-37）。

以上特点的原因分析，根据湖北省被调查者填写的夫妻共同遗嘱的民众观念之理由（见表6-36），（1）七成半以上的人赞同设立夫妻共同遗嘱，三成的地区也有该习惯，其原因是共同遗嘱为双方共同设立，反映了双方的共同意愿，理应为双方所遵守、共同遗嘱有利于为子女保留一定的遗产份额或可以避免纠纷；（2）二成以上的人不赞同设立夫妻共同遗嘱，近七成的地区也没有该习惯，其原因是共同遗嘱无法应对出现的新情况和新问题，限制了双方对自己财产的处分权。

关于夫妻共同遗嘱之我国立法，我国《继承法》对此无规定。我国《遗嘱公证细则》第15条规定："两个以上的遗嘱人申请办理共同遗嘱公证的，公证处应当引导他们分别设立遗嘱。遗嘱人坚持申请办理共同遗嘱公证的，共同遗嘱中应当明确遗嘱变更、撤销及生效的条件。"即规定并不提倡公民订立共同遗嘱，但对遗嘱人坚持订立共同遗嘱的，也有条件地承认其效力。

从域外立法例看，对于夫妻设立共同遗嘱，有的国家允许，有的国家禁止。一是允许设立夫妻共同遗嘱。例如，《德国民法典》第2265～2269条规定，夫妻可以订立共同遗嘱。夫妻双方在其据以相互指定为继承人的共同遗嘱中，规定生存配偶死亡后，双方的遗产应归属于第三人的，有疑义时，必须认为该第三人系就全部遗产而被指定为最后死亡的配偶的继承人。可见，德国立法承认共同遗嘱的效力，且共同遗嘱的主体仅限于夫妻。二是否定夫妻共同遗嘱，如《法国民法典》第968条规定，二人或二人以上不得以同一证书订立遗嘱。

从我国诸继承法学者建议稿看，"王稿""张稿""陈稿"等均没有规定夫妻共同遗嘱。部分学者建议稿承认夫妻共同遗嘱的效力，如"徐稿"第四分编第61条规定："夫妻共同遗嘱应采取夫妻共同自书遗嘱的形式。夫妻一方按照本分编第96条及以下数条的普通规则为自书遗嘱规定的形式表达他们共同的最后愿望，他方在这一共同文件上签名，遗嘱即告成功。签名的夫妻一方应注明签署遗嘱的时间和地点。"

我们认为，尽管从观念上七成半以上的湖北省被调查民众赞成设立夫妻共同遗嘱，但近七成的该省被调查者所在地区并没有该习惯。并且多数域外立法例和我国继承法学者建议稿并没有规定夫妻共同遗嘱，从尊重生存配偶对其个人财产的处分权考量，我国不宜规定夫妻共同遗嘱。

六、继承和遗赠的接受与放弃之特点与原因分析

（一）继承的接受与放弃的时间与方式之特点与原因分析

第一，关于继承的接受与放弃的时间之民众观念，统计数据显示的特点是，在被调查者中，继承人接受或放弃继承的意思表示，认为应当在遗产处理前作出的，占七成以上（71.78%）；认为应在知道继承开始的2个月内作出的，占近三成（28.22%）（见表6-38）。

以上特点的原因分析，根据湖北省被调查者填写的继承的接受与放弃的时间与方式的

民众观念之理由（见表6-39），（1）七成以上的人认为继承人接受或放弃继承的意思表示，认为应当在遗产处理前作出，其原因是这样既不影响其他继承人的利益，又可以保证继承人行使放弃继承的权利；（2）近三成的人认为继承人接受或放弃继承的意思表示，应在知道继承开始的2个月内作出，其原因是2个月的时间较为合适，可以让继承人有一定的时间去考虑是否放弃继承权，同时，又可以督促继承人积极行使权利。

第二，关于继承的接受与放弃的方式之民间习惯，统计数据显示的特点是，在被调查者所在地区，（1）通过书面或公证处公证表示接受继承的，合计占五成以上（51.30%）；（2）继承人接受继承无须作任何表示的，占近五成（48.70%）（见表6-40）。

以上特点的原因分析，在湖北省被调查者所在地区，（1）五成以上的地区有通过书面或公证处公证的方式作出表示的习惯，其原因可能是该种方式更为正规，便于保存和取证；（2）近五成的地区有继承人接受继承无须作任何表示的习惯，即继承人不作表示的可以被视为接受继承，其原因可能是受我国现行法之规定的影响。

关于继承的接受与放弃的时间与方式之我国立法，我国《继承法》第25条第1款规定，继承开始后，继承人放弃继承的，应当在遗产处理前，作出放弃继承的表示。没有表示的，视为接受继承。根据1985年《执行继承法意见》第49条、第47条规定，继承人放弃继承的意思表示，应当在继承开始后、遗产分割前作出。遗产分割后表示放弃的不再是继承权，而是所有权。继承人放弃继承应当以书面形式向其他继承人表示。用口头方式表示放弃继承，本人承认，或有其它充分证据证明的，也应当认定其有效。

从域外立法例看，《日本民法典》规定，在日本，继承人自知悉为自己的继承开始时起3个月内，应作出单纯承认、限定承认或放弃的表示。一旦继承人没有在法定期限内表示限定承认或放弃的，就被推定为单纯承认。① 继承人放弃继承的期限，自知悉为自己的继承开始时起3个月内，可由家庭法院依请求延长。放弃继承，由欲放弃继承者向家庭法院申述其意旨。②

从我国诸继承法学者建议稿看，“王稿”规定，继承人放弃继承的，应当在知道或应当知道继承开始2个月内，向遗产管理人、遗嘱执行人或人民法院作出书面的放弃继承的表示。到期没有表示的，视为接受继承。③ “陈稿”规定，继承开始后，自继承人知道自己为继承人时起或自遗嘱开启时起2个月内，继承人可以声明接受或放弃继承。以制作遗产清单方式接受继承的，制作遗产清单的期间一般为2个月，特殊情况下，经申请法院批准，可延长至3个月内。④ 继承人在国外的，此期限为6个月。⑤

我们认为，七成以上的湖北省被调查民众认为继承人接受或放弃继承的意思表示，认为应当在遗产处理前作出；近五成的该省被调查者所在地区有继承人接受继承无须作任何表示的习惯，即继承人不作表示的可以被视为接受继承。上述的观念与习惯与我国现行法的规定相一致，我国此方面立法可保持不变。

---

① 《日本民法典》第921条。
② 《日本民法典》第915条。
③ “王稿”第554条。
④ 参见“陈稿”第70条。
⑤ 参见“陈稿”第11条。

（二）遗赠的接受与放弃的方式与效力之特点与原因分析

关于遗赠的接受与放弃的方式与效力之民众观念，统计数据显示的特点是，在被调查者中，（1）受遗赠人未作表示应视为放弃遗赠的，占三成以上（31.94%）；（2）受遗赠人未作表示应视为接受遗赠的，占近七成（68.06%）（见表6-41）。

以上特点的原因分析，根据湖北省被调查者填写的遗赠的接受与放弃的方式与效力的民众观念之理由（见表6-42），（1）三成以上的人认为受遗赠人未作表示应视为放弃遗赠，其原因是乙有权选择是否接受甲的遗赠，如乙没有表示，就应该视为放弃遗赠，这也体现了对乙人格的尊重或接受遗赠应该当面表示；（2）近七成的人认为受遗赠人未作表示应视为接受遗赠，其原因是接受遗赠是一种纯获利行为，乙不表示，就应该视为接受或这也遵循死者意愿。

关于遗赠的接受与放弃的方式与效力之我国立法，我国《继承法》第25条规定："受遗赠人应当在知道受遗赠之日起两个月内，作出接受或者放弃受遗赠的意思表示。到期没有表示的，视为放弃受遗赠。"

从域外立法例看，有些国家规定受遗赠人未作表示的，应视为接受遗赠。例如，《意大利民法典》规定，遗赠不需要承认而取得，遗赠的标的，在遗嘱人死亡瞬间从遗嘱人移转于受遗赠人。①

从我国诸继承法学者建议稿看，"梁稿"认为："受遗赠人接受遗赠的，应当在知道受遗赠后两个月内作出接受遗赠的意思表示；逾期未表示的，视为放弃接受遗赠。"② "陈稿"第59条规定："受遗赠人在遗赠人死亡以后，可表示放弃接受遗赠，放弃的效力溯及至遗赠后1年内作出，1年内未作出的视为接受遗赠。"③

我们认为，我国《继承法》第25条的规定没有必要改动，现行立法是合理的，虽然根据湖北省被调查民众的调查数据来看，有近七成的被调查者认为放弃遗赠应明示，未作表示的视为接受遗赠，但我们认为维持我国现行立法更能够对继承人和受遗赠人的身份特性进行区分。对于受遗赠人来说，这也体现对出对他内心意思的尊重，即使是纯获利行为，受遗赠人并没有接受的表示，也应该视为放弃受遗赠。

（三）继承的放弃与债权人的撤销权之特点与原因分析

关于继承的放弃能否被债权人撤销的民众观念，统计数据显示的特点是，在被调查者中，继承人放弃继承的行为，（1）认为不可以被撤销的，占五成半以上（56.24%）；（2）认为可以被撤销的，占四成以上（43.76%）（见表6-43）。

以上特点的原因分析，根据湖北省被调查者填写的继承的放弃能否被债权人撤销的民众观念之理由（见表6-44），对于继承人放弃继承的行为，（1）五成半以上的人认为不可以被债权人撤销，其原因是这有利于照顾儿媳及其孙女的生活，她们是弱势群体，理应获得优先照顾或应遵循甲的意愿、放弃继承是继承人的自由；（2）四成以上的人认为可以被债权人撤销，其原因是甲的债权人利益也需要被考虑，这有利于保护债权人的利益。

关于继承的放弃与债权人的撤销权之我国立法，我国《继承法》对此无规定。

---

① 参见《意大利民法典》第649条。

② 参见"梁稿"第2008条。

③ 参见陈苇主编：《外国继承法比较与中国民法典继承编制定研究》，北京大学出版社2011年版，第494页。

从域外立法例看，主要有两种立法模式：一是肯定债权人有撤销权。例如，《法国民法典》第788条规定，继承人放弃继承有损债权人利益时，债权人可以请求法院准许其以债务人的名义，代替其地位接受继承，且得为债权人的利益，在债权额的限度内对继承人的放弃行为予以撤销。二是否定债权人有撤销权，代以财产分离的方式保护债权人的利益。例如，《日本民法典》第941条规定，在继承人可作出限定继承的期间，或者继承的财产与继承人的固有财产未混合期间，继承人的债权人可以向法院申请继承人的个人财产与遗产相互分离。

从我国诸继承法学者建议稿看，"王稿"规定，债权人在法定情况下享有对放弃继承的撤销权，即继承人放弃继承损害其债权人利益的，债权人可以在知道或者应当知道继承人放弃继承之日起6个月内申请法院撤销继承人的放弃行为。① "陈稿""张稿"均未规定债权人对放弃继承的撤销权。

我们认为，我国欠缺继承的放弃可否被债权人撤销之规定，这是我国立法之不足。实践中，在遇到这类案件时，法院通常采取的做法有三种：判决驳回债权人诉讼请求；依据1985年《执行继承法意见》第46条规定的"继承人因放弃继承权，致其不能履行法定义务的，放弃继承权的行为无效"处理；还有依据我国《合同法》第74条规定的债权人撤销权来处理，这样就容易导致出现这类案件时，法律适用出现了混乱。② 在理论界主要存在两种观点"肯定说"和"否定说"，持"肯定说"观点的人认为当继承人放弃继承危及债权人的利益时，债权人可以请求人民法院撤销，主要目的是在于维护交易安全。而持"否定说"观点的人认为继承权的放弃行为不得成为债权人撤销权的标的，主要理由在于，第一，该行为具有特定身份为前提；第二，接受或放弃继承中蕴含着继承人的人格自由与尊严；第三，继承人放弃继承利益，并没有损害其固有个人财产（这是其偿还个人债务的责任财产），因此，继承人放弃继承之行为，不应属于危及债权，不得被撤销。放弃继承行为因具有身份行为的特质，不能允许继承人之债权人撤销。③ 因此，上述主张债权人不享有撤销权的湖北省被调查民众的观念和域外立法例，可供我国立法参考。

七、继承权的丧失、被继承人的宥恕与代位继承之特点与原因分析

（一）继承权的丧失与被继承人的宥恕之特点与原因分析

关于继承权的丧失与被继承人宥恕的民众观念，统计数据显示的特点是，在被调查者中，对于继承人因欺诈或者胁迫而丧失继承权，可否因被继承人宥恕而恢复继承权，（1）可以恢复的占七成以上（73.27%）；（2）不可以恢复的占二成半以上（26.73%）（见表6-45）。

以上特点的原因分析，根据湖北省被调查者填写的继承权的丧失与被继承人宥恕的民众观念之理由（见表6-46），对于继承人因欺诈或者胁迫而丧失继承权，可否因被继承人宥恕而恢复继承权，（1）七成以上的人认为可以恢复继承权，其原因是乙有权处分自己的遗产，如果乙已经原谅了某甲，则可以恢复某甲的继承权或应当尊重父亲乙的最后决

① "王稿"第559、560条。

② 参见陈舒筠：《论放弃继承与债权人撤销权的立法平衡》，载《常州工学院学报（社科版）》2016年第1期。

③ 参见陈苇、王巍：《论放弃继承行为不能成为债权人撤销权的标的》，载《甘肃社会科学》2015年第5期。

定；（2）二成半以上的人认为不可以恢复继承权，其原因是某甲的行为造成恶劣影响，导致其丧失继承权，即使乙原谅了某甲，也不能恢复某甲的继承权或不能让别有用心的人有继承权。

关于继承权的丧失与被继承人的宥恕之我国立法，我国《继承法》第7条规定："继承人有下列行为之一的，丧失继承权：（一）故意杀害被继承人的；（二）为争夺遗产而杀害其他继承人的；（三）遗弃被继承人的，或者虐待被继承人情节严重的；（四）伪造、篡改或者销毁遗嘱，情节严重的。" 1985年《执行继承法意见》第13条规定："继承人虐待被继承人情节严重的，或者遗弃被继承人的，如以后确有悔改表现，而且被虐待人、被遗弃人生前又表示宽恕，可不确认其丧失继承权。"

从域外立法例看，关于继承权的丧失与被继承人的宥恕，《法国民法典》规定，被继承人需以遗嘱的形式明文申明其宽恕意愿①；《日本民法典》规定被继承人可随时请求家庭法院撤销对推定继承人的废除。②

从我国诸继承法学者建议稿看，关于继承权的丧失与被继承人的宥恕，"王稿"第532条规定，继承人有下列行为之一的，丧失继承权：（一）故意伤害被继承人；（二）为争夺遗产而杀害其他继承人；（三）遗弃被继承人或者虐待被继承人情节严重的；（四）伪造、篡改或者销毁、隐匿遗嘱的；（五）以欺诈或者胁迫的手段，迫使或者妨碍被继承人设立、变更或者撤销遗嘱，情节严重的。继承人因前款第（三）、第（四）、第（五）种情形丧失继承权，如经被继承人宽恕的，可不确认其丧失继承权。被继承人知道继承人除前款第（一）、第（二）项外的丧失继承资格的事由，仍然在遗嘱中指定其为继承人或对其为遗赠，视为宽恕。

我们认为，我国欠缺继承人因欺诈或者胁迫丧失继承权，获得被继承人宥恕后可以恢复继承权这一情形，这是其立法之不足。因此，上述主张该情形下可以恢复继承权的湖北省被调查民众的观念、域外立法例和我国学者建议稿的观点，可供我国立法参考。

（二）继承权的丧失与代位继承之特点与原因分析

关于继承权丧失的效力是否及于代位继承人的民众观念，统计数据显示的特点是，在被调查者中，（1）认为及于代位继承人的，占近五成半（53.82%）；（2）认为不及于代位继承人的，占四成半以上（46.18%）（见表6-47）。

以上特点的原因分析，根据湖北省被调查者填写的继承权丧失的效力是否及于代位继承人的民众观念之理由（见表6-48），关于继承权丧失的效力是否及于代位继承人，（1）近五成半的人认为效力及于代位继承人，其原因是乙已经丧失继承权，导致丙代替乙继承的前提丧失、伪造遗嘱等不正当手段，不受法律保护或丙的继承顺序靠后不得代位；（2）四成半以上的人认为效力不及于代位继承人，其原因是丙作为独立的民事主体，可以孙子的身份来继承祖父甲的遗产，与乙丧失继承权没有关系。

关于继承权丧失的效力是否及于代位继承人之我国立法，1985年《执行继承法意见》第28条规定："继承人丧失继承权的，其晚辈直系血亲不得代位继承。"即我国立法采取"代位权说"，认为继承人丧失继承权的，其子女亦不得代位继承。

---

① 参见《法国民法典》第728条。

② 参见《日本民法典》第894条。

从域外立法例看，关于继承权丧失的效力是否及于代位继承人，一些国家有规定，继承人丧失继承权的，其晚辈直系血亲仍可以代位继承。如《瑞士民法典》规定，继承资格的丧失，仅及于继承资格丧失人本人。继承资格丧失人的直系血亲卑亲属，视如继承资格丧失人先于被继承人死亡，继承被继承人的遗产。①

从我国诸继承法学者建议稿看，关于继承权丧失的效力是否及于代位继承人，“王稿”第572条规定，被继承人的子女在继承开始前先于或同时与被继承人死亡的或者丧失继承权的，由被继承人子女的直系血亲卑亲属代位继承。代位继承不受辈分的限制，但以亲等为序。

我们认为，我国有关继承权丧失的效力及于代位继承人之规定，是其立法之不足。因此，上述主张被代位继承人丧失继承权其子女仍可以代位继承的湖北省被调查民众的观念、域外立法例和我国学者建议稿的观点，可供我国立法参考。

八、继承协议之特点与原因分析

（一）继承协议的订立主体与方式之特点与原因分析

关于继承协议的订立主体与方式的民众观念，统计数据显示的特点是，在被调查中，（1）认为应由被扶养人与全部继承人共同协商签订的，占六成以上（63.72%）；（2）认为应由被扶养人与扶养人协商签订的，占近二成半（24.19%）；（3）认为共同继承人间协商签订即可而无须被扶养人知晓或同意的，占一成以上（12.09%）（见表6-49）。

以上特点的原因分析，在湖北省被调查者中，（1）六成以上的人认为继承协议应由被扶养人与全部继承人共同协商签订，其原因可能是由全部继承人协商签订的协议，便于执行，可避免纠纷；（2）近二成半的人认为继承协议应由被扶养人与扶养人协商签订，其原因可能是尊重当事人双方的合意，且遗赠为通过遗嘱处分个人财产，所以无须征求其他继承人同意；（3）一成以上的人认为继承人间协商签订继承协议即可，无须被扶养人知晓或同意，其原因可能是谁承担赡养义务谁有权决定扶养的具体方式，体现权利与义务一致性。

关于继承协议制度之我国立法，我国《继承法》对此无规定。但对遗赠扶养协议，在该法第31条规定：“公民可以与扶养人签订遗赠扶养协议。按照协议，扶养人承担该公民生养死葬的义务，享有受遗赠的权利。”我国学者认为，继承协议是指被继承人与继承人、其他自然人、法人和其他组织等就继承权或者受遗赠权的取得或消灭及相应义务承担等而达成的合意。② 可见，我国立法仅有遗赠扶养协议，并未规定适用于被继承人和继承人间的继承协议制度。

从域外立法例看，根据《德国民法典》“继承合同”章的相关条文之规定，被继承人仅能亲自订立继承合同，继承合同的一方当事人应当为被继承人，但并未限定另一方当事人之范围，另一方当事人既可以是夫妻、婚约当事人或同性生活伴侣中的一方，也可以是其他主体，甚至是财团。即该合同的另一方和第三人均可以被指定为合同所定的继承人或

---

① 参见《瑞士民法典》第541条。

② 陈苇主编：《外国继承法比较与中国民法典继承编制定研究》，北京大学出版社2011年版，第433页。

受遗赠人。①

从我国诸继承法学者建议稿看，“张稿”规定继承合同的当事人一方是被继承人，另一方是共同继承人，不仅仅是承担赡养义务的继承人。“张稿”采取继承合同与遗赠扶养协议并列的“双轨制”，对继承合同的订立形式应当以书面的形式订立，并从依法成立时起生效。

我们认为，我国欠缺继承协议制度，这是其立法之不足。因此，上述赞成设立继承协议的湖北省被调查民众的观念、域外立法例和我国学者建议稿的观点，可供我国立法参考。

（二）继承协议的变更方式及效力之特点与原因分析

关于继承协议的变更方式与效力的民众观念，统计数据显示的特点是，在被调查者中，（1）认为该协议可有条件继续履行，如原扶养人的子女有扶养能力的，在原扶养人的子女和被扶养人双方同意的情况下，可由原扶养人的子女继续履行该继承协议的，此即代位扶养的，占四成半（45.74%）；（2）认为该协议效力终止，须签订新的继承协议，由新的扶养人履行扶养义务并继承遗产的，合计占近四成（37.36%）。其中，认为需要对原扶养人的继承人补偿超过其扶养义务部分费用的，占近三成（29.92%），认为不需要对原扶养人的继承人补偿超过其扶养义务部分费用的，占不到一成（7.44%）；（3）认为该协议终止，应补偿原扶养人的继承人补偿超过其扶养义务部分费用后，由所有法定继承人共同扶养的，即实行法定赡养的，占一成半（15.97%）（见表6-50）。

以上特点的原因分析，根据湖北省被调查者填写的继承协议的变更方式及效力的民众观念之理由（见表6-51），（1）四成半的人认为该协议可有条件继续履行，其原因是由王二的儿子继续扶养王某，使继承协议继续履行，有利于维持被扶养人一贯的生活方式，使其安度晚年；（2）合计四成半的人认为应补偿原扶养人家人一定费用，其原因是赡养王某是其子女的法定义务，由于法律规定扶养义务人应平等承担赡养义务，故王一、王三应当补偿王二家人6万元；（3）不到一成的人认为对原扶养人的家人无须补偿，其原因是原签订的继承协议效力终止，故依据协议对原扶养人的家人无须补偿。

关于继承协议的变更方式及效力之我国立法，我国没有继承协议之变更方式及效力方面的规定。

从域外立法例看，关于继承协议的变更方式及效力，《瑞士民法典》规定，如果继承人或受遗赠人在被继承人之前死亡的，继承合同自动解除。继承合同因此而自动解除后，对于被继承人因该合同而获得的利益，已履行给付义务的继承人或受遗赠人的继承人可以请求利益返还，但继承合同另有约定的除外。②

从我国诸继承法学者建议稿看，关于继承协议的变更方式及效力，“张稿”第55条规定：“义务人不按约定履行赡养（扶养）义务，或者因为死亡或丧失赡养（扶养）能力而不能继续履行合同义务，被继承人可以解除合同。合同解除后，义务人已经支付的赡养（扶养）费用应当在共同继承人之间进行结算。”

我们认为，我国欠缺继承协议制度，这是其立法之不足。因此，上述主张规定继承协

① 《德国民法典》第2274、2275、1941条。

② 《瑞士民法典》第515条。

议制度的湖北省被调查民众的观念、域外立法例和我国学者建议稿的观点，可供我国立法参考。

九、遗产债务清偿之特点与原因分析

（一）遗产债务清偿责任的类型之特点与原因分析

关于遗产债务清偿责任的类型之民众观念，统计数据显示的特点是，在被调查者中，（1）主张实行自愿的无限清偿责任的，合计占六成半以上（66.87%）；（2）主张实行有限清偿责任的，占近五成（48.16%）；（3）主张对有侵害遗产违法行为者应当实行强制的无限清偿责任的，占四成以上（43.25%）（见表6-52）。

以上特点的原因分析，在湖北省被调查者中，对于被继承人生前欠下的所有债务，（1）六成半以上的人主张实行自愿的无限清偿责任，其原因可能是我国有“父债子偿”的传统习惯；（2）近五成的人主张实行有限清偿责任，其原因可能是受我国现行法的影响；（3）四成以上的人主张对有侵害遗产违法行为者应当实行强制的无限清偿责任，其原因可能是继承人隐匿、转移财产的违法行为应当予以一定惩罚。

关于遗产债务清偿责任的类型之我国立法，我国《继承法》第33条规定，继承遗产应当清偿被继承人依法应当缴纳的税款和债务，缴纳税款和清偿债务以他的遗产实际价值为限。超过遗产实际价值部分，继承人自愿偿还的不在此限。即我国实行无条件的有限清偿责任制度和自愿的无限清偿责任制度，但欠缺强制的无限清偿责任制度。1985年《执行继承法意见》第59条规定：“人民法院对故意隐匿、侵吞或者争抢遗产的继承人，可以酌情减少其应继承的遗产。”

从域外立法例看，《意大利民法典》规定的遗产债务的清偿责任类型包括三类：一是，有限清偿责任，希望按遗产清册接受继承的人，自按遗产清册接受继承的声明在继承开始地的不动产登记处完成登记之日起1个月后，如果债权人或受遗赠人未对遗产清册提出异议的，继承人也不准备提起清算程序的，则继承人在遗产价值范围内向债权人和受遗赠人实施清偿；[①] 二是，自愿的无限清偿责任，遗产可以单纯地简单接受，即无限责任继承，也可以享有遗产清册利益的方式接受；[②] 三是，强制的无限清偿责任，在遗产清册中故意隐瞒被继承人的财产或者谎报实际不存在债务的继承人，丧失遗产清册利益；债权人或受遗赠人对遗产清册主张异议的，如果继承人未遵守提出异议情况下的清算规定或者未在规定的期限内完成清算或编制清偿顺序表的，继承人丧失遗产清册利益。[③]

从我国诸继承法学者建议稿看，主张同时设立有限清偿责任、自愿的无限清偿责任和强制的无限清偿责任及损害赔偿责任。例如，“陈稿”第69条规定，继承人选择有条件限定继承且依法制作遗产清册的，仅以遗产为限清偿债务。继承人自愿选择无条件概括继承的，以继承的遗产和个人财产清偿遗产债务。已全部或部分处分遗产，或未在法定期间制作遗产清册的，或故意未将遗产计入遗产清册的，承担无限清偿责任。

我们认为，我国欠缺有限责任继承之条件和强制的无限责任继承制度，这是其立法之

① 《意大利民法典》第490、495条。
② 《意大利民法典》第470条。
③ 《意大利民法典》第494、505条。

不足。因此，上述主张增加遗产债务清偿责任类型的湖北省被调查民众的观念、域外立法例和我国学者建议稿的观点，可供我国立法参考。

（二）被继承人丧葬费的支付之特点与原因分析

关于被继承人丧葬费支付的民间习惯，统计数据显示的特点是，在被调查者所在地区，（1）由全体继承人共同支付的，占近六成（57.21%）；（2）从被继承人的遗产中支付的，占近四成（38.64%）（见表6-54）。

以上特点的原因分析，在湖北省被调查者所在地区，（1）近六成的地区有由全体继承人共同支付的习惯，其原因可能是子女担负着对老年人养老送终的责任，即子女对父母生前的赡养和死后的殡葬负责，这不仅是我国传统的家庭道德的要求，也是民间的习惯；（2）近四成的地区有从被继承人的遗产中支付的习惯，其原因可能是认为从遗产中支付丧葬费用对各继承人更为公平。

关于被继承人丧葬费的支付方式之我国立法，我国《继承法》对此无规定。

从域外立法例看，《德国民法典》第1968条规定，由继承人负担被继承人的丧葬费用。《俄罗斯联邦民法典》第1174条规定，遗产应首先清偿被继承人的疾病和丧葬费所支出的费用。

从我国诸继承法学者建议稿看，“王稿”规定，被继承人的、与其社会地位相称的丧葬费用，由继承人负担，即丧葬费用不属于被继承人的遗产债务。①“陈稿”规定，继承费用，包括合理的丧葬费用、制作遗产目录、发布公告继承的通知或公告、清点和保管遗产所必要的费用、遗产分割的费用、执行遗嘱的费用等属于被继承人遗留的个人债务，即遗产债务。②

我们认为，我国欠缺被继承人丧葬费的支付方式之规定，这是其立法之不足。因此，上述主张丧葬费由被继承人遗产支付的湖北省被调查民众的习惯、域外立法例和我国学者建议稿的观点，可供我国立法参考。

（三）遗产债务的清偿顺序之特点与原因分析

关于遗产债务的清偿顺序的民间习惯，统计数据显示的特点是，在被调查者所在地区，遗产债务按如下顺序清偿：第一顺序为丧葬费用；第二顺序为遗产管理等费用、欠付的工资；第三顺序为欠债；第四顺序为受被继承人扶养人的生活费、税款；第五顺序为对被继承人扶养较多的人之酌情分配遗产份额、遗赠扶养协议写明遗产的遗产（见表6-55）。

以上特点的原因分析，关于遗产债务清偿的清偿顺序，（1）丧葬费居于第一的原因，可能是利于被继承人“入土为安”；（2）遗产管理费、欠付的工资居于第二，可能是涉及共同继承人及遗产利害关系人的共同利益，或涉及生存权问题；（3）欠债居于第三，先于前款，可能是考虑私人债权优先；（4）受被继承人扶养人的生活费先于对被继承人扶养较多的人之酌分份额，可能是考虑优先保障受扶养人的生存需要。

关于遗产债务的清偿顺序之我国立法，我国《继承法》尚无条文明确规定。但我国《继承法》第19、33、34条分别规定，遗嘱应当对缺乏劳动能力又没有生活来源的继承

① “王稿”第651条。

② “陈稿”第68条。

人保留必要的遗产份额，继承遗产应当清偿被继承人依法应当缴纳的税款和债务，执行遗赠不得妨碍清偿遗嘱人依法应当缴纳的税款和债务。1985年《执行继承法意见》第61条规定："继承人中有缺乏劳动能力又没有生活来源的人，即使遗产不足清偿债务，也应为其保留适当遗产，然后再按继承法第三十三条和民事诉讼法第一百八十条的规定清偿债务。"

从域外立法例看，《德国民法典》规定遗产债务按下列顺序清偿：（1）临时扶养费；（2）遗产管理费；（3）有担保的债权；（4）普通债务、特留份遗赠等遗产的负担。①

从我国诸继承法学者建议稿看，"梁稿"规定的遗产债务清偿顺序如下：（1）继承费用；（2）必要的生活费；（3）遗产债务。②"王稿"规定的遗产债务清偿顺序如下：（1）继承费用；（2）遗产税；（3）被继承人生前欠下的债务；（4）遗产酌给债务；（5）因特留份扣减权、遗赠等产生的债务。对遗产享有担保物权的债权人可申请就担保物优先受偿。③

我们认为，我国欠缺被继承人遗产债务的清偿顺序之规定，这是其立法之不足。因此，以上有关遗产债务清偿顺序的湖北省被调查民众的习惯、域外立法例和我国学者建议稿的观点，可供我国立法参考。

十、遗产分割之特点与原因分析

（一）遗产分割的自由与限制之特点与原因分析

第一，关于遗产分割自由与限制的民间习惯，统计数据显示的特点是，在被调查者所在地区，（1）共同协商后分割遗产的，占八成半以上（86.80%）；（2）遗嘱禁止分割则不得分割的，占近七成（69.95%）；（3）只要有继承人要求分割遗产就得进行分割的，占不到二成（19.12%）（见表6-56）。

以上特点的原因分析，根据湖北省被调查者填写的遗产分割自由与限制的民间习惯之理由（见表6-57），（1）八成半以上的地区有遗产由各继承人共同协商后进行分割的习惯，其原因是遗产由各继承人共同所有，遗产分割关系各继承人的共同利益，故遗产的分割由各遗产继承人共同协商的；（2）近七成的地区有遗嘱禁止分割的遗产则不得分割的习惯，其原因是遗产是被继承人遗留的个人财产，所以有权通过遗嘱决定遗产的归属和分割；（3）不到二成的地区有只要有继承人要求分割遗产就得进行分割的习惯，其原因是每个继承人享有的继承权受法律保护，同时基于效率原则考虑，故继承开始后，基于继承人的要求就可以分割遗产。

第二，关于提出遗产分割请求时间的民间习惯，统计数据显示的特点是，在被调查者所在的地区，（1）子女不会提出遗产分割请求的的分割，占近七成半（75.19%）；（2）子女会提出分割其他遗产，但对其母正在居住的房屋需等其母去世后进行的，占一成半稍多（16.12%）；（3）仅有不到一成（7.60%）的极少数地区有子女会马上向其母亲提出分割遗产的习惯（见表6-58）。

① 《德国民法典》第1969、1971、1973、1978条。

② "梁稿"第2016、2018条。

③ "王稿"第650条。

以上特点的原因分析，根据湖北省被调查者填写的提出遗产分割请求时间的民间习惯之理由（见表6-59），（1）七成半的地区有子女不会提出遗产分割请求的习惯，其原因是根据当地观念，小王的父亲去世遗留下的财产就应该由其母亲全部继承；（2）一成半稍多的地区有子女会提出分割其他遗产，但对其母正在居住的房屋的分割需要等其母去世后进行的习惯，其原因是这有助于孝敬老人，保证老人的晚年生活；（3）不到一成的地区有子女会马上向其母亲提出分割遗产的习惯，其原因是遗产是由小王及其母亲共同继承，继承开始后，小王有权根据法律规定提出遗产分割的请求，并且有利于防止日后发生不必要的纠纷。

第三，关于遗嘱可否限制遗产分割的民众观念，统计数据显示的特点是，在被调查者中，（1）认为可以限制的占八成以上（83.02%）（见表6-60）；（2）并且认为该期限应在5年以内的占近三成半（34.39%）（见表6-61）。

以上特点的原因分析，在湖北省被调查者中，（1）八成以上的人认为遗嘱可以限制遗产分割，其原因可能是遗产是被继承人死亡时遗留下来的个人财产，所以有权通过遗嘱限制遗产分割；（2）近三成半的人认为遗嘱限制遗产分割的期限应在5年以内，其原因可能是从发挥物之效用的角度考量，遗嘱限制遗产分割的期限不宜过长，以5年以内为宜。

关于遗产分割的自由与限制之我国立法，我国《继承法》第15条规定："遗产分割的时间、办法和份额，由继承人协商确定。协商不成的，可以由人民调解委员会调解或者向人民法院提起诉讼。"但我国立法对于被继承人可否立遗嘱限制遗产分割、继承人间合意可否突破该限制等无规定。

从域外立法例看，《德国民法典》规定，每一个共有人可随时请求取消共同关系，其取消共同关系的请求权，不受消灭时效的限制。共同继承人的任何一人可以随时请求分割遗产。[①] 对遗产分割时间的限制有三类：第一类是遗嘱对遗产分割时间的限制。第二类是法律对遗产分割时间的限制，包括为保护胎儿利益不得分割；在继承人身份关系确定前不得分割；遗产债务必须先从遗产中予以清除。第三类是继承人的协议或请求对遗产分割时间的限制。[②]

从我国诸继承法学者建议稿看，"梁稿"规定，继承开始后，继承人可以随时请求分割遗产，但有下列情形之一的除外：其一，遗产债务尚未清偿完毕；其二，遗嘱指定遗产于一定期间内不得分割，但该期间不得超过5年；超过5年的，缩短为5年；其三，继承人协商同意于一定期间内不分割遗产；其四，胎儿未出生的，请求分割遗产时，应当为胎儿保留其应继份，出生后为死胎的，保留份额依照法定继承处理；其五，对特定遗产进行即时分割将会严重损害其价值的，人民法院经继承人申请，可以裁判暂缓分割。[③]

我们认为，我国有关遗产分割自由与限制条款之规定存在不足，因此，以上主张对遗产分割自由适当限制的湖北省被调查民众的观念与习惯、域外立法例和我国学者建议稿的观点，可供我国立法参考。

---

① 《德国民法典》第749条第1款、第758条、第2042条第1款。

② 《德国民法典》第2043～2047条。

③ "梁稿"第2021条。

（二）遗产分割瑕疵的担保责任之特点与原因分析

关于遗产分割的瑕疵担保责任的民间习惯，统计数据显示的特点是，在被调查者所在地区，对遗产分割的瑕疵，（1）共同继承人共同承担的合计占近六成（58.18%）；（2）由“乙自行承担”，即共同继承人间不会共同承担的占四成以上（41.32%）（见表6-64）。

以上特点的原因分析，根据湖北省被调查者填写的遗产分割瑕疵的担保责任的民间习惯之理由（见表6-65），（1）近六成的地区有共同继承人间会互担遗产瑕疵担保责任的习惯，其原因是50只羊是由甲和乙共同继承的，对于2只病羊的损失也应该由甲和乙共同承担；如果让乙一个人承担则有悖公平原则；（2）四成以上的地区有共同继承人间无互担遗产瑕疵担保责任的习惯，其原因是乙分得的25只羊是随机分配的，事先甲乙两人都不知道，因此，对于2只病羊的损失与甲无关，应由乙自己承担。

从域外立法例看，《法国民法典》规定，共同继承人仅就分割前的原因引起的对财产的侵害与追夺，互负担保责任。所有的共同继承人就某一共同分割人对于归入其财产份额中的债务在遗产分割前就已经显示的无支付能力负担保责任。如财产被追夺的情况属于遗产分割证书中明定的特别条款排除的情况，不发生前条款所指的担保责任；如共同继承人的财产被追夺是因其本人的过错引起，前项担保责任亦告停止。各继承人按其继承份额的比例对其他共同继承人因继承的遗产可能被追夺而受到的损失负补偿责任。如某一继承人无支付能力，应由其负担的部分，由被担保人和其他有清偿能力的共同继承人分担之。共同继承人之遗产担保责任之诉讼时效期间为2年，自财产被追夺或者发现侵害之日起计算。[①]

从我国诸继承法学者建议稿看，“梁稿”规定，遗产分割后各继承人以其所得的遗产份额为限，对其他继承人分得的遗产，承担与出卖人相同的担保责任。受遗赠人接受的遗产为种类物的，有权要求继承人承担前款规定的责任。[②]“徐稿”规定，实施分割后，每位相续人马上对分得的一切物件取得所有权，而被排除对遗产中的其他物件的权利。因此，如果共同相续人之一在分割中已分给了其他相续人的物件，可按本民法典第八分编第150条[③]关于出卖他人之物者的责任的规定处理。[④]

我们认为，我国欠缺遗产分割瑕疵的担保责任，这是其立法之不足。因此，以上主张共同继承人间共同承担遗产分割瑕疵担保责任的湖北省被调查民众的观念、域外立法例和我国学者建议稿的观点，可供我国立法参考。

十一、无人承受遗产之特点与原因分析

（一）无人承受遗产的归属之特点与原因分析

关于城镇居民无人承受遗产的归属主体的民众观念，统计数据显示的特点是，（1）城镇居民（72.53%）和农村居民（68.75%）认为无人承受的遗产应归社会公共组织的，各占七成左右；（2）城镇居民（27.47%）和农村居民（31.25%）认为无人承受

① 《法国民法典》第884~886条。

② “梁稿”第2025条。

③ “徐稿”第八分编第150条规定：“如果缔约之时出卖人不享有标的物的所有权，他应财产补救措施尽量使买受人取得所有权。买受人从出卖人取得所有权时起成为标的物的所有人。”

④ “徐稿”第四分编第433条。

的遗产应归自然人的，各占三成左右（见表6-66、表6-68）。

以上特点的原因分析，根据湖北省被调查者填写的城镇居民或农村居民无人承受遗产的归属主体的民众观念之理由（见表6-67、表6-69），（1）七成左右的人认为城镇居民或农村居民无人承受遗产应归社会公共组织所有，其原因是甲的遗产应归国家所有可以规范财产秩序，同时这也与部分国家的做法相一致或甲的遗产归甲生前所在地的集体经济组织所有，这有利于对遗产的清算、管理和利用等；（2）三成左右的人认为城镇居民或农村居民无人承受遗产应归自然人所有，其原因是甲的其他亲属是与甲有较密切联系的人，甲的遗产归其他亲戚所有，这符合情理。

关于无人承受遗产的归属主体之我国立法，我国《继承法》第32条规定："无人继承又无人受遗赠的遗产，归国家所有；死者生前是集体所有制组织成员的，归所在集体所有制组织所有。"

从域外立法例看，《日本民法典》规定，不存在主张作为继承人的权利的人，家庭法院认为适当时，可以根据曾与被继承人共同生活的人、对被继承人的疗养看护尽力的人及其他与被继承人有特别亲属关系的人的请求，将继承的全部或者部分配给此等人。在此之后，仍无法处分的遗产，归属于国库。①

从我国诸继承法学者建议稿看，"王稿"规定，对继承人、受遗赠人、债权人的公示催告期间届满，无继承人承认继承时，其遗产于清偿债务并交付遗赠物后，如有剩余，由遗产管理人移交有关部门上缴国库所有；如果死者生前是集体所有制组织成员的，则应移交所在的集体所有制组织并归其所有。②

我们认为，从保护和尊重自然人私有财产权角度出发，我国无人继承的遗产应尽可能分配给不是继承人的其他亲属所有。

（二）无人承受遗产的处理之特点与原因分析

第一，关于无人承受遗产管理人的产生方式之民众观念与民间习惯，统计数据显示的特点是，（1）在被调查者的观念上，认为应由居委会、村委会或所在单位指定的占五成以上（52.77%），认为应由人民法院或民政部门指定的，合计占近五成（47.23%）（见表6-70）；（2）被调查者所在地区的民间习惯是：由村委会、居委会或单位指定的，合计占近五成（48.44%），由人民法院或民政部门指定的，合计占五成以上（51.56%）（见表6-72）。

以上特点的原因分析，根据湖北省被调查者填写的无人承受遗产管理人的产生方式的民众观念之理由（见表6-71），（1）五成以上的人认为应由居委会或村委会或所在单位指定产生，近五成的地区也有该习惯，其原因是上述主体对死者及其遗产的情况比较清楚，由其指定遗产管理人，这有利于对遗产进行清算、管理和利用；（2）近五成的人认为应由人民法院或民政部门指定产生，五成以上的地区也有该习惯，其原因是人民法院通过法定程序，对遗产进行清算和管理，由其指定遗产管理人，有利于公平保护相关债权人的利益。

关于无人承受遗产的管理人的产生方式之我国立法，我国立法没有遗产管理人制度，

---

① 《日本民法典》第958条之三。

② "王稿"第666条。

亦没有规定遗产管理人的产生方式。

从域外立法例看，关于无人承受遗产的管理人，《法国民法典》规定，应任何债权人、为死者的利益负责管理其全部或一部概括财产的任何人、有利益关系的任何其他人或者检察院提出的申请，受理请求的法官委托负责公产管理的行政机关管理无人继承的遗产。①

从我国诸继承法学者建议稿看，“梁稿”规定，在没有继承人的情况下，须由人民法院依利害关系人的申请或自行指定管理人②；“王稿”规定，继承开始时，有无继承人不明时，由村委会或居委会作为遗产管理人。③

我们认为，我国欠缺无人承受遗产管理人的产生方式之规定，这是其立法之不足。因此，以上主张规定遗产管理人产生方式的湖北省被调查民众的观念与习惯、域外立法例和我国学者建议稿的观点，可供我国立法参考。

第二，关于无人承受的遗产之酌分请求权主体的民众观念与民间习惯，统计数据显示的特点是，(1) 在被调查者的观念上，认为依靠死者扶养的人（71.70%）、与死者关系密切且对其帮助较多的人（72.63%）、与死者共同生活的人（60.03%）均可以成为无人承受遗产的酌分请求权主体的，各占六成至七成以上（见表6-73）；(2) 被调查者所在地区的民间习惯是：与死者共同生活的人（20.00%）、照顾过死者的人（41.11%）、对死者有帮助的人（16.67%）和不是继承人的其他亲属（16.67%），均可以请求酌分无人承受遗产的，各占一成至四成以上（见表6-74）。

以上特点的原因分析，六成至七成以上的湖北省被调查民众认为依靠死者扶养的人、与死者共同生活的人、与死者有密切联系且对其帮助较多的人都可酌情分得遗产，一成至四成以上的该省被调查者所在地区也有该习惯，其原因可能是无人承受遗产之酌分请求主体较为广泛，有利于充分发挥遗产的经济扶养功能和可利用价值。

无人承受遗产的酌分请求权主体之我国立法，我国《继承法》第14条规定：“对继承人以外的依靠被继承人扶养的缺乏劳动能力又没有生活来源的人，或者继承人以外的对被继承人扶养较多的人，可以分给他们适当的遗产。”1985年《执行继承法意见》第57条规定：“遗产因无人继承收归国家或集体组织所有时，按继承法第十四条规定可以分给遗产的人提出取得遗产的要求，人民法院应视情况适当分给遗产。”

从域外立法例看，《日本民法典》第958-2条规定，法院认为适当时，可以根据曾与被继承人共同生活的、对被继承人的疗养看护尽力的人及其他与被继承人有特别关系的人之请求，将遗产的全部或部分分配给此人。

从我国诸继承法学者建议稿看，“陈稿”第87条规定，无人承受遗产的酌分遗产人为依靠被继承人扶养的人、对被继承人扶养较多的人、与被继承人一同生活的人或其他与被继承人有密切关系的人。

我们认为，我国无人承受遗产的酌分请求权主体较窄，这是其立法之不足。因此，以上主张扩大无人承受遗产的酌分请求权人范围的湖北省被调查民众的观念与习惯、域外立

---

① 《法国民法典》第809-1条。

② “梁稿”第2029条。

③ “王稿”第661条第1款。

法例和我国学者建议稿的观点，可供我国立法参考。

第四节 当代中国湖北省民众财产继承观念与遗产处理习惯对中国民法典继承编制定的立法启示

以上，我们针对湖北省被调查者的财产继承观念与遗产处理习惯的调查统计的汇总数据，分析归纳其特点，研究其特点的产生原因，考察和分析我国司法实践的相关案例，研究我国继承法律制度的适用情况，进而结合考察域外立法例和我国诸继承法学者建议稿的观点，剖析我国《继承法》相关制度存在的优点与不足。以下，我们将以湖北省被调查者的财产继承观念与遗产处理习惯为参考基础，借鉴域外立法例和我国诸继承法学者建议稿的有益观点，对我国“民法典继承法编”编纂中相关继承制度的修改完善或予以保留，提出立法建议，以供我国立法机关参考。

一、我国遗产范围界定制度之不足与立法完善建议

（一）我国遗产范围界定制度之不足

有关遗产的范围，我国立法之不足表现为：第一，欠缺遗产的反面排除规定。在湖北省被调查者中，有五成至七成以上的人认为家庭日常生活用品、欠债和交通事故死亡赔偿金属于遗产，此认识与现行法的规定不一致（见表6-4），这反映出我国立法欠缺对遗产的反面排除规定，这使部分被调查者对某些财产是否属于遗产的认识还不甚清晰。前述涉及遗产范围界定案例之司法审判实践中也反映出我国立法对遗产的反面排除规定之不足。第二，我国《继承法》没有规定被继承人生前特种赠与财产的归扣制度，不利于在继承人间公平地分配遗产。

（二）我国遗产范围界定制度之立法完善建议

针对以上立法之不足，我们提出以下两方面立法完善建议：

1. 遗产范围界定模式之立法建议

对于遗产范围的立法，建议采取正面概括与反面排除的立法模式，正面界定遗产是被继承人死亡时遗留的个人合法财产；反面明确规定邮箱、QQ账号等具有人身性的物、死亡赔偿金、欠款等不属于遗产。

2. 被继承人生前特种赠与财产归扣之立法建议

建议立法规定遗产归扣制度。遗产的归扣，除被继承人作出免除归扣的意思表示外，当接受被继承人生前特种赠与财产的继承人参加继承时，该生前赠与财产应计入遗产的总额中，然后计算出每一个继承人的应继份额进行分割，并从接受该赠与的继承人之应继份额中扣除该赠与份额。但被继承人生前表明其赠与的财产不适用遗产归扣的除外。

二、我国继承开始的通知和公告制度之不足与立法完善建议

（一）我国继承开始的通知和公告制度之不足

关于继承开始的通知与公告制度，我国立法之不足表现为：第一，我国欠缺继承开始的通知和公告主体不履行通知和公告义务的法律责任。前述涉及继承开始的通知与公告案例之司法审判实践中也反映出我国此立法之不足。第二，欠缺继承开始的通知与公告期间

之规定。合计六成以上的湖北省被调查者认为应在被继承人死亡后7日内发出继承开始的通知和公告（见表6-12）。

（二）我国继承开始的通知和公告制度之立法完善建议

针对以上立法之不足，我们提出以下三方面立法完善建议：

1. 继承开始的通知和公告的主体之立法建议

建议维持我国现行法中继承开始的通知和公告之主体，即继承开始后，知道被继承人死亡的继承人应该及时通知其他继承人和遗嘱执行人。继承人中无人知道被继承人死亡或者知道被继承人死亡而不能通知的，由被继承人生前所在单位或者住所地的居民委员会、村民委员会负责通知。

如果上述主体不履行法定通知或公告义务造成遗产损失的，应当承担相应的损害赔偿责任。

2. 继承开始的通知和公告的方式之立法建议

我们认为，对于继承开始的通知和公告的方式并没有必要予以明确规定，原因在于，随着科技水平的提高，通信方式在不断增多，法律的滞后性有可能限制了通知的方式的灵活和自由。负有通知义务的人或单位通过适当的方式及时履行通知到被继承人的法定继承人或遗嘱执行人即可。

3. 继承开始的通知和公告的期间之立法建议

建议立法应对继承开始的通知和公告的期间予以明确。凡负有通知与公告义务的主体，继承开始的通知应该于被继承人死亡15日内发出。在被通知对象不明、不知下落或用其他方式无法通知时，公告期间不少于60日。

三、我国遗产管理制度之不足与立法完善建议

（一）我国遗产管理制度之不足

关于遗产管理制度，我国立法之不足表现为：第一，我国欠缺遗产管理制度，没有规定遗产管理人的产生方式，只是在我国《继承法》和司法解释中原则性地规定了遗嘱执行人、遗产保管等内容。在湖北省被调查者所在地区，由死者的法定继承人作为遗产管理人的，占近九成（见表6-13）。前述涉及遗产管理案例之司法审判实践中也反映出我国此立法之不足。第二，我国欠缺遗产管理人的职责之规定，只是原则性地规定存有遗产的人应妥善保管遗产。五成至九成以上的湖北省被调查民众认为制作遗产清单、妥善保管遗产、查明被继承人生前的债权和债务等均是遗产管理人的职责（见表6-16）。第三，我国欠缺遗产管理人的报酬之规定。在湖北省被调查者所在地区，继承人担任的遗产管理人，五成的地区有管理人不能请求给付报酬的习惯；法院指定的遗产管理人，近五成半的地区有可以请求给付报酬的习惯；继承人选任的第三人作为遗产管理人，其中五成（50.97%）的地区有是否给付报酬应当由继承人决定的习惯；三成半的地区有一律有权请求给付报酬的习惯（见表6-17）。第四，我国欠缺遗产管理人的损害赔偿责任之规定。在湖北省被调查者所在地区，遗产管理人有故意或重大过失，才承担损害赔偿责任的占五成半以上（见表6-19）。

（二）我国遗产管理制度之立法完善建议

针对以上立法之不足，我们提出以下四方面立法完善建议：

1. 遗产管理人的确定之立法建议

遗嘱管理人必须具备完全民事行为能力。有遗嘱执行人的，由其担任遗产管理人；没有遗嘱执行人的，由继承人担任遗产管理人，如有多位继承人的，继承人间应进行协商推选遗产管理人；既没有遗嘱执行人也不存在继承人或无法确定是否有继承人的，或遗产债权人证实其权利受到继承人的损害或有损害危险的，经遗产利害关系人申请，由法院指定遗产管理人。

2. 遗产管理人的职责之立法建议

继承开始后，及时清点遗产，制作遗产清单；负责妥善保管遗产；查明被继承人是否留有遗嘱，并且确定遗嘱是否真实合法；查明被继承人生前的债权和债务，积极地追讨债权或清偿债务；以原告或被告的身份参加因遗产引起的诉讼；定期制作遗产管理报告，向继承人报告遗产管理的情况等都是遗产管理人应有的职责。

3. 遗产管理人的报酬之立法建议

关于遗产管理人的报酬，首先，继承人担任遗产管理人一般不给予报酬，但多个继承人同意支付报酬的除外。继承人担任遗产管理人确需要请求报酬的，可以向人民法院提出申请，由人民法院根据其遗产管理的工作量和难易程度，酌情决定是否给予报酬。其次，继承人外的其他主体担任遗产管理人的可以请求获得报酬。其中，遗嘱执行人的报酬以遗嘱的规定为准。如果遗嘱无规定的，遗嘱执行人可以请求人民法院裁定是否给予其报酬。

4. 遗产管理人的损害赔偿责任之立法建议

遗产管理人和继承人在管理过程中，如违背善良管理人的注意义务或法定程序使遗产权利人的利益遭受损害的，应负赔偿责任。

四、我国法定继承制度之不足与立法完善建议

（一）我国法定继承制度之不足

关于法定继承制度，我国立法的不足表现为，父母排在第一继承顺序中的立法模式不尽科学，易造成财产外流，这不符合财产向下传承的发展趋势。

（二）我国法定继承制度之立法完善建议

针对以上立法之不足，我们提出以下五方面立法完善建议：

1. 法定继承的范围与顺序之立法建议

我国现行《继承法》将父母和子女一并列为第一顺序法定继承人，其指导思想是死后扶养，即死者生前应当赡养父母、抚养子女，在死亡后，其财产应当继续发挥该作用。① 但一般来说，人们希望将财产留给子女并通过他们在自己的直系卑亲属中传递下去。若父母继承财产，该财产可能部分甚至全部归属于死者的兄弟姐妹以及他们的直系卑亲属。在有子女的情况下，人们自然不愿财产落入旁系血亲手中。尤其是在我国计划生育政策有所改变的情况下，独生子女越发减少，遗产流向旁系亲属的可能性更大。因此，建议将配偶、子女及其直系卑亲属为第一顺序继承人，父母不应排在第一继承顺序。

2. 配偶与血亲继承人的法定应继份之立法建议

配偶无固定顺序继承是一种更为细致的利益权衡，若配偶固定在第一顺序，则完全排

① 张玉敏：《继承法律制度研究（第二版）》，华中科技大学出版社 2016 年版，第 133 页。

除了其他顺序中血亲的继承权，形式上是偏向配偶一方的。但必须注意的是，如打破原有的广为民众接受的规则需要慎重考量。因此，尽管有学者主张学习他国关于配偶与血亲继承人的法定应继份的经验，但我们建议维持我国《继承法》的现有规定更适宜。

3. 配偶对遗产中的家庭住房的先取权与终生使用权之立法建议

我国《继承法》规定平均分配遗产的立法，体现公平的理念，并且已经深入人心。轻易改变可能会引起立法波动，因此建议维持现行法的规定，即不予增设该制度。

4. 后顺序特殊法定继承人对遗产中原使用的住房及日常生活用品的终生使用权之立法建议

无论从我国传统道德还是从婚姻家庭法的规定来看，民众一般都不会无视老人的晚年生活安排问题。因此关于后顺序特殊法定继承人对遗产住房的终身使用权，建议不纳入立法。

5. 尽了主要赡养义务的丧偶儿媳或女婿的遗产分配方式之立法建议

我国《继承法》第12条的立法目的在于，通过赋予丧偶儿媳、女婿继承权来激励其赡养老人。从调查统计情况看，近六成半的湖北省被调查民众对尽了主要赡养义务的丧偶儿媳或女婿可以作为第一顺序法定继承人是持赞同态度的（见表6-29），即被调查民众的认知与我国《继承法》的规定相契合。特别是在人口老龄化日益严重的情况下，老人的扶养将越发成为不容忽视的问题，社会化的扶养不可能一步到位，就必须借助于家庭内部的照顾。因此，对于尽了主要赡养义务的丧偶儿媳、女婿的遗产分配方式，立法应当积极维护他们的权益，建议维持现行规定。

五、我国遗嘱继承制度之不足与立法完善建议

（一）我国遗嘱继承制度之不足

关于遗嘱继承制度，我国立法的不足表现为，我国没有规定特留份制度，不利于防止被继承人权利的滥用。近七成的湖北省被调查民众赞同设立特留份制度（见表6-33）。

（二）我国遗嘱继承制度之立法完善建议

针对以上立法之不足，我们提出以下三方面立法完善建议：

1. 公证遗嘱与其他形式遗嘱的适用效力之立法建议

建议维持现行法规定，除公证遗嘱适用效力最高外，其他遗嘱应按照设立的先后顺序确定遗嘱的效力。

2. 遗嘱自由的限制——特留份之立法建议

建议我国立法应在现有必留份的基础上增加特留份制度，即遗嘱人以遗嘱处分财产，应当为配偶、晚辈直系血亲、父母保留特定的遗产份额，建议以遗产的二分之一为宜。

3. 夫妻共同遗嘱之立法建议

建议在他方配偶死亡后，为便于生存一方可以另行设立遗嘱处分其个人财产，我国立法不宜设立共同遗嘱。①

① 我们认为，夫妻可以采取公证、书面形式设立共同遗嘱。夫妻设立共同遗嘱的，一方在另一方死亡后，不得改变遗嘱中已死亡遗嘱人的遗嘱内容。生存一方可以另行设立遗嘱处分其个人财产，生存一方另行设立遗嘱的，视为改变了共同遗嘱中其个人财产的处分。也就是说，夫妻一方死亡后，生存的夫妻一方可以就其个人财产另立遗嘱，这实际上否认了共同遗嘱的效力。

六、我国继承和遗赠的接受与放弃制度之不足与立法完善建议

（一）我国继承和遗赠的接受与放弃制度之不足

关于继承和遗赠的接受与放弃制度，我国立法的不足表现为：第一，没有明确继承接受与放弃的应具体向哪些主体作出。第二，继承人放弃继承的行为，债权人是否享有撤销权，我国立法没有规定。然而在司法实践中，已多有类似案件的发生，给我国带来了一定的审判困境。在湖北省被调查者中，认为继承人放弃继承的行为不可以被债权人撤销的，占五成半以上（见表6-43）。

（二）我国继承和遗赠的接受与放弃制度之立法完善建议

针对以上立法之不足，我们提出以下三方面立法完善建议：

1. 继承的接受与放弃制度之立法建议

继承开始后，继承人放弃继承的，应当在遗产处理前，向其他继承人、遗产管理人、遗嘱执行人或者人民法院作出书面放弃继承的表示。到期没有表示的，视为接受继承。

2. 遗赠的接受与放弃制度之立法建议

建议维持我国《继承法》第25条之规定，即现行立法条文是合理的，没有必要改动。

3. 继承的放弃与债权人的撤销权之立法建议

继承人接受或放弃继承的意思表示，债权人不能撤销。

七、我国继承权的丧失、被继承人的宥恕与代位继承制度之不足与立法完善建议

（一）我国继承权的丧失、被继承人的宥恕与代位继承制度之不足

关于继承权的丧失、被继承人的宥恕与代位继承制度，我国立法的不足表现为：第一，继承权丧失的法定情形过窄，没有将以欺诈或者胁迫的手段，迫使或者妨碍被继承人设立、变更或者撤销遗嘱的情形作为丧失继承权的法定情形，不利于体现法的惩戒功能，维护被继承人和其他法定继承人和合法权益。认为继承人因欺诈或者胁迫而丧失继承权，获得被继承人宥恕后可以恢复继承权的湖北省被调查者，占七成以上（见表6-45）。第二，我国现行立法采取的是子女“代位权说”，即继承人丧失继承权的，子女的代位继承权亦随之丧失。域外相关立法例和我国学者立法建议稿多采取“固有权说”，我国“代位权说”不利于与国际立法相接轨。

（二）我国继承权的丧失、被继承人的宥恕与代位继承制度之立法完善建议

针对以上立法之不足，我们提出以下两方面立法完善建议：

1. 继承权的丧失与被继承人的宥恕之立法建议

继承人有下列行为之一的，丧失继承权：（一）故意杀害被继承人的；（二）为争夺遗产而杀害其他继承人的；（三）遗弃被继承人的，或者虐待被继承人情节严重的；（四）伪造、篡改或者销毁遗嘱情节严重的；（五）以欺诈或者胁迫的手段，迫使或者妨碍被继承人设立、变更或者撤销遗嘱，情节严重的。

有以上（三）（四）（五）丧失继承权行为的，如以后确有悔改表现，而且被继承人生前又表示宽恕的，可不确认其丧失继承权。

2. 继承权的丧失与代位继承权之立法建议

被代位继承人丧失继承权的，不影响其子女代位继承。

八、我国遗赠扶养协议制度之不足与立法增补建议

(一) 我国遗赠扶养协议制度之不足

如前所述，我国目前没有继承扶养协议制度，我国的遗赠扶养协议制度存在适用主体范围较窄的问题，即将受扶养人的法定继承人排除在协议主体之外，此与湖北省多数被调查民众的相关观念和处理习惯不符，不利于被继承人与其继承人协商处理自己的赡养和遗产继承问题。六成以上的湖北省被调查民众认为，被继承人可以与全部继承人共同协商签订继承扶养协议（见表6-49）。前述涉及继承协议案例之司法审判实践中也反映出我国此制度之不足。

(二) 我国继承扶养协议制度之立法增补建议

针对以上立法之不足，我们提出以下两方面立法完善建议：

1. 继承扶养协议的订立主体与方式之立法建议

被继承人与所有继承人协商一致的，可以签订继承扶养协议。

2. 继承扶养协议的变更方式及效力之立法建议

与被继承人签订继承扶养协议的继承人死亡的，原则上该协议效力终止。但如被继承人与死亡人的继承人双方协商同意继续履行原继承扶养协议的，该协议可以继续履行。被继承人也可以与其他继承人另行签订继承扶养协议。被继承人与其他继承人另行签订继承协议的，其他继承人应补偿死亡继承人已支付超过其扶养义务部分的扶养费。

九、我国遗产债务清偿制度之不足与立法完善建议

(一) 我国遗产债务清偿制度之不足

关于遗产债务清偿制度，我国立法的不足表现为：第一，关于遗产债务清偿的责任类型，我国立法采取无条件的有限清偿责任偏重于保护继承人的合法利益，但忽视了对遗产债权人的利益保护。现实中继承人往往也是遗产管理人，若其不妥善保管遗产则导致遗产的毁损灭失，或者故意藏匿、转移财产以损害债权人的利益，债权人的利益往往不能获得救济。这是我国无条件的有限责任继承制度之不足。在湖北省被调查者中，主张实行自愿的无限清偿责任的合计占六成半以上；主张实行有限清偿责任的占近五成；主张对有侵害遗产违法行为者应当实行强制的无限清偿责任的占四成以上（见表6-52）。前述涉及遗产债务清偿案例之司法审判实践中也反映出我国此制度之不足。第二，我国《继承法》未规定被继承人丧葬费的支付方式，不利于指导司法实践。关于被继承人丧葬费支付的民间习惯，由全体继承人共同支付的占近六成；从被继承人的遗产中支付的，占近四成（见表6-54）。第三，我国《继承法》未对遗产债务清偿顺序作出规定。目前，司法实践中多根据我国《继承法》、1985年《执行继承法意见》和我国《企业破产法》等的相关规定确定遗产债务的清偿顺序。在具体案件审理中，在有限遗产内如何确定被继承人债务清偿顺序，这往往成为司法实务中的难点。在湖北省被调查者所在地区，遗产债务按如下顺序清偿：第一顺序为丧葬费用；第二顺序为遗产管理等费用、欠付的工资；第三顺序为欠债；第四顺序为受被继承人扶养人的生活费、税款；第五顺序为对被继承人扶养较多的人

之酌情分配遗产份额、遗赠扶养协议写明遗产的遗产（见表6-55）。

（二）我国遗产债务清偿制度之立法完善建议

针对以上立法之不足，我们提出以下三方面立法完善建议：

1. 遗产债务清偿责任的类型之立法建议

被继承人的生前所有债务，继承人应先用所有遗产偿还债务。不足部分由继承人自愿以个人财产偿还。

继承人转移遗产、隐瞒遗产时，遗产应当重新分配，对有转移、隐瞒遗产的继承人应当少分或不分。

2. 被继承人丧葬费的支付之立法建议

死者的丧葬费用先由被继承人的遗产支付，不足部分由各继承人共同支付。

3. 遗产债务的清偿顺序之立法建议

建议遗产的债务的清偿，按照下列顺序进行：（1）丧葬费用、遗产管理费用；（2）欠债、欠付的工资；（3）遗赠扶养协议写明遗赠的遗产；（4）受被继承人扶养人的生活费；（5）税费；（6）对被继承人扶养较多的人之酌情分配遗产份额。

十、我国遗产分割制度之不足与立法完善建议

（一）我国遗产分割制度之不足

关于遗产分割制度，我国立法的不足表现为：第一，缺少对遗产分割自由的限制条款。近七成的湖北省被调查者所在地区有遗嘱禁止分割不可分割的习惯（见表6-56）。第二，欠缺遗产分割瑕疵的担保责任之规定，不利于在继承人间公平地分配遗产。合计近六成的湖北省被调查者所在地区对遗产分割的瑕疵，有共同继承人共同承担的习惯（见表6-64）。

（二）我国遗产分割制度之立法完善建议

针对以上立法之不足，我们提出以下两方面立法完善建议：

1. 遗产分割的自由与限制之立法建议

遗产由所有继承人共同协商后进行分割。

被继承人死后，未经被继承人配偶的同意的，不得对其居住的房屋进行分割。

被继承人可以在遗嘱中写明在其死后，其房屋在一定期间内不能进行分割。该期限不得超过5年。但在特殊情况下，可以允许继承人将遗嘱禁止分割的房屋进行分割。

2. 遗产分割瑕疵的担保责任之立法建议

遗产分割后，各继承人以其所得的遗产份额为限，对其他继承人分得的遗产，负与出卖人同样的瑕疵担保责任。

十一、我国无人承受遗产制度之不足与立法完善建议

（一）我国无人承受遗产制度之不足

关于无人承受遗产的处理，我国立法的不足表现为：第一，无人承受遗产的归属主体不足，应优先归属于被继承人的不是继承人的其他亲属。第二，我国欠缺无人承受遗产的管理制度，没有规定无人承受遗产管理人的产生方式。湖北省被调查者中，认为无人承受遗产的管理人应由居委会、村委会或所在单位指定产生的，占五成以上；认为无人承受遗产的管理人应由人民法院指定的，占三成半（见表6-70）。第三，我国无人承受遗产的酌

分请求权主体过窄。湖北省被调查民众认为参与酌分无人承受遗产的请求权主体并不需要达到“缺乏劳动能力又没有生活来源”的法定条件。在湖北省被调查者的观念上，六成至七成以上的人认为依靠死者扶养的人、与死者关系密切且对其帮助较多的人、与死者共同生活的人均可以成为无人承受遗产的酌分请求权主体（见表6-73）。

（二）我国无人承受遗产制度之立法完善建议

针对以上立法之不足，我们提出以下两方面立法完善建议：

1. 无人承受遗产的归属主体之立法建议

建议无人继承的遗产，可以归不是继承人的其他亲属所有。没有其他亲属的，才归国家所有。

2. 无人承受遗产的处理之立法建议

建议无人承受遗产的管理人，由被继承人住所地的村委会、居委会、所在单位或人民法院指定产生。

建议适当扩大无人承受遗产的酌分请求权主体。依靠死者扶养的人、与死者共同生活的人、与死者关系密切且对其帮助较多的人，可以请求酌情分得无人继承的遗产。

图书在版编目（CIP）数据

当代中国民众财产继承观念与遗产处理习惯实证调查研究/陈苇主编．—北京：中国人民公安大学出版社，2019.10

（家事法研究学术文库）

ISBN 978-7-5653-3770-3

Ⅰ.①当…　Ⅱ.①陈…　Ⅲ.①继承法—研究—中国　Ⅳ.①D923.54

中国版本图书馆 CIP 数据核字（2019）第 202232 号

当代中国民众财产继承观念与遗产处理习惯实证调查研究（上、下卷）

主编　陈　苇（课题负责人）

出版发行：中国人民公安大学出版社
地　　址：北京市西城区木樨地南里
邮政编码：100038
经　　销：新华书店
印　　刷：北京市泰锐印刷有限责任公司

版　　次：2019 年 10 月第 1 版
印　　次：2019 年 10 月第 1 次
印　　张：75
开　　本：787 毫米×1092 毫米　1/16
字　　数：1825 千字

书　　号：ISBN 978-7-5653-3770-3
定　　价：286.00 元（上、下卷）

网　　址：www.cppsup.com.cn　www.porclub.com.cn
电子邮箱：zbs@cppsup.com　zbs@cppsu.edu.cn

营销中心电话：010-83903254
读者服务部电话（门市）：010-83903257
警官读者俱乐部电话（网购、邮购）：010-83903253
法律图书分社电话：010-83905745